W9-BLF-239

Critical Issues in Education
A Dialectic Approach

Critical Issues in Education

A Dialectic Approach

THIRD EDITION

Jack L. Nelson
Rutgers University

Kenneth Carlson
Rutgers University

Stuart B. Palonsky
University of Missouri

The McGraw-Hill Companies, Inc.

New York   St Louis   San Francisco   Auckland   Bogotá   Caracas
Lisbon   London   Madrid   Mexico City   Milan   Montreal   New Delhi
San Juan   Singapore   Sydney   Tokyo   Toronto

This book was developed by Lane Akers, Inc.

This book was set in Palatino by The Clarinda Company.
The editor was Lane Akers;
the production supervisor was Margaret Boylan.
The cover was designed by Robin Hoffmann.
Project supervision was done by Hockett Editorial Service.
R. R. Donnelley & Sons Company was printer and binder.

CRITICAL ISSUES IN EDUCATION
A Dialectic Approach

This book is printed on acid-free paper.

4 5 6 7 8 9 0 DOC DOC 9 0 9 8 7

ISBN 0-07-046212-7

Library of Congress Cataloging-in-Publication Data

Nelson, Jack L.
    Critical issues in education: a dialectic approach / Jack L.
Nelson, Kenneth Carlson, Stuart B. Palonsky.—3d ed.
        p.   cm.
    Includes bibliographical references and index.
    ISBN 0-07-046212-7
    1. Education—United States.   2. Teaching—United States.
3. Educational evaluation—United States.   4. Critical thinking—
United States.   I. Carlson, Kenneth.   II. Palonsky, Stuart B.
III. Title.
LA217.2.N45   1996
370'.973—dc20   95-39695

About the Authors

JACK L. NELSON, a professor of education at Rutgers, obtained his doctorate from the University of Southern California. He is an experienced teacher in schools at the elementary, secondary, undergraduate, and graduate levels; his university teaching experience includes California State University, Los Angeles; the State University of New York at Buffalo; San Jose State University; and Cambridge University. Nelson has been a visiting scholar at the University of California, Berkeley; Stanford University; University of Colorado; and Curtin University and the University of Sydney in Australia. *Critical Issues in Education* is his sixteenth book; he has also published about 150 articles and reviews. He is listed in *Who's Who in America* and *Contemporary Authors.*

KENNETH CARLSON is a professor of education at Rutgers. After serving as a teacher of secondary school in New York State, he earned his doctoral degree at the State University of New York, Buffalo. Among his publications is the book, *Radical Ideas and the Schools,* and a variety of journal publications on educational topics. Carlson was principal investigator on a three-year National Institute of Education study of compensatory education; he has also conducted research on urban schools and on issues of educational equity, sexism, and censorship. He has served as associate dean for teacher education, president of the state council of the American Association of University Professors, and as chair of the Rutgers University Senate.

STUART B. PALONSKY is professor of education and director of the Honors College at the University of Missouri–Columbia. A former public school teacher in New York and New Jersey, Palonsky earned his doctorate at Michigan State University. His publications include *900 Shows a Year,* an ethnographic study of high school teaching from a classroom teacher's perspective. In addition, Palonsky has published numerous articles and reviews in educational and social science journals, and has presented scholarly and professional papers on educational issues at national association conferences.

Contents in Brief

PREFACE xv

1. Introduction: Unity and Diversity in Schooling 1

Part I
WHAT INTERESTS SHOULD SCHOOLS SERVE?

2. Welfare: Safety Net or Free Lunch 57

3. School Choice: For Family Choice or Against Vouchers 84

4. School Finance: Equity or Disparity 108

5. School Integration: Compulsory or Voluntary 132

6. Affirmative Action: Progressive or Restrictive 160

Part II
WHAT SHOULD BE TAUGHT?

7. Basic Education: Traditional Disciplines or Critical Thinking 203

8.   Multicultural Studies: Representative or Divisive   223

9.   Curriculum Control: National or Local   241

10. Values: Traditional or Liberational   262

11. Business Influence: Positive or Negative   281

12. Standardized Testing: Restrict or Expand   295

Part III
HOW SHOULD SCHOOLS BE ORGANIZED AND OPERATED?

13. School Leadership: Teacher Directed or
     Administrator Controlled   331

14. Academic Freedom: Teacher Rights or
     Responsibility   345

15. Teacher Unions: Detrimental or Beneficial   365

16. Privatization of Schools: Boon or Bane   379

17. School Violence: School or Social Responsibility   402

18. School Reform: Excellence or Equity   419

INDEX   435

Contents

PREFACE   xv

1. Introduction: Unity and Diversity in Schooling   1

Part I
WHAT INTERESTS SHOULD SCHOOLS SERVE?

2. Welfare: Safety Net or Free Lunch   57

Children from all social classes go to schools. Do
welfare programs help to level the playing field for
children of the poor, or do they lead to dependency
where human dignity and freedom are sacrificed?

Position 1: For More Welfare   57

Position 2: For Less Welfare   66

3. School Choice: For Family Choice or Against
Vouchers   84

Is choice of schools in the public interest, or is it
destructive of the ideals of the public schools?

Position 1: Family Choice in Education   84

Position 2: Against Voucher Plans   93

4. **School Finance: Equity or Disparity**   108

   Should taxpayer spending on schools be different in different communities? Are the interests of liberty or those of equity more served by differences in financing?

   Position 1: For Equity in Education   108

   Position 2: For Freedom in Financing Schools   117

5. **School Integration: Compulsory or Voluntary**   132

   De jure segregation in school is illegal; but how should integration be approached? Whose interests are served?

   Position 1: For Legal Integration   132

   Position 2: Against Legal Integration   142

6. **Affirmative Action: Progressive or Restrictive**   160

   Equality is a major goal for a democracy, and bias is restrictive. Whose interests, those of old victims or new, should prevail in moving toward equality and away from bias?

   Position 1: For Affirmative Action   160

   Position 2: Against Affirmative Action   171

Part II
WHAT SHOULD BE TAUGHT?

7. **Basic Education: Traditional Disciplines or Critical Thinking**   203

   What are the defining characteristics of fundamental knowledge? Who should decide this?

   Position 1: Teach the Basic Disciplines   203

   Position 2: Teach for Critical Thinking   211

8. **Multicultural Studies: Representative or Divisive**   223

   Diversity of population suggests diversity of education, but how can the United States remain united if schools stress the differences?

Position 1: For a Multicultural Perspective   223

Position 2: For the Common Culture   231

9. Curriculum Control: National or Local   241

Who should determine what constitutes knowledge for
students?

Position 1: For a National Curriculum   241

Position 2: For Local Determination   249

10. Values: Traditional or Liberational   262

Schools are directly involved in the transmission of
values. What values should be the focus of schools?

Position 1: Teach Traditional Values   262

Position 2: For Liberation   270

11. Business Influence: Positive or Negative   281

Business defines required knowledge as employable
skills and work values. Is the influence of business on
schools excessive or insufficient?

Position 1: For Increased Business Influence   281

Position 2: Limit the Influence of Business   287

12. Standardized Testing: Restrict or Expand   295

Testing is virtually universal in schools. Should the use
of standardized tests be increased or decreased?

Position 1: Restrict Testing   295

Position 2: Expand Testing   302

Part III
HOW SHOULD SCHOOLS BE ORGANIZED AND OPERATED?

13. School Leadership: Teacher Directed or
Administrator Controlled   331

Educational reform includes the idea of restructuring schools. Which groups should play the leading role in new, improved schools?

Position 1: For Teacher Directed Leadership   331

Position 2: For Administrator Control   336

14. Academic Freedom: Teacher Rights or Responsibility   345

Teaching involves risk taking; so does being a parent. Should teachers have increased or decreased rights to academic freedom?

Position 1: For Teacher Responsibility   345

Position 2: For Increased Academic Freedom   354

15. Teacher Unions: Detrimental or Beneficial   365

Collective bargaining in school districts has become common. Are teachers, students, parents, and taxpayers better off as a result of unionism?

Position 1: Teacher Unions Are Destructive   365

Position 2: Teacher Unions Are Beneficial   370

16. Privatization of Schools: Boon or Bane   379

Is education better when it is operated as a public or as a private enterprise? What criteria should be used to measure better education?

Position 1: Public Schools Should Be Privatized   379

Position 2: Public Schools Should Be Public   389

17. School Violence: School or Social Responsibility   402

Schools and society are plagued by violence. How should schools deal with violent or potentially violent students?

Position 1: Schools Can Curb Violence and Educate   402

Position 2: Schools Must Eliminate the Violence in Order to Educate   409

18. School Reform: Excellence or Equity 419

Excellence is a key term in school reform literature and a key element in democracy. Are these concepts in opposition in education?

Position 1: Excellence Is a Public Deception 419

Position 2: Excellence Is the Only Reform 425

INDEX 435

Preface

At the close of the twentieth century, education is still important and still controversial. From the earliest periods of recorded human history and across the civilized expanse of the earth, schooling has been a topic of great social concern and dispute. We can expect educational issues to remain important in the twenty-first century, becoming even more important to more people as the global information age develops.

It is possible to study about schooling by reading newspaper reports of test scores, finances, and school activities. These tend to ignore or gloss over basic conflicts and to sterilize issues, usually by presenting one unexamined view. That implies that there is one correct view, and it obscures the vital importance of education to society.

Schooling has a long history of conflicting ideas. Our effort is to explore a collection of pervasive and critical school issues by considering divergent views. Persistent school issues are related to basic disagreements over the kinds of individuals and society we desire. These issues deserve critical examination, which involves consideration of divergent ideas, including those with which one disagrees. Controversies, we claim, are at the center of active learning.

Alfred North Whitehead commented:

> Above all things we must beware of what I call "inert ideas"—that is to say, ideas that are merely received into the mind without being utilized, or tested, to be thrown into fresh combinations. . . . Except at rare intervals of intellectual ferment, education in the past has been radically infected with inert ideas. (1929; 13)

The issues presented here are far from inert; by presenting them in the form of opposing essays we intend to show how provocative and dynamic they are. We see the terrain of education as rugged and rocky with few clear paths, but with many roadsigns proclaiming truth while dismissing other roadsigns.

The introductory chapter presents a framework for examining critics and reform efforts in education. Three following parts each focus on a major question about schooling and are introduced with background material to provide a context:

Part I: What interests should schools serve?

Part II: What should be taught?

Part III: How should schools be organized and operated?

Every part contains chapters on specific critical issues in education which illustrate the theme question of the part. Each chapter contains two essays expressing divergent positions on that issue. Obviously, this does not exhaust the possible positions, but it does provide at least two views on each issue. References are provided to encourage further exploration. At the end of each chapter are a few questions to consider and a brief sample of data that relate to that issue.

This book presumes that education is a matter of great significance in modern society, and that critical examination of education is a necessary and worthwhile activity.

On the one hand, education is in deep trouble and getting worse; on the other hand, the schools are remarkably good, with excellent teachers and programs of high quality. If we had a third or more hands, we could add that many more ideas. New views emerge as debates over education stimulate rethinking of positions. Still, two views may be enough to establish an issue. Our hope is that these issues become the basis for lively discussion, further examination, and a dialectic which leads to new ideas about how to improve education.

The authors took major responsibility for this volume as follows: Nelson, Introduction to Part II and Chapters 1, 7, 10, 11, 14, 16, and 18; Carlson, Introduction to Part I and Chapters 2, 3, 4, 5, 6, and 9; and Palonsky, Introduction to Part III and Chapters 8, 12, 13, 15, and 17. After two previous editions and valuable responses from users of the book, we have revised and updated this edition and replaced some topics with three new chapters on current educational issues: welfare, privatization, and violence.

We have a great intellectual debt to the many who have taken seriously the relation of education to society, and who have expressed divergent ideas in the extensive literature. We are also indebted to students, colleagues, and others who provided criticism and assistance. In particular, we express appreciation to Lane Akers, our effectively critical editor, and to Gwen and Nancy for forbearance and encouragement. We especially appreciate the contributions of many good colleagues who reviewed the manuscript, criticized the work, or provided challenging ideas. Among these are: Donald Adams, Bucknell University; Ian Baptiste, Northern Illinois University; Thomas Caldwell, Middle Georgia College; James Daly, Seton Hall University; Emily de la Cruz, Portland State University; Russell Dennis, Bucknell University; Herbert Edwards, attorney, Harbor Springs, Michigan; Kenneth Eltis, University of Sydney, Australia; Corrine Glesne, University of Vermont; Lawrence Klein, Central Connecticut State University; Kevin Laws, University of Sydney, Australia; Nell Noddings, Stanford University; Glenn Pate, University of Arizona; Bonnie Rose, Riverside City Schools, California; Ron Rose, businessman, Riverside, California; Stephanie Shea, University of Washington; William Stanley, University of Delaware; Stan Talley, Middle Georgia College; Doris Terr, City Schools of New York; David Tyack, Stanford University; and Gerald Unks, University of North Carolina.

We further dedicate this effort to Megan, Jordan, Jonathan, Barbara, Mark, Steven, and others of the generation of students and teachers who are at the core of education into the twenty-first century.

Jack L. Nelson

Kenneth Carlson

Stuart B. Palonsky

CHAPTER ONE

Introduction: Unity and Diversity in Schooling

People are not bashful about noting school problems. Critics of schools are easy to find. But they disagree on what is wrong, who is responsible, and what should be done to correct the problems. Although there is significant diversity of opinion, there is some unity in the idea that schools need change. Criticism of schools and pushes for their reform seem to be constant activities in modern life.

Schools are a focus of public criticism and reform because attending school is among the most common of people's experiences and schools are the most public of institutions. Long periods of our lives are spent in schools, and they are a highly visible activity in both the smallest of communities and the largest of cities. In addition, the public has lofty expectations for schools, giving them wide and deep responsibilities. As a result, the school is seen as a source of both problems and solutions (Smith, 1995). Perceived problems include wasted tax money, as well as students with poor skills, low test scores, and rude behavior. Proposed solutions to social problems include such school programs as drug and sex education, moral training, and crime prevention. In sex education, for example, schools are the focus of heated, continued debate (Whitehead, 1994; Bernstein, 1995).

Education is among the most critical issues in society because it affects so many people, as well as society's future. Education, of course, actually occurs in many settings, including the family home, the workplace, religious institutions, the media, libraries, and friendships, in addition to school. Public and private schools, however, are the social establishments organized to provide formal education in modern nations, and involve nearly everyone at some time or another. Thus school is the focus of most disputes about education.

SCHOOL DISPUTES IN A POLITICAL CONTEXT

The harsh criticisms of schools and teachers that were evident during the 1980s have diminished. Claims in governmental and media reports that schools had put the nation at risk, were on a rising tide of mediocrity, and were responsible for declining American values and economic competitiveness made the 1980s very uncomfortable for educators (National Commission on Excellence in Education, 1983). More reasoned analyses of data indicate that the schools were not as bad as they had been portrayed to the public (Bracey, 1992, 1994, 1995; Berliner, 1993).

There is even evidence that a major government-sponsored study that showed that American schools were better than the Bush administration wanted to divulge was suppressed for two years (Tanner, 1993). Sandia National Laboratories, a widely respected research agency, was contracted in 1990 by the U.S. government to conduct a thorough study of American education (Carson, Huelskamp, and Woodall, 1992). The Sandia Report, submitted to the Department of Energy in 1991, showed that American schools were far better than the government and influential media had been reporting and that government-heralded school reforms were based on misinterpretations and misrepresentations of the data.

The main findings of the Sandia Report include the facts that: (1) scores on Scholastic Aptitude Tests (SATs) for comparable students have remained the same or have increased over time, but because many more students from the lower half of a class now take the test, the average score has declined as a result; (2) minority ethnic and racial groups have maintained or improved their SAT test scores since the late 1970s; (3) scores on National Assessment of Educational Progress tests have improved; (4) America has the highest rates of college enrollees in the world, and the highest percentage of women and minorities who receive degrees; although the numbers are larger, the average scores on the Graduate Record Exam have actually risen significantly; (5) high school dropout rates for all groups except Hispanics have decreased, and the Hispanic group includes a high proportion of immigrants who had dropped out of school before they came to the United States; (6) teacher beginning salaries, after adjustment for inflation, were essentially the same in 1990 as they were in the 1970s; and (7) school expenditures for all except special education students have not increased, in constant dollars, over two decades (Huelskamp, 1993; Tanner, 1993). Among its conclusions, the Sandia Report notes: "Much of the 'crisis' commentary today claims total system-wide failure in education. Our research shows that this is simply not true" (Carson, Huelskamp, and Woodall, 1992, p. 99).

Clearly, the findings and conclusions of the Sandia Report did not support the idea that American schools had suffered a significant decline, an idea fostered by U.S. government educational policy and prominently featured in the news media. In an apparent effort to change or suppress the Report, government agencies subjected it to extensive delays and revisions. These did not refute the major conclusion that the public schools were actually doing pretty well in educating American youth. Delays and revisions did, however, effectively suppress the Report from public view for over two years (Tanner, 1993, p. 292). The story of that government suppression placed it among the ten most censored stories of 1994 (Jensen, 1994).

Even with negative publicity about schools, survey evidence shows that the public rating of local public schools has actually been positive, and increasing, for over a quarter of a century. The twenty-sixth Annual Phi Delta Kappa/Gallup Poll (*Phi Delta Kappan,* 1994) showed a continuation from the 1993 Poll, which contained the largest one-year increase in the grades people give to their local public schools in over two decades. About 40 percent rated the schools A or B in 1992; almost 50 percent rated them that high by 1995. The ratings of local schools remain significantly higher than the ratings of schools across the nation (only 19 percent rating the nation's schools A or B, while almost 50 percent rate their local schools in the top two grades), continuing an interesting phenomenon in the Gallup data. When people rate the school that their oldest child attended, the rating is extremely high (over 70 percent rating it A or B). Gallup interpreted these data to suggest that the more the public knows about actual practices in schools, the better it rates them. The data also indicate that negative political and media treatment of schooling influences ratings of schools that people know least well.

The decreasing stridency in negative criticism of schools might suggest that school reforms in the past fifteen years have been successful, but that would be a misreading. No evidence about the reforms and their consequences is clear; they are still in dispute. Although there are many claims as to specific reforms, there are few comprehensive studies that show that schools are significantly better or worse now as a result of the 1980s reforms. Since recent evidence shows that the schools were never as bad as had been reported, one could make the case that some of the reforms hindered school progress by improperly blaming and alienating teachers and by forcing more testing and more government intervention in school requirements and operations.

The national Goals 2000 campaign and legislation press the schools to meet, by the year 2000, a strange mix of externally determined standards that are vague (students will come to school ready to learn) or unrealistic (American students will score highest in international mathematics tests). This reflects a political agenda based on unsupported assumptions that the schools have failed and government has to interfere (Clinchy, 1995; Resnick and Nolan, 1995). Goals 2000 does not meet the concerns of educational thinkers who propose a qualitatively different idea of progress for schools, one where caring, ethics, critical thinking, and creative imagination are worthy conditions for a liberal education (Noddings, 1995; Greene, 1995).

There are many arguments about the quality and value of shifts in schooling. These arguments are worthy of attention because they involve ideological, political, and personal interests. School reforms are subject to intense political pressures as politicians struggle to position themselves as saviors of education. It is not surprising that schools are the subject not only of public dispute, but also of partisan political interest. Schools are, among other things, both political agencies and handy targets for every side of party politics. Schools consume more local budget money than any other social agency, and are among the top consumers of state funds. Schools are a major responsibility under state legislation and local control, thus subjecting them to political pressures from those in office and from those who are candidates.

The national level has seen a rekindling of political interest in education since 1975. The Department of Education became a pulpit for strong views on schools when William Bennett was secretary, even though one of the goals of President Reagan's party was the abolition of the department. Presidential politics now include a strong focus on schools, and most candidates want to be the Education President.

Even though local schools are well received, schooling remains one of the most controversial topics in society. The evidence that schools are better than reported should not lead to complacency since schools always need good criticism and improvement, but the suppressed evidence about good schools should suggest some skepticism concerning news media reports and political statements about schools. The political nature of educational issues suggests the importance of schooling in contemporary society, as well as ideological differences over the direction of the society and its schools.

So it is not difficult to find an argument about schools. We share an interest in good schools, but we hold strongly felt, diverse views of what makes schools good or bad. These views are influenced by differing visions of the good society and how new generations should be prepared. Americans are reform-minded about all aspects of society and, as in our views of schools, we hold widely disparate views on what changes should be made. Historian David Tyack (1991), discussing the intertwining of school reform with social reform, says, "For over a century and a half, Americans have translated their cultural anxieties and hopes into demands for educational reform" (p. 1).

IDEOLOGICAL ROOTS OF SCHOOL CRITICISM

Schools are directly engaged in developing the society, and the individuals in that society, of the future. People care a great deal about what kind of individuals and society are to be developed. Apple (1990) states:

> The conflicts over what should be taught are sharp and deep. It is not "only" an educational issue, but one that is inherently ideological and political. (p. vii).

Ideologies are sets of beliefs that enable people to explain and justify a society they would prefer. An ideology includes assumptions about the nature and purpose of society and the related nature of individuals (Shils, 1968); it provides criteria against which one can judge human life and society (Lane, 1962); and it provides a means for self-identification (Erikson, 1960).

A set of beliefs that humans are essentially good, that society should provide expansive freedom and opportunity for individual development, and that individual creative energies should be encouraged provides criteria for the kind of schooling that is consistent with those beliefs. An opposing ideology might see individuals as naturally competitive and conniving, the purpose of society as exerting control over individuals and preserving order, and personal safety and well-being as dependent on obedience to authority—an entirely different view of schooling. Obviously, these are two among many ideological structures providing a basis for school criticism and reform.

Ideologies are basic rationales for divergent educational views to either sustain, alter, or overthrow the contemporary school (Christenson et al., 1971). Each ideology also provides grounds for unity around its beliefs. Thus, traditionalists share a general view that schools ought to follow time-honored ideas, practices, and authorities from a previous golden age of education. Progressivists share a different view—that schools must be flexible, child-centered, and contemporary. Radical educational ideologies from both the right and the left wing (e.g., liberationists, reconstructionists, abolitionists, and extreme elitists or egalitarians) provide their views of schooling, from advocating the abolition of public schools to espousing the use of the schools for social criticism and the overthrow of oppressors.

Divergent views of schooling and politics can be understood in terms of an ideological continuum: from elitist positions on the extreme right to egalitarian positions on the extreme left, with mainstream conservative and liberal positions in the center. Radical views are important to the disputes, since they present stark and clearly defined differences between egalitarian and elitist ideologies. But mainstream conservative and liberal ideas govern most reform movements because of their general popularity and their immense influence over the media and government. Liberals, conservatives, and radicals differ in their views of which mainstream position has the schools in its grip (Aronowitz and Giroux, 1993).

Plato, Dewey, and Counts: Three Positions

The importance of education in society is reflected in the controversies among divergent ideological positions. Plato, along with significant philosophers of every period, considered education one of the most important of social activities. Despite some ideas that were progressive for his time, Plato remains a prime example of the conservative ideology identified as traditionalism or essentialism in education. Traditionalism holds that there is essential or traditional knowledge that students must learn, that authority rests on tradition, that "wrong" ideas should be subject to censorship, and that the cultural heritage should be exalted. Interpretations of Plato's ideas have been used to justify school practices that Plato might not have actually supported. We doubt that Plato would have liked joyless schools run by stern teachers who do not permit deviation from the lesson, where rote memorization and recitation of useless information are the standard, and where such measures as SAT scores are used as prime indicators of learning. Traditionalists cannot be blamed for all bad school practices, but malformed traditionalist ideology can lead to dull and lifeless schools, repetitive drill, and memorization of trivial information to pass tests.

John Dewey, whose views provide an ideology on the liberal, progressive side, clearly recognized the power and importance of education in society. Dewey's *Democracy and Education* (1916) challenges Plato's concept of a fixed ideal for school and for society, arguing that society is dynamic and change dominant. Dewey argued strongly against Plato's idea that knowledge comes from outside the students' experiences and that students should only learn what previous generations learned. The Dewey view of learning entails reconstruction, where students are actively involved in learning, constantly reconstructing and reorganizing experience to gain a better understanding of life as it is happening. He made a case for individual differences and active participation in experiences and learning. Dewey, however, would not condone some things that go on in school under the label of progressive. We doubt that Dewey would support acquiescent teachers, chaos, and complete permissiveness in classrooms. Progressives, like traditionalists, cannot be blamed for all the ills in schools, but unthoughtful progressivist ideology can lead to lack of standards, free-form learning, and teacher irresponsibility.

George Counts extended Dewey's reconstructionism idea to a more radical view of schooling. Dewey used reconstructionism to refer to the reorganization of experience by students, but Counts argued that reconstructing the society should be the purpose of schools. Reconstructionists maintain that schools should criticize, change, and improve society, not merely reflect it (Counts, 1932; Brameld, 1956; Stanley, 1992). This view places schools at the center of social change, criticizing the evils in society and involving students in social action to correct, or reconstruct, society. Those who have power under the status quo are not likely to be enamored of reconstructionist ideas for schools. The radical elements in reconstructionism are obviously highly controversial. Reconstructionism developed some thoughtful advocates and remains an intriguing reform idea, but there have been few attempts at practicing these ideas in schools (Stanley, 1992).

Plato, Dewey, and Counts illustrate that wise thinkers can have thoughtful but divergent views on society and schools. Their conservative, liberal, and radical views are historic examples of divergent views of pervasive educational issues. Each of these views makes different assumptions about the nature of students, knowledge, and society. And each suggests a different kind of school, a different kind of teacher, a different society.

CONTEMPORARY CONSERVATIVE, LIBERAL, AND RADICAL VIEWS

Definitions of conservative and liberal may be slippery, but these terms are very commonly applied and widely understood to refer to divergent ideas and people of any period. Liberal ideas in one period may be seen as conservative in another, and vice versa. Neoconservative and neoliberal are more recent terms used to indicate a rethinking of conservative or liberal ideas. These are also loose terms (Steinfels, 1979; Rothenberg, 1984), but are in popular use to suggest modifications in diverse opinions.

Radical positions, from the right or left, offer highly divergent answers to pervasive educational issues. Radical critiques from the left and right wing influence the general debate by providing clear polarities that allow liberals and conservatives to take more popular positions in the center. Radical ideas tend to have limited credibility in mainstream discussions, but liberals and conservatives draw from those ideas in making reform proposals.

The Courage of a Conservative (1985), by the former and controversial Secretary of the Interior James Watt, is an example of a conservative view that argues that liberals and conservatives are in a moral battle for the life of the society and that schools are failing because they are controlled by the liberals. Watt claims that the failings include the abolition of moral teachings from the McGuffey *Eclectic Readers;* the substitution of the doctrine of evolution for that of creation; the elimination of school prayers; the insinuation of "humanism" into the school textbooks and curricula; the provision of sex education and contraceptives, which promote sexual promiscuity; and the teaching that abortion and homosexuality are acceptable (pp. 104–123).

In opposition to the conservative view, Henry Giroux and Paulo Freire (in Purpel, 1989) argue that the reform of public schooling is controlled by the right-wing conservatives. They submit that the right-wing agenda for schools is to hide basic social conflict, to return to a mythical past portrayed in such books as McGuffey's *Eclectic Readers,* to elevate elitist cultural uniformity, to impose a rigid view of authority and religion, and to reshape curricula in the interests of industrialists and big business.

There are deeper ideological roots of discord beyond the popular mainstream liberal–conservative dialogue. These include a variety of radical positions on what the society and its schools should be. Critical positions often are first expressed in the radical literature of a time, and then filter into the liberal and conservative rhetoric (Nelson, Carlson, and Linton, 1972). Those mainstream views sound much more reasonable at any point in history as bases for reform, but the radical ideas contain the seeds for longer-term and more significant change. In the age when kings were presumed to rule by divine right, democracy was a radical view. In a dictatorship, individual freedom is considered radical.

Radical right-wing ideas about schooling are not uniform; they come from different special interest groups. Some promote the teaching of fundamentalist religious dogma. Some seek to censor all teaching materials that deal with sex, socialism, atheism, or anything that they consider "anti-American." And some want to undercut public-supported schools in favor of elite schooling for a select group of students. Right-wing groups have attacked "secular humanism," feminism, abortion rights, sex education, global education, and values education in schools (Kaplan, 1994).

Members of the radical left wing also offer disparate views of school. Some see education as the way for the masses to uncover the evils of capitalism and the corporate state. Some advocate free schools where students may study whatever they want. And some propose education as the means for revolution, where all the institutions of society are subject to critique. Left-wing groups have attacked business-sponsored teaching materials, religious dogma in the public schools, and blind patriotic obedience teachings.

Conservative, liberal, and radical views of society and education provide different rationales for criticism of school and different proposals for reform. They are general frameworks that underlie individual and group discontent with school. We would like to include in this volume all viewpoints on each educational issue, but that is an obvious impossibility. We have limited the diverse presentations to ones that can illustrate the issue in the current society; some draw from liberal–progressive ideas, some from conservative–traditional ideas, and some from radical critiques. Additional references to conservative, liberal, and radical literature are included, and we encourage the exploration of those highly divergent views.

A TRADITION OF SCHOOL CRITICISM AND REFORM

Criticism and reform in education are not new phenomena. We have had advocates of educational reform for so long that it is impossible to identify when they began. Perhaps the first educational reformer, a member of a prehistoric group, rose up to protest that children in the group were not learning the basics the way he had. Or it could have been another member with a radical new plan to improve children's hunting and gathering skills. There are probably some bashed skulls lying about prehistoric sites, the results of arguments over education.

From the intensity and vigor of the public debate over schooling, a debate that has continued in western society at least since the time of Socrates, one would expect either dramatic changes in schools or their abolition in favor of an alternative structure. At least one critic has argued to abolish schools (Illich, 1971), and some have proposed very significant changes in schooling (Sinclair, 1924; Rafferty, 1968; Apple, 1990), but mostly the changes have been moderate and there have been no serious efforts at abolition.

In our written records, there is considerable evidence of efforts to use education to alter society and, thus, the recognition that divergent ideas about education can be very controversial. One of the two accusations leveled against Socrates in the indictment that brought him to trial, and to his death by hemlock, was "corruption of the young" through schooling. He may have paid the ultimate price for being an educational reformer in a political setting that was not ready for his reforms.

There are some school purposes that are commonly accepted, such as distributing knowledge and providing opportunity, but there are many controversies over what knowledge should be distributed, which children should get which opportunities, and who should be in charge of deciding. For more than 3,000 years, human societies have recognized the value of education—and have argued about what schooling should be and how to achieve it (Ulich, 1954). For some 300 years, Americans have agreed that education is among the most significant of social topics, but have engaged in arguments over what school should be.

Shifts in criticism and efforts at reform are common in American educational history (Cremin, 1961; Welter, 1962; Tyack, 1967; Karier, 1967; Katz, 1971), but the schools actually change only modestly. Traditional and progressive agendas differ, but the response of the schools to each seems to be to move very gradually in the direction proposed, with a few widely publicized examples of reform, and to await the next movement. Kaestle (1985) notes that the "real school system is more like a huge tanker going down the middle of a channel, rocking a bit from side to side as it attends to one slight current and then to another" (p. 423). Purpel (1989) considered the highly visible school reforms of the 1980s to be relatively inconsequential, a trivialization of the important educational issues of the time.

SCHOOL REFORM IN EARLY-TWENTIETH-CENTURY AMERICA

The United States has a long tradition of innovation in education, stemming from its pioneer role in providing popular education to large numbers of students at public expense. There are some major failures in this history, most notably in the lack of equal educational opportunities for African-Americans, native Americans, women, immigrants, and members of the lower classes. We have had, however, an expanding view of education as a major means for developing democracy and for offering some social mobility. We may not realize these ambitions, and the real intentions may be less altruistic (Katz, 1968), but the idealization of democratic reform through education is part of the traditional American rhetoric.

American schools, from the nineteenth century, were expected to blend immigrants into the American mainstream. This was to be accomplished by compulsory education with an emphasis on such subjects as English, American history, and civics. A history of racism, sexism, and ethnic prejudice was commonly ignored in American social life and schools, while we labored under the idea that everyone shared in the concept of a happy society made up of people who should all talk, think, and value in the same way. Schools were understood to be a primary social agency to meld students from divergent cultural backgrounds into the American ideal, which, not unsurprisingly, exhibited white, European, male characteristics and values. Standard use of the English language and belief in the superiority of western literature, history, politics, and economics dominated the schools. Schools were expected to be key institutions in "Americanizing" generations of immigrants.

In the early twentieth century, compulsory education laws became a primary reform agenda for schools, which were a part of a larger social reform movement. Urbanization and industrialization had created the need for different forms of school services. Large numbers of children from the working classes were now in schools in urban areas, and the traditional classical curriculum, teaching methods, and leisure-class approach to school were criticized by many.

Graham (1967) identifies the extensive development of vocational and technical courses as the most dominant change in schooling before World War I, with the broadening of the school's activities to include medical exams, health instruction, free lunch programs, open schools during vacation periods to accommodate working parents, and other community services. These reforms fit with the evolving sense of social progressivism.

The progressive education movement, from about 1920 to World War II, incorporated severe criticisms of traditional schooling ideas and practices. Those traditional practices included corporal punishment, rigid discipline, rote memorization and drill, stress on the classics regardless of student interests, and high failure rates.

Progressives offered a positive program that involved students in decisions of what was to be studied, in practical experiences and projects, and in community activities, and opened up the study of opposing opinions on controversial topics, established the practicing of democracy in the school, and organized the school as an embryonic society. Schools became more open to more students of all classes, and the curricula moved from more esoteric studies to courses with current social application, such as driver education, home economics, business and vocational education, current events, health, sociology, sex education, and consumer math.

There were sporadic and severe criticisms of progressive thought throughout that time, but a major reform movement from the right gained more public interest near the end of the Depression and again following the war. Graham (1967), summarizing the shift, states:

> Sometime between 1919 and 1955 the phrase "progressive education" shifted from a term of praise to one of opprobrium. To the American public of 1919, progressive education meant all that was good in education; thirty-five years later nearly all the ills in American education were blamed on it. (p. 145).

Gurney Chambers (1948) notes that after the stock market crash of 1929, education came under attack: "Teachers were rebuked for their complacency and inertia, and the schools, surprisingly enough, were blamed for the increasing crime and divorce rates and political corruption" (pp. 142–143).

RECENT CYCLES OF EDUCATIONAL REFORM

Attacks on the schools increased in intensity and frequency during the late 1940s and 1950s. The great school debates of this time involved many pervasive issues.

Church–state issues, including those of school prayer and the use of public funds for religious-school busing and other school services, were significant.

Racial issues, with the implications of the landmark Supreme Court decision in *Brown v. Board of Education of Topeka* (1954) and forced busing, were another focus of school controversy. Rapidly increasing tax burdens, to pay for new schools and teachers required by the baby boom, created many school critics. Rising expectations for education, exemplified by the thousands of "noncollege prep" veterans who went to college on the GI Bill, were applied to the lower schools. Curricular issues, including disputes over the most effective way to teach reading and the occasional story about test scores that showed students do not know enough history or math or science or English, filled the popular press. The McCarthy period, another "Red Scare," produced rampant public fear of a creeping communistic influence in American life, and created suspicions that schools were likely places for "communal" and progressive thought. These, and other factors, led to renewed criticism of schools. For many, there was simply a lingering sense that the schools were not doing their job.

Two books illustrate the criticisms: Albert Lynd's *Quackery in the Public Schools* (1950, p. 53) and Arthur Bestor's *Educational Wastelands* (1953). Each attacked progressive education, and the "educationists" who advocated it, for turning schools away from traditional discipline and subject knowledge toward "felt needs" of children. As historian Clarence Karier (1985) notes in his discussion of the impact of Bestor's book, "the educationist who spoke out for 'progressive education' and 'life adjustment education' appeared increasingly out of place in the postwar, cold war period" (p. 238).

Major foundations began to examine America's schools. The Ford Foundation stated that education had emerged as the focal point of its work. Grants were made to the Educational Testing Service to improve measures of student performance. The Carnegie Foundation asked James Bryant Conant, former president of Harvard and U.S. ambassador to West Germany, to conduct a series of studies of public education. There was much public criticism of academic failures of American schools. Then came the Soviet launch of *Sputnik* in 1957, ahead of the United States, and a new focus for educational reform. The *Sputnik* launch was a highly visible catalyst for conservative critics, illustrating a lack of American competitiveness they attributed to progressive reforms in schools during the pre-World War II period. They blamed the "permissive" atmosphere in schools for this deficiency.

Excellence and Discontents

This post-*Sputnik* reform included a reinstitution of rigor, discipline, traditional-subject teaching, and standards. That theme, to be repeated in the 1980s, was "excellence." In fact, there are some remarkable similarities in the language and rationales used in this reform movement and those used in current efforts to return the schools to traditional work. International competition, advancing technology, and the needs of business are rationales found in the literature of both periods.

Excellence, ill-defined and excessively used, is a main cue word that shows up in many reports and statements. John Gardner's prominent document for the Rockefeller Brothers Fund, *The Pursuit of Excellence: Education and the Future of America* (1958), is one illustration. Another term common to both periods is "mediocrity," a threat suggested in the title of Mortimer Smith's book *The Diminished Mind: A Study of Planned Mediocrity in Our Public Schools* (1954). The Conant Report, *The American High School Today* (1959), was a moderate book that proposed a standard secondary school curriculum, tracking by ability group, special courses for gifted students, improvements in English composition, better counseling, and other recommendations. It became a guide for many schools.

Federal funds for reform were dramatically increased. The National Defense Education Act (NDEA) responded to pleas that the schools are key to providing "national defense," and that *Sputnik* showed that the United States was vulnerable. Funds were provided to improve teaching in science and math, foreign languages, social studies, and English. These curricular projects were primarily devoted to having university scholars in the subject fields determine better ways for conveying the subject matter; and many projects attempted to make the curriculum "teacher-proof" (as in foolproof) to avoid having classroom teachers teach it incorrectly. Teacher education came in for its share of criticism, with blasts at the teachers' colleges, the progressive techniques advocated, and the quality of students going into teaching. All of this sounds hauntingly familiar to those who read current educational criticism.

As the public trend toward conservative educational ideas developed support and school practice turned back to standards and "rigor," criticism from the left began to emerge. This liberal criticism was a response to the rote memorization, excessive testing, lock-step schooling, and increased school dropout and failure rates that had begun to characterize schools. A number of writers, including Paul Goodman, George Dennison, Edgar Z. Friedenberg, A. S. Neill in England, Nat Hentoff, John Holt, Herbert Kohl, and Jonathan Kozol, attacked the schools for their sterility, bureaucracy, boredom, lack of creativity, rigidity, powerlessness of students and teachers, and inadequacy in educating disadvantaged youth. Holt (1964) stated:

> Most children in school fail. . . . They fail because they are afraid, bored, and confused . . . bored because the things they are given and told to do in school are so trivial, so dull, and make such limited and narrow demands on the wide spectrum of their intelligence, capabilities, and talents. . . . Schools should be a place where children learn what they want to know, instead of what we think they ought to know. (pp. xiii, xiv, 174).

This 1960s left-wing reform rebelled against conservative authoritarianism and the dehumanization of schools. Reforms included open education, nongraded schools, more student freedom, more electives, less reliance on standardized tests, abolition of dress codes and rigid rules, and more teacher–student equality. The Vietnam war and demonstrations provided the politics that stimulated much of the educational reform literature of the late 1960s.

Multicultural education was not on the educational agenda in early America because the main effort of school was to produce a melting pot in which various cultural strands were blended into the "new American." Consistent with ideas emerging from the 1950s and later civil rights movement, at a time of great social transition toward equality of opportunity for minorities, the melting-pot thesis about American society was judged to be a myth. This led to other approaches to the issue of diversity and unity in society and schools. One was the advocacy of separatism, where each major subcultural group would go its own way with separate social and school structures. Another was an effort to reconstitute a form of the melting-pot idea by integration in such institutions as housing, restaurants, and schools. Integration often led to resegregation through white flight and the establishment of private, all-white academies. Multicultural education, which aimed to recognize the positive contributions of a variety of national, racial, ethnic, gender, and other groups to American life, developed as a way to recognize both diversity and unity.

The effort was to correct a century of schooling that featured white male heroes who were Americans or Europeans from the middle and upper social classes. African-American, Hispanic, and female authors were added to the lists of standard readings in English classes. Contributions of native Americans, blacks, Chicanos, and women to American society were added to history and civics books. Equal physical education opportunities for boys and girls, compensatory education for the disadvantaged, and programs featuring minority and women role models developed.

Conservatism Revisited: The 1980s

In the early 1980s, reports of falling SAT scores, drug abuse, vandalism, and chaos in schools increased the public receptivity to reform. A nervousness about international competition, the resurgence of business and technology as dominant features of society, and questions about shifting morality and values provided a political setting in which the schools could be blamed for inadequacies. The presidentially appointed National Commission on Excellence in Education published a highly political document, *A Nation at Risk* (1983), that claimed that there was a "rising tide of mediocrity" in the schools. The ensuing public debate produced a flurry of legislation to develop "excellence" and raise the quality of schools. The key term, "excellence," suggests the competitive nature of schooling and the demand for increased standards.

Student protests of the 1960s had died and a negative reaction set in. Yuppies (young urban professionals) emerged as models for the dominant student style in the 1980s, featuring careerism and corporate fashion. There was an increasing perception of disarray in the American family, and a return to religion for many. The recurrence, under President Reagan, of open confrontation with communism subsided as the Iron Curtain collapsed in the late 1980s. Anticommunism, a major influence on conservative educational reform since the 1920s, seemed to be replaced by the drug war and character education. Schools not only are blamed for these strains in American life, but are expected to respond to them by becoming excellent.

Foundations and individual critics again undertook the study of schools and they published books. These include generally conservative reports from the Twentieth Century Fund (1983), College Entrance Examination Board (1983), and National Science Foundation (1983), as well as Mortimer Adler's *The Paideia Proposal* (1982). Also appearing were the more liberal works of John Goodlad, *A Place Called School* (1983), and a middle-ground book by Theodore Sizer, *Horace's Compromise* (1984). Ernest Boyer's moderate *High School* (1983) for the Carnegie Foundation was popular.

States pumped up school financing until the 1990s recession. State officials, having enacted myriad new regulations governing school matters, claim some credit for educational change (*Results in Education: 1990*, 1990; *The Education Reform Decade*, 1990; Webster and McMillin, 1991). In the main, jaw-boning by the federal government and increased regulatory activity in the states produced little in the way of dramatic change, but many adjustments have been made. Most of the underlying social problems, such as poverty, family disruption, discrimination, and economic imbalance, worsened during the 1980s, and schools are subject to the continuing effects. In the 1990s, the focus of educational criticism and reform has shifted from state regulation and test score worries to more diverse views of the national influence on schools, school choice, control of curricula, at-risk students, restructuring of schools to lead to more school-based management, teacher empowerment, parental involvement, interagency collaboration for community services, school district reorganization, and shared decision making. These ideas are potentially conflicting, some leading to increased centralization and others leading to increased decentralization. The core disputes of unity and diversity remain.

The idea of replacing the traditional canons of literature and social thought with modern multicultural material engendered other unity–diversity battles. Finn (1990a,b) and Ravitch (1990), high officials of the U.S. Education Department under former Secretary William Bennett, argue for teaching traditional content that emphasizes unified American views rather than diverse views of various segments of the society. The Organization of American Historians, however, supports the teaching of nonwestern culture and diversity in the schools (Winkler, 1991). Camille Paglia (1990), arguing against current feminist positions, states that her book "accepts the canonical western tradition and rejects the modernist idea that culture has collapsed into meaningless fragments" (p. xii). Unity and diversity in educational content were also in battle when Stanford University's faculty debated whether to substitute modern literature for traditional literature in its basic course, when New York State social studies curriculum revision stirred the New York governor to be "wary" (Safire, 1991), and when English-only resolutions passed in state legislatures.

Evaluation of the Reforms

There is general agreement that the results of the multiple reform efforts of the 1980s have been mixed. There is no clear evidence that the reforms have significantly changed educational practice. Analyses of the decade of well-publicized school reform show great diversity among viewpoints (Giroux, 1989; Finn, 1990b; Darling-Hammond, 1991; *U.S. News and World Report*, 1990; Fiske, 1991; Safire, 1991; Moynihan, 1991; *New York Times*, 1992). There are ideological chasms between the analysts in trying to explain why the reforms did not seem to work and what should now be done. Stories about drugs, shootings, and gang violence around schools compete with news articles stating that American students cannot read, are ignorant in math and science, and fail tests of common knowledge in history and geography (*Business Week*, 1990; Atkins, 1994; Hawley, 1990; Holt, 1989; Mandel, 1995; McEvoy, 1991: Novak, 1989; Sautter, 1995; Smith, 1995). The premise is that drastic changes need to be made in schooling.

One solution is to make school much tougher, requiring higher standards and expelling school deviants. More discipline, emphasis on basic skills, training in moral behavior, longer school days and school years, and nationally standardized curricula and testing are advocated to correct school problems.

From another view, schools are defective because they are too standardized, excessively competitive, and too factorylike. Students are measured and sorted in an assembly-line school atmosphere where social class, gender, and race determine which students get which treatments. Teachers are deprofessionalized, treated as servile workers. Critical thinking is punished; one kind of curriculum or classroom instruction fits all. Creativity and joy are excluded from the school lexicon because education is presumed to be hard, dreary, and boring work (Nathan, 1991; Fisher, 1991; Purpel, 1989). The need for drastic action to correct these defects is apparent. A proposed answer is to liberate schools, teachers, and students from the oppression of standardized tests, uncritical knowledge, and dehumanizing school operations. Making schools active, pleasant, student-oriented, and sensitive to social problems is the reform advocated.

Critics (Bastian et al., 1985; Giroux, 1988b; Presseisen, 1985) charge that the school reform movement of the 1980s was dominated by mainstream conservative thought. This conservative agenda included standardization, more testing, more rigor in school, a return to basics, more implanting of patriotic values, increased regulation of schools, more homework for students, fewer electives, less student freedom, renewed emphasis on dress codes and socially acceptable behavior for students and teachers, stricter discipline, and teacher accountability. The agenda enhanced changes already under way in schools in response to declining student test scores and a sense that respect for authority had been lost among the young.

Conservative reform of schools has been the main recent influence on schooling in America, but liberal and radical ideas have not been obliterated. Teacher empowerment, academic freedom, student rights, humane knowledge, and social participation are liberal ideas percolating in school reform to come. Reconstructionist ideas that place schools at the center of social change have not been entirely forgotten in the current surge of literature on schools and reform. William Stanley (1992) presents a rethinking of social reconstructionism and examines key ideas from the critical pedagogy movement in an intriguing book on educational possibilities for the twenty-first century. His focus is on practical reasoning that provides critical examination of social issues and stimulates social action toward social improvement. His book proposes a liberating role for schools in society, based on careful analysis of educational theory and practice.

Recent public arguments also include the topics of multicultural education and politically correct speech in schools (*National Review*, 1990; Kinsley, 1991; *Progressive*, 1991; D'Souza, 1991; Winkler, 1991; Strike, 1994; Banks, 1995). This conflict involves questions about knowledge and process. The interrelated questions are: Should the schools emphasize the positive influences of divergent minority cultures and women or traditional unifying themes from a traditional Eurocentric, white, male-dominated curriculum? And should we restrict racist, sexist, or other bigoted comments, or would that conflict with the right to free speech?

"Politically correct" speech, defined as speech that does not denigrate any minority group or gender or sexual preference, is attacked because it is equivalent to censorship, stifling free expression. The effort to make schools more civil places by controlling statements that could be offensive to some group was met by a storm of protest. Political correctness became a lightning-rod issue for schools at all levels as the 1980s passed. Protecting civil rights to free speech appeared to be at odds with protecting the civility of schools and protecting the "multiculturally diverse" from negative comments. The argument is that the free marketplace of ideas requires free speech, not courteous speech, and that the best response to epithets and slurs is reasoned argument and public disapproval. Although there are few who are open advocates of politically correct regulations in schools, there are many who would like to find a way to limit racist and sexist comments and graffiti.

There is no current shortage of school critics and reformers. They present a bewildering array of educational ideas, from left-wing to right-wing, moderate, and radical positions. Some want schools to emphasize classic, white, male, upper-class knowledge. Others would have schools focus on multicultural and contemporary ideas. Some would separate students into tracks and provide special treatment for academic students, whereas others want students of all abilities and talents mixed in classes. Some would allow students to determine much of their own education, whereas others would mandate substantial material for all to master. Some would target social problems that schooling should solve, whereas others would keep social problems out of school affairs. Some expect schools to emancipate students from oppressive aspects of society and economics, whereas others would have schools be training grounds for working in industry and developing national patriotism. New battles have arisen over "outcome-based education" and its potential for coddling youth (Manno, 1995).

Although polls continue to show general public support of local schools, most of us can identify one or more areas that need correction. Impatient or burned-out teachers, cloddish administrators, frazzled counselors, and outdated textbooks and curricula are examples. Most of us know the virtues, as well as the warts and blemishes, of schools from our direct personal experience. Some critics propose quick and simplistic reforms to improve schools. Fortunately, most people understand that change in schooling is more complex, and that the potential consequences of change need more thought.

Schools are controversial. Nearly everyone can find some fault with the way schools are organized and operated. Education, along with sex, religion, and politics, is one of the most debated topics in society. School, in fact, is the focus of much of the public debate over sex, religion, and politics. Sex education, religious study, and "anti-American" teaching materials are among the many controversial issues that swirl about schools. Should we distribute condoms and provide abortion-clinic information in schools, have sexually explicit films, examine issues of date rape and sexual abuse, or teach that homosexuality is a legitimate life-style? Should there be prayer in school, public financing of religious schools? Should we suspend students who refuse to salute the flag, censor school books that contain criticisms of America, require more patriotic exercises in schools? Should we change the canon of required literature to ensure that women and minority authors are represented, and require multicultural education?

Schools are seen by reformers either as the cause of some problem or as part of the cure. We are led to believe that schools are at fault when the Japanese economy is doing better than the American economy. We are also led to believe that schools can solve major social problems, such as racism, sexism, automobile accidents, AIDS, teenage pregnancy, and abuse of drugs.

Although there are few who advocate keeping schools exactly as they are, there are many who are relatively content with the way schools work and whose suggestions for change are very moderate. They may propose making a minor addition to the curriculum to enhance computer skills, increasing the time spent in school, cutting back on extracurricular activities, or assigning more homework for students. Modest though these proposals may be in their reform of education, they can be items of intense debate in communities and they represent another set of views of schools (Mandel, 1995). And some who accept the status quo believe that schools cannot change significantly because they are actually marginal institutions, with little power and no independence.

Among the conditions of human civilization is the tension between unifying and diverse ideas. We want to share a vision of the good life with others, and yet we recognize that human improvement depends on new ideas that may be in conflict with that vision. Unity provides a focus, but also complacency; diversity provides stimulation, but also dissension. Both comfort and discontent reside in unity or diversity. The tension between ideas of unity and diversity occurs in all parts of life, and it is most evident in such important matters as schooling.

DEMOCRATIC VITALITY AND EDUCATIONAL DIVERSITY

Criticism of schools is fully consistent with open democracy. Of all social institutions, the school should be the most ready for examination. Education rests on critical assessment and reassessment. That does not mean that all criticism is justified, or even useful. Some of it is simplistic, meanspirited, or wrong-headedly arrogant. But much of it is thoughtful and cogent. Although some criticism can be unjustifiably detrimental to education in a democracy, open debate can permit the best ideas to be revised and developed.

Over the long haul, schooling has been improved and civilization has been served by the debates over education. More people throughout the world now get more education of a better quality than did previous generations. Despite lapses and declines, the debates force reconsideration of schooling ideas and permit increased sophistication concerning schools and society.

Democratic vitality and educational criticism are good companions. Democracy, as Thomas Jefferson so wisely noted, requires an enlightened public and free dissent. Education is the primary means to enlightenment and to thoughtful dissent. It is to be expected that schooling would be among those fundamental social institutions subject to continuing public criticism in a society striving to improve democracy.

Dewey (1916) put school at the center of democracy:

> The devotion of democracy to education is a familiar fact. . . . Since a democratic society repudiates the principle of external authority, it must find a substitute in voluntary disposition and interest; these can only be created by education. (p. 87)

Bertrand Russell (1928) also noted that education is basic to democracy: "It is in itself desirable to be able to read and write, . . . an ignorant population is a disgrace to a civilized country, and . . . democracy is impossible without education" (p. 128).

Democratic vitality and educational criticism both require the open expression of diverse ideas, and both are based on an optimistic sense of unity of purpose. Diverse ideas and criticism provide necessary tests of the ideas we have. Criticism can easily appear to be negative, pessimistic, or cynical, but that is not its only form. Informed skepticism, the purpose of this book, offers a more optimistic view of criticism without becoming Pollyanna-like. Diverse ideas are sought because we think, optimistically, that things can be improved. Unity of purpose suggests that there is a bedrock of agreement on basic values, criteria against which to judge diverse ideas. Without diverse ideas, there is no vitality or opportunity for progress; without unity of purpose, diverse ideas can be chaotic and irrational.

However, diverse ideas combined with unity of purpose is an ideal that is not easily attained, and perhaps never will be. Diversity and unity are more commonly seen as contradictory. Some diverse ideas are too radical, too preposterous, or too challenging to deeply held beliefs for some people. Fundamental religions expect unity and do not accept diversity; criticism of religious dogma is considered heretical and sacrilegious. For those religions, just as for some people who believe they have the only truth, unity of belief is sacrosanct.

On the other hand, some question unity. One argument is that unity of purpose or values is a myth perpetuated by those in power to stay in power. Hard work, frugality, and acceptance of authority are seen as fictional values that are part of an effort by the powerful class to hide its oppressive actions and to maintain the social order and keep workers docile.

Another argument used against unity as a social requirement was made by Aldous Huxley in *Brave New World Revisited* (1958):

> The wish to impose order upon confusion, to bring harmony out of dissonance and unity out of multiplicity is a kind of intellectual instinct, a primary and fundamental urge of the mind [a Will to Order]. . . . It is in the social sphere, in the realm of politics and economics, that the Will to Order becomes really dangerous . . . [it] becomes the practical reduction of human diversity to subhuman uniformity, of freedom to servitude. . . . The beauty of tidiness is used as a justification for despotism. (pp. 22, 23)

Thus, diversity and unity can be seen as adversarial positions, bound to opposition. Those on the side of unity believe that diverse ideas can be censored, ignored, or disdained; those arguing for diversity consider unity to be a façade hiding the basic conflicts in society. It is also possible to understand diversity and unity as collateral positions, supporting and energizing. There is diverse opinion about the relation of diversity to unity.

It is this tension between diversity and unity, multiple views and common principles, that informs this book about schools. Among the current critical issues in education, those public and pervasive debates about the purposes and practices of schooling, are such matters as school choice, finance, racism, sexism, child welfare, privatization, curricula, business orientations, academic freedom, unionism, and testing. These issues reflect deeper social and political tensions between unity and diversity, liberty and equality, rights and responsibilities, consensus and conflict, individual and social development.

A Dialectic Approach

School is not only a subject of disputes, it is also the logical place for the thoughtful study of disputes. A setting where reasoned thought and open inquiry are advocated and practiced is most suitable for disputes about important issues. Important social issues are characterized by diverse opinions. Critical issues, those of the greatest significance, are subject to the most intense disputes. Indeed, debate is basic to the very definition of the word "issue." Critical issues deserve dialectical reasoning. A dialectical approach is a form of reasoning that involves disputes and divergent opinions in an attempt to arrive at a better idea. There are many complicated and twisting explanations of dialectical reasoning, and there is, as one might expect, philosophical dispute about what is dialectical and what is not. This is not a treatise on dialectics, and the subtle distinctions among forms of dialectical thinking are not our focus. We take a simpler and clearer approach, using the idea of a dialectic as a framework for a critical examination of issues.

A basic structure in dialectical reasoning is to pit one argument (thesis) against another (antithesis) to develop a synthesis that is superior to either. It is an inquiry into important issues that identifies the main points, important evidence, and logical arguments used by each of the proponents of at least two divergent views of the issue. A dialectical approach requires critical examination of evidence and argument from each side of a dispute, granting each some credibility in order to understand and criticize it. A dialectical approach is also dynamic; a synthesis from one level of reasoning can become a new thesis at a more sophisticated level, and the process of inquiry continues to spiral (Adler, 1927; Cooper, 1968; Rychlak, 1976).

Dialectical reasoning suggests a dialogue between competing ideas, not to defeat one and accept the other, but to find an improved idea. In this sense, a dialectical approach is optimistic—it assumes that there are better ideas to improve society and that examining diverse ideas is a productive way to develop them. Dialectical reasoning requires an openness to divergent views and a critical stance about evidence and argument. It also requires learning enough about each position to recognize the virtues and defects in each. Roth (1989) notes that dialectical study of educational issues can offer enlightenment for social improvement and support for reflective teachers.

We define dialectical reasoning as optimistic, dynamic, and disputational. As in any form of human discourse, dialectical reasoning does not necessarily lead to truth; it can merely repeat errors and bias. Thus, we also advocate a healthy skepticism in examining these disputes. Skepticism is not simply doubt, despair, or cynicism. In the ancient Greek tradition, it means to examine or to consider—it raises questions about reasons, evidence, and arguments. Without skepticism, we can easily fall into "complacent self-deception and dogmatism"; with it, we can "effectively advance the frontiers of inquiry and knowledge," applying it to "practical life, ethics, and politics" (Kurtz, 1992, p. 9).

We think dialectical reasoning, with prudent skepticism, is a thoughtful form of inquiry that should be applied to school issues. This book presents two differing views on each topic in each chapter. The views expressed are not always exactly opposing idealistic views, but they represent publicly expressed and divergent ideas about how schooling could be improved. Contrasting these views in terms of evidence presented and the logic of each argument offered can provide a realistic dialectic, affording an opportunity to examine issues in the way in which they arise in human discourse. You should note that divergent essays will sometimes use the same data or the same published works to make opposite cases, but will usually offer evidence from widely separate literatures. The search for improvement in society and in schooling is a unifying purpose; dialectical reasoning requires diversity.

The last years of the twentieth century and the first decade of the twenty-first may be placid for schools, another period of recuperation from the latest reforms. Even in placidity, however, educational issues are sure to arise, cause alarm, and enflame passions. Some of these will become elements of new school reforms; nearly all will be disputed.

References

Adler, M. (1927). *Dialectic*. New York: Harcourt, Brace.

Adler, M. (1982). *The Paideia Proposal*. New York: Macmillan.

Apple, M. (1990). *Ideology and Curriculum*, 2nd ed. London: Routledge & Kegan Paul.

———, and L. Weis, eds. (1983). *Ideology and Practice in Schooling*. Philadelphia: Temple University Press.

Atkins, A. (1994). "Violent Hallways." *Better Homes and Gardens*. **72**; 36+.

Aronowitz, S., and Giroux, H. (1993). *Education Under Siege: The Conservative, Liberal, and Radical Debate Over Schooling*, 2d ed. South Hadley, MA: Bergin & Garvey.

Banks, J. A. (1995). "The Historical Reconstruction of Knowledge About Race: Implications for Transformative Teaching." *Educational Researcher* **24**, 15–25.

Bastian, A., et al. (1985). *Choosing Equality: The Case for Democratic Schooling*. San Francisco: New World Foundation.

Berliner, D. (1993). "Mythology and the American System of Education." *Phi Delta Kappan* **74**, 632ff.

Bernstein, N. (1995). "Learning to Love." *Mother Jones*, Jan/Feb, pp. 44–49.

Besag, F., and Nelson, J. (1984). *The Foundations of Education: Stasis and Change*. New York: Random House.

Bestor, A. (1953). *Educational Wastelands*. Urbana: University of Illinois Press.

Boyer, E. (1983). *High School*. New York: Harper & Row.

Bracey, G. (1992). "The Second Bracey Report on the Condition of Public Education." *Phi Delta Kappan* **74**, 104–108ff.

——— (1994). "The Fourth Bracey Report on the Condition of Public Education." *Phi Delta Kappan* **76**, 115–127.

——— (1995). "Stedman's Myths Miss the Mark." *Educational Leadership* **52**, 75–78.

Brameld, T. (1956). *Toward a Reconstructed Philosophy of Education*. New York: Holt, Rinehart & Winston.

Brown, S. (1991). "Free Speech Undermined." *Civil Liberties* **373**, 1, 4.

Brown v. Board of Education of Topeka, Shawnee County, Kansas, et al. (1954). 74 Sup. Ct. 686.

Business Week. (1990). "Using Flash Cards and Grit to Defeat a Secret Shame." *Business Week*, July 16, pp. 22, 23.

Carson, C. C., Huelskamp, R. M., and Woodall, T. D. (1992). "Perspectives on Education in America," Final Draft. Albuquerque, NM: Sandia National Laboratories.

Chambers, G. (1948). "Educational Essentialism Thirty Years After." In *Secondary Education: Origins and Directions*. (1970), edited by R. Hahn and D. Bidna. New York: Macmillan.

Christenson, R. M., et al. (1971). *Ideologies and Modern Politics*. New York: Dodd, Mead.

Clinchy, B. Mc. (1995). "Goals 2000: The Student as Object." *Phi Delta Kappan* **76**, 383–385.

College Entrance Examination Board. (1983). *Academic Preparation for College*. New York: College Entrance Examination Board.

Conant, J. B. (1959). *The American High School Today*. New York: McGraw-Hill.

Cooper, D., Editor. (1967). *To Free a Generation: The Dialectics of Liberalism*. New York: Collier.

Counts, G. S. (1932). *Dare the Schools Build a New Social Order?* New York: John Day.

Cremin, L. (1961). *The Transformation of the School*. New York: Random House.

_____. (1965). *The Genius of American Education*. New York: Random House.

Darling-Hammond, L. (1991). "Achieving Our Goals: Superficial or Structural Reforms?" *Phi Delta Kappan* **72**, 286–295.

de Rugierro, G. (1959). *The History of European Liberalism*, translated by R. G. Collingwood. Boston: Beacon Press.

Dennison, G. (1969). *The Lives of Children*. New York: Random House.

Dewey, J. (1916). *Democracy and Education*. New York: Macmillan.

_____. (1933). *How We Think*. Boston: Heath.

D'Souza, D. (1991). *Illiberal Education: The Politics of Race and Sex on Campus*. New York: Free Press.

Elam, S. et al. (1994). "26th Annual PDK-Gallup Poll." *Phi Delta Kappan* **76**, 41–56.

Erikson, E. H. (1960). *Childhood and Society*. New York: Norton.

Finn, C. (1990a). "Why Can't Our Colleges Convey Our Diverse Culture's Unifying Themes?" *The Chronicle of Higher Education* **36**, 40, 1.

_____. (1990b). "The Biggest Reform of All." *Phi Delta Kappan* **71**, 584–593.

Fisher, E. (1991). "What Really Counts in Schools." *Educational Leadership* **48**, 10–15.

Fiske, E. B. (1991). *Smart Schools, Smart Kids*. New York: Simon & Schuster.

Freire, P. (1973). *Education for Critical Consciousness*. New York: Continuum.

Friedenberg, E. Z. (1965). *Coming of Age in America*. New York: Random House.

Gardner, J. (1958). *The Pursuit of Excellence: Education and the Future of America*. New York: Rockefeller Brothers Fund.

Giroux, H. (1988a). *Teachers as Intellectuals: Toward a Critical Pedagogy of Learning*. Granby, MA: Bergin & Garvey.

_____ (1988b). *Schooling and the Struggle for Public Life*. Granby, MA: Bergin & Garvey.

_____ (1989). "Rethinking Educational Reform in the Age of George Bush." *Phi Delta Kappan* **70**, 728–730.

Goodlad, J. I. (1983). *A Place Called School: Prospects for the Future*. New York: McGraw-Hill.

Goodman, P. (1964). *Compulsory Miseducation*. New York: Horizon Press.

Gouldner, A. (1970). *The Coming Crisis of Western Sociology*. New York: Basic Books.

Graham, P. A. (1967). *Progressive Education: From Arcady to Academe*. New York: Teachers College Press.

Greene, M. (1995). "Art and Imagination: Reclaiming the Sense of Possibility." *Phi Delta Kappan* **76**, 378–382.

Gurr, T. (1970). *Why Men Rebel*. Princeton, NJ: Princeton University Press.

Hawley, R. A. (1990). "The Bumpy Road to Drug-Free Schools." *Phi Delta Kappan* **72**, 310–314.

Hentoff, N. (1977). *Does Anybody Give a Damn?* New York: Knopf.

Holt, J. (1964). *How Children Fail*. New York: Pitman.

Holt, R. (1989). "Can We Make Our Schools Safe?" *NEA Today* **8**, 4–6.

Huelskamp, R. (1993). "Perspectives on Education in America." *Phi Delta Kappan* **74**, 717–720.

Huxley, A. (1958). *Brave New World Revisited*. New York: Harper & Row.

Illich, I. (1971). *Deschooling Society*. New York: Harper & Row.

Jensen, C. (1994). *Censored: The News That Didn't Make the News—and Why*. New York: Four Walls Eight Windows Press.

Johnson, C. (1966). *Revolutionary Change*. Boston: Little, Brown.

Kaestle, C. F. (1985). "Education Reform and the Swinging Pendulum." *Phi Delta Kappan* **66**, 410–415.

Kaplan, G. R. (1994). "Shotgun Wedding: Notes on Public Education's Encounter with the New Christian Right." *Phi Delta Kappan* **75,** K1–K12.

Karier, C. (1967). *Man, Society and Education.* Chicago: Scott, Foresman.

—— (1985). "Retrospective One." In A. Bestor, *Educational Wastelands,* 2d ed. Urbana: University of Illinois Press.

Katz, M. (1968). *The Irony of Early School Reform.* Cambridge, MA: Harvard University Press.

—— (1971). *Class, Bureaucracy, and Schools: The Illusion of Educational Change in America.* New York: Praeger.

Kerlinger, F. (1984). *Liberalism and Conservatism.* Hillsdale, NJ: Erlbaum.

Kinsley, M. (1991). "P.C.B.S." *The New Republic* **204,** 8, 9.

Kohl, H. (1967). *36 Children.* New York: New American Library.

Kohlberg, L. (1981). *The Meaning and Measurement of Moral Development.* Worcester, MA: Clark University Press.

——, and DeVries, R. (1987). *Child Psychology and Childhood Education.* New York: Longmans.

Kozol, J. (1967). *Death at an Early Age.* Boston: Houghton Mifflin.

Kristol, I. (1983). *Reflections of a Neoconservative.* New York: Basic Books.

Kurtz, P. (1992). *The New Skepticism.* Buffalo, NY: Prometheus Books.

Lane, R. E. (1962). *Political Ideology.* New York: The Free Press of Glencoe.

Lloyd, T. (1988). *In Defense of Liberalism.* Oxford: Blackwell.

Lynd, A. (1950). *Quackery in the Public Schools.* Boston: Little, Brown.

Mandel, M. et. al. (1995). "Will Schools Ever Get Better?" *Business Week,* Apr. 17, pp. 64–68.

Manno, B. (1995). "The New School Wars: Battles Over Outcome-Based Education." *Phi Delta Kappan.* **76,** 720–726.

McEvoy, A. (1991). "Combating Gang Activities in Schools." *Education Digest* **56,** 31–34.

McLaren, P. (1989). *Life in Schools.* New York: Longman.

Moynihan, D. P. (1991). "Educational Goals and Political Plans." *The Public Interest,* Winter, pp. 32–49.

Nathan, J. (1991). "Toward Educational Change and Economic Justice: An Interview with Herbert Kohl." *Phi Delta Kappan* **72,** 678–681.

National Commission on Excellence in Education. (1983). *A Nation at Risk.* Washington, DC: U.S. Government Printing Office.

National Review. (1990). "Academic Watch." *National Review* **42,** 18.

National Science Foundation. (1983). *Educating Americans for the 21st Century.* Washington, DC: National Science Foundation.

Neill, A. S. (1966). *Summerhill: A Radical Approach to Child Rearing.* New York: Hart.

Nelson, J. L., Carlson, K., and Linton, T. L. (1972). *Radical Ideas and the Schools.* New York: Holt, Rinehart & Winston.

New York Times. (1992). "Education Life," special supplement. *The New York Times,* Sect 4A, January 5, pp. 1ED–60ED.

Newsweek. **111,** 18–20.

Noddings, N. (1984a). *Awakening the Inner Eye: Intuition and Education.* New York: Teachers College Press.

—— (1984b). *Caring: A Feminine Approach to Ethics and Moral Education.* Berkeley: University of California Press.

—— (1995). "A Morally Defensible Mission for Schools in the 21st Century." *Phi Delta Kappan* **76,** 365–368.

Novak, M. (1989). "Scaring our Children." *Forbes* **144,** 167.

Paglia, C. (1990). *Sexual Personae*. New Haven, CT: Yale University Press.

Piaget, J. (1950). *The Psychology of Intelligence*. London: Routledge & Kegan Paul.

Plato. *The Works of Plato*, edited by Irwin Erdman. (1930). New York: Modern Library.

Presseisen, B. (1985). *Unlearned Lessons*. Philadelphia: Falmer Press.

Price, H. B. (1990). "The Bottom Line for School Reform." *Phi Delta Kappan* 72, 242–245.

Progressive. (1991). "The PC Monster." *The Progressive* 55, 9.

Purpel, D. (1989). *The Moral and Spiritual Crisis in Education: A Curriculum for Justice and Compassion in Education*. Granby, MA: Bergin & Garvey.

Rafferty, M. (1968). *Max Rafferty on Education*. New York: Devon Adair.

Ravitch, D. (1990). "Multiculturalism: E Pluribus Plures." *American Scholar* 59, 337–354.

Resnick, L., and Nolan, K. (1995). "Where in the World Are World Class Standards?" *Educational Leadership* 52, 6–11.

Results in Education: 1990. (1990). The Governors' Report on Education. Washington, DC: National Governors' Association.

Rickover, H. (1959). *Education and Freedom*. New York: Dutton.

Roth, R. A. (1989). "Preparing Reflective Practitioners." *Journal of Teacher Education* 40, 31–35.

Rothenberg, R. (1984). *The Neoliberals*. New York: Simon & Schuster.

Russell, B. (1928). *Sceptical Essays*. London: Allen & Unwin.

Rychlak, J. F., Editor. (1976). *Dialectic*. Basil, Switzerland: Karger.

Safire, W. (1991). "Abandon the Pony Express." *The New York Times*, April 25, pp. 140, A17.

Sautter, R. C. (1995). "Standing Up to Violence." *Phi Delta Kappan*. 76, K1–K12.

Shils, E. (1968). "The Concept of Ideology." in *The International Encyclopedia of the Social Sciences*, edited by D. Sills. New York: Free Press.

Sinclair, U. (1924). *The Goslings*. Pasadena, CA: Sinclair.

Sizer, T. (1984). *Horace's Compromise: The Dilemma of the American High School*. Boston: Houghton Mifflin.

Smelser, N. (1962). *Theory of Collective Behavior*. New York: Free Press.

Smith, F. (1995). "Let's Declare Education a Disaster and Get on With our Lives". *Phi Delta Kappan*. 76, 584–90.

Smith, M. (1954). *The Diminished Mind*. New York: Regnery.

Stanley, W. (1981). "Toward a Reconstruction of Social Education." *Theory and Research in Social Education* 9, 67–89.

_____ (1992). *Education for Utopia: Social Reconstructionism and Critical Pedagogy in the Postmodern Era*. Albany, NY: SUNY Press.

Steinfels, P. (1979). *The Neoconservatives*. New York: Simon & Schuster.

Sternberg, R. J. (1985). *Beyond I.Q.: A Triarchic Theory of Human Intelligence*. New York: Cambridge University Press.

Strike, K. (1994). "On the Construction of Public Speech." *Educational Theory* 44, 1–26.

Tanner, D. (1993). "A Nation Truly at Risk." *Phi Delta Kappan* 75, 288–297.

Tawney, R. H. (1964). *The Radical Tradition*. London: Allen & Unwin.

The Education Reform Decade. (1990). Policy Information Report. Princeton, NJ: Educational Testing Service.

Towns, E. L. (1974). *Have the Public Schools "Had It"?* New York: Nelson.

Twentieth Century Fund. (1983). *Making the Grade*. New York: Twentieth Century Fund.

Tyack, D. (1967). *Turning Points in American Educational History*. Waltham, MA: Blaisdell.

_____ (1991). "Public School Reform: Policy Talk and Institutional Practice." *American Journal of Education* 100, 1–19.

U.S. News and World Report. (1990). "The Keys to School Reform." *U.S. News and World Report*, February 26, pp. 108, 50ff.

Ulich, R. (1954). *Three Thousand Years of Educational Wisdom,* 2nd ed. Cambridge, MA: Harvard University Press.

Useem, M. (1975). *Protest Movements in America.* Indianapolis: Bobbs-Merrill.

Watt, J. (1985). *The Courage of a Conservative.* New York: Simon & Schuster.

Webster, W. E., & McMillin, J. D. (1991). "A Report on Calls for Secondary School Reform in the United States." *NASSP Bulletin* **75,** 77–83.

Welter, R. (1962). *Popular Education and Democratic Thought in America.* New York: Columbia University Press.

Whitehead, B. D. (1994). "The Failure of Sex Education." *The Atlantic Monthly* **274,** 55–80.

Winkler, K. (1991). "Organization of American Historians Backs Teaching of Non-Western Culture and Diversity in Schools." *The Chronicle of Higher Education* **37,** 5–8.

Part I

_____

What Interests Should Schools Serve?

Part I presents opposing viewpoints on the general theme of liberty versus equality.

You may think it strange to see these two values cast in competition with each other. After all, aren't they both basic American values? Liberty and equality were clarion calls of the American Revolution. The colonists felt that the British government was not treating them in a manner equal to that afforded its citizens in England, because it placed greater restraints on the colonists' liberty. Thus, liberty and equality are the values on which our nation was founded. The U.S. Constitution says that our government was formed to "promote the general Welfare, and secure the blessings of Liberty." Ask almost any American whether he or she believes in liberty and you will get a positive answer. Even children

like to remind each other that "it's a free country, isn't it?" Ask the same people whether they believe in equality, and you will get the same "of course" kind of answer. Better yet, ask yourself these questions.

The difficulty is that liberty and equality lie along the same continuum. At one end of the continuum is total liberty, and at the other, complete equality. Very few people wish to go all the way out on either of these limbs. They try to have it both ways by dancing back and forth from the center of the line.

Those whose steps take them more often toward the liberty (or right) end of the continuum are called "Republicans" or "conservatives" or "libertarians," in the order of their distance from the center, with libertarians being the most distant. Sometimes the people in these categories are identified with the generic label "right-wingers." Persons who incline more often to the equality (or left) side of the continuum are "Democrats" or "liberals" or "egalitarians," with the egalitarians being the farthest out. The generic label for these groups is "left-wingers."

Presidential elections are reminders of how skittish politicians can be about these terms, since most people pride themselves on their moderation and don't want to seem too far out in either direction. And the labels really are misleading, since most of us are an amalgam of conflicting urges: sometimes right-leaning, sometimes left, with a pendulumlike behavior depending on the particular issue or the context, or just the mood we are in at the moment. That explains why we can have such otherwise oxymoronic terms as "liberal Republican" and "conservative Democrat."

The reason why right- and left-wingers get into such bitter wrangles is that each wing believes that what it values is imperiled by the efforts of the other side to promote its own values. Right-wingers see liberty weakened with each increase in equality among Americans. That happens, in their view, because equality—even equality of opportunity—is produced by government actions that reduce our individual freedom and may hinder us from rising above the herd. Left-wingers, on the other hand, see equality—including equality of opportunity—as diminished when there is so much individual freedom that some people can rise up to exploit and oppress others. Fortunately, there are some values that right- and left-wingers hold in common, such as,

family stability and job opportunity. The disagreement is about whether the government is an effective agency for promoting the values (Kuttner, 1991).

Education is a good place to observe the liberty–equality battle. Education involves us all and has momentous consequences for our lives. Its pervasive influence commands the attention of both ends of the political spectrum. There is much at stake depending on whether education is made more equal for students of different backgrounds or whether it is left more to the varying fortunes of students' families. Because the stakes are so high, both the left and the right try to steer the government's education policies in their direction.

THE "LIBERTY" POSITION

In general, the right subscribes to the notion of the less government, the better. Parents should be free to find or develop the kind of education they want for their children. Parents can do this in cooperation with others who share their views, and most often they do so by living in communities with people who are like themselves. The government's role is to *allow* this to happen, to guarantee this freedom.

This position of the right in the matter of education is echoed in its attitude toward all the other areas of social policy. It fuels the centuries-old fervor about the extent to which government should interfere in people's lives to promote the welfare of the less fortunate. Those on the right argue that the government's attempts to help the disadvantaged do more harm than good to the very people who are supposed to benefit. The handouts these people receive, whether in the form of educational benefits or some other kind of benefit, sap initiative. As Irving Kristol (1978) puts it, "Dependency tends to corrupt and absolute dependency corrupts absolutely" (p. 242). Ira Glasser (1978), a liberal and the executive director of the American Civil Liberties Union, examined the process by which well-intentioned government officials end up imprisoning the people they had set out to help, and concluded: "Because their motives were benevolent, their ends good, and their purpose caring, *they assumed the posture of parents* toward the recipients of their largesse. . . . As a result, they infantilized those they intended to help, and denied them their rights" (p. 107). Charles Murray (1991, 1994a) argues that welfare benefits and the way they are apportioned cause lower-class women to stay single but still have children, and that this is the primary cause of family disintegration among America's poor. Lawrence Mead says that "no real progress in welfare is imaginable until government obligates needy adults to assume greater responsibility for their condition" (Mead, 1988, p. 52).

Moreover, the handouts the government provides do not materialize from thin air. They are pried from the pockets of hard-working, productive people, and that discourages these people in their industriousness. "The egalitarian seeks a collective equality, not of opportunity, but of *results*. He wishes to wrest the rewards away from those who have earned them and give them to those who have

not" (Simon, 1978, p. 200). It should be noted that one of the rewards that the right believes people in our society earn is the wherewithal to give their children a good education. If the children cannot benefit from their parents' effort, or can benefit no more than other people's children, a powerful work incentive has been taken from the parents.

Those on the right are therefore telling us of the signal advantage of inequality: that it makes us all work harder and realize ourselves more fully. When we do so, we not only help ourselves, but we automatically advance the whole of society. This is the "invisible hand" described by Adam Smith (1776/1976), the eighteenth-century Scottish economist.

> As every individual, therefore, endeavours as much as he can both to employ his capital in the support of domestic industry, and so to direct that industry that its produce may be of the greatest value; every individual necessarily labours to render the annual revenue of the society as great as he can. . . . He intends only his own gain, and he is in this, as in many other cases, led by an invisible hand to promote an end which was no part of his intention. (p. 477)

Mickey Kaus accepts the harsh reality behind this:

> You cannot decide to keep all the nice parts and get rid of all the nasty ones. You cannot have capitalism without "selfishness," or even "greed," because they are what make the system work. You can't have capitalism and material equality, because capitalism is constantly generating extremes

of inequality as some individuals strike it rich . . . while others fail and fall on hard times. (Quoted by Bluestone, 1994, p. 92)

Thus, each of us, by our own labors, helps those less fortunate simply by the sum we add to the *national* welfare. Those who help the most are the rich because they have money to invest in job-creating industries. George Gilder (1981) goes so far as to say that this is *the* function of the rich: "fostering opportunities for the classes below them in the continuing drama of the creation of wealth and progress" (p. 82). Indeed, Gilder asserts that in order for the poor to get richer, the rich must first get richer so they will have more to invest in opportunities for the poor (p. 86). This argument is too easily dismissed by do-gooders, says Milton Friedman, the foremost conservative economist of our time. The do-gooders prefer simple, emotional arguments for collectivism to subtle, rational ones for individualism (Friedman, 1994).

The subtle and rational argument was captured in a single paragraph written in 1835 by Alexis de Tocqueville, the French statesman and author famous for his insightful analyses of American society.

Any permanent, regular, administrative system whose aim will be to provide for the needs of the poor will breed more miseries than it can cure, will deprave the population that it wants to help and comfort, will in time reduce the rich to being no more than the tenant-farmers of the poor, will dry up the sources of savings, will stop the accumulation of capital, will retard the development of trade, will benumb human industry and activity, and will culminate in bringing about a violent revolution in the State, when the number of those who receive alms will have become as large as those who give it, and the indigent, no longer being able to take from the impoverished rich the means of providing for his needs, will find it easier to plunder them of all their property at one stroke than to ask for their help. (de Tocqueville, 1835/1968, p. 25)

This quote echoes a common concern of today's conservatives: that assistance to the poor becomes a bottomless sinkhole. The assistance is a magnet that attracts more and more people into dependency, and the level of assistance is never adequate to restore them to independence. A look at the price tags that liberals put on their pet programs can cause disbelief and alarm. The Committee for Economic Development (CED) calls for an annual outlay of $19.53 billion just for programs for poor kids under the age of 5 (*The Unfinished Agenda*, 1991). At that rate, the so-called peace dividend could be diverted entirely to the poor, with no investment in America's productive capacity, such as the infrastructure. If earlier investments in the poor had yielded better results, additional expenditures could be viewed as wise investments in human capital. Indeed, if the earlier investments had yielded better results, additional expenditures would not be necessary. The disappointing results may explain why the CED, in its 1994 report, has almost nothing to say about increased expenditures and much to say about effective management of existing resources (*Putting Learning First,* 1994).

Moreover, conservatives worry because additional expenditures are being demanded not just for children, but also for able-bodied adults who refuse to work. These are the passive poor who are content to watch while job opportunities are exploited by immigrants. The passive poor have been resistant to attempts to put them to work, and cutting them from the welfare rolls victimizes their hapless children. A way has to be found to make them assume the work ethic of their fellow citizens (Murray, 1991, 1994b).

THE "EQUALITY" POSITION

Those on the left do not want a hands-off government content merely to guarantee the freedom of the powerful. They demand a government that will guarantee that children everywhere have equally good schooling regardless of their parents' circumstances. This means taking power away from parents and giving it to the government, which is to act as a benevolent parent to all our children (Keniston and the Carnegie Council on Children, 1977, p. 204).

The purpose of government, as far as those on the left are concerned, was expressed eloquently by Abraham Lincoln in his first annual message to the Congress: "To lift artificial weights from all shoulders; to clear the paths of laudable pursuit; to afford all an unfettered start, and a fair chance in the race of life" (quoted in Grant Foundation Commission, 1988, p. 118).

This, of course, is a classic exhortation to equality of *opportunity.* As such, it invokes the approval of those on the right as well. However, those on the right disagree with those on the left about the extent to which equality of opportunity is synonymous with equality of *condition.* To those on the left, being poor means the same thing as having little opportunity. It means poor prenatal and neonatal care, poor early childhood development, poor homes, poor schools, and ultimately poor jobs or no jobs. Conversely, "the children of the rich [tend] to grow up rich and powerful far more often than mere talent or energy or morality could have guaranteed. . . . Power, privilege and prosperity [are] transmitted not only by the direct inheritance of wealth but also by the subtler route of acquired manners, learned skills, and influential friends" (Keniston and the Carnegie Council on Children, 1977, p. 40). "If we Americans wish children to reap the equality of opportunity that is so honored a goal of our society, we must address an issue that has, ironically, been obscured by our focus on equality of opportunity; we must attempt to create greater equality of social condition directly, not indirectly through children" (deLone, 1979, p. 25). In short, the distinction between opportunity and condition is not nearly as clear to those on the left as it is to those on the right.

Furthermore, the left sees governmental attempts to give the poor more opportunity by equalizing their condition to that of better-off people as being much too feeble. Ever since modern welfare reforms were begun in the sixteenth century, the purpose has been to keep the poor miserable enough that they would remain dependent on the niggardliness of employers to improve their condition beyond a subsistence level. "Efforts to shape relief arrangements so they would not intrude on market relations virtually define the history of social welfare. . . ." (Block et al., 1987, p. 12). Equal opportunity is not provided to the poor, but only continuing vulnerability to exploitation. That governmental relief is offered at all is to keep the poor from rioting, according to analysts on the left. Welfare is "a mechanism of social control, designed to pacify the poor and [serve] the interests of the business elite" (Block et al., 1987, p. 168). Moreover, there are two welfare systems: one for the poor and the other for the rich and the middle class. The first consists of such things as Aid to Families with Dependent Children (AFDC) and Food Stamps. It cost $117 billion in 1990. The second includes Social Security payments and tax breaks. It cost $1,265 billion (Huff, 1992, p. 38). Even the conservative columnist William Safire grants that the U.S. budget deficits "are being caused far less by helping the poor than by the aged and elderly of all incomes ripping off the young and middle aged" (Safire, 1995, p. A27). Barlett and Steele (1994) say that "America's most expensive social welfare program ever" was the "$200 billion in federal income tax money that Congress decided to return to the nation's most affluent individuals and families" between 1987 and 1994 (p. 17). Republican Senator William Cohen of Maine notes that the $90 billion spent on Aid to Families with Dependent Children in 1994 was less than the $100 billion in health care

fraud, where medical professionals were well represented among the cheats (Nelson, 1995).

Those on the left are not convinced that redistributing the wealth in America in such a way as to improve the living and educational conditions of the disadvantaged will backfire. They see the desperate situation of the poor as such social dynamite that more, not less, redistribution is imperative to defuse it. Naturally, they would like to see the redistribution schemes administered more wisely than in the past so that the intended beneficiaries do not suffer unintended consequences. The left also believes that equalizing the educational *conditions* of children from different social classes is a good public investment. "Our primary concern should be with the acute failure to provide a vast number of low-income and minority students with decent schools and skills" (Bastian et al., 1985, p. 117).

Finally, people on the left are not persuaded that the rich always invest their money in ways that benefit the rest of society. In recent years especially, tremendous wealth has been invested in stock speculation and corporate takeovers that have benefited rich insiders at the expense of everyone else (Bruck, 1988). How rich the insiders got is demonstrated by the fact that one brokerage house, Drexel Burnham Lambert, could afford to pay a $650 million fine for its confessed felonies (Cowan, 1992). That whopping amount was soon topped by a $700 million fine assessed against Prudential Securities for its Wall Street shenanigans (Eichenwald, 1994). About every six months, federal officials raise the estimate of how much it is going to cost the average taxpayer to bail out the savings and loan industry and honor the government's commitment to the above-average taxpayer who had insured deposits. Moreover, Americans have been made wise to the fact that the chief executive officers (CEOs) of corporations keep getting fatter compensation packages at a time when their employees are forced to take wage cuts or endure layoffs (Uchitelle, 1991). In 1992, "the total pay for the average CEO of a large U.S. corporation reached $3,494,296—a sizable 42% increase from the previous year" (Byrne and Hawkins, 1993, p. 57). Corporations try to conceal these exorbitant sums by not giving all of the money as salaries, but instead paying much of it in the form of bonuses and stock options (Hass and Nayyar, 1994). As Derek Bok, a former president of Harvard University and a labor economist, complains in his recent book, these extravagant levels of compensation are not tied to the CEOs' productivity but to an insider network of boards of directors whereby CEOs are on each other's boards and protect each other (Bok, 1994).

This is part of the generally widening gap between the rich and the rest of America. Since 1977, after-tax income has been dropping for the bottom 60 percent of the population, staying the same for the 60–80 percent bracket, and rising sharply for the top 20 percent (DeParle, 1991). Indeed, from 1977 to 1989, the pretax income of the top 20 percent increased by 29 percent, which was nothing compared with the 77 percent increase for the top 1 percent, but a lot more than the 9 percent *decrease*

for the people on the bottom (Nasar, 1992, p. A1). The wealth gap in the United States is wider than that of any other Western nation, making America the most economically stratified of industrialized nations (Bradsher, 1995). Kevin Phillips, a former Republican consultant, argues at book length that the *upward* redistribution of America's wealth was engineered by the policymakers in the Reagan administration. Reaganomics was a reduction of government services to the poor coupled with a reduction in taxes and regulations on the rich. It was *the* test of Gilder's theory that if the rich got richer, benefits would trickle down to the poor. The theory has not been proved by the facts (Phillips, 1990). That the situation has been worsening can be seen in statistics from the U.S. Bureau of the Census, which show the widest rich–poor gap since the Bureau began collecting this information in 1947. Top-fifth families now take in 44.6 percent of U.S. income compared with only 4.4 percent for the bottom fifth (Bernstein, 1994). The Census data reveal a large and increasing number of poor children, which grew by 1.1 million—to a total of 11.2 million—from 1980 to 1990. That's more than an 11 percent increase (*Child Poverty Up Nationally and in 33 States,* 1994). Of this number of children in poverty, more than half are less than six years old (*Young Children in Poverty,* 1995).

Perhaps the most significant difference between the right and the left lies in the matter of *psychological* needs. Karl Marx had always maintained that socialism could not come about until there was a technology of abundance to take care of our *material* needs. Such a technology was "an absolutely necessary practical precondition [of socialism], for without it one can only generalize *want*, and with such pressing needs, the struggle for necessities would begin again and all the old crap would come back again" (quoted in Harrington, 1973, p. 33). The United States now has a technology of abundance capable of satisfying everyone's basic material needs. The difficulty is that some people have a psychological need for more material goods than their neighbors have. This is often referred to as "conspicuous consumption," the practice of acquiring and flaunting material possessions. This psychological dynamic can be observed even in the kinds of schools that parents "purchase" for their children, and it is resistant to equalization efforts (Thurow, 1980, p. 198).

Of late it has become popular to talk about an emerging two-class society: those with education, technical skills, and good job opportunities; and those without any of these. Conservatives like Herrnstein and Murray (1994) are pessimistic about tempering this trend, but liberals like U.S. Secretary of Labor Robert Reich keep insisting that it is an imperative task of American education to prevent the development of a permanent underclass.

Let us now get a preliminary sense of how the theme of liberty versus equality is played out in the chapters of this section.

WELFARE

For this edition of *Critical Issues*, the authors decided to add a chapter on welfare. Many of the debates about schooling seem truncated when factors physically external to school buildings are ignored. Teachers are deeply aware of how much the conditions exogenous to the school control what goes on inside the building. While these conditions are heavily controlling of the educational process, educators do not have much control over the conditions. That is why the external environment of the schools is so often left out of the debates about education. Some people suggest that to introduce this factor is to make excuses for school failure.

Poverty is the most powerful of all the conditions that affect education. This point can be demonstrated easily when you consider that people preparing to be teachers pretty much know where they would like to teach and where they would not. The desirable and undesirable teaching sites are likely to be located on different sides of a wealth fault line. Good schools/bad schools mean rich communities/poor communities. It is the poverty in the home that wreaks the greatest havoc on attempts to educate in the schools.

A just and humane society tries to keep the disparities in wealth from becoming too extreme. Redistribution schemes are employed whereby those who have are taxed to support those who do not have. How much wealth should be transferred in this way is, of course, the nub of the great public policy debate on welfare.

But first it is necessary to understand that anyone whose personal wealth is enhanced by government action is a "welfare recipient" (Gordon, 1994a, p. 15). The phrase "welfare for the rich" is meant to denote all the government actions that serve to make the rich richer. These include *reductions* in the capital gains tax and in the tax rate for the highest tax brackets, as well as *deductions* for such things as the interest payments on a home and entertainment expenses related to one's business. They would also include government handouts in the form of Social Security payments and Medicare benefits to people who don't need them. The tax breaks are defended with the argument that they spur investment in the economy, thereby creating jobs for the poor. This is the "trickle-down theory." The handouts are defended on the basis that the receivers are only getting back what they paid in and so are entitled to it. The rebuttal to these arguments involves counting up the dollar value of the breaks and handouts and noting that it far exceeds the amount of welfare going to the poor. If a rich person can get so much help from the government, isn't it churlish for that person to complain about the paltry amount going to the poor?

This brings us to the most controversial of all the welfare plans: AFDC (Aid to Families with Dependent Children). What makes this program controversial is that the recipients are said to make virtually no contribution to the economy; they don't even hold jobs. And because they don't pay taxes, and may never have paid them, they are not getting back something they paid for. Moreover, unlike widows with young children, whose tragic circumstance people can sympathize with and wish the government to relieve, AFDC recipients are people whose dysfunction cannot be attributed to so devastating a trauma.

The questions that have been hassled over ever since the inception of AFDC in 1935 are: How much should the recipients be getting? How long should they get it? What should they have to do for it? How can they be weaned from this dependency? At its creation, AFDC was deliberately set up to be inadequate. The well-meaning, reform-minded women from a variety of charitable organizations of the period who designed AFDC did not want welfare mothers and their children to be independent of the need for male support at a time when the patriarchal family was the ideal (Gordon, 1994b). That rationale still permeates welfare policy.

What has made the questions more pressing is the increase in the number of names on the AFDC rolls, which is at an all-time high (Besharov and Fowler, 1993, p. 97). In New York State alone, there are 1.2 million people on AFDC, or about one in every twelve residents of the state. That is a 32 percent increase from 1989 to 1993 (Sack, 1994). New Jersey had a 25 percent increase from 1990 to 1994 ("Welfare Reform Won't Be Cheap," 1994). Nationwide, 4.8 million families, or 14 million people, were on AFDC in 1992, at a cost of $23 billion. The vast majority of these were single-parent families headed by women, meaning that about two-thirds of the AFDC recipients were children (Coughlin, 1994). The average amount received by a three-person AFDC family was $367 a month, well below the poverty level (Goodman, 1994).

By 1994, the cost of AFDC had risen to $34 billion, and the hard core of recipients was made up of teenage girls with children (Gibbs, 1994). The dollar cost is a number that can be used to stir alarm, but it should be noted that it is only 1 percent of annual government spending (Abramovitz and Piven, 1993). Moreover, by the end of 1994 the six-year increase in AFDC and Food stamps had finally leveled off (Pear, 1995b).

While welfare never goes away and the number of recipients predictably increases with each downturn in the economy, the costs have been contained in recent years either by a direct reduction in benefits in some states or by failing to adjust the benefits upward to keep pace with inflation (Dugger, 1994). The largest decline has been in Wisconsin, where the inflation-adjusted reduction was 30 percent between 1986 and 1994 (DeParle, 1994b). Officials in both the Bush and Clinton administrations have allowed states to do this as part of experimental programs. The states are now looked to for solutions, since the Family Support Act passed by Congress and signed by President Reagan in 1988 has failed to stem the rising tide of welfare cases. The act has provisions for job training and transition into jobs, but it has been funded at a level that allows only 20 percent of AFDC recipients to be covered by these provisions (Besharov and Fowler, 1993).

The paradox continues to be the public's demand for a reduction in welfare costs without the interim cost increase needed to bring about a long-term cut. President Clinton's welfare reform proposals call for short-term increases totaling billions of dollars, and creating millions of jobs (DeParle, 1994a). In addition, the Clinton plan puts a two-year lifetime limit on welfare benefits; provides for training and child care while a family is on welfare; requires recipients born after 1971 to join a work program, and eliminates benefits to those who do not; requires hospitals to establish the paternity of newborn babies; creates a national clearinghouse to track child support cases across state lines; denies occupational and drivers' licenses to fathers who fail to pay; allows states to deny additional benefits to women who bear children while on welfare; and provides $400 million in grants to schools and neighborhoods to discourage teenagers from having children (Jehl, 1994; Mink, 1994). In the spring of 1995 the Republican-controlled House of Representatives passed the Personal Responsibility Act, which (1) denies payments to unwed teen-age mothers and most legal immigrants, as well as additional children born to families already receiving AFDC, (2) cuts the amount for Food Stamps, and (3) gives governors more control by transmitting welfare funds to the states in block grants for states to spend as they think best (Pear, 1995a).

All of this has profound implications for education, and yet "public school leaders are curiously silent, or at best ineffective players, as the celebration over family and early-childhood initiatives grows louder. . . . The political hay accumulated by officeholders eager to look tough on welfare . . . may be the straw that breaks the back of America's preschool network" (Fuller and Holloway, 1994, p. 48).

CHOICE OR COMMON SCHOOLS

Chapter 3 presents arguments for and against allowing parents to pick the schools their children will attend. The traditional American pattern has been for a child to attend the school in his or her neighborhood. Where you live determines where you will be educated.

Giving parents choices beyond the traditional nonoption approach certainly enhances their liberty. The choices can be made possible in a variety of ways. Parents could have a choice among all the schools—public, private, and parochial—in a large geographic area, perhaps the size of a county. Or the choice could be limited to public schools, or still further to the public schools in an existing school district. Districts can create "magnet" or "theme" schools from which children and their parents can choose. Almost 90 percent of the large city districts in America now have magnet schools (Nathan, 1993). The choice might even be restricted to minischools within the same building, sometimes known as "schools-within-schools." A recent variation on these possibilities is the "charter" school—a public school that a group of parents and teachers or other interested people have been authorized to set up relatively free of the bureaucratic requirements for the other public schools in the area. If the local district itself is to be the authorizing body, it may be resistant to freeing anyone of its requirements. In Colorado, the state board of education had to order Denver to allow the establishment of a charter school (Stevens, 1994). A judge in Michigan has ruled that only the state board of education has the authority to charter schools (Walsh, 1994). The more limited the number and kinds of schools from which people can choose, the

less liberty there is, but limited-choice plans have the advantage of being more manageable administratively.

The administration of President Reagan gave rhetorical support to the idea of choice in education, but did nothing significant to bring this about. President-elect Bush, in the days before his inauguration, came out strongly in support of choice. He asserted that "choice has worked," and that he intended "to provide every feasible assistance to the states and districts interested in further experimentation with choice plans" (Weinraub, 1989, p. B28). After becoming president, Bush asked Congress to appropriate $100 million for magnet schools in order to increase parental choice of schools (Cohen, 1989). In 1986, the National Governors' Association (NGA) went on record in favor of choice within the public school sector (*Time for Results*, 1986, p. 13).

A leading member of the NGA at that time was Governor Clinton of Arkansas. As President Clinton, he still voices support for choice within the public school sector, but fostering it has not been a priority of his administration. The state that has gone the furthest in this regard is Minnesota, which allows interdistrict choice of schools for all students (*Choice in Public Education*, 1988).

Cities also can create choice plans. Milwaukee has a plan whereby 260 low-income children can attend private, nonreligious schools with state support of $2,500 each (Olson, 1991). Other cities have had choice plans for some time, and these provide for a choice among the "magnet" or theme schools, so that students can focus on their particular interests in schools that are centered on those interests. Even one of the community school districts in New York City— District 4, in the area commonly known as "Spanish Harlem"—has had a magnet school plan, with fifty-three different schools in twenty-two school buildings. These include a bilingual school, a music academy, an environmental science school, and a communication arts school (Fliegel, 1993; Kirp, 1992; Meier, 1991).

In Jersey City, the mayor has been fighting to have the state legislature permit a plan that will make public school students eligible for vouchers that can be used to pay tuition at the city's many private schools. The mayor sees this as triply beneficial: it will give students an opportunity to transfer out of the public schools, it will thereby relieve the pressure on the public schools, and it will reduce the cost of education to the taxpayers (Schundler, 1994).

All of this should suggest that "choice" is an idea that has taken firm root in education and will sprout lots of shoots over the next several years. This can be attributed to the way in which choice plans invoke the value of liberty. Their relation to the value of equality is not so clear-cut, however. Choice plans can increase equality, but they can also decrease it.

Equality is increased when people who previously had no choice are given some say about the school in which their children are to be educated. In this way, choice plans make these people more equal to those who can afford to send their children to private or parochial schools, or who can afford to live in communities that have good public schools. How equal these people have been made depends, of course, on how large a voucher they are given to pay the tuition at nonpublic schools. As Jonathan Kozol puts it:

> The advocates for vouchers nowadays pose the issue in a clever, but I think dishonest, manner. They say something like this: "The rich have always had the opportunity to send their kids to private school. Why shouldn't we give poor people the same opportunity?" But when you ask them what kind of vouchers they have in mind, the amount of money they propose varies from about $1,000 to at most the amount that is spent on an inner-city public school, maybe $5,000. None of them are suggesting the $10,000 or $15,000 voucher that it would take to send these kids to the prep schools the rich children attend. (Quoted by Kemper, 1993, pp. 25–26)

Kozol's opponents would obviously reply that this is still $1,000 or $5,000 more equality than the poor students had previously.

Equality is decreased if the particular choice plan gives the same amount of benefit to both the rich and the poor, thereby augmenting the advantage the rich already have. For example, if both rich and poor families are guaranteed a modest amount of government financial support to seek out schools to their liking, the rich can add this amount to what they already are spending on good private schools and get even better ones. The poor might only be able to afford the kind of schools they are getting under the present no-choice system. Voucher proposals like that of the Friedmans (1980), which would give the same amount to all families regardless of wealth, threaten to have this *disequalizing* effect. So, too, do tuition tax credit plans that grant all families the same tax credit for tuition they pay for their children's schooling. Only parents who can afford to pay tuition in the first place are eligible for the tax credit. Even more disequalizing would be a plan that allows parents a tax credit in the amount they actually pay for tuition, since the wealthiest people tend to send their children to the schools that charge the highest tuitions.

Choice that is disequalizing in this way was a major reason for the overwhelming defeat of the voucher proposal in Oregon in 1990, in Colorado in 1992, and in California in 1993. In California, for example, the proposal would have given a flat $2,600 to each student to spend on private school tuition, including to students who were already attending expensive private schools. Many voters viewed this as a $2,600 subsidy for the rich and a virtually useless pittance for the poor. Moreover, the $2,600 each private school student would receive would come out of money that would otherwise go to the public schools (Schorr, 1993).

Choice plans can also reduce equality if schools are allowed to refuse certain kinds of pupils. The "choice" in this situation is only that of trying to get into a desired school, and could result in finally having no choice left but the kind of school one had been attending previously. Former Secretary of Education Lamar Alexander said that private and religious schools were intended to be part of the Bush administration's choice plan, eligible for federal antipoverty funds, and that these schools could still deny children the opportunity to enroll (Pitsch, 1991; Shanker, 1991). Democrats, such as President Clinton, are generally unwilling to include private and parochial schools in publicly supported choice plans, or to allow "choice" schools many justifications for rejecting applicants. But even when a student does get into a desired school, he or she can be segregated into a *program* that is itself much like the old school. Some magnet schools segregate pupils according to ability, and the low-ability youngsters get less attractive programs (Moran, 1987).

Christopher Jencks and his colleagues at Harvard once designed a choice system that had safeguards against such inequalities (Jencks, 1970). For instance, poor families would get larger amounts of money than would rich ones; schools could not demand in tuition more than the amount of money a family received from the government; and schools would be limited in their latitude to refuse admission to applicants.

Ironically, the Jencks' kind of system provokes claims of another kind of inequality. If the poor are guaranteed as much choice as the rich, they have been given as much liberty as the rich. That means that the rich have lost in terms of *relative* equality. Their hard-earned wealth no longer entitles them to purchase greater liberty on behalf of their children than the poor can enjoy. By being made more equal to the poor, the rich are made less equal to their previous status.

Myron Lieberman (1994) has made an insightful comment on all of this, and it is worth keeping in mind for every chapter in this section.

For a century or more, two concepts of freedom have dominated political debate. One is that freedom consists of absence of government restraint. . . . The other understanding of freedom is that it consists of the power to do something. The first concept implies a minimal government and is the one most often embraced by conservatives. The latter concept is usually associated with activist and interventionist government. . . . This concept is very much in keeping with the philosophy of the left in the Democratic Party.

School choice has turned this political and intellectual line-up upside down. On this issue, it is conservatives who are asserting that the legal freedom to attend a private school is insufficient; government should provide "real freedom," that is, the same means that are available for the affluent. Meanwhile, liberals are insisting that the legal freedom to attend private schools is all that government should provide. . . . Whatever the political outcome, the philosophical winner is clearly Vilfredo Pareto, the Italian sociologist who observed that men find it easy to convert their interests into principles. (p. 34)

SCHOOL FINANCE EQUITY

The longstanding practice in America has been for the public schools to obtain their financial support from the communities in which they are located. The schools in Chicago are supported by the people of Chicago; the schools in suburban Winnetka,

Illinois, by the people in Winnetka. And the most common means the local residents have used to pay for their public schools is a tax on their property (Goertz et al., 1982, pp. 9, 44). In 1994, Michigan became a dramatic exception to this practice when its citizens voted to replace the historical reliance on property taxes with state sales and cigarette taxes (Celis, 1994). Since the sales tax is not as stable a source of revenue as the property tax, Michigan may have traded one set of problems for another. But it is too early to tell, so this edition of *Critical Issues in Education* will continue to focus on that almost universal form of school support, the local property tax.

Over time, this system of school finance has led to two kinds of disparities. The first is that people in poor communities who have low incomes (property tax is paid out of income) bear a heavier tax burden than do people in rich communities. A larger proportion of their income is spent on their property tax than is true for wealthier people. Since poor people don't have much income to begin with, this hits them especially hard. The second disparity is that even when poor people make the extra effort to support their schools, they come up with less money per pupil than do people in wealthier communities. The amount spent on each public school child in a poor community can be two or three times less than the amount spent per pupil in a wealthy community.

States have reduced these spending gaps by giving more aid to poor communities than to richer ones. For some poor communities, the state actually covers 75 percent or more of the school budget, since the local residents cannot afford to pay for more than a small portion. But even with all this state assistance, the poor communities still spend less on their students than do richer communities elsewhere in the state (Lefelt, 1988). And this continues to be true even after federal aid is added to the picture, belying the assumption of federal officials that the poor districts to which they are giving aid had some initial spending equality with rich districts (Taylor and Piche, 1991).

There are two further complications to this picture: educational overburden and municipal overburden. Educational overburden exists when a school has an unusually high number of students who require special services. These are students who are handicapped or disadvantaged in some way. City schools typically have educational overburden and suburban schools typically do not. Municipal overburden occurs when taxpayers have to support a lot of other public services in addition to the schools—such as police and fire departments, welfare offices, or housing authorities (Jordan and McKeown, 1980, p. 81; Levine and Havighurst, 1989, p. 302). Cities are much more likely to experience municipal overburden than are suburbs. What all this amounts to is the fact that cities in America, especially the large cities, have high educational costs but not good revenue bases. And even when states try to help, the children in poor communities get a less expensive education than do the children in rich communities.

The observable consequences of this situation in the cities are large class sizes, run-down buildings, beat-up and outdated textbooks, inexperienced and emergency-certificated teachers, and inadequate supplies and space all across the board. As scandalous as these conditions may sound at first, they beg a very basic question: How bad must things be before there is a legal obligation for the government to do something? How large a class size is too large? When is a beat-up textbook too beat-up? How inexperienced and unqualified is it permissible for teachers to be? When does inadequate become unacceptable? To put the questions another way, how identical must the schools of poor students be to those of rich students?

These questions have been brought before state and federal courts in a rash of litigation over the past two decades. The answers have been wide-ranging. Generally, the courts decline to deal with the questions in terms of specific school components. Judges do not feel competent to rule on such specifics as class size, textbook quality, and teacher qualifications. Moreover, the educational experts who appear before the courts contradict each other, and this leaves the judges even less inclined to get into these thickets. When they do, as Judge Skelly Wright did in *Hobson v. Hansen*, they have to withstand a barrage of criticism accusing them of going beyond their ability to comprehend the issues (Spring, 1988, pp. 161–166). Instead, the courts construe the issue in the simplest possible terms: dollars. That is, how equal is the amount of money spent per pupil in one school district to the amount spent in another district? Is the difference too large to be legally permissible?

The California Supreme Court ruled that the amount spent on a student could *not* be based on the wealth of the student's family or of the community in which the student lives. This meant that there had to be statewide equalization in California (*Serrano v. Priest*, 1971). It did not mean that the same amount had to be spent on every pupil, but only that the tax base from which education was funded had to be the same for all school districts. A district had some say about how much it wanted to draw on this base in the amount it was willing to tax itself. The New Jersey Supreme Court ruled that there did not have to be complete tax-base equalization, but rather a large reduction in the amount of the inequality (*Robinson v. Cahill*, 1973). Seventeen years after this ruling, the New Jersey court found it necessary to rehear the issues, since the gap between rich and poor districts had actually widened. It ruled that the amount spent per pupil in the thirty poorest districts had to be substantially equivalent to that being spent in the state's richest districts (*Abbott v. Burke*, 1990). The Georgia Supreme Court decided that the disparities in Georgia were not in violation of that state's constitution, so nothing had to be changed (*Thomas v. Stewart*, 1981). As of the spring of 1994, there were sixteen states in which the courts ruled against the funding systems and thirteen states where the funding system was upheld in state court, with the funding systems of eleven states still being challenged in court (Harp, 1994). Because the court decisions have been so divided among the states, no national pattern has developed. However, in those states where the funding formulas have been declared illegal, there is an emerging pattern to the court decisions. The decisions show a willingness on the part of the courts to define equity more broadly than in minimum dollar terms. Equity is coming to mean *equality* between the richest and poorest districts, as well as the *adequacy* of funding to provide a *quality* education (Verstegen, 1994).

In 1973, a case was brought before the U.S. Supreme Court on the basis of the U.S. Constitution. The Supreme Court ruled that the spending inequalities in the state of Texas did not violate the "equal protection" guarantee of the Fourteenth Amendment to the Constitution. This ruling obviously implied that such inequalities are constitutionally tolerable in other states as well, which is why the challenges to the inequalities are being brought in state courts under state constitutions. However, this did not mean that the justices of the U.S. Supreme Court approved of the inequalities, but only that they could find no justification in the Constitution for acting against them. Justice Potter Stewart wrote in his concurring opinion that the inequalities were "chaotic and unjust," but not illegal (*San Antonio Independent School District v. Rodriguez*, 1973). Since there was no Supreme Court ruling against the inequalities, each state, through its judicial and legislative branches, will continue to decide how much inequality it will permit. Texas itself has tried five different finance formulas in thirteen years, with the first four being rejected by the state supreme court and the fifth under challenge in the court as of this writing.

Even if a state decides that it will not tolerate differences in the taxable wealth available per pupil, it still has to decide whether it will allow the taxpayers in different communities to tax themselves so differently that one community raises a lot of money for its schools and another raises very little. In other words, states still have to decide how equal they want the *spending* to be. The state of Hawaii is one single school district, so it does not have this problem. A problem it does have in common with other states, however, is deciding how much additional money should be spent on students in each special category. For example, how much extra is needed for the education of a blind student, or a mentally retarded student, or a socially maladjusted student?

It is hoped that the foregoing overview of school finance issues has given you a good enough sense of them to see how the values of liberty and equality come into play. If complete liberty were to exist for each school district, the rich districts could raise large amounts of money and have lavish education programs. Poor districts might have the theoretical liberty to do this, but they would not have the practical liberty because they simply cannot raise much money from their limited resources.

> The shortage of funds in some districts actually minimizes local discretion in programming and in the ability to compete for the services of good teachers. School boards in poor districts cannot opt to institute special services when their budgets do not include adequate funds even for essentials. In this sense local control is illusory. It is control for the

wealthy, not for the poor. (*Robinson v. Cahill*, 1972, p. 64)

A state can increase the liberty of a poor school district by equalizing its resources up to the level of richer districts. The more it does of this, the more it will cost the state. That means that the state will have to collect tax money in rich communities and give it to poor communities. This brings equality to the poor at the expense of the rich. There is no other way. The rich can then claim correctly that the state has intruded on their liberty by confiscating their wealth, denying them the freedom to spend it as they see fit.

The major public policy question in school finance is: How much dollar liberty should be reserved for the rich and how much dollar equality should be conferred on the poor?

INTEGRATION: COMPULSORY OR VOLUNTARY

One of the truly epochal events in American judicial history was the 1954 decision of the U.S. Supreme Court in the case of *Brown v. the Board of Education of Topeka, Shawnee County, Kansas*. That decision began the long, turbulent, and still unfinished dismantling of racial segregation in America. It said that the government no longer could require that the education of blacks take place in schools separate from those of whites. Richard Kluger (1976), in his definitive history of the *Brown* decision, expressed its significance thus:

> At a moment when the country had just begun to sense the mag-

nitude of its global ideological conquest with Communist authoritarianism and was quick to measure its own worth in megaton power, the opinion of the Court said that the United States still stood for something more than material abundance, still moved to an inner spirit, however deeply it had been submerged by fear and envy and mindless hate. (p. 710)

Most of you who are now reading this are likely to have been born after 1954 and to have come of age after government segregation ceased to be taken for granted as part of the American way of life. Thus, it may be difficult for you to understand how the land of the free could ever have been officially racist. It may help to trace the judicial history of desegregation since 1954.

How determined people were to maintain a segregated society can be seen in the fact that there was not just one *Brown* decision. Rather, there was also what has come to be known as *"Brown II."* This decision was issued a year after the first one to direct local governments to eliminate their segregated schools "with all deliberate speed" (*Brown v. Board of Education*, 1955). There had been no speed after the first *Brown* decision, and the Court's vague exhortation hardly sped things up at all. The vast majority of black students in the south continued to attend all-black schools.

For thirteen years after *Brown II,* southern school districts found ways to continue segregation while appearing to be in compliance with the Court's directive. The most common way was to have "schools of choice,"

whereby black and white students were free to go to whatever school they wanted. Predictably, the black students stayed in their black schools and the white students in their white schools. In 1968, the Supreme Court declared that the time for "all deliberate speed" had run out (*Green v. County School Board of New Kent County*, 1968). Three years later, the Court began allowing lower federal courts to impose remedies to rid the south of segregation, and the most controversial remedy was forced busing (*Swann v. Charlotte-Mecklenburg Board of Education*, 1971).

After that, the Court turned its attention to northern school districts. It found that even though these systems had not been segregated explicitly by law, they had been so segregated through the deliberate actions of local officials (*Keyes v. School District No. 1, Denver, Colorado*, 1973).

The Supreme Court decision most directly related to the chapter you will be reading was issued in 1974. This decision said, in effect, that the suburbs of Detroit did not have to participate in a desegregation plan with the city of Detroit since it could not be shown that the racial segregation practiced within the Detroit city limits caused segregation throughout the whole metropolitan area. Detroit would have to desegregate its schools without the suburbs' being forced to help (*Milliken v. Bradley*, 1974). "The *Milliken* decision is surely the basic reason why Illinois, New York, Boston, Michigan, and New Jersey, each of which has a much lower share of African-American students than many Southern states, have been the most segregated states for black students for more than a decade" (Orfield,

1993, p. 2). "The goal of genuinely integrated schooling suffered a tragic setback in 1974 when the Supreme Court, in a case from Michigan, allowed the city line across which many whites had fled to set the boundaries of Detroit's efforts to desegregate its schools" ("Forty Years and Still Struggling," 1994, p. A22).

When Detroit and other northern cities tried to desegregate their schools, this provoked "white flight" to the suburbs, leaving the prospect of desegregating a system that had become mostly black. (White flight was inhibited in the south by the fact that many southern school districts are countywide, and include both a city and its suburbs.)

In several cases in the north, the lower federal courts found that an entire metropolitan region had, in fact, been segregated deliberately by state housing policies. The first such case was in the Wilmington, Delaware, area (*Evans v. Buchanan*, 1977). In these cases, the courts ordered plans for desegregation that involved both the cities and their suburbs.

One of the most bitter and protracted cases of court-ordered school desegregation took place in the cradle of American liberty, Boston. It pitted the working-class Irish, who were intent on preserving their ethnic enclaves in South Boston and Charlestown, against the blacks in Roxbury, who wanted schools that would give their children a chance to escape the ghetto. When the federal court tried to impose cross-neighborhood busing at the opening of school in 1974, years of violence began. Some children stayed out of school for as long as three years (Wilkinson, 1979, p. 208). There was even an

ironic sidelight: school officials from Boston traveled to Charlotte, North Carolina, for advice on how to handle racial integration. And now there is the melancholy postscript so common in these cases: *resegregation.* "A system that once had 85,000 students, 49 percent of them white, has about 64,000 students, 19 percent of whom are white" ("Boston Schools More Segregated," 1994, p. 18).

J. Harvie Wilkinson has traced five stages in the desegregation of America: absolute defiance, token compliance, modest integration, massive integration, and resegregation (Wilkinson, 1979, p. 78). We are well into the last stage now. The proportion of the minority population in large cities is growing daily, and many large cities are now overwhelmingly minority in population. The public schools of these cities are even more racially isolated than the cities themselves. In 1991, the Supreme Court gave a qualified endorsement to resegregation. It ruled that the Oklahoma City school district could discontinue busing, even though the discontinuance would mean a return to racially segregated neighborhood schools. The Court said this would be allowable if Oklahoma City had taken all "practicable" steps to eliminate the "vestiges" of past discrimination. The case was referred to a lower court for a finding of fact as to whether this condition was met (*Board of Education of Oklahoma City v. Dowell*, 1991). In 1992, the Court ruled in the Georgia case of *Freeman v. Pitts* that once a school district had made a good faith effort to comply with a desegregation order, it can be freed from further court control. If it has complied with only part of the order, it can still be released from court control over that aspect of its operations (*Freeman v. Pitts*, 1992). In 1993, the Supreme Court upheld a lower court ruling that the schools of Topeka, Kansas, still had not been desegregated. This was the school district at issue in the original *Brown* decision of 1954. That case was brought on behalf of a little schoolgirl, Linda Brown. She is now a 50-year-old grandmother (Turner, 1994). At this writing, the U.S. Supreme Court has just decided the Kansas City case. Improving the segregated schools of Kansas City so that they might attract white students from the suburbs and provide better education for all has cost $1.3 billion, most of which the Court ordered the state of Missouri to pay. The state then asked the Court to agree that it has done all it can to desegregate the Kansas City schools and make up for the past segregation. The Kansas City school officials argued that not all has been done until such time as the students' test scores have improved. The Court agreed with the state. (*Missouri v. Jenkins*, 1995).

The Supreme Court has also ruled on the matter of college segregation. Nineteen southern states historically had dual college systems, and while black students can now apply to the historically white colleges (and vice versa), the Court has said that more deliberate desegregation *and equalization* of these two sets of colleges must occur. State officials say they are not sure what it will take to satisfy the Court, and the black colleges worry that they might lose their identity altogether (Jaschik, 1992).

Even while resegregation is taking place in many cities, there are still attempts at desegregation elsewhere in the nation. In a very dramatic court case over school desegregation in the city of Yonkers, New York, the federal court for that jurisdiction ruled that Yonkers officials had enacted policies with the clear but unannounced intention of segregating both the schools and the housing of the city. Yonkers was ordered to desegregate its housing, as well as its schools. When the city officials refused to comply, the judge assessed fines that would soon have brought the city to bankruptcy, so instead brought years of foot-dragging compliance. The Yonkers crisis also had the school officials of a northern city going to the south for advice on successful integration (Foderaro, 1988).

In 1994, the Commonwealth Court of Pennsylvania ordered the desegregation of the Philadelphia schools. School officials contend that with 75 percent of the 191,000 students being black or Hispanic, desegregation is possible only if there is a metropolitan plan that includes suburban school districts. Since the case was brought under a state law and not the U.S. Constitution, the *Milliken* decision does not apply and the court could order desegregation across the entire metropolitan region (Hinds, 1994).

Once the court battles and the public tumult ended and integrated schools were established, scholars set about measuring the effects of the integration. Their main concern was with the consequences of integration for the children involved. How has it affected their academic performance? How has it affected their attitudes?

Unfortunately, the answers to these questions are not clear-cut or consistent. For example, Nancy St. John, in reviewing the relevant studies, found that the students whose academic performance was most enhanced by integration were the middle-class younger black students. She also found, however, that integration had a negative effect on the self-esteem and the aspirations of black students generally (St. John, 1975).

Laurence and Gifford Bradley reviewed twenty-nine desegregation studies and found that all of them had methodological weaknesses, limiting the faith that one could put in their findings. The better-designed studies were divided between those that showed improved academic performance for the black students and those that did not (Bradley and Bradley, 1977).

In a major study for the National Institute of Education, David Armor (1984) reached this conclusion:

> The very best studies available demonstrate no significant and consistent effects of desegregation on Black achievement. There is virtually no effect whatsoever for math achievement, and for reading achievement the very best that can be said is that only a handful of grade levels from the 19 best available studies show substantial positive effects, while the large majority of grade levels show small and inconsistent effects that average out to about 0. (See also Armor, 1995.)

An important statement on this question, signed by fifty-eight scholars, summarizes the research of the 1970s and 1980s. The conclusions are: (1) school desegregation can positively influence residential desegregation; (2) integration is associated with moderate academic gains for minority students and does no harm to

white students; (3) integration works best when the mechanism includes as many grades and as large a geographic area as possible, and when there are clearly defined goals; and (4) integration is most effective when linked to other types of educational reform (Coughlin, 1991).

The most recent analysis is the one that Wells and Crain (1994) did of studies of the long-term effects of school desegregation on the life chances of African-American students. As they conclude: "There is a strong possibility . . . that when occupational attainment is dependent on knowing the right people and being in the right place at the right time, school desegregation assists black students in gaining access to traditionally 'white' jobs" (p. 552).

One of the most interesting studies, in terms of attitude toward integration, was done by Leroy McCloud. He was the black principal of a black school in Englewood, New Jersey, when the Englewood schools were integrated in 1963, at which time he opposed the integration. In the late 1970s, he contacted his former pupils to assess the impact that integration had had on them and to learn their current opinions about integration. He hypothesized that both the impact and the opinions would be negative, given the turmoil and acrimony of the integration process. His findings clearly show the opposite to be true. His former students, who had since become young adults, overwhelmingly considered the integration experience to have been worth the pain and disruption that had marked its beginning. They said they felt that they were much better equipped to survive and thrive in a multiracial world than they would have been if their education had remained segregated (McCloud, 1980).

Those who believe that integration has positive effects for blacks, in terms either of academic gains or of improved attitudes, and either in the short term or over the long term, are willing to intrude on the liberty of its opponents to bring these benefits about. They are convinced that blacks deserve this equalization even if it has to be forced on an unwilling white community by court edict. To the extent that blacks themselves are reluctant to have their children integrated, the court edict can be seen as a violation of their liberty, too. People who see integration as necessary for a more just society believe that the advantages that black children would reap not only would make them more equal, but would give them resources to be used in the exercise of their liberty. Greater equality means greater liberty for those who are being equalized upward. Alas, one person's gain is another person's loss in a competitive society with a finite number of opportunities. This reality is what pits caring parents against each other in the matter of school integration.

AFFIRMATIVE ACTION

"Affirmative action" has become a highly charged term in the thirty-some years since its introduction. President Kennedy's 1961 Executive Order 10925 directed companies doing business with the government to take "affirmative action" to overcome racial, religious, and ethnic discrimination. Exactly what these federal contractors were expected to do was

not spelled out by the order, but it was clear that they were expected to do something positive and not just desist from discriminatory practices. As colleges, universities, and school districts receive significant amounts of federal money, they were included in Kennedy's order.

President Johnson's Executive Orders 11246 and 11375 were more explicit. Federal contractors were required to make attempts to recruit, hire, and promote minorities and women. Johnson believed that knocking down racial barriers was not enough. "You do not take a person who, for years, has been hobbled by chains and liberate him, bring him to the starting line of a race and then say, 'You are free to compete with all others' and still justly believe you have been completely fair" (as quoted by Mills, 1994, p. 7). But even Johnson's orders were not much more specific than Kennedy's. President Nixon ordered federal contractors to come up with goals stating the number of minorities and women who would be hired and giving deadlines by which the contractors expected to meet the goals. The government had authority to approve and monitor the goals and timetables. It was Nixon, then, who introduced the era of goals and good faith.

Terms such as "goals" and "good faith" raised skepticism among minorities and women. If a school district had goals and said it was really making a good faith effort to hire more minorities and women, but, in fact, it consistently fell short of its goals, suspicion arose that perhaps the district was playing a game. In this situation, the government's Equal Employment Opportunity Commission could charge the district with discrimination and take it to court. Major corporations, such as AT&T and the Bank of America, and Brown University were so charged, and they consented to hire more minorities and women.

This pressure from the government caused people to say that the goals had been turned into quotas. Once the government set an example with big fish like AT&T, Bank of America, and Brown University, everyone else knew the game was serious and became intent on avoiding a similar fate. The only way a company could guarantee that it would stay in the government's good graces was by meeting its own goals, and that made the goals the same as quotas. U.S. Attorney General Edward Levi acknowledged this when he stated that the goals were "said with great profoundness not to be the setting of quotas. But it is the setting of quotas . . . [even though] we will call quotas goals" ("In Job-Bias Test, Colleges Get Passing Grades," 1975, p. 73).

A danger seen by opponents of affirmative action is that in order to meet quotas, companies and government agencies will hire minorities and women even if they are not qualified to do the job. This will hurt the productivity of the enterprise and the American economy overall. Rather than going down this slope, the opponents urge us to rely instead on Title VII of the 1964 Civil Rights Act. This law forbids discrimination based on "race, color, sex, or national origin." A woman or a member of a minority group who believes that he or she was denied a job because of discrimination can take legal action against the employer. Title VII is designed to ensure that all *individuals* have equal opportunity; affirmative action calls for preferential treatment to ensure that *groups* who were historically denied equal opportunity will be brought into full economic and educational citizenship.

Affirmative action has led to some landmark Supreme Court decisions. The first was that of Allan Bakke. Bakke, a white man, was denied admission to the medical school at the University of California, Davis. He charged that he had a higher score on the Medical College Admissions Test than the sixteen minority students who were admitted. A deeply divided Supreme Court ruled that the medical school could not have a strict minority quota, but it could take an applicant's minority status into consideration (*Regents of the University of California v. Bakke,* 1978). Bakke had been excluded because of a minority quota, so the medical school was ordered to admit him. He is now a physician.

The second case was brought by Brian Weber, a white steelworker who was excluded from a company training program that would have upgraded his skills. He had more seniority than any of the black workers who got into the program. The Supreme Court ruled against Weber on the grounds that his situation was sufficiently different from that of Bakke as not to constitute illegal discrimination. The training program from which Weber was excluded had been established jointly by the United Steelworkers and Kaiser Aluminum Corporation for the specific purpose of allowing blacks to qualify for the skilled craft positions from which they traditionally had been barred.

Moreover, the Court said that Title VII did not prohibit "private employers and unions from voluntarily agreeing upon bona fide affirmative action plans" (*United Steelworkers of America v. Weber*, 1979).

In *Fullilove v. Klutznik* (1980), the Court ruled that Congress had acted properly in legislating that 10 percent of federal funds for public works projects had to be spent with minority-owned businesses. This is known as the minority set-aside program.

Ever since President Reagan succeeded in giving the Supreme Court a majority of conservative justices, there have been rulings against affirmative action plans. In *Richmond v. A. J. Crosson Co.* (1989), the Court decided that the city of Richmond, Virginia, had created its own minority set-aside program too broadly and without sufficient evidence that discrimination had existed prior to the program. In *Martin v. Wilks* (1989), the Court ruled that white firefighters in Birmingham, Alabama, could bring a case of reverse discrimination caused by an affirmative action plan that gave jobs and promotions to black firefighters. In the *Adarand Constructors v. Pena* case, the Court dealt another blow to affirmative action by ruling that Federal programs classifying people by race were presumably unconstitutional without a "compelling governmental interest" (Greenhouse, 1995).

Three major cases are being heard in the federal courts during the Clinton administration. In the first of these, *Taxman v. the Board of Education of Piscataway* (1993), the Clinton Justice Department actually reversed the position of the Bush Justice Department. The Bush officials agreed with Taxman that she had been wrongly dismissed as a teacher so that an African-American teacher with the same length of service could be kept on. The Clinton officials are arguing that the dismissal was justified on the grounds that it allowed the Piscataway high school business department to maintain racial diversity. The federal district court agreed with Taxman that she had been impermissibly dismissed.

The second case, *Hopwood v. Texas*, is against the University of Texas School of Law. The complaint is that the law school admitted African-American and Latino students whose Law School Admission Test (LSAT) scores were well below those of white applicants who were rejected. The federal district court has found that the law school did, indeed, violate the Fourteenth Amendment to the Constitution, which guarantees equal opportunity (Rossow and Parkinson, 1994).

The third case, *Podberesky v. the University of Maryland*, was brought by a white student who objected to the university's targeting some of its scholarships for black students only. The Supreme Court has upheld the federal appeals court in siding with the student plaintiff (Jaschik, 1995).

The three decisions together, plus the fact that the University of California system is considering the abolition of its affirmative action policy (Bernstein, 1995), suggest that affirmative action may be losing the allegiance in judicial and higher education circles that it once enjoyed.

All of the foregoing court cases illustrate the way in which the values of liberty and equality are involved in every affirmative action case. On the one hand, there is the liberty right of an employer or an educational institution to decide who comes through the door or gets promoted. On the other hand, there is the right of a minority or female applicant to equal opportunity. Affirmative action complicates the conflict between these rights even further because there is a third party involved: a white person, such as Bakke, Weber, Taxman, Hopwood, or Podberesky, who feels that his or her right to equal opportunity has been sacrificed so that society can make up for having denied this right to minorities in the past.

The complexity of affirmative action is reflected in Gallup poll results. When asked whether companies should be required to hire about the same proportion of blacks and other minorities as live in the surrounding community, the respondents were almost evenly divided, with 45 percent saying Yes and 50 percent saying No ("Racial Quotas in the Workplace," 1991). But when other respondents were asked whether women and minorities should be given preferential treatment in getting jobs and places in college, or whether their ability, as determined by test scores, should be the major consideration, only 10 percent favored preferential treatment, with 84 percent choosing ability. The latter results continue a trend that began in 1977 (Colasanto, 1989). The overall conclusion to be drawn from these disparate poll results is that Americans do not support the idea of racial proportionality in the workplace, but they are especially opposed to preferential treatment for either minorities or women. Unfortunately for race relations, such feelings of disapproval

are restricted to whites, 58 percent of whom decry racial preferences in hiring even when there has been past discrimination, whereas 66 percent of blacks think that preferential treatment is in order ("Views on Race: Progress Made, Needed," 1993).

Affirmative action cases are also good examples of the unintended consequences that can arise when the government attempts to right a wrong. Where two rights and three parties are involved, the government is in the unenviable position of trying to strike a balance among these several competing interests. Schools are one of the arenas in which this drama is frequently played out. The school setting adds an important new value to the struggle between liberty and equality: the value that cultural diversity has in the education of young people for a democracy.

References

Abbott v. Burke. (1990). Sup. Ct. N.J., Case A61, June 5.

Abramovitz, M., and Piven, F. (1993). "Scapegoating Women on Welfare." *The New York Times,* September 2, p. A23.

Armor, D. (1995). *Forced Justice.* New York: Oxford University Press.

———— (1984). *The Evidence on Desegregation and Black Achievement.* Washington, DC: National Institute of Education.

Barlett, D., and Steele, J. (1994). *America: Who Really Pays the Taxes.* New York: Simon & Schuster.

Barton, P., Coley, R., and Goertz, M. (1991). *The State of Inequality.* Princeton, NJ: Educational Testing Service.

Bastian, A., et al. (1985). *Choosing Equality: The Case for Democratic Schooling.* New York: New World Foundation.

Bernstein, A. (1994). "Inequality: How the Gap Between Rich and Poor Hurts the Economy." *Business Week,* August 15, pp. 78–83.

Bernstein, R. (1995). "Moves Under Way in California to Overturn Higher Education's Affirmative Action Policy." *The New York Times,* January 25, p. B7.

Besharov, D., and Fowler, A. (1993). "The End of Welfare as We Know It?" *The Public Interest,* No. 111, pp. 95–108.

Block, F. et al. (1987). *The Mean Season: The Attack on the Welfare State.* New York: Pantheon.

Bluestone, B. (1994). "The Inequality Express." *The American Prospect,* Winter, pp. 81–93.

Board of Education of Oklahoma City v. Dowell. (1991). 111 S. Ct. 630.

Bok, D. (1994). *The Cost of Talent: How Executives and Professionals Are Paid and How It Affects America.* New York: Free Press.

"Boston Schools More Segregated Than Before '74 Court Busing Order." (1994). *Newark Star-Ledger,* June 19, p. 18.

Bradley, L., and Bradley, G. (1977). "Academic Achievement of Black Students." *Review of Educational Research* **47,** 399–449.

Brown v. Board of Education of Topeka, Shawnee County, Kansas, et al. (1954). 74 Sup. Ct. 686.

Brown v. Board of Education. (1955). 349 U.S. 294.

Bruck, C. (1988). *The Predators' Ball.* New York: Simon & Schuster.

Celis, W. (1994). "Michigan Votes for Revolution in Financing Its Public Schools." *The New York Times,* March 17, pp. 1, 21.

Child Poverty Up Nationally and in 33 States. (1992). Washington, DC: Children's Defense Fund.

Choice in Public Education. (1988). New Brunswick, NJ: Eagleton Institute of Politics.

Cohen, D. (1994). "Making the Connection." *Education Week* **13**(31), 1–15.

Cohen, R. (1989). "Bush Details 7-Point Program for 'Educational Excellence.'" *Newark Star-Ledger,* April 6, pp. 1, 6.

Colasanto, D. (1989). "Public Wants Civil Rights Widened for Some Groups, Not for Others." *The Gallup Poll Monthly,* No. 291, pp. 13–22.

Coughlin, E. (1991). "Amid Challenges to Classic Remedies for Race Discrimination, Researchers Argue Merits of Mandatory School Desegregation." *The Chronicle of Higher Education* **38**(7), A9, A11.

_____(1994). "Experts Add Their Voice to Welfare-Reform Debate." *The Chronicle of Higher Education* **40**(48), A6–A7.

Cowan, A. (1992). "Milken to Pay $500 Million More in $1.3 Billion Drexel Settlement." *The New York Times,* February 18, pp. A1, D10.

deLone, R. H. (1979). *Small Futures: Children, Inequality, and the Limits of Liberal Reform.* New York: Harcourt Brace Jovanovich.

DeParle, J. (1994a). "Change in Welfare Is Likely to Need Big Jobs Program." *The New York Times,* January 30, pp. 1, 22.

_____(1994b). "Way Out Front on a Hot-Button Issue." *The New York Times,* October 20, p. A25.

_____(1991). "Richer Rich, Poorer Poor, and a Fatter Green Book." *The New York Times,* May 26, p. E2.

de Tocqueville, A. (1835/1968). "Memoir on Pauperism." In *Tocqueville and Beaumont on Social Reform,* edited by S. Drescher. New York: Harper Torchbooks.

Dugger, C. (1994). "Researchers Find a Diverse Face on the Poverty in New York City," *The New York Times,* August 30, pp. A1, B3.

Eichenwald, K. (1994). "Brokerage Firm Admits Crimes in Energy Deals." *The New York Times,* June 28, pp. A1, D15.

Evans v. Buchanan. (1977). 416 F. Supp. 328.

Fliegel, S. (1993). *Miracle in East Harlem.* New York: Time Books.

Foderaro, L. W. (1988). "In Yonkers, A Measured Integration of Schools." *The New York Times,* September 25, pp. 1, 42.

"Forty Years and Still Struggling." (1994). *The New York Times,* May 18, p. A22.

Freeman v. Pitts. (1992). Case No. 89-1290.

Friedman, M. (1994). "Once Again: Why Socialism Won't Work," *The New York Times,* August 13, p. 21.

Friedman, M., and Friedman, R. (1980). *Free to Choose.* New York: Harcourt Brace Jovanovich.

Fuller, B., and Holloway, S. (1994). "Why the Silence on Welfare Reform?" *Education Week* 14(4), 48, 40.

Fullilove v. Klutznik. (1980). 448 U.S. 448.

Gallup, A. M. (1986). "The 18th Annual Gallup Poll of the Public's Attitudes Toward the Public Schools." *The Gallup Report* 252, 11–26.

Gibbs, N. (1994). "The Vicious Cycle." *Time,* June 20, pp. 24–33.

Gilder, G. (1981). *Wealth and Poverty.* New York: Bantam.

Glasser, I. (1978). "Prisoners of Benevolence: Power vs. Liberty in the Welfare State." In *Doing Good: The Limits of Benevolence,* edited by W. Gaylin et al. New York: Pantheon.

Goertz, M., et al. (1982). *Plain Talk About School Finance.* Washington, DC: National Institute of Education.

Goodman, E. (1994). "Welfare Reform Will be Expensive, Even If It Works." *The Central New Jersey Home News,* April 24, p. C11.

Gordon, L. (1994a). "How We Got 'Welfare': A History of the Mistakes of the Past." *Social Justice* 21(1), 13–16.

———(1994b). *Pitied But Not Entitled.* New York: Free Press.

Grant Foundation Commission on Work, Family and Citizenship. (1988). *The Forgotten Half: Pathways to Success for America's Youth and Young Families.* Final Report. Washington, DC: Grant Commission.

Green v. County School Board of New Kent County. (1968). 391 U.S. 430.

Greenhouse, L. (1995). "Justices, 5 to 4, Cast Doubts on U.S. Programs That Give Preferences Based on Race." *The New York Times,* June 13, pp. A1, D25.

Gross, R., and Esty, J. (1994). "The Spirit of Concord." *Education Week* 14(5), 36, 44.

Hacker, A. (1992). *Two Nations: Black and White, Separate, Hostile, Unequal.* New York: C. Scribner.

Harp, L. (1994). "No Clear Trend Seen in Recent Finance Decisions." *Education Week* 13(32), 13, 16.

Harrington, M. (1973). *Socialism.* New York: Bantam.

Hass, N., and Nayyar, S. (1994). "Barbarians Break the Bank." *Newsweek,* May 2, p. 55.

Herrnstein, R., and Murray, C. (1994). *The Bell Curve.* New York: Free Press.

Hinds, M. (1994). "Schools Ordered to Desegregate in Philadelphia." *The New York Times,* February 5, p. 6.

Huff, D. (1992). "Upside-Down Welfare." *Public Welfare* 50(1), 36–47.

"In Job-Bias Test, Colleges Get Passing Grade." (1975). *U.S. News and World Report,* August 18, pp. 73–74.

Jaschik, S. (1992). "High-Court Ruling Transforms Battles Over Desegregation at Colleges in 19 States." *The Chronicle of Higher Education* 38(44), A16–A18.

———(1995). "'No' on Black Scholarships." *The Chronicle of Higher Education* 41(38), A25, A29.

Jehl, D. (1994). "President Offers Delayed Proposal to Redo Welfare." *The New York Times,* June 15, pp. A1, B7.

Jencks, C., et al. (1970). *Education Vouchers.* Cambridge, MA: Center for the Study of Public Policy.

Jordan, K. F., and McKeown, M. P. (1980). "Equity in Financing Public Elementary and Secondary Schools." In *School Finance Policies and Practices,* edited by J. W. Guthrie. Cambridge, MA: Ballinger.

Kemper, V. (1993). "Rebuilding the Schoolhouse." *Common Cause Magazine* **19**(1), 24–28.

Keniston, K., and the Carnegie Council on Children. (1977). *All Our Children: The American Family Under Pressure*. New York: Harcourt Brace Jovanovich.

Keyes v. School District No. 1, Denver, Colorado. (1973). 413 U.S. 189.

Kirp, D. (1992). "What School Choice Really Means." *The Atlantic Monthly*, November, pp. 119–132.

Kluger, R. (1976). *Simple Justice*. New York: Knopf.

Kristol, I. (1978). *Two Cheers for Capitalism*. New York: Basic Books.

Kuttner, R. (1991). "Notes From the Underground: Changing Theories About the 'Underclass.'" *Dissent*, Spring, pp. 212–217.

Lefelt, S. (1988). *Abbott v. Burke*. Initial Decision. Trenton, NJ: State of New Jersey Office of Administrative Law.

Lemann, N. (1991). *The Promised Land: The Great Black Migration and How It Changed America*. New York: Knopf.

Levine, D. U., and Havighurst, R. J. (1989). *Society and Education*. Boston: Allyn & Bacon.

Lieberman, M. (1994). "The School Choice Fiasco." *The Public Interest*, No. 114, pp. 17–34.

Martin v. Wilks. (1989). 490 U.S. 755.

McCloud, L. (1980). *The Effect of Racial Conflict in School Desegregation on the Academic Achievement and the Attitudes of Black Pupils in the Englewood Public Schools*. Doctoral dissertation, Rutgers University.

Mead, L. M. (1988). The new welfare debate. *Commentary* **85**, 44–52.

Meier, D. (1991). "Choice Can *Save* Public Education." *The Nation*, March 4, pp. 253, 266–271.

Miller, J. (1992). "Senate Rejects Private School Choice Proposal." *Education Week* **11**(19), 1, 26–27.

Milliken v. Bradley. (1974). 418 U.S. 717.

Mills, N. (1994). "Introduction: To Look Like America." In *Debating Affirmative Action*, edited by N. Mills. New York: Dell.

Mink, G. (1994). "Preface." *Social Justice* **21**(1), 2–3.

Missouri v. Jenkins. (1995). Case No. 93-1823.

Moran, B. (1987). *Inside a Gifted/Talented Magnet: An Analysis of the Enrollment and Curricular Patterns by Race and Gender in the Hillside School in Montclair, New Jersey*. Doctoral dissertation, Rutgers University.

Murray, C. (1994a). "Does Welfare Bring More Babies?" *The Public Interest*, No. 115, pp. 17–30.

_____(1994b). "What To Do about Welfare," *Commentary*, **98**(6), 26-34.

_____(1991). *Losing Ground: American Social Policy, 1950–1980*. New York: Basic Books.

Nasar, S. (1992). "The 1980's: A Very Good Time for the Very Rich." *The New York Times*, March 5, pp. A1, D24.

Nathan, J. (1993). "President Clinton, School Choice, and Education Reform in the 1990's." *Youth Policy* **14**(9), **15**(1), 6–10.

Nelson, L-E. (1995). "The Undeserving Poor." *The Newark Star-Ledger*, March 2, p. 19.

Olson, L. (1991). "Proposals for Private School Choice Reviving at All Levels of Government." *Education Week* 10(22), 1–10, 11.

Orfield, G. (1993). *The Growth of Segregation in American Schools: Changing Patterns of Separation and Poverty Since 1968*. Cambridge, MA: Report of the Harvard Project on School Desegregation to the National School Boards Association.

Paterson, J. T. (1986). *America's Struggle Against Poverty: 1900–1985*. Cambridge, MA: Harvard University Press.

Pear, R. (1995a). "G.O.P. Governors Urge Big Changes for Welfare Bill." *The New York Times*, April 13, pp. A1, B9.

_____(1995b). "Welfare and Food Stamp Rolls End Six Years of Increase." *The New York Times*, March 14, p. A18.

Phillips, K. (1990). *The Politics of Rich and Poor: Wealth and the American Electorate in the Reagan Aftermath.* New York: Random House.

Pitsch, M. (1991). "School-Choice Plan Could Endanger Entire Bush Proposal, Senators Warn." *Education Week* **10**(39), 31.

Putting Learning First (1994). Washington, DC: Committee for Economic Development.

"Racial Quotas in the Workplace." (1991). *The Gallup Poll Monthly,* No. 309, June, p. 35.

Regents of the University of California v. Bakke. (1978). 438 U.S. 265.

Richmond v. A. J. Crosson Co. (1989). 448 U.S. 469.

Robinson v. Cahill. (1972). Docket L-18704, Sup. Ct. of N.J., Hudson County.

Robinson v. Cahill. (1973). 62 N.J. 473, 303 A.2d 273.

Rossow, L., and Parkinson, J. (1994). "Introduction and Comment." *School Law Reporter* **36**(10), 1–2

Sack, K. (1994). "New York Shifting Focus of Welfare to Job Placement." *The New York Times,* May 21, pp. 1, 26.

Safire, W. (1995). "The Newt Deal." *The New York Times,* January 5, p. A27.

St. John, N. (1975). *School Desegregation: Outcomes for Children.* New York: Wiley.

San Antonio Independent School District v. Rodriguez. (1973). 411 U.S. 1.

Schorr, J. (1993). "California's Experiment on Your Schools." *The New York Times,* October 30, p. 21.

Schundler, B. (1994). *The Jersey City "Schoolchildren First" Education Act.* Jersey City, NJ: Save Our Schoolchildren.

Serrano v. Priest (1971). 96 Cal. Rptr. 601, 437 P.2d 1241.

Shanker, A. (1991). "Private Is Public." *The New York Times,* December 1, p. E7.

Simon, W. E. (1978). *A Time for Truth.* New York: McGraw-Hill.

Smith, A. (1776/1976). *The Wealth of Nations.* Edited by Edwin Cannan.

Chicago: University of Chicago Press.

Snider, W. (1988). "In Chicago, Implications of Reform Bill Please the Grassroots, Dismay Others." *Education Week* **8,** 6.

Spring, J. (1988). *Conflict of Interests: The Politics of American Education.* New York: Longman.

Stevens, M. (1994). "State Orders DPS to OK Charter Plan." *The Denver Post,* July 19, pp. 1, 8.

Swann v. Charlotte-Mecklenburg Board of Education. (1971). 402 U.S. 1.

Taxman v. Board of Education of Piscataway. (1993). 832 F.Supp. 836 (D.N.J).

Taylor, W., and Piche, D. (1991). "Fiscal Equity and National Goals." *Education Week* **10**(26), 26.

"The Threat to Welfare Reform." *The New York Times,* editorial, May 2, p. A16.

The Unfinished Agenda: A New Vision for Child Development and Education. (1991). Washington, DC: Committee for Economic Development.

Thomas v. Stewart (1981) No. 8275 (Ga. Super., Polk County).

Thurow, L. C. (1980). *The Zero-Sum Society: Distribution and the Possibilities for Economic Change.* New York: Basic Books.

Time for Results: The Governors 1991 Report on Education. (1986). Washington, DC: National Governors' Association.

Turner, R. (1994). "Round Two in Topeka." *Emerge,* May, p. 34.

Uchitelle, L. (1991). "No Recession for Executive Pay." *The New York Times,* March 18, pp. D1, D10.

United Steelworkers of America v. Weber. (1979). 443 U.S. 193.

Verstegen, D. (1994). "The New Wave of School Finance Litigation." *Phi Delta Kappan* **76**(3), 243–250.

"Views on Race: Progress Made, Needed." (1993). *The New York Times,* April 4, p. 16.

Walsh, M. (1994). "Charter Ruling Sends Schools in Mich. Reeling." *Education Week* **14**(13), 1, 16.

_____(1995). "Court Hears Arguments in K.C. Case." *Education Week* **14**(17), 1, 19.

Weinraub, B. (1989). "Bush Wooing Educators, Urges Choice in Schools." *The New York Times*, January 11, p. B28.

"Welfare Reform Proves Sluggish." (1992). *The New York Times*, April 4, p. 22.

"Welfare Reform Won't Be Cheap." (1994). *The Central New Jersey Home News*, February 1, p. A6.

Wells, A., and Crain, R. (1994). "Perpetuation Theory and the Long-Term Effects of School Desegregation." *Review of Educational Research* **64**(4), 531–555.

Wilkinson, J. H. (1979). *From Brown to Bakke: The Supreme Court and School Integration, 1954–1978.* New York: Oxford University Press.

Wilson, W. J. (1987). *The Truly Disadvantaged: The Inner City, the Underclass, and Public Policy.* Chicago: University of Chicago Press.

Young Children in Poverty: A Statistical Update. (1995). New York: National Center for Children in Poverty.

CHAPTER TWO

Welfare: Safety Net or Free Lunch

POSITION 1: FOR MORE WELFARE

Giving Schools a Fair Chance

There is a popular magazine in New Jersey called *New Jersey Monthly.* Annually, at the start of the school year, this magazine publishes a report on the best public high schools in the state. The schools are selected on the basis of such "objective" indicators as SAT scores and college-going rates. (Your state may have such a magazine that does the same thing.)

When New Jersey's college students are asked to guess which high schools made the list, they do a good job. They may not be able to name the specific schools, but they know that the "best" high schools are in the "best" towns, that is, the richest. You can be sure that the officials of these schools take a lot of pride in having their schools make the list. But even they are willing to admit privately that the pride is somewhat unwarranted. The list, after all, is really one showing the schools with the "best" *students,* and only indirectly and indeterminately is it a list of the best schools.

Officials at the schools that do not come close to making the list are quick to point out that the indicators of school quality are really indicators of pupil quality. These officials can easily convince themselves that, given the kinds of pupils with whom they have to work, they do a high-quality job. They intimate that if they were working in one of the "best" schools, they would be able to achieve even better results than those the incumbent officials boast about.

The real cause of school success (or failure) is the kinds of kids in attendance. Unfortunately, most people persist in praising (or blaming) the schools, just as most people lay responsibility for changes in the economy solely at the feet of whichever politicians happen to be in power at the moment. The praise and the blame are both largely misplaced if student quality is not taken into consideration. If a good way could be found to adjust for student quality, the conclusion might be that the "best" schools are those serving the state's poorest students.

A much better way to make the competition among schools less unfair is to make the gap among the students less wide. Narrowing the gap means dealing with the conditions with which so many students have to contend: hunger; substandard housing; residential transiency; lack of medical, dental, and vision care; unemployment of parents; single-parent households; absence of an adult caregiver for long periods each day.

These are conditions over which schools typically do not have control, so other government agencies have to become involved. Consider, for example, the danger of raising babies in a dwelling with peeling, lead-based paint. Exposure to this paint is linked to neurobiological disabilities in children, such as hyperactivity and depressed cognitive functioning. Slum landlords are reluctant to incur the costs of removing the paint, and cities have limited resources to monitor the problem and enforce compliance with clean-up laws (Brady, 1995; Purdy, 1994). Schools have nothing to do with this situation, but they get the damaged children in their classrooms.

This is only one of the many kinds of child dangers that result from poverty. Indeed, a recent study done at the University of Michigan found that "family income is a 'far more powerful' determinant of I.Q. at age 5 than whether a child lives with a single parent or how well educated the mother is" (Cohen, 1993, p. 4). The director of the study thinks that an increase in welfare benefits would be a wise *educational* investment.

Keep in mind that we are talking only about the basic conditions of life, not of such enhancements as computers and VCRs and Segas and the Internet. For the poor, the information superhighway is as remote as the yellow brick road in *The Wizard of Oz*. But unless the basics, at least, are made more equal among children, it will always be grotesque to compile a list of the best schools.

Rigging the Safety Net

Circuses have safety nets under the trapeze artists and tightrope walkers. Many nations have a social safety net under their populations to keep anyone from falling too far into destitution. How far anyone is allowed to fall depends, of course, on how high the net is rigged. The U.S. safety net is not rigged as high as are those of most industrialized nations. Thus, American citizens are guaranteed less of the survival basics than are the citizens of those other countries.

For example, in Sweden, Norway, Denmark, and Finland, all families receive child support payments from the government, and newly divorced mothers get additional assistance (Popenoe, 1994).

A recent report to the Carnegie Corporation shows that the United States is near the bottom of the list of industrialized nations in providing health care, child care, and work leaves for families with children under the age of 3. In addition, American children are the least likely of those in the developed countries to be immunized against disease. Correcting these social service deficiencies would be an investment in the production of children who are more robust physically and mentally (Chira, 1994b).

The need for an increase in social services is evident when one considers the prototypical poor child in America's most beleaguered schools. This is someone with an absentee father who sends no cash support; several siblings, often of different paternities; an unemployed mother with few, if any, job skills in an area with few, if any, jobs, and no good transportation to where many jobs are; a mother whose child care responsibilities make paid employment infeasible, anyway. The child's home is a vermin-infested, urine-reeking, drug-saturated killing zone called public housing. Not a very high or safe net.

Coming to Terms with the Genetic Suspicion

During the Vietnam war, General William Westmoreland, the commander of the U.S. troops in that country, became notorious for claiming that the Vietnamese do not value life as highly as do Americans. This dehumanizing of the enemy (even of the Vietnamese on our side) made American actions more palatable to the American conscience. The unintended service Westmoreland did by his remark was to get people thinking seriously about just how human the Vietnamese are. Westmoreland articulated a prejudice that the average soldier had only intimated with such terms as "gook" and "slopehead."

It would be hard to believe that anyone living in the United States for any length of time has not heard the equivalents of gook and slopehead that are used for welfare recipients. And there is a plethora of Westmorelands, people of prominence who blame welfare recipients for causing their condition. For these people, the fact that many welfare recipients remain in that condition for protracted periods—frequently across generations—is evidence of a genetic failure, not of a failure of the sociopolitical system. This is worse than the presumed subhumanness of the Vietnamese, which, after all, could be explained as a cultural deficit, self-correcting with exposure to the right cultural values. Welfare recipients have enjoyed exposure to mainstream American values, and yet many remain steeped in poverty. Unlike the circus performer who uses the safety net to get back on his or her feet, the chronic welfare cases just seem to lie in the net, distending their own condition further and further downward.

The arguable assumption here is that the social safety net provides sufficient bounce to get all but the most severely disabled or pathologically recalcitrant recipients back on their feet. But put yourself in the shoes of a welfare mother, especially one who wants to do what's best for her children. Being on the dole may mean guaranteed poverty, but the guarantee of this minimal assistance is one that you understandably would be reluctant to risk losing. It provides your children with some security, and it allows you to be around to protect them against the violence of their environment. You are not at work when they get ready for school or arrive home from school. If you were at work, it would probably be at a minimum-wage, dead-end, nerve-jangling job. And it would bring you home in a stressed-out condition with the same or more money worries as you have on welfare. If the job does not include medical benefits, you have lost those unless you can find some surplus in your minimum wage to buy your own policy. If your children are too young to be left alone and there is no kind soul who will care for them for free, you must now budget for child care. If, after considering all this, you conclude that it is not in your children's interest for you to get off welfare, can you still conclude that it is in society's interest for your children to be raised in even more extreme privation than they are already experiencing? If you cannot, in good conscience, worsen your children's condition, then you are not a "welfare cheat" or a "deadbeat." You are a responsible parent who has internalized the highest of American values. That is why Linda Gordon sees claiming welfare as an important part of the civil rights movement. "Claiming welfare [is] a strategy for upward mobility and especially for benefiting one's children, a move away from poverty and resignation" (Gordon, 1994a, p. 326). Assistant Secretary David Ellwood in the U.S. Department of Health and Human Services, and a former Harvard expert on welfare policy, says bluntly, "If you can't get a job that pays six, seven, or eight dollars an hour, if you can't get quality, inexpensive childcare, then you are deadlocked in the alternative, which is the welfare system" (Ellwood, 1994, p. 51). And the jobs are not available for welfare mothers who live in places like Harlem, as a recent study by the Columbia University anthropology department has detailed (Newman, 1995).

If welfare is the only viable alternative for many mothers, it is hardly a bad one for taxpayers. All the loose talk about packing kids off to orphanages would have vindictive taxpayers cutting off their noses to spite their faces. The Child Welfare League of America estimates that a child living with its mother on welfare costs the public $2,644 a year. In an orphanage, the cost would be $36,500 (Van Biema, 1994). It would be interesting to see if people unsympathetic to welfare mothers are that much more sympathetic to welfare children.

Breaking the Cycle of Dependency

Welfare mothers have a social as well as a parental obligation to stay on government assistance. Their children are more likely to mature into productive citizens if they are spared the traumas of extreme poverty. The government assistance programs are a frank recognition of this fact.

If people are to be weaned from welfare dependency, transition programs have to be created. Short-term, low-cost programs are the ones that will be most popular with taxpayers, and thus the ones with a good prospect of being enacted. The 1988 Family Support Act has been condemned by liberals as being too parsimoniously funded and by conservatives as demanding too little of recipients. The low funding and the low demand are directly related. Such programs are the ones with a predictably low success rate. The large number of failures revives the genetic suspicion about the programs' beneficiaries as much as they arouse skepticism about the design of the programs. The public has to be educated by courageous politicians to the fact that real welfare reform costs much more than current welfare programs.

Job training is a key component of a welfare-to-work program. It assumes that there are unfilled jobs "out there." Very often, the existing jobs do not require much training at all, and as a consequence are minimum-wage, part-time jobs with no medical coverage or other benefits. It is argued by business groups that such jobs are important as a way of giving high school and college students work experience and a little income. These jobs may serve the needs of students (and the business groups), but they are a step down from welfare. Thus, the greatest welfare reform measure is the creation of decent jobs. Simply taking welfare benefits away and forcing people into the job market does not miraculously cause new jobs to appear. It causes old jobs to pay less. "The net result of forcing welfare mothers to work will be a further decline in wages for everyone—as desperate women flood the work force. . . ." (Ehrenreich, 1994, p. 90).

In the 1970s and 1980s, the steel industry in the Pittsburgh area collapsed. Steelworkers, who had been the blue collar elite, with high-paying jobs and lucrative fringe benefits, suddenly were out of work. The job-placement programs that management and the United Steelworkers put in place to cope with this crisis were of limited use because the Monongahela Valley had become a jobless area. One would notice, but try to avoid eye contact with, former steelworkers who were bagging groceries at the local supermarket checkouts. It would be interesting to learn how this experience changed the steelworkers' attitudes toward welfare and welfare recipients.

In the past several years, there has been a lot of corporate downsizing. White collar workers at middle management levels in such giant behemoths as IBM, who thought that their futures were forever secure, have become middle-aged people looking for work. Like the steelworkers, they are being forced to accept the fact that their high-income years are behind them. Whatever contempt they may once have felt for welfare recipients has probably been tempered by their experience with "economic restructuring." The net result of this restructuring has been summarized by David Howell (1994): "Today, more workers are crowding into a pool of 'secondary' jobs that remained a fairly constant share of total jobs throughout the 1980s, tending to lower the wages of what were already the worst jobs in the labor market" (p. 88). So welfare recipients have more competition for jobs that may still leave them in poverty.

If there were an adequate supply of jobs that were more economically attractive than welfare, the training for these jobs would have to be reasonably matched to the requirements. It could take more time to complete this training than public sentiment will allow. For example, the long-term unemployed need such basic start-up skills as getting themselves on a workday and workweek schedule. They have to be able to calculate the amount of time it will take to get to the job site and the best mode of transportation to use. They need practice in dealing with bosses and customers without feeling "put down." This attitude problem is a major cause of women's cycling on and off welfare instead of staying with a job (DeParle, 1994f). Even after they have secured a job, they may need mentors to help them handle job-related stress.

The importance of these basic job skills and attitudes is seen on that rare occasion when a company locates one of its operations in a ghetto community. Local people are not as likely to be hired for the jobs as are outsiders because the locals are deemed to be riskier prospects (Klein, 1994). They need training that will instill confidence in a prospective employer, as well as in themselves. And the job training might be better targeted not to welfare mothers but to the unemployed men who impregnated and then abandoned them, so that these men could be encouraged (or coerced) to assume paternal responsibility.

It may also be necessary to extend the two-year limit for job preparation. Educators are concerned that the two-year limit will allow only for limited vocational training and not the longer-term education that will pay off in greater benefits to the individual and society (D. Cohen, 1994; Lively, 1994). An analogy that is often used is that of the G.I. Bill, which provided college financing for veterans of America's wars. That program was a great boon to the U.S. economy, as well as to the veterans, not all of whom had served in combat positions or had even gone overseas.

Child care is another component of welfare reform. The newly employed mother of young children is not likely to earn enough to afford child care. If she does, *quality* child care must still be available to her or her children's emotional and intellectual development will have been jeopardized for a paycheck. It is better that society continue to give her a welfare check to enable her to stay home and care for her kids. Needless to say, good child care outside the home can be expensive (Cost, Quality & Child Outcomes Study Team, 1995), and will be made more so as the demand increases and child-care workers become more professionalized. That is another cost of genuine welfare reform. Fortunately, it is a cost that the public might be willing to bear. A 1994 *Time*/CNN poll showed that 90 percent of those surveyed thought the government should provide day care so that poor mothers might work or get job training (Gibbs, 1994, p. 26). Researchers at Johns Hopkins University posit another reason why day care is a good social investment. In a study of 867 children nationwide, they found that children from the poorest homes who were placed in infant care achieved higher intellectual development than did a control group of children who were left in the nonstimulating environment of the home (Chira, 1994a).

Medical coverage will have to be continued through the welfare system if the employer does not provide it. (Universal health coverage is not yet a reality in the United States as this is being written.) A parent who gives up medical coverage in the hope that the emergency room of a municipal hospital will be able to meet her children's medical needs raises a serious question about her fitness to be a parent. Emergency rooms hardly provide the routine dental care or vision screening that children require. Employers who do provide medical coverage rightly count this as a labor cost, and that makes them more intent on keeping their employee count down, and thus there will be fewer jobs to absorb the welfare recipients.

Food stamps and rent subsidies may have to be continued, even if in reduced form, should the new jobs not pay well enough to cover the full value of these benefits. Rent subsidies may be especially crucial in enabling the new employee to locate closer to the place of work. Such relocation increases the chance of a good work-attendance record, and it is likely to mean a better community in which to raise children.

The experts and the politicians will always haggle about the cost of all this, and in truth no one can predict the costs with great certainty. When President Clinton presented his welfare reform package, he estimated the cost at $9.3 billion over five years, but the Congressional Budget Office (CBO) put the figure at $11.8 billion. The cost to the states was pegged by Clinton at $1 billion and by the CBO at $2.6 billion (DeParle, 1994a). The one thing on which all knowledgeable observers agree is that getting people off welfare will cost more than keeping them on, and the extent to which it can be done is exactly the extent to which the United States will have a full employment economy. Think of what the following means in that regard.

> Statisticians at the New York State Labor Department say about 20 percent of all job vacancies are listed with the State Employment Service. In October [1994], the service listed 7,991 openings in New York City. . . . That would mean there were about 40,000 job vacancies. . . . The city's official unemployment figure for October was 271,000. So the jobless outnumber the available jobs by about 7 to 1. (Harvey, 1994, p. A37)

Avoiding the Tragedy of Cold Turkey

Some people, most notably Richard Herrnstein and Charles Murray (1994), say that the costs of welfare reform, and of welfare itself, are unnecessary and undesirable. Welfare, they argue, is a highly addictive dependency. Welfare reform will be just another government-designed drug, likely to attract more users than it rehabilitates. The only real reform of the welfare system is its abolition. They maintain that we must break the welfare habit by going cold turkey.

Imagine the immediate consequences of such a draconian act. If poverty correlates with such crimes of assault as mugging and murder, can hunger and homelessness really be expected to lower the correlation? Desperate people do desperate things—or, as James Baldwin once wrote, there is nothing as dangerous as the person who has nothing to lose. Robbery to feed one's children might continue to be a crime, but religious authorities would be hard put to condemn it as a sin. More likely, they would praise it with faint damn as a necessary evil.

It is true that in the idealized era of small-town America, which Murray persists in invoking, friends and kin would rally around a family temporarily down on its luck. President Clinton's mother wrote about the assistance she got from these sources when young Bill's father died (Kelly and Morgan, 1994). But the ghetto and Appalachian America are not that idealized small town. There, entire communities are down on their luck. If the downtrodden residents of New York's Harlem and the South Bronx were wrapped in community wealth, they would not do their panhandling and mugging in midtown Manhattan. Much of the little wealth that does exist in those communities is concentrated in the hands of drug dealers, and only in a movie like *King of New York* is the drug kingpin going to become the savior of the slums. For the luckless in these areas, their friends are as needy as themselves; their relatives are apt to be needy also, or their whereabouts unknown. For many of their male friends and kin, jail is their habitat.

No longer able to get by on either public or private charity, the former welfare mother is expected to look to her bootstraps. She can work her way out of poverty as the immigrant hordes had to. Here again, unfortunately, an idealized past is being superimposed on current conditions. The United States had a frontier to accommodate past immigrant waves. At the time of the first waves, most territories in America had still not been admitted to the Union. There was also a burgeoning economy, with labor-intensive manufacturing industries. That meant jobs. The picture is idealized because of the parts that have been airbrushed out: the recurrent plagues, the high infant mortality rate, the alcoholism, the industrial illnesses, the sweatshop working conditions, the bloody suppression of strikes, the crimes of violence, the rise of organized criminal groups, the rampant political corruption.

And there remains the question of whether or not at least one parent should be at home during the earliest formative years of the children. Even if the welfare mother can be forced into the labor market or a job training program by the withdrawal of public assistance, is that a wise social policy? What makeshift arrangement for the kids could be as good as that of the mother's own presence? Is this work-or-starve choice going to force a lot of mothers into prostitution?

Court action in California may signal an end to the wholesale cutting of welfare benefits in that and every other state. (Nationwide, the value of the AFDC grant has eroded by 40 percent in the last twenty years, so that now it is less than 60 percent of the poverty line [Abramovitz, 1994].) The U.S. Court of Appeals for the Ninth Circuit ruled that California was wrong in reducing benefits, even though it did so with approval from both the Bush and Clinton administrations. California had been gradually reducing the benefits to all recipients statewide as part of an experiment in which only 5,000 recipients in four counties were being studied. The court said that reducing the benefits to everyone before the effects on the experimental few were known was "wholly unjustified by any legitimate experimental goal" (Levin, 1994, p. A12). The decision is a strong rebuke of cuts that are made solely for political purposes masquerading as "experiments."

In a few states, a less drastic measure has been enacted. This consists of withholding welfare aid for children conceived after a woman has begun receiving welfare. In New Jersey, it amounts to the denial of about $64 a month in additional aid that the mother would otherwise be receiving for the new child. Such groups as the National Organization for Women, the American Civil Liberties Union, and the Catholic Church are protesting the measure as punishment of an innocent newborn child and an inducement to abortion (Pear, 1995). It also can be viewed as punishment of all the children in the family, since the total assistance has not increased, but the number of children to feed, clothe, and shelter has. The notion that $64 a month is such a lordly sum that women will become baby mills to obtain it flies in the face of the simplest economic rationality. Welfare mothers are not so irrational as to find $64 a child to be an attractive cost–benefit calculus. The causes of their childbearing are much more complicated than that. Among such causes are a pathetic need by poor adolescent girls for some kind of status and someone to love them. As Sheldon Danziger says: "Researchers know a lot more about the effects of poverty on kids than we do about the effects of welfare on out-of-wedlock childbirth" (quoted by Coughlin, 1994, p. A6). Danziger and seventy-six other poverty researchers have signed a statement opposing the termination of benefits to young unwed mothers. In New Jersey, state officials stopped arguing that the $64 denial reduced childbearing, and frankly admitted that the effects cannot be measured with ease or confidence (Henneberger, 1995).

State-by-state welfare "experiments" put recipients at the mercy of politicians who try to one-up each other by showing how tough they can be. This is primarily posturing for the voters, since national studies by independent researchers have consistently found that "like other Americans, a single [welfare] mother and her children are much more likely to be drawn to a new place by job opportunities, family ties, warm weather, better schools and safer streets than by a few extra dollars in their welfare check" (Dugger, 1995, p. A1). Welfare bashing is too easy a political game to play, which is why the welfare system should be nationalized and not turned over to the states for fifty different programs. That would focus national media attention on the proposals and produce greater public awareness of the real nature of the problems. It would put an end to competition among governors for the title of Mr. or Ms. Crackdown.

Welfare Reform Means Better Benefits

Programs that result in decent-paying jobs for welfare mothers so that they can afford health care and child care, as needed, will fall far short of 100 percent success rates. It is in order, therefore, to think about those who remain in need. What are they entitled to receive? More important for society's long-range interest, what do their children deserve?

There are two answers: (1) the minimum you want guaranteed for your own children, and (2) the maximum you are prepared to pay for someone else's. The first answer is the more humane, and ethical philosophers, such as John Rawls (1983), argue that it is the better moral basis upon which to establish social policy. If people decided solely on this basis, welfare benefits would surely increase. They would include housing subsidies (and housing stock) to allow the poor access to safe neighborhoods and good schools. The housing would be sufficiently commodious so that each child would have some private space. There would be something that most of us take for granted: vaccinations. There would be eye care and dental care so that a child would not have to struggle through school with blurred vision and aching teeth. There would be compulsory parenting classes (also available to the nonpoor at cost) to keep the child's material sustenance from being nullified by the psychological damage that parents can do unwittingly. There would be cash incentives to keep teenage parents in school and on track toward gainful employment so that they would not become long-term wards of the state. In Ohio, the incentive is an extra $62 a month for attending school (and a deduction of that amount for not doing so). That is an effective inducement of $124, and has resulted in a 5.6 percent increase in the high school completion rate for teenage mothers on welfare (Chira, 1994c). There would be no automatic loss of benefits for getting married, nor would the income from part-time employment be subtracted in full from the welfare benefits. These penalties act as disincentives to marriage and work, the key ingredients of stable, self-sufficient families.

There would be genuinely empowered "enterprise zones." These would be established in the most blighted urban areas, and would include tax breaks to get businesses to locate there, as well as money for social services, job training, and transportation (Vobejda, 1994). The enterprise zones should also be permitted to charge a lower state sales tax than the rest of the state in order to attract customers to the zone and employ local people (Redburn, 1994).

Children Need Hope

There is a terrible beauty to a toddler playing in a slum neighborhood. The innocence and happiness are beautiful to behold, but the vision of the child's probable future makes one wince. What a well-designed and financed welfare system can do is delay the time when the prospect of a better future vanishes, perhaps delay it forever. Society cannot demand civility from children denied hope.

POSITION 2: FOR LESS WELFARE

The Era of Universal Suffering

The number of people claiming victimhood has been increasing in recent decades (Dershowitz, 1994; Sykes, 1992). It almost seems as though everyone in America is a victim of some sort, entitled to compensation for the injustices suffered. There are racial/ethnic groups, religious groups, women, gays and lesbians, the handicapped, victims of childhood trauma, victims of sex abuse or harassment, victims of police abuse, chemically damaged veterans of Vietnam and Desert Storm, victims of economic restructuring. This proliferation of self-proclaimed victims creates a paradox. Some of the victims may feel an obligation to compensate the others, but they all wish to be on the receiving end. Thus, there is a surfeit of compensatees and a paucity of compensators.

Welfare recipients constitute just one group of people who feel, or would like others to believe, that they have been the hapless victims of an unjust society. They have to take their place in line with all the other victims who are expecting redress. Among those other victims is a group commonly referred to as taxpayers. Their howls of protest at the mistreatment they have endured have been heard in every state in the Union. And because disgruntled taxpayers may well be the victim group with the largest bloc of votes, their howls have to be heeded by politicians. Alas, they are the victims who would be best able to help all the other victims, if only they did not feel so victimized themselves.

The taxpayer turnip may still be one from which a bit more blood can be drawn, but no politician is apt to approach it with a very large syringe, especially not when a *Time*/CNN poll shows that 53 percent of respondents think the government is already spending too much on welfare ("Vox Pop," 1994). The tectonic shift to the Republicans in the 1994 elections certainly reflects that sentiment. If taxes were to be raised or more money were to be siphoned from the defense budget, welfare recipients and their advocates would be only one voice in the clamor for it. In the antitax climate of current years, welfare recipients have been *losing* benefits. In New York City, for example, the dollar value of welfare benefits declined by 30 percent between 1975 and 1992, down to $2,206 per person for 1992 (Dugger, 1994b). It is naive for the welfare lobby to expect a sudden expansion of benefits, either as currently structured or as reconfigured under the guise of welfare "reform."

Don't Trash the Working Poor

There are physically and mentally disabled people who cannot perform even the simplest of jobs. They are already the victims of a cruel circumstance over which they have no control. That is why no one begrudges them their public assistance. Indeed, we are gladdened to see them get it because it assuages our guilt at our own relative good fortune.

The large welfare category at issue in this discussion, however, is that of "families with dependent children," and the issue is whether they are entitled to AFDC compensation. Anyone who has filed federal tax forms knows that virtually all minor children (and a lot of older ones) qualify as "dependents." Most of us think of these children as dependent on us—their parents or guardians and not on the government. We take responsibility for them because we created them and we love them. Given our parental obligations, the option of unemployment is unthinkable. Our children depend on *our* paychecks. That is why so many of us drag ourselves to jobs that long ago lost their lustre and from which advancement is almost beyond hope.

The authors of this book are university professors with tenure, good salaries, and no dependent children, so it would be overweening for us to pretend to a posture of noble self-sacrifice. Think instead about the working poor. You encounter them all the time, especially if you live in or near a city. They are the busboys in diners who stopped being boys years ago. They are the women you espy among the steam presses in the backs of laundries, even on hot summer days. They are the immigrant cab drivers so ubiquitous now in the big cities. They are the custodial staff and the cafeteria workers of the college you attend. You may think that they make a good enough wage, even though you have never wondered what exactly it was, but if they are the only working parent in a household with several dependent children, they may well meet the official federal criterion for being poor. In 1994, this was an income of less than $14,764 for a family of four, regardless of whether the family lived in San Antonio or San Francisco ("Poverty Is Unfairly Defined," 1994). But the working poor are not dependent. They have too much pride to go on the dole. They refuse to be dependent on the rest of us. It is we who depend on them to perform the essential jobs that cushion our lives. Their own lives do not know the cushioning effect of plentiful food, restaurant meals, nights at the movies, days at amusement parks, vacation excursions, or even the cushioning effect of good furniture. In some posh watering holes for the rich, such as Hilton Head, South Carolina, and Telluride, Colorado, the low-wage serving class live in ramshackle houses or tents because decent housing has been priced beyond their reach (Applebome, 1994; Jaynes, 1994). But they don't go on welfare.

The working poor make do; they hold their lives together and they raise their children in some stability. To many welfare recipients, the working poor are suckers. A sure way to make the working poor feel this way themselves is to increase benefits for welfare recipients and provide them with free education and job training. Pride may keep people working at poverty-level jobs, but when the sheer economic cost of this pride becomes too great, they are made to feel abused. They begin to fear that they are sacrificing their children on the altar of their pride. Welfare recipients should not be raised above the living conditions of the working poor unless you as a taxpayer are prepared to give more to the current population of welfare recipients and to see a sharp increase in the size of that population.

Welfare as Rip-off

There is Ronald Reagan's notorious "report" of the woman who drove a Cadillac to the welfare office to collect her check. Liberals shout foul when apocryphal reports such as this are used to discredit welfare recipients. To the chagrin of liberals, however, there is a long list of *documented* reports of welfare fraud. The abuses of the welfare system and their cost to taxpayers are so enormous that one cannot but conclude that welfare is easy pickings for unscrupulous people. And these are only the abuses that we know about.

For example, the African-American sociologist Elijah Anderson has documented cases of young men in Philadelphia persuading their girlfriends to have babies. The girlfriend continues living at home with her parents but collects $158 in public aid every two weeks, a lot of which goes to the aid of her boyfriend (Gibbs, 1994).

In Manhattan, a man living in a $4,000-a-month apartment in Trump Tower and riding around in a fleet of luxury cars was collecting $176 every two weeks on welfare (McFadden, 1994).

In Chicago, nineteen children of six mothers and seventeen fathers were found living in an apartment with rat droppings and dog feces. The six mothers had amassed $74,000 in public assistance in the previous year (Will, 1994).

In Boston, one welfare recipient has fourteen children, all of whom are themselves on welfare, as are most of the grandchildren and great grandchildren, or about 100 public wards from a single source (Will, 1994).

And, of course, there are the recurring cases of people who collect welfare payments in more than one state. One survey disclosed that 4,200 New York State recipients were also collecting in another state (Fisher, 1994). A check of

1,800 welfare recipients in Newark, New Jersey, revealed that 23 percent had also been collecting in Manhattan. The 425 cheats had collected more than $1 million illegally (Will, 1994). Fingerprint identification of collectors of welfare is needed to discourage this double dipping (Leusner, 1994; Mitchell, 1994a). Finally, there is even the rip-off by welfare clerks themselves, who arrange to have millions of dollars of unearned welfare checks mailed to accomplices with whom they split the money (James, 1995).

Rush Limbaugh, in his inimitable style, has expressed the exasperation of the American people with all the welfare cheating: "I am weary and near my wits' end at having to listen to the complaint that the American safety net has holes in it and too many people are slipping through. The problem is that too many people are using that safety net as a hammock" (Limbaugh, 1993, p. 50).

The Best Reform Is Self-Reform

All sides agree with President Clinton that "welfare as we know it" is a mess. The solution advanced by liberals is to inflate the mess, as though it could be expected to reach a state of destruct as certainly as a balloon will. Liberals would reform welfare additively, which would only make it more attractive to those who already are welfare junkies, and get a lot of others hooked in the bargain. The supposedly tough talk about providing benefits for only two years and then terminating them is just that, talk. At the end of the two-year period, all those AFDC mothers who have not found work, and many of whom will have continued to find inseminators, will make a case for extending their benefits indefinitely, and social workers, whose own livelihoods are dependent on having caseloads, will buy it. Those whose benefits do get terminated will be a small minority, not nearly enough to offset the costs of the "temporarily" expanded benefits. In the meantime, they will have been allowed two years to "sit on their butts" (Lawrence Mead as quoted by Coughlin, 1994). Moreover, there will be the cost of all those who have been lured to the welfare life by the expanded benefits.

The liberal version of welfare reform is based on a bewilderingly naïve notion of human nature. For example, liberals are hell-bent on "proving" that welfare does not cause single women to have babies, and that an increase in the amount of the benefit does not produce a corresponding increase in illegitimacy. Charles Murray has examined the liberals' "data" very carefully and found some interesting distortions. First, welfare is defined only as the AFDC payment itself, when it should include the whole welfare package: AFDC, food stamps, Medicaid, and housing allowance. Second, illegitimacy is measured as the average number of babies being born to unmarried women, not the average number of illegitimate babies in the total population. Unmarried women may be having fewer babies, on average, but unmarried women are now a decided majority of black mothers and are approaching a majority of white mothers. Welfare is certainly a plausible suspect in the vast increase of single women and illegitimate births overall (Murray, 1994). As Rutgers sociologist Ted Goertzel notes: "When a teenage mother has a baby, she gets a check and is set up in her own apartment while the girl who stays in school and doesn't have a baby gets nothing" (quoted in Kadish, 1994, p. 6).

A realistic conception of human psychology tells us that aversive stimuli are the most promising correctives for the welfare mess. Welfare benefits are incentives to get on welfare. Benefits have to be scaled back on a continuing schedule, starting now. Some states are already attempting to do this, if only by not making inflationary adjustments to the benefits. Unfortunately, welfare mothers may not be intelligent enough to understand the inflationary depreciation of their benefits. The reduction has to be more noticeable than that.

A good place to begin would be the benefits going to noncitizens, which would save billions and discourage undesirable types of people from coming to America. Californians passed Proposition 187 to keep benefits from going to illegal immigrants, a perfectly sensible thing to do. Not only did the welfare payments lure illegals across the border, but those who sneaked in and went on welfare had larger families than did their peasant compatriots who remained in Mexico. Welfare made the migration affordable (Linden, 1994).

The incremental reversal of benefits has to be detailed in law, leaving no room for bureaucratic discretion. This will give welfare recipients due notice and will force them gradually to assume responsibility for their own lives, until they are like the rest of us. It can be expected that churches and other local charities will provide stopgap assistance in emergency cases. As Murray says: "How does a young woman survive without government support? The same way she has since time immemorial. If she wants to keep a child, she must enlist support from her parents, boyfriend, siblings, neighbors, church or philanthropies" (quoted in Gibbs, 1994, p. 30).

Because these helping agencies will be community-based, even familial, and not anonymous government bureaucracies spending taxpayer money, the beneficiaries will feel pressure to stop freeloading on their friends and family. Deadbeat dads will know that it is no longer the government on whom they are getting over; it is folks who know them personally. The deadbeat father should be identified by the mother as a criterion for her to collect assistance, and he can then be persuaded to do his parental duty by such enforced threats as jail time or the revocation of his driver's and occupational licenses. Massachusetts now enforces the first regulation and Maine the second (Gibbs, 1994). If a father is unable to avoid his financial obligations, he may be willing to be paternal in other ways, perhaps to the point of being a presence in his children's lives. The fear by liberals that this forced involvement will lead to abusiveness (Ehrenreich, 1995) is overstated.

If welfare recipients continue to live off the public, they should, at the very least, be required to work for their benefits. They have caused cuts in such governmental services as sanitation and school safety by gobbling up a large piece of the tax pie. They can restore those services by performing the jobs themselves. They should welcome the chance to thank their benefactors by making the community cleaner, safer, and more civil. Moreover, "mandated community service may be the only way to build the job skills and work habits of those who cannot support themselves in the regular job market. Inactivity is bad for everyone; it can be devastating for those only loosely connected to the labor market" (Besharov and Fowler, 1993, p. 104). The effects on young children when their mothers go to work can be beneficial. Assistant U.S. Secretary for Health and Human Services Mary Jo Bane concedes that working can ease a mother's social isolation, give her pride and self-confidence, and overcome her depressive slumps (Chira, 1994a).

Obviously, there will still be some sociopathically indigent people who will hustle anyone they can. Such people are hardly good moral exemplars for their children, let alone good providers. By their behavior they will have condemned themselves as unfit for parenthood. If welfare advocates are genuinely concerned about the fate of children, they will support measures to remove children from the care of such people, as advocated by former U.S. Education Secretary William Bennett (Gibbs, 1994). A variety of child-care arrangements could be created to replace the unfit biological parents. Foster homes already exist, but their number could be increased. Year-round boarding schools are another possibility. A network of community hostels for needy kids and their mothers might be a last-resort measure to get the mother healthily involved in her children's lives before she loses them (Magnet, 1994). To make any of these arrangements truly wholesome and nurturing environments will cost money, but taxpayers will have the satisfaction of knowing that it is being spent on real victims and in ways that can be easily monitored. The prospect of losing their children should cause parents who claim to care, or don't want the stigma of being proved uncaring, to alter their behavior. It should also cause a lot of cavalierly prospective parents to think twice about conceiving children.

Race and Sex Are Smokescreens

Those who would reduce AFDC benefits to ultimate total extinction are regularly branded as racist or sexist. African-Americans are represented disproportionately among welfare recipients, although not by enough to be a majority, and welfare mothers are by definition women. It is, therefore, easy to twist an argument for reduced welfare benefits into an attack on African-Americans and women. The accused are sometimes let off "easily" by the smug suggestion that their racism or sexism is subconscious, becoming manifest only in the form of acute insensitivity. Poor dears, they just don't get it.

The labels of racist and sexist are today's form of the old McCarthyism, and they are just as hard to defend against. How could one prove that one was not a communist when communists were expected to misrepresent themselves? How does one prove that one is not racist or sexist if only the most retrograde redneck or misogynist is expected to acknowledge this? The labels are ad hominem/feminem attacks that don't even have the merit of being based on demonstrable truth. They are cheap-shot ways of ducking the issue by defaming the opponent.

The imputation to another of base motivation is in order when there is an array of evidence to support the suspicion. The simple fact that one advocates a legitimate public policy that someone else does not like is no evidence at all of nefarious intent. To make it so is to engage in the politics of intimidation. This can have a tremendously chilling effect on the exercise of free speech. And because free speech is so essential to democracy, any form of political correctness that curtails it is anti-American.

Let us assume for the sake of argument that a person who inveighs against welfare recipients is someone who is frequently heard uttering racist and sexist slurs. The person's prejudices are trumpeted from his or her own mouth. If such a person is nonetheless capable of analyzing the welfare system and constructing an argument for an alternative, the analysis and the argument have to be judged on their merits. Human progress would never occur if good ideas were allowed to emanate only from invariably virtuous sources. The bigot dismisses the arguments of welfare advocates by caricaturing the advocates as "woolly-headed, bleeding-heart liberals." If we want the bigot to listen seriously to such arguments, we must insist that his or her arguments be given a respectful hearing, as well.

African-American Leaders as Welfare Scolds

In recent years, there has been a refreshing amount of candor on the part of leaders of the African-American community concerning the welfare issue. These leaders are prepared to go beyond the defensive cant that says that all African-Americans in trouble got there solely, or even primarily, because of racism. They acknowledge the progress that has been made toward the elimination of institutionalized racism and the compensation that has been won by many of its victims. They also recognize the advances resulting from affirmative-action policies and case law. They know that the last vestige of racism will not disappear from the American landscape for a long time, if ever, but that there is enough race fairness now to make full participation in American life possible.

This involvement is not guaranteed to be untroubled, however. Quite the contrary: racial tenseness, slights (real or imagined), awkward interpersonal relations, and mutually wary distancing are guaranteed to produce psychological trouble. Numerous African-Americans have detailed these phenomena in autobiographical accounts of their passage through the white world (for example, McCall, 1994; Staples, 1994; Steele, 1991). The point is that it is time to get on with that struggle and not desist from it. Opportunities do exist, and every opportunity explodes an excuse for copping out. As Supreme Court Justice Clarence Thomas, himself an African-American, has said, to treat African-Americans as victims and not hold them responsible for their actions is to treat them like children, "or even worse, to treat them as animals without a soul" (quoted in Lewis, 1994, p. A14).

It was an African-American and a Democrat, Wayne Bryant, who introduced legislation in New Jersey to withhold additional child support from women who have a child while on AFDC. His legislative district is a poor one with a lot of welfare families. That he felt compelled to introduce his bill says much about his exasperation with the proliferation of welfare babies. He had not given up on defusing this population time bomb, but he had obviously abandoned hope that exhortation alone would do the job. By denying a cash inducement to childbearing, he was assigning the responsibility for the act directly to the parents, and not to any amorphous racist "system." His willingness to assess this penalty against the parents can be questioned for its effect on the children themselves, but it honors the parents by treating them as free agents in determining their fate and not as witless pawns. It can also be seen as a salute to working-class parents who have their babies without turning to the government teat. As the black journalist Stanley Crouch has noted, there was a time in the not-too-distant past when teenage pregnancy "was not acceptable behavior" and "those girls became pariahs. . . . They saw that they were the ones left holding the bag and if that meant they had to abstain from sex, they did" (quoted by Will, 1994, p. 84).

Another African-American state assemblyman, Democrat Antonio Riley, Jr., of Wisconsin, introduced a bill to abolish that state's welfare program as of midnight, December 31, 1998. The legislature passed the bill and the Republican governor signed it. Whether the federal government will allow Wisconsin to be without a welfare system is not yet known, but as Riley says, "Welfare is the jailer of our people" (quoted by Cooper, 1994, p. 33). And as the Democratic mayor of Milwaukee says, "AFDC is an incentive not to work. . . . Individuals may indeed continue to act irresponsibly, but we will not design a system around them. . . . You don't solve this problem by giving more money to the mothers, you solve it, if necessary, by building more orphanages" (quoted by Cooper, 1994, pp. 35–36). For liberals who lament Wisconsin's efforts to get welfare under control, it is worth noting that by the spring of 1995 Wisconsin's welfare benefits were $200 more a month than in Chicago, and Wisconsinites had to cope with hundreds of Chicago welfare cases coming across the state line for the added benefits (Johnson, 1995).

What assemblymen Bryant and Riley and other African-American leaders are trying to do is restore the most crucial of child-rearing institutions, the intact family. This is the springboard from which children enter school and the support system for all their school years. A large fatherless family is fraught with perils to a child's development, and thus to his or her school success.

The Nation of Islam, or Black Muslims, assigned responsibility for family stability to mothers and fathers and to the Nation's own support network years ago, at a time when other minority groups were still externalizing family failure. However abhorrent the rhetoric of the Nation's leaders might be to some Americans, they were ahead of their time in saving families. They showed that it can be done, but whether it can be done as successfully outside the confines of the Nation's strictures and zealotry remains to be seen.

Bad Beyond Reform

In a book on education intended for educators and prospective educators, it is usual to emphasize human malleability. People can be changed, and educators are the ones who can change them for the better. The more changeable people are and the less socialized they are, the more work there is for the educators, and the greater the glory that redounds to them. Preparing welfare recipients for jobs and responsible parenthood are educational tasks premised on the belief in human perfectibility.

This mind-set about malleability may, however, be a form of fanaticism. That is to say that it may be adhered to beyond evidence to support it—indeed, despite evidence to the contrary. There is a burgeoning literature on the fixity of individual human nature. For example, psychologists now question whether certain kinds of sexual deviance can be cured or only controlled. Other psychologists assert that there are fixed parameters to each person's intelligence, which set limits on the person's success. Some psychologists extend these individual differences to group differences between racial and ethnic groups (Gottfredson, 1994; Herrnstein and Murray, 1994). In other areas where behavior is not absolutely fixed and predictable, there are still powerful genetic predispositions and abilities to act in a certain way (D. Cohen, 1994; Gallagher, 1994; Kagan, 1994).

The word that captures all this for our purposes is "incorrigibility." Educators who bump up against troublesome students for whom nothing seems to work begin, in violation of their professional faith, to suspect that the student is incorrigible, "bad beyond reform" (*Random House College Dictionary*, 1982, p. 674). A percentage of welfare recipients is certainly incorrigible. It would be a waste of time and money to keep trying until every recipient has been reformed. There are, after all, limits to both public patience and the public purse. Those welfare recipients who insist on testing these limits and make no serious attempt at self-improvement should be removed from the welfare rolls, or at least have their temporary continuation made contingent on voluntary sterilization so that they don't add to a new generation of welfare dependents. The serious attempt at self-reform could be demonstrated by the welfare recipient's providing evidence that he or she was applying for at least six jobs a week. New York State is experimenting with this requirement to determine if an able-bodied, childless welfare applicant is even eligible to go on welfare (Sack, 1994).

Earning the Benefits

If welfare benefits continue to be doled out, their recipients should be required to do something in return. Many recipients live in cities that are plagued by graffiti and litter. The recipients should *earn* their benefits by cleaning up *their* cities. When winter comes, there is all that snow to be removed from pedestrian walkways. Spring is the season for sprucing up the municipal parks and readying the swimming pools. A signal advantage to having people work at these jobs is that it prevents them from working at concealed jobs and collecting welfare fraudulently.

Westchester County, just north of New York City, has been requiring such services from its welfare recipients for the past five years (Dugger, 1994a; Dugger and Hernandez, 1994). Only twenty hours a week have to be worked, which is not much to expect, and is far from being the "forced" or "slave" labor that some liberals allege.

The Westchester program has been successful enough that Mayor Giuliani has proposed its adoption by New York City (Mitchell, 1994b). It should be noted that in neither case are welfare mothers required to participate, but only able-bodied childless individuals on that form of welfare known as Home Relief. But welfare mothers whose children are old enough not to require constant supervision could reasonably be expected to join in, if only for a few hours a week. The children themselves could be enlisted. This would give some common purpose to the families, as well as instill some work ethic. A nation that wishes to be competitive cannot afford the free lunches of the welfare state.

For Discussion

1. Here is a list of benefits people receive from the government and the percentage of families getting them. What does this listing tell you about welfare (AFDC) as compared with other government benefits?

Handouts for Everyone
(The proportion of all families receiving government transfer payments of some type in 1992)

Benefit	Families
Social Security	26%
Medicare	24
Medicaid	12
Food stamps	9
Unemployment compensation	9
Subsidized school lunch	8
Government retirement	5
Aids to Families with Dependent Children	4
Supplemental Security Income	4
Energy assistance	4
Educational assistance	3
Public housing	3
Veterans benefits	2
All benefits	52%

Source: Robert J. Samuelson, "Sowing More Cynicism," *Newsweek*, October 24, 1994, p. 45.

2. This map shows how the amount of welfare benefits varies state by state. What explains the variation? What behavior is encouraged by the interstate differences? Is the variability an argument for uniform national benefits?

The Welfare Patchwork

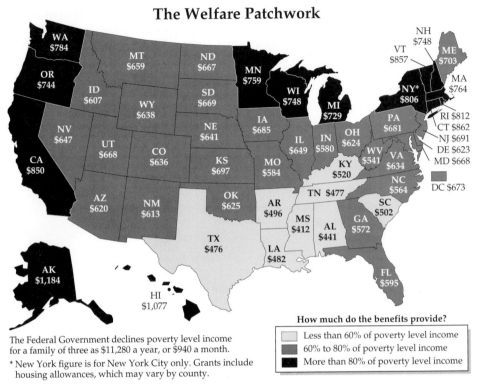

The Federal Government declines poverty level income for a family of three as $11,280 a year, or $940 a month.

* New York figure is for New York City only. Grants include housing allowances, which may vary by county.

How much do the benefits provide?

- Less than 60% of poverty level income
- 60% to 80% of poverty level income
- More than 80% of poverty level income

Source: "The Welfare Patchwork," *The New York Times,* July 5, 1992, p. 16.

3. Here are two graphs that Herrnstein and Murray use to demonstrate the influence of IQ and family background on welfare status. What do the graphs tell you? More important, what *don't* they tell you?

Socioeconomic background and IQ are both important in determining whether white women become chronic welfare recipients

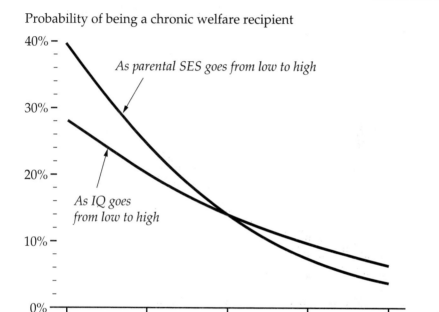

Probability of being a chronic welfare recipient

As parental SES goes from low to high

As IQ goes from low to high

Very low (–2 SDs)   Very high (+2 SDs)

Note: For computing the plot, age and either SES (for the black curves) or IQ (for the gray curves) were set at their mean values. Additional independent variables of which the effects have been extracted for the plot: marital status at the time of first birth, and poverty status in the calendar year prior to the first birth.

Even after poverty and marital status are taken into account, IQ played a substantial role in determining whether white women go on welfare

Probability of going on welfare within a year after birth

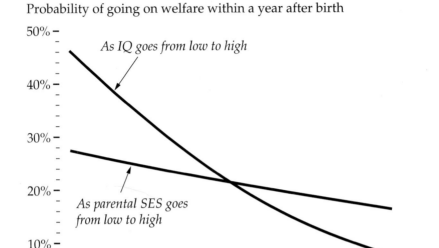

As IQ goes from low to high

As parental SES goes from low to high

Very low
(–2 SDs)

Very high
(+2 SDs)

Note: For computing the plot, age and either SES (for the black curves) or IQ (for the gray curves) were set at their mean values. Additional independent variables of which the effects have been extracted for the plot: marital status at the time of first birth, and poverty status in the calendar year prior to the first birth.
Source: Richard Herrnstein and Charles Murray, *The Bell Curve,* New York: Free Press, 1994, pp. 195, 198.

4. Read the following paragraph and see how many of the questions you can answer.

As we listen to the daily life experiences of these women and those of count-less other single mothers across the nation, we hear about recurring unmet needs, gaping public policy holes that actually structure family poverty. How do you hold down a full-time job when there is no available, accessible, or affordable childcare? This is well-illustrated in the 1993 "Report of the National Law Center on Homelessness and Poverty," where in 63% of the 19 cities surveyed, the market cost of two children in childcare actually exceeds one's total earnings from a full-time, minimum-wage job. How do you pay rent when, according to the same National Law Center, the fair market rent for a two-bedroom apartment exceeds the maximum AFDC allowance for a family of three in 100% of the surveyed cities? How do you get into public hous-ing or Section 8 when in many areas the wait is two to 10 years? How do you survive as a single mother with young children in public housing when you and your children are prey to sexual violence and physical assaults as drug dealers and gangs stake out territory? How do you take care of your family on welfare when in 1992 your AFDC grant, according to the Children's Defense Fund, amounted to only 41% of the poverty line? How do you get immunizations when free clinics are only open twice a week and the bus fails to run when your older child is ill? How can you ever escape poverty even when you attend job training and do miraculously find a job among the few available, when the job itself pays minimum wage, offers no benefits, and you are a single parent with two young children?

Source: Valerie Polakow. (1994). "Welfare Reform and the Assault on Daily Life: Targeting Single Mothers and Their Children," *Social Justice* **21**, 30.

5. Have the welfare rolls in your state been expanding or contracting? Each state has an agency responsible for welfare, so it should be easy for you to get the overall numbers. However, you will want to go beyond those to see the kinds of people who are most likely to be coming onto, or going off, the welfare rolls. What is it about these groups that makes them vulnerable or fortunate? In what parts of the state are these groups concentrated? What can be done to decrease the vulnerability and increase the good fortune?

6. The following article suggests that the opposition to welfare is selfishly motivated. Do you think the author has captured the essence of that opposition?

Our Forked Tongue
By John Kenneth Galbraith

Cambridge, Mass.

In these last years, and notably in these past months, we have heard much of the burden imposed by government on the citizen. Nothing has been more emphasized in speech and possibly also in thought. This comment is not meant to regret this concern, as some might suppose: rather, it is to clarify the way the word "burden" is now employed. It has a very special connotation, of which all who cherish good or anyhow accepted English usage should be aware.

As now used, "burden" applies only to a very specific range of government activities. Many are not a burden and are not to be so described. Defense

John Kenneth Galbraith, professor emeritus of economics at Harvard, is an adviser on English usage for the American Heritage Dictionary.

expenditure is definitely not a burden; indeed, increases therein are now being proposed. That there is now no wholly plausible enemy does not affect the situation. Similarly, in recent years large sums, in a range upward from $50 billion, have been appropriated to bail out failed financial institutions, specifically the savings and loan associations. This was not a burden. A clear distinction must be made between a burden and an admittedly unfortunate and costly financial misadventure.

Social Security is not a burden; in no politically acceptable discourse is it so described. Nor are farm price and income supports, although recipients regularly command incomes of a hundred grand or more. Medicare is basically not a burden and is not to be so described. There are many lesser items of expenditure that are not a burden,

continued

Our Forked Tongue (continued)

including health care for members of the Congress.

On the other hand, some functions of government are a heavy burden. Notable are welfare payments, especially those to unmarried mothers and their children. Likewise expenditures for food stamps and child nutrition. While Medicare is not a burden, Medicaid is a real burden.

Education is a somewhat special case. While private education is not a burden, public education, especially in our cities, can be a very heavy load. Here, as elsewhere, burden bears no necessary relation to cost.

And here one sees the rule by which students of contemporary English usage should be guided. Whether a public function or service or regulation is or is not a burden depends on the income of the individual so helped or favored.

As with all linguistic rules there can be exceptions. The National Endowment for the Arts, support to public broadcasting, a few other items not specifically designed for the poor, are a burden. The exceptions, as ever, make the rule.

It is the generally accepted purpose of language to convey meaning. All who use or hear the word "burden" should know the precise and subtle meaning that it conveys. Basically something is a burden when it is not for the rich, not for the merely affluent, but for the poor.

Source: The New York Times, February 6, 1995, p. A17.

---

7. Kathryn Edin, a Rutgers sociologist, studied 214 mothers on welfare and 165 low-wage, single working mothers. Below is a table of the typical expenses and income for each group. What does this tell you in terms of the (a) incentive to go to work, and (b) most responsible course of action for a single mother with children and few job skills?

WELFARE

The Bottom Line

Monthly Income
  A.F.D.C. payments: $485
  Food stamps: $400
  Odd jobs (baby-sitting, selling trinkets
    and perfume door to door): $200
Monthly Expenses
  Rent (in public housing): $100
Net: $985 a month.
  (All figures estimated for a mother of
  four.)

WORK

The Bottom Line

Monthly Income
  Wages (includes overtime for two 13-
    hour shifts per week): $1,645, after
    taxes.
Monthly Expenses
  Rent (income-adjusted): $300
  Transportation to and from work
    (averaged cost to buy and repair two
    cars): $300.
  Car insurance and gas: $100.
  Child care: $100.
  Student loan payment: $61.
  Beeper: $9.
Net: $775 a month.

Source: J. DeParle (1994). "Better Work Than Welfare, But What If There's Neither," The New York Times, December 18, 1994, pp. 46–47. See also K. Edin, (1994). "The Myths of Dependency and Self-Sufficiency: Women, Welfare, and Low-Wage Work," Working Paper No. 67, Piscataway, NJ: Rutgers University Center for Urban Policy Research, p. 15.

References

Abramovitz, M. (1994). "Challenging the Myths of Welfare Reform From a Woman's Perspective." *Social Justice* **21**, 17–21.

————, and Piven, F. (1993). "Scapegoating Women on Welfare." *The New York Times,* September 2, p. A23.

Applebome, P. (1994). "Tourism Enriches an Island Resort, But Hilton Head Blacks Feel Left Out." *The New York Times,* September 2, p. A18.

Besharov, D., and Fowler, A. (1993). "The End of Welfare as We Know It?" *The Public Interest* **111**, 95–108.

Brody, J. (1995). "Despite Reductions in Exposure, Lead Remains Danger to Children." *The New York Times,* March 21, p. C3.

Chira, S. (1994a). "If Welfare Mothers Must Go to Work in Clinton Plan, Will Children Gain?" *The New York Times,* August 9, p. B8.

———— (1994b). "Study Confirms Some Fears on U.S. Children." *The New York Times,* April 12, pp. A1, A13.

———— (1994c). "Teen-Age Mothers Helped by Ohio Plan, Study Finds." *The New York Times,* September 20, p. A16.

Cohen, D. (1993). "New Study Links Lower I.Q. at Age 5 to Poverty." *Education Week* **12,** 4.

———— (1994). "Welfare Panel Leaves Open Education Questions." *Education Week* **13,** 18.

Cohen, L. (1994). "The Puzzling Case of Jimmy 'the Greek,'" *Society* **31,** 43–50.

Cooper, M. (1994). "Overthrowing the Welfare State." *Village Voice,* May 31, pp. 33–37.

Cost, Quality & Child Outcomes Study Team. (1995). *Cost, Quality and Child Outcomes in Child Care Centers, Executive Summary.* Denver: Economics Department, University of Colorado at Denver.

Coughlin, E. (1994). "Experts Add Their Voices to Welfare-Reform Debate." *The Chronicle of Higher Education* **40,** A6–A7.

DeParle, J. (1994a). "Analysis Increases the Cost of Clinton's Welfare Plan." *The New York Times,* December 3, p. 11.

———— (1994b). "Change in Welfare is Likely to Need Big Jobs Program." *The New York Times,* January 30, pp. 1, 22.

———— (1994c). "Momentum Builds for Cutting Back Welfare System." *The New York Times,* November 13, pp. 1, 30.

———— (1994d). "States' Eagerness to Experiment on Welfare Jars Administration." *The New York Times,* April 14, pp. A1, B10.

———— (1994e). "Way Out Front on a Hot-Button Issue." *The New York Times,* October 20, p. A25.

———— (1994f). "Welfare Mothers Find Jobs Are Easier to Get Than Hold." *The New York Times,* October 24, pp. A1, A14.

Dershowitz, A. (1994). *The Abuse Excuse.* Boston: Little, Brown.

Dugger, C. (1995). "Exodus Over Welfare Cuts?" *The New York Times,* May 1, pp. A1, B4.

———— (1994a). "Fish Story Ends in 'Workfare' and Sweet Smell of Success." *The New York Times,* October 8, p. 26.

———— (1994b). "Researchers Find a Diverse Face on the Poverty in New York City." *The New York Times,* August 30, pp. A1, B3.

————, and Hernandez, R. (1994). "Often-Cited Workfare Effort Provides Cautionary Lessons." *The New York Times,* November 25, pp. A1, B4.

Ehrenreich, B. (1995). "Battered Welfare Syndrome." *Time,* April 3, p. 82.

———— (1994). "Real Babies, Illegitimate Debates." *Time,* August 22, p. 90.

Ellwood, D. (1994). "Welfare Reform and the Clinton Administration." *Social Justice* **21,** 50–59.

Fisher, I. (1994). "Albany Study Finds Fraud in Welfare." *The New York Times*, August 3, pp. B1, B2.

Gallagher, W. (1994). "How We Become What We Are." *The Atlantic Monthly* **274,** 39–55.

Gibbs, N. (1994). "The Vicious Cycle." *Time*, June 20, pp. 24–33.

Gordon, L. (1994a). "Welfare Reform: A History Lesson." *Dissent*, Summer, pp. 323–328.

_____ (1994b). *Pitied But Not Entitled*. New York: Free Press.

Gottfredson, L. (1994). "Egalitarian Fiction and Collective Fraud." *Society* **31,** 53–59.

Harvey, P. (1994). "Plenty of Jobs? Where?" *The New York Times*, November 25, p. A37.

Herrnstein, R., and Murray, C. (1994). *The Bell Curve*. New York: Free Press.

Henneberger, M. (1995), "State Aid Is Capped, but to What Effect?" *The New York Times*, April 11, pp. A1, A18.

Howell, D. (1994). "The Skills Myth." *The American Prospect* **18,** 81–90.

James, G. (1995). "Welfare Clerks Held in $2 Million Benefits Fraud." *The New York Times*, May 12, pp. A1, B6.

Jaynes, G. (1994). "Down and Out in Telluride." *Time*, September 5, pp. 60–61.

Johnson, D. (1995). "Larger Benefits Lure Chicagoans to Wisconsin." *The New York Times*, May 8, p. A11.

Kadish, J. (1994). "Limits on Extra Welfare Payments for Newborns Questioned." *The New York Times*, September 11, Sec. 13, pp. 1, 6.

Kagan, J. (1994). *Galen's Prophesy: Temperament in Human Nature*. New York: Basic Books.

Kelly, V., and Morgan J. (1994). *Leading With My Heart*. New York: Simon & Schuster.

Klein, J. (1994). "A Tale of Two Cities." *Newsweek*, August 15, p. 57.

Leusner, D. (1994). "Fingerprinting to Counter Welfare Fraud Clears." *The Newark Star-Ledger*, June 10, p. 18.

Levin, T. (1994). "Appeals Court Overturns California's Welfare Cut." *The New York Times*, July 15, p. A12.

Lewis, N. (1994). "Justice Thomas Assails Victim Mentality." *The New York Times*, May 17, p. A14.

Limbaugh, R. (1993). *The Way Things Ought To Be*. New York: Pocket Books.

Linden, E. (1994). "Population: The Awkward Truth." *Time*, June 20, p. 74.

Lively, K. (1994). "Wary of Welfare Reform." *The Chronicle of Higher Education* **40,** A25–A26.

Magnet, M. (1994). "Problem No. 1: The Children." *The New York Times*, November 25, p. A37.

McCall, N. (1994). *Makes Me Wanna Holler*. New York: Random House.

McFadden, R. (1994). "Big Spender Is Charged with Fraud on Welfare." *The New York Times*, October 7, pp. B1, B6.

Mitchell, A. (1994a). "Fingerprinting for Welfare Is Defended." *The New York Times*, June 8, pp. B1–B2.

_____ (1994b). "Giuliani Plans to Require Work From Able Welfare Recipients." *The New York Times*, October 8, pp. 1, 26.

Murray, C. (1994). "Does Welfare Bring More Babies?" *The Public Interest* **115,** 17–30.

Newman, K. (1995). "What Inner-City Jobs for Welfare Moms?" *The New York Times*, May 20, p. 23.

Pear, R. (1995), "Catholic Bishops Challenge Pieces of Welfare Bill." *The New York Times*, March 19, pp. 1, 26.

Popenoe, D. (1994). "Scandinavian Welfare." *Society* **31,** 78–81.

"Poverty Is Unfairly Defined." (1994). *The New York Times*, Editorial, August 7, p. E16.

Purdy, M. (1994). "Cost of Lead Cleanup Puts More Poor Children at Risk." *The New York Times*, August 25, pp. B1, B3.

Random House College Dictionary. (1982). New York: Random House.

Rawls, J. (1983). *A Theory of Justice.* New York: Oxford University Press.

Redburn, T. (1994). "A City in the Enterprise Zone." *The New York Times,* May 18, pp. B1, B4.

Sack, K. (1994). "New York Shifting Focus of Welfare to Job Placement." *The New York Times,* May 21, pp. 1, 26.

Staples, B. (1994). *Parallel Time.* New York: Pantheon Books.

Steele, S. (1991). *The Content of Our Character.* New York: St. Martin's Press.

Sykes, C. (1992). *A Nation of Victims.* New York: St. Martin's Press.

Van Biema, D. (1994). "The Storm Over Orphanages." *Time,* December 12, pp. 58–62.

Vobejda, B. (1994). "Gore Unveils Antipoverty Strategy." *The Washington Post,* April 1, p. A3.

"Vox Pop." (1994). *Time,* June 27, p. 26.

Will, G. (1994). "Orwell in New Jersey." *Newsweek,* March 21, p. 84.

CHAPTER THREE

School Choice: For Family Choice or Against Vouchers

POSITION 1:
FAMILY CHOICE IN EDUCATION

Some time ago, during the first administration of President Nixon, a proposal emerged from the U.S. Office of Economic Opportunity that provoked a heated debate. The initial excitement passed after a few years when the proposal did not bear much fruit in terms of implementation. However, the debate continued on a back burner of public policy discussion. In recent times, during the administrations of Presidents Reagan and Bush, the flame was turned up by proposals from the U.S. Department of Education. The Nixon, Reagan, and Bush proposals are called either "family choice" or "vouchers." Although "family choice" is the longer name, it captures the spirit better, and so it is the term that will be used in this argument. The family choice idea merits consideration for three reasons: (1) it will not go away; (2) it gives many people, including officials at the highest levels of local, state, and national government, great hope for the future of American education; and (3) it is an idea of such intrinsic promise that it cries out for a fair test. Moreover, as Lynn Cheney, former chairperson of the National Endowment for the Humanities, has said: "Critics of choice are fond of saying that it is not a panacea, and they have a point; nevertheless, simply because of the forces it sets in motion, choice does have primacy among reforms. It is, as well, a change that seems long overdue" (Cheney, 1990, p. 24).

Family choice means that the family chooses the school its children will attend. The family can make this choice from among *all* of the *approved* schools within a reasonable commuting distance. Approved schools would be those that met minimum standards, such as building safety and fiscal accountability. Public, private, and parochial schools could all participate. That would include literally scores of schools in the more populous areas of the United States. But even if there were only five schools in a less populous area, that would be five times more choice than families have now.

To pay for the school of its choice, the family would be given a check (or voucher) by the government. The government would get the money for these checks from the taxes it collects. In other words, schools would still be supported by taxes, but a family would be able to get its hands on its share of the tax money and use that to buy the kind of education it *really* wants. All families would get the same amount of money per child, depending on the needs of the child. For example, the amounts of the checks (or vouchers) for handicapped children would be more than those for children without handicaps because it costs more to educate the handicapped. For all children in the same educational category, the amounts of the checks would be the same.

Breaking the Educational Monopoly

Obviously, none of this would make any sense if the family could choose only from among schools that were all the same. That is why the idea doesn't make much sense in today's school market, where the vast preponderance of schools are interchangeable clones of each other. "If we first implement choice, true choice among schools, we unleash the values of competition in the education marketplace" (*Time for Results*, 1986, p. 6). What the idea is intended to do, therefore, is replace that amorphous mass of jelly that passes for education in America with some really solid alternatives from which families can select.

Under family choice, the neighborhood school will no longer be forced on families until they have the money to buy their way out. "There's something galling about the idea that you're stuck in a particular school that's not working for you unless you are rich enough to buy yourself out of it" (Meier, 1991, p. 271). The captive clientele of today's schools will be set free. Family choice in education is a liberating act of the twentieth century. And just as indentured servants of the eighteenth century who had worked off their period of servitude could either remain with their former owners or strike out on their own, families can stick with the neighborhood school or go off to some school that has deliberately fashioned itself to be attractive and interesting. Indeed, the neighborhood school will probably refashion itself in an effort to keep families from fleeing.

The possibilities for attractive and interesting schools are everything that you can imagine, plus much more that may not even occur to you. For example, one of the public schools in the East Harlem section of New York City is a maritime academy, with the East River serving as a natural laboratory. There is a talented and gifted school, a performing arts school, a career academy, and a key (basic skills) school. The last four schools share space in what was once a large impersonal, one-size-fits-all school (Fliegel, 1993; Kirp, 1992). It is remarkable that these public schools in one of the worst sections of New York City have been made so attractive that they enroll 1,000 students from other parts of the city (Snider, 1990, p. 19)! Cleveland has an aviation high school whose curriculum includes flying lessons. Or a school could be truly "user friendly" by using the experiences of the kids in the neighborhood as the building blocks of the curriculum (Raywid, Tesconi, and Warren, 1984, p. 24). The choice will be especially rich if families can select not just from among the public schools of an area, but also from among the private and parochial schools. This variety of schools already has some diversity to offer, but the choices will be multiplied many times as *all* schools scurry to attract parents with vouchers. With declining patronage, a school will have decreasing income and will have to lay off staff. With few, if any, vouchers, a school will not have adequate resources to stay in operation and will have to shut down. These dismal prospects will cause schools to work harder than ever to attract customers and keep them satisfied. Up until now, a public school has not had to work hard at all because it has had a virtual monopoly on the education in its neighborhood. "Under a real competitive system of choice, what would a school board do if a school lost 40 percent of its students and 40 percent of its money? They'd give the principal a year to turn the damn place around or get out the door. There would finally be a reason why somebody had to care about these schools. It would work for the kids left behind even more than for the kids who move" (Clark, 1993, p. 53).

The Rights of Parents

In the United States, parents have extensive and legally sanctioned control over their children. The theory that justifies this legal authority is that parents are the people who are most likely to understand the needs of their children, and are also the ones most concerned about their welfare. "In its unique opportunity to listen and to know and in its special personal concern for the child, the family is his most promising champion" (Coons and Sugarman, 1978, p. 53).

The rights of parents over their children are not unlimited, and should not be. There are needs of children that parents simply are not competent to meet and for which they have to rely on expert help. Medical care is one example. Education is another. Parents may lack pedagogical skills and have to turn to professional educators for assistance. However, professional educators have transitory relationships with children and never acquire the intimate knowledge and concern that parents have. Moreover, they do not have to live with the consequences of having a miseducated and unhappy child. Therefore, parents should always be the senior partner of the educational team for their child. And they should certainly have the most to say about the primary educational decision: the school the child will attend.

Or not attend. Parents' rights in the education of their children have been recognized by the courts as including the right to educate children at home. Parents need only demonstrate their competence to deliver the basic education expected by the state. Home schooling is not widespread yet, but if parents could cash in the "choice" voucher themselves instead of signing it over to some school, it would become financially feasible for more parents to do what they've always wanted—create family schools.

Escaping Secular Humanism

In addition to having the right to choose something good for their children, parents have a right to protect their children against things that are bad. One of the things that most worries parents is having their children come under "evil influences." Parents forbid their children to play with certain other children because they fear that their children will be led astray.

For many parents, especially among those who are devoutly religious, the public school itself is an evil influence. It is evil because it is so nonreligious. In its attempt to avoid indoctrinating children into any religion, the public school shuns all but the most neutral presentation of religion, treating religious faiths as purely historical phenomena. It presents all religions as being equally good and equally arbitrary manifestations of people's search for meaning. This obviously suggests to students that their family's religion is just one among equals and that it is no more divinely inspired than any of the others, and maybe not at all.

Parents believe that the noncommittal approach of the public schools weakens their children's religious commitment. It turns children from spiritual sources of certain truth and guidance to merely human ones that are uncertain and relative. Naturally, parents whose own lives are made meaningful by religion and whose own behavior is guided by it dread having their children weaned away from religion by the nonreligion of the public schools. Some parents go so far as to say that because the public school's approach has consequences for their religion, it is, in fact, a form of religion itself. They call this form "secular humanism," meaning a religion that elevates human beings to the highest moral realm. And that means that their children are in a school where a competing and hostile religion is being taught, subtly and insidiously.

Choice is the way to allow these parents the right to protect their children's salvation as they see fit. It is a violation of religious freedom to require parents to send their children to an institution that undermines the parents' religious values.

The liberal reaction to this is to say that the comprehensive, "melting pot" school is such a good thing that it is worth maintaining even if everyone in it is offended in some way. Indeed, offensiveness itself is presumed to have educative value. However, Nathan Glazer, a leading scholar of religious and ethnic conflict, articulates a much more realistic position:

> I am convinced the conflict of values in this country today, between the religious and the secular, the permissive and the traditional, those seeking experience and those seeking security and stability, between the culture of the coasts and the culture of the heartland, between the cosmopolitans of Los Angeles and New York and the staid inhabitants of smaller towns and cities (as well as most of the inhabitants of Los Angeles and New York), are so great that the vision of a truly common school, in which all are educated together, simply will not work . . . a decent opportunity for withdrawal to a more homogeneous and educationally effective environment is necessary and can be provided without destroying our democracy and/or our multiethnic society. (Glazer as quoted by Lieberman, 1993, p. 38)

The Benefits for Students

One of the recurring and most common complaints about American education is that it leaves students bored out of their skulls. You can judge for yourself how much this complaint echoes your own experience. The complaint has been around a long time, but school officials have never had to do anything about it because there has been no choice for children or their parents. Children had to go to school; they had to go to the school that some authority mandated; and they could end up in reform school if they did not attend the prescribed school. Well, youngsters may have to receive an education for their own and society's benefit, but they at least should be able to go to a school they like.

The literature of professional education contains some truths that remain remarkably absent from the *practice* of education. One of these truths is that different children have different needs and interests. That's so obvious as to be a truism. Another truth is that students learn more when they are motivated than when they are longing desperately for the bell to ring. That, too, is a truism. Family choice means that at long last these two fundamental truths of education will actually be *applied.*

As a matter of fact, the truths are being applied already, but for only a few students—those whose families can afford to send them to a school beyond the control of the local authorities. Family choice will give all of us a right that now exists in reality only for the well-to-do. It is true that the poor can scrimp and save to send their children to parochial schools, but parochial schools for the poor are not markedly better, and from the student's point of view may be much worse, than the local public schools. Why should only the rich be allowed to have effective control over their children's education? Bret Schundler, as mayor of Jersey City, has fought to get a voucher program for the poor children of his constituency. As he puts it:

> School choice has been a reality for the rich. They can move to suburban districts where the public schools are decent. Or if, like Bill Clinton, occupational requirements compel them to live in a city, they can send their children to high-quality private schools. The poor are largely denied that opportunity. They are compelled by law to attend government schools, even when some of these schools are dysfunctional. (Schundler, 1993, p. A27)

If a poor family can pick a school outside of its neighborhood, then minority families will be able to integrate their children into majority schools. As it stands now, American schools are notoriously and thoroughly segregated (Orfield, 1993). It is easy to find a school that is populated overwhelmingly by minority students. It is just as easy to find an almost lily-white school. A tragedy of our times is that these schools can be found in such close proximity to each other. They are on opposite sides of an arbitrary and artificial line known as the school district boundary. Family choice on a nondiscriminatory basis offers real promise of getting past this disgraceful condition. It might mean that the student body of Phillips Academy, the elite boarding school in Andover, Massachusetts, will be as racially diverse as that of the Andover Public High School (Boaz, 1993).

Racial and social-class integration of schools, to the extent that it has been tried in the United States, has had a rocky history. There are many cases in which it seems to have done more harm than good, and to have been a huge waste of time, energy, money, patience, and kids' lives. Such cases have all involved legally forced integration. With family choice, the integration will come about naturally, that is, voluntarily. The kids in a given school will not have race or social class in common, but they will have common interests and needs. Those commonalities are more important to children than are the superficial characteristics of race and class that adults worry so much about.

Family choice is a way to honor the good sense of children to everyone's advantage. The Hervey School in Medford, Massachusetts, did just that by offering such interesting programs that it attracted a multiracial student body (Bastian et al., 1985, p. 76). It is even possible to have a "choice" school whose theme is integration. "Educational alternatives can be based on a newer conception of integration—multicultural education, which establishes cultural diversity as its founding principle" (Fantini, 1973, p. 229). There is something paradoxical about the push for multicultural education in today's racially segregated schools.

The Benefits for Teachers

Family choice does not sit well with teacher unions because it is thought to pose a threat to their members' job security. Every family that pulls out of a school brings the teacher's job closer to extinction. If families are not allowed to pull out, the teacher can bask in the assurance of guaranteed employment— at least when birth rates are not falling. That is the negative attitude toward family choice, and it paints teachers as wanting nothing more than to be civil service lifers. It is a demeaning portrait of teachers, and it ignores the positive aspects of family choice for them.

Family choice frees teachers to design schools as they wish. The deadening uniformity and ritualism of schools can be as enervating to teachers as to students. Most teachers would like to do something to make school exciting for themselves and their students, but they have no chance to do so because they are locked into the bureaucratic monolith. The "something" may be little more than a series of interest-arousing community explorations that are outside the standard organization of the school day. What the teachers would like to do cannot be done because it does not fit into the "system." David Kearns, former chairman and chief executive officer of the Xerox Corporation, as well as a U.S. Assistant Secretary of Education, says that America's public school system has to be broken up just as business corporations had to be in recent years, and for the same reason: they have become bureaucratic dinosaurs that impede the productivity of their employees. Choice is the way to disassemble them (Kearns and Doyle, 1988). If one of the most powerful corporations in the world, IBM, has been forced to acknowledge the necessity to do this, it is not too much to expect that public education will have to do the same. All teachers can do now is struggle around the periphery of the dinosaur until they become exhausted, and then content themselves with going through the motions until retirement or get out of teaching altogether. Read this description of the idealistic teacher who has become burned out and imagine what "choice" could mean for such a person.

> The classic example of Type II burnout is a young, well-educated, socially idealistic, politically involved young man or woman who comes to an impoverished inner-city or rural school brimming with ideas, enthusiasm, and confidence and who, after several months (or perhaps even years) of giving more and more—of depriving him- or herself of sleep and/or a relaxing social life, of trying to find new, creative ways to motivate and teach children—senses that these efforts are not paying off, that he or she is ineffective and perhaps even mistrusted. (Farber, 1991, p. 91)

Family choice will give the bolder and more creative teachers an opportunity to break loose and start their own schools. A school could be created on the basis of a shared enthusiasm for a particular approach to education. It could be formed out of friendships among teachers, with the particular educational approach being hashed out collegially, and revised the same way (Raywid, 1987). If the school is small, the teachers will still be able to maintain their standard of living while saving a lot of the cost of administrative overhead. A sufficiently small school could be operated out of a home or store, so that both capital and custodial costs could be kept to a minimum.

Less adventurous teachers could redesign the schools in which they have been working, perhaps dividing them into minischools. The school administrators who might be rendered superfluous by this action need not be fired. They could take on more strictly educational duties, and they should welcome this prospect if they are truly committed to working with children.

Family choice, then, will have the effect of *empowering* teachers. Not only will they remain in direct contact with students, but there no longer will be a bureaucratic Maginot line between them and the parents, or the school policies. Schooling will become a cooperative venture among the three parties essential to it: students, teachers, and parents. This does not mean that all of the new schools will be better than any of the present schools. It means that students, teachers, and parents will be able to have the kind of school in which they feel the most comfortable and have the most confidence.

These prospects could in themselves solve the problem of a teacher shortage. People who would not deign to teach in the present system would be excited enough by the chance to be true educational professionals that they would make career switches. The Friedmans report that people have told them: "I have always wanted to teach [or run a school] but I couldn't stand the educational bureaucracy, red tape, and general ossification of the public schools" (Friedman and Friedman, 1980, p. 169).

The "charter schools" movement is especially promising. The goal is to allow teachers and parents to take over the operation of their local public schools, relatively free of control by local boards of education or the state. This truly local control would be exercised within only the most general and minimal guidelines. At least eleven states have already passed legislation permitting the establishment of charter schools, and another dozen states have legislation pending (General Accounting Office, 1995).

Respecting Differences

Teaching children to respect differences among people is supposed to be a goal of today's public schools. However, the schools betray this goal in two major ways. First, they are segregated along racial and social-class lines. The message that this sends to students is that some people are more worthy of avoidance than of respect. Second, the public schools are like giant food blenders, where differences are ground into mush. It's all right for the teachers to talk about tolerance, but the kids don't get much chance to assert anything about themselves that could require toleration.

Religion, politics, esthetic sensibilities, and expressive styles are all carefully constrained in the public school of today. No one is allowed to get "too far out of line" or be "too radical." Everyone walks on eggshells. Genuine self-expression is like a time bomb that has to be defused. Eccentricity is a scandal, and in today's frantically vanilla schools it does not take much to be eccentric. The norms in urban poor schools may be different from those in suburban affluent schools, but they are just as limiting and oppressive. The frantically chocolate school leaves no more breathing room than does the one that is frantically vanilla.

Family choice means freedom for the misfits in today's schools. That they are misfits reflects not on them, but on the intellectual and social rigidity of the schools. They are as likely to be supernormal as subnormal. Their only crime lies in falling outside a field of tolerance that is not very wide. The only choice they have now is for an education that is either painful or inauthentic, and often both. If they display their true selves, they suffer rejection and ridicule on the part of their peers and constant badgering by the school authorities. If they dissemble to get by, they feel false and dishonest, which can cause them to reject themselves. Family choice can widen the field of tolerance *across* schools, so that the misfits, some of whom are misfitted unto suicide, begin to belong. It may not increase the tolerance within a school, and could even reduce it, but at least children would know that society respected them enough to find places for them all.

What choice does, then, is allow the creation of communities of interest and mutuality, as opposed to the current school communities of coercion. The genuine community nature of choice schools is their essential element, and that is what most guarantees the success they enjoy.

> What can choice be, then, if it finds support in so many different, ordinarily antagonistic quarters? The common element—for community organizers, for Catholics, for free marketers—is that in each case proponents of choice are arguing for the creation and support of *communities*. This may seem far-fetched with regard to the current choice movement—after all, the free market dissolves communities, it doesn't create them. But free choice in a free market environment for schooling does indeed permit the expression, creation, and maintenance of communities. And if choice is effective, as its advocates hope, in raising academic achievement, the primary reason will be because it re-creates community in schools in which the maintenance of community had become difficult or impossible. (Glazer, 1993, p. 650)

Building in Safeguards

Family choice, of course, is vulnerable to abuse, with hucksterism the abuse that usually leaps to people's minds first. Schools-for-profit are permitted—indeed, encouraged—by family choice. Some of the profiteers are going to be hucksters willing to do some unscrupulous things to attract and bilk families. False advertising, misrepresentation, inflated claims, hidden charges, and bait-and-switch schemes are some of the practices that have to be prevented. As with other businesses, the best way to circumvent these white collar crimes is through a monitoring mechanism that can detect them, and then impose swift and severe penalties on their perpetrators. Dishonest educational practices are among the worst kinds of consumer fraud because the victims are children and the harm can be long lasting. A well-staffed agency should be able to keep the abuses to a minimum and to catch quickly any that do occur.

Another potential abuse of the family choice system is discriminatory admissions practices. A school might want to make itself attractive to both families and teachers by excluding certain students, such as black students, low-achieving students, handicapped students, or students from a minority religious group. It might be permissible to exclude students who perform poorly on a test that is related to the purpose of the school, or students who are so profoundly handicapped that the school is not equipped to help them. There will be other schools that specialize in such problem students, so their needs can be met in a variety of ways. And academically elite schools, such as Boston's Latin School, should be allowed to continue their mission of serving those students who are most talented academically without considering their nonacademic characteristics (Glenn, 1991). However, exclusion on the bases of race and religion and other illegitimate criteria are abuses that the fair practices agency should be charged to prevent. In this regard, public support for choice, as measured by a *Time*/CNN poll in the spring of 1991, strongly indicates that the public wants more choice even if it means that some schools will be nearly all white and others all black, with 48 percent of those polled agreeing to this, whereas 42 percent did not (Shapiro, 1991, p. 57). Equally noteworthy is the result of a Gallup survey showing that 64 percent of those polled believe that parents should receive governmental financial support to send their children to religious schools (*The People's Poll on Schools and School Choice*, 1992). In sum, the public is prepared to have racially and religiously segregated schools if that is what people freely choose.

A third form of abuse would be the failure to provide the minimally adequate education expected for all normal children regardless of the school they and their families choose. A school may attract students because it is warm and friendly and fun to attend, but then not assist them in acquiring the academic skills needed for gainful employment and useful citizenship. Society has a right to establish minimum standards of achievement and to test students to ascertain that they are meeting these standards. Many states already have statewide standards and tests, so it is simply a matter of maintaining these under the family choice system.

A fourth problem is the cost of transportation. Students should be transported at public expense to any school in the region covered by the family choice system. Otherwise, a family's choices will be circumscribed by the cost of transportation. For poor families, this cost can be prohibitive, so they will have no real choice apart from the school(s) in the neighborhood. It is not likely that suburban students would be attracted to an urban school if that school were nearly crammed to capacity with kids who are trapped in the neighborhood. Without a transportation allowance, the family choice system will offer a lot less choice, and may bring about very little integration racially and socially. Obviously, if private schools are allowed to be part of a publicly funded choice system, they will have to play by these rules. They can't take government money and be free of government regulation. They will have to compete for students under the same constraints as those imposed on public schools. The line between private and public will largely be erased (Kemerer, 1992; Weinberg, 1992).

A fifth form of abuse has been alleged in Wisconsin. Milwaukee's Parental Choice Program is the only publicly financed private school choice experiment, and its success (or failure) will greatly influence the future of choice. Thus, the research on this program is studied closely by the advocates, the opponents, and policymakers generally. The advocates claim that the researcher doing the "official" analysis is biased against choice and is rigging the research to discredit the Milwaukee program (Lindsay, 1994; McGroarty, 1994). This points up the need to make the program data widely available for independent analysis by any interested researcher.

Once a choice system is under way, other dangers may appear and other safeguards will have to be devised, but human ingenuity should be able to cope with these problems. It is possible to protect everyone's legitimate interest while expanding everyone's freedom. The result will be education characterized by harmonious pluralism. "The ability to get the kind of education one wants for oneself or one's children serves both as a reward for those with a pedagogical interest and as a means of defusing fights between interests over who should have the ability to impose universal requirements on the system" (Kerchner, 1988, p. 390).

POSITION 2:
AGAINST VOUCHER PLANS

Defining the Terms

"Family" and "choice" are powerful words in the American lexicon. They carry a lot of emotional baggage. Both the Democratic and Republican national parties invoke the word "family" as though it were a sacred mantra. And choice is something we instinctively associate with democracy as opposed to tyranny, which is characterized by the denial of choice. So when the words are combined into the term "family choice," the unwitting listener or reader is disposed to agree with the proposal itself.

It's a good debate tactic to give your side of the argument an appealing label. If the debate were just an intellectual exercise, no harm would be done by this, and one side would rack up a few points in the category of "best label." However, the issue under discussion here is one that has momentous implications for us all. The two sides to the debate are not nearly as important as the great in-between, the American public. For the American public to judge the debate fairly and make a well-informed decision about the future direction of American education, it is imperative that it not be blinded by debaters' tricks. Therefore, we will not use the loaded term "family choice," which plays into our opponents' hands, nor will we employ a loaded term of our own. Instead, we will use a term that is so neutral that when people hear it they say, "Huh?" The word "voucher" has practically no value connotations, except perhaps to accountants, and it is a word that does not even exist in most people's working vocabularies. The use of this word will not cloud the debate, but will allow it to be judged on its substantive merits. Moreover, a voucher is simply a mechanism by which choice is effected: parents get a voucher (or check) from the government, which they use to pay for their child's education at the school of their choice. While vouchers are but one form of choice, they are the logical end to which the truncated forms lead. It is for this reason that the more limited forms of choice are suspected of being stalking horses for vouchers.

Preserving Diversity

A voucher system has many practical problems, and they will be addressed in later sections. The overriding problem, however, is a philosophical one. The American public school now functions as a crucible of democracy. This is especially true of the comprehensive high school, where students from a good-sized geographic area and with a wide range of interests and abilities are brought together.

In today's comprehensive high school, there is choice—not a choice of school, but a choice of curricula within the school. Students with different interests and abilities have programs that are tailored to them. They also can easily switch from one program to another since all the programs are in a single school. Thus, the individual has both choice and ease of choice, and there is also the benefit of heterogeneity for the individual and for society. Students from different programs in the high school can mingle and engage in common activities. The *extra*curricular activities of the school are open to all regardless of their curriculum program. But even some of the academic courses mix students from different programs. For schools that have programs but not ability grouping (or tracks) within the programs, the commingling is even greater.

The net result of this arrangement is that different kinds of people get practice at living together. The practice may, on occasion, be unsettling, even painful. However, it cannot be forestalled forever, and school is a semiprotected environment in which to gain the experience of democratic living. It is a relatively safe place for learning how to get along with others. In the comprehensive high school, "others" does not just mean others like oneself; it also means others with whom one does not have much in common. Students who develop the ability to interact smoothly with a variety of other people are likely to be successful and happy as adults. They will know when to compromise and what behaviors are offensive to what sorts of people. They will also understand the value of reciprocity in relationships. These abilities can only be developed where there is a variety of other people—that is, in the comprehensive high school.

A voucher system, by whatever euphemism and in whatever form, would replace the crucible that is the comprehensive high school with a spice rack on which differences are physically isolated and separately contained. That may be snug and comfortable for the students in each little container, but it is poor preparation for the real world. For American students, it is poor preparation for citizenship in a democracy. "The unifying function is not simply an ideal of the comprehensive high school model; it reflects an ideal central to our democratic republic. It is, in effect, an effort to act upon the motto of the United States, *E Pluribus Unum*—out of many, one" (Wraga, 1992, p. 42). Learning how to socialize with people who share your interests and abilities is relatively easy, but hardly enough. There are all those other kinds of people out there, and you cannot hide from them forever if you wish to have a rich and full life. A voucher system would cripple students socially and breed a divisive defensiveness among groups of people who have never been able to know each other. At a time when states are trying to develop more truly multicultural curricula in recognition of the value of multiple perspectives in an interdependent world, it is ironic that some people are trying to make the school itself more unicultural.

Choosing When Ready

Thus far the focus of this discussion has been on the high school and why a voucher system is both unnecessary and undesirable at that level of education. It may seem that a voucher system is justified at the elementary school level because students (and families) now have virtually no choice there at all. There is the single neighborhood school, with its single curriculum for everyone. Moreover, that single curriculum is supposed to have a stranglehold on elementary education in America. It *is* our elementary education. Voucher advocates imply that this situation was developed conspiratorially by people who are indifferent to the needs of children. The American elementary school system is a gulag archipelago, they suggest—nothing more than a national system of prisons for children.

This characterization is a gross slander of elementary school educators and an insult to the intelligence of the American people. The elementary schools of America are, in reality, the places where the *common* needs of children are met. The schools are similar precisely because children's needs are common. *All* children who are going to survive and thrive in our society need to learn the academic basics of reading, writing, and arithmetic. These are generative skills; they are used as tools for further learning. The fact that all schools teach these skills, along with the social studies and science needed by future voters and workers, as well as art and music for life enrichment, simply reflects the good sense of Americans. Computer literacy is being added to the list because its importance has become obvious, and elementary schools are flexible and prudent enough to accommodate such a significant cultural adaptation. Do we really want to allow families to decide whether their children should have to learn things that are of transparent benefit to them and the rest of society?

Just how important and widely approved those things are can be seen in the national tests now being developed under federal auspices. Tests in the core school subjects and grade-by-grade standards are being designed so that Americans will have a good gauge of how well their children are doing relative to those standards and to other children. National standards have already been promulgated in English, mathematics, science, American history, world history, and civics. By the winter of 1995, a seventeen-state project was under way to translate the standards into performance objectives, which can be the basis for national tests (Olson, 1995). National testing will make the elementary school curriculum even more standard across the country and further weaken the case for a voucher system.

Children's needs and the corresponding academic subjects are the same from school to school, and to some extent from grade to grade, which enables children to transfer between schools without disrupting their academic progress. This portability has to be an important consideration for a people as mobile as are Americans. It does not mean, however, that all children are expected to learn the basic academic skills in exactly the same way. Different schools have different teaching styles and materials, and this is true for students of different abilities within the same school. The styles and the materials are matters best left to the judgment of trained professionals. Without denigrating the intelligence of parents and children, the indisputable fact is that they have not been trained to make the professional judgments of educators. Moreover, parents may wish to send their children to school outside the neighborhood just because it has become fashionable to do so, much as some college students wish to go to an out-of-state college. If the cost of transportation is only a dollar each way, that could amount to $400 a year per student, or millions of dollars for the transportation system that then would not be available for the education system. Moreover, parents of even young children are apt to defer to their children's choice, and as the president of the American Federation of Teachers predicts, "What most kids—and most adults—want is not to have to work very hard" (Shanker, 1993, p. E7). This certainly is not the best basis on which to choose.

Voucher advocates argue that the differences in styles and materials to be found in today's elementary schools aren't different enough. Not even the differences that a school district creates when it makes each school a magnet site with its own unique theme are enough to satisfy the voucherites. They insist on a veritable multitude of choices, in the naive belief that children and parents are capable of wading through this wild abundance and making an intelligent selection. Elementary school children are too young to have this responsibility imposed on them, and most parents lack the time and expertise to make distinctions among a host of closely competing alternatives. The voucher proponents subscribe to the silly notion that there can't be too much of a good thing. Choice is a good thing, but too much of it can be as paralyzing as taking too much cough medicine for a cold. If more choice is desired by the public, it should be brought about gradually and cautiously within an already proven system.

Inequality of Choice

Should a voucher system succeed in bringing about a wide variety of schools, choosing is going to be difficult for even the most intelligent and assiduous parents. Ploughing through the promotional material and independent assessments of the many schools could entail an enormous amount of reading. Interpreting this material could require technical expertise not possessed by the ordinary parent. Visiting schools that look good on paper to check out the reality is a task that many parents don't have time to carry out. Other parents lack the self-confidence to embark on such a bold venture.

What this brief consideration makes obvious is that not all parents are equal when it comes to choosing. The most educationally disadvantaged students are likely to have parents whose own poor education did not equip them to make wise choices for their children. Recent news disclosures have shocked us with the revelation that many parents brutalize their children and it may be unwise to trust them with their children's welfare in any way. Thus, the already educated and concerned parents will be able to take advantage of a choice system in ways that won't even occur to the ignorant or the indifferent.

Making the choosing situation equal will require considerable money for the production of reliable and cognitively accessible information packets, in more than one language, and for a goodly number of qualified counselors. This money may have to be subtracted from the value of the vouchers, leaving less for the actual education of children. Mario Fantini's blithe suggestion that those who lack the ability to choose well can simply continue doing so on a trial-and-error basis until they get it right (Fantini, 1973, pp. 74–75) ignores the huge educational and psychological cost for youngsters who wander from school to school, year after year.

The propagation of low social status across generations is something in which poor parents engage unwittingly. And in a voucher system, "parents will be able to send their children to schools that [may] reinforce in the most restrictive fashion the family's political, ideological, and religious views. That is, school will be treated as a strict extension of the home" (Levin, 1980, p. 251). The upshot will be that working-class parents will pick schools that stress discipline, basic skills, and following orders, while middle-class parents will select schools that foster independence and higher-order thinking skills. Working-class kids will learn how to be low-wage workers; middle-class kids will be readied for high-salaried professions. The working-class students will be limited by their parents' constrained conception of success.

Since minorities are represented disproportionately among the poor, social-class tracking by school will mean racially segregated schools. It is instructive to recall that the south used "schools of choice" as a way to guarantee the continuation of a dual school system, and it worked. Now that we know how fiercely northern communities have resisted desegregation, "it is fatuous to believe that the white community will permit a voucher system to operate so as to remove the barriers that they have laboriously erected to protect themselves and their children from what they consider to be the undesirable behavior patterns of the disadvantaged" (Ginzberg, 1972, p. 106). Whites will fight to make sure that "choice" is intradistrict only, leaving them safe to choose from among schools that will remain predictably white. New Jersey trumpets its "choice" initiatives, but they are intradistrict plans, posing no threat to the suburbs of Newark or Trenton or Camden.

The same result is possible with interdistrict choice if schools are allowed to choose students after the students have indicated their choice of schools. Schools could establish admission criteria that would predetermine the composition of the student body, not just in terms of academic ability, but also socioeconomically and racially. An example of how this might work is the New York City school system, where there are four tiers of high schools: academic schools, theme schools, vocational schools, and neighborhood schools. The top tier schools cream off the most able and manageable students, leaving the most needy, and therefore least desirable, students to the neighborhood schools (Bastian et al., 1985, p. 75). The choice for the disadvantaged is to stay put.

The segregative potential of "choice" plans is so great that it has been recommended that choice and vouchers be granted only to students who are failing in their present school. That should help to ensure that vouchers have an overall positive effect on students (Elconin and Holahan, 1990). Moore and Davenport looked at the way choice operated in New York, Chicago, Philadelphia and Boston, and concluded:

> School choice has, by and large, become a new improved method of student sorting, in which schools pick and choose among students. In this sorting process, black and Hispanic students, low-income students, students with low achievement, students with absence and behavior problems, handicapped students, and limited-English-proficiency students have very limited opportunities to participate in popular-option high schools and programs. Rather, students at risk are proportionately concentrated in schools which . . . characteristically exhibit low levels of expectations for their students, deplorable levels of course failure and retention, and extremely low levels of graduation and basic skill achievement. (Moore and Davenport, 1989, quoted in *Public Schools of Choice,* 1990, pp. 12–13)

Even in the much-touted District 4 of East Harlem, "creaming" has been found to occur in subtle ways. Bad students are encouraged to go elsewhere. The junior high schools annually recruit the best sixth graders. Such practices explain why the highly esteemed Central Park East School in the district had so few children from welfare families (Tashman, 1992). Robert Peterkin, director of the Urban Schools Programs at Harvard, has remarked on the "subtly selective" nature of the choice schools in Cambridge, Massachusetts, another district whose choice program has garnered a lot of favorable publicity (Peterkin, 1994). That kind of sorting is now taking place in Great Britain, where "choice" was made national policy in the late 1980s. British schools, desperately seeking to assure themselves of a student body, are screening out less desirable students, whether they are handicapped, troubled, or slow learners (Chira, 1992b). Their reasoning is that having undesirable students gives a school a poor reputation, and the only families willing to patronize such a school are those with no other choice, perhaps because their children are among those deemed undesirable.

The Interests of Society

It is interesting to note how the voucher proposal is pitched to the self-interests of different groups. Parents are told of the latitude it will give them in deciding where their children go to school. Students are regaled with visions of candy store education where they will be able to go on shopping sprees. Teachers are led to believe that, finally, they will have total job control. Very little emphasis is placed on the *responsibilities* that these groups will acquire—time-consuming, anxiety-provoking, selfishness-inducing responsibilities. Worse yet, no attention is paid to the interests of the whole, the common good. As a society, we have interests that transcend the self-interests of individuals, and that cannot be left to individual whims. The more legitimate such interests society has, the less freedom each individual or group can be allowed. The public interest requires that we be constrained in the exercise of our selfish interests.

What are society's interests in education? First, all children are to acquire the communication skills and the knowledge of government necessary for full and active citizenship. When these have been spelled out in detail by the state authorities whose responsibility this is, a good part of the K-12 curriculum has been specified. This becomes more and more the case as democracy demands greater and greater sophistication of its members.

Society's second major interest is in preparing young people for effective functioning in the world of work. This involves the development not only of marketable skills, but also of work habits and attitudes. This should eliminate from any "choice" equation those schools whose principal attraction for students is low expectations. In addition to having high expectations of its schools, the state has an obligation to monitor the schools to ensure a satisfactory level of fulfillment.

Society's third interest is a negative one. The state has a definite interest in keeping every school it pays for free of religious and ideological indoctrination. Public schools—and all voucher schools would be publicly funded—are not places for brainwashing students into the agenda of any interest group. As the U.S. Supreme Court said in the Epperson case, involving the teaching of Darwinian theory in Arkansas:

Judicial interposition in the operation of the public school systems of the Nation raises problems requiring care and restraint. Our courts, however, have not failed to apply the First Amendment's mandate in our educational system where essential to safeguard the fundamental values of freedom of speech and inquiry and of belief. By and large, public education in our Nation is committed to the control of state and local authorities. Courts do not and cannot intervene in the resolution of conflicts which arise in the daily operation of school systems and which do not directly and sharply implicate basic constitutional values. On the other hand, "The vigilant protection of constitutional values is nowhere more vital than in the community of the American Schools." (*Epperson v. State of Arkansas*, 1969)

Preserving freedom of speech and inquiry and of belief will mean that a lot of people are going to find themselves ineligible for voucher money with which to impose their personal convictions on youngsters. Otherwise, we are going to see public subsidization of socially divisive and miseducative institutions, such as white supremacist and black nationalist schools. Such cities as Detroit, Milwaukee, and New York have given serious thought to the establishment of public academies for black males (Chmelynski, 1990). Should such academies come into being, their curricula are likely to be Afrocentric as a way of promoting the self-esteem of the black male students. The goal will be laudable, but the instruction itself might amount to the myth mongering found in other Afrocentric programs.

Keeping Teachers Sane

Teacher unions get a bum rap for being opposed to vouchers. The unions are accused of an attitude of protecting the jobs of teachers above all else and let the public be damned. If the voucher system is adopted, the public *will* be damned, just as surely as there will be a dramatic drop in the number of teachers.

No one wants to work in an insecure environment. Everyone seeks stability and predictability in employment. To ask teachers to subject themselves to *no-guarantee* jobs for the rest of their working lives is to expect of them a sacrifice that no other workers would willingly make. Each summer, teachers would have to wait for word that their schools had attracted enough students for them to return to work in September. Their anxiety would then end only briefly, since student transfers during the year (another choice in the voucher radical choice scheme) could put them back out on the street. It might be possible for a teacher in a low-drawing school to transfer to a high-drawing school, but this could require that he or she abandon a sincerely held teaching philosophy. The teacher's effectiveness would be seriously impaired by such coerced insincerity. Certainly, job satisfaction would be diminished.

Over time, the constant tensions inherent in a voucher system are bound to have an insidious effect on even the most dedicated of teachers. They will know that their livelihoods are at stake in every interaction with their pupils. Dissatisfied pupils (and parents) will have the choice of pulling out even if their dissatisfaction is not justified. There will be a lot of shopping around for a good deal, not for a good education. Grade inflation, already at a scandalous level in American education, will render teacher judgments meaningless. Teachers will be in the untenable position of being the direct employees of the very people they are expected to evaluate. "Without an external incentive system that demands a certain kind of quality, success will be based on popularity rather than quality" (Shanker, 1994). *Caveat vendor* should not be the watchword of education.

This is not a call for the continuation of the tenure system for teachers. It is much more modest, and thus should be much less controversial, than that. It is only a call for some continuity and independence in the professional lives of teachers so that they can do their jobs honestly. Vouchers will drive teachers into other careers, and the first teachers to go are likely to be those who value honesty the most.

Controlling Temptation

This brings us to another consideration of honesty or, rather, dishonesty. Voucher schools will be public schools insofar as they are to be funded publicly and to be open to the public. However, a salient feature of public schools historically is that they have also been nonprofit institutions. Budgets are subject to public approval, including the budget items for employee salaries, and there are no stockholders to receive dividends or capital gains. In short, the opportunities for public school officials to make a profit from their positions are severely limited, and in many cases such profiteering can be exercised only through illegal or unethical conduct. Even then, the amount to be gained may be so small that no one would take the risk of being detected and punished.

The voucher system will put public education in the for-profit category. People who run the schools will be allowed to earn as much as they can wring from the public. The thickness of their wallets no longer will be limited to the amount of their previous salaries. Public education will be transformed into just another capitalist venture. "Supply-side competition introduces strong incentives for providers to present superficial or inaccurate information on effectiveness, to package information to promote their product, and to protect as proprietary certain types of information that would be useful in making client choice" (Elmore, 1986, p. 34). If college recruiting brochures have only a coincidental relationship to the actual institution they supposedly portray, imagine all the misleading fluff that will go into the promotional material of voucher schools.

Some idea of this can be gleaned from California's open enrollment law, which allows parents to send their children to any public school within their school district. Schools are now running television commercials and placing newspaper advertisements to attract students (Newman, 1994). Even if the hype is restrained, the money and personnel time consumed in producing it could have been spent directly on education.

We should make sure the American public does not have to bail out an array of corrupt voucher schools as it has had to bail out corrupt savings and loan associations. A corrupt–practices control board for the voucher system will have its hands full. Its first order of business will be to figure out what constitutes a corrupt practice in this strange new form of business. No doubt it will encounter, among other abuses, those that have been so rife among proprietary schools: inflated claims of graduate placement; inflated projected earnings for graduates; elastic definitions of success, such that a person who becomes a file clerk in a public defender's office is credited with a career in law enforcement. The prohibited practices will necessarily be defined in general terms, so there will be large gray areas where all kinds of shady practices can take place. The number of independent public schools will increase geometrically, and just conducting paper audits of each one of them could take up all the time of a well-staffed control board. On-site inspections would take place perhaps once every five years. The years between inspections would be the stealing time.

Voucher schools will either conduct or commission studies of their own effectiveness. This is not a reassuring prospect, given the record to date of evaluations of choice programs. What the public has been getting is a welter of conflicting research results. The Carnegie Foundation for the Advancement of Teaching captures page 1 of *The New York Times* with its report questioning the effectiveness of choice programs (Chira, 1992a). The data used by this prestigious source are then challenged by prestigious researchers, such as Paul Peterson of the Harvard University government department (Lindsay, 1994). District 4 in East Harlem is acclaimed nationally for raising test scores and reducing dropout rates, but then Princeton University Press publishes a book demonstrating that both the test scores and the retention rates were misrepresented, if not deliberately rigged (Henig, 1994). This data battle over choice programs does not give the public much basis on which to choose. Imagine what it would be like if voucher programs were enacted on a wide scale, with all the jobs and money at stake. The only group guaranteed to do well in such an environment would be the researchers-for-hire.

What makes these prospects all the more horrendous is that the families that are especially presumed to benefit from a voucher system—the poor—are most likely to be the victims of its abuses. They will be sold a bill of goods by sleazy operators who prey on their ignorance. The poor may even be sold a bill of ideological and racial goods so that they end up rallying to the defense of the people who stole their money and their children's futures.

If the profits to be made from voucher schools are large enough, members of the control board may find themselves looking the other way in order to get their piece of the action. In other words, all the sickening travesties of corporate America and its regulatory bodies will be visited upon public education. For centuries now, the young have been shielded from that danger by a public school system that has controlled corruption by controlling temptation. We must not throw teachers and students to the wolves of the profit system.

Fortunately, the danger may have passed. The defeat of voucher proposals in California, Colorado, and Oregon is one sign that the public has become skeptical. Nationwide, 54 percent of Americans now oppose vouchers, according to the 1994 Gallup poll on this issue (Elam, Rose, and Gallup, 1994). And nonpublic schools are beginning to rethink the wisdom of participating in a government-run operation that will prohibit some of the things they are now doing and impose other demands on them (Corwin and Dianda, 1993; Trowbridge, 1993). Vouchers, which not long ago were said to be in everyone's interest, are beginning to look as though they are in no one's interest.

For Discussion

1. Randomly select any two public schools with the same grade levels and get information on their curricula, scheduling of class periods, average class size, and instructional methods. Compare the two schools for significant differences and similarities. Does it really matter which of the two schools a student attends?
2. If there are different kinds of schools (with different goals, teaching styles, governance structures, and organizational arrangements), should there be different kinds of teacher training programs in the colleges in order to prepare people to fit well into a particular kind of school?
3. Will having a wide variety of school types force college admissions officers to rely much more heavily on standardized test results (for example, the Scholastic Aptitude Test), since they will have no clear sense of all the kinds of schools from which applicants are coming?
4. The following table shows different ways choice can be built into a school system. There are four different ways of *financing* a choice system. There are also four ways of *selecting the students and teachers* who will be assigned to a school. And there are

Illustrative Choice Options

School organization			
Local centralization	School-site decentralization	Cooperative contracting	Regulated market
Finance			
Payment to districts; centralized budgeting	Lump-sum payment to schools; decentralized budgeting	Contracting with consumer or producer cooperatives	Payment to clients
Attendance and staffing			
Central assignment with centrally administered exceptions	Centrally administered matching	School-level selection; minimum regulation	School-level selection; minimum regulation
Content			
Central rule making; decentralized implementation	School-level planning; decentralized rule making and implementation	Examination-driven	Consumer-driven

Source: Adapted from R. F. Elmore, *Choice in Public Education,* East Lansing, Mich.: Center for Policy Research in Education, 1986, p. 20.

four ways of *deciding on the curriculum*. Which components do you think would make for the best choice system?

5. Below are reasons that people in Europe and the United States give for choosing a school. Do these reasons seem like good ones to you? Do they persuade you that school choice will be of educational benefit to children?

TABLE 1. Reasons for Choosing a Swedish Compulsory School
(Entry ages: 7, 10, 14)

Reason for Choosing a School Other than the Nearest	Percentage of Parents
Friends/good peer atmosphere	34
Quiet/not violent/small classes	21
Good teachers/school leadership	16
Social factors/attention to pupils	15
Special pedagogical character (Waldorf, Montessori, etc.)	12
Geographical factors	10
Better equipment/facilities	8
Attention to pupils with problems	7
Special subject character (music, art, foreign language)	5
Good reputation	5
Possibility of parent influence	4
Special religious character	2

TABLE 2. Reasons for Choosing an English Secondary School (%)
(Entry age: 11)

	An Influential Reason	One of the Three Most Important Reasons
Child preferred school	59.2	23.3
Near to home/convenient for travel	57.3	23.7
Children's friends will be there	56.1	14.5
Standard of academic education	55.7	21.0
Facilities	55.7	20.6
School's reputation	54.6	20.6
Child will be happy there	49.2	21.0
School atmosphere	44.7	5.0
Policy on discipline	42.0	11.5
Standard of education in non-academic areas	40.8	6.5
Examination results	38.9	11.1
What school teaches/subject choices	37.4	6.9

TABLE 3. Reasons for Choosing a French Lycée (%)
(Entry age: 15)

	Most Important Reason	One of Three Most Important Reasons
Success at *baccalauréat*	6.2	10.4
Quality of teaching	15.0	20.3
Reputation	13.7	25.1
Discipline	0.7	3.3
Total of above 4 motives	35.6	59.1
Smaller classes	2.0	4.3
Subject option	14.7	20.9
Atmosphere	1.0	6.9
Continuity	10.7	16.2
Closeness	27.0	51.7
Sibling(s)	2.6	10.1
Child's preference	6.5	12.4
Total	100.0	181.6

TABLE 4. Factors Considered as Important in Choosing a School, by United States Parents

Very or Fairly Important Factors	Percentage Agree
Quality of teaching staff	96
Maintenance of school discipline	96
Curriculum/courses offered	95
Size of classes	88
Grades/test scores of students	88
Close proximity to home	74
Extracurricular activity	68
Athletic programme	53
Racial or ethnic composition	32

Source: School: A Matter of Choice, Paris, France: Organisation for Economic, Co-operation and Development, 1994, pp. 26–27.

References

Bastian, A., et al. (1985). *Choosing Equality: The Case for Democratic Schooling.* New York: New World Foundation.

Boaz, D. (1993). "Five Myths About School Choice." *Education Week* **12**(18), 24, 36.

Cheney, L. (1990). *Tyrannical Machines.* Washington, DC: National Endowment for the Humanities.

Chira, S. (1992a). "Research Questions Effectiveness of Most School-Choice Programs." *The New York Times,* October 26, pp. A1, B8.

_____ (1992b). "Schools Vie in a Marketplace: More 'Choice' Can Mean Less." *The New York Times,* January 7, pp. 1, 12.

Chmelynski, C. (1990). "Controversy Attends Schools with All-Black All-Male Classes." *The Executive Educator,* October, pp. 16–18.

Clark, J. (1993). "Pro-Choice." *Mother Jones.* September, pp. 52–54.

Coons, J. E., and Sugarman, S. D. (1978). *Education by Choice: The Case for Family Control.* Berkeley, CA: University of California Press.

Corwin, R., and Dianda, M. (1993). "What Can We Really Expect From Large-Scale Voucher Programs?" *Phi Delta Kappan* **75**(1), 68–74.

Elam, S., Rose, L., and Gallup, A. (1994). "The 26th Annual Gallup Poll of the Public's Attitudes Toward the Public Schools." *Phi Delta Kappan* **76**(1), 41–56.

Elconin, M., and Holohan (1990). "Education Vouchers: A Win–Win Plan." *The New York Times,* May 9, p. A-31.

Elmore, R. F. (1986). *Choice in Public Education.* Madison, WI: Center for Policy Research in Education.

Epperson v. State of Arkansas (1969). 393 U.S. 97.

Fantini, M. D. (1973). *Public Schools of Choice.* New York: Simon & Schuster.

Farber, B. (1991). *Crisis in Education: Stress and Burnout in the American Teacher.* San Francisco: Jossey-Bass.

Fliegel, S. (1993). *Miracle in East Harlem.* New York: Times Books.

Friedman, M., and Friedman, R. (1980). *Free to Choose.* New York: Harcourt Brace Jovanovich.

General Accounting Office (1995). *Charter Schools.* Report to Congressional Requesters, Washington, DC: U.S. General Accounting Office.

Ginzberg, E. (1972). "The Economics of the Voucher System." In *Educational Vouchers: Concepts and Controversies,* edited by G. LaNoue. New York: Teachers College Press.

Glazer, N. (1993). "American Public Education: The Relevance of Choice." *Phi Delta Kappan* **74**(8), 647–650.

Glenn, C. (1991). "Controlled Choice in Massachusetts Public Schools." *The Public Interest* No. 103, 88–105.

Henig, J. (1994). *Rethinking School Choice: Limits of the Market Metaphor.* Princeton, NJ: Princeton University Press.

Kearns, D. T., and Doyle, D. P. (1988). *Winning the Brain Race: A Bold Plan to Make Our Schools Competitive.* San Francisco: Institute for Contemporary Studies.

Kemerer, F. (1992). "The Publicization of the Private School." *Education Week* **11**(16), 42, 56.

Kerchner, C. T. (1988). "Bureaucratic Entrepreneurship: The Implications of Choice for School Administration." *Educational Administration Quarterly* **24**(4), 381–392.

Kirp, D. (1992). "What School Choice Really Means." *The Atlantic Monthly,* November, pp. 119–132.

Levin, H. (1980). "Educational Vouchers and Social Policy." In *School Finance Polices and Practice: The 1980's, a Decade of Conflict,* edited by J. Guthrie. Cambridge, MA: Ballinger.

Lieberman, M. (1993). *Public Education: An Autopsy.* Cambridge, MA: Harvard University Press.

Lindsay, D. (1994). "Wis. Blocking Voucher Data, Researcher Says." *Education Week* **14**(15), 14.

McGroarty, D. (1994). "School Choice Slandered." *The Public Interest* **117,** 94–111.

Meier, D. (1991). "Choice Can Save Public Education." *The Nation,* March 4, pp. 253, 266–271.

Newman, M. (1994). "California Schools Vying for New Students Under a State Plan for Open Enrollments." *The New York Times,* May 25, p. B9.

Olson, L. (1995). "17-State Project Hammers Out Own Standards.' *Education Week* **14**(17), 1, 8.

Orfield, G. (1993). *The Growth of Segregation in American Schools: Changing Patterns of Separation and Poverty Since 1968.* Cambridge, MA: Report of the Harvard Project on School Desegregation to the National School Boards Association.

Peterkin, R. (1994). "Strategies in Choice: The Cambridge and Milwaukee Experiences." Presentation to the Urban Superintendents' Issues Conference, Edison, NJ, November 14.

Public Schools of Choice. (1990). Alexandria, VA: Association for Supervision and Curriculum Development.

Raywid, M. A. (1987). "The Dynamics of Success and Public Schools of Choice." *Equity and Choice* **4**(1), 27–31.

_____, Tesconi, C. A., and Warren, D. R. (1984). *Pride and Promise: Schools of Excellence for All the People.* Washington, DC: American Educational Studies Association.

Schundler, B. (1993). "The Simple Logic of School Choice." *The New York Times,* October 28, p. A27.

Shanker, A. (1994). "Charter Schools." *The New York Times,* June 26, p. E7.

_____ (1993). "Students as Customers." *The New York Times,* August 8, p. E7.

Shapiro, W. (1991). "Tough Choice." *Time,* September 16, pp. 54–60.

Snider, W. (1990). "Convergence on Choice." *Teacher Magazine,* February, pp. 18–20.

Tashman, B. (1992). "Hobson's Choice: Free-Market Education Plan Voucher for Bush's Favorite Class." *Village Voice* **37**(3), 9, 14.

The People's Poll on Schools and School Choice: A New Gallup Survey. (1992). Princeton, NJ: Gallup Organization.

Time for Results: The Governors 1991 Report on Education. (1986). Washington, DC: National Governors Association.

Trowbridge, R. (1993). "Vouchers: Devil's Bargain for Private Schools." *The Wall Street Journal,* October 20, p. A20.

Weinberg, H. (1992). "For School Choice: Let's Follow the F.A.A." *Education Week* **11**(21), 40.

Wraga, W. (1992). "School Choice and the Comprehensive Ideal." *Journal of Curriculum and Supervision* **8**(1), 28–42.

CHAPTER FOUR

School Finance: Equity or Disparity

POSITION 1:
FOR EQUITY IN EDUCATION

Gauging the Gap

The American system of free public education is touted as being the great equalizer of opportunity. It exists for all children regardless of their parents' station in life. In virtually every state, the child and the parents have no choice but to take advantage of this educational opportunity, since school attendance is required by law up to a certain age, usually 16. Moreover, the guarantee of a public school education is good for several years beyond the school-leaving age. Because attending school is compulsory, and because the guarantee extends over so many years, the United States can justly pride itself on giving all its children an education, even those whose parents are residents only and not citizens.

This educational birthright for America's youth, however, is a prize that comes in many different dollar amounts, depending on various factors. For the child in an affluent suburb, it can be worth about $12,000 a year, the amount actually spent on his or her education in the local public school. For a child in a large city or a rural area, the prize may be worth only half that amount, or $6,000. The $6,000 difference multiplied over the twelve years of school adds up to $72,000 more education for the suburban child than for his or her urban or rural counterpart, not counting inflation or interest. All American children are guaranteed an educational opportunity, but there is no guarantee that the opportunity will be equal for all—and in reality, it is quite unequal. No wonder that James Conant, a former president of Harvard University, was moved to write that "the contrast in money available to schools in a wealthy suburb and schools in a large city jolts one's notion of the meaning of equality of opportunity" (Conant, 1961, pp. 2–3). What appalled Conant over thirty years ago is appalling still.

The inequality is even more pronounced than these numbers indicate. The child in the plush suburb is likely to begin school with much greater educational advantages than the urban or rural child. The suburban child may have traveled abroad with his or her parents even before entering first grade, and foreign travel may be part of every summer vacation. The child may have been "prepped" for first grade by attendance at an expensive nursery school. Books, including a variety of costly and up-to-date reference works, may abound in the child's home. The parents are likely to be proficient readers. Educational toys will probably be plentiful. A personal computer is becoming a standard possession of children in suburbia, and they are making their exploratory forays onto the information highway. Attending summer camps that feature specialized educational programs is an annual rite for many suburban kids. The very conversations that a suburban child has with his or her well-educated parents are intellectually enriching. "There is no mystery about it: the child who is familiar with books, ideas, conversation—the ways and means of the intellectual life—before he begins consciously to think, has a marked advantage. He is at home in the House of Intellect just as the stableboy is at home among horses or the child of actors on the stage" (Barzun, 1959, p. 142). Add to all this the robust good health that proper nutrition and medical attention can assure.

Contrast this bountiful life with the austere life of the child from the inner city. The contrast starkly reveals an accumulation of privations for that inner-city child. There has been no foreign travel, and perhaps not even intracity travel. There are adolescents who have grown up in Brooklyn, for example, who have never been to Manhattan. The poor child sees no books other than comic books, and a few superficial magazines left lying around by adults. A personal computer is as removed from possibility as a private spaceship. Perhaps the child might be allowed a brief vacation at a charity summer camp, such as those sponsored by the Fresh Air Fund and the St. Vincent de Paul Society. Conversations with adults who use English badly put the child at a *disadvantage* in school. Actually, there are few conversations with adults at all, and these are necessarily abrupt, because the only adult permanently in the home is a badly harried mother trying to hold her life together. Increasingly, neither a mother nor a father stays at home. Between 1970 and 1990, the proportion of American children without a mother or father at home rose from 6.7 percent to 9.7 percent (Gross, 1992). And that "home" may be a room in a welfare hotel (Kozol, 1988). The television set is the child's constant companion, purveying visions of distorted reality and false hopes. The diet is one of junk food, or no food, and any medical attention is the perfunctory medical care that one receives in a municipal hospital emergency room. Moreover, many serious injuries are never reported or treated because they are the result of child abuse, including sexual abuse. And, of late, there is the injury for which there may be no cure: the brain damage suffered by the fetuses of crack-addicted women. Many children born on crack are now of school age (Daley, 1991; Treaster, 1993).

Outside the home, the ghetto child lives under the threat of becoming a victim or witness of a murder. Kotlowitz has recorded this situation in ghastly detail. The Chicago mother of the family he studied pays $80 a month for burial insurance on her five children, knowing the odds of collecting. This was the experience of one of her children.

> At the age of ten, Lafayette had his first encounter with death; he saw someone killed. . . . The first victim was a young Disciple nicknamed Baby Al, who was shot with a .357 Magnum, not far from [the building in which Lafayette lived]. Wounded, he ran into the high-rise, where, while trying to climb the stairs, he fell backward and lost consciousness. Lafayette came running out of his apartment to see what all the commotion was about. He watched as Baby Al bled to death. Two years later, his blood still stained the stairwell. . . . A couple of weeks later, as Lafayette and Pharaoh played on the jungle gym in midafternoon, shooting broke out. A young girl jumping rope crumpled to the ground. . . . They watched as paramedics attended to the girl, who luckily had been shot only in the leg. (Kotlowitz, 1991, pp. 39–40)

No wonder that when Kotlowitz asked the mother if he could write about her children, she replied, "But you know, there are no children here. They've seen too much to be children" (p. x).

Or read this poem scrawled on the side of a building in the South Bronx.

> I am the boy who lives in a slum surrounded by problems with no where to
> go
> I am the boy who has no hope, who solves his problems with a bag of smoke
> I am the boy who lives next door, whose father is a drunk and whose mother
> is a whore
> I am the boy who lives a rough life, who has to depend on a push-button knife
> I am the boy who must take the first swing
> I am the boy who must pull the trigger
> I am the boy who whitey calls nigger.
> (Vergara, 1991, p. 805)

Adolescent boys in Camden, New Jersey, spend a lot of time imagining their own, presumably imminent, funerals (Previte, 1994). And in Chicago, 11-year-old Yummy Sandifer became famous as a gang shooter who was shot to death by his own gang (Gibbs, 1994).

Poor children require more than the rich when they get to school because they have so much less at home, and so much trauma with which to cope. They come to school undereducated in the things that schools consider important, so they need *compensatory* education to bring them to the same starting line as the rich. What happens, instead, is that the disadvantage poor children bring to school is aggravated by the underfunding of their formal education, whereas the advantage of the rich is augmented by the generous funding for their schooling. In short, the American system of education uses public money to favor the already favored. It is the great *disequalizer* of opportunity.

Understanding the Cause

Before giving specifics concerning the educational advantages that taxpayer money can buy in schools, it would be well to explain why such glaring inequality exists between the schools of the rich and those of the poor. The answer, in two words, is *local control.* To the extent that rich communities pay for their own schools and poor communities pay for theirs, there will be inequality. The rich can afford to pay more, so they have better schools. State governments try to smooth over the gaps by giving more state money to the poor schools than they do to the rich ones. But except for Hawaii, where all public schools are funded by the state government, the gap between rich and poor schools is never closed completely. In many states, it is a yawning chasm.

You should be able to obtain from the education officials in your state a breakdown of how much is spent per pupil in each of the school districts in the state, including the one where you went to school. For example, in 1990, New York City spent an average of $6,644 per pupil. This was $22,814 less than the amount spent in Pocantico Hills, directly to the north in suburban Westchester County, and $39,330 less than the amount spent on Fire Island, off Long Island (Barbanel, 1992). If Pocantico Hills and Fire Island are dismissed as extreme examples, there was still a difference (in 1993) of $8,448 between New York City and Great Neck, Long Island (Winerip, 1993). In Texas and Illinois, the highest-spending districts spend almost seven times as much as the lowest-spending districts ("States' School Spending Disparities," 1992). In looking at the disparities from an interstate perspective, we see that New York spends two and a half times what Utah spends, even after adjusting for estimated cost-of-living differences (Barton, Coley, and Goertz, 1991, p. 24). "We must also take note of the fact that children from rich families stay in school longer than children from poor families. When we take this into account, we estimate that America spends about twice as much on the children of the rich as the children of the poor" (Jencks et al., 1972, p. 27). Such information for your own state may bring you to the realization that you yourself have already been denied an equal educational opportunity, as compared with other young people in your state. Of course, that same information also could reveal that the inequality was in your favor.

Local control explains the inequality in American education. It does not, however, explain the continuing American allegiance to that inequality. That explanation is to be found in the unequal power arrangements between rich and poor.

> We must recognize the ways in which powerful groups are able to arrange better opportunities for their children, despite the rhetoric of standard and therefore equal education. Families with the economic and political power to give their children an advantage are unlikely to relinquish that advantage willingly. Most people with influence over public education have at least some measure of such an advantage and are surrounded by associates who share it as well. They are likely to share a perspective that makes the maintenance of separate schools with superior human and material resources for the white middle class seem natural and necessary. Their vested interests are served by muting the recognition of differences in the opportunities offered by school accessible to children of different races and social classes. (Metz, 1988, p. 60)

The rich have reason to rig the system in their favor. "Significant changes toward a more equal educational system . . . would be associated with equally significant changes in the statistical relationship between education and the distribution of economic rewards . . . unequal schooling perpetuates a structure of economic inequality which originates outside the school system" (Bowles and Gintis, 1976, p. 248).

Specifying What the Gap Means

There are people who say that money cannot buy a good education. So let us see what it is that money can buy. You get some idea of this even before entering a school building. The building's exterior tells you whether the building is new, attractively designed, and in good repair, or old, fortresslike, and ramshackle. Many old city school buildings not only are ugly, but are in such disrepair as to be safety hazards. "Many schools have rundown physical facilities that are, in some cases, safety and health hazards. . . . If this sample of schools is any indication, the physical plants of many of the nation's urban schools need substantial rehabilitation and modernization" (*City High Schools,* 1984, p. 68). However, it costs so much to renovate old buildings or replace them with new buildings that they are made to do year after year. Inside, a building may be bright with windows and fluorescent lights, cheery with decorative touches, and comfortable with carpeting and the latest in school furniture. Or it may be Gothic in style and gloomy. City (and rural) school buildings, because they are on average much older than suburban schools, are more likely to fall into the latter category. One elementary school in the city of Camden, New Jersey, occupies a three-story building, but it has only one boys' and one girls' lavatory, both on the first floor. The building is so crowded that two of the classes have to be held in the cafeteria of another school (Lefelt, 1988, p. 32). The fact that situations like this are more likely to be corrected as a result of adverse publicity does not keep others from constantly cropping up.

More important than the buildings are the educational materials they house. Poor schools have small libraries with few recent additions to the book collection, only a few magazine subscriptions, and very little audiovisual equipment and software. The audiovisual equipment may be so old and unreliable that the teachers have given up on it in order to spare themselves awkward delays in trying to adjust or just restart it. The libraries themselves serve mostly as study halls, but don't even have comfortable chairs. The libraries of suburban schools are much more richly endowed, and some are absolutely alluring in their architectural splendor and provision of creature comforts, not to mention the wide array of multimedia material available.

The auditorium of a poor school may be little more than a cavern with chairs and a stage. For the rich school, it is a professional theater, with all the technical paraphernalia needed for live productions. These lavish productions not only instill school spirit among the students, but also inspire parental pride and support.

The suburban school is much more likely to have a swimming pool and a fully equipped gym, perhaps with a weight room, as well as a basketball court with spectator stands. The spacious grounds on which the school is located allow for regulation-size athletic fields, which are well maintained by professional groundskeepers.

The vocational shops and the home economics rooms in a suburban school have all the latest gadgets, whereas their counterparts in the urban school contain equipment that has been used by generations of students. New equipment is acquired in an incremental fashion, so that only a small part of it is ever really new. Poor vocational education prepares teenagers for jobs that no longer exist, or underprepares them for the new types of jobs on the scene.

The labs of many urban schools would be laughable to someone seriously trying to teach science, with some test tubes, a few bunsen burners, a couple of microscopes, some old jars of chemicals, and a washbasin making up the entire inventory of supplies. Students do not have a variety of materials from which to learn, and what they do have is so limited in quantity that they have to wait their turn to share it. Suburban schools, in contrast, are likely to approach a state-of-the-art lab station for each student in the class.

Computers—the communication tool of our common tomorrow—are much more in evidence in the rich schools of today than in the poor ones. In some fortunate schools, each child is assigned his or her own computer, much as a textbook is assigned at the beginning of a course. Those are the schools whose students also have computers at home.

The textbooks used in English and social studies classes in some poor schools have been through thirty years of page turning, according to the president of the New York City teachers' union (Weiss, 1988, p. 60)—and not all the pages in these beat-up and out-of-date books are there to be turned. Supplementary reading consists of a desultory book collection approaching antiquity on a bookshelf in the back of the room. The pages of those fossils remain intact because no one ever turns them. Rich schools have spiffy new texts that catch your eye even if they don't hold your attention. There is a cornucopia of new paperback books for supplementary reading. Of course, the students in these schools have no trouble creating their own paperback libraries at home.

Jonathan Kozol has visited city schools and observed the privations under which they function. East St. Louis Senior High School is just one example. Sewage backs into the school, including the school kitchen. The teachers run out of chalk and paper. The football field does not have goalposts. The football uniforms are nine years old and are washed at a local laundromat. The science labs are not hooked up for water. The heating system and the building's insulation are so bad that it costs thousands of unnecessary dollars each year to maintain them (Kozol, 1991, pp. 23–32).

The saddest commentary of all is that even the teachers in rich schools tend to be better than those in poor schools. They are better educated, having attended superior colleges and universities, and remained long enough to acquire advanced degrees. That is why they receive job offers from the rich schools. And such offers are eagerly sought because teaching in these schools means working with students who are relatively docile and pliable, and who, by and large, come prepared to learn regardless of the teacher's communication skills. Rich schools also have higher salary ranges than poor schools, just another of the things they can afford to buy. When teacher salaries are computed by the number of students a teacher has, the teacher in the poor school fares even worse because poor schools control costs by having large classes. The higher salaries mean higher pension costs for teachers in rich schools. In New Jersey, where the state pays for all teacher pensions, the total amount in the affluent community of Millburn averages out to $1,066 per pupil, whereas in the poor community of Camden it is only $522 (King, 1992).

Equalizing Educational Opportunity

Those who say that money cannot buy a good education live in good neighborhoods with good schools on which a lot of money is spent. Some of these people do not deign to use even the good public schools in their neighborhoods; they send their children to private schools in an effort to buy what they say cannot be bought. If they are correct that money cannot buy a good education, then it would seem that the poor have as much right to be disappointed by this fact as the rich (Coons, Clune, & Sugarman, 1971, p. 30). Some of the rich who patronize private schools are candid enough to admit the relation between money and quality education. The chairman of the board of trustees of the Peddie School says that "as one would expect, the more assets the better the education. . . . Funds are necessary to employ able teachers, to provide reasonable facilities and to provide a reasonable student-faculty ratio. If you achieve that, you can have a very fine education" (van Tassel, 1988, p. NJ3). The Peddie School should offer a fine education, indeed, since it recently received a $100 million donation from the billionaire philanthropist Walter Annenberg.

Educational opportunity can be equalized simply and straightforwardly by equalizing the money spent among pupils. It is necessary to do this within as well as between school districts because single districts often spend more on schools in the better neighborhoods (Sexton, 1961). The parents in the better neighborhoods may be more demanding, and so they succeed in getting for their children materials and programs, and even teachers, not available to schools in the poorer parts of town. Jonathan Kozol (1991) describes the heavy allocation of resources to the relatively affluent Riverdale section of the Bronx as compared with poorer schools elsewhere in the borough. The inequality extends from the number of computers to the quality of the teachers (pp. 84–85). In Los Angeles, parents in the poor neighborhoods won a court case, *Rodriguez v. Los Angeles Unified School District,* in which they alleged that the teachers assigned to their schools had less experience and were more likely to be unlicensed or to be substitutes than were the teachers in other Los Angeles neighborhoods. They also demonstrated the obvious overcrowding of their schools and the dilapidation of the facilities (Bradley, 1994). Such disparities can develop almost imperceptibly, so it is important for school districts to be on the watch for them.

This does not mean that districts cannot spend different amounts for students in different educational categories, for example, handicapped versus nonimpaired students or high school versus elementary school students. These differences result from real differences in the costs of educating different kinds of students. They are not the same as spending different amounts on students who are in the *same* educational category.

Equalizing educational opportunity *across* school districts is a responsibility of the state. Under our constitutional system, education legally is a prerogative of state government, so states already have the authority to intervene in local school operations. What better justification for intervention could they have than to redress elemental fairness? The unfairness is so egregious that it forces the question of why states have allowed it to exist for so long. As already indicated, the answer is a political one: the people who profit from the unfairness are the rich, and the rich have more political power than do the poor. If the rich are going to continue exercising their power at the expense of the poor, then they should stop pretending that justice and fairness and equality are characteristic of American education. If the children of the poor are going to be treated shabbily by the state simply because of the plight of their parents—a plight for which the children will suffer enough as it is—then the state is an oppressor of its people just as a Latin American oligarchy is.

It is desirable to equalize educational opportunity not just among schools and districts within a state, but also among the fifty states of the union. There are wide variations from state to state in the amount of dollars spent per pupil, even taking into account cost-of-living differences. So even if there were full equalization within states, the poor states would still be spending less than would the wealthier ones. John Fischer, when president of Columbia University Teachers College, once said: "If we really mean it when we say that every American child—rather than every Californian or every Arkansan—is entitled to equal educational opportunity, we must be prepared to use federal means to bring about such equality" (quoted in Herbers, 1972, p. E3). Only the federal government has the capacity to deal with inequality on this level, but the Constitution gives it no clear warrant to do so, and the political clout of the rich can be as intimidating to members of the U.S. Congress as to the members of a state legislature. Perhaps the most that can be expected from our national leaders is that they be more restrained in their rhetoric about the greatness of the American educational system. There is as much reason to be ashamed of that system as there is to be proud of it.

Something the government could do immediately would be to increase the funding for Chapter I, the major federal program for poor students. It could also retarget the money so that it goes to districts with the highest concentrations of poor students. The money cannot be expected to do much good when it is spread around almost half of the elementary schools in the country, in some of which poor children account for as little as 10 percent of the student body (Rotberg, 1994). The funding for Head Start should also be increased now that the accumulated evidence shows that the gains students make are longer lasting than previously thought and that any fade-out is likely to be a result of poor subsequent schooling (Barnett, 1993; Viadero, 1994). Unfortunately, at a time of tax-cut fever and middle-class paranoia, making these changes is an uphill struggle.

The Benefit to Society

John Donne's insightful statement that "no man is an island, entire of itself" is truer in today's interdependent world than it was when he wrote it. Its application to American education at the end of the twentieth century has been captured by Lester Thurow: "I am willing to pay for, indeed insist upon, the education of my neighbor's children, not because I am generous but because I cannot afford to live with them uneducated" (Thurow, 1985, p. 187).

As Thurow correctly understands, educating the children of the poor is in the interest of us all. It saves corporations the costs of searching extensively for minimally qualified employees or of minimally educating those who come unqualified. It gives people legal opportunities so that they desist from taking illegal courses, with the corresponding cost in human and property loss.

Educating the poor necessarily entails some additional costs to compensate for the disadvantages they bring to school with them. For example, urban communities have unusually high percentages of students whose native language is not English, and these students are from literally scores of different language groups. There is a debate about how best to make such students proficient in English, but, as generally agreed, it requires extra resources regardless of the approach used. Urban districts also have security costs just to keep the schools safe enough for students to venture into them. Guards have to be paid, and their walkie-talkies cost about $1,000 each. Suburban schools are spared these costs.

Philanthropies and corporate leaders have recognized the need and have some appreciation of the cost of successfully educating the poor and minorities. The Ford Foundation, after completing a national study of city high schools, came up with a list of twenty "lessons" it had learned. At least twelve of these lessons involve more money, and four of them specifically mention the need for more funds (*City High Schools,* 1984, pp. 66–68). The Carnegie Foundation for the Advancement of Teaching has issued a more recent report on urban schools, which concludes with a call for a national urban schools program. All eight of the points in this program are high-cost ones (Carnegie Foundation, 1988, pp. 37–38). The Institute for Educational Leadership examined the working conditions of teachers in thirty-one schools distributed among five large cities. The conclusion was that "urban teachers . . . labor under conditions that would not be tolerated in other professional settings. This is true of teaching in general, but the compounding of problems in urban schools creates extremely difficult and demoralizing environments for those who have chosen to teach" (Corcoran, Walker, and White, 1988, p. xiii). This study, too, emphasizes the lack of resources available to urban teachers. Imagine the following generalization being applied to suburban teachers: "Urban teachers often do not have even the basic resources needed for teaching. There are serious shortages of everything from toilet paper to textbooks; teachers have limited access to modern office technologies, including copiers, let alone computers" (Corcoran, Walker, and

White, 1988, p. xiii). The Committee for Economic Development, composed of chief executive officers of various American corporations, in true business fashion presents a list of "cost-effective programs" and "investment strategies" for helping the educationally disadvantaged. All of these recommendations cost money, and more than is now being spent (*Children in Need,* 1987). Wehlage et al. (1989) describe fourteen dropout prevention programs that have had marked success in keeping at-risk youngsters in school. A common feature of these programs is the intensive personal attention the students get. That requires additional professional personnel, whose salaries must be paid. Lucas, Henze, and Donato (1990) report on successful programs for Latino students, all of which have associated costs.

To be blunt, urban schools need more money. Moreover, they need more money per pupil than do suburban schools just to afford an equally good chance at an effective education. Currently, they are struggling to make do with less money. This condition is not in our interest as an interdependent society, and the socially deleterious consequences should be obvious to all. The money spent on schools in poor neighborhoods can be an especially good social investment since formal education has a greater impact on poor students than it does on their better-off peers, as was demonstrated over twenty years ago in the largest study of education ever undertaken (Coleman et al., 1966). But perhaps the best reason for doing something now is to make us a more honest society. It will reduce not only the opportunity gap between rich and poor, but also the gap between our lofty rhetoric and the grim reality (Bell, 1976, p. 263).

As to the question of whether we can afford it, it is instructive to compare our effort with that of fourteen other industrialized nations. We rank eleventh in terms of the percentage of gross domestic product devoted to public spending on elementary and secondary schools. Our average expenditure of $3,398 per pupil puts us in sixth place in that regard (Nelson, 1991, p. 2). The Quality Education for Minorities Project of the Massachusetts Institute of Technology has come up with twenty-five programs the federal government could fund. Some of these programs are already in place, but with inadequate funding. Full funding of all the programs would cost $27.31 billion (*Education That Works,* 1990). This is an amount that should be borne in mind by federal officials when they try to decide what uses can be made of the "peace dividend" and whether a tax cut for the middle class should be a high priority at this time in America's history.

POSITION 2:
FOR FREEDOM IN FINANCING SCHOOLS

Gauging the Gain

There is, to be sure, a strong undercurrent of capitalism in American education. But instead of fretting over this fact and becoming defensive about it, people should assess the benefits it brings.

In education, as in the free enterprise system generally, inequality is both inevitable and desirable. The prospect of getting to the top and the possibility of falling to the bottom are what motivate us as individuals to do our best. That is just basic human nature. And when all of us are working hard to get to the top or to avoid falling to the bottom, the whole ship of state is buoyed up. America is made stronger, and we as a people are enriched materially.

Government-guaranteed equality denies people their drive. What's the point of striving if you can't advance beyond the level of the person who sits around doing nothing? Even communist countries, most notably those that made up the former Soviet bloc, have come to appreciate the motivating force of capitalist inequality. Inequality not only is a great goad to human effort, but it is a just way to distribute the blessings of liberty. You get what you earn, or, as the Bible says, you reap what you sow. To earn something is to *deserve* it. Capitalist inequality is intended to ensure that everyone is rewarded appropriately in the fair competition of the free marketplace. We are all aware that the system does not work perfectly, but what Churchill (1947) said about democracy as a political system is also true of capitalism as an economic system: "No one pretends that democracy is perfect or all-wise. Indeed, it has been said that democracy is the worst form of government except all those other forms that have been tried from time to time." And despite its imperfections, the free enterprise system has created a wealth of opportunities for upward mobility. Millions of successful people have come from humble beginnings, so that the top ranks of government, the arts, the professions, business, and the military are filled with people whose origins were no more auspicious than those of Ronald Reagan or Whitney Houston or Jonas Salk or Famous Amos or Colin Powell or Bill Clinton or Ross Perot or Bill Gates.

Education is a right of all Americans, and it is guaranteed to all Americans because it is essential to our progress as a nation and our fulfillment as individuals. However, the guarantee is only for a minimally adequate education. There is no unanimity as to how high the guaranteed amount of education should go. There is a general consensus that public education should be free through high school, but no agreement on what a student should have learned by graduation. The higher the expectation, the more it will cost taxpayers to bring every student to that level. Frankly, it does not seem that the level need be very high to satisfy the needs of society.

> Our definition of a basic education is considerably . . . restricted. It consists of those things necessary for minimal effective functioning in a democracy. This includes the ability to read, write, and do basic arithmetic, and knowledge of our democratic government. These goals are relatively clear-cut, and accomplishment is more easily measured than in other curricula. Most people would agree that they form the core of education, while few would agree on other curricular objectives. It should be possible to complete this basic education by the end of the eighth grade. (Garms, Guthrie, and Pierce, 1978, pp. 241–242)

There need be no guarantee that everyone will graduate from high school, let alone go to medical school and become a doctor or to law school and become a lawyer. Education beyond the minimum eighth-grade guarantee is something that has to be earned, just like any other valued commodity. More-over, society creates social dynamite by educating people beyond its capacity to absorb them into careers that are congruent with their education. It is fashionable now to talk about the education needed for the cybernetic society of the twenty-first century. The implication is that everyone will be on the information superhighway, but no one will be there as part of a minimally skilled janitorial crew. Not only will there be many low-skill jobs in the information systems world, but this world will be but a small part of the overall job market in which low-skill jobs predominate. People who are overeducated for the jobs they hold are discontented workers, which makes them ripe for revolutionary appeals. Hayek (1944) found this condition to have been a cause of Hitler's success: "The resentment of the lower middle class, from which fascism and National Socialism recruited so large a proportion of their supporters, was intensified by the fact that their education and training had in many instances made them aspire to directing positions and that they regarded themselves as entitled to be members of the directing class" (p. 117). The three occupations with the greatest projected *percentage* growth between 1992 and 2005 are those of home health aides, human services workers, and personal and home care aides. The occupation projected to have the greatest *numerical* growth is that of retail sales clerk. None of these four occupations requires more than a two-year college education, if that (Krugman, 1994).

The commodities children value are sometimes earned directly by the children. A child can use the money from a paper route to buy a bicycle. Another child can study and earn a scholarship to a private school. But mostly it is the parents who earn the commodities for their children. They buy the bike and they pay the private school tuition. The most common way in which parents buy their children an education beyond the state's minimum guarantee is to buy a home in a community that has good schools.

Good schools are one of the most cherished blessings of liberty, and parents struggle very hard to earn a good education for their children by living near good schools. One of the great (if not the greatest) motivators for parents is being able to provide a good education for their children. One parent has written movingly of his decision to relocate his family to a small town so that his children would have good schools. He realized that in abandoning the city he violated some of his own convictions, but he concluded that *"no one is willing to sacrifice their children on the altar of their social principles"* [author's emphasis] (Nocero, 1989, p. 30). Real estate agents are well aware of this fact, which is why they reveal (or conceal) the quality of local schools as a selling point in their pitch to prospective home buyers. To deny parents the right to influence the quality of their children's education in this way is worse than denying them a basic right as citizens in a free society; it is to deny them a *natural* right as parents. And it is to deny society the benefit of the parents' highly motivated labor.

Equalizing How?

Egalitarians espouse noble sentiments that we all endorse to some extent. However, they avoid discussing those troublesome specifics that gravely weaken their case. When they exhort us to equalize per-pupil spending throughout an entire state, they fail to tell us in which direction and how far this should be done. These are hardly minor details! Suppose the following is the situation in your state:

Highest-spending districts	$10,000 per pupil
Average-spending districts	$ 7,000 per pupil
Lowest-spending districts	$ 4,000 per pupil

Should the state allocate money to equalize everyone up to the top level of $10,000 per pupil? That's going to cost the state and its taxpayers, including poor folks who pay taxes, a lot of money. It may be more than the taxpayers are willing to provide, and they'll make their reluctance known at the ballot box in good democratic fashion. Former Governors Florio of New Jersey, Weicker of Connecticut, and Cuomo of New York can tell you all about taxpayer revolts. Besides, it will mean to the family already living in the $10,000 district that it has to pay additional taxes for the benefit of someone else's children. It is already paying stiff taxes to guarantee its own children a good education, and those children will not benefit from the additional taxes it pays to help poor school districts. In fact, their education will become relatively devalued.

Perhaps the state should equalize everyone *down* to the level of the $4,000 districts. That would require putting a ceiling on how much the affluent districts could spend on their children and forbidding them to spend any more. The poor districts would not get any more money; they would just have the spiteful satisfaction of knowing that everyone else was as bad off as they are. (Many conservative commentators have remarked on the symptoms of envy and greed among egalitarians; see, for example, Hayek, 1944, p. 139, and Kristol, 1978, p. 220.) The $10,000, and even the $7,000, districts would have to make major adjustments. Their budgets would be slashed by 60 percent and 42 percent respectively. These are enormous reductions, and even if they were phased in gradually, the ultimate result would be a huge decline in the quality of education. People will not sit still and let something that disastrous happen to their children. If they cannot stop it from becoming law, they will surely find ways to get around the law. They would probably arrange all kinds of ways of making "voluntary" contributions to their schools to make up for the loss in official revenue. There would be bake sales galore. That sort of thing is already happening in Manhattan's better neighborhoods, where parents of public school children use their own money to hire teachers' assistants and buy supplies and equip the playgrounds (Chira, 1992; Freeman and Pollitt, 1991). In other communities, educational foundations are being established. These will allow the public schools to engage in private fund-raising on a grand scale, and the grandest communities will obviously be the ones to do so on the grandest scale. Public equality will once again, and inexorably, be nullified by private inequality.

The middle ground is a compromise that avoids all of one approach while including a bit of both. The affluent districts could be equalized down to the $7,000 level while the poor districts are equalized up to it. However, the affluent districts might not be much more willing to suffer a 30 percent reduction in their budgets than a 60 percent one, even though 30 percent is twice as easy to make up in bake sales. To avoid the problem of affronting the affluent, they could simply be left alone at their $10,000 level. However, egalitarians would no doubt declare this to be a cop-out, and people in the average districts would feel that the poor had been thrown into the same pot with them while the rich escaped the soup altogether.

There is another hitch to all this that should be noted. The poor tend to be in large urban districts with lots of students. If they were fewer in number, the cost of equalization would be more bearable. The actual cost when one multiplies the per-pupil increase by the number of pupils who would be eligible is outrageously high.

At any rate, it is not up to people who value educational liberty to work out a politically viable means of vitiating that liberty. It is up to the egalitarians. Even if they can come up with a scheme that the citizens will support, it will prove to be a failure in the long run because it will contradict human nature and the values that have made America great. Those values were upheld by the U.S. Supreme Court when it refused to strike down the Texas system of local financing of schools and found that system to be "rational" (*San Antonio Independent School District v. Rodriguez*, 1973). Unfortunately, people were not content to leave well enough alone after the Supreme Court ruled. Another case was brought, this time in the Texas state court system. It resulted in a victory for the egalitarians, and a court order that school financing be equalized in Texas. That led to a years-long battle over exactly how this was to be done, ending in a crazy "Robin Hood" scheme with which both the rich and the poor are unhappy (Celis, 1994; Suro, 1991).

Pouring Money Down Ratholes

All but one of the schemes discussed under Position 1 have something in common: they would all inject a large infusion of cash into poor school districts, in addition to the huge amounts of financial aid already given to those districts over the past twenty years. Unfortunately, the recipient districts have a dismal record for spending money unwisely, and even illegally. The poor performance of their students is due as much to mismanaged money as it is to insufficient money. For example, there is money that never gets spent on the pupils for whom it is targeted. "Entitlement funds have frequently been treated as discretionary monies, and have been diverted from their original purposes" (Bastian et al., 1985, p. 30). Urban districts have taken state compensatory education money intended for remedial programs and used it to pay regular classroom teachers to continue doing what they had been doing all along. They justified this diversion of funds by pointing to the money they were saving their taxpayers. The result was that suburban districts, with few remedial pupils, were spending roughly $150 on additional services for each of their neediest children, whereas one urban district was spending only $7 on each of its many needy youngsters (Carlson and Rubin, 1979).

Even when the money is spent on the targeted population, coordination is inadequate. How do we ensure that the expenditure approved by some assistant superintendent results in a teaching tool that actually becomes known to and used by the teachers? Fancy instructional hardware gathers dust in the storerooms of poor school districts. Moreover, there are simply too many assistant superintendents and other administrators, all busying themselves with things that never percolate down to the classroom. After the late Richard Green became chancellor of the New York City schools, he announced that he intended to clean out the board of education headquarters and send a whole bunch of people out to the schools, where they might finally be able to do some good for the children. The fact that his successors, Joe Fernandez and Ramon Cortines, have tried to do the same thing means that there is still bloat. Cortines found that the personnel of the central headquarters had been badly undercounted. The previous count had 3,468 people working in the central office; Cortines' count put the number at 7,078 (Barbanel, 1994a). The bloat is largely responsible for the fact that of the $7,000 per pupil spent in the New York City schools, only $3,500 gets to the pupil for instruction (Barbanel, 1993).

Besides allowing people to spin their wheels for no apparent educational purpose, poor school districts, and urban districts in particular, are pestholes of corruption. The poor citizens who live in these districts lack the expertise to detect the corruption and the political skills to attack it. They are at the mercy of slick operators with education certificates who exploit them and their children, and who themselves are likely to live in suburbs where their own children are getting a decent education. These parasites who prey on the poor have a lot of taxpayer money to spend, and much of it they keep for themselves in the form of kickbacks. They do business with the companies from which the most money can be extorted, whether it benefits the students or not. They manage to give their friends and relatives no-show jobs on the district payroll, and then they take a share of the unearned paycheck. They treat themselves to lavish perks, such as expensive dinners when they're in town and luxurious travel accommodations when they're out of town (ostensibly on school business), and they're out of town a lot.

New York City witnessed the spectacle of an elementary school principal being arrested on the street near his school for making a drug purchase. He turned out to have a record of absenteeism from his job. A detailed report on the front page of the *New York Times* began: "Members of a community school board in Brooklyn formed an interlocking power base to secure jobs and promotions for relatives and friends and advance a major private development project, according to school employees, parents and personnel records" (Lewis and Blumenthal, 1989, p. 1). Lest it be thought that this is the behavior of minorities, it should be noted that all the board members were white. In another report, on the business practices of the Jersey City school district, a nationally known accounting firm listed a host of irregularities in the awarding of contracts, the maintenance of payrolls, and the operation of the personnel office (Peat Marwick Main & Co., 1988). These irregularities were one of the major reasons why the state of New Jersey took over operation of the Jersey City schools. In Newark, a member of the board of education admitted that he offered to secure school principalships for people who were willing to pay him. In a school district in the Bronx, central office administrators, including the superintendent himself, "rarely bothered to visit the schools they were charged with improving," and three board members pleaded guilty to various criminal charges (Berger, 1991, pp. B1–B4). The principal of a Queens public school for handicapped youngsters pleaded guilty to stealing more than $20,000 by faking bills for goods that he never ordered and skimming money from fundraisers (Berger, 1992a). In the Bronx, teachers who hoped to be appointed to principalships were expected "to work in the election campaigns of members of their school board, calling voters and chauffering election workers" (Berger, 1992b). In Brooklyn, a principal was charged with stealing nearly $10,000 in school funds and with coercing teachers into joining a political club (Fried, 1994, 1995). In the poorest districts of the Bronx and upper Manhattan, school board members were running up huge travel expenses to such places as Las Vegas, Honolulu, and the Virgin Islands (McKinley, 1994). Retired New York City teachers have been allowed to collect their pensions while being retained as "consultants" making $200 a day (Barbanel, 1994b). One consultant was paid $4,000 to make a recommendation as to whether another consultant should be hired (Dillon, 1994). Since all these examples come from a small geographic area, one shudders to think of the scope of the problem nationwide.

Until such time as honest and effective people take control of poor school districts, it would be foolish for the taxpayers of a state to be sending care packages to crooks and incompetents in the form of extra revenue. As Henry Levin (1976) put it after studying the impact of expenditure increases on school effectiveness: "Spending increases will have a much greater effect on the economic status and employment of educational professionals than they will on the educational proficiencies of children" (p. 194). In the decade after Levin wrote this, school spending increased by 33 percent, not counting inflation, and student academic performance still did not improve (Chira, 1991). William Bennett, a former U.S. Secretary of Education, has noted that between 1960 and 1993, spending on elementary and secondary schools increased more than 200 percent and SAT scores dropped 73 points (Bennett, 1994, p. 82).

Throwing Dollars in the Dark

We know how we do not want to spend school money: on waste and corruption. But we are not sure how we do want to spend it. Educational research and past experience do not tell us clearly what works.

> Research currently available in this arena is deficient in both focus and rigor; findings often are nonconfirmatory or contradictory. For example, teaching

experience and advanced degrees are major determinants of teachers' salaries, but these variables are not clearly related to improvements in school outputs. . . . Education has not been able to provide cost/benefit data as readily as have some other public services, and the citizenry appears less sanguine about the efficacy of public schools than was true in the past. (McCarthy and Deignan, 1982, p. 102)

Detailed research spanning two decades and observing performance in many different educational settings provides strong and consistent evidence that expenditures are not systematically related to student achievement. (Hanushek, 1989, p. 49)

Hanushek's work is often cited by those who would reduce school spending, but, to be fair, it should be noted that his statistical methods have been challenged by others (Hedges, Laine, and Greenwald, 1994). In the further interest of fairness, it should also be noted that Hanushek (1994) claims that his critics themselves use dubious methods. Policymakers with authority to legislate on school finance have an obligation to study both sides of the debate, and not just cite the data that bear out their own positions. If they do, they may be forced into the agnostic approach that other researchers reach when they review the evidence. As James Guthrie puts it:

Everybody's arguing for more school decision-making, and the school finance people and the economists say they don't know how to advise them on the appropriate spending of resources. What the field needs is to better understand how money is spent inside a school, what are we buying, and what is it we ought to buy, and what leads to more learning. (Guthrie, quoted in Colvin, 1989, p. 13)

The so-called effective schools research that yielded a list of nostrums has itself come under attack for the narrow assumptions on which it is based, for example, that a successful school is one whose students score well on standardized tests in math and reading. There are now whole books devoted to critiques of the effective schools research (Knapp and Shields, 1990). Some research results are presented in such turgid detail that they defy comprehension by school personnel who are supposed to make use of them. One research report entitled "Early Schooling of Children at Risk" (Reynolds, 1991) would be of obvious interest to urban school officials, but they might abandon the effort to fathom it about halfway through. Researchers tend to write for other researchers, not for the people who are in a position to implement the research recommendations. As Ralph Tyler (1988) has said: "Researchers are accustomed to looking to the university for guidance and rewards. Practitioners are accustomed to looking to school and community leaders for guidance and rewards. It is therefore difficult to get them together and establish a tradition of working together" (p. 177).

Some of the things that seem to work in poor schools peter out in effectiveness after a while. It is as though what really works is novelty. But even then, some novelties do not work as well as others, or at all. Some of the things that are said to work either are beyond the control of schools or cannot be bought. Good families and stable neighborhoods are said to work, and this makes intuitive sense, but these conditions are largely the responsibility of other government agencies and private charities. Parental participation in school affairs is said to work, but suburban schools are able to get this without paying for it. Principals who take an interest in the quality of classroom instruction are said to be more effective, but this does not cost more money, only a reordering of the principal's priorities. Aligning the curriculum with the tests by which student achievement will be assessed should not cost much money, and it is so commonsensical that it should have been done long ago. Keeping students on task and not distracting them with silly administrative interruptions is something else that does not cost money and is patently desirable.

Given all this uncertainty about the things that cost money and the much greater certainty about the things that don't, spending more money on poor schools is like throwing dollars in the dark and hoping that they will land someplace where they can do some good. The uncertainty is not restricted to poor schools; rich schools spend money on a lot of things that have no demonstrated effect on the schools' goals. An Olympic-size swimming pool is certainly nice to have, but it is hardly essential. Luxuriantly carpeted and paneled offices create an elegant ambiance, but their relationship to staff or student productivity is elusive. The same is true for beautifully manicured grounds surrounding the school building. The difference is that rich schools spend (or waste) their own money; poor schools are asking for money from people who don't use these schools and don't live anywhere near them. Poor schools cannot expect anyone to invest in them before they establish a record for getting results with their own money.

It is not at all impossible that poor school districts already have enough money to do the job. They may have only half as much per pupil as a rich district, and their students may have a lot of educational handicaps, but by emphasizing a few really important goals they could concentrate their staffs' energy on accomplishing those goals. If the vast majority of the students are deficient in the basic skills of reading, writing, and arithmetic, the poor districts should focus their time and money on those areas. Full-fledged art and music programs may be luxuries that poor districts cannot afford and that detract from the students' real needs. Robert Slavin and his colleagues at the Johns Hopkins University have been operating an intensive primary grade reading program in five Baltimore schools and achieving well-documented success as compared with the other Baltimore schools. They are using the same Chapter 1 money from the federal government that the other schools get. The difference is that they spend the money in a concentrated, systematic way, with a focus on what little children need most to learn: reading (Madden, et al., 1993).

Dedicated urban educators can get results without waiting for more largesse from the state or federal treasury. Jaime Escalante, a math teacher in California, got such startling results that his story has been made into the movie

Stand and Deliver. Joe Clark, a New Jersey high school principal, was lionized in a *Time* magazine cover story and in the movie *Lean on Me.* And surely every state has its Jim Caulfield, a district superintendent whose schools spend less, have proportionately fewer administrators and teachers, and still get higher student test scores than other districts with the same kinds of students (O'Neill, 1994). Whatever one thinks of these individuals' tactics, the fact is that they had latitude for action that did not cost money, and they acted.

The simple fact that a rich district spends twice as much money per pupil as a poor district could mean that the rich district is wasting half its money on frills that its students don't need. However, it could also mean that the students are so educationally advanced that they require expensive programs and materials in order to continue their intellectual development. When a school has a sizable number of students who are able to handle expensive laboratory equipment and learn from doing so, buying that equipment is a legitimate educational expense. But to buy that equipment for students who are incapable of comprehending it is to pay for a foolish equality. Educationally backward students don't need sophisticated equipment, and they are not likely to have much respect for equipment that they find frustratingly difficult. The propensity of students from poor communities toward destructive behavior often leads to schools with expensive, unused, and *damaged* equipment. Equal education for rich and poor students does not mean the same education; it means equally appropriate education. Rich students tend to do better in school than do poor students, so it is a good social investment to spend more on them. These students *earn* the additional expenditure by dint of their hard work and better-developed ability.

Making Students Responsible

Society gives students a free start in life but not a guaranteed finish. Students are the adults of the future, and one of the things they must learn in school in order to assume their adult roles is responsibility. They must learn and act on the conviction that they are the major determiners of their fate.

A society that insists on excusing the transgressions of students does a tremendous disservice to young people. It gives them the notion that others are always to blame for their behavior. In the case of poor students, it is society itself that is supposed to be at fault. These children are pitied to the point of being denied all free will. That attitude, however charitably it is grounded, is insulting and damaging to poor children. It will have the effect of maintaining them in their poverty and dependency. The lesson these children must learn is that society simply cannot afford to give everyone an unending free ride. After going a certain distance, some payment has to be made by the riders. The ability and willingness to make such payments are traits of responsible, self-sufficient individuals. Students in poor schools may not be able to make cash payments toward their education, but they can certainly make payments of effort. If they do, they will find their own children attending suburban schools, just as so many earlier generations of the poor worked their way out of poverty.

This may already be happening, if minority student performance on standardized tests is an indicator. The scores are getting higher on a variety of tests. For example, the Scholastic Aptitude Test, one of the most consequential, is being taken by an increasing number of minority students, and they are doing better all the time. Between 1979 and 1989, black students' scores rose by 49 points, Mexican-Americans' scores by 31 points, and Puerto Ricans' scores by 33 points. Anglo students' scores rose by only 10 points. Thus, minorities were catching up during a period when they were supposed to be increasingly discriminated against economically (*Education That Works*, 1990, Table 2).

For Discussion

1. Find out the current per-pupil expenditure for your home school district, and then do in-class comparisons with other members of your class. Or get the official expenditure numbers from the state education department (in some states this is called the department of public instruction) and then make in-class comparisons of several school districts. How tolerable are the spending disparities across school districts?
2. The Committee for Economic Development* lists the following as major reasons why children do poorly in school. Try to devise cost-free or inexpensive means of dealing with these conditions. Is it really necessary to spend more money on schools where these conditions are endemic?

   They may come to school poorly prepared for classroom learning or not yet ready developmentally for formal education.

   Their parents may be indifferent to their educational needs.

   They may be children of teenagers who are ill-equipped for parenting.

   They may have undiagnosed learning disabilities, emotional problems, or physical handicaps.

   They may have language problems or come from non-English-speaking homes.

   They may experience ethnic or racial prejudice.

   They may have access only to schools of substandard quality.

   *Children in Need: Investment Strategies for the Educationally Disadvantaged, New York: Committee for Economic Development, 1987, p. 8.
3. It is often said that the one who pays the piper picks the tune. States that start giving more money to poor school districts will try to exercise more control over these districts to make sure the money is spent well. Make a list of the areas over which states should be exercising direct, prescriptive, uniform control. Then make a list of the areas that should be left to the judgment of local officials, no matter how much money the state is contributing. Items on your lists might include the hiring and evaluation of personnel, the determination of curriculum content and teaching materials, the testing of student achievement, the requirements for a high school diploma, the length of the school year, and the safety standards for buildings. Do your lists indicate that you prefer a centralized statewide school system or a localized system?
4. Below is a breakdown of the budget for the Reynoldsburg, Ohio, School District, for 1991–1992. How do you explain the differences in the amount spent per pupil from

Central-Office Costs by Function				School-Level Costs by Function			
Central-Office Functions	Cost Per Pupil	% of Central-Office Costs	% of Total District Costs	School-Site Functions	Cost Per Pupil	% of School Costs	% of Total District Costs
Administration	$200	71.30	4.57	Administration	$265	6.50	6.08
Operations and Building Support	$54	19.39	1.24	Operations and Building Support	$683	16.72	15.65
Teacher Support	$1	0.39	0.02	Teacher Support	$50	1.22	1.14
Pupil Support	$23	8.07	0.53	Pupil Support	$514	12.58	11.77
Instructional Support	$2	0.85	0.05	Instructional Support	$2,571	62.98	58.94
Total	$280	100.00	6.41	Total	$4,083	100.00	93.59

Total Cost Per Pupil: $4,363

Instructional expenditures per student by school

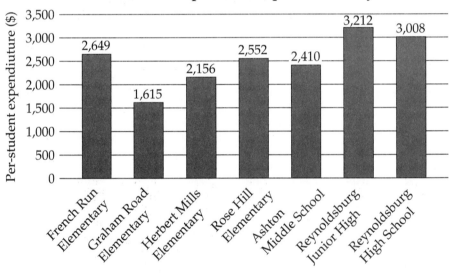

Source: Education Week **12**(27), 12.

school to school? Can you justify these differences? Is too large a portion of the district budget going to noninstructional expenditures?

References

Baker, K. (1991). "Yes, Throw Money at Schools." *Phi Delta Kappan* **72**(8), 628–631.
Barbanel, J. (1992), "Long Island District Illustrates Paradoxes of School Financing." *The New York Times,* February 12, p. A23.

Barbanel, J. (1993). "School Financing Not Less for the Poor, Study Says." *The New York Times,* October 5, p. B3.

———— (1994a). "Cortines Says Board Payroll Was Misstated." *The New York Times,* February 11, pp. B1, B3.

———— (1994b). "Some Retired Teachers Evade Income Restrictions." *The New York Times,* March 15, p. B3.

Barnett, S. (1993). "Does Head Start Fade Out?" *Education Week* **12**(34), 40.

Barton, P., Coley, J., and Goertz, M. (1991). *The State of Inequality.* Princeton, NJ: Educational Testing Service.

Bastian, A., et al. (1985). *Choosing Equality: The Case for Democratic Schooling.* New York: New World Foundation.

Barzun, J. (1959). *The House of Intellect.* New York: Harper & Row.

Bell, D. (1976). *The Cultural Contradictions of Capitalism.* New York: Basic Books.

Bennett, W. (1994). *The Index of Leading Cultural Indicators.* New York: Simon and Schuster.

Berger, J. (1991). "Report Sharply Rebukes School District in the Bronx." *The New York Times,* April 23, pp. B1, B4.

———— (1992a). "Principal Admits Misusing School Funds." *The New York Times,* February 21, p. B3.

———— (1992b). "Trade-off in the Schools: Principals Pay Political Dues to Get Jobs." *The New York Times,* February 7, pp. B1, B4.

Bowles, S., and Gintis, H. (1976). *Schooling in Capitalist America: Educational Reform and the Contradictions of Economic Life.* New York: Basic Books.

Bradley, A. (1994). "Equation for Equality." *Education Week* **14**(2), 28–32.

Carlson, K., and Rubin, L. (1979). *Analysis of the Development and Implementation of Local and Statewide Standards in Basic Skills in the State of New Jersey: A Final Report.* Washington, DC: National Institute of Education.

Carnegie Foundation for the Advancement of Teaching. (1988). *An Imperiled Generation: Saving Urban Schools.* Princeton, NJ: Princeton University Press.

Celis, W. (1994). "A Long-Running Saga Over Texas Schools." *The New York Times Education Life,* April 10, pp. 30–31.

Children in Need: Investment Strategies for the Educationally Disadvantaged. (1987). New York: Research and Policy Committee of the Committee for Economic Development.

Chira, S. (1991). "Money's Role Questioned in Schools Debate." *The New York Times,* May 4, pp. 1, 9.

———— (1992). "Quality Time for Quality Schools." *The New York Times,* March 30, pp. B1, B4.

Churchill, W. (1947). Address to House of Commons, November 11, 1947.

City High Schools: A Recognition of Progress. (1984). New York: Ford Foundation.

Coleman, J. S., et al. (1966). *Equality of Educational Opportunity.* Washington, DC: Government Printing Office.

Colvin, R. (1989). "School Finance Equity Concerns in an Age of Reforms." *Educational Researcher* **18**(1), 11–15.

Conant, J. B. (1961). *Slums and Suburbs.* New York: McGraw-Hill.

Coons, J. E., Clune, W. H. III, and Sugarman, S. D. (1971). *Private Wealth and Public Education.* Cambridge, MA: Harvard University Press.

Corcoran, T. B., Walker, L. J., and White, J. L. (1988). *Working in Urban Schools.* Washington, DC: Institute for Educational Leadership.

Daley, S. (1991). "Born on Crack and Coping With Kindergarten." *The New York Times,* February 7, pp. 1, D24.

Dillon, S. (1994). "School Board Said to Misuse Consultants." *The New York Times,* August 10, pp. B1–B2.

Education That Works: An Action Plan for the Education of Minorities. (1990). Report of the Quality Education for Minorities Project. Cambridge, MA: Massachusetts Institute of Technology.

Freeman, J., and Pollitt, K. (1991). "Islands of Quality, Sea of Decay. *The New York Times,* March 16, p. 23.

Fried, J. (1994). "Principal Charged With Stealing Funds." *The New York Times,* May 19, p. B3.

Fried, J. (1995). "More Corruption Charges Against Former Principal." *The New York Times,* March 1, p. B3.

Garms, W. I., Guthrie, J. W., and Pierce, L. C. (1978). *School Finance: The Economics and Politics of Public Education.* Englewood Cliffs, NJ: Prentice-Hall.

Gibbs, N. (1994). "Murder in Miniature." *Time,* September 9, pp. 54–59.

Gross, J. (1992). "Collapse of Inner-City Families Creates America's New Orphans." *The New York Times,* March 29, pp. 1, 20.

Hanushek, E. (1989). "The Impact of Differential Expenditures on School Performance." *Educational Researcher* **18**(4), 45–51, 62.

———— (1994). "More Money Might Matter Somewhere: A Response to Hedges, Laine, and Greenwald." *Educational Researcher* **23**(4), 5–8.

Hayek, F. A. (1944). *The Road to Serfdom.* Chicago: University of Chicago Press.

Hedges, L., Laine, R., and Greenwald, R. (1994). "Does Money Matter? A Meta-Analysis of Studies of the Effects of Differential School Inputs on Student Outcomes." *Educational Researcher* **23**(3), 5–13.

Herbers, J. (1972). "School Financing: A New Way to Foot the Bill." *The New York Times,* March 12, p. E3.

Jencks, C., et al. (1972). *Inequality: A Reassessment of the Effect of Family and Schooling in America.* New York: Basic Books.

King, W. (1992). "Florio's Educational Panel Offers Many Changes, at a Hefty Price." *The New York Times,* January 9, p. B7.

Knapp, M., and Shields, P., eds. (1990). *Better Schooling for the Children of Poverty: Alternatives to Conventional Wisdom—Volume II: Commissioned Papers and Literature Review.* Menlo Park, CA: SRI International.

Kotlowitz, A. (1991). *There Are No Children Here.* New York: Doubleday.

Kozol, J. (1988). *Rachel and Her Children: Homeless Families in America.* New York: Crown.

———— (1991). *Savage Inequalities: Children in America's Schools.* New York: Crown.

Kristol, I. (1978). *Two Cheers for Capitalism.* New York: Basic Books.

Krugman, P. (1994). "Technology's Revenge." *The Wilson Quarterly* **18**(4), 56–64.

Lefelt, S. (1988). *Abbott v. Burke.* Initial Decision. Trenton, NJ: State of New Jersey Office of Administrative Law.

Levin, H. M. (1976). "Effects of Expenditure Increases on Educational Resource Allocation and Effectiveness." In *The Limits of Educational Reform,* edited by M. Carnoy and H. M. Levin. New York: David McKay.

Lewis, N. A., and Blumenthal, R. (1989). "Power Base vs. Schools in Brooklyn District," *The New York Times,* February 10, pp. 1, B4.

Lucas, T., Henze, R., and Donato, R. (1990). "Promoting the Success of Latino Language-Minority Students: An Exploratory Study of Six High Schools." In *Strategies for Success: What's Working in Education Today.* Cambridge, MA: Harvard Educational Review.

Madden, N., et al. (1993). "Success for All: Longitudinal Effects of a Restructuring Program for Inner-City Elementary Schools." *American Educational Research Journal* **30**(1), 123–148.

McCarthy, M. M., and Deignan, P. T. (1982). *What Legally Constitutes an Adequate Public Education?* Bloomington, IN: Phi Delta Kappa.

McKinley, J. (1994). "School Districts Assailed on Travel Expenses." *The New York Times,* February 11, p. B3.

Metz, M. H. (1988). "In Education, Magnets Attract Controversy." *Issues '88,* special edition of *NEA Today.*

Nelson, F. (1991). *International Comparison of Public Spending on Education.* Research Report of the American Federation of Teachers. Washington, DC: American Federation of Teachers.

Nocero, J. (1989). "The Case Against Joe Nocero." *The Washington Monthly,* February, pp. 22–31.

O'Neill, T. (1994). "Where Schools Work." *New Jersey Reporter* **23**(6), 30–34.

Peat Marwick Main & Co. (1988). *Executive Summary of Jersey City Schools Investigation.* Trenton, NJ: New Jersey Department of Education.

Previte, M. (1994). "What Will They Say at My Funeral?" *The New York Times,* August 7, p. E17.

Reynolds, A. (1991). "Early Schooling of Children at Risk." *American Educational Research Journal* **28**(2), 392–422.

Rotberg, I. (1994). "Separate and Unequal." *Education Week* **13**(24), 44.

San Antonio Independent School District v. Rodriguez, (1973). 411 U.S. 1.

Sexton, P. C. (1961). *Education and Income: Inequalities in Our Public Schools.* New York: Viking.

"States' School Spending Disparities." (1992). *Education Week* **11**(39), 28.

Sullivan, J. (1989). "School Official Admits Guilt in Bribery Case." *The New York Times,* January 24, p. B3.

Suro, R. (1991). "Equality Plan on School Financing Is Upsetting Rich and Poor in Texas." *The New York Times,* October 9, p. B9.

Thurow, L. C. (1985). *The Zero-Sum Solution.* New York: Simon & Schuster.

Treaster, J. (1993). "For Children of Cocaine, Fresh Reasons for Hope." *The New York Times,* February 16, pp. A1, B4.

Tyler, R. (1988). "Utilization of Research by Practitioners in Education." In *Contributing to Educational Change: Perspectives on Research and Practice,* edited by P. Jackson. Berkeley, CA: McCutchan.

van Tassel, P. (1988). "Keeping the Peddie School's Aims Alive." *The New York Times,* December 11, p. NJ3.

Vergara, C. (1991). "New York's New Ghettos." *The Nation* **252**(23), 804–810.

Viadero, D. (1994). "'Fade-Out' in Head Start Gains Linked to Later Schooling." *Education Week* **13**(30), 9.

Wehlage, G., et al. (1989). *Reducing the Risk: Schools as Communities of Support.* London: Falmer Press.

Weiss, P. (1988). "The Education of Chancellor Green." *The New York Times Magazine,* December 4, pp. 42–44, 60–62, 81, 92–94, 109.

Winerip, M. (1993). "America Can Save Its City Schools." *The New York Times Education Life,* September 7, pp. 16–18.

CHAPTER FIVE

School Integration:
Compulsory or Voluntary

POSITION 1:
FOR LEGAL INTEGRATION

Assessing the Damage of Segregation

The major and most often quoted reason for outlawing racial segregation in American schools, as given by the U.S. Supreme Court in 1954, is that such segregation does psychological damage to black students. The damage may be so severe that it can never be repaired, said the Court. In the Court's exact words: "To separate them [blacks] from others of similar age and qualifications solely because of their race generates a feeling of inferiority as to their status in the community that may affect their hearts and minds in a way unlikely ever to be undone" (*Brown v. Board of Education of Topeka*, 1954). The Court, however, could only look at "legal" segregation, that is, segregation imposed by law. The Court ruled that this segregation by law was, in fact, illegal: It violated the highest law in the land, the U.S. Constitution.

The Supreme Court ruling against legal segregation has caused profound changes in society over the past forty years. The civil rights movement was given tremendous momentum by the ruling; schools throughout the nation were desegregated; blacks were afforded opportunities for better education, employment, and housing. Some blacks were even given preferential treatment over whites in securing these benefits. The progress of blacks during the forty-year period may be symbolized most dramatically by the presidential campaigns of Jesse Jackson, Douglas Wilder, and Allan Keyes and the much-anticipated presidential bid of Colin Powell.

And yet, after all the tumult and all the genuine progress of the past forty years, where does the United States stand today? It is still a racially segregated society. Several American cities now have majority black populations, including Atlanta, Baltimore, Birmingham, Detroit, Memphis, Newark, New Orleans, and Savannah, as well as Washington, D.C. (*Statistical Abstract of the United States*, 1994, pp. 44–46). In many areas of the country, the segregation in schools is more extensive than it was twenty years ago. In 1972–1973, the percentage of blacks and Latinos attending predominately minority schools was 64 percent and 57 percent respectively. By 1991–1992, these percentages had increased to 66 percent and 73 percent. Ironically, the most segregated states in the union are now those in the north and the west: Illinois, Michigan, New York, New Jersey, and California. Segregation of black students is worse now than it was before the Supreme Court's first busing decision in 1971. Latino students are far more likely than black students to be in segregated schools (Orfield, 1993). Moreover, "both African-American and Latino students are much more likely than white students to find themselves in schools of concentrated poverty. Segregation by race is strongly related to segregation by poverty" (Orfield, 1993, p. 1). The segregation is so extreme in the urban areas of the north that social scientists have new names for people trapped in the ghettos: "the underclass" and "the truly disadvantaged." The underclass and the truly disadvantaged are worse than poor; they are without hope. They can see no legitimate way out of their poverty, either for themselves or their children. The attempted way out for many of them is the illegitimate route of crime, which often leads only to prison, or death.

The plight of these people is passed from generation to generation because they are isolated in the ghetto without role models. When there was total racial segregation, successful blacks lived in the ghetto and could serve as guides and role models for black children. Now they are able to escape to residences in the suburbs, leaving the black children who are still in the central cities with nothing but models of defeat. William Julius Wilson, in examining the cities of New York, Chicago, Los Angeles, Philadelphia, and Detroit, found the following.

> Although the total population in these five largest cities decreased by 9 percent between 1970 and 1980, the poverty population increased by 22 percent. Furthermore, the population living in poverty areas grew by 40 percent overall, by 69 percent in high-poverty areas (i.e., areas with a poverty rate of at least 30 percent), and by a staggering 161 percent in extreme poverty areas (i.e., areas with a poverty rate of at least 40 percent). It should be emphasized that these incredible changes took place within just a 10-year period . . . the significant increase in the poverty concentration in these overwhelmingly black communities is related to the large out-migration of nonpoor blacks. (Wilson, 1987, pp. 46, 50)

The result of this massive and sudden dislocation for people left behind is that:

> people experience a social isolation that excludes them from the job network system that permeates other neighborhoods and that is so important in learning about or being recommended for jobs . . . in such neighborhoods the chances are overwhelming that children will seldom interact on a sustained basis with people who are employed or with families that have a steady breadwinner . . . the relationship between schooling and postschool employment takes on a different meaning. . . . In such neighborhoods, therefore, teachers become frustrated and do not teach and children do not learn. (Wilson, 1987, p. 57)

The schools of the underclass are a national disgrace. They catch the contagion of hopelessness from the ghettos in which they are located. As a result, they add to the despair and hostility the students bring in off the streets. The U.S. Department of Education reports the following differences between black and white students in elementary and secondary schools in America. While the numbers include students in integrated schools, it is a simple fact that relatively few black or white students attend such schools.

	White %	Black %
Enrollment	16	70
Suspensions	30	59
Corporal punishment	31	60
Educable mentally retarded	35	58
Trainable mentally retarded	27	60
Seriously emotionally disturbed	27	65
Learning disabled	17	71
Gifted and talented	8	81

Source: *A Special Analysis of 1986 Elementary and Secondary School Civil Rights Survey Data,* National Coalition of Advocates for Students, 1988.

Black students make up 16 percent of the total school enrollment nationwide, whereas white students are 70 percent. However, black students account for much more than 16 percent of those in the problem categories, and for only 8 percent in the nonproblem category of gifted and talented. Thus, black students are not being served well by the schools they attend, and most of them attend segregated schools.

The acuteness of the problems of urban schools led the National Governors Association to adopt the position that states should be prepared to take over their urban school districts that are locked in a cycle of failure (*Time for Results*, 1986). The state of New Jersey has already taken over the Jersey City and Paterson school systems, on the grounds that the residents of these cities have demonstrated repeatedly that they are unable to give an adequate education to their own children. The state has replaced the boards of education and the chief school administrators of these cities with its own appointees. It is now on the verge of taking over Newark, the largest school district in New Jersey. In the Chelsea school district in Massachusetts, the local authorities asked Boston University to assume management of the schools because they felt powerless to overcome the impact of poverty on their schools. The Hartford, Connecticut, board of education has signed a contract to let a private firm, Educational Alternatives, Inc., run the Hartford public school system, all else having failed to improve the beleaguered schools.

Obviously, the plight of the American underclass has reached crisis proportions. The newsmagazines are doing cover stories on it; the *New York Times* carries periodic front-page reports; and the television networks run prime-time specials. This means that the problem has risen to the top of the national political agenda. When the answers are being formulated, it is the U.S. Supreme Court's words forty years ago that should be heeded first.

Focusing on Effects, Not Intentions

It was four decades ago that the Supreme Court spoke of the possibly permanent damage done to youngsters by racial segregation. The Court's answer at that time was to outlaw various forms of "legal" segregation. If the segregation was not being imposed by some law, and it just happened to come about as a result of private choices that individuals made, then it was all right. But that did not mean that the psychological harm caused by this second kind of segregation was any less.

Moreover, it can be impossible to tell whether the segregation is due to official action or just to a series of innocent acts. For example, the United States is now largely divided into cities and suburbs. Blacks tend to be clustered in the cities and whites in the suburbs. When the suburbs were being established by state incorporation laws after World War II, it might have been an *intention* of the lawmakers to create racially segregated communities. They must certainly have known that racial segregation would result from their action. Indeed, the federal courts, including the Supreme Court, found this to have been the case in several metropolitan areas of the north (for example, *Keyes v. School District No. 1*, 1973; *Evans v. Buchanan*, 1976). If segregation was brought about *deliberately* in other metropolitan areas of the north—and this seems probable given the prejudices of the period during which the suburbs were being developed—none of those responsible would admit it today. Thus, all we can know with certainty is the *effect* that the state incorporation laws have had: white suburbs and black cities, white schools and black schools. "Requiring proof of intentional segregation before calling for any remedy is . . . not the most sensible [policy]. The injury that children suffer from racial separation has nothing to do with its cause" (Kirp, 1982, p. 285).

The answer to America's apartheid, then, is to integrate our country. The constitutionality of the segregation we now have may be debatable, but the harm it is doing is not. There are some obvious strategies that we can (and must) use to bring about an integrated society.

Integrating the Schools

The first and cheapest strategy is to redraw school district boundaries. One of the reasons why the south has had more success with school desegregation than the north has had is that southern school districts are countywide. The districts cover areas large enough to include a good mix of students from both races, although busing may be necessary to get children from their respective neighborhoods to a common school. When a state has large, racially mixed school districts, the ease of fleeing to a lily-white district is reduced. And the desire to flee is also reduced, since the integration is spread out enough to allay white panic.

The north has many racially segregated and economically inefficient little school districts that could be consolidated profitably into large integrated districts. Getting students of the different races to the same school may require some busing, but not as much as opponents claim. Black (and Hispanic) students who live on the periphery of the city may already be closer to the nearest suburban school than they are to the city school they are now forced to attend. The reverse is true for some suburban students whose homes are near the city line.

Interdistrict integration is the only kind of integration that is feasible now that city schools have become predominantly black and suburban schools almost exclusively white. "Desegregation in a society where whites have run to the suburbs to establish a 'white noose' around decaying, predominantly minority central cities requires metropolitan desegregation" (Mahard and Crain, 1983, p. 124). There is also evidence that integration in a limited area engenders more resistance than does large-scale integration (Hochschild, 1984, pp. 54–70, 147). This may be due to the fact that large-scale integration has effects that are popular with whites as well as with blacks. "A range of desirable goals for an effective school desegregation program—such as furthering genuine integration, cost and transportational efficiency, equity, and parental choice—can all be more effectively advanced within a metropolitan context" (Pettigrew, 1981, p. 163).

Even if there were better racial proportions within the cities, it is fairer to integrate over a larger geographic area. When the schools of the working-class Irish and blacks in Boston were integrated under court order, the noted Harvard psychiatrist Robert Coles had the following reaction:

> The busing is a scandal. I do not think that busing should be imposed like this on working-class people exclusively. It should cross these lines and people in the suburbs should share it. . . . [Working-class whites and blacks] are both competing for a very limited piece of the pie, the limits of which are being set by the larger limits of class which allow them damn little, if anything. (Coles, quoted in Lukas, 1985, p. 506)

Metropolitan desegregation of schools does not guarantee integration of classrooms, however. Even well-intentioned communities with magnet schools designed to promote integration find that, over time, the classrooms of these integrated schools become segregated (McLarin, 1994). This raises delicate questions regarding ability grouping and maintaining the support of high-status parents, who happen to be the wealthier and whiter parents in town. Ways can be found to meet the needs and abilities of all children in integrated classrooms, and thereby give all students the added benefits of integration itself. Now that the federal government's Magnet Schools Assistance Program requires the schools getting this assistance to demonstrate how they have increased interaction among students of different racial and social backgrounds (Schmidt, 1994), the government itself should be monitoring the situation to make sure that a good amount of the interaction is taking place *within* classrooms.

The Benefits for Students

People typically want to know what educational rewards will result from such large-scale reorganization and the added time and cost of busing. Those who ask this question usually think of educational benefits in terms of such things as math and reading and SAT scores. They do not seem to be aware of the learning that children can realize through associating with children from other backgrounds. This kind of knowledge can contribute to their success in later life, and it is absolutely indispensable for nullifying the poison of America's racial past and present. Such an attitudinal change may not be as easy to measure as are gains in academic achievement, but it is no less important for the future of America.

We know that schools can be integrated successfully. Traditional academic achievement need not be sacrificed in order for children to reap the benefits of a multiracial, multicultural environment. "White children almost never experience declines in performance on standardized achievement tests as a result of desegregation. Minorities benefit academically from desegregation much more often than they experience negative effects" (Hawley, 1981, p. 151).

This is especially likely to be the case for minority students if they are given the "wise" schooling about which Claude Steele writes. Schooling of this kind overcomes the double fear that minority students have—the fear of failing and the fear of being devalued. It allows them to relax and achieve by being encouraged to undertake successively more difficult tasks (Steele, 1992).

We are also sophisticated enough to realize that the *process itself* of creating an integrated school can be a valuable learning experience. Integration has to happen not just in the school, but also in its classrooms. Classroom integration permits cooperative learning tasks, with black and white students working together toward common goals. This usually has a positive effect on the racial attitudes of both groups (Conard, 1988; Schofield and Sagar, 1983, pp. 78–85). Adults are somewhat sheepishly aware that young people are more adaptable in these matters. But what we should understand most keenly of all is the necessity of preparing the next generation to handle the vicissitudes of a multiracial world better than we have. It is a world in which Anglo-Americans are becoming a smaller and smaller proportion (or percentage), both worldwide and in the United States itself.

A large integrated school district can afford the best of both worlds. Because it is large, it can purchase school supplies and equipment in quantity at discount prices. It can offer special programs, such as four years of Russian or Chinese, because it has enough students to make these programs economical. And yet a large district does not have to be a bureaucratic nightmare. Indeed, it should require fewer administrators than would several small districts serving the same overall number of pupils, and the savings in administrator salaries can be put to instructional purposes. A large district can be broken down into fairly independent units, with each school having considerable self-governance. There can even be schools-within-schools to give students a greater sense of belonging, such as the Central Park East Schools in New York

City (Bensman, 1987). Thus, a large district makes racial (and cultural) integration possible; it makes a richer education program possible; and it does not preclude the existence of decentralized control.

Integrating the Neighborhoods

School integration can accomplish only so much. Its benefits for all groups end each day when the students are bused back to their segregated neighborhoods. And not only do the black and Hispanic students return to segregated neighborhoods, but they are likely to return to poor neighborhoods as well. Many of these neighborhoods are crime- and drug-ridden, which discourages the students who live there from doing well in school. It is difficult for them to concentrate on homework assignments because of the turmoil around them. They are told by neighborhood hoodlums that it is not cool to be a good student, or to attend school at all. They are under constant threat of physical harm because of the rampant violence in a neighborhood marked by desolation and hopelessness. And very often, and tragically, these conditions have seeped into the home as well.

The abolition of ghettos is the only way fully to liberate the youngsters living in them so that they can lead successful and lawful lives. But abolishing ghettos will require that the people now trapped in them be given the means to live elsewhere. They will need housing allowances, since their meager incomes do not permit them to buy or rent decent housing now. They also will require *available* housing outside the area. Fortress suburbia has to be opened up to make room for our fellow citizens. The fair housing law passed by Congress makes this goal explicit. It stipulates that all federal agencies "shall administer their programs and activities relating to housing and urban development in a manner affirmatively to further the purposes of this title [housing integration]" (quoted in Orfield, 1978, p. 436).

Suburban communities have erected barricades against the poor. The barricades are called "zoning laws." One zoning law says that no house can be built on a lot smaller than two acres in size. The cost of such a lot alone would drive up the price of the house beyond the reach of poor people. Another zoning law says that no house can be occupied by anyone but the immediate nuclear family. This requires that grandparents be abandoned to live elsewhere, and it assumes that separate housing can be afforded for the grandparents or for other relatives who are not in the immediate family. Another zoning law says that no house can be smaller than so many thousand square feet: the larger the house, the greater the cost. Still another law forbids apartment housing and mobile homes in the area, often the only kind of housing the poor can afford.

These laws are defended with the argument that they keep the community "nice." Nice means rich and, mostly, white. It is as though being poor means you are not entitled to live in a nice neighborhood. This is true even if you are a full-time worker performing a vital job, but at a poverty wage.

These artificial barriers can be broken down, as the state of New Jersey has shown. The New Jersey Supreme Court ordered the state's suburban communities to change their zoning laws to permit the construction of housing for people with low and moderate incomes. Builders have agreed to put up low- and moderate-income housing, even though they will not make much profit from it, because they are also allowed to build expensive and profitable housing. Unfortunately, even the low-income housing is too expensive for many families, which is why housing allowances are needed. In the absence of housing allowances, court rulings may not effect much change. The ultimate ineffectiveness of the New Jersey court ruling was reflected in remarks made by the chief justice:

> New Jersey today, like much of this country, is a collection of islands, not happy with each other at all, potentially hostile, a black and Hispanic population overwhelmingly and disastrously poor, a white population trying to make ends meet, not having it easy at all. Our separateness is frightening: The public school enrollment of our biggest cities is more than 90 percent minority. (Wilentz, 1991, p. 7)

To accomplish neighborhood integration on a national level requires greatly expanded government intervention in the housing market, with much more government control of what the housing industry is allowed to do, and many more incentives to get the industry to do the right things (Downs, 1973; U.S. Commission on Civil Rights, 1974). The city of Hartford, Connecticut, has considered forcing the issue by razing some of its low-income housing projects, thereby pressuring the state to order construction of low-income housing in some of the surrounding suburbs. This would distribute the poverty population more evenly throughout the metropolitan area (Johnson, 1991).

It is ironic that rich folks want to keep the poor folks out, and yet rich folks themselves are now invading the neighborhoods of the poor. They are engaged in a process called "gentrification," whereby they purchase city dwellings in poor neighborhoods, evict the poor or hire thugs to terrorize them, expensively refurbish the dwellings, and then sell or rent them to other rich folks. The reason rich people want to live in cities like New York is to be close to where they work and to the cultural events of the region. Alas, the poor who get pushed out to make room for the rich cannot afford to go to the suburbs. Many of them end up in welfare hotels or in abandoned buildings without heat or running water. Others take to living on the streets as part of America's growing population of homeless people.

Those who maintain that the races will not be reconciled during our lifetimes and so neighborhood integration is a dream, should look to the city of Shaker Heights, Ohio, where the dream has been a reality for thirty years. That reality exists because the city is determined to have it so. For example, it provides low-cost loans to black or white families who move into neighborhoods dominated by the other race. The elementary schools offer race sensitivity training. There are even attempts to make sure that block parties are integrated. Shaker Heights is an affluent community that decided that it could become integrated without losing that affluence. And it was sophisticated enough to realize that integrating in a racist nation would have to be a continuing effort (Wilkerson, 1991a).

In a similar vein, the town of Matteson, Illinois, 40 miles south of Chicago, launched a $37,000 advertising campaign to attract affluent white families and stabilize the town's racial balance ("Illinois Town, Fearing Racial Imbalance, to Advertise for Whites," 1995).

Unless the suburbs, too, are integrated, the pattern of Boston will remain the national pattern:

> So desegregation does not get pushed very far—instead, we get a little, but not too much. Virtually no scholar looking at Boston and lacking any personal interest in defense of the desegregation process there has failed to see that the lower classes did the desegregating, the middle classes did the fleeing, either immediately or after a short trial (some stayed because their children traveled on insulated or relatively "safe" tracks to the sixth grade and then escaped into the six-year Latin schools), while the affluent were exempt from the start. (Formisano, 1991, p. 232)

Making the Only Choice

It might seem too costly to integrate the schools and communities of the United States. The busing costs for school integration might be low enough for the taxpayers to take on this burden, but the cost of housing allowances for residential integration could demand too much sacrifice. Given the federal budget deficit, housing allowances could also be what former President Reagan referred to as "budget busters." Taxpayers might well resent having to use part of their own hard-earned income to subsidize the housing of people they consider unworthy. Resentment toward the poor has been successfully exploited by politicians who got elected on the promise of "rolling back all those government handouts." The 104th Congress is set to do the rolling back as this is being written.

To a large extent, in fact, that is what happened at the end of the 1970s. There was a political backlash against the poor by the middle and upper classes. It became popular to think that the problems of poverty could be dealt with *cheaply*. In some circles, increased misery was even considered the most effective way to snap the poor out of their poverty. In addition, there was the genetic argument. It was said that the poor were poor because they were "naturally" dumb and shiftless. They had been born that way, just as though they had been born with an incurable disease. Nature *meant* them to be poor, and they were too brutish even to resent it much.

This kind of thinking has resurfaced in the writings of people like Herrnstein and Murray (1994), but it is an indulgence that the United States no longer can afford. It is selfish thinking, and the best answer is selfish thinking that is more realistic. It is unrealistic to think that the problems of the poor do not affect the rest of us.

We may not want to incur the costs of school reorganization and busing, but those costs can still be less than the property and insurance losses due to urban crime, and productivity losses due to high rates of joblessness. We may not want to bear the costs of integrated housing, but such housing can still be cheaper than building prisons for criminals whose breeding ground is the ghetto. We may wish we could forego the initial tensions, suspicions, and hostility of intergroup association, but these are still easier to cope with than are the riots and physical assaults—as well as the constant threat of them—that result from intergroup alienation. We may want our children to acquire a competitive edge in the occupational marketplace against the children of the poor, but with the American workforce declining numerically, with the structure of future work so difficult to predict, and with a growing elderly population to be supported, it might well be in our mutual interest to have *everyone's* talents fully developed. We might wish to treat our minority citizens as though they were citizens of a developing country, but we can hardly expect to be spared Los Angeles–type rioting if we do.

We can choose to ignore the problems of segregation in our society and hope that they will vanish in time. We can do as we've been doing for so long: treat the problems with Band-Aids and lip service. Or we can determine that the problems must be eliminated. The last choice is the one most clearly in our self-interest, and in the interest of our consciences. Moreover, public opinion is swaying in this direction. In 1971, 43 percent of the public thought that integration improved education for black children and 23 percent thought that it also helped white children. In 1988, 55 percent thought that it helped blacks and 35 percent believed that white students benefit, too. Over the seventeen-year period, the percentages went up by 12 points regarding both black and white children. Additionally, in 1973, 30 percent of the public thought that more should be done to integrate the schools; in 1988, it was 37 percent (Gallup and Elam, 1988, p. 39). This was at the end of the Reagan era, after a long federal retreat from integration as a goal for America. In 1993, a majority of both blacks and whites said in a *New York Times*/CBS poll that they favored full integration for America (Jones, 1994). Obviously, some will define the term more restrictively than others, but the general sentiment that integration is good and just reveals the angels to whom the appeal for full integration should be addressed.

In 1994, the *New York Times Magazine* carried an article entitled "We're All Racist Now" (Bissinger, 1994). The title quote is from a white woman who sent her daughters to the newly integrated school in her community, and who worked to make that school a success. Her discouragement at the behavior of the black students and the indifference of their parents is what prompted her remark. You may think that her experience and reaction would be better left to Position 2 of this chapter. But they are the cautionary note on which this side of the debate must end. The struggle to end slavery was long and difficult, as was the struggle for civil rights 100 years after—and the last struggle, for a fully integrated society, will be as well. There is no choice but to get on with it, patiently and persistently, and to leave a legacy for which future generations will be profoundly grateful.

POSITION 2:
AGAINST LEGAL INTEGRATION

Keeping Government off Our Backs

Let's not mince words. "Legal" integration is simply a euphemism for *forced* integration. Integration forced on us by law is as objectionable as segregation forced on us by law. "Legal" integration is as contrary to the freedoms guaranteed to Americans by the U.S. Constitution as "legal" segregation was.

One can be an integrationist without being rabidly so. The rabid integrationist is willing to invoke all the forces of government to bring about a goal that is *not* guaranteed in the Constitution. A racially integrated society was not even envisioned by our slave-owning Founding Fathers, let alone guaranteed (Higginbotham, 1978). However desirable a racially integrated society may be, it is not the role of the government to force such a society on free individuals, black and white. If an integrated society is to emerge in the United States, it must be through the *uncoerced* interaction of individuals.

Federal Judge John Parker, "a moderate jurist who had issued several racially progressive rulings" (Wilkinson, 1979, p. 81), interpreted the *Brown* decision in the only reasonable way:

> A state may not deny to any person on account of race the right to attend any school that it maintains . . . but if the schools which it maintains are open to children of all races, no violation of the Constitution is involved even though the children of different races voluntarily attend different schools, as they attend different churches. Nothing in the Constitution or in the [*Brown*] decision of the Supreme Court takes away from the people the freedom to choose the schools they attend. The Constitution, in other words, does not require integration. It does not forbid such discrimination as occurs as the result of voluntary action. It merely forbids the use of governmental power to enforce segregation. (*Briggs v. Elliott*, 1955)

Exactly 40 years later, Judge Parker's opinion was echoed by the black Supreme Court Justice, Clarence Thomas, in his concurring opinion in the *Missouri v. Jenkins* case (1995).

The freedoms the Constitution guarantees us are largely freedoms *from* government. The Founding Fathers had fought a war to rid themselves of the restraints of a repressive British government. They wanted a government that would itself be restrained from interfering in the affairs of its citizens. As Thomas Jefferson said, "That government governs best which governs least."

Tyranny can creep up on us in small steps, and so government must be prevented from taking any steps that are not absolutely essential for the common good. Even when the proposed government action appears benevolent, the question must be raised as to whether the result of that action will be worth the loss of individual freedom that will inevitably occur.

For example, in 1974, members of the U.S. Congress became dismayed at the number of deaths resulting from automobile accidents. They then passed a law requiring all newly manufactured cars to contain an alarm system that would continue sounding until a car's occupants had fastened their seat belts. For people who hated to buckle up, the sound might drive them crazy as they drove, but "better nuts than dead" was Congress's reasoning. Others reasoned differently: that however benign its intention, Congress was protecting a large number of people against their will and had thereby abrogated too much basic human freedom in return for too little added automobile safety. The law was soon rescinded, at the urging of both liberals and conservatives. (The increasing cost of automobile insurance may have caused people to be more forbearing concerning state laws requiring the use of seat belts.)

The next time you are tempted to support government interference in the private lives of your fellow citizens for their own good—perhaps in the form of a government ban on all tobacco smoking—pause to consider some of the many ways the government could compel you to do things that it considers to be in your best interest. The government could control most of your waking hours in the sincere belief that it was making you a better person. But each time the government is allowed to control you at all, it acquires an argument for controlling you further. People who are behaving well *under duress* have hardly been ennobled.

Giving Government Manageable Tasks

Nothing breeds disrespect for government so much as its failures. We have become used to hearing such expressions as a "government mess" and a "real government foul-up." The messes and foul-ups often occur because the government arrogantly decides to take on a task that is beyond its capability. Even if it does so reluctantly in response to public pressure, the result may be the same. The job may be so complicated that it cannot be done well by any human agency. If it cannot be done well, whoever undertakes it is foredoomed to failure.

Sometimes the government invites predictable disasters, which then make it such an object of ridicule that people start breaking the law out of contempt for the government's bungling. A good example of this is the widespread practice of tax cheating, which many people rationalize on the basis that the government's tax collection system is conceded even by officials of the Internal Revenue Service to be unnecessarily confusing and unfair. At other times, the law so tramples on a cherished right that breaking the law becomes an honorable pastime. Prohibition violated people's assumed right to drink alcohol, and they defied it with zest. Exceeding the 55 m.p.h. speed limit on highways is another example. In instances such as these, the government is reduced to ignoring or repealing its own laws in order to avoid the public defiance that would make enforcement a nightmare.

The right of association is a cherished American right, and one that is actually addressed in the freedom of assembly clause of the First Amendment of the Bill of Rights. The government has already curtailed this right by forcing people who engage in most forms of commerce to do so on a nondiscriminatory basis. This government action is designed to prevent a harm: the denial of opportunity to minorities. For the government to go the next step and insist that people integrate (associate) with groups they dislike is to provoke wholesale defiance of the law. "Most groups (racial and ethnic) prefer to live among their own kind. While this may look and have the same effects as prejudice, it really is different. For one thing, it may affect blacks in the same way as whites. For another, the housing decision is not one based on prejudice against a specific group" (Glazer, 1981, p. 138). How rich and emotionally fulfilling life can be for blacks in a segregated community has been captured by Henry Louis Gates in his memoir of growing up in such a community in West Virginia (Gates, 1994). As another black, one who grew up in Alabama, puts it: "We had our own doctors, our own soda shops. We didn't have the psychic pressure of feeling uncomfortable, of feeling less than. We didn't have or need a Jesse Jackson on the national level saying 'I am somebody,' because it came from our teachers, our churches, the man who ran the movie theater" (Nellie Hester-Bailey as quoted by Jones, 1994, p. 40). Moreover, people, both black and white, who live in the suburbs consider their residence a reward for achievement. They will not tolerate government intrusion into that hard-earned sanctuary. If a person's home is his or her castle, the neighborhood around it is the moat. And to maintain the dollar value of the castle, it is necessary to maintain the quality of the moat.

The task of enforcing compulsory integration would be monumental even if it were tolerated. Many, many more government officials would have to be hired to carry out this task alone. They would have to keep track of racial proportions community by community to ensure that the "correct" balances were being achieved. They would, of course, first have to decide what the correct balance should be for each community and school. As the proportions got out of the proper balance, adjustments would have to be made continually to restore the right racial mix. School attendance patterns would be redrawn regularly—perhaps every year—to keep the numbers to the satisfaction of some bureaucrat. Housing allowances for families and construction permits for builders would be subject to constant government manipulation. Altogether, it would be a tremendous task of social engineering—one that government already has proved itself unable to handle, and one that would cause endless exasperation for everyone concerned. It might succeed in uniting blacks and whites, but only in their disgust with the government. A good example of how the best-laid plans of government can go awry in large-scale social planning is to be found in Daniel Patrick Moynihan's aptly titled book *Maximum Feasible Misunderstanding* (1969). He details consequences of the War on Poverty program that *no one* intended.

How difficult the task of metropolitan school integration would be was suggested by a series of questions the U.S. Supreme Court raised when it rejected the attempt to integrate the Detroit metropolitan region:

> Entirely apart from the logistical and other serious problems attending large-scale transportation of students, the consolidation would give rise to an array of other problems in financing and operating this new school system. Some of

the more obvious questions would be: What would be the status of authority of the present popularly elected school boards? Would the children of Detroit be within the jurisdiction and operating control of a school board elected by parents and residents of other districts? What board or boards would levy taxes for school operations in these 54 districts constituting the consolidated metropolitan area? What provision could be made for assuring substantial equality in tax levies among the 54 districts, if this were deemed requisite? What provisions would be made for financing? Would the validity of long-term bonds be jeopardized unless approved by all of the component districts as well as the State? What body would determine that portion of the curricula now left to the discretion of local school boards? Who would establish atten-dance zones, purchase school equipment, locate and construct new schools, and indeed attend to all the myriad day-to-day decisions that are necessary to school operations affecting potentially more than three-quarters of a million pupils? (*Bradley v. Milliken*, 1974)

These questions suggest the tumult that will ensue if metropolitan desegrega-tion is attempted, a tumult that has no Constitutional imperative and is likely to thwart any educational rationale.

It is important to bear in mind that the compulsory integrationists do not limit their benevolence to blacks. They are more altruistic than that. They also seek to integrate into the American mainstream Hispanics and the poor in gen-eral. The grander the goals of the integrationists, the greater will be the gov-ernment action needed to achieve them. So all the difficulties we have been discussing are going to be made even worse. Moreover, the huge expansion of the public, or government, sector of society called for by the integrationists' ambitious agenda will necessarily reduce the size of the private, or productive, sector. In other words, the *revenue-producing* sector of society will be reduced in favor of the *revenue-consuming* sector. This obviously will have negative con-sequences for the health of the U.S. economy, but just how negative they will be will depend on how zealously the compulsory integrationists pursue their dreams.

The Kansas City, Missouri, schools are a case in point. The federal judge presiding over that district has not *compelled* metropolitan integration, but he has been hell-bent on fostering it. He has succeeded in forcing the people of Missouri to pay a sharply higher tax so that the schools in Kansas City can be made more attractive, with the hope that these schools will then lure suburban whites to attend them. More than $1.3 billion have been spent on this effort, with no significant effect either on integration or on the performance of the black students (Celis, 1995). Surely Missouri has pressing economic needs that would have been much better served by leaving this money in the hands of the taxpayers. The judge's gamble, like all overweening government schemes, is but one example of the danger of know-it-all government. The judge's most recent ruling that the Kansas City schools would remain under his desegrega-tion order until the students' test scores had improved was a horrible conflation of racial neutrality with academic performance. Fortunately, the parties have agreed to try to work their way out of this quagmire through negotiations (Schmidt, 1995), and the Supreme Court has curtailed the district judge's control of the Kansas City schools (*Missouri v. Jenkins*, 1995).

We can get some sense of the risk by looking at the state of the former Soviet economy. The Soviets had a centrally planned society with a massive government bureaucracy, and their budget deficit got to be as high as 20 percent of their national income (Shelton, 1989). Our deficit has been kept below 6 percent, which explains why former communists are trying to become capitalists and be more like us. Their society has fallen into such disarray that they cannot be called "Soviets" any more, but there is no new name by which to identify them. We should not be adopting practices that they are rejecting after long and bitter experience, practices from which it is a nightmarish experience to become disentangled.

Challenging the Integrationist Assumptions

All the aggravation and pervasive government control of our lives might be worth bearing if the results could be predicted, with some certainty, to be beneficial. However, we cannot know beforehand whether the results will be beneficial at all, let alone how beneficial. The compulsory integrationists act as though their *assumptions* about the benefits are already proven facts accepted by all. In making their assumptions, the integrationists may be guilty of nothing more than excessive optimism about human nature. But even so, to base social policy on their Pollyanna-like attitudes is to take a big and dangerous gamble.

The first assumption of the integrationists, and one of the most obvious, is that different groups will grow to respect each other if they are forced to live and work in close contact. The danger is that they might, in fact, grow to dislike each other so much that instead of having a productive relationship, they will spend all of their time in bitter enmity. It is true that some cases of forced integration have turned out reasonably well. Unfortunately, these cases are more than counterbalanced by cases in which physical violence was a recurring event, and even now, years later, there is mutual antagonism and tension between the groups. A series of studies on the interactions that occur between blacks and whites in integrated schools in both the south and the north reached the following conclusions:

> The racial cleavage reported time and again in these studies suggests that while the student populations may have been desegregated, they were not integrated . . . For most participants, school desegregation spelled trouble, and to keep it at arm's length was thought to be success enough. . . . Violence was thought to be just below the surface of daily behavior . . . the racial attribute of being 'white' carried high status, while that of being a member of a racial minority carried low status. Given that so many members of the minority groups were also economically poor meant that status characteristics were reinforced with class characteristics. (Rist, 1979, pp. 8–10)

What worked in the happy cases of integration may be unique to the contexts in which they unfolded, and since we cannot be sure what *that* was, we cannot know whether or how to apply it to all other situations. But we do know that there are a lot of unhappy cases. One truly sad situation was the one that developed with regard to the senior prom a few years ago at Brother Rice High School, an integrated Catholic school in Chicago. The black students, who constituted only about 12 percent of the senior class, felt so excluded from the prom planning that they held their own, separate prom (Wilkerson, 1991b). There is just too much at stake for us to rely on government by guess and wishful thinking in the matter of integration. As a California newspaper said in opposition to the forced integration of the Berkeley schools: "The board of education is destroying a city to test a theory" (quoted in Kirp, 1982, p. 161).

The second assumption of the compulsory integrationists is that the downtrodden will respond to kindness with gratitude. "Just give 'em a chance and they'll come around," is their thinking. However, it's possible that the downtrodden will perceive kindness as a weakness to be exploited. During the high-tide years of the War on Poverty in the late 1960s and early 1970s, the poor and minorities spent a good deal of time not in reforming themselves, but in ripping off the system that was trying to help them (Lemann, 1988–1989). If the abuses are not as great today, it's because the benefits have been cut back and so there are fewer opportunities for abuse than there once were. The integrationists may have naive notions about human nature, or, at least, notions that cannot be generalized to *every* human being. At any rate, it is possible that some people's personalities have become so warped, either by genetic predisposition or life experience or both, that kindness is a medicine that will no longer work. The bleeding-heart integrationists refuse to acknowledge that such a grim situation is even possible.

The Affront to Blacks

A third assumption of compulsory integrationists is so offensive that it demands discussion in a section by itself. This is the belief that blacks long for the chance to live and work among whites. This assumption brings the integrationists close to being racists. Behind it is the further assumption that blacks *should* want to live and work with whites. The reverse assumption is not made: that whites should want to live and work with blacks. Thus, the compulsory integrationist position is insulting and condescending to blacks because it fails to represent their real feelings. The last Gallup poll to sample people's opinions about the use of busing to integrate the schools showed that fully 31 percent of blacks were opposed to it (Gallup, 1988). The fact that 78 percent of whites were also opposed to busing can be interpreted to mean that both races want good schools for their children, period. They do not crave the chance to mingle with each other.

By 1988, the Gallup organization no longer was asking about busing, but just whether enough was being done to integrate the schools. Fifty-four percent of the respondents thought it was ("Special Report on Education," 1988). By 1989, Gallup had switched to asking what could be done to improve inner-city schools, a recognition of a reality that Americans accept. The 1994 Gallup poll had no questions on integration or urban schools, reflecting how much these issues have been superseded by other educational concerns among the public (Elam, Rose, and Gallup, 1994).

It is true that much of the school desegregation litigation has been initiated by black organizations, particularly the National Association for the Advancement of Colored People (NAACP). However, it is false to infer from this that it is integration per se that blacks want.

> Blacks and Mexican-Americans who supported desegregation did so primarily because they believed that desegregation would enable their children to receive the same kind of education as white children. The underlying black assumption . . . is that chances are greater that their children will receive equal or quality education if they attend the same classes with white children. Many parents said that in a desegregated school, classroom minority and white children would be exposed to the same curriculum materials and other resources and would most likely be treated alike by teachers and other school personnel . . . *the perspective on the desegregation situation given by these parents is not the same as that held by social scientists* [emphasis added]. (Ogbu, 1986, p. 40)

Thus, what blacks want is not integration but equal educational opportunity. This is what Kenneth Clark, the black psychologist whose evidence was so influential in the Supreme Court's *Brown* decision, meant when he argued for equal schools regardless of integration (Clark, 1965). It is what the advocates of Afrocentric schools mean when they demand equality of resources while recognizing that Afrocentrism itself is a powerful antidote to the paucity of resources.

> The biggest problem with Afrocentrism, at least as it's practiced at the grade school level, is that it has distracted attention from far more pressing issues like overcrowding, crumbling facilities, the violence in and around schools, lagging technology, the dearth of even the most basic supplies. . . . In these circumstances, tinkering with the curriculum can help when it lifts spirits, motivates teachers, parents, and children, and inspires a commitment to excellence. (Mosle, 1993, p. 82)

This is not a call for integration, and it echoes the pride felt by Vern Smith when he recalls the segregated school he attended in Mississippi: "By the conventional wisdom of the day, we were the lowest of the low: black kids in a segregated school in the poorest, most violent of the Southern states. But we never saw ourselves as powerless victims; [our] teachers drummed into us that it was possible to overcome, but it took preparation. Knowledge was power, so we strove to empower ourselves." The success rate for the graduates of that segregated school is remarkable (Smith, 1994, p. 53).

The pride that blacks take in their own schools and the success they enjoy through these schools are now becoming evident at the collegiate level. In the push for integration, the federal courts are threatening the existence of historically black colleges in the southern states. The continuation of these colleges has become a major goal among blacks, who see in them a nurturing environment absent from integrated institutions (Constantine, 1994; Smothers, 1994; Ware, 1994).

John Ogbu notes that blacks are often disappointed by desegregated schools. They find that the schools become segregated inside, with the black children being shunted disproportionately into special classes for problem students (Ogbu, 1986, p. 41). After all the agony Bostonians endured to integrate their schools so that children would have a better chance at an education, what was the result? "Far and away the gravest failures in the Boston story concern the continuation of generally poor instruction. The number of students denied promotions is still significant, and it reveals a sorry state of affairs. Academic achievement has been improved in a few schools but such is not the case in most" (Dentler and Scott, 1981, p. 233).

For integration to be palatable to whites, their children have to constitute a large majority of the students in an integrated school. When white representation drops below 75 percent of the student body, the "tipping point" is said to have been reached, after which the whites start pulling out. Therefore, the usual integration pattern is for black youngsters to go from segregated schools where they are a majority to integrated schools where they are a distinct minority. Metropolitan integration is intended to keep blacks in this minority status so that whites will not become unduly alarmed. The predictable result for black children—for any children—when they are put into a strange and hostile environment is that their self-esteem drops. "Many researchers have found that black children tend to indicate a higher degree of self-esteem than white children, but that desegregation often has a discouraging effect . . . desegregation tends to threaten the self-esteem of minority children" (St. John, 1981, p. 91).

> The desegregated experience, then, is one of enhanced awareness of the broader society's negative attitudes towards one's race. . . . In segregated settings, the self-esteem of black children from separated or never-married families is just as high as that of children from intact families; but in the desegregated setting it is substantially lower. In addition, in desegregated settings black children are more likely to be poorer than those around them than in the segregated settings. In several important respects, social comparisons tend to be more unfavorable in desegregated than in segregated settings. (Rosenberg, 1986, pp. 186–187)

What black parent should be expected to subject his or her child to the psychological torment attendant on integrated education? Some might find this a reasonable price for their children to pay in exchange for improved academic performance. Unfortunately, the evidence for the effect of integration on black academic achievement is not at all clear. The data are "mixed and ambiguous" (Granovetter, 1986, p. 99). "The very best studies available demonstrate no significant and consistent effects of desegregation on Black achievement" (Armor, 1984, p. 58). Is this indeterminacy worth the price paid in lower self-esteem?

The most recent comprehensive study of this issue is that of Meier, Stewart, and England (1989). They looked at what they call "second-generation discrimination," that is, discrimination that occurs in desegregated schools. They examined schools in 174 districts, with each district having at least 15,000 students. They found that black students were overrepresented in classes for the educable mentally retarded and the trainable mentally retarded; among students receiving corporal punishment, suspensions, and expulsions; and among dropouts. Black students were *underrepresented* only among those in gifted classes and those graduating. The more desegregated the school, the higher is the level of resegregation. A school that has a high percentage of black teachers and relatively affluent black families is much less likely to experience this internal segregation. Should black parents in the 1990s be expected to relegate their children to in-school conditions that may well be as damaging as the between-school conditions that existed prior to 1954?

Now that they are familiar with the alleged benefits of school integration, blacks themselves have lost enthusiasm for it. In Louisville, Kentucky, a proposal to eliminate school busing and return to racially segregated neighborhood schools was unopposed by the local chapter of the NAACP, which in previous years had been an ardent advocate of busing (Marriott, 1991). The Urban League in Oklahoma City is also prepared to abandon busing. The issue for many blacks in Oklahoma City is quality education, regardless of student body composition (Traub, 1991).

Sparing the Innocent

That the United States has a horrible history of racism is a matter beyond dispute. In recent decades, however, remarkable progress has been made in removing its overt manifestations. This progress has affected attitudes as well, so that racism no longer constantly lurks in the American mind as it once did. The laws that forbade racist behavior among the older generations of Americans have gradually caused those generations to purge themselves of racist attitudes, which are now looked back on with shame. The younger generations, with a few well-publicized exceptions such as Howard Beach, are generally free of racist behavior, and they have learned from schools and the media that racist attitudes are discreditable.

And yet it is the younger generations from whom the compulsory integrationists expect the greatest sacrifice in their bold experiment. It is young married couples and their children who are being asked to redeem the United States from its legacy of racism. School integration will involve them directly; all the trauma will be visited upon them as though they personally must make restitution for the crimes of others. Worse, it will be visited on them by people who arrange to avoid it for themselves, as Nathan Glazer has noted.

> The leading advocates of transportation for integration—journalists, political figures, and judges—send their children to private schools which escape the consequences of these legal decisions. This does raise a moral question. The judges who impose such decisions, the lawyers who argue . . . for them

would not themselves send their children to the schools to which, by their actions, others poorer and less mobile than they are must send their children. Those not subject to a certain condition are insisting that others submit themselves to it, which offends the basic rule of morality in both the Jewish and Christian traditions. (Quoted in Wilkinson, 1979, p. 210)

If we could be sure that the school integration experiments would go smoothly, it would be reasonable to subject innocent children to the inconveniences involved, for the long-term good of society. The resistance is not to an integrated society per se, or to the use of children in bringing about that goal. The resistance, the absolute refusal, stems from fear of gratuitous harm to the innocent of both races.

This harm can take several real forms, as past experiments with integration have shown. First, gentle and well-bred children will be forced into close and constant association with children with violent tendencies. For whites to connect violence with black youngsters is not irrational when the number of firearm homicides among blacks aged 19 or younger is greater than that for their white peers even though there are far fewer adolescent blacks than adolescent whites (*The State of America's Children*, 1994, p. ix). How the violent children got that way is beside the point; they threaten and sometimes inflict physical harm on children who have done nothing to provoke it. And the possibilities of this physical harm do not stop short of killing. The innocent child may not even be an intended victim but just someone who got in the path of a stray bullet. Second, the threat of physical harm will be used to extort money from frightened children. Some schoolchildren have gone without lunch for long periods of time because their lunch money was being extorted and they were too terrified to tell even their parents. Third, the availability of drugs in or near the school is likely to increase, as are the pressures to engage in drug abuse. This risk is made all the more intolerable as newer drugs are formulated, some of which irreparably damage the body. Fourth, the school's academic mission will become more diffuse as students of different abilities have to be accommodated. As the school's focus becomes blurred, energy and resources will be spread more thinly than when they were concentrated on single-purpose efforts. Everyone will lose. Fifth, a less homogeneous (less segregated, if you will) school community will cause a loss of school spirit. Neither students nor parents will be able to identify with the school as they did when it more fully reflected their own values and aspirations.

The list of the harms that can and do result from school integration experiments indicates that blacks as well as whites run the risk of a worse educational experience. For blacks who are transported from a predominantly black school near their homes to an overwhelmingly white school miles away, the sense of being an unwelcome outsider can be most dispiriting. Just as there are innocent white children who ought not to be victimized by the integrationists' grand schemes, there are innocent black children whose most valuable possession is their sense of self-worth. Putting that in jeopardy is a serious matter, and something that should not be done in our present state of social policy forecasting.

Finally, the fundamental difference between the compulsory integrationists and those who oppose them is not the goal they want to achieve. We should all wish for an integrated society. The difference lies in each group's sense of the possible, and in the opposing group's conviction that good intentions are not enough. It would be wonderful to have a better society but, given the fragility of human relationships, it would be quite easy to create a worse one.

It is fitting that some final word be given to William Bradford Reynolds, the U.S. assistant attorney general for civil rights during the Reagan administration, who fought so hard, in the face of so much slander, to restore morality and common sense to American education:

> We have learned something from this unfortunate social experiment, which has led needlessly to the sacrificing of quality education on the altar of racial balance. It is a lesson that should not soon be forgotten, with respect to school desegregation or civil rights generally. We must always be aware of the danger to an individual's civil rights that lurks in group-oriented policies grounded on racial preferences, racial-balancing, and proportionality. If we ever succumb to this threat, the great civil rights movement will have tragically, and unnecessarily, exhausted all credibility. Once the noble ideal of equal opportunity is compromised, it is not easily retrieved, and all Americans suffer. (Reynolds, 1986, p. 13)

All in Due Course

Integration is taking place in America owing to the natural goodwill of the American people. "From 1980 to 1990, the black population in the suburbs grew by 34.4 percent, the Hispanic population by 69.3 percent and the Asian population by 125.9 percent. By contrast, the white population in the suburbs increased by 9.2 percent" (DeWitt, 1994, p. 1). Moreover, "the percentage of all black families earning incomes of $50,000 or more (as adjusted to 1992) dollars rose from 10.2 percent in 1970 to 16 percent in 1992 . . . . The percentage of blacks in professional or managerial jobs rose from 10 percent to 16.8 percent in the same period. And the percentage of blacks 25 to 29 years old who had completed at least four years of college more than doubled, from 6 percent in 1970 to 12.7 percent in 1989" (Jones, 1994, p. 40). The percentage of blacks 18 to 24 years old enrolled in college in 1993 was 33, which compares favorably with the 42 percent for whites (Bennett, 1995, p. 9).

Our generation of Americans is well-motivated in matters of race. We can be trusted to do the right thing. Big Brother schemes that attempt to accelerate progress beyond its natural flow create eddies and currents that only make the progress more difficult and may reverse its course.

The great black leader and educator, W. E. B. DuBois, said it best 60 years ago:

> To sum up this: theoretically the Negro needs neither segregated schools nor mixed schools. What he needs is Education. What he must remember is that there is no magic, either in mixed schools or in segregated schools. A mixed

school with poor and unsympathetic teachers, with hostile public opinion, and no teaching of truth concerning black folk, is bad. A segregated school with ignorant placeholders, inadequate equipment, poor salaries, and wretched housing, is equally bad. Other things being equal, the mixed school is the broader, more natural basis for the education of all youth. It gives wider contacts; it inspires greater self-confidence; and suppresses the inferiority complex. But other things seldom are equal, and in that case, Sympathy, Knowledge, and the Truth, outweigh all that the mixed school can offer (DuBois, 1935, p. 335).

For Discussion

1. If, as William Julius Wilson contends, black children in the inner city are isolated from good role models as well as from good job contacts, how can this isolation be broken?

2. Louise Day Hicks, the chairperson of the Boston School Committee, justified her resistance to the court's desegregation order in the following terms:

> Why is there resistance in South Boston? Simply stated, it is because it is against your children's interest to send them to schools in crime-infested Roxbury. . . . There are at least one hundred black people walking around in the black community who have killed white people during the past two years. . . . Any well-informed white suburban woman does not pass through that community alone even by automobile. Repairmen, utilities workers, taxi drivers, doctors, firemen, all have refused at one time or another to do what Judge Garrity demands of our children on a daily basis. (quoted in J. A. Lukas, *Common Ground*, New York: Knopf, 1985, p. 412)

If you were Judge Garrity, how would you have answered Mrs. Hicks?

3. The following graphs show arrest rates for violent crimes, broken down by race. How might these graphs be used as an argument against integration? How might they constitute an argument for integration?

Distribution of Arrests: 1992

People under the age of 18 arrested for violent crimes, and in the general population

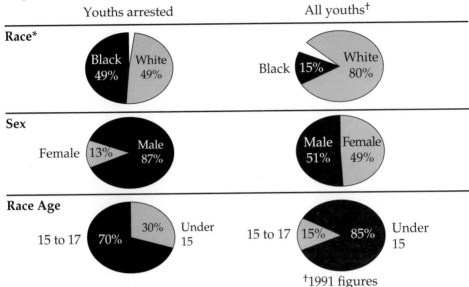

Youths arrested   All youths†

†1991 figures

Arrest Rates and Race

Rate, per 100,000, at which people under 18 were arrested for violent crimes.

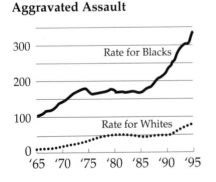

Aggravated Assault

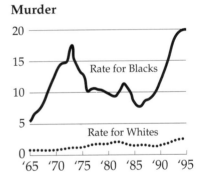

Murder

Racial breakdown of youths arrested for each offense in 1992*

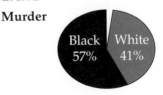

Aggravated Assault   **Murder**

Source: The New York Times, May 16, 1994, p. A-14.

4. The map below shows that schools 1, 2, and 3 have large populations of minority students. Schools 4, 5, and 6 have small percentages of minority students. If these two sets of schools are to be integrated, what is the best way to do it to enhance the education of all the children and keep families from pulling out of the schools?

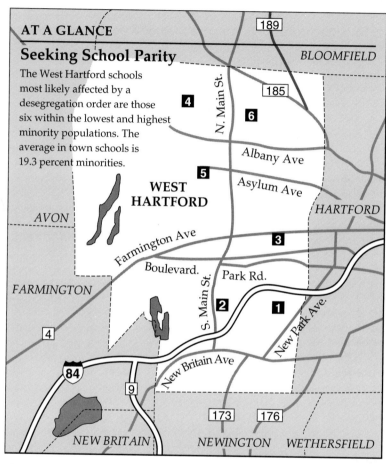

AT A GLANCE

Seeking School Parity

The West Hartford schools most likely affected by a desegregation order are those six within the lowest and highest minority populations. The average in town schools is 19.3 percent minorities.

1 Charter Oak School
46.3% minorities

2 Webster Hill
Elementary School
33.5% minorities

3 Whiting Lane Elementary School
31.8% minorities

4 Norfeldt Elementary School
5.9% minorities

5 Lloyd H. Bugbee
Elementary School
9.0% minorities

6 Aiken Elementary School
9% minorities

Source: Judson, G. (1995). "West Hartford Tries to Cope As Its Schools Are Integrated." *The New York Times,* January 23, B5.

5. The table below is for Primary Metropolitan Statistical Areas (PMSA). These are major cities and their surrounding suburbs. The "black isolation" within a PMSA means the percent of blacks who are living in neighborhoods where blacks are more than 90 percent of the population. Are blacks becoming more or less isolated within America's major metropolitan areas? For which areas is this the trend and for which is the trend in the opposite direction?

TABLE 1. Isolation of Blacks in America's Largest Metropolitan Areas

Primary Metropolitan Statistical Area (PMSA)	1990 Black Population (1,000)	1990 Total Population (1,000)	Blacks Isolated (%)		
			1980	1990	Change
New York	2,250	8,547	28	31	+3
Chicago	1,333	6,070	80	71	−9
Washington, DC	1,042	3,924	46	37	−9
Los Angeles	993	8,863	20	7	−13
Detroit	943	4,382	57	61	+4
Philadelphia	930	4,857	53	53	0
Atlanta	736	2,834	49	43	−6
Baltimore	616	2,382	58	53	−5
Houston	611	3,302	50	30	−20
New Orleans	430	1,239	50	47	−3
St. Louis	423	2,444	73	70	−3
Newark	423	1,824	44	41	−3
Dallas	411	2,553	51	29	−22
Memphis	399	982	59	58	−1
Norfolk	398	1,396	40	24	−16
Miami	398	1,937	41	33	−8
Cleveland	356	1,831	67	67	0
Oakland	304	2,083	16	5	−11
Charlotte	232	1,162	33	32	−1
Boston	210	2,871	25	19	−6
Kansas City	201	1,566	50	44	−6
Milwaukee	197	1,432	49	42	−7
Nassau–Suffolk	194	2,609	20	14	−6
Ft. Lauderdale	193	1,255	64	34	−30
Cincinnati	190	1,453	35	34	−1
Tampa–St. Petersburg	186	2,068	41	30	−11
Riverside	179	2,589	0	0	0
Indianapolis	172	1,250	45	39	−6
Pittsburgh	168	2,057	34	32	−2
Columbus	165	1,377	26	20	−6
San Diego	159	2,498	0	0	0
Nashville	152	985	35	30	−5
Ft. Worth	144	1,332	50	23	−27
Orlando	133	1,073	54	32	−22
San Francisco	122	1,604	6	2	−4
Buffalo	110	969	48	51	+3
Bergen–Passaic	106	1,278	14	6	−8
Sacramento	102	1,481	1	0	−1
Denver	96	1,623	10	7	−3
Rochester	94	1,002	14	14	0
Minneapolis–St. Paul	90	2,464	1	1	0
San Antonio	89	1,302	34	15	−19
Seattle	81	1,973	0	0	0
Phoenix	74	2,122	5	2	−3
Middlesex	71	1,020	3	0	−3
Monmouth	59	986	17	10	−7
San Jose	56	1,498	0	0	0
Anaheim	43	2,411	0	0	0
Portland	39	1,240	0	0	0
Salt Lake City	10	1,072	0	0	0
Average for 50 PMSAs	342	2,261	44	37	−7

Source: Turner, M. (1992–93). "Discrimination in Urban Housing Markets: Lessons From Fair Housing Audits." *Youth Policy*, **14 & 15** (9 & 1), 35.

References

Armor, D. (1984). *The Evidence on Desegregation and Black Achievement.* Washington, DC: National Institute of Education.

Bennett, C. (1995). *The Black Population in the United States: March 1994 and 1993.* Current Population Reports P20-480, Washington, DC: Bureau of the Census.

Bensman, D. (1987). *Quality Education in the Inner City. The Story of the Central Park East Schools.* New York: Central Park East Schools.

Bissinger, H. (1994). "We're All Racist Now" *The New York Times Magazine,* May 29, pp. 27–33, 43, 53–56.

Bradley v. Milliken (1974). 418 U.S. 717.

Briggs v. Elliott. (1955). 132 F. Supp. 776.

Brown v. Board of Education of Topeka. (1954). 347 U.S. 483.

Celis, W. (1995). "Kansas City's Widely Debated Desegregation Experiment Reaches the Supreme Court." *The New York Times,* January 11, p. B7.

Clark, K. (1965). *Dark Ghetto: Dilemmas of Social Power.* New York: Harper & Row.

Conard, B. D. (1988). "Cooperative Learning and Prejudice Reduction." *Social Education* **52**(4), 283–286.

Constantine, J. (1994). "The 'Added Value' of Historically Black Colleges." *Academe* **80**(3), 12–17.

Dentler, R. A., and Scott, M. B. (1981). *Schools on Trial: An Inside Account of the Boston Desegregation Case.* Cambridge, MA: Abt Books.

DeWitt, K. (1994). "Wave of Suburban Growth Is Being Fed by Minorities." *The New York Times,* August 15, pp. A1, B6.

Downs, A. (1973) *Opening Up the Suburbs: An Urban Strategy for America.* New Haven, CT: Yale University Press.

DuBois, W. E. B. (1935). "Does the Negro Need Separate Schools?" *Journal of Negro Education,* July, pp. 328–335.

Elam, S., Rose, L., and Gallup, A. (1994). "The 26th Annual Phi Delta Kappan Gallup Poll of the Public's Attitudes Toward the Public Schools." *Phi Delta Kappan* **76**(1), 41–56.

Evans v. Buchanan. (1976). 416 F. Supp. 328.

Formisano, R. (1991). *Boston Against Busing: Race, Class, and Ethnicity in the 1960s and 1970s.* Chapel Hill, NC: University of North Carolina Press.

Gallup, A., and Elam, S. (1988). "The 20th Annual Gallup Poll of the Public's Attitudes Toward the Public Schools." *Phi Delta Kappan* **70**(1), 33–46.

Gates, H. (1994). *Colored People.* New York: Knopf.

Glazer, N. (1981). "Race and the Suburbs." In *Race and Schooling in the City,* edited by A. Yarmolinsky, L. Liebman, and C. S. Schelling. Cambridge, MA: Harvard University Press.

Granovetter, M. (1986). "The Micro-Structure of School Desegregation." In *School Desegregation Research: New Directions in Situational Analysis,* edited by J. Prager, D. Longshore, and M. Seeman. New York: Plenum.

Hawley, W. D. (1981). "Increasing the Effectiveness of School Desegregation: Lessons From the Research." In *Race and Schooling in the City,* edited by A. Yarmolinsky, L. Liebman, and C. S. Schelling. Cambridge, MA: Harvard University Press.

Herrnstein, C., and Murray, C. (1994). *The Bell Curve.* New York: Free Press.

Higginbotham, A. (1978). *In the Matter of Color, Race and the American Legal Process: The Colonial Period.* New York: Oxford University Press.

Hochschild, J. L. (1984). *The New American Dilemma: Liberal Democracy and School Desegregation.* New Haven, CT: Yale University Press.

"Illinois Town, Fearing Racial Imbalance, to Advertise for Whites" (1995). *The New York Times*, April 30, p. 36.

Johnson, K. (1991). "Take Our Poor, Angry Hartford Tells Suburbs." *The New York Times*, February 12, pp. 1, B5.

Jones, C. (1994). "Years on Integration Road: New Views of an Old Goal." *The New York Times*, April 10, pp. 1, 40.

Keyes v. Denver School District No. 1. (1973). 413 U.S. 189.

Kirp, D. L. (1982). *Just Schools: The Idea of Racial Equality in American Education.* Berkeley, CA: University of California Press.

Lemann, N. (1988–1989). "The Unfinished War." *The Atlantic Monthly* **263**(1): 37–56; January 1989, pp. 53–68.

Lukas, J. A. (1985). *Common Ground: A Turbulent Decade in the Lives of Three American Families.* New York: Knopf.

Mahard, R. E., and Crain, R. L. (1983). "Research on Minority Achievement in Desegregated Schools." In *The Consequences of School Desegregation*, edited by C. H. Rossell and W. D. Hawley. Philadelphia: Temple University Press.

Marriott, M. (1991). "Louisville Debates Plan to End Forced Grade School Busing." *The New York Times*, December 11, p. B13.

McLarin, K. (1994). "Specter of Segregation Returns." *The New York Times*, August 11, pp. B1, B9.

Missouri v. Jenkins. (1995). Case No. 93-1823.

Meier, K., Stewart, J., and England, R. (1989). *Race, Class and Education: The Politics of Second-Generation Discrimination.* Madison, WI: University of Wisconsin Press.

Mosle, S. (1993). "Separatist But Equal?" *The American Prospect*, No. 15, 73–82.

Moynihan, D. (1969). *Maximum Feasible Misunderstanding: Community Action in the War on Poverty.* New York: Free Press.

Ogbu, J. U. (1986). "Structural Constraints in School Desegregation." In *School Desegregation Research: New Directions in Situational Analysis*, edited by J. Prager, D. Longshore, and M. Seeman. New York: Plenum.

Orfield, G. (1978). *Why Must We Bus? Segregated Schools and National Policy.* Washington, DC: Brookings Institution.

———— (1993). *The Growth of Segregation in American Schools: Changing Patterns of Separation and Poverty Since 1968.* Cambridge, MA: Report of the Harvard Project on School Desegregation to the National School Boards Association.

Pettigrew, T. F. (1981). "The Case for Metropolitan Approaches to Public-School Desegregation." In *Race and Schooling in the City*, edited by A. Yarmolinsky, L. Liebman, and C. S. Schelling. Cambridge, MA: Harvard University Press.

Reynolds, W. B. (1986). "Education Alternatives to Transportation Failures: The Desegregation Response to a Resegregation Dilemma." *Metropolitan Education* **1**, 3–14.

Rist, R. C. (1979). "Introduction." In *Desegregated Schools: Appraisals of an American Experiment*, edited by R. C. Rist. New York: Academic Press.

Rosenberg, R. (1986). "Self-Esteem Research: A Phenomenological Corrective." In *School Desegregation Research: New Directions in Situational Analysis*, edited by J. Prager, D. Longshore, and M. Seeman. New York: Plenum.

St. John, N. H. (1981). "The Effects of School Desegregation on Children: A New Look at the Research Evidence." In *Race and Schooling in the City*, edited by A. Yarmolinsky, L. Liebman, and C. S. Schelling. Cambridge, MA: Harvard University Press.

Schmidt, P. (1995). "Accord Set in Desegregation Case in K.C." *Education Week* **14**(23), 1, 4.

_____ (1994). "New Magnet-School Law Emphasizes Desegregation." *Education Week* **14**(13), 20.

Schofield, J. W., and Sagar, H. A. 1983. "Desegregation, School Practices, and Student Race Relations." In *The Consequences of School Desegregation,* edited by C. H. Rossell and W. D. Hawley. Philadelphia: Temple University Press.

Shelton, B. (1989). *The Coming Soviet Crash: Gorbachev's Desperate Search for Credit in the Western Financial Market.* New York: Free Press.

Smith, V. (1994). "We Wanted to Be the Best." *Newsweek,* July 18, p. 53.

Smothers, R. (1994). "Mississippi's University System Going on Trial." *The New York Times,* May 9, p. A10.

"Special Report on Education." (1988). *The Gallup Report* No. 276, pp. 41–53.

(A) Special Analysis of 1986 Elementary and Secondary School Civil Rights Survey Data. (1986). Boston: National Coalition of Advocates for Students.

Statistical Abstract of the United States. (1994) (114th edition). Washington, DC: U.S. Bureau of the Census.

Steele, C. (1992). "Race and the Schooling of Black Americans." *The Atlantic Monthly,* April, pp. 68–78.

The State of America's Children (1994). Washington, DC: Children's Defense Fund.

Time for Results: The Governors 1991 Report on Education. (1986). Washington, DC: National Governors Association.

Traub, J. (1991). "Separate and Equal." *The Atlantic Monthly* **268**(3), 24–37.

U.S. Commission on Civil Rights. 1974. *Equal Opportunity in Suburbia.* Washington, DC: Government Printing Office.

Ware, L. (1994). "Will There be a 'Different World' After *Fordice*?" *Academe* **80**(3), 7–11.

Wilentz, D. (1991). Commencement Address to Rutgers University School of Law, Newark, June 2.

Wilkerson, I. (1991a). "One City's 30-Year Crusade for Integration." *The New York Times,* December 30, pp. 1, 11.

_____ (1991b). "Separate Proms Reveal an Unspanned Racial Divide." *The New York Times,* May 5, pp. 1, 36.

Wilkinson, J. H. (1979). *From Brown to Bakke: The Supreme Court and School Integration, 1954–1978.* New York: Oxford University Press.

Wilson, W. J. (1987). *The Truly Disadvantaged: The Inner City, the Underclass, and Public Policy.* Chicago: University of Chicago Press.

CHAPTER SIX

Affirmative Action: Progressive or Restrictive

POSITION 1:
FOR AFFIRMATIVE ACTION

The Persistence of Prejudice

A question often asked about affirmative action is: How long must we put up with it? Opponents of affirmative action answer this question with a rhetorical question of their own: Hasn't affirmative action lost whatever usefulness it may have had?

Both questions miss the primary point. We should start not with a question about affirmative action, but ask about the phenomena that gave rise to affirmative action (Bond and Reed, 1991). The real question, then, is: Do racial, ethnic, and sexual prejudices still exist in America, and do these prejudices keep people from having equal opportunity?

Not only do the prejudices still exist, but they have resurfaced in recent years in more and more overt forms. The prejudices have been given a patina of acceptability by being published in "respectable" journals, such as *Commentary* and *The Public Interest*. The prejudices have also been the subject of a lot of mush-mouthing by intellectual and government "leaders." These high falutin variations of prejudice consist of blaming victims for their situation. Anyone who thinks it is only racial prejudice we are writing about here is advised to read Susan Faludi's *Backlash* (1991) for its extended description of the forces undermining feminism, or David and Myra Sadker's *Failing at Fairness: How America's Schools Cheat Girls* (1994) for a host of examples of the sexism from which girls still suffer.

Politicians have seen the value of appealing to bigots, with the notorious Willie Horton commercial of the 1988 Bush presidential campaign being the most obvious example. The Bush administration long delayed enactment of the 1991 Civil Rights Act on the grounds that it would result in racial quotas, even though these were expressly prohibited by the bill. The administration did not capitulate until Bush desired to distance himself from the demagoguery of David Duke, the Louisiana politician with a long history of race-baiting, who was only saying what the White House had been saying.

Although the Clinton administration's position on affirmative action and performance have been an improvement, Clinton himself has shown a willingness to back off when resistance begins to coalesce. His nominee to be the assistant attorney-general for civil rights, Lani Guinier, was abandoned by Clinton after the *Wall Street Journal* dubbed her a "quota queen." All she had suggested was that people *consider* some voting changes to ensure that minorities are not completely powerless in our democracy. For example, if a town had six openings on the town board, instead of having to vote for one candidate for each opening, a voter could cast all six of his or her ballots for a single candidate. This "cumulative" voting would increase the chance that the town's minority citizens would win at least one of the six slots and not be utterly unrepresented on the town board (Guinier, 1994).

It is strange indeed that affirmative action is challenged at a time when prejudice is becoming much more palpable. Although challenge often comes from sources that seem well-intentioned, it also comes from sources with a lengthy record of hostility toward minorities. The election of 1994 turned control of the Congress over to the Republicans for the first time in many years. Among the Republicans elected or reelected were many whose positions are contrary to the interests of minorities. Abolishing affirmative action is but one of these positions (Holmes, 1995a). These attacks on so much that is of benefit to minorities, including affirmative action, are a manifestation of the prejudice—or, at the very least, the insensitivity—that makes affirmative action necessary.

Expressions of racial, ethnic, and gender-based prejudice are demonstrably on the increase, as the popularity of hate-filled radio talk shows so readily attests. Thus, the case for abandoning affirmative action has to be made on the basis that prejudice is unrelated to educational and employment opportunity. In fairness, the case is not as brazenly illogical as that sounds. The argument is that laws are now in place to prevent prejudice from having a controlling effect on school admissions or on hiring and promotion decisions. However, anyone who has ever had to make such a decision knows the effort involved in keeping personal prejudices out of the picture, even when race, ethnicity, or gender is not at issue. The success of the effort can never be known for certain.

It is ridiculous to expect judges to understand the thought processes of an admissions officer or an employer better than that individual does himself or herself. The most that judges can determine is whether the negative decision is completely at odds with the rejected candidate's qualifications (and those of the accepted candidate). Admissions officers and employers no longer are likely to make decisions that are so patently unsustainable. For that, the antidiscrimination laws are to be thanked. Alas, below that jurisprudential threshold there is plenty of room for prejudice to be exercised subtly and indiscernibly. Without affirmative action to promote some positive results for them, minorities and women would be left at the mercy of the antidiscrimination laws, which, at best, can guard them only against the grossest displays of prejudice.

Moreover, an antidiscrimination law can provide justice for a person who has been victimized by prejudice only if that person invokes the law. The cost of doing so can be huge, greater even than the value of the opportunity that was unfairly denied. There are time costs, which translate into lost-work (or wage) costs. There are direct dollar costs of legal assistance, especially now that free legal aid to the poor has been sharply reduced with the general slash in government services. There are emotional costs, which mount as the case drags on month after month, year after year. Recent rulings by the conservative majority on the U.S. Supreme Court have made it more difficult to bring a case, and to win a case once brought (*Patterson v. McLean Credit Union*, 1989; *Wards Cove Packing Co., Inc. v. Atonio*, 1989).

It takes a determined and persevering nature to embark on such a journey. All those who lack the heart, and all those who start but then stop, forsake press coverage, as well as justice. We know only about the stalwart few who persist and ultimately prevail. The publicity given to their victories makes the law seem more efficacious than it is. Affirmative action gives the unheralded losers another small chance at justice.

Cornel West, professor of Afro-American Studies and the Philosophy of Religion at Harvard University, captures well the prophylactic nature of affirmative action:

> Progressives should view affirmative action as neither a major solution to poverty nor a sufficient means to equality. We should see it as primarily playing a negative role—namely, to ensure that discriminatory practices against women and people of color are abated. Given the history of this country, it is a virtual certainty that without affirmative action, racial and sexual discrimination would return with a vengeance. Even if affirmative action fails significantly to reduce black poverty or contributes to the persistence of racist perceptions in the workplace, without affirmative action, black access to America's prosperity would be even more difficult to obtain and racism in the workplace would persist anyway. (West, 1994, p. 95)

The Value of Inclusiveness

For a long time, colleges and private schools, especially those whose reputations allowed them to be very selective in admissions, tried for a geographically diverse student body. This diversity, it was believed, would yield a variety of perspectives, which would enrich the education of all the students. Diversity had educational value. The student who could provide it was considered to have an extra qualification for admission.

Geographic diversity is only one kind of *cultural* diversity. With the mass media homogenization of America, the white, male, middle-class student from Washington State may not differ significantly from his Pennsylvania peer. The two will probably share a lot of cultural referents and values. Educationally enriching differences are more likely to be found between blacks and whites, Latinos and Anglos, males and females. "Affirmative action," then, is simply a catchall term for attempts to give students the benefits of diversity. It is certainly as defensible to apply affirmative action to racial, ethnic, and gender differences as to geographic differences. There would be a strange inconsistency if geographic origin were the only desirable kind of difference, as indeed it was when American education was officially racist and sexist.

Chang-Lin Tien is an Asian-American. He is also the chancellor of the University of California at Berkeley. He has no trouble thinking of ways in which a diverse student body enriches the education of all students.

> The medical student who plans to set up practice in East Los Angeles needs to learn how to interpret the way her patients perceive and describe symptoms, patients whose families come from Mexico, Guatemala, El Salvador, Korea, China, Taiwan, and Japan.
>
> The journalism student who aspires to one of California's major dailies— such as the *Los Angeles Times, San Jose Mercury News*, the *San Francisco Chronicle*, or others—must be versed in interviewing and reporting on all constituencies. The story about flooding in a Central Valley farm town will be based on accounts from Mexican field hands. The story about new directions in Silicon Valley will require interviews with engineers born in Taiwan and India.
>
> The business administration major who hopes to climb the corporate ladder will head a work force predominated by women and ethnic minorities. The education student will one day teach classes populated by youngsters of different ethnic and language backgrounds. The law student whose sights are set on political office must become familiar with the needs of a multicultural electorate in order to win votes. (Tien, 1994, pp. 239–240)

Cultural diversity is at least as desirable in K–12 schools as it is in higher education. It can prevent prejudices from being formed at an age when students are especially suggestible. A mixed student body is the focus of the chapter on integration. Suffice it here to say that affirmative action serves to integrate a school's *staff*. Ghetto students are already likely to have white teachers, so the benefit of affirmative action is to students in suburban schools who would not otherwise have a black or Hispanic teacher. There is a benefit to students in both kinds of schools who might otherwise think that only men can be school principals or superintendents.

A case now wending its way to the U.S. Supreme Court highlights this matter well. A New Jersey high school had to dismiss one of the teachers in its business department because of declining pupil enrollment. The two most junior teachers both had the same length of service. Ordinarily, the decision would have been made by tossing a coin. In this case, however, one of the teachers was black in an otherwise all-white department. It was decided to keep her on in the interest of diversity. As the school superintendent explained, "Piscataway High is 52 percent minority. We think that students need to have both role models for them in the school. We also feel we have to have faculty members who represent the cultural differences in the school when we make judgments, policy and decisions about student programming and services" (Philip Geiger, as quoted by Gladwell, 1994, p. 33). The Bush administration argued in court against this action; the Clinton administration decided to support the action because it recognizes that cultural diversity is a legitimate *educational* interest (Rosen, 1994).

Apart from educational settings, inclusiveness has value in the workplace generally. Indeed, it can have a direct dollar value. That is, it can have a positive effect on the major focus of the workplace: profits. A company that excludes, or denies advancement to, people solely on the basis of their skin color or sex can hardly have good public relations with the groups from which these people come. The company may even run the risk of being boycotted by those potential customers. By threatening such a boycott, Jesse Jackson was able to persuade several major corporations that the mix of their personnel should better reflect that of their customers. It is, therefore, in a company's bottom-line interest to have a diverse workforce. Awareness of this business reality is one of the reasons why the National Association of Manufacturers has given affirmative action a ringing endorsement (Urofsky, 1991, pp. 36–37). "Market penetration" is not the noblest of motives, but it serves a good cause if it broadens employment opportunities. If a company's marketing staff, salespeople, and advertising personnel comprise a representative mix of the American population, the company can easily gear its product image to a variety of subgroups. Its own employees will tell it what the subgroups are likely to respond to.

Who now thinks it strange or off-putting that Jane Pauley should be among NBC's senior news broadcasters, or Cookie Roberts among those at ABC? Both women are convinced that their careers would never have taken off if there had not been affirmative action pressure on the networks (Reeves, 1995).

What does *employment* opportunity have to do with education, the focus of this book? Actually, the two are powerfully linked. The prospect of qualifying for a good job is a great inducement for students to stay in school and study. Students for whom school and study promise no occupational dividends can be expected to drop out. If students believe their sex or skin color vitiates the value of education, they will not see much point to spending time in school, other than for the social life it affords.

The employment–education link is of interest to society, as well as to the individual. Society seeks to get as much productivity out of individuals as possible. The bigger the boost an individual can give to the national economy, the better. The key employment consideration should be the ability to do the job. To subvert this consideration with petty prejudice is as injurious to the society as it is to the individual. For a long time in history, ending only in the latter half of the twentieth century, and then far from completely, whole classes of people who had done well in school were kept from making the most of their education. We will never know how much more advanced and secure the national economy would be today if so much talent had not been suppressed.

The Long History of Preferential Treatment

Affirmative action was first made federal law in 1961 by an executive order of President Kennedy. Whatever preferential treatment women and minorities have received as a result can only have been since that year. The 174 years of U.S. history prior to 1961 were the era of preferential treatment for white men of European (and Christian) ancestry. In terms of years alone, white European men have received about six times as much preferential treatment as the groups that are now said to be benefiting from it. Whatever preferential treatment accrues to minority groups or women does so with a good deal of fanfare. The preferential treatment that still redounds to white men is given no attention at all.

One of the most obvious and ongoing forms of this historical preference is that of the Ivy League "legacies." The legacies are students who are given preference in admission to the Ivy League colleges because they are the children of alumni. "For more than forty years, an astounding one-fifth of Harvard's students have received admissions preference because their parents attended the school. . . . Offspring of [Yale alumni] are two and a half times more likely to be accepted than their unconnected peers. Dartmouth this year admitted 57 percent of its legacy applicants, compared to 27 percent of nonlegacies. At the University of Pennsylvania, 66 percent of legacies were admitted last year" (Larew, 1994, p. 248). And the practice is not limited to the Ivy League; fully 25 percent of Notre Dame students are legacies (Lamar, 1991; Leslie, Wingert and Chideya, 1991). The legacies contribute affluence and Anglocentricity to the student body, so one has to look to affirmative action for other ingredients.

Another common form of preference for children of the favored has been guaranteed job slots in such industries as the printing and construction trades, as well as in municipal services, such as police and fire departments. These father–son job arrangements long continued in force with the blessings of the labor unions. This preferential treatment was perforce a form of discrimination since employment, like college admission, is a zero-sum game. Antidiscrimination laws were used to break down these barriers in several notable cases. However, affirmative action programs were also valuable tools since they could get results much more quickly than would a years-long court case based on an antidiscrimination law. President Nixon used an affirmative action decree, known as the Philadelphia plan, to set numerical goals and enforcement procedures for the desegregation of the construction trades (Urofsky, 1991, p. 18).

Try to imagine how civil harmony would be disrupted if police and fire departments had not been integrated to reflect the communities they serve. Would ghetto communities want to be "protected" by people they have come to perceive as an invading force, a colonial power? If the Los Angeles police officers who repeatedly clubbed Rodney King had been of his race, their behavior would have been no more excusable, but the community reaction would likely have been nonviolent. The integration of the municipal services was brought about, in large measure, by affirmative action plans. And schooling was one of the affected municipal services. No longer were minority families required by law to entrust the education of their children to people from outside the community who were unfamiliar with and hostile to its ways—so hostile, in fact, that they could not even use the community's traditions as building blocks in the education of its children. All the outsiders did was instill in the children a sense of shame for their roots, and rage eventually erupted from the shame.

The Myth of Potential

There is a widely held belief that it is possible to measure a person's potential for success at some endeavor, and that it is possible to calibrate this potential with a high degree of precision. There are all kinds of "ability tests" that are supposed to do just that. The readers of this book no doubt have acquired a good deal of personal experience with such tests. The Scholastic Aptitude Test (SAT), the American College Test (ACT), and the Graduate Record Exam (GRE) are ability tests, or tests of potential. So are all those screening tests that business, government, and the military use to decide who gets in the door and to which slot the successful applicant is assigned.

If one believes in the validity of these tests, that they really tell us what they claim to tell us, then it would be both stupid and cruel not to rely on them in making decisions about a person's fate. It would be stupid because talent would go unused and activities would be carried out by incompetents. It would be cruel because both the talented and the incompetent would suffer frustration and despair. By overriding the results of ability tests, affirmative action is said to be both stupid and cruel.

But is it? It is only if one shares two common assumptions about ability tests. The first is that these tests measure something innate that is unaffected by the environment, even though it may interact with the environment. For a long time, the Educational Testing Service (ETS) made that claim for the SAT, saying that coaching could not change one's predestined score, which reflected innate ability, or at least knowledge that was obtained over a long period and could not be quickly acquired. In recent years, the ETS has conceded that coaching can raise the score considerably; it even sells its own SAT coaching products (Crouse and Trusheim, 1989; "SAT Coaching," 1991; "Ten Myths About the SAT," 1989). This, of course, had long been obvious to parents who paid a lot of money to have their children coached. The SAT, like all so-called ability tests, is really an *achievement* test. Achievement is a product of native endowment plus experience, and coaching is just one experience that affects the score. Another factor is school experience, and to the extent that women and minorities score lower than white males on the SAT, one should look to differential school experience for an explanation.

The second assumption one has to make in order to conclude that affirmative action is wrongheaded is that an ability or achievement test allows us to target a person to the place where he or she can perform best. The U.S. Supreme Court, in *Griggs v. Duke Power Company* (1971), struck a heavy blow against this assumption. The Duke Power Company had used a general intelligence (IQ) test to determine who got hired and where they would work. Blacks, on average, scored lower than whites because they had received poorer educations, so they were either rejected or consigned to the low-paying jobs.

The Court recognized the experiential component of an IQ score. More important, the Court found that the test was not job-related. The general intelligence test does not predict how well someone will perform a particular job, any more than SAT scores are good predictors of how well people, especially women, will do in college (Wainer and Steinberg, 1992). What tests like this do is make screening decisions easy, not wise.

When the assumptions about test validity as related to job or school performance are challenged successfully, affirmative action ceases to seem stupid and cruel. What is stupid is giving people tests on which they are doomed to do poorly because of past discrimination, and not taking the discrimination into account when interpreting the test scores. What is cruel is denying people an opportunity to overcome the effects of past discrimination, and instead using those effects to justify further discrimination. Affirmative action is intended to break what otherwise would be an unending cycle of discrimination.

One way to avoid the unfair use of screening tests, other than to prohibit their use altogether, is to conduct differential "norming" of the results. For example, SAT scores should be adjusted to take into consideration their lesser predictive validity for women. The women could be compared (normed) with each other and not lumped together with the men. For a while, such norming was actually being done for racial and ethnic groups. An employer was allowed to hire the top-ranked black even if the black's score was lower than that of the top-ranked white; it was recognized that the black had overcome obstacles to get to that point and would probably do well on the job. The Civil Rights Act of 1991 banned further norming of this type, but Robyn Dawes (1993) is right in her conclusion about race norming:

> Yes, racial norming does involve unfairness to some majority applicants, but there is no way to treat everyone fairly at once. Is it fair to penalize a minority applicant from a poor background who had few opportunities to develop a relevant aptitude by interpreting test scores in a color-blind manner? Is it fair to penalize the majority applicant who scores higher for lacking a poor background by race-norming our test results? As President Kennedy once said, "Life is not fair." Reality prohibits fairness. What we can do is minimize unfairness. Racial norming of tests, which adversely affects only those majority group applicants with the lowest scores, is a coherent way of minimizing unfairness. The problem with racial norming is that it is also explicit, and therefore open to objections and alternative proposals that are not coherent. I argue, however, that social policy should be coherent. (p. 34)

Much Ado about Little

Affirmative action has become a blackjack for beating up women and minorities. That might be sufferable if the size of the blackjack were proportional to the actual impact affirmative action has had.

A good way for you, the reader, to get a firsthand sense of this impact is to ask a working parent, "How has affirmative action affected your place of employment?" (If you have work experience of your own, you can ask your-self this question.) You may have to push the parent (politely) for some actual evidence, since affirmative action is the subject of countless unfounded and horrific rumors.

The truth is that the government simply does not have, nor can it afford to have in a time of budget deficits, enough monitors to check on the thousands and thousands of businesses and educational institutions that fall under affirmative action requirements. The lukewarm enforcement and nonenforce-ment of these requirements were widespread even during the years of the Carter presidency (Stasz, 1981). During the Reagan and Bush presidencies, the executive branch of the federal government was ideologically opposed to affirmative action, hardly an attitude conducive to strict enforcement. Indeed, the U.S. attorney general's office was openly engaged on the side of interests opposing the civil rights laws. An ideological shift occurred with the advent of the Clinton presidency. Clinton's assistant attorney-general for civil rights, Deval Patrick, is actively supportive of affirmative action, to the point of reversing hostile decisions made by his predecessor ("Affirmative Action Without Fear," 1994).

This is not to suggest that no minorities or women benefited from affirma-tive action in the 1980s. They certainly did, but it is impossible to know the extent to which this benefit was *undeserved*. And that, after all, is the crucial question. Ask your working parent, or yourself, "Are your female and minor-ity co-workers incompetent at their jobs? How is their competence judged?" If they are as competent as the other workers, then they were entitled to the jobs all along. If it took some pressure from the government to get them preferen-tial treatment so that they could be afforded long-delayed *equal* treatment, that is not *their* fault and they should not be beaten with a blackjack for it. "When reverse discrimination does *not* lead to visible differences in performance, the clear implication is that the selection criteria on which blacks ranked lower than whites were inappropriate to begin with and should be abandoned" (Jencks, 1992, p. 63).

Something we can know for sure at this time is the economic and educa-tional status of minorities relative to that of whites. The data show that black progress was halted, and in some cases reversed, during the 1980s (Jaynes and Williams, 1989). In 1969, black men earned $694 for every $1,000 earned by white men. By 1989, the figure for black men had increased by only $22, to $716 (Hacker, 1992b, p. 101). As for black representation in the professions, from 1970 to 1990, the percentage of black physicians increased from 2.2 per-cent to only 3.0 percent; of lawyers, from 1.3 to 3.2 percent; and of professors, from 3.5 to 4.5 percent (Hacker, 1992a, p. 24). In answer to the question "So what, why should blacks get special treatment?" one can quote Jim Sleeper:

> Blacks who demand preferments on the basis of past oppressions have more right behind them than do other interest groups, whose justifications are far more specious. Therefore, it is hypocritical for us to hold blacks, even those who trade irresponsibly on their status as special creditors, to standards of social reciprocity we certainly don't apply to savings-and-loan sharpies who

come to us for bailouts and civil servants who demand pension increases. (Sleeper, 1990, p. 309)

There are also data showing that progress for women has been halted as well. Women bump up against the "glass ceiling," that level in the hierarchy of a firm below which they are kept. For example, women hold 43.5 percent of the low-level jobs in state and local government, but only 31.3 percent of the high-level jobs. They hold only 6 percent of the top jobs in the largest American corporations ("Few Women Found in Top Public Jobs," 1992). These numbers were compiled by the Federal Glass Ceiling Commission, which has since found that white men are now circling the wagons to keep themselves as the controlling group in corporations. They do this through mentoring and shared life-styles (Kilborn, 1995a, 1995b).

These objective data for blacks and women indicate that affirmative action was never a forceful federal program. That is why the outcries against it seem especially churlish. Nevertheless, those outcries reach the ears of poll takers and thus of politicians. The politicians are also aware of the popularity that conservatives such as David Duke, Jesse Helms, Michael Huffington, and George Pataki garnered by opposing affirmative action, even though they repudiate their more extreme statements. A good gauge of the gutlessness of politicians concerning the affirmative action issue can be found in the statements of the Democratic contenders in the 1992 presidential race. And this does not augur well for Democratic platforms in the future.

All this reveals what everyone knows: there are large elements of racism and sexism in the opposition to affirmative action, and politicians are prepared to pander to those elements. This may make affirmative action a losing cause, but it also makes clear the necessity for affirmative action.

Acceptable Costs

The most painful aspect of affirmative action is the unavoidable hurt that it causes innocent people. If someone with a higher score on the Medical College Admissions Test is passed over for admission to medical school in favor of a person with a lower score, there is bound to be disappointment, if not bitterness. The rejected applicant may realize that both test scores are within the range deemed acceptable by the medical school, that the lower scorer had been handicapped by an impoverished education, and that the lower scorer will use his or her medical training to serve a poor community in dire need of doctors. And yet the rejected applicant is also aware that he or she was in no way responsible for the conditions that justify the affirmative action acceptance. Bearing no responsibility for the wrongs of the past, the rejected applicant cannot help but wonder why it is he or she who must bear the burden of rectifying those wrongs. Nevertheless, the zero-sum nature of medical school enrollments demands that some individual do penance for society's sin. The old victims are replaced with new ones.

The policymakers who create affirmative action requirements are not personally inconvenienced thereby. Their hopes are not shattered, and they may even be able to assuage their consciences at little personal cost. They pass the cost on to someone else, usually someone much younger than they and much less implicated in the evil being redressed. It is often said by the opponents of affirmative action that it substitutes one wrong for another, and that two wrongs don't make a right. Alas, social order among all species is a series of trade-offs in which the interests of some are sacrificed to the interests of the whole. It is in America's self-interest to progress beyond the injustices of the past. And there is no way to do this without providing compensatory justice to the victim groups. They deserve to be made as whole as it is now possible for us to make them. Their plight is real; it is without redeeming purpose; it is a disgrace that demeans us all. Those relatively few persons whose aspirations are being thwarted by affirmative action should at least have the satisfaction of knowing that they are taking part in a historic struggle toward establishing a victimless society.

We should all be able to take satisfaction in the successes of that struggle. Read the words of Stephen Carter (1991), an unapologetic beneficiary of affirmative action:

> I got into law school because I am black. As many black professionals think they must, I have long suppressed this truth, insisting instead that I got where I am the same way everybody else did. Today I am a professor at the Yale Law School. I like to think that I am a good one, but I am hardly the most objective judge. What I am fairly sure of, and can now say without trepidation, is that were my skin not the color that it is, I would not have had the chance to try. (p. 11)

What Carter graciously avoids adding is that for *centuries* the color of his skin would have been enough to keep him out of law school.

Finally, we may all admire the reaction of Paul Spickard, a white man with degrees from Harvard and Berkeley in Asian history, after he was twice turned down for college teaching jobs because the colleges wanted a person from a minority:

> My family came over on the *Mayflower* and made money in the slave trade. Doctors, lawyers, judges, and comfortable business people go back several generations in my clan. . . . I am standing on the shoulders of my ancestors and their discriminatory behavior.
>
> Contrast my experience with that of a Chicano friend, whose immigrant father had a fourth-grade education and ran a grocery store. Without affirmative action and the social commitment it symbolizes, my friend might not have gone to Amherst, nor to Stanford Law School. . . . Our society would be poorer for the loss of his skills. . . . Affirmative action may not always be fair. But I'm willing to take second best if overall fairness is achieved. After all, for biblical Christians, fairness—often translated in our Bibles as "justice" or "righteousness"—is a fundamental principle by which God calls us to live. And affirmative action is an appropriate program aimed at achieving the godly goal of putting others' welfare before our own. (Spickard, quoted in Urofsky, 1991, pp. 28–29)

Meanwhile . . .

Progress does continue to be made. There is action, and it is affirmative. The examples are numerous, but space allows only two to be given here.

Texas Southern University has created the Black Male Initiative, a program that intervenes in the lives of high school students to get them on the college-bound track and keep them at Texas Southern until they graduate. The fact that almost 3,000 students attended the recruitment meetings in 1994 is evidence of the program's value (Zook, 1994).

The Compact for Faculty Diversity is a thirty-six-state consortium working to get 200 minority students a year into doctoral programs. These students will be among the college faculty members of the future, serving as role models and mentors to the minority students of that era (Mercer, 1994).

Do these programs amount to preferential treatment? Yes. Is it a preferential treatment from which we will all benefit? Absolutely.

POSITION 2: AGAINST AFFIRMATIVE ACTION

The Problem of the Protected Category

Affirmative action is inherently corrupted by the terms in which it must deal. Unlike the antidiscrimination laws, which relate to *individuals* who have been discriminated against and have to prove it in court, affirmative action refers to whole *categories* of people, all of whose members are presumed to have been discriminated against and none of whom has to prove anything. This immediately raises the sticky problem of deciding what these lucky categories are to be. For the federal government, the protected categories have been blacks, the Spanish-surnamed, Asians, native Americans, and women. Government at other levels has been free to decide what categories to include in affirmative action programs. If there are a large number of Italians in a town, the town officials can decide that the historical discrimination against Italians in America warrants preferential treatment for Italian-Americans. This happened when the City University of New York added Italians to its preferred hiring list (Hacker, 1990, p. 7). Such self-serving mischief is called affirmative action. More and more we hear about others who would like to put themselves on board the affirmative action bandwagon, for example, the overweight, the elderly, the short. Northeastern University has announced its intention to give hiring preference to gays, lesbians, the disabled, and veterans (Cage, 1994), so it is only a matter of time before other institutions will succumb to pressure to do the same. If there is no end to this, everyone will eventually belong to an affirmative action category and we will all be back to square one.

Thinking only in terms of the five federal categories does not make matters much more palatable. Consider, for a moment, the Spanish-surnamed category. An Anglo woman who took the last name of her Hispanic husband would qualify for special treatment in that category. So would a person of mixed parentage, both of whose parents were well-to-do. So, for that matter, would Linda Chavez (1991, 1994), the most vociferous Spanish-American opponent of affirmative action. Chavez's counterpart in the Asian community is Dinesh D'Souza (1991). The group mistakenly thought to have the largest number of beneficiaries of affirmative action—African-Americans—includes such prominent opponents as Thomas Sowell (1990). Sowell has studied the disastrous consequences of affirmative action programs in countries around the world, and he sees much more harm than good flowing from these programs. Other black scholars, such as Glenn Loury (1989) and William Julius Wilson (1987, 1991), are not ready to abandon affirmative action at this time, but have serious reservations about its efficacy and make a case for race-neutral programs to help all the poor. It is bizarre for supporters of affirmative action to insinuate that its opponents are bigots when so many of those opponents are among the putative beneficiaries.

What the opponents all share is an uneasiness about the sweeping nature of the categories. *Every* African-American and *every* Spanish-surnamed person and *every* Asian-American and *every* native American and *every* woman are treated as victims entitled to special government protection. This broad labeling is but another kind of stereotyping that ignores individual differences. It allows the wealthy Ivy League graduates in these groups to be accorded preferential treatment on the assumption that they have been victims of oppression. Some oppression! By this all-encompassing definition of oppression, the wife of the chief executive officer of the Cable News Network—Jane Fonda, as of this writing—is as much a victim of oppression as is a woman in Appalachia raising a family on her own. Indeed, it is a melancholy fact of affirmative action that the people who have best been able to take advantage of it are those who were already relatively advantaged. Affirmative action operates to widen the gap between these people and the less advantaged members of their category.

The five federal categories are problematic for what they exclude as much as for what they tolerate. Homosexuals, for example, are not included and have to depend solely on antidiscrimination laws just to get fair treatment, not preferential treatment. And yet it is obvious that homosexuals historically have been much more maligned as a group than women. Given the voters' rejection of state initiatives designed to safeguard homosexuals against discrimination, it can be argued that gays and lesbians continue to be at greater risk than heterosexuals of whatever affirmative action category. Neither do the poor constitute a protected category, even though they are the neediest group in terms of sheer survival. Poverty is considered to be a less compelling case for government intervention than is membership in one of the five official categories. Poverty is not an immutable—that is, unchangeable—characteristic, but race, ethnicity, and gender are. Therefore, the government assumes that the poor person is free to change his or her status with a little effort. In a recession economy, even a lot of effort may not be enough to do the trick, especially if the poor person has to wait for whatever, if any, jobs are left after the affirmative action placements have been made. An employer, when forced to choose between hiring an unemployed white man with several young children or an already employed African-American woman with no dependents, is on notice that giving the job to the white man could cause trouble with the government. Giving the job to the African-American woman will improve his hiring profile, if the government should come looking.

In fact, hiring the African-American woman is a double bonus since the employer will have satisfied two of the categories in a single stroke. For that reason, a needy African-American *male* applicant is not going to be as attractive to an employer as a Spanish-surnamed female applicant with an independent source of income. There is some small feeling of amusement to be derived from thinking of the ideal affirmative action hire in the near future, perhaps a Puerto Rican lesbian of African ancestry.

The important point is that the opponents of affirmative action are champions of the poor. It is their very concern for the needy that causes them to oppose a program that so often bypasses the poor in favor of those who already have taken a step up. The opponents of affirmative action as it now operates are the supporters of a means-tested program targeted to the truly disadvantaged, regardless of race, gender, ethnicity, sexual orientation, age, body shape, or veteran status. Paul Starr, a liberal, notes the static affirmative action creates in the antipoverty campaign:

> With the positive effects of racial preferences have come many unhappy ones—sustaining racism, stigmatizing much minority achievement as "merely" the result of affirmative action, creating a sense of grievance among whites who then feel entitled to discriminate, and blocking the formation of bi-racial political alliances necessary to make progress against poverty. (Starr, 1992, p. 14)

From Goals to Quotas

In its earliest incarnation, affirmative action was only a reach-out program. Federal contractors were expected to reach out to minorities and women in order to make sure that these groups knew about available jobs and had a chance to apply. The reach-out effort added to employer costs and raised the question as to why these job hunters could not learn about job openings the way everybody else always has. Even so, the initial version of affirmative action was fairly benign.

Then the ominous mutations began. The employer's good faith efforts at reaching out, which were easy to document, were not enough if they did not lead to actual hires of women and minority group members. The employer was expected to establish hiring goals and timetables for reaching the goals. Employers knew that they would be suspected of bad faith if they reached out and set goals and timetables, but the composition of their workforce did not change. The goals inexorably mutated into quotas as employers felt more and more pressure to meet them and became more and more determined to do so.

U.S. Representative Edith Green of Oregon testified to her colleagues in Congress about how irrational the pressure on employers could be. A Portland company was told by federal officials that it would receive no federal contracts until it had 15 percent minority employees in every single job category. It was impossible for the company to meet this demand unless it was willing to give jobs to highly unqualified people just for the sake of show (Maguire, 1980, p. 34).

For large companies such as Coca-Cola, there was more than government pressure. Jesse Jackson's Operation PUSH (People United to Save Humanity) threatened to boycott these companies' products if hiring demands were not met. There was also the pressure that came from comparisons. One company would contrast the composition of its workforce with that of other companies in the same industry. Colleges and universities developed sets of tables and graphs to show how well they were scoring in the affirmative action contest as compared with their competitors. To score well meant getting out from under a lot of pressure from Big Brother. It also meant a public relations victory.

The victories proved somewhat Pyrrhic when the price at which they were achieved became known. At the Georgetown University Law Center, a student who was hired to file student records began to notice some anomalies. He then did an analysis of a random sample of the records. He found:

> The average white student accepted by GULC had a score of 43 on the Law School Aptitude Test (LSAT) out of a possible 48 on the scale then in use; his average black counterpart had a score of 36. The average white student accepted by the school had maintained an undergraduate grade-point average (GPA) of 3.7; for the average black the figure was 3.2. (Maguire, 1992, p. 50)

It is numbers like these that impelled a white student to bring a suit against the University of Texas Law School. The case of *Hopwood v. Texas* is now on its way to the U.S. Supreme Court. Institutions determined to get the affirmative action numbers up are being embarrassed by the disclosure of these other numbers, which are way down.

The sundry pressures that transform official goals into unofficial quotas will continue to exist under the Civil Rights Act of 1991. The law itself may contain language prohibiting quotas, but it has other language that will make employers anxious to meet their "goals" (Holmes, 1991). The distinction between a goal and a quota vanishes in these circumstances. A goal that is treated as a quota is, for all intents and purposes, a quota by whatever euphemism it is called. The *Hopwood* case may finally put an end to this charade.

Fabricating Ability

Employers and colleges are caught on the horns of a dilemma in pursuing their affirmative action interests. On the one hand, they cannot blatantly fill openings with people who are unqualified. Nor can they justify giving an opening to an affirmative action applicant who is well below the standard of other applicants. They need *relatively qualified* affirmative action applicants.

These constraints put employers, colleges, the government, and affirmative action applicants in collusion to pad the applicants' abilities. The most common way by which this is done is to interpret low ability in the most positive light. An applicant's low score on a screening test may be explained away by saying that the score is remarkable given the inferior education to which the applicant was subjected in a racist (sexist) society. That the applicant scored even this well, it is said, is a sign of perseverance against obstacles, a trait that surely means that the person will perform well on the job.

This kind of score interpretation was formally institutionalized in the practice known as race norming. The General Aptitude Test Battery (GATB) is a screening test whose use is encouraged by the U.S. Department of Labor. This battery was originally accepted as a reasonably valid way to predict how someone would do at a particular job. It was a job-related test. The problem was that minorities scored lower on the test than others did. Thus, if an employer were to be guided by the scores alone, minorities would be hired at a much lower rate than other people, and at a rate much lower than would seem warranted by their percentage of the population.

Therefore, it was decided that two adjustments had to be made. First, the raw scores were converted into percentile scores. This is a common practice and is not objectionable on the face of it. But in this case the percentile scores were computed *by category*. The percentile score for African-American test takers was figured only against other African-Americans who had taken the GATB. The percentile score for Hispanics was calculated against other Hispanics. All the other test takers were lumped into a third category called "other." The result of this race norming of the test scores was that an African-American could have a much lower raw score than a white ("other") but be in the same percentile. A low test score could put someone at the 70th percentile among African-Americans; a high score could put someone at the 70th percentile among "others" (Blits and Gottfredson, 1990a, 1990b). The employer would be free to hire the lower-scoring applicant, and would be under government pressure to do so.

The 1991 Civil Rights Act prohibits further use of race norming (Clymer, 1991). However, given the ingenuity behind this practice, one cannot be sure that a new scheme for inflating low scores will not soon emerge. Besides, now that employers cannot use the GATB to satisfy their affirmative action interests, they may well turn to more congenial screening devices.

One such device is to discount the value of test scores in the light of "other considerations." A low-scoring student can be redeemed by the benefit the student is presumed to bring to his or her classmates simply by being a member of an approved minority. Or it might be anticipated that the minority student will use the education to advance the interests of his or her "people." The most common way of adding value to the applicant is to say that he or she is entitled to preference in compensation for past sufferings.

None of these justifications is an empirical proposition. They are all faith statements. And the faith can be shattered easily by empirical data. Consider the last statement about compensation. As Lino Graglia (1993), the Cross Professor of Law at the University of Texas, notes:

> Persons who have been unfairly disadvantaged should undoubtedly be made whole to the extent feasible, but race is neither an accurate nor an appropriate proxy for such disadvantage. It is inaccurate because not all and not only blacks have suffered from disadvantage. Indeed, racially preferential admissions to institutions of higher education ordinarily help, not those most in need of help, but middle-class and upper-middle-class blacks. (pp. 29–30)

Thus, there is a large amount of wishful thinking in these rationales, and their nebulousness allows almost anything to be done in the name of affirmative action. Tests and test scores, for whatever problems they may have, also have a comprehensibility that permits them to be discussed meaningfully.

Perpetuating Prejudice

Affirmative action is marked by many ironies, several of which we have just discussed. The most tragic is that it exacerbates the very condition it was designed to help the country transcend. Racism is on the rise in America, and affirmative action provides much of the fuel. Those who rightly resent the unfairness of affirmative action go beyond attacking the program to attacking the groups covered by the program. This is a terrible mistake, but one that was predicted when the program was set up. As government pressure to force results increased, the prediction became more and more true. Affirmative action became an albatross hung around the necks of the people it was supposed to help, the vast majority of whom did not benefit at all. Those who have benefited from affirmative action have done so at the cost of increased hostility toward all those who have not. Affirmative action is now used by the likes of Rush Limbaugh and Jesse Helms as an attack weapon against minorities. Mainstream politicians use it more sneakily, but to the same end. Affirmative action has created a backlash against minorities. The way this backlash evolved and the ways in which the Republican party instigated it, and has capitalized on it, are spelled out at book length by Thomas and Mary Edsall (1991). The 1994 election gives their book a genuinely prophetic quality.

The prejudice engendered by affirmative action can directly affect the beneficiaries themselves. They may feel great about being hired for this job or admitted to that school, but they immediately are confronted by the animosity of their co-workers or of other students. Often they also have to contend with the condescension of supervisors or faculty. Whereas the government treats them as victims entitled to special treatment, their co-workers and fellow students *react* to them as political extortionists undeserving of the concessions they have been granted. Those women and minority group members who earned their jobs or college placements without special consideration cannot wear sandwich boards advertising this fact; they themselves may not even be sure of it. That's how insidious affirmative action is. Thus, they are stigmatized as the *woman* forklift operator or the *black* Ph.D. candidate, with everyone understanding what that implies about their right to be where they are.

Because of the unwelcoming work environment, the minority employee will either remain aloof or quit. Either behavior reinforces the prejudice that precipitated it. The psychodynamics of these situations are explored in fascinating detail by Shelby Steele (1991). And gripping books have been written on the trauma experienced by two young blacks who were admitted to the exclusive St. Paul's and Phillips Exeter Academy prep schools (Anson, 1987; Cary, 1991).

On college campuses, the result is segregation. The college may have succeeded in assembling a mixed student body, but the minority and majority students don't mix with each other outside the classroom. When minority students choose "minority majors," such as African-American or Puerto Rican studies, even the in-class mixing is kept to a minimum. Minority clubs and minority fraternities or sororities further institutionalize the separation. The diversity rationale for affirmative action is nullified by reality.

The worst cases are those of the employer or college administration who maintains a "good" hiring or admissions record by using the "revolving door" policy (Jacobs, 1989). A high-risk person is let in, at which point all special assistance stops. Studies show that colleges have lowered their admission standards so that they could admit minority students, who are likely to fail out without remedial help, and yet the help has not been forthcoming (Hacker, 1989). Moreover, there is little or no preparation of co-workers or fellow students, and there are no spelled-out sanctions against bigoted behavior toward the newly admitted minority. The speech codes that some universities developed to protect minorities against verbal assault have been overturned by the courts as undue infringements on a bigot's First Amendment rights. The minorities are left to swim or sink in a sea of taunts. After a drowning, another hapless newcomer is admitted to the company or college. That person will constitute a body to be counted toward an affirmative action target until he or she goes under and someone else is brought in. The company or college or school district has invested virtually nothing in ensuring the success of the individual; it has cynically exploited him or her to win a numbers game it plays with the government. And every time an affirmative action prospect fails, the failure is attributed to others in the same category, tarring them all.

Jay Walker's case is emblematic of the syndrome. Walker was one of three black lawyers in a 200-member law firm. He was never told he was an affirmative action hire, but he was always made to feel like one.

> You always want to believe you were hired because you were the best. You work seven days a week, you wear Brooks Brothers suits, you play golf. But

everything around you is telling you were brought in for one reason: because you were a quota. No matter how hard I worked or how brilliant I was, it wasn't getting me anywhere. It's a hell of a stigma to overcome. There are only 24 hours in a day.

When he left the firm, another black took his place. "It's a revolving door," Walker concluded (Walker, quoted by Wilkerson, 1991, p. 28).

Women, too, must contend with the stigma of affirmative action. From 1960 to 1990, the proportion of women earning doctorates increased from 11 percent to 36 percent (Stimpson, 1992). That was literally thousands of women in 1990 alone. For all these women to realize that the value of their doctoral degrees has been cast in doubt by affirmative action policies that benefited very few of them is a terrible cruelty. In business, the proportion of senior vice presidencies held by women went from 14 percent in 1982 to 23 percent in 1992, and women now occupy more than 40 percent of all managerial positions (Ingraham, 1995). As these presumed beneficiaries of affirmative action become increasingly aware of the extent to which they, too, have been victimized by it, it will pass into history as a sincere but misguided attempt to bring justice into the picture.

The Emerging Dismantlement

The affirmative action edifice is being taken down, and with little protest. The keystones were laid by the federal government, and those will probably be the last to be removed—although such action already is occurring in the state and local levels.

New York City Mayor Rudolph Giuliani has discontinued the practice of steering city contracts to female- and minority-owned businesses. "This administration believes in hiring the best person or best company irrespective of race, color, creed or sexual orientation. All such decisions are based solely on merits" (Giuliani, as quoted by Hicks, 1994, p. B1).

In California, the voters will get to decide in 1996 whether to abolish the state's affirmative action program. Before that happens, the University of California board of regents may act on a request that the school discontinue its affirmative action policy. The request was made by a member of the board who is black. He would do away with ethnic outreach and replace it with economic outreach to the poor (Klein, 1995). Were this to occur, the Caucasian proportion of the freshman class at Berkeley would climb from 30 percent to perhaps 37 percent, while the African-American proportion would drop from 6 percent to 2 percent. There would also be a significant increase for Asian-Americans and a significant drop for Hispanics (Lubman, 1995).

Nationally, the Republican contenders for the Presidency in 1996 lined up in opposition to affirmative action, and President Clinton announced a review of all 160 federal programs to determine which have outlived their usefulness.

The Supreme Court is looking more skeptically at affirmative action. In the *Adarand Constructors v. Pena* case, the Court decided that all affirmative action programs are suspect and must be strictly scrutinized to see if they really serve a "compelling government interest" (Greenhouse, 1995). The Court also let stand a lower court ruling in the *Podberesky v. University of Maryland* case that race-based scholarships given by public universities are unconstitutional (Holmes, 1995b).

Affirmative action was always a delicate balance between need and merit. Basing it on such categories as race and gender confused both sides of the issue. If it is to be continued, it should be recast in terms that more clearly capture its purpose. "Need" and "disadvantage" have to be defined in ways with which most Americans can agree and which they can endorse, even if reluctantly.

For Discussion

1. Stephen Carter considers affirmative action analogous to taxation. Do you agree with Carter's analogy, as presented in the following quote, or do you believe that Carter has overlooked some important distinctions between affirmative action and taxation?

> The costs of affirmative action differ from the costs of taxation only in degree, not in kind. People are routinely taxed for services they do not receive that are deemed by their government necessary to right social wrongs they did not commit. The taxpayer-financed "bailout" of the weak or collapsed savings-and-loan institutions is one example. Another is the provision of tax dollars for emergency disaster assistance after a hurricane devastates a coastal community. The people who bear the costs of these programs are not the people who caused the damage, but they still have to pay. (Carter, 1991, pp. 17–18)

2. It is often said that one college or another has an "underrepresentation" of blacks or Hispanics or women.
   a. What are the percentages of these groups in the student body of your college? (The dean of students should be able to tell you.)
   b. What are the percentages among the faculty? (The director of personnel or the affirmative action director should know.)
   c. Are the percentages of blacks, Hispanics, and women "high enough," and how is "high enough" determined?

3. Andrew Hacker claims that if affirmative action is applied only on the basis of economic need, minority students will have less chance of getting into college than they have now. That is because minority students in economic need have lower SAT scores than do poor white students, as the following table shows (Hacker, 1991, p. 18). What do you make of Hacker's logic and his table?

Average SAT Scores of Students from Low-Income Families (1990)

	Number	Score*
White	65,599	881
Asian	18,729	832
Hispanic	21,291	738
Black	32,738	692

Based on a high of 1600.

4. Below are two tables showing the admissions to the University of California at Berkeley, broken down by ethnicity. Does the first table show that affirmative action is working at Berkeley at a cost that you deem acceptable? Does the second table change your opinion in any way?

Lewis Jones: Ethnicity and Admissions at Berkeley (1988–1989)

	Blacks	Hispanics	Whites	Asians
Ethnicity of California High School Graduates (1)	8.1%	19.9%	63.0%	9.0%
Proportion of Each Group Eligible for University (2)	4.5	5.0	15.8	32.8
Proportion of Total in Eligible Applicant Pool (3)	2.56	6.97	69.78	20.69
Ethnicity of Students Accepted by Berkeley (2)	11.4	19.6	38.9	27.5
Percent of Eligible Group Members Accepted (4)	71.4	45.0	8.9	21.3
Graduation Rate (2)	37.5	43.5	71.5	67.3

(1) Derived from table in Andrew Hacker's *Two Nations*, p. 137. Hacker's figures are adjusted to take the "other" category out. The four groups listed account for 97 percent of the high school graduates.

(2) From table in *Two Nations*. The UC system defines eligibility for regular admissions as the top 12.5 percent of California high school graduates. Apparently, this represents high school grade point average with some minimum amount of college preparatory course work. This would seem to imply that an easier grading high school would offer an advantage to a Cal applicant.

(3) Derived. First row data multiplied by second row data divided by the sum of the products. Thus for blacks, the percent in the universe of high school graduates multiplied by the proportion of that group that makes the top 12.5 percent of California high school graduates as defined in (2) is divided by the sum of the similar products for blacks, Hispanics, whites, and Asians. This represents the percent of the total number actually eligible for UC admission. Thus whites, for example, who make up 63 percent of high school graduates, represent 70 percent of the eligible pool of potential applicants.

(4) Derived from figures above and from a statistic presented in Karen Paget's "Diversity at Berkeley: Demagoguery or Demography?" (TAP Spring 1992). This statistic indicated that 16 percent of Berkeley applicants were accepted in 1989. The admitted figures in this row assume that the members of each group are no more likely to apply to Berkeley than the members of any of the groups. I then took the "accepted" divided by the "eligible" and multiplied the result by 16 percent.

Jerome Karabel: A Second Look At Berkeley Admissions (1988–1989)*

	Blacks	Hispanics	Whites	Asians
Ethnicity of Cal High School Graduates	7.7%	19.3%	58.2%	8.6%
Percent of Group Eligible for UC	4.5	5.0	15.8	32.8
Percent of Eligible Applicant Pool	2.6	7.3	70.0	21.1
Ethnicity of Accepted Students	11.2	19.0	41.2	17.2
Percent of Group Accepted**	75.0	85.0	28.0	25.0
Graduation Rate (after 5 years)	37.5	43.5	71.5	67.3
Graduation Rate** (after 6 years)	51.0	53.0	77.0	75.0

Source: Office of Student Research, University of California, Berkeley.
*This is a revised version of Lewis Jones's table with the addition of 6-year retention rates.
**Figures rounded to the nearest percentage point.
Source: L. Jones (1993). "Admissions Omissions." J. Karabel (1993). "Berkeley and Beyond." *The American Prospect* No. 12, 154, 157.

5. Below are two tables, one for racial difference in IQ among college students, and the other for racial difference in IQ among workers. The second table gives the difference in terms of "standard deviation." That is a unit of measurement, with anything larger than a single "standard deviation" being quite significant. How do these two tables make you feel about affirmative action?

Ethnic composition of the student body on an average campus

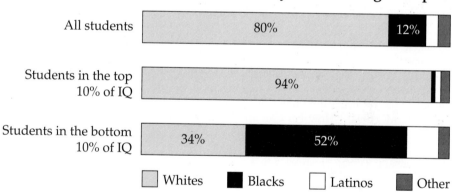

All students: 80% / 12%
Students in the top 10% of IQ: 94%
Students in the bottom 10% of IQ: 34% / 52%

Whites   Blacks   Latinos   Other

The Black–White IQ Difference by Job Category, 1990

Job Category	Mean White IQ	Black–White Difference, in Standard Deviations
Professions	114	1.3
Managerial	108	1.1
Technical	113	1.5
Sales	106	1.4
Clerical	104	1.1
Protective services	103	1.4
Other service jobs	97	1.4
Craft	99	1.1
Low-skill labor	96	1.1

Source: R. Herrnstein and C. Murray (1994). *The Bell Curve.* New York: Free Press, pp. 472, 488.

References

"Affirmative Action Without Fear." (1994). *The New York Times,* September 19, p. A16.

Anson, R. (1987). *Best Intentions: The Education and Killing of Edmund Perry.* New York: Random House.

Blits, J., and Gottfredson, L. (1990a). "Employment Testing and Job Performance." *The Public Interest* No. 98, 18–25.

――――. (1990b). "Equality or Lasting Inequality?" *Society* **27**(3), 4–11.

Bond, J., and Reed, A. (1991). "Equality: Why We Can't Wait." *The Nation* **253**(20), 733–737.

Cage, M. (1994). "Diversity or Quotas?" *The Chronicle of Higher Education* **40**(40), A13–A14.

Carter, S. (1991). *Reflections of an Affirmative Action Baby.* New York: Basic Books.

Cary, L. (1991). *Black Ice.* New York: Knopf.

Chavez, L. (1994). "Just Say Latino." In *Debating Affirmative Action,* edited by Nicolaus Mills. New York: Dell.

――――. (1991). *Out of the Barrio: Toward a New Politics of Hispanic Assimilation.* New York: Basic Books.

Clymer, A. (1991). "Senate Passes Civil Rights Bill, 95–5, Ending a Bitter Debate Over Job Bias. *The New York Times,* October 31, p. A–20.

Crouse, J., and Trusheim, D. (1989). *The Case Against the SAT.* Chicago: University of Chicago Press.

Dawes, R. (1993). "Racial Norming: A Debate." *Academe* **79**(3), 31–34.

D'Souza, D. (1991). *Illiberal Education: The Politics of Race and Sex on Campus.* New York: Free Press.

Edsall, T., and Edsall, M. (1991). *Chain Reaction: The Impact of Race, Rights, and Taxes on American Politics.* New York: Norton.

Faludi, S. (1991). *Backlash: The Undeclared War Against American Women.* New York: Crown.

"Few Women Found in Top Public Jobs." (1992). *The New York Times,* January 3, p. A–12.

Gladwell, M. (1994). "How Far Can an Affirmative Action Plan Go?" *The Washington Post National Weekly* **11**(49), 33.

Graglia, L. (1993). "Affirmative Discrimination." *National Review* **45**(13), 29.

Greenhouse, L. (1995). "Justices, 5 to 4, Cast Doubts on U.S. Programs That Give Preferences Based on Race." *The New York Times,* June 13, pp. A1, D25.

Griggs v. Duke Power Company. (1971). 401 U.S. 424.

Guinier, L. (1994). *The Tyrrany of the Majority.* New York: Free Press.

Hacker, A. (1990). "Affirmative Action: A Negative Opinion." *The New York Review of Books,* July 1, p. 7.

――――. (1989). "Affirmative Action: The New Look." *The New York Review of Books,* October 12, pp. 63–68.

――――. (1991). "Playing the Racial Card. *The New York Review of Books,* October 24, pp. 14–18.

――――. (1992a). "The Myths of Racial Division." *The New Republic,* March 23, pp. 21–25.

――――. (1992b). *Two Nations: Black and White, Separate, Hostile, Unequal.* New York: Scribner's.

Hicks, J. (1994). "Giuliani Is Halting or Scaling Back Affirmative-Action Efforts." *The New York Times,* August 23, pp. B1, B3.

Holmes, S. (1995a). "Backlash Against Affirmative Action Troubles Advocates." *The New York Times,* February 7, p. B9.

_____ (1995b). "Minority Scholarship Plans Are Dealt Setback by Court." *The New York Times,* June 23, p. B9.

_____. (1991). "Lawyers Expect Ambiguities in New Rights Law to Bring Years of Lawsuits." *The New York Times,* December 27, p. A20.

Hopwood v. State of Texas. (1994). 861 F. Supp. 551.

Ingraham, L. (1995). "Enter, Women." *The New York Times,* April 19, p. A23.

Jacobs, J. (1989). *Revolving Doors: Sex Segregation and Women's Careers.* Stanford, CA: Stanford University Press.

Jaynes, G., and Williams, R., eds. (1989). *A Common Destiny: Blacks and American Society.* Washington, DC: National Academy Press.

Jencks, C. (1992). *Rethinking Social Policy.* Cambridge, MA: Harvard University Press.

Kilborn, P. (1995a). "White Males and Management." *The New York Times,* March 17, p. A14.

_____. (1995b), "Women and Minorities Still Face Glass Ceiling." *The New York Times,* March 16, p. A22.

Klein, J. (1995). "The End of Affirmative Action." *Newsweek,* February 13, pp. 36–37.

Lamar, J. (1991). "Whose Legacy Is It, Anyway?" *The New York Times,* October 9, p. A–25.

Larew, J. (1994). "Who's the Real Affirmative Action Profiteer?" In *Debating Affirmative Action,* edited by Nicolaus Mills. New York: Dell.

Leslie, C., Wingert, P., and Chideya, F. (1991). "A Rich Legacy of Preference." *Newsweek,* June 24, p. 59.

Loury, G. (1989). "Why Should We Care About Group Inequality?" In *The Question of Discrimination: Racial Inequality in the U.S. Labor Market,* edited by S. Shulman and W. Darity, Jr. Middletown, CT: Wesleyan.

Lubman, S. (1995). "Campuses Mull Admissions Without Affirmative Action." *The Wall Street Journal,* May 16, pp. B1, B10.

Maguire, D. (1980). *A New American Justice: Ending the White Male Monopolies.* New York: Doubleday.

Maguire, T. (1992). "My Bout With Affirmative Action." *Commentary* **93**(4), 50–52.

Mercer, J. (1994). "Ambitious Program Aims to Produce Minority Ph.D.'s." *The Chronicle of Higher Education* **40**(35), A36.

Patterson v. McLean Credit Union. (1989). 491 U.S. 164.

Reeves, R. (1995). "Affirmative Action Does America Good." *The Newark Star-Ledger,* May 10, p. 18.

Rosen, J. (1994). "Is Affirmative Action Doomed?" *The New Republic* **211**(16), 25–36.

Sadker, D., and Sadker, M. (1994). *Failing at Fairness: How America's Schools Cheat Girls.* New York: Macmillan.

"SAT Coaching: Reality vs. Cover-up." (1991). *FairTest Examiner* **5**(4), 1–2.

Sleeper, J. (1990). *The Closest of Strangers: Liberalism and the Politics of Race in New York.* New York: Norton.

Sowell, T. (1990). *Preferential Policies: An International Perspective.* New York: Morrow.

Starr, P. (1992). "Civil Reconstruction: What to Do Without Affirmative Action." *The American Prospect* No. 8, 7–14.

Stasz, C. (1981). *The American Nightmare: Why Inequality Persists.* New York: Schocken Books.

Steele, S. (1991). *The Content of Our Character: A New Vision of Race in America.* New York: St. Martin's Press.

Stimpson, C. (1992). "It Is Time to Rethink Affirmative Action." *The Chronicle of Higher Education* **38**(19), A48.

"Ten Myths About the SAT." (1989). *FairTest Examiner* **3**(4), 8–9.

Tien, C. (1994). "Diversity and Excellence in Higher Education." In *Debating Affirmative Action,* edited by Nicolaus Mills. New York: Dell.

Urofsky, M. (1991). *A Conflict of Rights: The Supreme Court and Affirmative Action.* New York: Scribner's.

Wainer, H., and Steinberg, L. (1992). "Sex Differences in Performance on the Mathematics Section of the Scholastic Aptitude Test: A Bidirectional Validity Study." *Harvard Educational Review* **62**(3), 323–336.

Wards Cove Packing Co., Inc. v. Atonio. (1989). 109 S. Ct. 2115.

West, C. (1994). *Race Matters.* New York: Vintage.

Wilkerson, I. (1991). "Remedy for Racism of Past Has New Kind of Shackles." *The New York Times,* September 15, pp. 1, 28.

Wilson, W. (1987). *The Truly Disadvantaged: The Inner City, the Underclass, and Public Policy.* Chicago: University of Chicago Press.

_____. (1991). "Racism and Race-Conscious Remedies." *The American Prospect* No. 5, 93–96.

Zook, J. (1994). "Recruiting Black Males." *The Chronicle of Higher Education* **41**(13), A34.

Part II

What Should Be Taught?

INTRODUCTION

The idea of knowledge is the focus of Part II. It is generally agreed that knowledge is the core purpose of schools, but there is considerable disagreement over what constitutes knowledge and how it should be taught. Significant disputes arise over such issues as:

What knowledge is most valuable?

Which knowledge should be taught, and in what sequence?

Who gets to decide what knowledge is to be taught?

Who gets access to which kinds of knowledge?

How is knowledge to be expressed in school?

These issues are basic to an evaluation of the school curriculum, giving rise to practical school questions. Should schools emphasize classics of western literature, or technology, or basic skills, or moral behavior, or employable skills, or test taking, or citizenship, or the arts, or science, or language? Do we want to produce broadly educated people, social critics, book learners, workers, college material, athletes, specialists, consumers, patriots, or something else? Should all students be required each year to take courses in English, social studies, math, science, and the arts? Who should be selected to take law, medicine, auto mechanics, flower arranging, or accounting?

Obviously, the most valuable knowledge should be taught in school, but that begs the question of who gets to decide what is worth knowing. The struggle to control what is accepted as knowledge is inevitably a struggle for power. To control people's minds is to control their expectations, their behavior, and their allegiance. And decisions on which students get which knowledge can lead to more social egalitarianism, more elitism, more social-class separation, or more integration. Such decisions can enable or restrict individual achievements, and enhance or detract from democracy. These decisions have enormous implications for the individual and for society.

In ancient times, when magic and witchcraft were socially credible, sorcerers enjoyed great power and status. Their pronouncements were often translated into law and policy. Learning their secret rites was reserved for a select few. Later, when witchery came to be viewed as evil knowledge, sorcerers were burned. In modern society where scientific knowledge is prized, "sorcerers" are seen as interesting eccentrics. A major difference among these situations is the way in which we have changed our definition of knowledge. Postmodern society suggests possible new definitions, and a new school curriculum (Stanley, 1992; Greene, 1994).

Knowledge incorporates the concept of literacy. In a time of belief in witchery, a literate person is one who shares the language and values of that form of knowledge. In an age of technology, a literate person may be defined as one who shares the language and values of that knowledge. Thus, the term "literate" may be thought of as a verbal badge given to those who possess knowledge considered socially valuable. Schools provide literacy credentials in the form of diplomas, degrees, and various types of professional certificates.

The school curriculum of each society reflects the definitions of knowledge prevalent in that society and in that time. The content of the school curriculum is shaped by what a society's leading groups consider valuable knowledge. These definitions are often in conflict—the arts versus the sciences, the practical versus the theoretical, social cohesion versus individual independence. More typically, the traditional school subjects coexist in the curriculum until a new topic arises that challenges that emphasis. When test scores revealed a deficiency in the basic skills of reading, writing, and arithmetic, many elementary schools decreased the curriculum time spent on science, social studies, and the arts and shifted it to reading and arithmetic. When computer education became socially valuable, the schools made time in a crowded school curriculum to fit it in.

The specific mix of courses and the emphasis within the curriculum depend on the prevailing visions of the "good" individual and the "good" society. In every age there are disparate views on what kinds of individuals and society are most desirable.

Some want to assist individuals to be free, independent, and critical; others advocate behavior modification to control deviation and to ensure social conformity. Some want to mandate that each person acquire specific, standard information; others recommend unlimited variety and creativity. Some demand that schools instill prescribed moral values and beliefs; others demand release from moralisms and prescriptions. Some desire respect for authority; others prefer challenges to authority. Some would use schooling to supply society's needs for workers, managers, engineers, and doctors; others would promote broad schooling with no vocational orientation. In each of these competing views are concepts of the "good" individual and the "good" society.

PRACTICAL, THEORETICAL, AND MORAL SCHOOLING

The literature of all societies is filled with disputes over how school should develop the good individual and the good society. Aristotle considered the state the fulfillment of our social drives and saw education as a state activity to provide social unity. He said that "education is therefore THE means of making it (the society) a community and giving it unity. . . . education should be conducted by the state." (Aristotle, 1962, pp. 51, 333) In his introduction to and discussion of Chapter 2, Book 8, of *The Politics*, Aristotle also recognized the continuing curriculum issue of whether schools should teach practical knowledge, moral character, or esoteric ideas:

> The absence of any clear view about the proper subjects of instruction: the conflicting claims of utility, moral discipline, and the advancement of knowledge. . . . At present opinion is divided about the subjects of education. All do not take the same view about what should be learned by the young, either with a view to plain goodness or with a view to the best life possible; nor is opinion clear whether education should be

directed mainly to the understanding, or mainly to moral character. (pp. 333–334)

Contemporary curriculum debate continues to focus on the relative emphasis that should be given to practical, theoretical, and moral schooling. What type of knowledge will best fulfill the needs of individuals and society for (1) developing the skills for doing the practical work; (2) pursuing advanced, theoretical knowledge in such areas as mathematics, literature, logic, and the arts; and (3) providing a set of moral guidelines and ethical values for judging right from wrong?

Disputes over emphasis and the kinds of knowledge to be presented in schools have not been resolved. Contemporary comprehensive public schools offer some useful applied educational programs, such as reading, writing, music, wood shop, home economics, computer operation, physical education, and vocational training. They also offer the study of theoretical and more esoteric material in English, math, social studies, the arts, and science. And schools provide various forms of moral education, including the study of selected literature and historical material that convey ideas of the good person and the good society, and learning from school rules and teachers to be respectful, patriotic, loyal, and honest. The mix of these forms of education varies as different reforms become popular and as local communities make changes.

The school reform literature of the 1980s and the reactions of the 1990s again were marked by arguments over whether to emphasize practical, moral, or higher knowledge in the schools. The National Commission on Excellence in Education, the lightning rod of the reform movement, proposed a high school graduation requirement of four years of English, three years of mathematics, three years of science, and a semester of computer science (National Commission on Excellence in Education, 1983). It is significant that vocational education, a prominent feature of the school reforms of the 1930s and 1940s, was ignored in this 1983 report. Physical education, part of major school reforms between 1910 and 1920, was also dismissed. The arts received only passing reference in the National Commission Report, but the proposed emphasis on computer science was actually a practical course, not unlike business education proposals of the 1920s and 1930s. The entire report was framed as a way to restore America's competitive edge in international business and national defense. These are practical purposes, and suggest that the required core of courses should tend toward knowledge useful in business.

Boyer's High School, an influential 1980s reform book from the Carnegie Foundation for the Advancement of Teaching, describes four essential functions of a high school. It should help students:

1. Develop critical thinking and effective communicating.
2. Learn about themselves, the human heritage, and the interdependent world.
3. Prepare for work and further education.
4. Fulfill social and civic obligations. (Boyer, 1983)

These functions incorporate practical, moral, and higher knowledge. Boyer's curriculum proposal includes required courses in writing, speech, literature, the arts, foreign language, American and world history, civics, science, technology, and health, and a seminar on work and a senior-level independent applied project. This was an effort to cover as many bases as possible to help students cope with an "interdependent, interconnected, complex world." It included some of each of the practical, moral, and esoteric topics that Aristotle had posed as disputable in education.

In the 1990s, opinion is increasing that the reforms of the 1980s were essentially mechanistic and "top-down." The presumption was that the president, governors, legislators, and national commissions could tell the schools what and how to teach and that would correct educational ills. Prescriptions for increased course requirements, longer school days and school years, more homework, more testing, and the forced feeding of knowledge to students by employee-teachers in factorylike schools have not proved their curative abilities.

Edward B. Fiske (1991), former education editor for the *New York Times,* argues:

> The time for tinkering with the current system of public education is over. After a decade of trying to make the system work better by such means as more testing, higher salaries, and tighter curriculums, we must now face up to the fact that anything short of fundamental structural change is futile. We are trying to use a nineteenth-

century institution to prepare young people for life in the twenty-first century. (p. 14)

Fiske argues against highly centralized school authority, standardization, and bureaucracy. He presents a case for students who can think for themselves; for decentralized and shared school decision making, with teachers taking responsibility for making the most important school decisions; for cooperative learning; and for moving beyond multiple-choice standardized testing to measure student knowledge. These views suggest a significantly different approach to questions of knowledge than did the prescriptions for particular subject field courses, test score improvement, and imposed requirements that were a feature of the 1980s school reform movement. In the Fiske proposal, knowledge is much more holistic and integrating, and is determined by those closest to the classroom.

Still, the formal curriculum in American schools is largely determined by external forces. Since Colonial times, it has evolved from a rather narrow interest in teaching religious ideals to the current multiple, and often conflicting, interests in providing broad knowledge, skills, and values with regard to nearly every aspect of social life. In American schools, the medieval curriculum of "seven liberal arts"— rhetoric, grammar, logic, arithmetic, astronomy, geometry, and music— has been replaced by a list of subjects too long to include here. And the formal curriculum is certainly not all that students are expected to learn in school.

THE HIDDEN CURRICULUM

In addition to the formal school curriculum, which is composed of the various courses that are prescribed or offered to students, there is also a hidden curriculum consisting of unexpressed and usually unexamined ideas, values, and behaviors that are conveyed to students through informal means. These are the subtle, often unintended, things that are learned by students (and teachers, too) as they go about their lives in school. They represent underlying ideologies, root ideas about human values and social relations.

At its simplest level, the hidden curriculum can be illustrated by two brief examples. Students are told by teachers to be independent and to express their own ideas, but the student who exhibits independence and expresses ideas the teacher doesn't like is often chastised or punished. What is learned? Students are taught in history courses that justice and equality are basic American rights, yet they recognize that compliant and well-dressed students get favored treatment. What is learned? The hidden curriculum is a vast, relatively uncharted domain that is often much more effective than the official formal curriculum in determining what students actually learn in school.

At a deeper level, the surface hypocrisies between such things as what a teacher says and what that teacher does blend into a more significant concern with competing ideologies. Examination of a hidden curriculum shows these basic conflicts with the stated purposes of the visible curriculum. A stated purpose of schools is to protect diversity; however, the hidden curriculum expects conformity. The stated curriculum advocates critical thinking; the hidden curriculum supports docility. The visible curriculum professes equal opportunity; the hidden curriculum separates students according to social-class background, gender, race, or other factors.

Recent critical literature examines the hidden curriculum and its ideological bases (see, for example, Anyon, 1979, 1980; Apple, 1990; Cherryholmes, 1978, 1988; Giroux, 1988; Giroux and Purpel, 1983; Popkewitz, 1987; Stanley, 1992; Young, 1970). From this critical view, the so-called great debates about schooling that are extensively covered in the media and the mainstream educational literature are actually narrowly constructed differences between liberals and conservatives that do not raise ideological concerns about the control of knowledge and its social consequences. That is the reason, it is argued, that superficial school reforms do very little to change schooling, and neither mainstream liberals nor conservatives really want much change.

At the surface level, where much school reform debate occurs, a discussion about whether to spend more school time on computers, math, and English and less on the arts and social studies is a trivial matter; it hides more fundamental disputes about whose interests are served and whose are maligned. Shallow arguments about whether the curriculum should stress the basics, provide vocational courses, allow electives, or emphasize American values, when critically examined in depth, should lead to

more fundamental disputes involving who controls the school curriculum and the consequences of that control. In mainstream discourse, those basic issues (class, gender, race, age controls) are hidden.

CURRICULUM CONTROL

Control of knowledge, with regard to the school curriculum, is a product of both prevailing social goals and prevailing social structures. During most of America's formative years, religion was the basis for the school curriculum. Although there were differences among the colonies, it was expected that all young children would be taught religious precepts at home or at dame or writing schools. The purpose was to thwart the efforts of "that ould deluder, Satan," who sought to keep human beings from knowledge of the scriptures. After learning to read and write, however, most girls were not permitted further education and returned home to learn the art of homemaking, while boys from more affluent homes continued their schooling at Latin grammar schools. African-Americans and native Americans were virtually excluded from the schools.

Historically, the struggle for the control of knowledge has paralleled social-class differences. Practical knowledge was presumed to be needed by the workers, higher knowledge by the privileged class, and moral knowledge by both, but with great disparity in the kinds of moral knowledge they required. Craft apprenticeships to acquire practical knowledge were for the masses. Formal schooling to learn critical thinking and to study philosophy, science, and the arts was for the aristocratic class. In terms of moral instruction, the masses were to gain the moral character to obey, to respect authority, to work hard and be frugal, and to suffer with little complaint. Members of the privileged class were supposed to gain the moral character to rule wisely, justly, and with understanding.

One of the central purposes of schooling is to prepare the leaders of the society. But schooling is controlled by those of the powerful class, and is responsive to their interests in what is taught.* Within an elitist society, the essential curricular question is: What should members of the ruling class know? In more democratic societies, where there is an effort to educate the masses, the curricular questions revolve around what all members of the society should be expected to know.

Even in democratic societies, however, special attention is given to the additional curricular needs of those identified as potential leaders. This can be seen in the higher academic tracks and honors programs that characterize many modern high schools. The correlation between social expectations, social-class structure, and what is taught is obvious and deserves ongoing examination. Marrou (1956/1982), for example, notes that in ancient Arabia the "upper class is composed of an aristocracy of warriors, and education is

*There is an extensive body of literature on this topic. See the reference list for works by Anyon, Apple, Bernstein, Bourdieu, Carnoy, Bowles and Gintis, Freire, Giroux, Oakes, and Young.

therefore of a military kind . . . training character and building up physical vigour rather than developing the intelligence." He found similar conditions in old oriental, Indian, and western educational systems (pp. xiv, xv).

R. H. Tawney (1964), observing that "educational policy is always social policy," criticized the elite "public boarding-school" tradition of the wealthy in England, and advocated improvements in the developing system of free schools for the working classes. He saw how the very nature of the elite system was a part of the hidden curriculum, teaching the sons of the wealthy "not in words or of set purpose, but by the mere facts of their environment, that they are members . . . of a privileged group, whose function it will be, on however humble a scale, to direct and command, and to which leadership, influence, and the other prizes of life properly belong" (Tawney, 1964, p. 83).

Social class is not the only major factor lying behind curricular decisions. Race, gender, national origin, and religion have been identified as other conditions that influence what knowledge is given to which people in society. The concept of privilege, and the education that privilege brings, has included racism and sexism in American and other national histories. Educational discrimination against racial minorities, women, Jews and Catholics, native Americans and Eskimos, and others is a sorry tradition in a democratic society.

A quarter of a century ago, psychologist Kenneth Clark, whose studies had been a significant factor in the Supreme Court decision that found segregated schools unconstitutional

(*Brown v. Board of Education*, 1954), put the case clearly:

> The public schools in America's urban ghettos also reflect the oppressive damage of racial exclusion. . . . Segregation and inferior education reinforce each other. . . . Children themselves are not fooled by the various euphemisms educators use to disguise educational snobbery. From the earliest grades a child knows when he has been assigned to a level that is considered less than adequate. . . . "The clash of cultures in the classroom" is essentially a class war, a socio-economic and racial warfare being waged on the battleground of our schools, with middle-class and middle-class-aspiring teachers provided with a powerful arsenal of half-truths, prejudices, and rationalizations, arrayed against the hopelessly outclassed workingclass youngsters. (Clark, 1965, pp. 111–117)

Similar expressions of educational discrimination based on religion, nationality, and gender are common in the critical literature (Hofstadter, 1944; Clark, 1965; Katz, 1971; Feldman, 1974; Spring, 1976; Apple, 1979, 1990; Sadker and Sadker, 1982; Walker and Barton, 1983; Grimshaw, 1986; Lather, 1991; Weiler, 1991; Giroux, 1991). As Rosemary Deem (1983) comments: "women have had to struggle hard against dominant patriarchal power relations, which try to confine women to the private sphere of the home and family, away from the public sphere or production and political power" (p. 107). Weiler (1991) essentially agrees in a critique of the western system of knowledge, arguing that feminist pedagogy is rooted in a

vision of social change that is critical, oppositional, and activist. Schooling in which different types of knowledge and skills are given to students who differ only in race, gender, class, religion, or nationality contributes to a continuation of inequality of treatment and to stereotypes.

The chapters of Part II examine some of the current curriculum disputes that have emerged as part of the reform movement in education. These disputes are clearly tied to the question of what knowledge is most valuable in our society, a question that, in turn, is tied to our differing visions of what constitutes the good individual and the good society.

SOCIAL EXPECTATIONS: BASIC EDUCATION VERSUS CRITICAL THINKING

Chapter 7 poses a question about what should be taught: should it be subject knowledge of historic and socially approved value, or material that encourages critical thinking and student interest? It raises the issue of external versus internal determination of what is to be learned. If individual students are expected to develop independent and critical judgment so they can participate actively in improving the democratic society, we should expect schooling that leads to that goal, and we can expect those individuals to have an impact on the society. If society values a structure in which only a few people have power and most people are expected to be docile and to conform to social norms, we should expect schooling that leads to that end, and the resulting society.

Those two hypothetical statements seem to suggest that the choice is simple; it is not. There are complex and changing relations among the kinds of individuals we desire, the society we want to develop, and the schooling we provide. These relations often lead to conflicting signals for schools, and the conflicts become enshrined in the school curriculum. Society wants students to become self-sufficient individuals, but not too self-sufficient too early, so students are allowed little latitude in deciding what to study until they reach college. What is desired is a society that is democratic and inspires voluntary loyalty, but open inquiry is not trusted, so required courses stress nationalistic patriotism.

"Individual-making" provides for self-development and fulfillment, and "society-making" instills social values and socially valuable knowledge and behavior. Arguments over what we should expect students to learn in school are related to the twin goals of individual-making and society-making, because critics differ in their views of the kinds of individuals and society we should have. This reflects the potential power of the school in influencing succeeding generations.

Some people enjoy mathematics, even word problems. For others, reading history or literature is a great joy. There are those who like to dissect white rats in biology class, to saw wood in the wood shop, or to exercise in the gym. Yet others are completely baffled or utterly bored by textbooks and teachers. Different strokes, as they say, for different folks. But aren't there some things that everyone should know, whether they enjoy it or not? Is there a set of skills that all

should master? Should we require that anyone who graduates from high school be literate? Who should decide the criteria for literacy? What does it take to be educated in this final decade of the twentieth century?

MULTICULTURAL STUDIES OR WESTERN CLASSICS?

Essays in Chapter 8 express two views of the curriculum question of whether to stress diversity or unity in schools. On one side of the issue are those who note the increasing diversity of peoples in the United States. Population studies indicate that by the beginning of the twenty-first century, more than one-half of the nation's population will be able to claim that they are members of an ethnic minority; we will have a majority of minority groups. That is not the only reason for changing the schools to reflect cultural diversity, but it is a strong reason. People should be able to have schools that reflect their experience and knowledge. Among other reasons offered for multicultural education are:

1. The increasingly global nature of affairs
2. The need to understand peoples of varying backgrounds and values
3. To correct Americans' appalling ignorance of other cultures' high-quality contributions to literature, science, history, and the arts

One of the concerns of those who advocate multicultural studies is that the traditional western heritage is made up almost entirely of the works of white men. The domination of this western tradition in schools perpetuates the discrimination against the fine works of women and minorities.

In opposition to those who support multicultural education are those who argue that national unity is more important. Essentially, they say, the emphasis on diversity decreases unity and places the nation at risk of developing factions. Multicultural education, it is argued, merely reinforces each subgroup's myths without any unifying core of knowledge for all. Basic to this position is the idea that separationist education, stressing the differences among groups, easily leads to factions and conflicts. In contrast, the historic standards of western civilization, which have been the common root of American education, have provided generations of immigrants with the knowledge that strengthens national unity. Further, the western tradition of literature, history, politics, and ethics that undergirds democratic life in this country contains the major ideas common to all humans. People who oppose multicultural studies hold that we are a western society and have a heritage that each new generation must learn. If that heritage is diminished or ignored, our society suffers. At the least, Americans should know about our Founding Fathers, political traditions, historic social values, and western literature.

This critical issue in education is among the most volatile in current debates. It has appeared on the front pages of leading newspapers and in popular newsmagazines, and has been the subject of disputes on college campuses, of discussions about changing state and local school curricula, and of arguments in national politics.

LITERACY: NATIONAL MANDATE OR LOCAL OPTION?

The essays in Chapter 9 focus on the value of a national curriculum as a way of establishing national standards for literacy. The formal curriculum is one of the most visible parts of a school, and it indicates the relative value the school puts on various forms of knowledge. Actually, every school does not make a separate determination of the relative value of parts of the curriculum; a number of factors influence what is taught in most schools and contribute to a relatively standard curriculum in U.S. schools.

The various states mandate certain courses that state legislatures believe are necessary for all students, such as English and American history, and many states encourage other courses, such as drug and alcohol education, by providing special funding or applying political pressure. Accrediting agencies in each region examine schools periodically, and the curriculum is one area that undergoes review for conformity. A school that does not have a standard curriculum or its equivalent is threatened with loss of accreditation. Publishers, aiming at a national market, produce teaching materials that fit a national curriculum. A school that deviates from that pattern will have trouble finding textbooks. And school district curriculum coordinators and department heads attend national conferences and read common journals that stress standard curricular structures. So there exists the outline of a general national curriculum based on common practices, even though that of each state could be different.

There are many political permutations to the question of a national versus a local curriculum, but we can agree on a basic social interest in this aspect of the struggle over control of knowledge: the concern for and definition of literacy. Schools have become the major means for access to socially approved knowledge, and literacy, defined in differing ways, has become the goal of schooling. This goal statement, however, is far from simple because the definition of "literacy" changes. Should we prescribe a national curriculum for all students, or should local communities be able to define the nature of literacy and the schooling needed to develop it?

TRADITION VERSUS LIBERATION

A central issue in the struggle for the control of knowledge is whether traditional knowledge is enduring wisdom or social oppression. Chapter 10 illustrates two views of what should be taught—traditional values or liberating knowledge.

Religious literacy and values dominated the school curriculum in early America. In the earliest secondary schools, boys of the wealthy class were taught Latin, Greek, catechism, and the Bible to prepare them to go to college, where many would prepare for the ministry. The religious motif continues to influence schooling, primarily in parochial schools, but it is also a basis for many of the values taught in public education today.

Prior to the American Revolution, religion was waning as the primary social glue. National political interests emerged. The schools changed to meet changes in frontier life, city development, and more secular and sectional economic interests. After the Revolution, and into the nineteenth century, nationalism replaced religion as an educational force. Literacy became important not for religious salvation, but for patriotism, the preservation of liberty, and participation in democracy.

The political-nationalistic tradition remains strong in American schools, with a renewed emphasis each time social values seem threatened. During the period of overt racism in America, and as a reaction to the technical abolition of slavery, literacy tests became one of the devices used to restrict voting rights in some areas. Since slaves had been prohibited, by law in some states, from being educated, these tests were intended to keep former slaves and the poor from voting. They were also used to limit participation by immigrants. An imperial wizard of the Ku Klux Klan is quoted by David Tyack (1967) as saying, "Ominous statistics proclaim the persistent development of a parasitic mass within our domain. . . . We have taken unto ourselves a Trojan horse crowded with ignorance, illiteracy, and envy" (p. 233).

The "red scare" of the 1920s, McCarthyism in the 1950s, and anti-communist political rhetoric in the 1980s were also threats; their effect on curriculum was to strengthen a nationalist viewpoint on history, government, literature, and economics. International competition in technology and trade threatens Americans and translates into increased curricular emphasis on mathematics; science; technological subjects, such as computers; and foreign languages.

In opposition to the traditional use of literacy as a tool to separate and control the masses is the idea of literacy for liberation, Paulo Freire's revolutionary concept (Freire and Berthoff, 1987). It upends the use of literacy as a weapon for the dominant class, and makes it a political tool by which the oppressed can overcome the oppressors. Freire, born in one of the most impoverished areas of Brazil, came to know the plight of the poor. He vowed to dedicate his life to the struggle against misery and suffering, and his work led to what he defined as the "culture of silence" of the disadvantaged. As Shaull (1970) notes, Freire recognized that "ignorance and lethargy were the direct product of the whole situation of economic, social, and political domination—and of the paternalism—of which they were victims."

Freire realized the power of knowledge and recognized that the dominant class used education to keep the culture of silence among the victims. He developed a program to teach literacy to adults in order to liberate them from their situation. As a professor of education in Brazil, he experimented with this program to erase illiteracy, and his ideas became widely used in literacy campaigns by private groups there. He was considered a threat to the government and was jailed after a military coup in 1964. Forced to leave his native country, he went to Chile to work with UNESCO, came to the United States, and then joined the World Council of Churches in Geneva as head of its educational division.

Freire's program involves the development of critical consciousness. It uses communication that exposes oppression. Teacher and student are "co-intentional," equally sharing in dialogues on social reality and developing critical understanding that can liberate them from the culture of silence.

Henry Giroux, citing Freire, argues that we need a redefinition of literacy in order to focus on its critical dimensions. Mass culture via television and other electronic media is under the control of dominant economic interests, and it offers only immediate images and unthoughtful information. This creates a "technocratic" illiteracy, and is a threat to self-perception, to critical thought, and to democracy. Giroux (1988) states:

> Instead of formulating literacy in terms of the mastery of techniques, we must broaden its meaning to include the ability to read critically, both inside and outside one's experiences, and with conceptual power. This means that literacy would enable people to decode critically their personal and social worlds and thereby further their ability to challenge the myths and beliefs that structure their perceptions and experiences. (p. 84)

Should schooling emphasize traditional values or liberation? What are the other options?

BUSINESS AND EDUCATION

Chapter 11 examines the issue of whether or not business and industrial views should dominate the struggle for control of ideas expressed in schools. The movement toward common schools in America has included support from business and labor leaders. Preparation for employment is now considered one of the basic purposes of schools. Vocational education evolved as a major response to the dual problem of the needs of business and the dropout rate among nonacademic students. Many parents want schools to give their children the skills that will make them employable. In many families, there is pressure on children to study material that will pay off in economic terms. The question is: What will help get the student into the right law school or medical school to ensure the proper job placement?

Even the organization of schools and their operation are the products of business organization and ideas. Members of school boards are often elected because they promise to bring "businesslike efficiency" to the schools. Business people are often members of blue-ribbon boards and committees that are asked to review school operations. School administrators are required by state licensing laws and university degree requirements to study management material taken from the literature of business schools and translated into school management practices. Textbooks on school administration advocate business management techniques.

Businesses provide considerable financial and other support for schools. School districts are pleased to have "ratables," taxable businesses that pay for schools but produce no students. Businesses also give large sums of money to local schools for various programs and teaching materials and for the sponsorship of school events.

One major social factor influencing the school curriculum is the traditional American interest in practical innovations within the ethos of capitalism. Benjamin Franklin serves as a stereotype of the American captivated by invention and utility. Andrew Carnegie, John D. Rockefeller, Jay Gould, J. Paul Getty, and Donald Trump, among others, illustrate the American belief in entrepreneurship and the values of "free enterprise." The idea of rugged individualism that permeated our early national literature glorified the combination of survival by wits and invention and a determination to succeed at any cost.

The idealization of capitalism in American society creates a need for adequately prepared engineers, technicians, assembly-line workers, maintenance and secretarial personnel, salespeople, and managers, as well as eager and knowledgeable consumers of new products. The schools are pressured to prepare people with skills and attitudes that enhance capitalism, just as they were earlier used to prepare people for religious and nationalistic loyalty. Schools are expected to train people in the skills necessary for employment, and in attitudes that will help them succeed in the workplace; television and videotape equipment is widely available in most schools; and personal computers are provided free or at very low cost to stimulate mass computer education and entice eager consumers.

In curricular terms, the industrial revolution assisted in the demise of the classical curriculum and in the rise of applied subjects. Latin, Greek, ancient history, philosophy, and many of the arts are not considered useful knowledge, whereas vocational subjects, commercial courses, the physical and biological sciences, and economics are useful. More current examples are the emphasis on computer literacy for all students, courses in reading and writing for employment purposes, "free enterprise" course requirements in some states, and the development in colleges of entrepreneurial programs and management science.

Industrialization creates social problems that also influence the school curriculum. Urbanization and suburbanization follow employment opportunities and social-class patterns, and this creates social and individual difficulties that schools are often expected to ameliorate. Violence, crime, alcohol and drug abuse, broken families, suicide, unemployment, prejudice, dislocation, and financial chaos are among the many examples of such issues.

The stress associated with late-twentieth-century life in a capitalistic society is the subject of books, lectures, and a new industry of human resource development. The school curriculum has changed since 1900 to provide courses in sociology, psychology, urban problems, financial planning, family studies, drug education, sex education, and death and dying.

At the college and university level, businesses provide major funding for many research and teaching projects. Grants from businesses to education total many millions of dollars per year. Business people are often the strongest advocates of schools, offering speakers, part-time employment for students, educational material, and myriad other subsidies.

Although these business relations with schools may seem worthwhile, they pose some obvious and subtle threats to education. The influence of business on what is taught is enormous. The visible and hidden curricula are subject to business manipulation. And business is not without blemish itself; it is scarcely an ideal model for social values and ethics. Should corporate interests dominate the definition of proper knowledge and literacy? Chapter 11 presents two of the many divergent views on what the relation between business and the schools should be.

STANDARDIZED TESTING AND WHAT IS TAUGHT

Standardized testing has become the most commonly used device to determine attainment and proficiency, the measure of what is taught in schools. Chapter 12 considers the role and impact of standardized testing as a critical educational issue.

As many as 300 million standardized tests are administered each year, most of them to public school students. A typical high school graduate will be subjected to six batteries of standardized achievement tests in twelve years of schooling (Mehrens and Lehmann, 1987, p. 2). Test taking is one of society's more widely shared phenomena; it is unusual to find anyone who has not taken at least one such exam.

Proponents of standardized tests argue that machine-scored multiple-choice tests are the best available measures of academic merit and educational quality. Well-designed and well-used tests, they note, can provide schools with the information needed to make curricular decisions. Test programs can inform educators about the effectiveness of their teaching methods, comparing the test takers with students of earlier times or other places. Standardized testing can also be used for accountability, to demonstrate that the money spent on education is being used prudently.

Opponents maintain that the tests are crude, imprecise measures that reward superficiality, ignore creativity, and penalize those test takers who read too much into the questions. Instead of informing the public, it is argued, test makers confuse people with test results shrouded in mathematics. Rather than offer accountability, testing mistakenly applies the simpleminded methods of cost accounting to the complexities of the teaching–learning process. To meet the demands for a large-scale testing program, testing and measurement experts have had to design instruments for a machine-scored, multiple-choice format. Critics claim that few things of significance can be reduced to discrete bits and measured by a series of short-answer, timed questions.

Standardized tests are one of the more controversial applications of social science to education, and despite the extent to which they have permeated every level of school experience, they represent a relatively recent development in this regard. Civil service examinations were first administered centuries ago in China, but it was not until the nineteenth century that standardized exams became a common part of social and economic life. Nineteenth-century Britain, in the throes of an expanding domestic economy and of becoming an international empire, found that the demand for large numbers of middle-class managers could not be satisfied by the traditional patronage appointments. Worldwide vacancies could not be filled by tapping privileged males—the sons of civil servants, members of Parliament, or others of wealth and connections. Competitive exams were introduced to open the civil service to a broader range of male applicants.

The United States also used testing as a means of democratizing the selection of government workers. Political abuse, through patronage, was rampant in the late nineteenth century. Civil Service reform began with the Pendleton Act of 1883, which established competitive exams for prospective government employees.

Standardized tests were introduced in Boston's public schools in 1845 to measure student knowledge and to determine who was eligible for secondary education (Travers, 1983). In many ways, performance on standardized tests still controls access to education and power in society (Eggleston, 1984).

Chapter 12 presents two competing perspectives on standardized testing in assessment. Position 1 argues against testing, maintaining that little of value can be measured in that way and that such testing is biased, stifles student creativity, and perpetuates social injustice (Broadfoot, 1984; Crouse and Trusheim, 1988; Owen, 1985). Position 2 argues that formal and objective evaluations can measure worthwhile educational achievements and can be used to measure school accountability (Mehrens and Lehman, 1987).

References

Anyon, J. (1979). "Ideology and U.S. History Textbooks." *Harvard Educational Review* 7, 49–60.

_____. (1980). "Social Class and the Hidden Curriculum of Work." *Journal of Education 162*, 67–92.

Apple, M. (1979, 1990). *Ideology and Curriculum*, 2d ed. New York: Routledge.

_____ (1982). *Education and Power.* London: Routledge & Kegan Paul.

Aristotle. (1962). *The Politics of Aristotle*, translated by E. Barker. Oxford: Oxford University Press.

Bernstein, B. (1977). *Class, Codes, and Control*, volume 3. London: Routledge & Kegan Paul.

Broadfoot, P., ed. (1984). *Selection, Certification and Control: Social Issues in Educational Assessment.* London: Falmer Press.

Brown v. Board of Education of Topeka, Shawnee County, Kansas et al. (1954). 74 Sup. Ct. 686.

Bourdieu, P., and Passeron, J. (1977). *Reproduction in Education, Society, and Culture.* London: Sage.

Bowles, S., and Gintis, H. (1976). *Schooling in Capitalist America.* New York: Basic Books.

Boyer, E. L. (1983). *High School.* New York: Harper & Row.

Butts, R. F. (1955). *A Cultural History of Western Education.* New York: McGraw-Hill.

Carnoy, M. (1975). *Schooling in a Corporate Society: The Political Economy of Education in the Democratic State*, 2nd ed. New York: McKay.

_____ and Levin, H. (1985). *Schooling and Work in America.* Stanford, CA: Stanford University Press.

Cherryholmes, C. (1978). "Curriculum Design as a Political Act." *Curriculum Inquiry* 10, 115–141.

_____ (1988). *Power and Criticism: Poststructural Investigations in Education.* New York: Teachers College Press.

Clark, K. (1965). *Dark Ghetto.* New York: Harper & Row.

Crouse, J., and Trusheim, D. (1988). *The Case Against the SAT.* Chicago: University of Chicago Press.

Deem, R. (1983). "Gender, Patriarchy and Class in the Popular Education of Women." In *Gender, Class and Education,* edited by S. Walker and L. Barton, London: Falmer Press.

Eggleston, J. (1984). "School Examinations—Some Sociological Issues." In *Selection, Certification and Control,* edited by P. Broadfoot. London: Falmer Press.

Feldman, S. (1974). *The Rights of Women.* Rochelle Park, NJ: Hayden.

Fiske, E. B. (1991). *Smart School, Smart Kids.* New York: Simon & Schuster.

Freire, P. (1970). *Pedagogy of the Oppressed,* translated by M. B. Ramos. New York: Herder & Herder.

_____ and Berthoff, D. (1987). *Literacy: Reading and the World.* South Hadley, MA: Bergin & Garvey.

Giroux, H. (1981). *Ideology, Culture, and the Process of Schooling.* Philadelphia: Temple University Press.

_____ (1988). *The Teacher as Intellectual.* South Hadley, MA: Bergin & Garvey.

_____, ed. (1991). *Postmodernism, Feminism and Cultural Politics.* Albany: SUNY Press.

_____ and Purpel, D. (1983) *The Hidden Curriculum and Moral Education.* Berkeley, CA: McCutchan.

Greene, M. (1994). "Postmodernism and the Crisis of Representation." *English Education* 26, 206–219.

Grimshaw, J. (1986). *Philosophy and Feminist Thinking.* Minneapolis: University of Minnesota Press.

Hanson, F. A. (1993). *Testing, Testing: Social Consequences of the Examined Life.* Berkeley: University of California Press.

Hofstadter, R. (1944). *Social Darwinism in American Thought.* Philadelphia: University of Pennsylvania Press.

Katz, M. B. (1971). *Class, Bureaucracy, and Schools.* New York: Praeger.

Langer, J., ed. (1987). *Language, Literacy and Culture: Issues of Society and Schooling.* Norwood, NJ: Ablex.

Lather, P. (1991). *Getting Smart: Feminist Research and Pedagogy With/in the Postmodern.* New York: Routledge.

Marrou, H. (1956/1982). *A History of Education in Antiquity,* translated by G. Lamb. Madison: University of Wisconsin Press.

Mehrens, W. A., and Lehmann, I. J. (1987). *Using Standardized Tests in Education,* 4th ed. New York: Longman.

National Commission on Excellence in Education. (1983). *A Nation at Risk.* Washington, DC: U.S. Department of Education.

Nelson, J., Carlson, K. and Linton, T. (1972). *Radical Ideas and the Schools.* New York: Holt, Rinehart and Winston.

Oakes, J. (1985). *Keeping Track: How the Schools Structure Inequality.* New Haven, CT: Yale University Press.

Owen, D. (1985). *None of the Above.* Boston: Houghton Mifflin.

Popkewitz, T. (1977). "The Latent Values of the Discipline-Centered Curriculum." *Theory and Research in Social Education* **13,** 189–206.

——— (1987). *The Formation of School Subjects.* New York: Falmer Press.

Sadker, P., and Sadker, D. M. (1982). *Sex Equity Handbook for Schools.* New York: Longman.

Soltow, L., and Stevens, E. (1981). *The Rise of Literacy and the Common School in the United States.* Chicago: University of Chicago Press.

Spring, J. (1976). *The Sorting Machine.* New York: McKay.

Stanley, W. (1992). *Education for Utopia: Social Reconstructionism and Critical Pedagogy in the Postmodern Era.* Albany: SUNY Press.

Tawney, R. H. (1964). *The Radical Tradition.* London: Allen & Unwin.

Travers, R. M. W. (1983). *How Research has Changed America.* Kalamazoo, MI: Mythos.

Tyack, D. (1967). *Turning Points in American Educational History.* Waltham, MA: Blaisdell.

UNESCO. (1957). *World Illiteracy at Mid-Century: A Statistical Study.* Paris: UNESCO.

——— (1976). *The Experimental World Literacy Programme: A Critical Assessment.* Paris: UNESCO.

Walker, S., and Barton, L. (1983). *Gender Class and Education.* London: Falmer Press.

Watts, A. (1960). *The Spirit of the Zen.* New York: Grove Press.

Weiler, K. (1991). "Freire and a Feminist Pedagogy of Difference." *Harvard Educational Review* **61,** 449–474.

Young, M. F. D., ed. (1970). *Knowledge and Control.* London: Collier-Macmillan.

CHAPTER SEVEN

Basic Education: Traditional Disciplines or Critical Thinking

POSITION 1:
TEACH THE BASIC DISCIPLINES

Schools have failed at the one thing they are charged to do for the society—provide students with a basic education. Declining test scores and the painfully obvious evidence of basically illiterate citizens demonstrate the serious deficiencies in American schooling. Academically, the United States ranks with the developing nations. Despite the enormous amount of money poured into our schools, our students do not compare favorably with students in Japan, Germany, or most of the modern nations.

We are a third-rate nation producing generations of graduates who can't read, write, compute, or respond intelligently to questions about history, geography, economics, or literature. Our 17-year-olds are incompetent in the humanities (Ravitch and Finn, 1987); in science and math, they are even worse, and in general information about society and contemporary affairs students do poorly (*National Review,* 1990; *USA Today,* 1990; *Fortune,* 1990; Samuelson, 1991; Perry, 1993; Peltzman, 1994; Finn, 1995).

The basic purpose of schools is to teach fundamental knowledge and skills to the young, including the body of important information and values from our cultural heritage. Fundamental skills, such as mature reading, writing, and computation, are necessary to survive and be productive in contemporary society. Our cultural heritage has evolved over time and has served society well. It incorporates history, literature, and the elements of national character that make America. Yet, even in the basic task of schools, there is failure.

School Failure in the Basics

Despite more than a decade of increased funding and more attention, the "rising tide of mediocrity" in American schools reported by a national panel in a devastating analysis of educational performance (National Commission on

Excellence in Education, 1983) has not been stemmed. That report identified thirty-seven different study findings, including the following:

Average academic achievement test scores are lower than in 1957, when *Sputnik* was launched.

SAT test scores were in continual decline from 1963 to 1980.

Test scores in science steadily declined from 1969 to 1977.

College remedial math courses increased by almost 75 percent.

In comparison with students in other industrialized nations on nineteen academic achievement tests, American students were never first or second, and they were last seven times.

The amount of homework has decreased.

Textbooks have been written at lower levels ("dumbing down") to accommodate students' declining reading abilities.

About half of the new teachers of math, science, and English are not qualified to teach these subjects.

Average school grades rise, however, as real student achievement falls.

Since the publication of the National Commission's *A Nation at Risk,* school funding and teacher salaries have been increased and some states have set forth requirements to improve the schools, but there has been no actual move to return the basics to their rightful place in the curriculum (*Time,* 1989; Shaw, 1993; Perry, 1993). Shaw (1993) points out that despite the failure of schools, Americans have become educated through the media and interaction with their families and peers; industrial growth has occurred in America even though there has been a steady decline in reading scores since 1930. Consider what might have happened if the schools were doing their job. Just as with the pretense that average school grades were going up whereas real student achievement was in decline, there is a superficial idea that schools have improved. Evidence of a return to basic education and solid improvement in student knowledge simply is not there, but there are many new much-heralded fads that hide this underlying erosion of school quality. Schools move like sludge, and the 1990s so far have shown no better overall student performance in academic subjects.

Schools just do not have enough time or resources to deal with every possible topic. We need to decide which things are important, and then focus our schools' energies on doing them well. That means we have to decide what to jettison and what to improve. This leads to a consideration of what has happened in our schools.

The Dumping-Ground School

It is clear that schools have taken on far too many tasks, have failed in the most significant ones, and have been put in the position of replacing parents, church, and society. The president of the Xerox Corporation charges that American schools have put the society "at a terrible competitive disadvantage" by producing workers with a "50 percent defect rate." He argues that a fourth of the students drop out and another fourth are "barely able to read their own diplomas" (*New York Times*, 1987).

Instead of teaching students the necessary skills, today's schools are seen as places to learn how to

Drive a car

Be a parent

Avoid drugs and alcohol

Gain self-respect

Get along with others

Adjust to society

Get a job

Have safe sex

Appreciate the arts

Behave in public

Learn secular morality and values

Do whatever is the next fad of the educationists

The schools' attempt to fulfill these more frivolous tasks has not been successful, and it has taken energies away from the basic purpose of education. Some people may desire to have the schools take over all responsibilities for children, but they don't recognize the threat that represents to our free society. Government-operated or -supervised schools have a limited capacity to know what's best, and financing those behemoth operations strains the tax budget.

Unfortunately, the school curriculum has become a dumping ground for every special interest group's pet idea for solving a human problem. If we have a problem with crime, we think it will be solved by teaching about crime in schools. The topics of teen-age sex and pregnancy show up on the front pages of the newspapers, and a new course is proposed for schools. A war occurs somewhere in the world, and we find calls for "peace education" in schools; we presume to stop the threat of nuclear war by teaching a class on peace. A student commits suicide, and there is an effort to develop antisuicide classes to deal with "improving self-concept." Some students fail, and the schools respond by taking up curricular time with courses on study habits and how to take tests. The AIDS epidemic leads to special courses and instructions on using condoms; meanwhile, the epidemic of school failure is essentially ignored.

If one could find evidence that these frill courses actually eliminated crime, teen-age pregnancy, war, suicide, failure, and AIDS, there might be some grounds for including them in the curriculum. But the simpleminded idea that the schools should use their valuable time to address each problem, or that they could actually deal effectively with social problems, has put the real curriculum in danger. While students are starved for quality academic work, schools crowd their time with frills and foolishness. Some of these topics are important social issues, but the school is ill-equipped to address them.

There are several reasons to get the schools out of the social welfare business and back into teaching students the basics. First, schools have limited time and have other, more significant, purposes. Second, these topics are heavily laden with values, and our children should not be subjected to a teacher's interpretation of them. And third, it is folly to believe that students who have difficulty reading and calculating, or lack basic knowledge and experience, can adequately deal with such topics as crime and nuclear war.

Then there are the courses that have no important social value but which pander to fads and fun while taking up students' time and absorbing their interest. School time should not be devoted to classes on such absurd topics as Being Me, Making Conversation, Informed Shopping, Hairstyling, and All About Cars. Underwater Basket Weaving may only be a satirical course title to illustrate the silliness of some schoolwork, but there is a heavy layer of nonacademic school time in virtually every school. Spending curricular time on driver's education, school safety, baton twirling, school newspaper production, marching band, sports, home maintenance, and the like drains valuable time and energy from the study of literature, history, geography, math, and science.

Schools Fail Even in the Nonessentials

Even if we agreed that schools were appropriate places in which to study society's problems or make students feel good, have those problems been solved? If anything, we have even more social problems. The school has not been successful in teaching fundamentals, nor has it been successful in the misguided effort to correct all of society's ills or to produce "happy campers."

In examining the list of excessive tasks taken on by schools, we find only one that has been performed moderately well—and that at great cost. Driver's education may help young drivers slightly in gaining lower insurance premiums, but that has been accomplished by sacrificing valuable and limited school time, using expensive teachers in very inefficient settings with a small number of students, eliminating an area in which parents can pass on a skill to their children, and saddling school budgets with unnecessary costs for automobiles, insurance, equipment, and teaching time.

This is not a diatribe against teaching students how to drive well, but is an example of limited and costly success in a mistaken school curriculum enterprise.

Consider other items on the list. Is school the best, or even a good, place for children to learn parenting, self-respect, drug avoidance, safe sex, and morality? Daily newspaper stories show that parenting, self-respect, and morality have declined in American society, even as the schools teach these subjects. It is also clear that drug usage has not abated after school efforts to teach its dangers, and various types of unsafe sex practices seem to be at epidemic levels. The backbone of American society, the family, is eroded because these educative activities are given over to schools. The historic and suitable purposes of families include security and nurturing. The nurturing purpose is essentially educative, with families providing guidance and values for the young.

It is not by chance that family life has declined in the twentieth century as schools have begun to take over many family responsibilities. Contemporary family life, in the homes where parents still live together, appears to consist of a place in which to sleep and eat, to watch television, and to wave good-bye as the parents go to work or the child goes to school. How can children gain respect for their parents and other relatives when basic family responsibilities are given over to a government institution, where they are homogenized. And those families in which nurturing is taken seriously run the risk of a different set of values being taught in school. Obviously, this is particularly a problem for religious families.

Adjustment and Conformity

Among other items on the list of extraneous school responsibilities are adjustment to society, getting along with others, obtaining a job, behaving in public, and appreciating the arts. This listing smacks of Big Brother. One of America's claims to world leadership rests in our diversity. Who is to decide what adjustment, behaviors, and arts are to be honored? Do we want monolithic schooling that requires each student to adjust to whatever the school determines to be the good of society?

Life adjustment education, brought in by the "progressives" just after World War II, assumed that educators knew what society needed and would determine how students would adjust. It was a form of social engineering that failed. The emphasis was on vocational courses to prepare people for work, not to provide intellectual or cultural enrichment. It was based on the false premise that over half of America's students could not benefit from traditional learning, and were destined to have a working-class existence. This movement opposed academic study and substituted such trivial activities as learning to dance, playing party games, selecting good movies, and relieving the tensions of young people. This period of silly curricula has passed, thankfully, but some remnants remain in the schools.

A school curriculum built on current fads and the latest social issues is one that has no lasting value and cannot hope to prepare young people for productive lives. Similarly, a curriculum designed simply to make students feel better about themselves does not develop maturity; rather, it is likely only to exaggerate personal problems and dependency on others. Meanwhile, these kinds of curriculum rob students of important time and teacher energy that should be devoted to real education. There are many truly important things that students should be learning in schools, things that are more consistent with the basic purposes of education. We need to identify the essential skills needed for learning and the time-tested knowledge that all educated citizens should acquire. This is the basic rationale for compulsory schooling; otherwise, why require all children to attend school?

In a well-reasoned book, published almost half a century ago, historian Arthur Bestor (1953) called attention to this educational issue:

> The disciplined mind is what education at every level should strive to produce. . . . The idea that the school must undertake to meet every need that some other agency is failing to meet, regardless of the suitability of the classroom to the task, is a preposterous delusion that in the end can wreck the educational system without in any way contributing to the salvation of society. . . . The school promises too much on the one hand, and too little on the other, when it begins to think so loosely about its functions. (pp. 59, 75–76)

Bestor further proposed identification of the fundamentals needed in schools: "Educational reform must begin with the courageous assertion that all the various subjects and disciplines in the curriculum are *not* (author's emphasis) of equal value. Some disciplines are fundamental. . . ." It is those fundamental studies, the basic disciplines in science, math, language, and history, that should be returned to primacy in the schools. Bestor directed his attack to the progressive educationists who claimed not to "teach history," but to "teach children." He correctly pointed out the inanity of this claim and stated that children must be taught something, and he argued strongly for intellectual content. Bestor supports public education, but not education about nothing, or about everything but with no intellectual focus.

In more recent times, Gilbert Sewall, education editor of *Newsweek*, visited about thirty schools in eight states and reviewed all the current writings about schools. In summarizing his findings, he wrote of the contemporary American schools:

> For youngsters of all backgrounds and capabilities, academic outcomes are low and, at least until very recently, have been shrinking. Why? To begin with, few pupils at the secondary level are required to take courses in the basic subjects—language, math, history, science—in order to qualify for a high school diploma. . . . Even more disturbing, curricular revisions have steadily diluted course content. New syllabuses in basic subjects have appeared, purged of tedious or difficult units. Vacuous electives have proliferated, allowing some students to sidestep challenging courses altogether. . . . Endless courses in family life, personal adjustment, consumer skills, and business have crowded out more rigorous subjects, notably in science and foreign language. (Sewall, 1983, pp. 6, 7)

Sewall concludes his book with strong support for the teaching of fundamental disciplines and basic subjects, with high expectations and clear standards for student performance. He argues that the schools have taken on "new and distracting duties to care for every unfortunate and antisocial child, increasingly acting as flunkies and surrogates for self-absorbed, overburdened, or negligent parents" (p. 177). The schools should return to their primary purpose, allow other social institutions to conduct their proper social welfare functions, and recognize that the best route to vocational education is solid preparation in fundamental knowledge.

The depressing and distressing list of curricular failures in areas of fundamental knowledge indicates that the nation is at risk. We must move to correct the accumulated problems of education by a refocus on basic education.

Stress the Basics and Necessary Skills

There is no solid argument against the traditional skills of reading, writing, and arithmetic. Disputes arise in such matters as how these skills should be taught, for how long, and how to measure their mastery, but even hard-core "happy children" advocates agree that children need to be able to communicate in language and numbers.

That would seem sufficient to guarantee strong emphasis on these skills in schools. But there are serious problems. Large numbers of students are not acquiring these skills, and will suffer as they try to make their way in society. The society will suffer as well, since these otherwise productive workers will not have the capability to survive in employment (Szabo, 1992). And there are many other students who manage to pick up some fundamental skills, but not enough to be competitive. These young people are destined to have marginal positions in society, and to be recipients of social welfare programs.

One of the reasons the schools fail in even this basic curriculum is that insufficient time is spent to ensure that children master these skills. There are too many distractions in school, including the dumping-ground problems. A second reason for the failure is that the skills are taught in isolation from the disciplines of knowledge that students will confront as they go through school. Instead of reading literature or history, children learn to read from texts especially designed to avoid ideas and to present only insipid stories using "a limited vocabulary." A third reason, tied to the second one, is that schools do not expect enough of many students, and the children become bored and shut out education. Students in earlier periods could read complicated material that stretched their minds. Texts that are "dumbed down" to meet a minimal standard are demeaning to students and stultify their development.

Beyond the Fundamental Skills

Not only do we need to reemphasize the fundamental skills in elementary schools, but we need to insist upon rigorous evaluation of those skills before we allow students to continue in school. The purpose for stressing skills early, and requiring that students obtain them, is to permit full use of those skills in further study of important knowledge. Thus, we do a disservice to students who have not mastered the skills, as well as to those who have, if we merely pass them on to higher grades.

The knowledge we have acquired over a long period, and with great effort, is stored in the major disciplines that have traditionally been taught in schools. This is the intellectual and cultural heritage that all new generations must learn in order to preserve and extend the culture. The development of disciplines has assisted in establishing categories of knowledge and methods of study that make access to the cultural heritage easier and more systematic. Learning is difficult work, and should be, but study of the basic disciplines provides logical avenues that help in understanding.

The disciplines represent differing ways that humans have organized wisdom, and they offer the means to intellectual power. Among these basic disciplines are:

Math, because we live in a world where quantity and numerical relationships are important

Language, because accumulated knowledge is set down in various languages

Sciences, because they provide understanding of our environment and its workings

History, because an understanding of current life requires study of the past

Of course, there are other disciplines that one can study in becoming an educated person, but these are the basic ones that deserve focus in schools. These are the liberal arts disciplines, the purpose of which is to liberate people from ignorance. Although the liberal arts have changed over time, they still represent the storehouse of knowledge that an educated person requires. Modern society needs citizens who are prepared in math, language, science, and history in order to take on the responsibilities of democratic governance.

A thorough understanding of mathematical and scientific principles is necessary for life in a technological world. A thorough understanding of the humanities, represented by literature and history, is necessary if we are to comprehend the human condition and to communicate effectively. This combination is the essence of education. To proceed with schooling otherwise is to short-circuit the educative process and to condemn our children to ignorance.

Summary

The program of basic school studies takes time and concentration to follow. One cannot master fundamentals and our cultural heritage on a part-time basis, while devoting considerable time to such things as "getting along with others," "improving self-respect," and "learning how to learn." The focus on current fads and personal problems trivializes our heritage, consumes precious school time, and compromises the futures of our citizens. Furthermore, it is clear that schools have not solved social problems and, as a result of the time taken up with them, are not very successful in doing what they should be doing.

The most valuable education for individual students and for society is to build basic skills and emphasize the liberal arts disciplines.

POSITION 2:
TEACH FOR CRITICAL THINKING

Amid the turmoil that has accompanied school reform over the past twenty years, the most important purpose of schooling has been lost. In the clamor to improve student test scores on information recall, we have ignored the need to develop critical inquiry. A democratic nation cannot long survive on simple math and reading skills, or on a body of memorized standard information, when the world requires critical examination of issues and policies. It is absurd to argue that one should not be able to read, write, and calculate numbers, but it is equally absurd to argue that that should be the limit of a good education. The effort to return American schools to a period when memorization, recitation, and skill drill were the main activities is misguided and intellectually restrictive.

The primary purpose of schooling is to stimulate critical thinking in order for young people to improve themselves and the society. How can we hope to accomplish this lofty ideal if we continue to burden students with learning material irrelevant to their lives and to the future society, and rob them of the opportunity to raise questions about that material and the society?

Much of the past decade's school reform craze has focused on learning sterile trivia in order to pass tests designed by and for an earlier generation of students. We are so driven by silly concepts of competition for test scores that we limit the time left for creativity, innovation, and reflection on matters of importance to the child and to our future. Critical thinking has been abandoned by the one social institution that should most defend it. In an educational absurdity, students must seek opportunities to develop critical thinking by looking outside the school (Caywood, 1994).

A backward-looking curriculum and lack of mental stimulation combine to rob contemporary students of their right to a liberating education. School has become an onerous period of separation from reality. What is learned does not prepare students for understanding or reflecting on life. As Howard Gardner (1991a) expresses it: "Specifically, school knowledge seems strictly bound to school settings" (p. 119). Gardner's studies show that school teaching may show up in students' scores on school-related tests, but that has limited relation to improved knowledge of the real world (Gardner, 1991b).

Basic Education Is Not Critical Thinking

"Basic education" has become a code term to describe a sterile and conformist environment in which externally defined skills and lists of information are fed to children. It depends heavily on indoctrination and regurgitation; there is, presumably, one right way to learn and one set of right knowledge to obtain.

Critical thinking, however, is defined by Robert Ennis (1991) as "reasonably reflective thinking that is focused on deciding what to believe or do" (p. 6). It depends on engagement of the thinker in the process. You can't just tell someone to do critical thinking the same way that teachers in traditional schools try to explain history or science by lecturing. Critical thinking requires active involvement in the reflective act and goes well beyond the mechanical recitation of information imparted by a teacher or textbook. This means that the interests of students must be stimulated to activate their participation. Students, then, have a serious stake in critical thinking, and their interests and motivations cannot be ignored. Critical thinking cannot operate in top-down schooling, which has no regard for the learner or for real learning situations.

The artificiality of traditional basic education in schools is obvious. These schools are disconnected from society, from the lives of children, from families, and from reality. Bells signal when one is supposed to start learning. Children are drilled to memorize terms that have no meaning for them. Tidiness and punctuality substitute for thought. Platitudes about a life that is not recognizable in the children's existence are common. Students are required to learn categories of information that do not relate to their experience, and they are tested on trivial details. It is then falsely presumed that the students' scores represent what they know about the world. We pretend that this is preparation for life. School takes children who are living a real life and gives them artificiality, claiming that it is education.

Thus, school becomes something to be dreaded, a regimen of rules, boredom, inert ideas, and stuffiness. We all start with immense curiosity about the world, and most of us are eager to start school. That curiosity is stifled and that eagerness is dulled as we progress through schools that deny critical thinking. Isn't that an incredibly ironic situation? The institution intended to stimulate learning about the world is, instead, the institution that presents the most obstacles to that learning.

The academically successful student in such schools is usually not the most curious or creative, but the one best able to follow the teacher's directions and to take tests on what the books say. The schools reward conformity and obedience, not diversity and independence. Schooling becomes training, not education. Students become passive receptacles for accumulations of adult ideas, and student learning is defined by adult-constructed measures. The student is a bystander in schooling. Sizer's (1984) study of high school students showed them to be compliant and docile and to lack initiative. He attributed this to the heavy emphasis on getting right answers and to too little emphasis on being inquisitive. Goodlad (1983), after examining data from observations in over 1,000 classrooms, documented the high degree of passivity among students and the lack of time or concern given to student interests and opinions.

Students need, and deserve, to participate actively in the process of learning, and they require materials that test their imaginations, their prexisting conceptions, and their intellectual capacities (Duckworth, 1987; Bamberger, 1991; Begley, 1993; Tice, 1994). These are basic elements in developing critical thinking. School reform at the end of the twentieth century has glossed over this necessity in favor of the old-fashioned basic skill drill. We continue to suffer from this backward stance.

Students were the most hidden part of the school reform movement of the 1980s; in fact, they were essentially nonexistent. And the most ignored curriculum concern was critical thinking. Virtually every report, government statement, and proposed legislation focused on basic skills, the school organization, or the school officials. The concern was to make some organizational or operational change in the structure of the institution. No interest was shown in the students and their lives in school, and the idea of developing critical judgment as a primary school goal was lost in the pages of data on test scores. More tests, higher standards set by adults outside the school, longer school days and years, more homework, more stress on teachers and administrators, and less enjoyment in learning were the major educational achievements of the 1980s. Students and critical skills were ignored once again.

In a particularly clear-headed review of the 1980s reform movement, English teacher Susan Ohanian (1985) summarized the point:

> We must be ever wary of wasting some youngster's life just because of a dubious notion that a rigorous, regimented curriculum will help restore to the U.S. a better balance of trade. . . . At best, the recommendations of the commissions and task forces on school reform are hallucinatory; at worst, they are soul-destroying. Let us teachers not succumb to the temptation of asking what we can do for General Motors; let us continue to ask only what we can do for the children. (p. 321)

Wrong First Question

The essential concern in education should not be what is taught, but what is learned. For too long, we have posed the wrong question in considering the school curriculum. Certainly we need to consider what is, or should be, taught, but that is a secondary issue. The primary focus should be on what is, or should be, learned. We can't properly address what we want to have taught in schools without first determining the nature of learning and of the learners. The beginning of curriculum artificiality is the presumption that we can ignore the needs and interests of children and their long-term development in favor of a set of traditional pronouncements on what subjects must be taught.

The statement that children must learn to read and write and do arithmetic is a code phrase that satisfies some members of an older generation who believe that all must suffer what they suffered in learning useless information by rote. There is no doubt that communication and mathematics are necessary parts of an education, but they are too limited to be the main goal of schooling. These skills are important, but they are important because of their value to individual children in their experience and in the critical thinking necessary for social improvement. They are not important simply because previous generations had to learn them. The view that everyone has to learn the same information in the same way leads to a stultifying standardization, but one that is easily measured. Information is essential, but why must everyone know the same things? The pronouncement that only that knowledge considered important by certain adults can be important to children only satisfies those adults. However, it is not adult satisfaction but human experience that determines what knowledge is of value.

The pronouncement that school should be a place of devotion to discipline and high test scores is satisfying to those who would restrict freedom and control others. Discipline and high standards are nothing more than means to ensure social conformity and restriction. Individual creativity, human development, and rational social purposes should be the goals of schools, not externally required discipline and standards. This is not a new school problem, but it has recurred in the current age of educational repression.

Half a century ago, John Dewey's remarkably cogent book, *Experience and Education,* differentiated between traditional and progressive education on the basis of a history of educational theory that "is marked by opposition between the idea that education is development from within and that it is formation from without. . . ." (Dewey, 1938, p. 17) He notes that traditional education consists of information and skills that "have been worked out in the past," that standards and rules of conduct are prescribed by adults, and that the school operates as though it were separate from the lives of children and the rest of society. The subject matter and the rules of conduct are imposed on children, and the attitude of pupils must "be one of docility, receptivity, and obedience" (p. 18).

Progressive education, Dewey says, arose as a product of discontent with this traditional approach to imposition from above and outside the child. This discontent is expressed as opposites:

> To imposition from above is opposed expression and cultivation of individuality; to external discipline is opposed free activity; to learning from texts and teachers, learning through experience; to acquisition of isolated skills and techniques by drill, is opposed acquisition of them as a means of attaining ends which make direct vital appeal; to preparation for a more or less remote future is opposed making the most of opportunities of present life; to static aims and materials is opposed acquaintance with a changing world. (p. 20)

Unfortunately, the schools have never taken progressive education seriously. Cosmetic changes have made schools appear more humane, but they have not shed their basic, misplaced authoritarian and traditional efforts to impose selected information and morals on children. Traditional education sought to pour information into students, discouraging critical thinking and creativity. Schools continue to teach as though education were not life, but preparation for some later event. They ignore individual children in favor of standardization of curriculum and test scores.

The premise for education must be the child's development, not the adult's categories of knowledge, values, and proper behavior. When we focus on subjects that must be taught, we are inclined to forget about the students and thinking. We are more likely to produce lists of things we were taught that we wish to impose on students. We introduce the teacher as an authority, rather than as a wise guide. And we structure the schools to destroy systematically the creative interests of children by forcing all to learn the same material.

A focus on what is to be learned permits consideration of the learner. Of course, it is possible to avoid that consideration by assuming that what is learned is what is taught, but that only continues the artificiality of the school. What is learned is what has meaning for the student, no matter what is taught and what is on the examination. It is this focus on the learner that makes what is learned the primary question.

Natural and Unnatural Learning

There is a substantial battle in the long history of educational thought between those who think that people learn naturally from within and those who believe that external force must be brought to assure learning. This battle is illustrated currently by the difference of opinion between those who want freedom in school for students to pursue their natural inclinations to learn and those who want to impose a set of conditions and ideas on the minds and actions of students. It can also be illustrated by a quote from a book by Nat Henthoff (1977):

> One afternoon as we were walking down the street, Paul Goodman turned to me and said, "Do you realize that if the ability to walk depended on kids being taught walking as a subject in school, a large number of citizens would be ambulatory only if they crawled." (p. 53)

The first position, freedom, does not mean license for students to do whatever they please. Among the false criticisms of progressive education, and of John Dewey's work, is that the child determines everything. That is either a misreading or a calculated attempt to discredit the position. Dewey insisted that the most mature person in the classroom, the teacher, must ultimately have responsibility for what is taught, but that the teacher's decision must be predicated on the needs and interests of the child. It is the child, or learner, who determines what is learned. Thus, the child-centered, or learner-centered, curriculum is designed first with the child's development in mind. The teacher must, in this curriculum, remain sensitive to the learner. License to do whatever one pleases, whether teacher or learner, is inconsistent with this view. Freedom encourages innovations and stimulates critical thinking.

The learner-centered curriculum is in opposition to the subject- or discipline-centered curriculum, where the decision on what is taught starts with consideration of how the discipline is organized. The traditional discipline-centered curriculum represents the imposition of information, categories, and ideas without regard to the learner. In these terms, it is an unnatural and external structuring of what is learned. The learner-centered curriculum rests on the conviction that students want to learn. What destroys that natural curiosity is the authoritarian nature of traditional approaches to schooling.

Defects in the Traditional Structure of Schooling

The discipline-centered school has several defects. It imposes an externally determined body of information on children, it ignores natural learning interests and stifles curiosity and creativity, and it requires schools to be places of authoritarianism. This last point, the authoritarianism of schools, deserves further discussion. If one starts with the premise that children are curious, imaginative, and eager to learn, then what happens to make schools become places of restriction and stultification for many students? There are many reasons, but they focus on the fact that schools traditionally have been expected to homogenize individual children into an adult view of what society should be.

The structure of traditional schooling is consistent with the old-fashioned view that schools should be cheerless places where the young are trained to become adults by learning what adults think they should know and behaving in the way that adults think they should behave. Schools are expected to impart to the younger generation skills and information that are based on the past; they are expected to train students to behave according to a set of rules and standards; and they are to do it all as efficiently as possible in order to save time and tax money.

Perceived in this manner, schools are organized to distill the adult world for children, to impose a set of ideas and morals on them, and to require them to undergo processing as though they were in a food-packing or auto-assembly plant. As a result, schools classify students by grade and test scores to make teaching more efficient, set up severe time schedules, and rely on teacher or textbook presentation of standard information, required courses, and excessive testing to ensure that all have been trained the same way.

As a result, traditional schools are static institutions that stress conformity and adult concepts that have limited meaning in the lives of students. Yet students are dynamic, growing, and concerned about their own individuality. It is remarkable that the resilience of youth permits them to survive in such a stifling environment. Good teachers recognize this paradox between traditional schooling and the needs of youth, and they try to find ways to match static material with a changing society. They also ameliorate the requirements for conformity by trying to recognize the individual differences among students. And they attempt to enlarge the students' horizons by building on their experiences. But these efforts by good teachers are undermined by the traditional structure of schooling, by standardized tests, and by pressure from vocal advocates of the past.

In traditional schools, we reward those who do as we tell them to do whether or not it involves thinking. The main purpose of much schooling is to have students get "right answers," not to have them engage in critical thinking. The thinking student might challenge the way the school operates, the uninteresting material, the stress on conformity, and why certain answers are "right." Schools are not usually designed to respond to such challenges, and the teachers and administrators often resort to fear, ridicule, repression, and isolation to squelch them. Students learn quickly that it does not pay to raise serious questions, and they withdraw into the safer haven of going along.

Schools present artificial barriers to learning, and they stimulate fear and repression. The typical student responds to school in one of the following ways:

Drop out

Slip through

Fail

Find satisfaction in extracurricular activities

Learn teacher-pleasing behavior and do well

Ignore the school rules and suffer penalties

Wait for something more interesting

None of these responses represents the best form of intellectual development. Do we think our schools are excellent when large numbers of students drop out, fail, or turn off their curiosity?

Student and Teacher Experiences

The primary way that people learn, as opposed to being taught, is through experience. It is an active process, not a static one. When we are involved in some physical activity, such as organizing a group project, building a model village, playing a game, or measuring a room, we are learning. We make errors, seek advice, modify actions, and gain understanding in a real situation. Most teachers will admit, for example, that they learned the most about a subject when they had to teach it, not when they were sitting in a college class. We learn more about cars by trying to fix them than by being told how to fix them.

Not all experiential learning involves physical activity or actual situations. Such vicarious experiences as reading a book or listening to a speaker can provide pertinent learning. And, of course, it is impossible, and not even desirable, for students physically to experience all situations in which learning could occur. Active engagement, mental or physical, is what produces learning.

Curiosity, interest, or the need to resolve a problem makes reading or listening a learning situation in which active engagement can take place. Simply being told that something is important, or that something must be learned for a test, does not necessarily stimulate active engagement. Perfunctory reading of a book or listening to a teacher may appear to be learning, but the active mind of the student may be off on a different tangent. The teacher teaches and assigns readings; the student appears to be listening and reading, but what is learned? The student has learned to cope with dry and uninteresting material in a school of boring routine and hourly tasks. That is not the experience that good teachers desire, and many are themselves tired of the dullness and boredom. Certainly, it is not the experience the students desire. But it is the way that traditional schools operate in too many places.

It is clear that not all experiences are equally beneficial as learning situations; some are actually detrimental. We may like the taste of excessively fatty and salty foods, but that can lead to poor nutritional habits. The smoking of cigarettes may lead to health problems. It may take only one experience of jumping out of a window to stop learning entirely. It is not simply experience that matters, but the quality and developmental nature of that experience. The teacher's role, then, becomes one of seeking and providing experiences for students that stimulate their interest and enrich their learning. Success, of course, depends on the wisdom and knowledge of the teacher and on the teacher's sensitivity to the students. As noted previously, it is in a learner-centered curriculum that the teacher's role is one of guiding and challenging rather than of acting as an authority and keeper of the truth.

The Subjects Learned

The learner-centered curriculum might appear to have no content, to be so loose and free that nothing intellectual is accomplished. Actually, the opposite is true. In the tightly organized and past-oriented traditional curriculum, the meticulously structured content is largely without meaning in the lives of students, and memorizing material for a test is scarcely intellectual. A properly developed learner-centered curriculum, however, requires the intellectual involvement of students in examining topics those students can comprehend and utilize in their own development. What is lacking in the learner-centered curriculum are what Alfred North Whitehead so eloquently derided in his 1929 classic, *The Aims of Education*, as "'inert ideas'—that is to say, ideas that are merely received into the mind without being utilised, or tested, or thrown into fresh combinations" (Whitehead, 1929, p. 13). He goes on to note that education is "overladen with inert ideas." And he states that "education with inert ideas is not only useless: it is, above all things, harmful. . . ."

The traditional school is filled with inert ideas, those bits and pieces of information that fit no pattern and have no vitality for most students. Consider the standard school day: students go from English class, with a mixed lesson on spelling, vocabulary, and story reading; to history, where they hear about America's victory in some past war; to science, where they watch the teacher mix chemicals; to math, where they put answers on the chalkboard; to art, where they draw; and to gym, where they do calisthenics and study the rules of a game. Every period of inert ideas is followed by another period of different, and apparently unrelated, inert ideas. Each teacher acts as though his or her ideas are very important, and will be on the test, and the student goes through the expected motions. Schools are like giant jigsaw puzzles, except that the box cover with the picture of the completed puzzle is missing.

The material taught—which is different from what is learned—is a series of disconnected and lifeless bits of information that have little meaning to students. The student learns that English is separate from history, which is separate from economics and science and math and the arts and physical education. And the student learns that school is separate from life, and certainly from social and individual problems. How can a student understand and try to resolve a personal or a social problem using traditional school subjects? Are shyness, feelings of failure, apprehension, death in the family, and acne the kinds of problems that traditional subjects can address? Does the student see problems of poverty, alcoholism, war, and human rights as resolvable by using the bits and pieces learned in math or science or history or English as taught in the schools? Is it reasonable for students to suffer school, and look forward to life outside of school? That is an inversion of what school should be, and what knowledge should provide.

Subjects taught in the traditional manner are not intellectual; they do not stimulate thinking and the consideration of diverse ideas. Intellectual vitality arises out of life, not out of the unrelated segments of knowledge we throw at students. We need to abolish this disconnectedness and restore the vitality of learning. That does not mean that we ignore or destroy the information gained from scholarly study of a subject; it means that we need to help students understand the connections that make knowledge valuable and learn how to utilize that knowledge in solving problems.

Knowledge and Problems

We need to focus on what knowledge is important for students to use in dealing with human problems. Thus, we must start with those problems and find what knowledge exists that can help us understand and address them. That is certainly different from the old-fashioned approach, which starts with categories of subjects and presumes that they need to be learned regardless of their value to the learner. Real human problems cannot be treated simply as literature or history or chemistry problems. Under the traditional curriculum, teachers resort to contrived "problems" in each of the subjects in an attempt to motivate student interest. Standard math story problems are notoriously unreal; American history usually presents problems that the student sees as already resolved and unrelated to current life. Why not start with a problem the students can easily identify, and then find knowledge—regardless of the subject field from which it comes—that can be utilized in solving that problem? This method recognizes knowledge as interrelated and useful, not as compartmentalized and ornamental.

The adult and traditional manner of organizing knowledge into apparently discrete categories, such as English and American literature, physics, political science, drawing, biology, algebra, European and American history, botany, geometry, economics, psychology, chemistry, and drama, may work well for those who devote their careers to advanced study in these areas. (Interestingly, some of the most advanced thinkers in each of these fields recognize the connections among subjects and seek to find theories that draw fields together rather than separate them.) These distinct categories may not be as useful for students in elementary and secondary schools, where there is a greater need to see that knowledge is seamless and valuable in examining life's problems.

The identification of problems to study should be a mutual process, with students and teacher jointly engaged. Some pervasive human problems revolve around such values as justice, equality, freedom, democracy, and human rights. And there are myriad individual problems that are related to these. They require knowledge from such fields as math, science, history, economics, psychology, literature, the arts, and politics. They also require skills in reading, writing, calculating, organizing, categorizing, and critical thinking. As students mature, they develop interests in different problems, types of knowledge, and levels of skills. An active problems approach to learning, based on student interests and freedom, leads to the development of critical thinking.

Summary

Traditional schooling continues to emphasize rote memory, achieving high scores on tests on relatively trivial material, and amassing information taught for its own sake. There is a lack of connection to students and their lives, and critical thinking is suppressed because it disrupts the teacher's authoritarian role. Schooling should, instead, open ideas that stimulate students to examine their own experiences and to engage in a critical examination of social problems. That requires a new focus on students and critical thinking.

Students come in a variety of personalities, backgrounds, and interests. We need a curriculum that recognizes this variety as an opportunity and sees the students as a dynamic resource. The static traditional curriculum pushes them into molds and stamps them with a list of subjects studied. The learner-centered critical thinking curriculum enhances the student's curiosity and energy, and utilizes knowledge in addressing human problems.

For Discussion

1. Construct and defend a hypothetical school curriculum that you believe would assure that:
   a. Graduates could be able to operate successfully in society.
   b. Individual students' rights and interests would be given credible expression.
   c. Critical thinking would have as high a priority as you think appropriate.
2. The Children's Defense Fund, a nonprofit national organization that lobbies for the improvement of services for children, notes that the United States gives about $8 billion in military aid to countries that our undereducated children can't even find on a map.

   The implication is that either we should cut back on military aid or we should improve basic education in geography. Are there other implications? Are these collateral or competing ideas? Would you conclude that the Children's Defense Fund is in support of basic education or of critical thinking?

   Would you expect strong supporters of increased basic education to support the use of military or defense funds to pay for that increase?

   Source: The State of America's Children, 1991. Washington, DC: Children's Defense Fund.

3. Given your experiences as a student in different levels of schooling, which of the following potential school topics would you identify as a frill? Which are fundamentals? On what basis do you make the distinction?

   Athletics
   Group play
   Penmanship
   Landscaping
   American history
   Writing letters
   Games and rules
   Movies, newspapers, television
   Literary classics
   Balancing a checkbook
   Advanced science and math
   Japanese, Russian, Chinese, and Spanish languages
   Astrology
   Myths and legends
   Latin and Greek
   Social living
   Economic theory
   Parts of speech
   Clothing design

   What would you add that is clearly a frill? What could be added that is obviously a fundamental?

4. If the roles of adults and children were reversed to allow children to determine what adults should know for a basic education, what would be the likely curriculum?

References

Bamberger, J. (1991). *The Mind Behind the Musical Ear.* Cambridge, MA: Harvard University Press.

Begley, S. (1993). "Doin' What Doesn't Come Naturally." *Newsweek* **122,** 84.

Bestor, A. (1953). *Educational Wastelands.* Urbana: University of Illinois Press.

Caywood, C. (1994). "Critical Thinking: A Critical Need." *School Library Journal* **40,** 46.

Dewey, J. (1938). *Experience and Education.* New York: Macmillan.

Duckworth, E. (1987). *The Having of Wonderful Ideas and Other Essays.* New York: Teachers College Press.

Elias, M., and Kress, J. (1994). "Social Decision-Making and Life Skills Development." *Journal of School Health* **64** (2), 62–66.

Ennis, R. (1991). "Critical Thinking: A Streamlined Conception." *Teaching Philosophy* **14,** 5–24.

Finn, C. (1995) "The School." *Commentary* **99,** 6–10.

Fortune. (1990). Special Issue: "Saving Our Schools." Spring, p. 121.

Gardner, H. (1991a). "The Tensions Between Education and Development." *Journal of Moral Education* **20,** 113–125.

———— (1991b). *The Unschooled Mind.* New York: Basic Books.

Goodlad, J. (1983). *A Place Called School.* New York: McGraw-Hill.

Henthoff, N. (1977). *Does Anybody Give a Damn?* New York: Knopf.

National Assessment of Educational Progress (1994). *NAEP 1992 Trends in Academic*

Progress. National Center for Educational Statistics. Washington, DC: US Department of Education.

National Commission on Excellence in Education. (1983). *A Nation at Risk.* Washington, DC: U.S. Department of Education.

National Review. (1990). "Knowing So Much About So Little (Poor Performance of American Schools)." *National Review* **42,** 14–15.

Ohanian, S. (1985). "Huffing and Puffing and Blowing the Schools Excellent." *Phi Delta Kappan* **66,** 316–321.

Peltzman, S. (1994). *USA Today.* **122,** 22–25.

Perry, N. J. (1993). "School Reform: Big Pain, Little Gain." *Fortune* **128,** 130–135.

"Political Factors in Public School Decline." (1994). *The American Enterprise* **4,** 44–49.

Ravitch, D. and Finn, C. (1987). *What Do Our 17-Year-Olds Know?* New York: Harper & Row.

Richburg, R. (1994). "Jump-Start Thinking." *The Social Studies* **85** (2), 33–35.

Rosenberg, A. (1994). "Futurescape." *Instructor* **103** (6), 44–45, 84.

Samuelson, R. J. (1991). "The School Reform Fraud." *Newsweek* **117,** 44.

Sewall, G. T. (1983). *Necessary Lessons: Decline and Renewal in American Schools.* New York: Free Press.

Shaw, P. (1993). "The Competitiveness Illusion: Does our Country Need to Be Literate in Order to Be Competitive? If Not, Why Read?" *National Review* **45,** 41–45.

Sizer, T. (1984). *Horace's Compromise: The Dilemma of the American High School.* Boston: Houghton Mifflin.

Szabo, J. C. (1992). "Boosting Workers' Basic Skills." *Nation's Business* **80,** 38–41.

Tice, T. N. (1994). "Critical Plus Open." *Education Digest* **59,** 42–44.

Time. (1989). "Mixed Review: Some Progress, More Needed." *Time* **133,** 68.

USA Today. (1990). "Skills Lacking for Tomorrow's Jobs." *USA Today* **119,** 11+.

Whitehead, A. N. (1929). *The Aims of Education.* New York: Macmillan.

CHAPTER EIGHT

Multicultural Studies: Representative or Divisive

POSITION 1:
FOR A MULTICULTURAL PERSPECTIVE

When I am asked to talk about the opening of the American mind, or the decentering of the humanities, or the new multiculturalism . . . I have to say my reaction is pretty much Mahatma Gandhi's when they asked him what he thought about Western civilization. He said he thought it would be a very good idea. (Gates, 1992, p. 105)

Curricula are not simply *there*, natural objects that somehow arise from the accumulated wisdom of the past. Rather, curricula are often the results of political settlements, compromises over what is important to know. Spencer's question—What knowledge is of most worth?—has been expanded to include another—Whose knowledge is of most worth? (Goodson, Meyer, and Apple, 1991, p. iii)

The Best That Is Thought and Known?

The multiculturalist movement reminds us that the study of school subjects is not the study of neutral knowledge. Schooling is never without political messages or political purpose. Curriculum writers choose certain heroes, events, and values to praise, and, at the same time, they shift other people, other events, and other values to the margins of academic consideration or ignore them altogether. Students are likely to hear more about the fictionalized childhood experiences of George Washington and Abraham Lincoln than about the real lives of people like themselves. No matter what their color, gender, or ancestry, students in English and social studies are more likely to read books by western white Christian men than by any other group of authors. Asian-American students, African-American students, Puerto Rican students, and Mexican-American students will learn to prize the activities and ideas of European Americans. What is often lost to these students is attention to the cultural variations of other groups, including their own (Takaki, 1993). Teaching a narrow view of our cultural heritage is done at the expense of the self-concept of each student, whose identity goes unrecognized and undervalued in the process.

Multiculturalists argue that groups previously marginalized or excluded because of gender, class, race, or sexual orientation must be given representation in the school curriculum. Public schools should be places where the stories of many different groups are heard. The curriculum should represent the perspectives of women as well as of men, of the poor as well as of the rich, and schools should celebrate the heroism not only of generals, but also of those who are victorious in the struggles of everyday life. In a multiculturally reconfigured curriculum, the voices of all Americans would find legitimacy and academic consideration (Apple, 1979, 1982). The nation would be united by examining its citizens' commonalities as well as their diversities. Unfortunately, not many schools offer a multicultural curriculum. Most follow a curriculum that is a standardized presentation of the dominant culture. Instead of being tailored to reflect the varied needs and aspirations of the children in the classroom, the curriculum is, by design, an idealized, uncritical account of what society believes children should know.

Borrowing from Matthew Arnold, traditional curriculum writers characterized schools as beacons of a single, high culture, passing on the best that is thought and known in the world. Writing in the late nineteenth century, Arnold, a literary critic, poet, and educator, fretted about what he saw as the "vulgar" tastes of the economically powerful but culturally unformed middle classes of England. He believed—as do many of those who now control the curricula of public schools—that appropriate tastes, judgments, and appreciations could and should be dictated from above. Members of the English upper class of Arnold's day, although losing their economic dominance, considered themselves culturally superior, possessing the most appropriate tastes, habits, and virtues. Arnold believed the middle classes would be better off if they followed the lead of their social betters. Those in power defined the behaviors, knowledge, and virtues that the schools were to celebrate and pass on to the next generation. Reflecting traditional values rather than actual merit, one body of literature came to dominate. One set of writers, poets, artists, and musicians was judged superior to others. One body of knowledge was taught in the schools, and other forms were ignored. Politically powerful minorities, in Europe and the United States, imposed their views on everyone else.

Different Voices

By the late 1980s, increasing numbers of parents and their children demanded that, in recognition of our pluralistic society and our democratic ends, American schools open the curriculum to wider representation. The United States comprises a wide range of cultural perspectives based on race, religion, class, exceptionality, geography, and ethnic origin (Gollnick and Chinn, 1983; Banks, 1993). No one viewpoint is assumed to be better than the others, and all viewpoints can make a claim to legitimacy. In order that students understand the complex mix of perspectives found in the United States, they must be encouraged to view American society through various cultural lenses. The schools must be open to the widest presentation of competing views.

Curricula are political as well as academic, and curriculum change is always a slow-moving process characterized by widespread disagreements. Be careful—the argument between multiculturalists and traditionalists is not a simple academic debate about textbooks or approved reading lists: the struggle over the curriculum is a political battle about the control of knowledge. Sort through the rhetoric carefully. Assess the arguments by asking which groups would benefit if a particular curricular orientation were pursued. Read the critics skeptically. If you were to believe the critics of multiculturalism, you might conclude that its proponents are bent on destroying not only the schools, but the whole of western civilization. E. D. Hirsch (1987), for example, tried to convince his readers that the nation would disintegrate unless schools required all students to study a common curriculum. Allan Bloom (1987) warned that multiculturalism poses the threat of cultural relativism, a disease that would likely cause the decline of the west. Another critic of multiculturalism, Diane Ravitch, asks you to recall the elementary school curriculum of what she clearly believes to have been a better time, the first decade of the twentieth century.

> Most children read (or listened to) the Greek and Roman myths and folklore from the "oriental nations" . . . The third grade in the public schools of Philadelphia studied "heroes of legend and history," including Joseph; Moses; David; Ulysses; Alexander; Roland; Alfred the Great; Richard the Lion Hearted; Robert Bruce; William Tell; Joan of Arc; Peter the Great; Florence Nightingale. (Ravitch, 1987, p. 8)

This represents a rich literature, to be sure, but, like the canon championed by Hirsch and Bloom, it is skewed toward a white, western, male orientation. No people of other races were represented in classroom readings during the "good old days," and in order for women to find their way into the curriculum, they either had to be burned at the stake or to pioneer as nurses! Henry Louis Gates, Jr., refers to this as the antebellum aesthetic position, "when men were men, and men were white . . . when women and persons of color were voiceless, faceless servants and laborers, pouring tea and filling brandy snifters in the boardrooms in the old boys' clubs" (Gates, 1992, p. 17).

Multicultural Perspectives

What do the multiculturalists want? Are they a threat to the social cohesion of the country? Are they trying to impose a political correctness on all Americans? Consider some of the multiculturalist arguments for curriculum change in the schools and decide for yourselves.

It should be understood from the beginning that multiculturalists are a diverse group that includes feminists, Afrocentrists, social critics, and a lot of people who defy labels but who simply want the variety of American culture to be transmitted more faithfully to their children. The charge that multiculturalists want to purge the school curriculum of western culture is false. Multiculturalism is not designed to eliminate the contributions of white men from the curriculum and substitute the experiences of women, gays, African-Americans, and other exploited and disadvantaged persons (Sobol, 1993). Multiculturalists are asking for a fair share of curricular attention, for an honest representation of the poor as well as the powerful, and for the reasonable treatment of minority as well as majority cultures. The United States is a multicultural country, and our ethnic and religious mix is becoming increasingly diverse owing to recent changes in the immigration laws and the influx of people from non-European countries. Whatever the outcome of the current struggle over cultural representation in the curriculum, the world of our students is already multicultural (Gates, 1992, p. xvi). The curriculum must reflect the society or become irrelevant to the students' lives.

The multiculturalist reaction against the traditional curriculum can be thought of as a "victims' revolution," a repudiation of the top-down approach to literature, art, music, and history. It is a demand for change by those who have been discounted and otherwise harmed by traditional approaches to schooling. Multiculturalism demands a more inclusive telling of the tale, one that weaves the experiences of the disadvantaged and the marginalized into the tapestry of America's rise to prominence. Multiculturalism is a call for fairness and for a better representation of the contributions of all Americans. Multiculturalists do not discount the role that the curriculum plays in developing a cohesive, national identity. At the same time, however, schools must guarantee that all students can preserve their ethnic, cultural, and economic identities (Banks, 1994).

Schools must teach multiple perspectives, in the name of fairness and historical accuracy. For example, school textbooks typically emphasize the roles played by the white abolitionists of the nineteenth century and the struggles of white people to achieve integration in the twentieth century. This is, of course, appropriate. Many white people have played vital and significant parts in the battle for social justice. But these same textbooks typically minimize the ways in which African-Americans resisted slavery, as well as their efforts to achieve integration and equality (Asante, 1991). These omissions alienate young African-American students and present an unfair picture to white students. The story of slavery must be told from many sides. A multiculturally educated person would be able to see the slave trade from the view of the white slave trader, as well as from the perspective of the enslaved people. Similarly, schools should ask students to consider westward expansion in the United States from the point of view of native Americans, as well as from that of the pioneers. Urban issues should be seen from the perspectives of social reformers, landlords, and inner-city residents.

Multiculturalism should find its way into every corner of the curriculum and at every grade level and not be restricted to high schools or to classes in social studies. Research indicates that young children come to school with many misconceptions about outside ethnic groups, and the schools are particularly effective in modifying these attitudes, especially in the earlier grades (Banks, 1993). Professor Ladson-Billings recommends that primary grade teachers, when presenting the story of "Cinderella," teach it fully, incorporating its many versions. They might begin with the familiar tale from the brothers Grimm, but they also should include variations in the story from China, Egypt, and Zimbabwe (Ladson-Billings, 1994, p. 23). By examining varying standards of beauty and differences in character behavior and plot, teachers can encourage young students to appreciate the ways in which culture produces similarities and differences in values and behavior. The point is not to replace one group's story with another, but to tell the story more fully. To include women, the poor, and minorities is not to be out of step with the lessons of culture or history; it is only a departure from the ways in which these lessons traditionally have been presented to schoolchildren.

Monoculturalism = Minority Alienation

Anyone familiar with schools knows that the most effective way to teach is to make the students' experiences central to the interpretation of school knowledge. A curriculum has more meaning when students find characters like themselves in the books they read, and instruction has a better chance of engaging students when the subject matter speaks to the cultural experiences of the students and their families. Exclusion of particular students and their history from the school literature alienates the students and destroys educational achievement. New immigrants from Asia and Latin America need to know about the lands they left, their new home, and their varied new neighbors. They need to examine the cultural baggage they have brought with them so that they can better understand how it fits in with the cultures that shape America. These children need to know that a pluralistic society welcomes cultural differences, and that they do not have to distance themselves from their families and traditions to be considered "good Americans." Schools in a democratic society have no choice but to be multicultural. Children who find themselves and their culture underrepresented in the school curriculum cannot help but feel lost and resentful. Without a multicultural emphasis, minority children are made to feel like outsiders. As Asante (1991) writes:

> The little African American child who sits in a classroom and is taught to accept as heroes and heroines individuals who defamed African people is being actively de-centered, dislocated, and made into a nonperson, one whose aim in life might be to one day shed that "badge of inferiority": his or her Blackness. (p. 171)

If the multiculturalist argument sounds like the rhetoric of the 1960s, it is. In the 1960s, high school students and teachers proposed new courses, and teachers encouraged greater latitude in reading and writing assignments. As a result of the civil rights movement, universities opened their doors to African-American students, and curriculum reform was not far behind. Other under-represented minority groups followed, and together "they developed courses on the Harlem Renaissance, rediscovered Zora Neale Hurston, Virginia Woolf, and the history of working people" (Perry and Fraser, 1993, p. 11). African-American courses, Latino studies, and Women's studies flourished. Then, in the 1970s and 1980s, a conservative school agenda, couched in the rhetoric of the "excellence" movement, stripped students and teachers of their control over the curriculum (Aronowitz and Giroux, 1991). Locally developed curricula focusing on the community and its cultural needs were sacrificed to statewide programs. There was a national, collective handwringing about what students did not know and what they could not do. A new call for "excellence" and a narrowly focused core curriculum forced multicultural approaches to instruction to be shelved before their effectiveness could be given a fair test.

Multiculturalism has been revitalized in the 1990s. School critics have come to realize that something is needed to reinvigorate the curriculum to make it more attractive to all students. Schools are being asked to attend to the learning styles of their students and their special needs. Subject matter is not to be passed on uncritically from one generation to another. The nature of what is studied must be broadened to include the experiences of those from varied cultural backgrounds, and no matter what textbook is used, its content must be examined for the cultural messages it contains and omits. Textbooks must relate to the experiences of the students who must be encouraged to give meaning to the texts, as well as to derive knowledge from them. School readings are to be unlocked for the messages they contain, but they also should be susceptible to the students' interpretations. When students are assigned *Romeo and Juliet*, for example, they are asked to read it as a romantic tragedy, but also to consider it in relation to their own experiences with forbidden love and to examine various courtship traditions. The goal of the multiculturalists is to bend education around the lives of the students so that all students can have a real chance at school success.

A Bold Step Toward a Multicultural Curriculum

Several years ago, the New York State commissioner of education invited scholars and curriculum writers to review the appropriateness of the state's K–12 social studies curriculum and recommend changes, if needed.* Reviewers were asked to examine the curriculum and address questions about its fairness and balance. Did this curriculum speak to the needs of female students as well as male students, of African-Americans and Asian-Americans as well as

---

*For a more detailed examination of multicultural curriculum reform in New York and California, see Cornbleth, C. and Wauch, D. (1995). *The Great Speckled Bird: Multicultural Politics and Educational Policymaking.* New York: St. Martin's Press.

European Americans, of the disadvantaged as well as the advantaged? On the basis of the reviewers' recommendations, New York developed a new curriculum that promises to bring a fresh focus to the treatment of all students in the state.

The New York curriculum writers recognized that minorities were not being fairly represented. Although the nation had opened its doors to millions of new immigrants, their ways of life, their food, their religions, and their histories were not to be found in the curriculum. Instead, the new immigrants were being socialized according to an "Anglo-American model" (New York State, 1991). Despite demographic projections that by the middle of the next century white Anglo-Saxon Protestants will be a minority in this country, we are still asking new immigrants to exchange their family's rituals for a homogenized American culture. The unstated curricular message is that new immigrants must abandon the culture of their forebears and learn to prize the literature, history, traditions, and holidays of the Anglo-American Founding Fathers.

This is a familiar model of cultural assimilation. Proponents of state-funded education in the nineteenth century had encouraged schools to teach immigrants social behaviors and patriotic rituals that were designed to encourage "Americanization." Such assimilation worked reasonably well for the white Europeans who came to this country in the nineteenth century, but it did not work for other immigrants, and now, in the face of new immigration patterns, it seems to be an untenable ideal. A significant demographic difference distinguishes today's immigrants from those of the last century. In the nineteenth century, most of the nation's voluntary immigrants were from Europe, and socialization toward an Anglo-American model of behavior may not have been terribly discontinuous with their heritage. Now, in the twentieth century, the majority of immigrants are from Asia and South America. People newly arrived from Korea and Colombia are less likely to find cultural resonance in the Anglo-American cultural ideal than did those who came to the United States from Ireland, Germany, and Italy.

The revised New York State curriculum report acknowledges the importance of socialization and nation-building for America's increasingly diverse population, but it also fosters respect for the right to cultural diversity. No longer should immigrants—old or new—be encouraged to abandon their cultural past in order to be considered Americans. If the report's recommendations are implemented, schools will be asked to reflect the cultural diversity of the nation by helping students develop a multicultural perspective. As defined by the report:

> A multicultural perspective, then, means that all of the applicable viewpoints of the historical and social protagonists should be explored, paying special attention to the ways in which race, ethnicity, gender and class generate different ways of understanding, experiencing, and evaluating the events of the world. Because interpretations vary as experiences differ, a multicultural perspective must necessarily be a multiple perspective that takes into account the variety of ways in which any topic can be comprehended. (New York State, 1991, p. 17)

Social Construction of Reality

The New York curriculum report recognizes that reality is socially constructed. Social reality—those taken-for-granted beliefs about life, such as who we are and how we should behave—is shaped by the books we read, the ways in which we discuss ideas, and the cultural perspectives of our schools and families. The subject matter that is taught in schools should be treated as provisional, as is all knowledge. "Knowledge," as the New York report reminds us, "is the product of human beings located in specific times and places; consequently, much of our subject matter must be understood as tentative" (New York State, 1991, p. 29).

In a pluralistic society, students must learn that there are many and varied sets of socially constructed realities. We believe what we do, in part, because of who we are and how we were raised. Knowledge about the social world is not objective, but is a human product that differs in composition for different groups of people, based on their cultural differences and unique histories. Schools must encourage students to develop a broad understanding, often from competing viewpoints. Students must be taught to appreciate the different social realities stemming from human differences, such as in language, gender, socioeconomic class, religion, sexual orientation, and age, and from being physically challenged. One of the guiding principles in the New York plan is that teaching "should *draw and build on the experience and knowledge that students bring to the classroom.*" The authors of the New York report argue that "such pedagogy not only validates a student's sense of worth, but also fosters developmentally appropriate and meaningful learning" (New York State, 1991, p. 29).

The New York State plan seeks to remedy the single perspective formerly presented in schools. The older New York curriculum, like that in most schools, was Eurocentric and unidirectional. That is, it tended to reflect what Europeans thought and believed and did to others. The New York curriculum designers have gone a long way toward promising children that the material they will be asked to study will be a fair representation of America's story. Students will be asked to consider social and historical phenomena from many perspectives. This is a lesson that other states should consider. It promises to change the ways in which we define education.

> In modern societies the changing conception of what it means to be an educated and intelligent person includes our capacity to entertain and understand phenomena from perspectives different from our own, on our way to arriving at wise judgments and the reconciliation of differences. (Gordon and Roberts, quoted in Sobol, 1993, p. 265)

The multiculturalist argument is not that Eurocentric views are wrong or evil or that children of Asian or African descent should not be taught about America's European cultural legacy. Multiculturalism rests on one simple educational truth: tolerance cannot come without respect; respect cannot come without knowledge (Gates, 1992, p. xv). The goal of education is to pass on knowledge fully and completely. Multiculturalism begins by recognizing the cultural diversity of the United States, and it asks that the school curriculum explore that diversity. A multicultural education does not concentrate on the accomplishments of one group of immigrants at the expense of learning about others. To be well educated, in a multicultural sense, means to learn about the history and literature and contributions of the various people who have fashioned the complex tapestry of American life. All students should be encouraged to sample broadly from all the cultures and all the ideas that have contributed to the making of America.

POSITION 2:
FOR THE COMMON CULTURE

> Educators often stress the virtues of multicultural education. Such study is indeed valuable in itself; it inculcates tolerance and provides a perspective on our traditions and values. But however laudable it is, it should not be allowed to supplant or interfere with our schools' responsibility to ensure our children's mastery of American literate culture. (Hirsch, 1987, p. 18)

> What happens when people of different ethnic origins, speaking different languages and professing different religions, settle in the same geographical locality and live under the same political sovereignty? Unless a common purpose binds them together, tribal hostilities will drive them apart. Ethnic and racial conflict, it seems evident, will now replace the conflict of ideologies as the explosive issues of our times. (Schlesinger, 1992, p. 10)

Schools and the Cultural Heritage

For the past 150 years, public schools have had three broad objectives: to educate individual citizens for democratic participation and thereby protect the nation from the threat of tyrants and despots; to encourage individual achievement through academic competition; and to promote, encourage, and teach the values and traditions of the American cultural heritage. Through the years, the role of the schools in achieving these lofty and far-reaching goals has been criticized. Recently, the part the schools play in dispensing the common cultural glue has drawn the most fire.

The United States has been enriched by every ethnic and racial group to land on these shores, and the immigrants, in turn, have been served well by the nation and the nation's schools. The public schools have their share of detractors, to be sure, but the latest attack on the schools' curriculum seems misguided. A fair assessment would find it difficult to fault the success schools have had in passing on to new generations of Americans—immigrants and native-born citizens alike—the common culture of the United States. No mean accomplishment, the transmission of the cultural heritage requires an appreciation for the complex aspects of American history, literature, and political traditions (Ravitch, 1990; Schlesinger, 1992). American culture is, after all, a hybrid of cultures—European, Asian, African—and it is the job of the schools to transmit this cultural legacy faithfully in all its complexity. The school's role in cultural transmission has been one of its brilliant successes for well over a century.

The nineteenth-century proponents of public education recognized that the United States was a dynamic nation, changing and being invigorated by succeeding waves of immigrants. The new arrivals came from every part of the world, and they brought with them a mixture of energy, talents, and cultural variations never before found in one nation. When they arrived in the United States, they spoke different languages, they were of many races, and they practiced many religions. What they shared was an eagerness to succeed economically and politically, and to learn how to become American, to fit into a unique, unprecedented cultural amalgam.

The common schools of the nineteenth century, influenced by the western ideas of philosophic rationalism and humanism, were an expression of optimism concerning human progress and democratic potential. Advocates of mass public education saw the schools as a vehicle of social progress, and they shared a common belief in education, "an education, moreover, which was neither a privilege of a fortunate few nor a crumb tossed to the poor and lowly, but one which was to be a right of every child in the land" (Meyer, 1957, p. 143). The common schools succeeded beyond anyone's expectations. Public education was provided for the children of the poor as well as those of the rich; the children of immigrants read the same texts and learned the same lore as the children of native-born Americans. The mix of immigrants coming to the United States in the 1990s is even richer and more diverse than could ever have been envisioned by the founders of the common schools. The need for the schools to transmit the common culture has never been greater; the preservation of democratic tradition has never been more difficult.

The United States has always been a haven for those seeking political freedom and expression. In the nineteenth century, millions of immigrants came to this country, in large measure, to enjoy the fruits and accept the burdens of participating in a democratic society. This is still true, but unlike the immigrants of former times, today's new arrivals typically have had little or no direct experience with democratic traditions. For example, in the 1840s, after the collapse of the Frankfurt diet, immigrants from Germany flocked to America seeking the democratic political expression they had been denied in their homeland. Today's immigrants may want democracy, but coming from autocratic regimes in Asia and South America, they have had no experience with the responsibilities of democratic living. They are less prepared for assuming a role in a democratic society than was any previous generation of immigrants. It is clearly up to the schools to induct the children of the new immigrants into the complexities of the American democratic culture.

Although the schools should expose children to the common culture, they are not to be asked to pretend to a cultural homogeneity or to deny the ethnic experiences of individual students. Schools are obligated to represent the range of cultural voices—male and female, African-American, Asian-American, and European American—but these voices must be trained not for solo performances, but to be part of a chorus. Schools must encourage individual identification with one central cultural tradition or the United States might fall prey to the same ethnic tensions that are undermining the sovereignty of Lebanon and the nations of Eastern Europe and Africa. Students should be taught the common western ideals that have shaped America and that bind us together as a nation: democracy, capitalism, and monotheism.

Particularism

The United States stands to benefit—economically, politically, and socially—from the infusion of talent of the new immigrants, as it has in the past. Assimilated new immigrants pose no threat to American growth or nationhood. The United States is threatened instead by those who deny that a common American tradition should be taught in the schools or that a common culture exists! Diane Ravitch calls these people particularists; they argue that teaching a common culture is a disservice to ethnic and racial minorities. "Particularism," writes Ms. Ravitch, "is a bad idea whose time has come" (Ravitch, 1990, p. 346).

Particularists demand that the public schools forsake attempts to teach the commonalities of cultural heritage in favor of a curriculum that centers on the specific ethnic mix represented in a given school or its community. Students in predominantly white schools would receive one focus, children in a predominantly African-American school another, and so on. It is not at all clear where the particularists would stop in the Balkanization of the curriculum. Would a school with a predominantly Asian population have an Asian-focused curriculum, or would they further divide the curriculum into Korean, Chinese, Vietnamese, Filipino, and Cambodian focuses (Fox-Genovese, 1991)?

The arguments of the particularists are extreme and unhelpful to the unifying and democratic ends envisioned by the founders of the common schools. Asante, for example, advocates an Afrocentrist curriculum that would teach young African-American children their African cultural roots at the expense of teaching them about western traditions. He denounces those African-Americans who prefer Bach and Beethoven to Ellington and Coltrane. An African-American person, he believes, should be centered on his or her cultural experience; anything else is dismissed as an aberration. Asante argues that majority as well as minority students are disadvantaged by the "monoculturally diseased curriculum." He writes that few Americans of any color "have heard the names of Cheikh Anta Diop, Anna Julia Cooper, C. L. R. James, or J. A. Rogers," historians who have contributed to an understanding of the African world (Asante, 1991, p. 175). He is probably right, but for better or worse, the most enduring of mainstream white historians—for example, Spengler, Gibbon, Macaulay, Carlyle, and Trevelyan—are not likely to enjoy greater recognition by Americans.

The cultural focus of the curriculum is a serious matter, and although petty and irrational arguments exist on all sides, the real issue is the role the schools must play in transmitting the common cultural heritage. Schools must teach children that regardless of race, gender, or ethnicity, great achievement is possible. Such is the record of the past and the promise of the future. The curriculum of the public schools should be configured in such a way that it allows all children to believe that they are part of a society that welcomes their participation and encourages their achievements. As Ravitch (1990) writes, "In their curriculum, their hiring practices, and their general philosophy, the public schools must not discriminate against or give preference to any racial or ethnic group. . . . They should not be expected to teach children to view the world through an ethnocentric perspective that rejects or ignores the common culture" (p. 352).

Schools cannot fulfill their central mission as transmitters of the common culture while they cater to particularist demands for teaching the perspective of every minority group. Ravitch argues that, in the past, generation upon generation of minorities—Jews, Catholics, Greeks, Poles, and Japanese—have used private lessons, after school or on weekends, to instill in their children ethnic pride and ethnic continuity. These may be valuable goals, but they have never been the job of the public schools, nor should the schools now take on these responsibilities. The public schools must develop a common culture, "a definition of citizenship and culture that is both expansive and *inclusive*," one that speaks to our commonalities not our differences (Ravitch, 1990, p. 352). The public school curriculum must not succumb to particularists' demands to prize our differences over the celebration of our common good.

Anticanonical Folly

Among the greatest absurdities produced by the particularists is their attack on the canon, denouncing it as racist, sexist, Eurocentric, logocentric, and politically incorrect. Before we put these distortions to rest, let us say a few words about the nature of the canon. The term "canon" (from the Greek word *kanon,* meaning a measuring rod), which originally referred to the books of the Hebrew and Christian Bibles, meant Holy Scripture, as officially recognized by the ecclesiastic authority. Today, it has taken on secular and political meanings. The canon represents, first of all, the major monuments to western civilization, great ideas embodied in books that form the foundation of our democratic traditions. The "Great Books" of the western tradition (for example, the writings of Plato, Aristotle, Machiavelli, and Marx) have shaped our political thinking, whether we trace our origins to Europe, Africa, or Asia; Homer, Sophocles, George Eliot, and Virginia Woolf inform our sense of literature whether we are male or female. Every major university offers courses in the western canon, sometimes referred to as the Great Books, and as the late Alan Bloom noted, students have always enjoyed these works. He wrote, "Wherever the Great Books make up a central part of the curriculum, the students are excited and satisfied, feel they are doing something that is independent and fulfilling, getting something from the university they cannot get elsewhere. . . . Their gratitude at learning of Achilles or the categorical imperative is boundless" (Bloom, 1987, p. 344).

The particularists' attack on the canon is new and somewhat surprising. The value of the canon as the cornerstone of quality education had long been taken for granted. As Searle (1990) writes, in educated circles it was accepted, almost to the point of cliché, that

> there is a certain Western Intellectual tradition that goes from say Socrates to Wittgenstein in philosophy, and from Homer to James Joyce in literature, and it is essential to the liberal education of young men and women in the United States that they receive some exposure to at least some of the great works in this intellectual tradition; they should, in Matthew Arnold's overquoted words, know the best that is thought and known in the world. (p. 34)

In the past, support for the canon was taken as an article of faith, not belabored or examined at length. These works and the ideas they contained were considered to be of enduring worth, part of a timeless literary judgment—as Samuel Johnson spoke of it—and quite apart from the hurly-burly of politics. Canonical authors were acknowledged representatives of the triumphant march of western civilization, "an unbroken crescendo from Plato to NATO" (Perry and Williams, 1991, p. 55). No longer. The canon is being attacked by particularists and multiculturalists of every hue. Searle writes that the cant of the anticanonicals runs something like this:

> Western civilization is in large part a history of oppression. Internally, Western civilization oppressed women, various slave and serf populations, and ethnic and cultural minorities, generally. In foreign affairs, the history of Western civilization is one of imperialism and colonialism. The so-called canon of Western civilization consists of the official publications of the system of oppression, and it is no accident that the authors in the "canon" are almost exclusively Western white males. . . . [The canon] has to be abolished in favor of something that is "multicultural" and "nonhierarchical." (p. 35)

The particularists and multiculturalists are trying to do to the public school curriculum what they tried unsuccessfully to accomplish at universities: to politicize the curriculum. In the name of justice and equity, universities were encouraged to broaden the curriculum and include nonwestern as well as western authors. Of course, curriculum is a zero-sum game; that is, if something is to be added, something has to be left out. The case of Stanford University is instructive. In the late 1980s, Stanford proposed adding authors from developing countries and both women's and minority perspectives to the curriculum of the Western Culture course. These changes would have come at considerable cost. Plato's *Republic* and Machiavelli's *Prince* would have been replaced by such works as *I, Rigoberta Menchu*, the story of the political coming of age of a Guatemalan peasant woman, and Franz Fanon's *Wretched of the Earth*, a book that encouraged violent and revolutionary acts among citizens of developing countries (D'Souza, 1991). Although campus radicals demonstrated in support of the proposal, chanting, "Hey, hey, ho, ho, Western Culture's got to go," cooler heads won the day. The required course in Western Culture kept its reading list, but added some optional assignments that provided a nonwestern focus.

Misguided Curriculum Reform

Most universities have successfully resisted the ratiocinations of multicultural-ists; the public schools have been less successful. New York State unfortu-nately has plunged headlong into the maelstrom of multiculturalism in reac-tion to a report critical of the state's social studies curriculum. One of the guiding principles of the report is that "[t]he subject matter content should be *treated as socially constructed* and therefore tentative—as is all knowledge." The document goes on to assert that "[k]nowledge is the product of human beings located in specific times and places; consequently, much of our subject matter must be understood as tentative."

This is distressing. As Searle (1990) writes, "If you think that there is no reality that words could possibly correspond to, then obviously it will be a waste of time to engage in an 'objective and disinterested search for truth' because there is no such thing as truth" (p. 40). What is it that we are passing on to succeeding generations if not the fruits of our culture's pursuit of truth? Why should parents be required to send their children to school, and why should taxpayers be expected to fund such tentative and subjective ends?

New York State's 1991 curriculum report ("One Nation, Many Peoples: A Declaration of Cultural Independence") has been criticized for its intellectual dishonesty and its potential for divisiveness. Albert Shanker, president of the American Federation of Teachers, argues that "multiculturalism" is an appeal-ing phrase, but in classroom application it is likely to degenerate into stereo-typing:

> For a teacher presenting a historical event to elementary school children, using multiple perspectives probably means that the teacher turns to each child and asks the point of view about the event. To the African-American child this would mean, "What is the African-American point of view?" To a Jewish child, "What is the Jewish point of view?" And to the Irish child, "What is the Irish point of view?" (Shanker, 1991, p. E7)

Shanker points out that multiculturalism is, in practice, a racist approach to teaching; it assumes that there is one perspective shared by every African-American child and a single perspective shared by all members of each reli-gious or ethnic group. The rhetoric of cultural relevance and curricula centered around the sociocultural experience of the child is, on the surface, attractive. However, it assumes that culture is a heritable characteristic. This is a cruel distortion. Culture is learned, much in the same way that language is learned. To assume otherwise is, as Ravitch reminds us, a form of cultural Lysenkoism. "It implies a dubious, dangerous form of cultural predestination" (Ravitch, 1990, p. 346).

Political Correctness

The New York State curriculum report enshrines the shrillest voices of the political correctness choir. No doubt you have heard of political correctness. It refers to the forced adherence to the political attitudes and social mores of the liberal left. Notoriously unsuccessful at the polls for the past thirty years, the liberal left has moved its assault from American college campuses to the public schools. American professors, many of whom were radical activists in the 1960s, are seeking to enforce a mandatory conformity on issues of race, ethnicity, feminism, and human relationships. They are less interested in teaching the great ideas of the western tradition than they are in ridiculing those ideas. Classes in American government have become pulpits for attacking America; literature classes seem less concerned with the reading of great works than they are with attacks on the alleged political messages of the canon; students are less likely to learn about the glories of Greece and Rome than they are to learn how the west enslaved and exploited the nonwestern world. Ironically, all across America the radicals on the left have created a climate of intolerance not seen since the days of Senator Joseph McCarthy, the bête noire of the left forty years ago.

Political correctness is not entirely bad; it has made us all more sensitive about the language we use. Political correctness should be credited with making people realize the inappropriateness of referring to mature women as "girls" and black men as "boys." However, there seems to be no stopping the tidal wave of "correctspeak" and demands for politically correct behavior. You no doubt have heard some wag report that it is no longer correct to call people "short"; instead, they are referred to as "people who are vertically challenged." Dead people may be said to be "permanently horizontal." This could be taken lightly if it were not such a serious matter. Political correctness, which has become the enforcement arm of the multiculturalists, has enriched the American lexicon with such neologisms as "ableism," "heteroism," and "lookism." One college defines these terms in the following ways:

Ableism: Oppression of the differently abled by the temporarily able.

Heteroism: Oppression of those of sexual orientation other than heterosexual . . . ; this can take place by not acknowledging their existence.

Lookism: The belief that appearance is an indicator of a person's value; the construction of a standard of beauty/attractiveness; and oppression through stereotypes and generalizations of both those who do not fit that standard and those who do. (Schlesinger, 1991, p. 115)

One shudders to think what would happen if lookism and ableism were ever deemed violations of the Constitution. Would medical schools be forced to accept applicants independent of ability? Would Miss America contests be decided by a lottery?

Consider another example of a misguided adventure into the world of political correctness. In 1994, a New Jersey high school decided that at senior commencement the names of graduates would not be announced in alphabetical order because to do so would group together the school's large number of Asian-Indian students. It seems that during past commencement ceremonies, members of the audience would snicker at the large number of graduates with the last name of Patel. "As each got up, some people would yell 'Patel number one,' 'Patel number two,' and so on," reported one school administrator. The school superintendent said, "We were teaching students about sensitivity to race and ethnic background. [We] were grouping the students by last names. It was a type of segregation. It didn't make sense" (Jaffe, 1994, p. 14).

The whole business does not make sense. Why was there a need for the new policy? What happens in schools where the most common surnames are Smith, Jones, and Johnson? Do administrators there consider calling names randomly at commencement? Or does political correctness force a new and unnatural attention to these matters?

Political correctness is clearly an example of a good idea that, pursued to its extreme, rapidly becomes an absurdity. The state of New York, for all its good intentions, appears to have fallen victim to the extremes of political correctness. In its most recent curriculum report, the word "slaves" has been replaced by "enslaved persons," so as to "call forth the essential humanity of those enslaved, helping students to understand from the beginning the true meaning of slavery (in contrast to the sentimental pictures of contented slaves, still found in some texts)" (New York State, 1991, p. 43). Textbooks have been scrutinized for potentially offensive language. References to the "Far East," a western term, are to be struck in favor of "East Asia," which is assumed to be less offensive to the people who live there. In a similar vein, the "Middle East" will be known as "Southwest Asia and North Africa," and references to the western hemisphere as the "New World" will be eliminated. (The last example is considered potentially offensive to native Americans.)

In a dissenting opinion appended to the New York State report, historian Arthur Schlesinger argued that the defining experience for Americans has not been ethnicity or the sanctification of old cultures, "but the creation of a *new* national culture and a *new* national identity." It is foolish, he argues, to look backward in empty celebration of what we were. Instead, the schools need to look forward and to blend the disparate experiences of immigrants into one American culture (New York State, 1991, p. 89). As they have in the past, schools should continue to serve the nation by passing on to children the elements of the common culture that defines the United States and binds its people together. This is not to say that the schools should be asked to transmit the culture as unchangeable or to force students to accept it without question. The culture of a nation changes as a reflection of its citizens. American culture will continue to change. School curricula of necessity will expand and sample more broadly from the various influences that have shaped American culture. However, to turn the schools away from the western ideals of democracy, justice, freedom, equality, and opportunity is to renounce the greatest legacy ever bequeathed by one generation to the next. No matter who sits in American classrooms—African-Americans, Asian-Americans, Latin Americans, or European Americans—and no matter what their religion or creed, those students and their nation have been shaped by the democratic and intellectual traditions of the western world, and they had better learn those traditions or risk losing them.

For Discussion

1. According to John Searle (1990), a well-educated person should be characterized by the following abilities:

   a The person should know enough about his or her cultural traditions to know how they evolved.

   b The person should know enough of the natural sciences that he or she is not a stranger in that world.

   c The person should know enough of how society works to understand the trade cycle, interest, unemployment, and other elements of the political economy.

   d The person should know at least one other language well enough to read the best literature in the original that the language has produced.

   e The person needs to know enough philosophy to be able to use the tools of logical analysis.

   f The person must be able to write and speak clearly and with candor and rigor.

   Do you agree or disagree with Searle's listing? Who should decide these matters? The individual? The school and the parents? The state? The federal government?

2. Opponents of multiculturalism claim that canonical authors such as Dickens, Hawthorne, Homer, Milton, Plato, and Shakespeare have been replaced by their leftist critics (for example, Lacan, Derrida, and Foucault, among others). However, the Modern Language Association (MLA) did not find this to be true. The MLA surveyed English professors on 350 campuses to determine the nature of the reading lists in three commonly taught courses: nineteenth-Century American literature, the nineteenth-Century British Novel, and Renaissance Literature (Mooney, 1991). On the basis of the survey, the MLA concluded that the canon was intact. Canonical authors were still the standard fare in the English classes surveyed. Review the range of required humanities texts in your required courses. Do the texts reflect a multicultural or a traditional curriculum?

3. Population demographers predict that by the year 2020, one of every three people in the United States will be a member of a group now labeled a "minority." By the middle of the next century, if current trends continue, white Anglo-Saxon Protestants will be the new minority.

   Assuming that these projections are correct, do they offer support for the multiculturalists' arguments that schools should teach many cultural perspectives and histories? Or do the projections support the arguments of those calling for a reemphasis on teaching the common culture? Is there a middle ground, a position that could satisfy both sides?

References

Apple, M. W. (1979). *Ideology and Curriculum*. Boston: Routledge and Kegan Paul.

———— (1982). *Education and Power*. Boston: Routledge and Kegan Paul.

Aronowitz, S., and Giroux, H. A. (1991). *Postmodern Education, Politics, Culture and Social Criticism*. Minneapolis: University of Minnesota Press.

Asante, M. K. (1987). *The Afrocentric Idea*. Philadelphia: Temple University Press.

————(1991). "The Afrocentric Idea in Education." *Journal of Negro Education* **60**(2), 170–180.

Banks, J. A. (1993). "Multicultural Education: Historical Development, Dimensions, and Practices." In *Review of Research in Education, 1993*, edited by L. Hammond. Washington, DC: American Educational Research Association.

_____(1994). "Transforming the Mainstream Curriculum." *Educational Leadership* **51**(8), 4–8.

Bloom, A. (1987). *The Closing of the American Mind.* New York: Simon & Schuster.

D'Souza, D. (1991). "Illiberal Education." *The Atlantic Monthly,* March, pp. 51–79.

Fox-Genovese, E. (1991). "The Self-Interest of Multiculturalism." *Tikkun* **6**(4), 47–49.

Gates, H. L., Jr. (1992). *Loose Canons: Notes on the Cultural Wars.* New York: Oxford University Press.

Gollnick, D. M., and Chinn, P. C. (1983). *Multicultural Education in a Pluralistic Society.* St. Louis: Mosby.

Goodson, I., Meyer, J. W., and Apple, M. W. (1991). "Introduction," Special Issue on Sociology of the Curriculum. *Sociology of Education* **64**(1), iii–iv.

Hirsch, E. D., Jr. (1987). *Cultural Literacy: What Every American Needs to Know.* Boston: Houghton Mifflin.

Jaffe, J. (1994). "Flunking Bigotry." *The Newark Star Ledger,* June 22, p. 14.

Ladson-Billings, G. (1994). "What Can We Learn From Multicultural Education Research?" *Education Leadership* **51**(8), 22–26.

Meyer, A. E. (1957). *An Educational History of the American People.* New York: McGraw-Hill.

Mooney, C. J. (1991). "Study Finds Professors Are Still Teaching the Classics, Sometimes in New Ways." *The Chronicle of Higher Education* **38**, 2.

New York State Social Studies Syllabus Review and Development Committee. (1991). "One Nation, Many People: A Declaration of Cultural Independence." Albany: State Education Department, University of the State of New York.

Perry, R., and Williams, P. (1991). "Freedom of Hate Speech." *Tikkun* **6**(4): 55–57.

Perry, T., and Fraser, J. W., eds. (1993). *Freedom's Plow: Teaching in the Multicultural Classroom.* New York: Routledge.

Ravitch, D. (1983). *The Troubled Crusade, American Education, 1945–1980.* New York: Basic Books.

_____ (1987). "Tot Sociology, Grade School History." *Current,* December, pp. 4–10.

_____ (1990). "Multiculturalism, E Pluribus Plures." *American Scholar,* Summer, pp. 337–354.

Schlesinger, A. M. (1992). *The Disuniting of America.* New York: Norton.

Searle, J. (1990). "The Storm Over the University." *The New York Review of Books,* December 6, pp. 34–41.

Shanker, A. (1991). "Multiple Perspectives." *The New York Times,* October 27, p. E7.

Sobol, T. (1993). "Revising the New York State Social Studies Curriculum." *Teachers College Record,* Winter, pp. 258–272.

Takaki, R. (1993). *A Different Mirror: A History of Multicultural America.* Boston: Little, Brown.

CHAPTER NINE

Curriculum Control: National or Local

POSITION 1: FOR A NATIONAL CURRICULUM

Providing Accountability

A national curriculum will give the public some assurance that students are learning *something*. Naturally, this means that there will have to be national tests to measure how well students are mastering the national curriculum. As things stand now, students are not judged by how many nationally significant things they have learned, but by how many things they have learned that the particular teachers in their particular schools think are important. Not all teachers can be trusted to make sound judgments about what is genuinely important. Some teachers emphasize trivial things that happen to interest them personally, and even then they don't expect their students to learn very much of the trivia. Teachers are professionals, to be sure, but they are no more infallible than any other professionals. The American public is entitled to hold teachers to some uniform standards, and to check on how well the teachers are meeting these standards. "Once you have a curriculum on which everyone agrees, you have an answer to the question of how to train teachers: They have to be able to teach the common curriculum. You also have an answer to the question about the level of understanding and skill student assessments should call for because you can base assessments on the common curriculum" (Shanker, 1991).

There are entire schools that emphasize trivial things—the notorious Mickey Mouse courses like basket weaving. There are other schools where students get what appears to be a straightforward academic curriculum, but where the course content is so watered down that very little material is covered. In some schools, the content is "covered" but students are not expected to master much of it to pass the course. A recent study by the U.S. Department of Education found that students in high-poverty schools get A's and B's for mastering no more of the content than students in suburban schools who get C's and D's (Shanker, 1994). Students graduate from the poor schools with impressive transcripts but little knowledge.

The public is entitled to more accountability than that, and the only way to get it is to have a national curriculum with which all schools must comply and against which all students are assessed. The public agrees, as indicated by the twenty-sixth annual Gallup poll. A whopping 73 percent of those polled think it is very important or quite important to have national tests based on a national curriculum that students must pass for grade promotion and high school graduation (Elam, Rose, and Gallup, 1994).

Poor performance on the tests should disqualify a student for federal aid toward a college education (Samuelson, 1991). The tests could even replace the Scholastic Aptitude Test (SAT) and the American College Test (ACT) as measures of whether a person is admitted to college (Finn, 1991). The SAT and ACT are not subject-specific and so are less valid measures of a student's academic ability than national subject-matter tests would be. For students not going on to college, the test results could be used by prospective employers to make their hiring decisions (Kean, 1991).

Promoting Economic Competitiveness

As a nation whose economic competitiveness with the rest of the world depends on how well educated our people are, we simply cannot afford to be slack any longer. It is important that we be an economically competitive nation so that we can provide all of our citizens with a decent standard of living.

To be truly competitive, we need people with highly useful technical expertise, but these people must also be educated broadly enough to understand the appropriate uses of their skills. They need an understanding of the society on whose behalf they labor. Human robots need not apply. Mortimer Adler, the renowned philosopher and founder of the Great Books program, puts it in the following terms:

> There is no question that our technologically advanced industrial society needs specialists of all sorts. There is no question that the advancement of knowledge in all fields of science and scholarship, and in all the learned professions, needs intense specialization. But for the sake of preserving and enhancing our cultural traditions, as well as for the health of science and scholarship, we need specialists who are also generalists—generally cultivated human beings, not just good plumbers. We need truly educated human beings who can perform their special tasks better precisely because they have general cultivation as well as intensely specialized training. (Adler, 1988, p. 43)

Although Adler thinks this can be accomplished through a prescribed set of required courses, E. D. Hirsch correctly recognizes that required courses do not guarantee the teaching of specific content. The content has to be specified so that children across America will learn things in common. Hirsch believes that content is preliminary to problem solving. "Yes, problem-solving skills are necessary. But they depend on a wealth of relevant knowledge. Meanwhile, street-smart children in the Bronx and elsewhere demonstrate outside school that they already possess higher-order thinking skills . . . what these students lack is not critical thinking but academic knowledge" (Hirsch, 1993). Hirsch and his colleagues have made a major contribution to this effort by creating *The Dictionary of Cultural Literacy* (Hirsch, Katt, and Trefil, 1988). Since then Hirsch has also developed a recommended curriculum for the elementary grades (Hirsch, 1991).

Easing Geographic Mobility

A national curriculum is especially important for a geographically mobile society like the United States. It may be personally satisfying to learn about the history of your own town, West Overshoe, or your own ethnic group, Transylvanians, and there still will be time to do that. But young people have to be prepared to move in the larger world, because they probably will. Before they die, they are likely to have lived in several towns and in more than one state. They need a broad perspective, one that they can share with the people they will encounter along their way. This broad perspective, this common frame of reference, this similar knowledge base will vastly facilitate social and business communication. It will hold us together as a people, serving as the cultural cement of our society. It will reduce for all of us the culture shock and the period of adjustment we face in moving from one locale to another. Indeed, the national geography standards will assure that we know how to get from one place to another, and have a sense beforehand of what the new place will be like in terms of topography, climate, and natural resources (The Geography Education Standards Project, 1994).

Without a common culture, the United States can become dangerously pluralistic. The danger in too much diversity is that groups have so little in common that they become strange to one another. The strangeness breeds suspicion, which, in turn, leads to hostility, and the hostility can degenerate into a descending spiral of intergroup violence. We do not have to look to the Middle East or Eastern Europe for examples of this phenomenon. We need look no farther than the Howard Beaches and Crown Heights and Los Angeles Centrals of America, and wherever else the next cross-ethnic explosion occurs.

A national curriculum will certainly ease geographic mobility for students. As the president of the American Federation of Teachers argues: "National curriculums mean that kids moving from one school district to another do not have to waste time by repeating the material they already know or struggle to catch up on stuff they've missed" (Shanker, 1992). The American Federation of Teachers is now calling for the United States to adopt a common academic curriculum and a national exam for high school students ("Largest Teachers' Union . . .," 1995).

Building National Cohesion

It is not enough simply to smooth interpersonal encounters. No nation can long survive if its people lack a sense of nationhood. The history of the nation is a vehicle by which to instill this sense of unity. The stirring examples of our nation's leaders, the enormous obstacles overcome in times of national peril, the daily struggles of ordinary people, the evolution of social institutions—a knowledge of all these awakens us to our common heritage and our shared destiny. "Indeed, we put our sense of nationhood at risk by failing to familiarize our young people with the story of how the society in which we live came to be. Knowledge of the ideas that have molded us and the ideals that have mattered to us function as a kind of civic glue" (Cheney, 1987, p. 7). President Reagan spoke to this concern in his farewell address when he commented that patriotism, which he defined as an informed love of country, can be promoted by having students learn of America's great triumphs, such as General Doolittle's bombing raid over Tokyo in World War II. For the dean of Yale College, the common culture of Americans is the "system of laws and beliefs that shaped the establishment of the country, a system developed within the context of Western civilization. It should be obvious, then, that all Americans need to learn about that civilization to understand our country's origins and share in its heritage, purposes and character" (Kagan, 1991).

Another way to bring a people together in national unity is through their literary past. The great works of prose and poetry—the canon of American literature—unite us with a shared delight. These literary treasures give us rich insights into ourselves, making it impossible to escape a recognition of the humanity we have in common with our fellow citizens. "Something of value is lost when there is no coherent literature curriculum. . . . Such a curriculum, beginning in the early grades, helps young people understand how the culture came to be what it is, how it was shaped, which writers defined it and thereby changed the way we see ourselves" (Ravitch and Finn, 1987, p. 10).

This "cultural" curriculum can be honest about America's past by acknowledging the shameful episodes and giving credit to groups whose contributions have thus far been ignored. The national standards for United States history are an attempt to do just that, by giving numerous examples of minority cultures and heroes and travails. Imagine elementary school students now reading the diaries of Harriet Tubman, *Tales From the Gold Mountain* by Paul Yee, and *The Cat Who Escaped From Steerage* by Evelyn Meyerson to vicariously experience the lives of slaves and of Chinese and Jewish immigrants (Crabtree and Nash, 1994, pp. 126, 146). At the same time, the curriculum can avoid the America-bashing and ethnic breast-thumping of multiculturalism. It can be a curriculum that unites us through mutual understanding and shared appreciation (Schlesinger, 1992).

Improving Reading Ability

One of the reasons why so many adults cannot, and will not, read even the local newspaper is that it contains too many terms with which they are unfamiliar. They don't have the time or patience to look up the meaning of these terms in dictionaries, encyclopedias, and atlases.

> The recently rediscovered insight that literacy is more than a skill is based upon knowledge that all of us unconsciously have about language. We know instinctively that to understand what somebody is saying, we must understand more than the surface meaning of words; we have to understand the

context as well. The need for background information applies all the more to reading and writing. To grasp the words on a page we have to know a lot of information that isn't set down on the page. (Hirsch, 1987, p. 3)

If students have been educated thoroughly in the general culture of their country, this information will be stored in their heads and they can draw on it as needed. A passing newspaper reference to the First Amendment or the Korean War, for example, will not create confusion and uncertainty. Such references will not cause the daily newspaper to take on the esoteric quality of a technical journal. Rather, the references will be readily grasped and put into context by readers who know the history of their country. Without this information, readers will become discouraged from reading, which will cause them to fall farther and farther behind in their understanding of things. The job of schools, then, is to give children the start-up information they need to get going on their lifelong intellectual development.

Enlightening the Electorate

If Americans are not able to *keep* informed because they have never been informed, then there is not much hope for democracy. People will turn off altogether to public affairs because they don't have the background to understand them. Or worse, they will vote without knowing the issues well enough even to realize what is in their own interest. Politicians will be able to manipulate the people with slick slogans. Lies will be as credible as truths. More and more ruthless demagogues will get into power, until eventually a despot inveigles the ignorant masses into letting him or her take control. "True enfranchisement depends upon knowledge, knowledge upon literacy, and literacy upon cultural literacy. To be truly literate, citizens must be able to grasp the meaning of any piece of writing addressed to the general reader" (Hirsch, 1987, p. 12).

Recent presidential campaigns may have underscored this point for you. With as many as seven candidates in a single debate during the primaries, and all of them trying to score points with high-sounding rhetoric and claims to expertise, the viewer needed a lot of background knowledge not to be completely flummoxed. Persons lacking this knowledge probably gave up trying to understand what the election was all about, and voted for no good reason or did not bother to vote at all.

The issues on which the electorate is expected to pass judgment are becoming more complex. The numerous technical details are difficult to comprehend, and the consequences of any course of action are less predictable than they were when the world was a simpler place. A cursory review of the several national health care and welfare reform proposals is all it should take to drive this point home. Thus, it is imperative that voters be able to fathom the issues in some depth if democratic decision making is not to become as random as a lottery drawing.

R. Freeman Butts (1995) has expressed these concerns in the following way:

It will not be easy, but a gigantic effort must be launched to counteract the superficial political opinions of citizens now molded by TV attack ads, by radio squawk-talk, and by organized floods of faxes—what *New York Times* reporter Michael Wines has called the "electronic din" of a "500-channel democracy." The public is so easily influenced by negative campaigning because they know less than they need to about what government is and should do. The only long-term hope of revivifying a cynical electorate is serious and sustained study and learning of basic principles of constitutional democracy like those invoked by Jefferson. (p. 48)

Butts was a senior consultant and advisor to the national civic standards project. Those standards now exist, and schools across America should adopt them to assure the vitality of democracy in the twenty-first century (*National Standards for Civics and Government*, 1994).

Uplifting the Poor

Americans will be better off when all citizens are well-informed. The ones who will reap the greatest benefits, however, are those who now are the least well-informed. The poor, especially the poor minorities who are so ignorant of mainstream culture, will be given the vocabulary needed to converse on equal terms with the higher social classes. There no longer will be a communication block to their upward mobility. The feeling of being outsiders who are resented and ridiculed will be reduced because a major reason for the resentment and ridicule will have been removed. Cultural literacy will give *power* to the poor so they will be able to compete in the job market and the political arena on a more equal footing. The black Harvard historian and sociologist Orlando Patterson expressed this view:

> The people who run society at the macrolevel must be literate in this culture. For this reason, it is dangerous to overemphasize the problems of basic literacy or the relevancy of literacy to specific tasks, and more constructive to emphasize that blacks will be condemned in perpetuity to oversimplified, low-level tasks and will never gain their rightful place in controlling the levers of power unless they also acquire literacy in this wider cultural sense. (Patterson, quoted in Hirsch, 1987, pp. 10–11)

Minority cultures certainly add to the richness of the United States, so there is no secret plot to drown these cultures in the mainstream. In fact, the intention is to make minorities themselves truly bicultural. They will retain their original cultures but will no longer be *trapped* in them. Furthermore, they will not be patronized by having celebrated that about their cultures which is simply meretricious, on the misguided notion that minority cultures deserve equal treatment with the mainstream culture in the curriculum. If there is no Tolstoy of the Zulus, there should be no attempt to inflate a minor writer to that status. Better that minorities be given the tools with which to "cross over" into the dominant culture as they choose. If there is an evil plot, it is on the part of those who pretend to honor minorities by keeping them "pure" (and poor) in their lack of literacy and mainstream culture. They are making ghettos of children's minds.

Escaping Indoctrination

A national curriculum will surely mean a loss of local control over the curriculum, and this alarms many people. However, the national curriculum not only will get children beyond the parochial and often trivial knowledge they are taught at the local level, but also will give them a broader *value* perspective. Instead of being indoctrinated only in the values of the fundamentalist Christian or Jewish or liberal or conservative community where they happen to live, they will be exposed to the positions of all these groups. If the *National Standards for United States History* (Crabtree and Nash, 1994) were to be adopted nationally, there would be some guarantee that students in Podunk were learning more about the minority cultures of America. Their own values and perspectives would be challenged and strengthened by this exposure. It is also possible that the exposure would cause students to rethink and modify some of their values and perspectives. This possibility is what alarms the elders in a community. They worry that the children will be corrupted by outside influences.

These fears are understandable, but the reaction is not. The reaction is to impose an ostrichlike education, with everyone's heads stuck in the sand. That kind of education is designed to keep children ignorant; it is not an education at all. It tells young people that the only way we can get them to believe what *we* tell them is to keep them from hearing anything else. Truth, however, arises in competition with other "truths," not in silence. Besides, with all the mass communications systems in the United States, it is futile to try keeping kids in a soundproof darkroom. Fiber optics and satellite dishes are giving us so many television channels that "surfing" will be the new labor-intensive activity. Who is to block the screen and drown the sound whenever something heretical appears? Computers put kids on the information highway, which, to be sure, is often strewn with litter, but who is to stand astride it waving warning flags? Even to attempt to do so would be counterproductive. Every new sight or sound that breaks through will have a special allure for youngsters because they will recognize it as something they're *not* supposed to see or hear.

The national curriculum, therefore, will help to save children from the narrow-mindedness of their communities. The elders in a community might still refuse to have certain topics taught to their children, but this enforced ignorance will be reflected in the youngsters' national test scores. The elders will soon realize that their attempts to preserve an unknowing innocence are being made at the expense of the youngsters' educational and occupational mobility. That realization should at least cause them to reconsider the values they took for granted for so long.

A Modest Proposal

Nothing really radical is being proposed here. There is not a suggestion that American schools be overhauled completely. Indeed, this is the most modest of proposals because it will result in so little change. A national curriculum already exists for American schools. In his book *Horace's Compromise* (1984), Theodore Sizer has a chapter entitled "What High School Is." His book would not have sold so well if the readers wondered which high school he was talking about. It was *their* high school, and the high schools with which they were familiar, because the American high school in so many respects is a constant. This is especially true for the curriculum, as you and your college friends can quickly establish by compiling and comparing lists of the high school courses you took.

Or imagine that you were kidnapped and blindfolded and then parachuted out of an airplane somewhere over the United States. Wherever you landed, the institution that would seem the least strange would be the local public school. The students might talk in strange accents and wear odd-looking clothes, but the things they were being taught would be pretty much the same as what you were taught when you were at that level in school.

There is a national curriculum because there are national textbooks. "Given that most teachers rely on textbook content for course content, and given that the large majority of textbooks are nationally distributed, how local could curricula be in practice? Sure, some states require unique course content. Requirements for social studies courses on a state's history or constitution provide an example. But, that's a pittance" (Phelps, 1993). There are also national college entrance exams and national teacher conferences and a national culture. The present proposal would simply make more systematized and deliberate that which is now somewhat random and coincidental. The reason for making it more systematic and deliberate is to plug the knowledge gaps from which so many students now suffer. The reason, in other words, is to *guarantee* that all students will be taught the crucial components of our cultural heritage.

Not a Task for the Weak

Drafting the national standards and developing the tests in a variety of subject areas is not an easy job. Enormous time is spent just getting input from a broadly representative array of constituencies. Sifting and assembling the input into a coherent document is another time-consuming task. The final product is certain to be second-guessed by those whose input is not reflected or who were not consulted at all.

Criticism of the national standards (and tests) will be keenest in the subject areas that are the most subjective—the social sciences and the humanities. The United States history standards, and, to a lesser extent, the world history standards, have provoked a firestorm of criticism. It would have been strange had they not. The U.S. Senate denounced the United States history standards by a vote of 99 to 1 (Johnston and Diegmueller, 1995). The standards were discredited for being illustrated with teaching activities that emphasized minorities and their oppression.

Had the suggested teaching activities been more traditional, they would have been criticized for that reason. Striking a universally popular balance is probably not possible. However, the authors of the standards are responding to the criticisms by seeking further input and displaying a willingness to compromise.

What this should tell you is that the creation of national standards is itself both a democratic and an educational process. And since it is the supporting activities and not the standards themselves that have come under attack, a consensus on the latter appears to have been reached.

> The standards represent an impressive breakthrough in linking the subject matter of history with new understanding of how children can and do learn at different stages of their development . . . these standards make available to elementary- and high-school students—our future citizens—the analytical tools and skills they need to come to their own understanding of history, skills that will enable them to differentiate between historical facts and historical interpretations and to consider historical events and characters from multiple perspectives. The standards offer nothing less than an escape from the rote learning of factual matter that has bedeviled the introductory study of history in this country for more than a century. (Jones, 1995)

In short, the process of creating national standards in history has worked. If it can work in an area as sensitive as history, it can work everywhere. And it has worked in the best American tradition: "The new standards are sprawling, messy, both too little and too much, just like the process that produced them. Focus groups do not create elegant, coherent curriculums, but they do keep the democratic juices flowing" (Gluck, 1994).

POSITION 2:
FOR LOCAL DETERMINATION

Maintaining Local Interest

Granted that there already is a haphazard national curriculum, it would be a disaster to solidify this further through national mandates and testing. Nothing is more certain to depress local interest in schools than to take away local control of what goes on in the schools. In recent years, local control has been severely eroded by all kinds of state requirements and monitoring. Specific courses are required; state achievement tests are given in these courses, as well as in basic skill areas such as math and reading; and all of this keeps getting added to rather than subtracted from. "If the school day weren't so overcrowded already by the pressure of the factologists, maybe there would be more time for teachers to teach and students to learn" (Ohanian, 1987, p. 21).

"It seems as though every journal or newspaper education section either reports on or calls for new standards. The calls and reports are always written by professors of education, politicians, federal or state education-department officials, or people with a special interest in a discipline like mathematics or biology. Can you imagine a group of teachers indignantly rising up to demand more standards? Sounds like material for a stand-up comic to me" (Schwarz, 1994, p. 44). It is worth noting that Schwarz is the codirector of the highly acclaimed Central Park East Secondary School in Harlem.

To carry the logic of the accountability schemes to the national level is to repudiate the wisdom of the Founding Fathers. Education is a power reserved to the states, according to the U.S. Constitution. Even within states there is wisdom in allowing local school districts to maintain the limited amount of curricular control they have left. First of all, the *informal* national curriculum that we already have ensures that no local district will get too far out of line. Second, the recent spate of state incursions into the curriculum created fairly rigid prescriptions that local districts must follow. What local districts need, then, is not more direction from above, but continued discretion over those few areas of the curriculum that they can still tailor to their particular needs. Harold Howe II, a former U.S. Commissioner of Education, recommends that national standards "be as vague as possible" so that teachers will continue to "have the freedom that will motivate them to take on the burdens of becoming true professionals" (Howe, 1995, p. 376).

It is not enough to let local people do their thing in the time that remains to them after the central government has done its thing. The educational program fashioned by the local people must be treated as seriously as that of the central government. Otherwise, the message that will be sent is that the local education program is merely a frill, and teachers should concentrate their time and energy on satisfying the national and state bureaucrats. This message effectively repudiates the legitimacy of determining curricula locally.

The message will come across loud and clear if the national tests have "high stakes," meaning that a lot will be riding on them in terms of students' careers and schools' reputations. There is not much point in having the tests if these consequences do not follow. That is why the National Coalition of Advocates for Students is opposed to national tests ("Steps Toward Improving Student Assessment," 1992).

> Furthermore, when tests are wired to an official curriculum and scores carry heavy consequences for individual students, teachers, and schools, the official district curriculum will narrow to what is on these high-stakes tests. Even this freezing and narrowing of the curriculum pales next to compelling evidence of test-score pollution that has occurred in schools responding to high-stakes state tests. "Test-score" pollution means that standardized-test scores rise because students practice with questions similar to ones that will be on the test. (Cuban, 1993, p. 25)

One need not speculate that the national standards and tests will narrow the curriculum, as other countries already have experienced that (Celis, 1993).

Greater control of curricula at the national level may be part of the conservatives' agenda for American schools, but it contradicts another part: parental choice of schools. If all the schools are bent on teaching one version of cultural literacy, there won't be much from which parents can choose (Henig, 1988).

Preventing Mediocrity

A national curriculum and tests necessarily mean a national set of standards. How obliged local school people will feel to focus on those standards will depend, of course, on what the payoffs are. If the chances of getting their graduates into good colleges, and with financial aid, are increased, local officials will take the national standards very seriously. The national curriculum will become the local curriculum, and a lot of time will be spent preparing students for the national tests. This will narrow what students learn to that which a single level of government has ordained. Since the national standards on which everyone will be focusing are likely to be arrived at through consensus by national committees, these will be *compromise* standards.

For some schools, the national standards will be higher than what they now have, so their students will be challenged to reach new heights. Alas, for a lot of schools the compromise standards will be lower than what they have now. The expectations for these students will drop. As Lorie Shepard has said about the new math standards of the National Assessment of Educational Progress: "If all 50 states have to agree to them, I can bet you you'll get a lower set of standards than if you let ambitious states go off on their own. . . . You'll get lowest common denominator standards, not world-class standards" (Shepard, quoted in Rothman, 1991b).

A pressure to weaken the standards arises from the standards mania itself. Every subject area wants to get in on the act. That means national standards and tests in English, social studies, mathematics, science, and foreign languages. And since each of these subjects breaks down into component subjects, the efflorescence will be boggling. In social studies alone, there is already a set of U.S. history standards and a set of world history standards and a set of civics and government standards and a set of geography standards and an umbrella set of social studies standards that tries to include all the subfields. The U.S. history standards themselves total 271 pages! Soon every social studies subject will have weighed in with its standards, as not to have national standards is to risk being dislodged from the curriculum.

The chairman of the social studies department in Gloucester, Massachusetts, has reacted to this wild abundance: "I have a major concern about being held accountable for all this. I'm already trying to fit 10 pounds into a five-pound bag. If all these documents come out this way, somebody's going to have to take a sabbatical to read it all" (Richard Aieta, quoted in Viadero, 1994, p. 25).

Thus, every subject area will come under pressure to be less piggish with its standards so that there will be room in the pen for the standards of every other subject. The new pared-down standards will be couched in such all-embracing terms that they will mean everything and nothing. Paul Schwarz gives a good example of a doozy: "Students will value the principles and ideals of a democratic system based on the premises of human dignity, liberty, justice, and equality" (Schwarz, 1994, p. 44). Sweeping generalities like that cause one to yearn for the mediocre.

Deciding What Is Important

If students lack the cultural literacy that people like Hirsch, Finn, and Ravitch think is important, it may be that the students have yet to be convinced of that importance. The only other possibility is that it is not being taught to the students, which means that teachers are not themselves persuaded of its importance. But this does not mean that students learn nothing in school, or that teachers teach nothing. All it means is that they are not learning or teaching what someone else has decided is important.

Let's take an example from Hirsch's book. One of the terms that Hirsch thinks should be in the vocabulary of a literate person is "Occam's razor." That's a wonderful philosophical term going back to the fourteenth century. As you probably know, it means that the assumptions used to explain something should not be multiplied beyond what is necessary. If you are given an explanation for a stock market crash that does not make sense unless you first assume the existence of ten prior conditions, and if an alternative explanation requires only five such assumptions, the alternative is more likely to be true because it entails fewer assumptions, which must also be true. Students would certainly not be *harmed* by learning the term "Occam's razor." But here's another philosophical term of even more ancient vintage: "Anselm's ontological argument." That is an argument for the existence of God, surely no small matter. It posits that an attribute of perfection is existence; since God, by definition, is that which is all-perfect, God must exist. This term is not on Hirsch's list.

Obviously Hirsch thinks the first term is important and the second one is not. That's his right, but in exercising it, he has engaged in arbitrariness. He has tried to impose his personal preference on other people. Thus, the issue is not whether schools should make students culturally literate. Of course they should. The issue is what constitutes cultural literacy. For Hirsch, one of the crucial items is Occam's razor. For someone else of a more theological bent, it would be Anselm's argument. (For a teenager, it might be Jim Carrey.)

Hirsch has a biased view of American culture, as do we all. "One could waste many happy hours looking things up in Hirsch's tome in an effort to characterize the American culture he imagines. He includes William Faulkner but not Zora Neale Hurston, the Beatles but not the Rolling Stones, Bob Hope but not Lenny Bruce, Chappaquiddick but not SDS, the Monroe Doctrine but not the Truman Doctrine, Solidarity but not the Wobblies" (Margaronis, 1989, p. 14). Hirsch's vision of American culture has a marked conservative bias. If Hirsch attempts to overcome this criticism, he will fulfill the prophesy of Neil Postman (1992): "We may be sure that Hirsch will continue to expand his list until he reaches a point where a one-sentence directive will be all he needs to publish: 'See the *Encyclopedia Americana* and *Webster's Third International*'" (p. 176).

After witnessing the seemingly interminable debate among math educators concerning national standards, Lauren Resnick noted that other disciplines are even more contentious than math. "It's going to be very difficult in this country to deal with the concept of a canon, to say which knowledge and pieces of the culture are going to be considered the nation's culture" (Resnick, quoted in Rothman, 1991a, p. 25). Thus, the effort at a national curriculum may be a fool's errand foredoomed to failure.

Avoiding the Merely Ornamental

You might wonder why such terms as "Occam's razor" and "Anselm's ontological argument" are worth learning at all. It might suddenly have occurred to you that you rarely come upon these terms in your schoolwork or general reading. Even rarer are the occasions on which you yourself employ the terms.

But wait a moment. Now that your memory of these terms has been refreshed, you might find yourself deliberately dropping them in a term paper (no pun intended) or a class discussion. Wouldn't that impress the professor and intimidate your classmates? It should, but only if the point you were trying to make, and into which you slipped the terms, was itself impressive and intimidating. Otherwise, all you have done is dazzle people momentarily with a sheen of culture that has no subsurface. This is called dilletantism, another term that, interestingly, does not appear on Hirsch's list. Your "literacy" is only ornamental. Its utility consists in dazzling people as a way of distracting them from your shallowness. No matter how high you pile the baubles, bangles, and beads of this ornamentation—even if you adorn yourself with *all* the terms in Hirsch's dictionary (Hirsch, Kett, and Trefil, 1988)—it is by your own good thinking that others will judge you in the long run, and not too long a run at that. You may be culturally literate in Hirsch's terms, but you will be a functional illiterate in the real world unless you can think well. Good thinking consists of locating relevant data and synthesizing them into meaningful wholes toward the solution of problems. Mere terms alone do not enable you to think. They only enable you to sound like a deep thinker for a while before people get wise to your superficiality. Knowing Hirsch's terms is no better than knowing the answers in Trivial Pursuit or Jeopardy.

The argument thus far may have been congenial because you think of yourself as liberal and Hirsch is being derided for his conservatism. But there are liberal lists, too. A good example is the *National Standards for United States History* (Crabtree and Nash, 1994). This tome is so skewed to the left that it has nineteen references to McCarthy and McCarthyism, but no mention of Soviet aggression in Eastern Europe (Ravitch, 1994). Harriet Tubman is cited far more often than George Washington (Winkler, 1995). In time, we may have not just one set of national standards per subject area, but a set for each ideological persuasion within each area. Perhaps there should be multiple versions of Trivial Pursuit and Jeopardy for the dilletantes of each ideological camp.

Shunning Elitism and Imperialism

It is likely that the average assembly-line worker in a Detroit auto factory would have trouble understanding Hirsch, who is a professor of English at the

University of Virginia, or the authors of the national history standards, who are professors at UCLA. The autoworker would lack familiarity with the terms being tossed around by the professors. One solution to this communication problem would be to drill into the autoworker's head the language of the professors. This, in fact, is the kind of solution being offered by the professors and others like them. They are saying that people should be taught to understand *them*. If the rest of us are taught the cultures of academe, human communication will be enhanced.

No doubt it will. But communication would also be enhanced if academics were taught the culture of the autoworker, or even the culture of the colleague whom they dismiss so cavalierly. The idea that "My culture is better than yours, so you should learn mine, but I don't have to bother with yours" is called cultural imperialism. The autoworker would probably use a shorter term: snobbery. To say that my culture is more important than yours because my group is more powerful than yours is to talk power politics. It is saying that you have to please me because I am one of the people in charge of running things. That's not education; that's domination. Education is about learning to understand *each other*.

Granting for the sake of argument that it is desirable for the poor to learn the culture of the better-off, the $400 million or so that it will cost to design and administer national tests would be better spent on upgrading the education of the poor rather than demonstrating once again what we already know to be its inadequacy (Schwebel, 1994). This is why such groups as the National Education Association, the National Association for the Advancement of Colored People, the National Parent-Teacher Association, and the American Association of School Administrators have urged that national testing not be done at this time (Neill, 1991). The Clinton administration has tried to defuse this opposition by proposing that there also be opportunity-to-learn standards to ensure that poor kids have been given a fair chance to do well on the national tests (Massell and Kirst, 1994). Working out these standards, which are sure to entail large costs and increased federal involvement in education, may be a politically impossible task.

If national tests are not to be elitist and imperialistic, does this mean we have to learn all the terms of the academics' culture(s) and all the terms of the autoworker's culture and every other group's culture, including those of blacks, Hispanics, women, and gays? That is obviously impossible. The most that can reasonably be expected is that these many major cultural groups be dealt with, and respectfully. What the major groups are will depend, to some extent, on the particular community. For example, a Texas coastal community with a large influx of Vietnamese refugees should include the culture of these people in the curriculum. In order to do this, the Texas town needs some control over the curriculum of its own schools. That is why a national curriculum with a lot of spelled-out details would be unwisely restrictive. "Students should have thorough exposure to the core of basic skills, but they should also have a curriculum which is relevant to their social environment . . . and which recognizes cultural diversity as a resource, not a deficit, in learning"

(Bastian et al., 1985, p. 47). A national curriculum without a lot of detail but just lofty rhetoric is not worth the paper to publish it.

One group whose culture should always be taken seriously in schools, but seldom is, is youth. The youth culture of the United States (and the local community variation on it) is a most appropriate subject of study in school. The fact that this culture is constantly changing does not mean that its current manifestations can be brushed off as frivolous. On the contrary, these manifestations are responded to eagerly by young people, who are, after all, the clients of schools. Schools should let their clients know that their culture is an important matter, and not something to be ignored until it is outgrown. Schools should cease suggesting to students that people become important only after they get out of school.

Having a Common Culture

The concern that local control will produce too much diversity and keep children from learning a common culture necessary for communication and career success is unwarranted. In the United States, the common culture is learned not only in school, but also through the mass media. There are only a handful of major television networks, including the cable ones. Syndicated radio talk shows like that of Rush Limbaugh are national town halls. The number of newspapers in the United States has been dwindling for a long time now, and there is even a national paper, *USA Today*. There are few newsmagazines, and Hollywood makes fewer movies than in the past. What all of this amounts to is a centralization and homogenization of culture by the media. This situation fosters a mass culture, even if it is not the high culture that appeals to Hirsch and others.

The mass culture is the primary basis upon which people relate to each other. Its terms are commonly understood. The subcultures people need to know in depth in order to get by in the world are the subcultures of their own jobs, religions, ethnic groups, and so on. People learn about these subcultures by living in them. It is the height of arrogance to insist that one's subculture be made the common culture.

> What standardized cultures are meant to do is distinguish their owners from the barbarians . . . by classifying the knowledge "we" have and "they" don't . . . it marks the difference between those for whom cultural literacy comes "naturally"—i.e., those who absorb the information and its context from home and social circles—and those who must acquire it, who feel the rift between their lived experience and what is considered important at school. (Margaronis, 1988, p. 14)

Avoiding Big Brother

In his classic novel *1984*, George Orwell warns against a society in which total control is exercised by the few over the many. The few who have total control (totalitarians) are referred to as Big Brother. If all the schools in the United

States are going to teach a single notion of cultural literacy, then the United States will need a Big Brother to spell out the details of that notion for the rest of us. Who should it be? Hirsch? You? Us? A committee of really, really smart people? A committee of people from every important cultural group? A bunch of members of Congress?

Before this question can be answered, there is a preliminary question that has to be answered: Who decides who gets to decide? If someone or some group is going to be America's cultural czar, then the people who get to pick the czar have to be selected very carefully.

As you can see, this all becomes very complicated and fraught with danger. The risks and effort might be worth it if we really needed national standards and tests, but we don't. The Republican-controlled 104th Congress may put an end to the effort by refusing further funding. If it is determined to cut unnecessary costs and keep the national government off our backs as much as possible, the national standards movement is a good place to begin. The left-leaning U.S. history standards have given the Republicans an added incentive for scuttling the movement (Diegmueller, 1995).

The spectre of Big Brother has been limned by the president of Rutgers University in his concern over national standards for higher education:

> The standard response of government to a public crisis is not friendly admonition to those responsible for its solution. Governments are made of much sterner stuff. The Department of Education has already floated more than once the idea of setting national standards by means of a national college test. It is just a series of short, easy steps, then, to crafting minimum student performance criteria. Since the government could not in good conscience allocate taxpayers' money to institutions whose students failed to meet the minimum criteria on the national test, the test would very shortly be required for all institutions and a specified pass rate would become a requirement for federal funding. Next, since many institutions obviously would be in need of guidance in order to reach the specified pass rate, the Department of Education would propose a standard curriculum to fulfill the standard criteria for the standard national test. You can be sure that the curriculum would be extremely specific, right down to the most minute detail, and that it would not be long before we would have an army of government inspectors monitoring the curriculum to make certain that it was being taught precisely as specified by the Ministry—oops, the Department of Education. (Lawrence, 1994, p. 5)

Teaching for Critical Literacy

Instead of giving students a false sense of culture by having them memorize a lot of big words, we should be making them *critically* literate. This notion is expressed by the Brazilian educator Paolo Freire (Freire and Macedo, 1987) and his North American colleagues, including Stanley Aronowitz and Henry Giroux (1985). It means helping people to understand and cope with the real world in which they live. People are taught how to think about their lives by being helped to do this intelligently. Their own culture is taken seriously through the process of analyzing it. But, in turn, they also have to analyze the larger culture for its impact on their lives. This critical literacy is functional literacy of the highest sort. It not only enables people to survive in their culture, but it empowers them to change the negative aspects of the culture.

If young people were to analyze American culture critically, they would surely find that the kind of cultural literacy being advocated by academics of whatever stripe bears faint resemblance to the kind of literacy that pays off with good jobs and high salaries in our society. They would quickly realize, if they don't already, that their elders are much better at preaching than practicing.

> We honor ambition, we reward greed, we celebrate materialism, we worship acquisitiveness, we commercialize art, we cherish success and then we bark at the young about the gentle arts of the spirit. . . . Kids just don't care much for hypocrisy, and if they are [culturally] illiterate, their illiteracy is merely ours, imbibed by them with scholarly ardor. They are learning well the lesson we are teaching—namely, that there is nothing in all the classics in their school libraries that will be of the slightest benefit to them in making their way to the top of our competitive society. (Barber, 1987)

A good way to come at *critical* literacy would be to involve students in the debate over *cultural* literacy. In the process, they would learn a lot of terms, but the real value would be in having them decide and defend for themselves the essentialness of these terms and whatever learning they deem to be more important than the terms. As Gerald Graff argues: "The best way to deal with the conflicts over education . . . is to *teach them*—teach the conflicts themselves" (Graff, quoted in Greene, 1989).

The standards movement may be well on the way to self-destructing because of its driven quality. So many groups have been beguiled by it that we now have national standards for arts, civics, economics, English, foreign languages, geography, health, history, mathematics, physical education, science, and social studies. This plus the fact that all the states are weighing in with their own versions (Struggling for Standards, 1995) means such a wild efflorescence of standards that people will soon get lost amid this and head for a clearing.

For Discussion

1. In 1859, John Stuart Mill, the English philosopher, issued the following warning in his classic work *On Liberty:*

> All that has been said of the importance of individuality of character, and diversity in opinions and modes of conduct, involves, as of the same unspeakable importance, diversity of education. A general State education is a mere contrivance for molding people to be exactly like one another; and as the mold in which it casts them is that which pleases the predominant power in the government . . . in proportion as it is efficient and successful, it establishes a despotism over the mind. . . .

How would you relate this quote to the cultural literacy movement?

2. It has often been said that schools are supposed to optimize each child's educational experience by individualizing instruction according to the child's background and abilities. How is this compatible with the goal of uniform cultural literacy for all?

3. At the end of his book *Cultural Literacy: What Every American Needs to Know*, E. D. Hirsch, Jr., has a sixty-four-page appendix of terms that every American should know. Following are several of these terms. How many of the terms do you know, and what do you make of your relative "knowledge" and "ignorance"?

Potato famine, Irish	primrose path
pragmatism	probation
precipitate (chemistry)	Procrustes' bed
premier (prime minister)	Prohibition
pre-Raphaelite	Prokofiev, Sergei
Presley, Elvis	proletariat
Pretoria	Prometheus
Pride and Prejudice (title)	Promised Land
prima donna	pro rata
primate	prose

4. The individuals honored as state teachers and principals of the year for 1988 compiled a list of recommended books for children of preschool to high school age.

   The educators made their selections at the "In Honor of Excellence" symposium held in October 1988. The event was sponsored by the Burger King Corporation in cooperation with the Council of Chief State School Officers and the National Association of Secondary School Principals.

   Following are the titles on the reading list. Do you think it would be a good idea to make this a required reading list for all schools in the United States? Are there any ways in which you would modify the list?

Preschool

Dr. Seuss series, Dr. Seuss
Mother Goose Stories
The Little Engine That Could, Watty Piper
Where the Wild Things Are, Maurice Sendak
Make Way for Ducklings, Robert McCloskey

Primary School (K–3)

The Velveteen Rabbit, Margery Williams
Alexander and the Terrible, Horrible, No Good, Very Bad Day, Judith Viorst
Ira Sleeps Over, Bernard Waber
The Tale of Peter Rabbit, Beatrix Potter
Winnie-the-Pooh, A. A. Milne
Charlotte's Web, W. B. White
Where the Wild Things Are, Maurice Sendak

Elementary School (4–6)

Charlotte's Web, E. B. White
Tales of a Fourth Grade Nothing, Judy Blume
Where the Red Fern Grows, Wilson Rawls
The Laura Ingalls Wilder series, Laura Ingalls Wilder
Little Women, Louisa May Alcott

Junior High School (7–9)

Where the Red Fern Grows, Wilson Rawls
Anne Frank: The Diary of a Young Girl, Anne Frank
The Red Badge of Courage, Stephen Crane
The Call of the Wild, Jack London
Huckleberry Finn, Mark Twain
Treasure Island, Robert Louis Stevenson
The Outsiders, S. E. Hinton

High School (10–12)

The Grapes of Wrath, John Steinbeck
To Kill a Mockingbird, Harper Lee
Huckleberry Finn, Mark Twain
The Scarlet Letter, Nathaniel Hawthorne
A Tale of Two Cities, Charles Dickens
Macbeth, William Shakespeare
The Catcher in the Rye, J. D. Salinger

Source: Education Week, October 19, 1988, p. 30.

5. Lynn Cheney, as chair of the National Endowment for the Humanities, funded the development of national standards for U.S. history. The final document has made her unhappy, however, because of what she thinks is the overrepresentation of some topics and the underrepresentation of others. The following graph illustrates her concerns. Do you share the concerns?

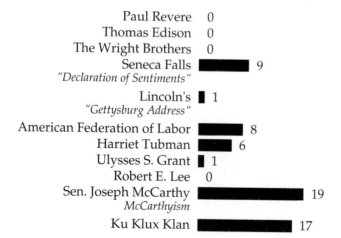

What midnight ride?

*The number of times certain historical
subjects are cited in the text of
"National Standards for U.S. History."*

Paul Revere	0
Thomas Edison	0
The Wright Brothers	0
Seneca Falls *"Declaration of Sentiments"*	9
Lincoln's *"Gettysburg Address"*	1
American Federation of Labor	8
Harriet Tubman	6
Ulysses S. Grant	1
Robert E. Lee	0
Sen. Joseph McCarthy *McCarthyism*	19
Ku Klux Klan	17

Source: L. Cheney (1994). "Hijacking America's History." *The Wall Street Journal*, October 20.

References

Adler, M. (1988). "The Paideia Proposal: Rediscovering the Essence of Education." In *Innovations in Education: Reformers and Their Critics*, edited by J. M. Rich. Boston: Allyn & Bacon.

Aronowitz, S., and Giroux, H. A. (1985). *Education Under Siege: The Conservative, Liberal and Radical Debate Over Schooling*. South Hadley, MA: Bergin & Garvey.

Barber, B. (1987). "What Do 47-Year-Olds Know?" *The New York Times*, December 26, p. 23.

Bastian, A., et al. (1985). *Choosing Equality: The Case for Democratic Schooling*. New York: New World Foundation.

Butts, R. (1995). "Antidote for Antipolitics: A New 'Text of Civic Instruction.'" *Education Week* **14**(17), 38, 48.

Celis, W. (1993). "The Fight Over National Standards." *The New York Times Education Life*, August 1, pp. 14–16.

Cheney, L. (1987). *American Memory: A Report on the Humanities in the Nation's Public Schools*. Washington, DC: National Endowment for the Humanities.

Crabtree, C., and Nash, G. (1994). *National Standards for United States History*. Los Angeles: National Center for History in the Schools.

Cuban, L. (1993). "A National Curriculum and Tests." *Education Week* **12**(39), 25, 27.

Diegmueller, K. (1995). "Backlash Puts Standards Work in Harm's Way." *Education Week* **14**(16), 1, 12–13.

Elam, S., Rose, L., and Gallup, A. (1994). "The 26th Annual Phi Delta Kappa Gallup Poll of the Public's Attitudes Toward the Public Schools." *Phi Delta Kappan* **76**(1), 41–56.

Finn, C. (1991). "Education Reform vs. Civil Rights Agendas." *The New York Times*, May 18, p. 23.

Freire, P., and Macedo, D. (1987). *Literacy: Reading the Word and the World*. South Hadley, MA: Bergin & Garvey.

Gluck, C. (1994). "History According to Whom?" *The New York Times*, November 19, p. 23.

Greene, E. (1989). "'Teach the Conflicts, Teach the Conflicts,' Preaches This Humanist." *The Chronicle of Higher Education* **35**(22), A3.

Henig, J. R. (1988). "Which Way, Mr. Bennett?" *The Washington Post National Weekly Edition*, September 12–18, p. 27.

Hirsch, E. D. (1987). *Cultural Literacy: What Every American Needs to Know*. Boston: Houghton Mifflin.

_____ (1993). "Teach Knowledge, Not 'Mental Skills.'" *The New York Times*, September 4, p. 19.

_____, Kett, J. F., and Trefil, J. (1988). *The Dictionary of Cultural Literacy: What Every American Needs to Know*. Boston: Houghton Mifflin.

_____ (1991). *What Your 1st Grader Needs to Know*, and *What Your 2nd Grader Needs to Know*. New York: Doubleday.

Howe, H. (1995). "Uncle Sam Is in the Classroom!" *Phi Delta Kappan* 76(5), 374–377.

Johnston, R., and Diegmueller, K. (1995). "Senate Approves Resolution Denouncing History Standards." *Education Week* **14**(18), 14.

Jones, A. (1995). "Our Stake in the History Standards." *The Chronicle of Higher Education* **41**(17), B1–B3.

Kagan, D. (1991). "Western Values Are Central." *The New York Times*, May 4, p. 23.

Kean, T. (1991). "Do We Need a National Achievement Exam? Yes." *Education Week* **10**(31), 28, 36.

"Largest Teachers' Union Calls for National High School Exam" (1995). *The New York Times,* July 6, p. A15.

Lawrence, F. (1994). Remarks to Meeting of National Association of State Universities and Land-Grant Colleges. Chicago, November 8, p. 5.

Margaronis, M. (1989). "Waiting for the Barbarians: The Ruling Class Defends the Citadel." *Village Voice Literary Supplement,* January/February, pp. 12–17.

Massel, D., and Kirst, M. (1994). "Determining National Content Standards: An Introduction." *Education and Urban Society* **26**(2), 107–117.

National Standards for Civics and Government. (1994), Calabasas, CA: Center for Civic Education.

Neill, M. (1991). "Do We Need a National Achievement Exam? No." *Education Week* **10**(31), 28, 36.

Ohanian, S. (1987). "Finding a 'Loony List' While Searching for Literacy." *Education Week,* **6**(5), 21–22.

Phelps, R. (1993) "The Weak and Strong Arguments Against National Testing." *Education Week* **12**(34), 30.

Postman, N. (1992). *Technopoly: The Surrender of Culture to Technology.* New York: Knopf.

Ravitch, D. (1994). "Standards in U.S. History: An Assessment." *Education Week* **14**(14), 40, 48.

_____ and Finn, C. (1987). *What Do Our 17-Year-Olds Know? A Report on the First National Assessment of History and Literature.* New York: Harper & Row.

Rothman, R. (1991a). "On the Road to National Standards, Math Educators Debate Assessments." *Education Week* **10** (32), 1, 25.

_____ (1991b). "Researchers Say Emphasis on Testing Too Narrow, Could Set Back Reforms." *Education Week* **10**(38), 25.

Samuelson, R. (1991). "Why School Reform Fails." *Newsweek,* May 27, p. 62.

Schlesinger, A. (1992). *The Disuniting of America: Reflections on a Multicultural Society.* New York: Norton.

Schwarz, P. (1994). "Needed: School-Set Standards." *Education Week,* **14**(12), 34, 44.

Schwebel, M. (1994). "Educational Pie in the Sky." *The Nation,* May 2, pp. 591–592.

Shanker, A. (1994). "All 'A's' Are Not Equal." *The New York Times,* September 11, p. E7.

_____ (1991). "Developing a Common Curriculum." *The New York Times,* February 24, p. E7.

_____ (1992). "National Standards and Exams." *The New York Times,* March 1, p. E7.

Sizer, T. (1992). "A Test of Democracy." *The New York Times,* January 30, p. A21.

_____ (1984). *Horace's Compromise.* Boston: Houghton Mifflin.

"Steps Toward Improving Student Assessment." (1992). *New Voices* 2(1), 3.

Struggling for Standards. (1995). *Education Week Special Report,* April 12.

The Geography Education Standards Project. (1994). *Geography for Life.* Washington, DC: National Geographic Research and Exploration.

Viadero, D. (1994). "Standards in Collision." *Education Week* **13**(17), 25–27.

Winkler, K. (1995). "Who Owns History?" *The Chronicle of Higher Education* **41**(19), A10–A11, A18.

CHAPTER TEN

Values: Traditional or Liberational

POSITION 1:
TEACH TRADITIONAL VALUES

Among the results of an educational philosophy that emphasizes selfishness, personal freedom, and permissiveness is a decline in social and family values (Sowell, 1992). An increase in crime and abuse of others is a natural outcome of schooling that preaches self-indulgence. Where can one gain a deep respect for other people, property, and social traditions if the schools assume the relativist stance that these things do not matter? The liberal view of schooling—that students should decide basic values for themselves, without guidance from educators or parents—has an eroding effect on the cornerstones of American society. It does not take a rocket scientist to recognize that the civility, manners, and courtesies once dominant in America have been replaced by greed, destruction, and fear of others. This erosion has been the companion of permissive attitudes fostered in schools since the 1930s (Bennett, 1994).

It is no wonder that family values have declined in the face of an educational philosophy based on individualism and libertine life-styles (Anderson, 1994; Roberts, 1994). Evidence of a moral disaster is all around us: extraordinarily high divorce rates, child and spouse abuse, lack of ethics in business and government, drug and alcohol addiction, out-of-control teen-age pregnancy rates, excessive reliance on child care outside the home, acceptance of immorality on television and in the arts, and cheating scandals in schools (Colson, 1994). This is a snapshot of life when we do not provide a strong education in traditional values. Schools have lost their moral quality and, thus, their leadership.

Efforts to bring schools and society back to their moral base have begun to yield positive results. In 1990, a combination of groups supporting family values and school morality were successful in elections in San Diego County in California, putting strong citizens in about two-thirds of the open seats on school boards and city councils. Pat Robertson's Christian Coalition described

San Diego as a model of what can be done in local communities to reestablish morality in schools and society. Local agendas now include maintaining traditional values in the school curriculum; stemming the tide of antifamily education, such as birth control classes; and fighting to bring back religion as basic to schooling (Rabkin, 1995).

The 1994 national elections, which replaced liberal politicians with more conservative ones, reflect the general discontent with the direction America was taking. Among the items in the Republican "contract with America" was the restoration of religion to American schools. Oliver North founded a national organization, the Freedom Alliance, to restore American first principles: traditional morality, close and strong families, free enterprise, solid schools, and vigorous national defense. This organization recognizes the tight relationship between good families and good schools in a society based on common values. These efforts illustrate the increasing disillusionment felt by many Americans concerning the drift of the nation and the decline of schools.

Bryce Christensen (1991), director of the Rockford Institute Center on the Family in America, argues persuasively that schools have become ideological centers for crusades against family and traditional values. He buttresses his points with numerous quotations, including one from sociologist Kingsley Davis: "one of the main functions of [the school system] . . . appears to be to alienate offspring from their parents" (p. 6). Christensen raises important questions about teachers who presume to supersede parents in implanting moral values in children. Further, he cites the work of Paul Vitz and Michael Levin, who document an aggressive feminist bias in school texts and teachings—a feminist bias that is in opposition to traditional American family values. Traditional parenthood and family life are virtually censored from school materials, while the same materials convey romantic images of adventurous single women. Similarly, reports Christensen, traditionalist parents have good reason to worry about amoral messages in literature that denounce religion and espouse adultery or other antifamily values.

America's Schools Are Rooted in Moral Values

Schools in America were founded to provide a moral foundation, and they were effective. Colonial schools had as their core a firm commitment to morality, ethics, and traditional values. Basic to these values was a firm belief in religion, even though the denominations differed among the various religions in the colonies.

The first school laws, in Massachusetts in 1642 and 1647, mandated that communities provide schools for young people, and that those schools preserve religious and social values. The *New England Primer,* the colonial schoolbook most used to teach the alphabet and reading, incorporated moral virtues in its teaching of basic skills. This was a pattern among all books used in schools for many generations. The necessary link between a good society and solid religious, family, and school values was clearly recognized in early America.

Religions afford a good moral base for young people, but they aren't the only source of traditional values. Ethical personal behavior also derives from deep-rooted family and social values. The good society depends on citizens who have developed keen concern for others, awareness of personal responsibility, and habits of moderation (McFarlane, 1994). These character traits are necessary in a civil society, but they have been forsaken in much of the modern selfish and individualistic world. Charles Colson (1994) makes the important point that the secularization of American society is responsible for the increase in violent crime. Not all families or social groups exhibit values that are conducive to the good society because they are themselves in moral decay. That is why schooling to preserve and protect traditional values is so essential. Schools, unfortunately, have fallen prey to the same selfish and corrupting ideas that have destroyed some families and some segments of society.

Secular Humanism and the Loss of Values

Schools no longer lead in the reaffirmation of traditional family and religious values, but have been taken over by secular humanism and its selfish pursuits. Secular humanism, with its relativistic and narcissistic values, has corrupted much of public life. Secular humanism has permeated the public schools; it has fostered permissiveness and kept students from developing a personal core of values. That is certainly one reason why family life has come apart and why religious involvement has declined. Most young people of the post–World War II generation were indoctrinated with secular humanism in school, even though they may not have recognized its perniciousness. Thus, it is easy to understand how family and religious life would suffer as that generation became parents. Now at least two generations have gone through that program, and American society is reaping the social discontent that secular humanism can produce.

Secular humanism is a view that the state is more important than religion, and that humans can create and change their values without reference to a greater being. This means that whatever is a current fad is the ethical code for the society. If enough people want to do something, they simply do it, no matter the damage to society or moral law. If what they want to do is illegal, they flout the law and put pressure on public officials to ignore higher values. In some instances, they have the law altered to erode basic values further. The rapid expansion of legalized gambling, easy abortions, alcoholism, drug abuse, and crime are examples of this in practice.

Secular humanism, and the relativistic values it promotes, caters to the basest of human desires. It provides no guidelines for behavior or thought. It is permissiveness at the highest level. Secular humanism is now the dominant view in the public schools.

Jerry Falwell (1980) described the destruction of American education:

> Until about thirty years ago, the public schools in America were providing . . . support for our boys and girls. Christian education and the precepts of the

Bible still permeated the curriculum of the public schools . . . Our public schools are now permeated with humanism . . . children are taught that there are no absolute rights or wrongs and that the traditional home is only one alternative. (pp. 205, 210)

Senator Strom Thurmond, a strong constitutionalist, wrote a ringing criticism of Supreme Court decisions that "assault the Constitution." Among the decisions he protests as leaving the country open to communism, collectivism, and immorality are the Court's actions to prohibit prayer and Bible reading in public schools. He asserts:

They [parents] ought to have a right to insist that their children are educated in the traditions and values of their own culture. Above all, they have a right to see that their children are not indoctrinated in a secular, Godless point of view which contradicts the values that are taught at home. (Thurmond, 1968, p. 28)

How Schools Destroy Values

Children are taught that the values they learn in the home or at church are a matter of choice. Through teachings such as "values clarification," children are led to believe that their individual opinions of what is right and wrong are perfectly satisfactory. There is no moral guideline for conduct or thought. In "values clarification," the teacher may ask a child to publicly identify situations at home where the father or mother was wrong, and to present his or her own view of what should have been done. The teachers ask children personal questions about their family lives and private thoughts. And they present lists of antisocial behaviors and ask the children to rank them according to their own opinions of whether the behaviors are "good" or "bad." The teacher does not present correct responses or try to explain why a particular view is the right one. There are no criteria against which children can weigh right and wrong. Instead, the teacher encourages each child to determine his or her own set of values.

In class discussions of values, children who present their personal opinions with conviction can influence other children, and the teacher is not supposed to intercede for fear of impeding the "clarification" of values. That is how it is possible for an entire class to agree that tying cans to a cat's tail, euthanizing people who are old or ill, or remaining seated during the salute to the flag may be acceptable behavior. Children also learn to report on their parents, and to ridicule those who hold traditional values of discretion and privacy.

Dr. Elmer Towns, in a hard-hitting book, documents the failures of public education and the resulting threat to American society. In a chapter entitled "The Smell of Deterioration," he writes:

What has "had it" in public schools? Bible-reading and prayers are not legal; they have "had it." The Puritan/Protestant ethic as a style of life has been edged out by the new morality; it has "had it." Dedication to academic pursuits is no longer prized by the majority of educators; it has "had it." Correct behavior, according to respected society norms, is no longer enforced; it has "had it." . . . the question that screams for an answer is, "Has our nation 'had it'?" (Towns, 1974, p. 23)

It is a blind belief that young children can exert self-restraint and make critical judgments without proper training. The government requires school attendance, but neglects and undercuts the moral basis required for proper education in values.

Confusing Values in the Current Curriculum

The school curriculum and textbooks now used present a wide array of relativistic values that only serve to confuse children. Secular humanism is not defined as a school subject, and there are no courses in it. Instead, it filters into nearly all courses and is often unrecognized, even by the teachers. Because there is no specific curriculum stressing traditional morals and values, it is easy for teachers and courses to present differing ones, and to lead students to believe that there are no eternal values, only personal ones. If the courses and the teachers do not attest to a common core of morality, students are left rudderless in school. This spawns confusion or self-indulgence at best, and scorn for morality at worst.

The teaching material presented to children is either vapid, without any connection to moral thought and behavior, or confusing, because it displays multiple values of supposedly equal weight. Current reading material in school includes nonsensical stories that lead nowhere, trash that directs attention to the values of the worst elements of society, and adult stories well beyond the moral development of children. In civics and history, the focus is on political power, not virtue. Children are taught how to manipulate others, and how interest groups get things their way. History texts are bland and noncommittal concerning basic values, and religion is ignored or treated with disdain. Sex education instruction is inclined toward promiscuity and sexual freedom, not toward abstinence and responsibility (Whitehead, 1994). Science ignores religious views and substitutes the idea of being value-free; any scientific experiment is OK. And the arts include study of depraved artists and music, rather than uplifting and positive arts. Innocence, instead of being protected and encouraged, is savaged and debased (Rafferty, 1968).

The results of this permissive and selfish education are apparent. We are subject to increasing abuse in contemporary life. There has been a startling increase in child abuse, so prevalent we have twenty-four-hour telephone "hot lines" to report it. Spouse abuse is another item reported almost daily in the newspapers. Animal abuse is so common that it no longer makes news. And sex and drug abuse have become epidemic.

There are other abuses in the current world. We abuse our ideals, our respect, our heroes, our national honor, and our religious base. Political and business leaders abuse the public trust through cheating and corruption. It is no longer clear to young people why we fought wars to protect our liberties. Some children refuse to recite the Pledge of Allegiance or to sing the "Star-Spangled

Banner." Graffiti covers many of our national monuments and our statues of heroes. Children no longer honor their parents or respect their elders.

What is the reason for this decline in American values? There are many reasons, but the foremost is that the schools have foresaken the teaching of solid values. Instead, they have substituted highly relativistic opinions that undermine parental and religious authority. Children are taught that all values are equal, so whatever they value is fine. We can't hold children responsible for this travesty on common morality because their natural tendency is to be selfish. Parents must teach children to share and to have respect for normal social values. Historically, we have relied on the school to reinforce and extend the basic ethical code taught in families and churches. In those unfortunate circumstances when parents are unable, or refuse, to teach children right from wrong, the school has usually supplied this important function. Those who now run the schools have forgotten their history, and people who forget will repeat the mistakes of the past.

With the current high divorce rates and parents' lack of attention to their children's moral development, the schools should be expected to play an even more significant role in conveying American values to children. It is in times of family and social stress that the schools should exert expanded influence to ensure the continuation of our heritage. Active membership in religions is beginning to increase as people recognize the insidious vacuum in morality created during the most recent period of permissiveness. But many of our young parents grew up during the 1960s and 1970s, when there was a sharp decline in religious participation and a significant increase in immorality. Without the value base that strong religious and national traditions provide, America will be in trouble. Schools must assume an increased responsibility for training students in the traditional values needed in society.

What Should Be Taught

Clearly, schools need to rediscover their proper role and function in a moral society. America was founded on Judeo-Christian ideals. We have survived, and thrived, because of these ideals. They form the basis of our concepts of justice and democracy. Schools were established to transmit those values to the young as a way of preserving the values and the society.

Early American schooling was deliberately intended to instill a belief in God and support for traditional values. There was a clarity of purpose and a solid direction for schools. Children did not receive mixed messages about morality and behavior, and they did not get the impression that they could make up and change their values on a whim.

Traditional Values as the Focus

The curriculum should include a prominent focus on traditional values at all levels. In elementary school, reading material should emphasize ideals (Anderson, 1994). Stories of great heroes, personal integrity, resoluteness, loyalty, and the productivity of hard work should be dominant. The main emphasis should be on the positive aspects of American history and literature, showing how individuals working together toward a suitable goal can succeed. Teachers should stress and expect ethical behavior, respect, and consideration. Various religions should be studied with the purpose of understanding their common values and the application of those values in life. Providing time in school for children to come into contact with their religious beliefs would be appropriate.

Signs and symbols in school should reinforce American values. Pictures, displays, and assemblies on morality offer students a chance to see how important those values are to the school. Inviting speakers into classes, showing films, and taking students to see significant monuments to American values are techniques that can help. Teachers can emphasize good values by providing direct instructions on moral precepts and rewarding students for good citizenship.

At the secondary level, the emphasis on traditional values should continue with more sophisticated material and concepts. There is no need for a special course on sex education if family values are covered well in other courses. A student honor roll, citing acts of outstanding school citizenship, might be as prominently displayed as the athletic trophies that now typically dominate glass cabinets near the principal's office. Libraries are good places for special sections containing books and displays that feature the kinds of thoughts and behaviors we seek.

Literature classes should present American and foreign literature that portrays the rewards of moral behavior and the negative consequences of immorality. Schools might sponsor essay contests on subjects that convey a concern for morality. American history classes should express the ideals for which we stand, and our extraordinary historical achievements. Science courses should feature stories of hard work and success in making scientific discoveries, as well as stories of how basic values and religious views have guided many scientists in their work.

The arts are a rich place to show values through the study of paintings, compositions, sculptures, and other art forms that express the positive aspects of human life under a set of everlasting ideals. Not only can religious music and art be used, but there are thousands of examples of nonreligious art that idealize such things as the golden rule and personal virtue. The vocational subjects afford numerous ways to present good attitudes toward work, family, responsibility, loyalty, decency, and respect. Sports are an especially important place in which to reaffirm these same values; numerous professional and college teams pray together before matches, and many players are leading figures in setting high standards of moral conduct.

Teachers for American Values

The kinds of teachers we need are those who themselves have a strong commitment to traditional values, and whose behaviors and lives exhibit that commitment. These teachers are the key to improved schooling in values. Changes in curriculum or teaching materials will have no impact if the teachers who work directly with the young do not meet our moral criteria. Obviously, the determination of moral beliefs goes beyond examining transcripts of college courses, since the subjects a person studied bear little relation to his or her moral conduct and beliefs.

In order to preserve and protect American values in schools, states have a right to require high moral standards from those who obtain state licenses to teach in the public schools. Colleges that prepare teachers should be required to examine potential students' records and deny entry to those with criminal or other socially offensive backgrounds. Applicants for teaching credentials should be expected to submit references that speak to their moral character. As this is expected of lawyers who take state bar exams, why shouldn't it be expected of people going into teaching? As a part of the application procedure for teaching positions, schools should require applicants to prepare essays stating their beliefs. Clearly, the period of student teaching and the first few years of full-time teaching provide ample opportunity to screen young teachers in their school and public lives to ensure that moral standards are upheld. If these criteria are clearly and publicly stated, there is fair warning. Teachers found wanting in their morality would need to find employment in some other occupation. They should not be retained in positions where they can influence the ideals of young people.

With a strengthened corps of teachers in the schools, there will be a rebuilding of American values. These teachers will demand better curricula, better teaching materials, and better student behavior. There will be an infectious quality about this rebuilding that will influence parents, government, and the media. The schools have a rich opportunity.

It is possible to restore basic American values to the schools, and to our young people. But being possible is not enough. It is crucial that we move quickly to reinvigorate our school leaders with a resolve to do it. There is a crisis of values in society, and that is reflected in our schools. Our society is extremely vulnerable. The school must reassume the responsibility for moral teachings that was its original purpose.

From the *New England Primer* through McGuffy's *Readers*, the content studied in school was consistent with America's traditional values. There is much to be learned from the moral stories presented in these old works. Children learned that it was wrong to misbehave at home, in the community, and at school. They learned the consequences of affronting the common morality by reading about what happened to those who did. They gained respect for proper authority in families, churches, society, and school. We need to reject the permissiveness and valuelessness of the current schools and return to an emphasis on moral precepts and proper behavior. That will require considerable effort in rethinking the curriculum and redirecting teaching. The crisis in education has the same origin as the crisis in society: a decline in basic values. Correction in the schools is the main avenue to corrections in the society.

POSITION 2:
FOR LIBERATION

School is not a neutral activity. There is no school that is value-free; the very essence of school expresses a set of values. The social and individual decisions to provide and to undertake education are based on a set of values, and the daily activity of education is a value-laden one. We educate for some purpose we consider to be good, and what we teach is what we think is a good thing. To do otherwise is an absurdity.

Schools, then, are heavily involved in a series of value-based decisions related to the kind of person and the kind of society that should be produced. The issue is not whether or not schools should be engaged in values education, since all are; rather, the issue is what kinds of values should be central to schoolwork. Teachers, textbooks, and the general operation of school all teach some set of values to young people. Schools can be organized and operated in ways that develop conformity, obedience to external authorities, and passive and docile behavior by students. Schools can also work to develop thoughtful critics of society's problems; students who are willing to challenge social norms and pursue the continued improvement of humankind into the future (Kidder, 1994; Haydon, 1995). There are many variations of these purposes for school in either socializing students to conform to social values or liberating them to engage in social improvement. Unfortunately, much of the activity in many contemporary schools is devoted to producing docile and passive students—and the schools are often successful.

Much of the focus of school life is on conformity, with extreme pressure on all students to think, behave, and view life in the same way. The "standard model" approach to values in schools leads to a stultifying school life based on moral pronouncements and outdated slogans. This not only is hypocritical, since many adult citizens and educators do not adhere to the moralistic standards prescribed, but it destroys the creativity and energy of our young people.

In traditional schools, students are force-fed moralisms and value precepts that are not consistent with what students see for themselves in society. Honesty is preached by poorly paid teachers while Wall Street financiers, bankers, and politicians loot the public. Persons who commit so-called white-collar crimes are seldom punished, although a few may be sent to luxurious detainment centers for brief stays, whereas small-time criminals from lower-social-class backgrounds are given long and debilitating sentences in the worst pits, where they learn more criminal behavior. Consider similar examples in regard to the moralisms taught students about cheating, selfishness, greed, and discourtesy.

This is not an essay in favor of abandoning the civilizing characteristics of human society, including decency, respect, responsibility, courage, and magnanimity. Indeed, it is the opposite—a view in favor of values that give students the power to develop and enhance civilization without hypocrisy. We cannot impose traditional and external values on children in schools without allowing those values to be criticized. Students learn to conform in school in order to avoid problems, and, as a result, they learn to ignore social injustice and inequality. Instead of questioning and acting to improve society, students are expected to sponge up moralisms and be quiet. This essay agrees with philosopher Maxine Greene (1990) that moral choice and ethical action should be the products of careful and critical thought. That occurs when the community provides freedom for individual students and teachers to engage in it.

The primary purpose of education is liberation. Freedom from slavery, from dictatorship, and from domination are based on freedom from ignorance. The freedom to think and the freedom to act are based on the freedom to know. Any society that intends to be free and democratic must recognize that elemental schooling equation: liberation = education. Schools that restrict and contort the minds of the young are in opposition to that principle, and democratic civilization is the victim.

John Stuart Mill (1859/1956), in his classic essay *On Liberty*, defines the commonplace education as conformist:

> A general State education is a mere contrivance for moulding people to be exactly like one another; and as the mould in which it casts them is that which pleases the predominant power in the government—whether this be a monarch, a priesthood, an aristocracy, or the majority of the existing generation—in proportion as it is efficient and successful, it establishes a despotism over the mind, leading by natural tendency to one over the body. (p. 129)

Mill's comments are still appropriate today.

Liberation Education

Liberation education is obviously not a prescribed set of teacher techniques, a specific lesson plan, or a textbook series for schools to adopt. There is no mechanistic or teacher-proof approach to students that will produce liberation. Devious and robotlike schooling ideas, such as behavioral objectives and mastery learning, are not part of liberation education. Indeed, liberation is in direct opposition to the conformist mentality that produced such ideas. Liberation is the emancipation of students and teachers from the blinders of class-dominated ignorance, conformity, and thought control (Shor, 1987; Clark, 1990; Ahlquist, 1991). It is dynamic, seeing students and teachers as active participants in opposing oppression and improving democracy (Giroux, 1991).

Liberation education is complex, because the social forces it addresses are complex. The central purpose is to liberate the individual and society from oppressive domination and to provide a broad distribution of liberating power. That, of course, requires a set of values, including justice and equality, to serve as ideals in opposition to oppression. It further requires critical understanding of the many cultural crosscurrents in contemporary society and the mechanisms of manipulation that hide ideological purposes. Liberation education uncovers the myths and injustices evident in the dominant culture, especially for the disadvantaged. It also includes an expectation that the powerless can, through education, develop power. This requires a recognition that the forms of knowledge and of schooling are not neutral, but are utilized by the dominant culture to continue its power.

Schools must be seen as sites where we examine the manifold conflicts of humankind, in increasing depth, in order to understand the ideological and cultural bases on which societies operate. The purpose is not merely to recognize those conflicts or ideologies, but to engage in actions that constrain oppression and expand personal power. This profound and revolutionary educational concept goes to the heart of what education should be. Schools themselves are subject to this liberating critique, and we should take actions to make them more truly democratic. Other social institutions are also necessary subjects of examination and action. It is obvious that "liberation education," a redundant term, is controversial in contemporary society and in education. Liberated people threaten the traditional docility and passivity that are now imposed by schools.

Mainstream Mystification

There is too little in popular educational literature that speaks to liberation, the opposition to oppressive forces, and the improvement of democracy. Most mainstream educational writing raises no questions about the context within which the school sits; it seems to accept the conservative purposes and operations of schools and merely intends to "fine-tune" them a bit. Standard educational writing does not see schooling as a problematic issue subject to critical examination of roots, ideologies, and complexities. Instead, teachers and teachers-in-training read articles on teacher techniques and slight modifications in school curriculum. There is nothing critical in these pieces, and there is no liberation of the mind from the strictures of a narrow culture. The dominant concern is to make the school more efficient, more mechanical, more factorylike, more conformist.

Mainstream educational literature rests on a mainstream of thought in American society that is bound by a narrow band between standard conservative and liberal ideas. It is not considered good form to read material, pose ideas, or raise criticism from outside this band. Those who do are labeled radical or "un-American" and are viewed with suspicion. The outside ideas and criticisms are not given public credibility. The effort to improve the way democracy works by subjecting it to critical evaluation is disdained, and neither conservatives nor liberals are pleased to have American democracy critically examined in schools.

Conservatives and liberals do seem to agree in their writings that schools in America should be related to democracy. Numerous platitudes about schools preparing citizens for democracy, or about the school as a minidemocracy, fill the standard mainstream literature. This literature can be classified as mystification in that it uses high-sounding phrases to cover its ideology of status quo, a continuation of the power of the already dominant class. It is not active democracy, with its liberation values, that this literature commends. The real purpose is keep the masses content as uncritical workers, believing themselves to be free but actually being powerless. The function of mainstream writing is to mystify readers with a rhetoric of freedom while maintaining domination by the powerful.

Schooling terms, such as "excellence," "mastery," "humanistic," and "progressive," fill mainstream periodicals. Although the terms can be useful in discussing education, they are often used as camouflage. Conservatives use the terms "excellence" and "mastery" to mask the interests of dominant classes in justifying their advantages, and the interests of business in the production of skilled and docile workers. Liberals use the terms "humanistic" and "progressive" to hide a soft and comfortable individualism that ignores basic problems and conflicts in society. The combination continues the business ideology that dominates schools and society, and the narcissism that prevents groups from recognizing the defects in that ideology. That is mystification—an effort to mystify the public and keep hidden the real agenda in schools.

That agenda is to maintain what Joel Spring (1976) calls a "sorting machine," whereby the different social classes are given different treatment and sorted into various categories of citizenship. Raymond Callahan (1962) documents this agenda as a business orientation in schools, designed to prepare the masses to do efficient work and the elite to manage. Jean Anyon (1980) exposes the actual curriculum of docility and obedience taught to the lower classes. Henry Giroux (1988) describes the hidden curriculum that imposes dominant class values, attitudes, and norms on all students. And Aronowitz and Giroux (1991) identify the need for a strong schooling in criticism to buttress students against the crippling effects of traditional imposed social values.

Much is made in the mass media of the conservative and liberal arguments about schooling, but, in fact, there is little that separates them. The schools can and do, by slight modifications every few years, accommodate each side for a while. The pendulum swings in a narrow arc from the center, but schools remain pretty much the same, with only cosmetic changes. When conservatives are in power, there is more concern about competition, grading, passing tests, and knowing specific bits of information. Liberals try to make students feel happy, to allow more freedom in the curriculum, and to offer more student activities.

With regard to democracy and schooling, the differences between the conservative and liberal views lie in how narrowly democracy is defined, and at what age democracy is to be practiced. The conservative rhetoric calls for a narrower definition and the forming of good habits and values by students before they can participate. That usually means that the school is a place to learn the narrow definition and to learn loyalty to American democracy without practicing it. Liberals write about a somewhat broader definition, and about the schools as places where a form of democracy should actually be practiced.

Neither the conservative nor the liberal mainstream view raises basic questions about the nature of democracy or the means used to achieve it. Neither view is critical of existing class domination of knowledge and schools.

Neither sees democracy as problematic, deserving of continuing critical examination in order to improve it. Both views assume that there is a basic consensus on what democracy is, and that the schools are merely an agency for obtaining it. As a result, there is very little basic difference between conservative and liberal views about schooling in a democracy. There are only shallow differences in what subjects are emphasized and how much limited freedom students are given. Those may sound like important differences, but debates over such matters as how tough grading practices should be or whether extra time is needed for reading drill do not address serious and significant issues of democratic life. Ideologically, conservatives and liberals share basic beliefs.

Reactionary Indoctrination and Cultural Reproduction

Only the reactionary fringe, the far right, appears on the surface to desire schools and a society that are basically undemocratic in purpose and operation. At least the far-right wing is honest and direct, if wrong. These reactionary groups, including religious fundamentalists, are clear that there is a natural hierarchical social order that must be imposed on children in schools. There is nothing democratic in that premise. Right-wingers are open advocates of indoctrination and censorship. If you know the *truth*, why let other ideas be presented? Dissent, of course, should be stifled because it confuses children of all ages. And deviation cannot be tolerated. It is refreshing to see such clarity and determination in the face of general uncertainty in the modern world, but this view has potentially disastrous consequences for any democracy and its schools.

Interestingly, conservative and liberal views also expect indoctrination, but they are loath to tell anyone, because it sounds undemocratic. Instead, since they control the schools and the society, they can impose their dominant views by more subtle means. By virtue of state laws, this coalition controls the school curriculum, textbook selection, school operation, and teacher licensing. State agencies—for example, a state department of education—monitor schools and prescribe limits. The news media, under similar domination by mainstream conservative and liberal forces, persuade the public that the democracy and the schools are working relatively well. There is very little basic criticism of either in the media; the news mainly reports minor disagreements on tactics and personalities. Ideological disputes are not confronted because there are no such disputes between standard conservative and liberal views.

So schools are expected to indoctrinate students into the mainstream, and the mainstream has the power to require this conformity. "Cultural reproduction" means that each generation passes on to the next the dominant cultural ideology that was imposed on it. In America, this cultural reproduction takes two forms: (1) a set of positive beliefs that America is a chosen country, with justice and equality for all and the best of economic systems; and (2) a set of negative beliefs that any views that raise troubling questions about American values automatically are anti-American. This two-fold reproduction ensures that teachers and students do not engage in serious critical thinking, but merely accept dominant ideologies. Thus, the very nature of democracy, and the means for improving it, are not seen as problematic; instead, they are perceived as naturally existing and beyond the school's examination.

In school, students read mainstream literature, hear mainstream views from teachers and peers, see mainstream films, listen to mainstream speakers, and engage in mainstream extracurricular activities. The school library carries only mainstream periodicals and books. It is virtually impossible to find an examination of highly divergent ideas. When students are not in school, they read the mainstream press, watch mainstream TV, and live in families of people who were educated in the same manner in previous generations. Teachers are prepared in colleges where they study mainstream views of their subjects and of the profession of teaching. It is no wonder that schools are prime locations for cultural reproduction. There are no other sources of ideas. To have mainstream ideas broadly represented in schools is certainly not improper, but to deny critical examination of those ideas, and to limit students to such a narrow band of ideas, is not liberating.

Students are often surprised to stumble on a radical journal or book that legitimately challenges basic assumptions about capitalism and American politics and their impact on justice and equality. Those students are rightfully concerned about an education that did not permit consideration of opposing values and ideologies. Unfortunately, the vast majority of students never come across radical materials, or they automatically and unthoughtfully reject any divergent views because the schools have been effective in sealing off their minds.

Mainstream Control of Knowledge

Not only do schools sort and label students, and limit the range of views permitted for examination, but the kind of knowledge available to differing groups of students also is class-biased. Michael F. D. Young (1971), a British sociologist, has argued that "those in positions of power will attempt to define what is taken as knowledge, how accessible to different groups knowledge is. . . ."

Essentially, those in power in schools guard the knowledge that they consider "high status" and use it to assist them in retaining power and in differentiating themselves from the masses. High-status knowledge is determined by those who already have power. Although the work of some auto mechanics, for example, involves complex skills and knowledge, it is not considered high-status knowledge. Law and medicine, which also utilize complex skills and knowledge, are considered of high status and access to them is restricted.

As Michael Apple (1990) notes, there is a relation between economic structure and high-status knowledge. A capitalist, industrial, technological society values the knowledge that most contributes to its continuing development. Math, science, and computer study have demonstrably more financial support than do the arts and humanities. A master's degree in business administration, especially if it is from a "prestigious" institution, is more valuable than a degree in humanities. Technical subjects, such as math and the sciences, are more easily broken down into discrete bits of information, and are more easily testable than are arts and humanities subjects. This leads to easy stratification of students, often along social-class lines. The idea of school achievement is to compete well in those "hard" technical subjects where differentiation is easiest to measure. Upper-class students, however, are not in the competition, since they are protected and usually do not attend public schools. The upper middle class provides advantages for its children; the working-class child struggles to overcome disadvantage.

The separation of subjects in the discipline-centered curriculum serves to legitimatize the high status of hard subjects and the academic preparatory sequence. The organization of knowledge is not examined or understood as class-based or problematic. Instead, information is presented in segments and spurts, with testing on detail and ranking on how well one accepts the school's definition. We pretend that knowledge is neutral, that the numerous subject categories and titles are merely logical structures to assist in understanding. This separates school learning from social problems, reinforces the domination of existing authority over what is identified as important to know, and maintains students as dependent and uncritical thinkers.

What Should Be Taught

Liberation education requires the blending of curriculum content with pedagogy. What is studied cannot be separated from how it is studied. The basis of this approach to schooling is to have students engage in critical study of the society and its institutions with the dual purpose of liberating themselves from simple cultural reproduction and liberating the society from oppressive manipulation of the masses. Critical study is both method and content. It expects open examination and critique of diverse ideas, and sees the human condition as problematic. That places all human activity as potential curriculum content and makes all such activity subject to critical scrutiny through a dynamic form of dialectic reasoning.

Obviously, students cannot examine all things at all times. Thus, the selection of what topics are to be studied at any one time depends on several factors, including whatever has been previously studied, and the level of those investigations; which contemporary social issues are significant; the interests and maturity level of the students; and the knowledge of the teacher. There is no neatly structured sequence of information that all students must pass through and forget. Knowledge is active and dynamic; it is complex and intertwined. Students should come to understand that, and to examine the nature of knowledge itself. That can lead to liberation.

Among the topics of early and continuing study should be ideologies. Students need to learn how to strip away layers of propaganda and rationalization to examine root causes. Ideology, in its most literal sense, is the study of ideas. Those ideas may be phrased in a language intended for mystification to persuade people. Critical study looks below the surface expression to find the roots of ideas.

Ideology can also mean basic, undergirding values and beliefs. Racism and sexism are not considered proper public views in America, and yet they often lie behind high-sounding pronouncements and policies. Using test scores from culturally biased tests to segregate those to be given favored treatment from those to be excluded can be rationalized in neutral-sounding nonracist and nonsexist terms, but the basic causes and the consequences may well be racist or sexist. Engaging in imperialism is not considered proper behavior in current international relations, but powerful nations do attempt to control other nations through physical or political-economic means while calling their actions defensive or "freedom fighting." Ideological study can help students situate events in historic, economic, and political settings that are deeper and richer than the surface explanations.

The Dynamic Dialectic

Liberation education requires teachers and students to engage in a dynamic form of dialectic reasoning to uncover ideological roots. A dialectic involves analyzing ideas by considering opposing ideas and delving deeper into the basis of each to attempt a more reasoned understanding of the issue. There are at least two forms of dialectic reasoning. One, as proposed by Plato, structures and limits the discourse to lead students to one fixed idea of truth. For example, Socrates knew the truth and led students to it by subjecting their answers to questions to further questions until the students came to accept Socrates' view. That is an authoritarian form of dialectic that is false in its application.

A dynamic dialectic opens topics to examination. It is not a set of absolutes with a known truth, but operates more like a spiral, digging deeper into rationales. It involves seeing the topic in its total social context, not in segments as studied in the discipline-centered curriculum. And it requires a vision of liberation that allows students to go beneath the surface or obvious parts of the topic to see its basic relationships to the structure of society and to dominant interests. The purpose of the dialectic is for students to transcend their traditional nonactive and sterile role and to accept active roles as knowledgeable participants in the improvement of civilization. In theory, the dialectic is never-ending, since civilization is in continual need of improvement. In practice in schools, the dialectic is limited by time, energy, interest, and the topics under study.

Liberation education expects that highly divergent ideas will be examined in schools. That, in itself, is insufficient. These divergent ideas must be examined in a setting where they can be fully developed and can be perceived as legitimate, rather than as strange or quaint. Adequate time and resources must be available, without censorship and authoritarianism.

For a truly liberated society, one cannot expect less of schools than education for liberation. An emancipatory climate in schools will regenerate students and teachers to full use of their intellects and increasing creativity. Those are fitting and proper goals for schools, unachievable under the restricted mainstream forms of schooling now practiced.

For Discussion

1. If you could appoint ten members to a state-wide advisory council with the charge to list and define a common core of values that should be taught in the schools because they are deemed essential to our society:

   a. What kinds of people would you select? Why?
   What educational background should be required?
   What occupations should be represented?
   What groups or agencies should be represented?
   What age, gender, or ethnic categories should be important?
   What other characteristics would you look for?

   b. What kinds of people would you want to exclude? Why?

   c. What list would you expect to get from this advisory group?

   Compare your list with the following list of values produced by such an advisory council in New Jersey.

   Civic responsibility, based on:
     acknowledgment of authority
     global awareness
     justice, fairness
     patriotism
     property rights
   Respect for the natural environment, based on:
     care and conservation of all living inhabitants
     care and conservation of land, air, water
     conduct based on interdependence of environment
   Respect for others, based on:
     compassion and service
     courtesy and cooperation
     honesty
     loyalty
     moderation
     recognition and understanding of various religions
     regard for human life
     tolerance
   Respect for self, based on:
     accountability
     courage
     diligence, commitment, reliability
     frugality, thrift
     knowledge, learning
     moral courage
     self-esteem, pride

   Can the schools convey these values? Should they? Are there inconsistencies or conflicts among the values? How should these be addressed? Whose interests are served by the values in this list? Are the values listed more consistent with traditional views or liberation education?

2. Paulo Freire, advocating liberation education, claims that traditional teaching is fundamentally "narrative," leaving its contents "lifeless and petrified." Freire writes:

   > The teacher talks about reality as if it were motionless, static, compartmentalized, and predictable. Or else he expounds on a topic completely alien to

the existential experience of the students. His task is to "fill" the stu
dents with the contents of his narration—contents which are detached from
reality . . .

The more completely he fills the receptacles, the better a teacher he is.
The more meekly the receptacles permit themselves to be filled, the better
students they are. (Freire, 1970, pp. 57, 58)

Does this description fit your experience in schools? Criticize Freire's view of this
"banking" form of education. Has he properly characterized what goes on in
schools? Should it go on? What are the social costs of changing to liberation education? What are the costs of not changing?

3. Many people agree that we should teach values in school, but there is disagreement
about which values and who decides. There is disparity among those who propose
everlasting and universal values, those who propose utilitarian and short-term values, those who propose general and vague social values, and those who propose values based on individual or immediate circumstances. What is a reasonable way to
approach these questions to determine what kind of values education should be
taught in American schools? What possible social consequences can you foresee for
the various forms of values education?

4. Examine textbooks and other teaching material used in a local school to determine
the major values being expressed to students. How could these values be catego-
rized? Are students expected to accept the values or to examine them critically?
How do the texts treat disparity in values?

References

Ahlquist, R. (1991). "Critical Pedagogy for Social Studies Teachers." *Social Studies
Review* **29,** 53–57.

Anderson, D. (1994). "The Great Tradition." *National Review* **46,** 56–58.

Anyon, J. (1980). "Social Class and the Hidden Curriculum of Work." *Journal of Education* **162,** 67–92.

Apple, M. (1990). *Ideology and Curriculum,* 2d ed. London: Routledge & Kegan Paul.

Aronowitz, S., and Giroux, H. A. (1991). *Postmodern Education: Culture, Politics, and
Social Criticism.* Minneapolis: University of Minnesota Press.

Bennett, W. J. (1994). "America at Risk." *USA Today* **123,** 14–16.

Callahan, R. (1962). *Education and the Cult of Efficiency.* Chicago: University of Chicago
Press.

Christensen, B. (1991). "Pro: The Schools Should Presume that Parents have the Primary Authority to Determine the Cultural Traditions to Be Transmitted to Pupils."
Debates in Education. *Curriculum Review* **31,** 6–10.

Clark, M. A. (1990). "Some Cautionary Observations on Liberation Education." *Language Arts* **67,** 388–398.

Colson, C. (1994). "Begging for Tyranny." *Christianity Today* **38,** 80–81.

Falwell, J. (1980). *Listen America!* Garden City, NY: Doubleday.

Giroux, H. (1988). *Teachers as Intellectuals.* Granby, MA: Bergin & Garvey.

——— (1990). "Curriculum Theory, Textual Authority, and the Role of Teachers as Public Intellectuals." *Journal of Curriculum and Supervision* **4,** 361–383.

——— (1991). "Curriculum Planning, Public Schooling, and Democratic Struggle."
NASSP Bulletin **75,** 12–25.

Greene, M. (1990). "The Passion of the Possible." *Journal of Moral Education* **19,** 67–76.

———— (1991). "Con: The Schools Should Presume that Parents have the Primary Authority to Determine the Cultural Traditions to Be Transmitted to Pupils." Debates in Education. *Curriculum Review* **31,** 6–10.

Haydon, G. (1995). "Thick or Thin: The Cognitive Content of Moral Education." *Journal of Moral Education* **24,** 53–64.

Kidder, R. (1994). "Universal Human Values." *The Futurist* **28,** 8–14.

Mill, J. S. (1859/1956). *On Liberty,* edited by C. V. Shields. Indianapolis: Bobbs-Merrill.

Lather, P. (1991). *Getting Smart: Feminist Research and Pedagogy With/in the Postmodern.* New York: Routledge.

McFarlane, A. (1994). "Radical Educational Values." *America* **171,** 10–13.

Rabkin, J. (1995). "Let us Pray." *The American Spectator* **28,** 46–7.

Rafferty, M. (1968). *Max Rafferty on Education.* New York: Devon-Adair.

Read, L. (1968). *Accent on the Right.* Irvington-on-Hudson, NY: Foundation for Economic Education.

Roberts, S. V. (1994). "America's New Crusade." *U.S. News and World Report* **117,** 26–29.

Shor, I. (1987). *Pedagogy for Liberation.* South Hadley, MA: Bergin & Garvey.

———— (1989). "Developing Student Autonomy in the Classroom." *Equity and Excellence* **24,** 35–37.

Sowell, T. (1992). "A Dirty War." *Forbes* **150,** 63.

Spring, J. (1976). *The Sorting Machine: National Educational Policy Since 1945.* New York: McKay.

Thurmond, S. (1968). *The Faith We Have Not Kept.* San Diego, CA: Viewpoint Books.

Towns, E. T. (1974). *Have the Public Schools "Had It"?* New York: Nelson.

Weiler, K. (1991). "Freire and a Feminist Pedagogy of Difference." *Harvard Educational Review* **61,** 449–474.

Whitehead, B. D. (1994). "The Failure of Sex Education." *The Atlantic Monthly* **274:** 55–80.

Young, M. F. D. (1971). *Knowledge and Control.* London: Collier-Macmillan.

CHAPTER ELEVEN

Business Influence: Positive or Negative

POSITION 1:
FOR INCREASED BUSINESS INFLUENCE

Business people, from the small shopkeeper to the executive of a major corporation, recognize that there may be no more important work in American society than the improvement of schools. America's vitality and the health of our economy depend on schools. Good schools are simply good business. Consistent with their beliefs, business leaders are in the forefront of reform efforts to improve schools (Ramsey, 1993). America 2000, the national strategy to improve schools, identifies the business community as basic to such improvements—business will "jump-start" the design of the new American schools, will use new national tests to aid in hiring, and will provide resources to lead the changes (*America 2000,* 1991, p. 23). Business stands ready to take on this task (Szabo, 1990; Miller, 1991).

A recent report of the Business Roundtable, an organization of major corporations, showed that 186 member businesses had formed school partnerships for educational improvement. These corporate-supported school activities took place in such diverse areas as academic instructional improvement, career awareness, civic and character education, drug prevention, dropout prevention, and programs for the disadvantaged. The activities were a response to a school partnership initiative of the education committee of the Business Roundtable. Corporations help schools in these key areas because they recognize the value of helping students reach their full potential. This is not a new role for business leadership in American schools; business–education relations have a long and positive history. What is new is the level of crisis in American education.

Serious problems confront America because schools fail to provide students with solid skills and workplace values. Significant numbers of employees are illiterate or disdain required work habits. Those who are unemployed often have inadequate skills or attitudes. They are the people the schools have missed. In addition to directly supporting schools, American business spends $25 billion annually on remedial education for employees ("Saving Our Schools," 1990). The United States is losing its competitive advantage because the workforce is undereducated. This crisis is particularly important in a time of rapid change in technology, and when workers' skills are improving in other nations. A dramatic shift has already occurred in the production of electronics, automobiles, furniture, and other consumer goods. High-quality products are now manufactured in Japan, Taiwan, Korea, and other places where school and business have become more obvious partners.

We need people who are competent in basic skills, who can understand technical manuals and operations, and who can work with management in a cooperative effort to strengthen this nation's economy. In far too many schools, students have trouble with simple written forms and directions, with understanding low-level technical information, and with maintaining interest in their work. As *Newsweek* education editor Gilbert Sewall (1984) describes it:

> For at least 23 million Americans, the instructions in a laundromat are mystifying; reading a repair manual or filling out a job application accurately is impossible. Bluntly stated, these citizens do not have the survival skills to compete in a highly specialized service economy that values, above all, mental agility and reliability. Consequently, they have little or no stake in the future of democratic capitalism. These functional illiterates are condemned to live on the fringe of the polity as menial laborers, as welfare recipients, as outlaws, as the emotionally tortured and spiritually broken. Doomed to insecure, insolvent, and possibly violent futures, they are what society considers failed people. (pp. 3–4)

In addition to the general need to improve instruction in basic skills and workplace attitudes for all young people, there is a special need to better prepare non-college-bound students for employment. A considerable part of the current school reform movement has been directed at improving the academic quality of schools for those who plan to go to college. The majority of students, however, take jobs immediately after graduating from high school, or they drop out before graduation and try to find employment.

The Forgotten Half (1988), a report of a Commission on Work, Family and Citizenship sponsored by the W. T. Grant Foundation, examines this issue of work and non-college-bound youth. Among the criticisms is that "a larger percentage of them are finding it harder than ever to swim against the economic tide" (*The Forgotten Half*, 1988, p. 410). The commission agrees "with those who say that America needs to 'work smarter' and raise productivity in order to be competitive with other nations" (p. 412).

The commission recommends a number of ways to "bridge the gap from school to work," including intensive training in basic skills, a monitored work experience of apprenticeships and preemployment training, improved vocational education, incentives from businesses and mentors to do well in school, and better career counseling.

An important recommendation of the commission is to foster stronger alliances between employers and schools. Business leaders can come into the schools to teach, to talk with students, and to help teachers and guidance counselors develop programs to improve student skills and attitudes. In addition, students can visit places of future employment. The alliances can establish work–study arrangements for students, produce teaching material, and obtain financial support from business for improving school technology and career guidance. Many businesses participate in "Adopt-a-School" programs that enrich the school's ability to prepare students for employment. Other businesses invite teachers to visit, provide summer employment and other opportunities for teachers to learn about their operations, and prepare free teaching materials. Business has strong interests in the improvement of education (Gilbert, 1993; Crain, 1994). Industries cannot survive without a well-prepared workforce, and they recognize this.

The Boston Compact, for example, established a partnership between Boston's schools and the Boston Private Industry Council. Businesses promised jobs to students if the schools were able to raise test scores and to decrease dropout rates. This alliance has provided jobs for over 1,000 graduates, and reading and math scores have improved (Fiske, 1988, p. B8).

Mann (1987) examined school–business partnerships and concluded that "partnerships between businesses and the schools have made positive contributions to the public schools . . . [they] have offered concrete assistance to the schools in a number of ways" (p. 228). These contributions included cash, services, sympathy, and assistance in political and economic coalitions. Mann notes several problems in business alliances with schools, but cites a large number of examples where businesses have been particularly helpful in improving local schools.

The Grant Foundation commission is also concerned with changes in the kinds of employment available and the need for schools to modify their programs to better prepare students for work. Prominent changes in the nature of employment in American society have had major implications for schools. Historically, the shift was from agricultural to manufacturing jobs; now the shift is from manufacturing to service. In the short space of the last fifty years, the proportion of farmers and farm workers has declined from almost 20 percent of the workforce to only 3 percent; since 1950, manufacturing jobs have declined from 32 percent to 27 percent of total employment, whereas service jobs have increased from 53 percent to 69 percent. The service sector has grown primarily in social and producer services (for example, health, medical technology), rather than in personal services (for example, hairdressing, domestic work) or distributive services (for example, sales, delivery). The most prominent change has been in the kinds of jobs. White-collar jobs went from about 45 percent of the labor force in 1940 to over 70 percent by the mid-1980s. Blue-collar jobs have declined from about 42 percent in 1940 to about 27 percent now.

In educational terms, this means a need for more and better schooling. Many agricultural jobs no longer demand just sheer physical labor, but involve technical work that requires strong academic skills. White-collar jobs typically require increased education. In a report on economic trends in America, a group of Oxford scholars commented: "Indeed, it is well documented that over recent decades a person's job and level of income have become influenced more and more by his or her level of education and formal qualifications" (Oxford Analytica, 1984, p. 68). Blau and Duncan (1967), in a classic study of the relation of education to jobs, reported high correlations between job status and education. Social class and occupational experience were also considered influential in employment status, but education had the greatest effect.

In earlier times in American history, basic literacy could be recommended purely for its inherent values; it had no special relation to people's work requirements. In a period when most citizens lived rural and farming lives, reading, writing, and calculating were considered nice to know, but not necessary for securing employment. Even in those times, however, there were obvious links between education and employment. A study conducted in 1867 by the Commonwealth of Pennsylvania, for example, showed that income was directly related to literacy: those who could not read averaged $36 per month; those who could read, but were otherwise poorly educated, averaged $52 a month; and those who were well educated averaged $90 a month (Soltow and Stevens, 1981). Other studies have continued to corroborate this point. But literacy for business purposes does not mean just proficiency in reading and writing. Soltow and Stevens, in examining the history of literacy in the United States, note: "To be literate, as we have seen, did not simply mean to be competent at a specific level of reading mastery. It meant, perhaps more importantly for the employer, exposure to a set of values compatible with a disciplined work force" (pp. 127–128). There is clear evidence that schools should give more importance to basic skills and workplace values.

For all students, college-bound or not, we need to improve our teaching of knowledge and attitudes that contribute to the society. Permissive education has led to indolence, narcissism, and a rebellious attitude against all forms of authority. The mistaken notion that we can do as we wish, and the equally mistaken ideology of socialism, has caused our society to suffer. Schools need to redirect their energies toward developing students' pride in workmanship, increasing productivity, and fostering good citizenship in a nation where competition and free enterprise offer the most opportunities for all.

The strength of American society lies in the fortuitous combination of democracy and capitalism. We not only offer freedom and opportunity in politics (the democratic concept), but also in economics. The freedom to engage in enterprise, without obstructive governmental interference, provides opportunities and motivations for everyone. Free enterprise is a basic condition for releasing the entrepreneurial spirit in humans, and entrepreneurs built and developed this great nation. People of merit and ideas of merit rise to the top. In order for the meritorious to stay at the top, the free marketplace requires continual improvement. That is how this nation has moved from being a minor colony to assuming its place as a world power. It is also why so many other nations have tried to emulate American entrepreneurship.

The complete breakdown of most communist countries at the end of the 1980s illustrates the flawed nature of socialism. The death of communism will find the early twenty-first century a world of competing capitalist nations. This new scenario requires even more American commitment to education relevant to business enterprise. We cannot afford to lose among capitalist nations after overwhelming the socialist countries. Schooling that will maintain our nation as a leader in international business competition is a top priority. Schools have not demonstrated their ability to produce qualified students in the quantity required for international leadership. Business must enter into new and more intertwined partnerships with schools to ensure that America keeps its competitive edge in global markets.

Business Approaches Are Also Good for School Operation

Not only do schools fail to give students basic skills and good workplace attitudes, but a corollary problem arises in the operation of the schools themselves. Schools are inefficient. Their organization and operation have not changed during the the twentieth century, while industry has made remarkable progress in becoming more efficient and more productive. If American industry had been as stultified as the schools, it would have failed long ago. In fact, those businesses that have not improved their efficiency and productivity have failed. Private enterprise cannot survive in stagnation. Yet we have protected our schools from this necessary competition, and they now lack motivation to show improvement. Schools are sheltered organizations; they consume significant amounts of tax money but have little accountability. They have not been required to show the improvements that would be expected of any contemporary business.

Improved technology and increased productivity could limit the need for costly employees. School budgets represent the biggest expense in local communities, and staff salaries constitute about 80 percent of that expense. Savings here could be used to bring better technology into schools to improve student skills, or to reduce taxes. The ratio of students to teachers has been stable, about 25 to 1, in comprehensive school districts for years. In many suburban schools, the ratio is less than 20 students to each teacher. There is no evidence that fewer students per class means a better education. And much of what a teacher does in a classroom could be accomplished more efficiently with larger groups of students by using video or computer equipment.

It is important for a teacher to guide the general teaching of students, but it is very expensive in money and teacher time to have each teacher work with a small number of students. The teacher could instead present material to larger groups, and individual students could work on computers under the general guidance of the teacher or a teacher's aide. This would mean that schools would be organized very differently, but that is what is needed. Businesses are constantly reorganizing to achieve better productivity because competition demands it. Schools should not be exempt from similar requirements to increase productivity.

The proportion of school administrators has actually increased, while the total student population has declined. Schools also employ large numbers of other workers to provide services that could be carried out more economically by contract with private industry. Such employees are usually on some form of civil service and keep their jobs regardless of reorganization. Teachers have tenure and lifetime security, and union contracts limit their workdays and working years.

School buildings are often large, inefficiently utilized, and costly to build and maintain. In districts where student enrollment has declined, expensive school buildings have been sold, destroyed, or renovated at great public financial loss. And school buildings are used less than half of the year and then for only one-third of the day. The debt for building these behemoths has been passed on to future generations by issuing bonds.

Many small schools, with separate buildings and school staffs, could be reorganized into less costly regional districts if business concepts were used. Individual school districts purchase millions of dollars' worth of books, equipment, and teaching material at high cost, when a coordinated effort could decrease such expense considerably. Small, expensive schools operate out of pride, not economy.

Meanwhile, businesses have shown that they can train large numbers of employees by using video and computer systems, lectures, programmed materials, self-study, and other devices that do not consume the high level of precious human resources that the schools use. Furthermore, this training occurs in facilities that are used extensively for the whole of each year. The educational activities of these businesses are the result of failings of the schools, and business has shown that it can train people better and more economically.

If schools could prove that expensive buildings and personnel increase productivity, there would be no problem. In fact, however, student test scores have been declining, students do not have work values that enhance their employment, and student social behavior is a public disgrace in many locations.

This is not a time for schools to continue the failures of the past. It is a time to change schools, and there are many business-proven techniques that must be used. The structure of business based on a competitive marketplace has withstood the most severe tests of war, depression, and dislocation. We need to introduce contemporary business management into education—management that is concerned with improved efficiency and demands improved productivity.

A reordering of our school purposes to give students solid skills and good, positive workplace values is a social and educational necessity. A reordering of our school operations more closely to approximate good business practices is an economic necessity. These are completely compatible and complementary reforms to which schools must attend.

All in all, business has much to offer education, much more than just the money schools need to continue their work (Feulner, 1991; Mandel, 1995). Financial support alone would do little to deal with the crisis in education. To develop basic skills, to improve workplace attitudes and values, to increase the productivity of American business, to enhance our competitive stance in international markets, and to make schools more efficient are goals common to business and to schools.

POSITION 2:
LIMIT THE INFLUENCE OF BUSINESS

Business should mind its own business first. If businesses could boast a tradition of ethics and quality in their operation, then there might be something to the claim that education should follow that example. However, the traditions of shoddy products, shady operations, and shaky ethics continue to haunt American business. Obviously, not all businesses share these unfortunate traditions, but too many concentrate on making profit, with little regard for ethics and justice. This casts strong doubt on the wisdom of allowing business leaders to influence how students are educated. The strong self-interest of corporations overwhelms their altruistic rhetoric about good schools for all children. Schools exist for society's benefit; society is not served by having business interests control the schools (Marina, 1994).

"America 2000" and "Goals 2000" are two names for the same strategy offered by two presidents, Bush and Clinton. These strategies call upon the business community to jump-start education reform by financing teams to design new schools, to use new national tests for hiring personnel, and to "catalyze needed changes in local schools, communities and state policies" (*America 2000*, 1991). This rhetoric emphasizes intrusion into the schools by business interests. Such ideas raise a menacing cloud over education in America and reflect an ignorance of the social and human injuries inflicted by business interests in the past.

Imagine allowing American corporations to design the new models of schools for the twenty-first century. What values would be expressed? It is certain that humane values, protection of the environment, caring and mutual support, skeptical consumerism, health and safety, and positive images of labor unions would not be in the curriculum. Teacher and student freedom to study diverse views of American society, economics, politics, and history could be severely curtailed. Would examination of the robber barons, the savings and loan fiasco, excessive cost overruns allowed business in government contracts, industrial pollution, unjustifiably high salaries for corporate executives, corruption of corporate officials, and related information about business operations be part of the curriculum in these corporate-sponsored schools?

Next, think of businesses which use national test scores in hiring workers. Those executives whose lives are determined by "the bottom line" are likely to seize on a single test score as the essence of each worker's talents and abilities. Test scores would become even more oppressive in covering up the multifaceted personalities of students and employees. Business would also insist on significantly influencing the tests themselves, including their production and sale. As Carnegie and other notorious industrialists showed us, whoever controls all elements of an industry also controls prices and profits. The same can happen with industry-controlled schooling. Those who control test manufacturing and use can manipulate employment levels, wages and benefits, labor contracts, and profits. They would also come to control the school curriculum through the tests.

Finally, consider asking business to "catalyze" educational reform. That assumes that business knows what needs reform. Most of the negative statements corporate leaders make about schools refer to lacks in basic skills and workers' values. Basic skills are certainly needed, but who should decide which basic skills are needed? Must they be employment-related? And the idea of educating for workers' values imposes a misguided and improper burden on schools. Human values and ethical conduct are proper goals of education, but employer values often contradict human and ethical values. Schools are not the place to insist on "worker" values.

The record of American business in its own domain has not been exemplary. A partial list of business contributions to the detriment of individuals and society includes sweatshops, child labor, virtual slavery of migrant workers, unhealthy and unsafe workplaces, pollution, linkages with corrupt politicians, secret coalitions to set falsely high prices, anticonsumer tactics, untruthful advertising, dissolution of pension funds, bankruptcy laws that permit executives to retain major assets while middle-class stockholders lose their life savings, taxpayer subsidies to cover up inept corporate management, and corporate lawyers and corporation-influenced laws that remove corporations from accountability or responsibility for their wrongdoing. Are these the ideas and values we want to emulate in schooling?

American business has had a grasping and greedy history, whereas American education serves essentially civilizing purposes. Among the schools' most positive goals is to enable students to improve the society in terms of increasing justice and expanding social ethics to incorporate a stronger concern for others. This speaks to the future of American democracy and poses a significant challenge to schools to strive continually for social development. And that requires knowledge, critical thinking, cooperative endeavor, and a set of values based on justice.

Unfortunately, students in American schools have been shortchanged and American society has been deluded by the imposition of business views on education for the past century (Apple, 1984, 1990; Callahan, 1962). It is deceptive to train the masses to conform to business interests while providing the elite with increased privileges. This is the most insidious educational trick in the new reform movement. Millions of students are relegated to nonthinking menial work as preparation for poor jobs, and the schools are expected to make them think that they are happy and are well educated.

Historian Christopher Lasch (1984) says there is:

> a new system of industrial recruitment, centered on the school. The modern system of public education, remodeled in accordance with the same principles of scientific management first perfected in industry, has replaced apprenticeship as the principal agency of training people for work. The transmission of

skills is increasingly incidental to this training. The school habituates children to bureaucratic discipline and to the demands of group living, grades and sorts them by means of standardized tests, and selects some for professional and managerial careers while consigning the rest to manual labor . . . a willingness to cooperate with the proper authorities offers the best evidence of "adjustment" and the best hope of personal success, while a refusal to cooperate signifies the presence of "emotional problems" requiring more sustained therapeutic attention. (pp. 48–49)

American schools have been dominated by the values of business and industry since the beginning of the twentieth century, and have lost their primary purpose of enlightenment for the improvement of social justice. Rather than being liberating, schools are indoctrinating institutions. They serve to provide docile and hard-working employees on whom business can rely to gain a profit. Further, these future employees are taught an ideology that supports business regardless of ethical considerations and conditions them to accept unquestioningly the authority of a managerial elite.

Reform movements in education in the United States have often victimized the underclasses, on the pretext of making them "fit for work and for democratic citizenship" by forcing them into schooling that tells them to be obedient, punctual, frugal, neat, respectful, and content with their lot in life. There is a duality, a dialectic, here between what is good for business and what is good for society. The work ethic, drawing from Puritan views in the colonies, is of great value to industrialists who desire uncomplaining and diligent workers. This ethic has become the school ethic. Employment has become the curriculum of the schools, enabling business to sustain a receptive workforce. The carrot of democratic citizenship, however, is mythological, since the economic facts of life are that the elite remain in power while the masses do the work. Education for democratic participation, in the pursuit of justice and equality, is still in the rhetoric of school literature, but is not acted on in the schools.

This disparity in the schools' purposes—preparation of students for participation as workers versus participation as equal citizens in striving for justice in society—is overlooked in much of the reform literature. As historian Barbara Finkelstein (1984) notes:

Nineteenth century reformers looked to public schools to instill restraint in increasingly large numbers of immigrants and native children, while at the same time preparing them for learning and labor in an industrializing society. . . . They saw no contradiction in the work of schools as economic sorting machines and enabling political institutions . . . . Contemporary calls for reform reflect a retreat from historic visions of public education as an instrument of political democracy, a vehicle of social mobility, a center for the reconstruction of community life . . . . Rather the educational visions of contemporary reformers evoke historic specters of public schools as crucibles in which to forge uniform Americans and disciplined industrial laborers. (pp. 276–277)

Finkelstein also identifies the role of corporate leaders in expanding their influence on public education in order to assure a competent and compliant workforce. She illustrates this with examples from a business–education alliance at George Washington Carver High School in Atlanta, where business conducts the daily activities of the school with work-study in semiskilled jobs in local businesses, moral pronouncements to promote industrial discipline in students, and public rituals, such as celebration of "Free Enterprise Day" and "passports to job opportunity." This, and other business intrusions into schools, leads to "an effective transfer of control over education policy from public school authorities to industrial councils. . . . For the first time in the history of school reform, a deeply materialistic consciousness seems to be overwhelming all other concerns" (Finkelstein, 1984, p. 280).

Is Business a Good Model for Schools?

The 1990s have shown the truth of Finkelstein's insight. We have become very good at teaching students to be avaricious, greedy, selfish, and conniving. Academic students are especially eager to get good grades in order to get into the right colleges in order to get high-paying jobs. They seem uninterested in intellectual development that does not pay off in employment and salaries. They seem uncaring about the homeless, the starving, and others who are disadvantaged, as well as the rest of the world. They are excessively competitive with each other and press for competitive advantage over other groups. Ethical considerations, including the pursuit of justice, do not seem to pose an obstruction to their efforts. Cheating, buying term papers, using parental influence, taking drugs to enhance performance temporarily, paying someone to take a college admission test, and falsifying a résumé are part of the process. Those who aspire to be yuppies understand that winning is important in order to secure high pay; how one wins is not important.

Interestingly, this is a pattern of beliefs drawn from big business. Wall Street companies have engaged in securities fraud, insider scandals, and various scams. Banks and insurance companies appear to have taken advantage of deregulation and loose public control to plunge the country's banking and insurance systems into serious trouble. Calavita and Pontell (1991), after reviewing government documents and material from congressional hearings on the savings and loan and insurance industries, described many actions of the top management as "collective embezzlement." Major corporations, including Chrysler and Lockheed, conducted business in a most unbusinesslike manner, leading to virtual bankruptcy. They then were bailed out by taxpayers, which turned the principles of "free enterprise" upside down.

Big business "sweetheart" contracts negotiated with current and former officers of government agencies have fattened profits and increased taxpayer costs exorbitantly. The Pentagon's extravagant contracts for military supplies are the obvious example, but many other federal, state, and local government contracts also overpay for work and supplies. The widely publicized Pentagon padding scandals are not the only example of questionable alliances between big business and government. Sematech, formed in 1986, presumably to regain America's competitive edge in semiconductors, was a consortium of fourteen major semiconductor corporations funded by the federal government. Taxpayers contribute about $100 million per year to this operation. In 1980, the United States had 75 percent of the worldwide semiconductor market; by 1991, we had only 45 percent of that market. Sematech neither has made any technical breakthroughs nor has it regained the competitive edge.

The big business of professional athletics, until the public became outraged, condoned and supported the taking of drugs by athletes to improve their performance. Fraud, misrepresentation, cheating, using or peddling improper influence, falsifying or hiding records, and abusing drugs for business purposes appear to be acceptable ethical standards for many in business. This curriculum is one that many students have picked up.

The unethical operations of business are manifold, and they are reported often enough to suggest that business is not the place to look for educational views on ethics. Even if one grants that the unethical is not the standard but the exception in business, there remains a serious concern about the business view of social justice and responsibility. Industrial waste pollutes the land, water, and air, but industry does not accept the responsibility to clean it up. Strong protests by the corporate world have been effective in slowing and stultifying the public regulation of worker health and safety, consumer protection, and improvement in public utilities and services. As Michael Apple (1990) describes it, "Economic and cultural power is being increasingly centralized in massive corporate bodies that are less than responsive to social needs other than profit" (p. 12).

The corporate takeover of schooling affects everyone, but the greedy and already advantaged stand to benefit most. Those who are not going to college, and are less likely to share the American business dream of success, are subjected to second-class treatment in schools and in careers. The industrial curriculum is designed to give them skills, not thinking, and is intended to make them believers, not thinkers. Industrial-strength education increases the gap between these groups, and is meant to produce workers willing to be manipulated.

Business leaders criticize the schools because new employees do not possess basic skills and do not have proper work attitudes. The basic skills business wants do not include critical judgment or skills of persuasion that could be useful in reconstituting the moribund union movement or challenging manager dictates. Rather, business basic skills are fundamental reading and computation that make one more efficient in carrying out management's policies. A job candidate who demonstrates the ability to read radical left-wing literature and to raise questions about worker safety, environmental hazards caused by industry, and the excessive salaries and disparate benefits provided to owners and executives as compared with workers is not likely to be hired. A candidate who can calculate the differences in value between the worker's effort and the pay received, or between labor and management perks in health care and leisure provisions, is not likely to be hired. It is the moral curriculum rather than the academic that is of most interest to business. Managers want workers who believe that what is good for business is good for the nation, and that management knows what is good for business.

Several states now require a high school course in "free enterprise," not in economics. Obviously, this course is not neutral, but is an advocacy course intended to indoctrinate youth. English is taught by using job application forms and having students answer help wanted ads. General math is turned to preparing students for working in stores and making change. History classes incorporate myths about the virtues of American business leaders, the appropriate power of corporations, and the threat of governmental interference in business. And, as Harty's (1980) study of business-produced teaching materials showed, students are given biased material that supports business views of environmental, social, and governmental actions. Harty (1989) more recently updated her analysis of the attempt by corporations to sell their wares by manipulating school materials, and found the practice continuing. Throughout the schools, students are treated as junior workers required to be punctual, to have good "work habits," to show deference to management, and to not engage in critical thought. This hidden curriculum of business has been very successful.

Business has been a major influence on education for a long time, yet there are still complaints about the product of an institution and a curriculum dominated by a business ethos. Raymond Callahan (1962) conducted a historical study of what most influenced the development of contemporary public education in its most formative period in the early twentieth century:

> At the turn of the century America had reason to be proud of the educational progress it had made. The dream of equality of educational opportunity had been partly realized . . . the basic institutional framework for a noble conception of education had been created . . . . The story of the next quarter century of American education—a story of opportunity lost and of the acceptance by educational administrators of an inappropriate philosophy—must be seen . . . the most powerful force was industrialism . . . the business ideology was spread continuously into the bloodstream of American life. . . . It was, therefore, quite natural for Americans, when they thought of reforming the schools, to apply business methods to achieve their ends. (pp. 1, 5)

Callahan considered the business influence tragic for education and society because it substituted efficiency for effectiveness. We got cost control at the sacrifice of high-quality schooling for all. The business dominance stuck, and in the last decade of the twentieth century, schools are still controlled by a corporate value system. This explains the factory mentality of schools. That is why teachers are so poorly paid and badly used, and are considered laborers. It is why students are treated as objects in the process of being manufactured on school assembly lines. It explains the conformity and standardization, the excessive testing, and the organization and financing of schools. It also explains the lack of concern for social justice and ethics, issues on which the schools were making progress until business gained influence.

Upton Sinclair, who is best known for his devastating criticism of the meat packing industry for ignoring public health and worker safety (*The Jungle*, 1906, 1938), which resulted in federal legislation to regulate food products, also published two books that showed the detrimental effects of the influence of business and industry on education. *The Goose Step* (1922) detailed how major industrialists determined educational policies and controlled who got appointed and promoted to professorships in the most important universities in America. Leaders of big business dominate the boards that govern most colleges and universities, a point made long ago by Thorstein Veblen (1918), who found that business practices and values detracted from the primary purpose of academic institutions: to liberate students. Sinclair also spent two years studying the public schools and found similar heavy-handed control over school policies and practices by business leaders across the United States. In *The Goslings* (1924), he stated, "The purpose of this book is to show you how the 'invisible government' of Big Business which controls the rest of America has taken over the charge of your children" (p. ix).

There is considerable evidence that things have not improved in the seventy years since Sinclair wrote about schools and business. What is taught in schools is what business wants. What should be taught is what society needs and justice requires. We need to return to the civilizing purposes of schooling—justice and ethics—and to wrench control over the schools away from those who see the school as just another agency to support the interests of big business. Certainly, the role of business in society should be studied, but not as a subject to be whitewashed, as it is now. Critical examination of business values and practices, in terms of social justice and human ethics, are of great import. We need to invert the current situation in which business controls schools, to one in which education will influence business values and practices in the direction of responsibility and enlightenment. That would put education in a proper position of monitoring the improvement of society by examining various social institutions, including business. It would certainly improve education, and it might improve business.

References

America 2000, (1991). Washington, DC: US Department of Education.

Apple, M. (1984). *Education and Power.* New York: Routledge & Kegan Paul.

———— (1990). *Ideology and Curriculum.* New York: Routledge, Chapman & Hall.

———— (1991). "The New Technology: Is it Part of the Solution or Part of the Problem in Education?" *Computers in the Schools* **8**, 59–80.

Blau, P., and Duncan O. D. (1967). *The American Occupational Structure.* New York: Wiley.

Calavita K., and Pontell, H. (1991). "Other People's Money Revisited: Collective Embezzlement in the Savings and Loan and Insurance Industries." *Social Problems* **38**, 94–112.

Callahan, R. (1962). *Education and the Cult of Efficiency.* Chicago: University of Chicago Press.

Crain, F. (1994). "Saving our Schools: Our Highest Priority." *Advertising Age* **65**, 28.

Finkelstein, B. 1984. "Education and the Retreat from Democracy in the United States, 1979–1980?" *Teachers College Record* **86**, 276–282.

Fiske, E. (1988). "Lessons." *The New York Times*, December 21, p. B8.

Feulner, E. J. (1991). "What Business Leaders Can Teach the Educators." *Chief Executive*, September, pp. 16–17.

Gilbert, T. (1993). "Corporate Influence by 2010." *Education Digest* **59**, 25–27.

Harty, S. (1980). *Hucksters in the Classroom*. Washington, DC: Center for Responsive Legislation.

────── 1989. "U.S. Corporations: Still Pitching After All These Years." *Educational Leadership* **47**, 77–79.

Lasch, C. (1984). *The Minimal Self*. New York: Norton.

Mandel, M. et al. (1995). "Will Schools Ever Get Better?" *Business Week,* Apr. 17, pp. 64–8.

Mann, D. (1987). "Business Involvement and Public School Improvement, Part 2." *Phi Delta Kappan* **69**, 228–232.

Marina, A. (1994). "Can the Private Sector Save Public Schools?" *NEA Today* **12**, 10–12.

Miller, W. H. (1991). "Bush Bucks It to Business: The President's Education-Reform Plan Relies on Business to Attain Goals." *Industry Week* **240**, 70–72.

Oxford Analytica. (1986). *America in Perspective: Major Trends in the United States Through the 1990s*. Boston: Houghton Mifflin.

Ramsey, N. (1993). "What Companies Are Doing." *Fortune* **128**, 142–150.

"Saving Our Schools." (1990). *Fortune,* Special Issue, Spring, p. 121.

Sewall, G. T. (1984). *Necessary Lessons: Decline and Renewal in American Schools*. New York: Free Press.

Sinclair, U. (1906, 1938). *The Jungle*. London: Cobham House.

────── (1922). *The Goose Step*. Pasadena, CA: Sinclair.

────── (1924). *The Goslings*. Pasadena, CA: Sinclair.

Soltow, L., and Stevens, E. (1981). *The Rise of Literacy and the Common School in the United States: A Socioeconomic Analysis to 1870*. Chicago: University of Chicago Press.

Szabo, J. C. (1990). "Grass-Roots Education Reform." *Nation's Business* **78**, 65–67.

The Forgotten Half: Non-College Bound Youth in America (Interim Report) (1988). Washington, DC: W. T. Grant Foundation.

Veblen, T. (1918). *The Higher Learning in America*. New York: Heubsch.

CHAPTER TWELVE

Standardized Testing: Restrict or Expand

POSITION 1: RESTRICT TESTING

A young Ojibwa student . . . was tested by several professionals and classified as having certain learning and behavioral problems. In part, this classification was based upon his staring into space, completing tasks very slowly, and giving "non-reality based" responses to questions. As it turned out, the boy had a special relationship with his traditional Ojibwa grandfather, who encouraged his dreaming . . . . In Ojibwa thought and language *ga-na-wa-bun-daw-ming*, which means seeing without feeling (objectivity), carries less value than *mu-zhi-tum-ing*, which means feelings that you do not see (subjectivity). (McShane, 1989, cited in Madaus, 1994, p. 80)

Vexed Tests

In a witty attack on standardized testing, Banesh Hoffmann (1962) recounted a debate that was played out on the pages of the *Times* of London. A letter to the newspaper's editor asked for help in solving a multiple-choice problem from a battery of school tests taken by the letter writer's son. At first glance, the question seemed to be straightforward and not surprising to anyone who has taken school tests. It asked, "Which is the odd one out among cricket, football, billiards, and hockey?"

The letter writer believed that the answer must be billiards because it is the only one of the four games played indoors. He admitted to being less than sure of his answer, and he reported that there was no agreement among his acquaintances. One of his neighbors argued that the correct choice was cricket because in all of the other games the object was to put a ball in a net. The

295

writer's son had selected hockey because it was the only one that was a "girl's game." The letter writer asked readers of the *Times* for help.

Ensuing letters and arguments succeeded only in muddying the waters, since the logic supporting one choice was no more compelling than the logic supporting any other. For example, billiards could be considered the odd one out because it is the only one of the four games listed that is not a team game. It is the only one in which the color of the ball matters. It is the only one in which more than one ball is in play, and it is the only one played on a green cloth rather than a grass field. Unfortunately, equally convincing briefs could be submitted in behalf of the other choices.

Hoffmann fumed about the inherent cultural bias in the question. He assumed that the test was designed to measure reasoning ability and not knowledge of sports, but he argued that the test taker might be disadvantaged by too little experience with athletics. For example, not all students with good reasoning skills may know how cricket is played. Test takers who know too much about sports might also be disadvantaged. They might choose hockey as the odd one out because it is really two different games that share the same name: in England and in several other countries, hockey is a game typically played on grass by players who receive no salary; elsewhere it is a game played on ice, often by professional athletes.

The language of this test item may trip up students, preventing it from measuring reasoning ability. For example, many working-class students are not familiar with either cricket or billiards. This item tends to reflect the language and culture of the middle and upper middle classes, and low scores may reflect social standing more than they do achievement or ability (Neill and Medina, 1989). Americans could also be at a disadvantage, confused by the language of test directions, which asks test takers to select the "odd one out." The question stem more commonly found in the United States is, "Which of the following does not belong?"

Test questions of this sort seem silly. There is no readily apparent "right answer," and test takers have no opportunity to demonstrate the thought processes that led to their decisions. As Hoffmann noted, "What sense is there in giving tests in which the candidate just picks answers, and is not allowed to give the reasons for his choice?" (Hoffmann, 1962, p. 20) Multiple-choice questions are an unnatural problem-solving format that is discontinuous with the way in which real-life problems present themselves. Rarely are life's dilemmas accompanied by four answers, one of which is guaranteed to be correct. Good problem solvers in the real world are seldom locked away; deprived of books, computers, and human contact; and told to respond to a set of timed, multiple-choice questions that have no practical meaning.

If multiple-choice questions, such as the one that vexed readers of the *Times*, were nothing more than a parlor game, a form of Trivial Pursuit played for amusement, there would be little objection to them. However, as everyone knows, standardized testing has serious consequences, and for public school students, the stakes are particularly high. On the basis of scores on standardized multiple-choice exams, decisions are made about placement in reading groups, and about who should be admitted to the college track programs in public high schools, who should go to elite colleges, who should be awarded scholarships, who should be admitted to medical and law schools, and who should be allowed to practice a profession or trade.

If Testing Is the Answer, What Was the Question?

In the early twentieth century, defining "native intelligence" and attempting to measure it through the use of standardized examinations instigated one of the most controversial legacies of the testing movement (Gould, 1981). Sir Francis Galton in England and Alfred Binet in France attempted to measure mental capacities through standardized tests (Cremin, 1961). Binet developed his test at the request of the French government, in order to identify those children who were "mentally subnormal" and not able to function adequately in regular classrooms. Louis Terman translated Binet's tests into English for American students, and he and his colleagues adjusted the tests to comport with their own sense of how intelligence was distributed. For example, Terman believed that men are more intelligent than women and that rural people are less intelligent than urban dwellers. Therefore, when girls outscored boys, test items on which girls scored unusually well were changed. On items where urban children outscored rural children, no changes were made (Garcia and Pearson, 1994).

Terman argued the intelligence tests make schools more efficient. He claimed that the tests could be used to sort children into differentiated curricula designed to prepare them for their appropriate lot in life:

> Preliminary investigations indicate that an I.Q. below 70 rarely permits anything better than unskilled labor; the range of 70–80 is pre-eminently that of semi-skilled labor; from 80–100 that of skilled or ordinary clerical labor; from 100–110 or 115 that of semi-professional pursuits; and that above all of these are grades of intelligence which permit one to enter the professions or other large fields of business. (Terman, quoted in Wolf et al., 1991)

Psychologists working for the United States government during World War I introduced the first wide-scale use of intelligence tests. The army was interested in classifying all new recruits, with special attention given to two groups: those of exceptional ability and those unfit for military service. Binet and Terman had used individual IQ tests that were not well suited to large-scale testing; under the direction of American psychologists, the army developed the first mass testing program in history (Gumbert and Spring, 1974, pp. 87–112).

The army used the tests to answer questions about the placement of soldiers: Who would best fit where? How could the army best use the varied talents and abilities recruits brought with them? After the war, colleges and universities bought the surplus exams. The language of the army tests required only slight modification for use in the schools. The original instructions given to soldiers read:

> Attention! The purpose of this examination is to see how well you can remember, think and carry out what you are told to do in the army . . . . Now in the

army a man often has to listen to commands and carry them out exactly. I am going to give you these commands to see how well you carry them out . . . .

In schools, these instructions were changed:

Part of being a good student is your ability to follow directions. . . . When I call "Attention," stop instantly what you are doing and hold your pencil up— so. Don't put your pencil down on the paper until I say "Go." . . . . Listen carefully to what I say. Do just as you are told to do. As soon as you are through, pencils up. Remember, wait for the word "Go." (Gumbert and Spring, 1974, p. 94)

For many years, schools used IQ tests to track children on the basis of their test performance. Intelligence was viewed as the "raw material" required for schooling, and students judged to have less intelligence were given less education. Educators' reliance on IQ tests produced the unintended result of limiting students' educational access (Darling-Hammond, 1994). Students performing at the lowest levels on IQ tests received an education designed to prepare them to be tractable, unskilled laborers. Complex skills would be introduced into the curriculum of only the highest-achieving students. Intellect was viewed as a biological trait much like height or eye color: it was thought to be inherited, measurable, and fixed. IQ tests allowed schools to sort students into appropriate curricula, and thus their later place in society (Callahan, 1962; Wolf et al, 1991). Too frequently, these tests excluded most students from the best opportunities the school had to offer. More often than not, the best education and the most promising futures were reserved for those who performed well on standardized tests.

IQ Tests Are Biased Against Poor

Standardized IQ tests have been shown to discriminate against the poor. In the United States, Americans of European descent score more than 15 points higher on average than do African-Americans. There is also a significant gap between the standardized test scores of European-Americans and of Mexican-Americans and native Americans. Some advocates of standardized testing believe that most of the differences in IQ scores are attributable to genetic endowment (Jensen, 1969; Herrnstein and Murray, 1994). However, many in the academic community view intelligence as more than a single biological trait that can be measured by paper-and-pencil tests, and IQ tests are often challenged because of their bias, as well as their failure to capture the test taker's range of abilities (Gardner, 1983; Gould, 1981). Anthropologists and educational sociologists, for example, argue that IQ is more reflective of a child's socioeconomic status than of his or her native ability (Ogbu, 1978). They point out when children are grouped according to family background and academic experiences, the differences in achievement scores tend to disappear (Garcia and Pearson, 1994). Some researchers claim that there is bias in the tests themselves. They argue that the tests "reflect the language, culture, or learning style of middle-to-upper-class whites. Thus scores on these tests are as much measures of race or ethnicity and income as they are measures of achievement, ability, or skill" (Neill and Medina, 1989, p. 691).

Teachers of poor and minority children report that they spend more time teaching the children how to take the test than do teachers of students from moderate- and high-income families, and are more likely to rely on data from standardized tests (Garcia and Pearson, 1994). Poor and minority children spend more time on workbook exercises and busy-work assignments. They are less likely than are middle-class students to have access to classes where they can discuss what they know, read real books, write down their thoughts, or solve problems in mathematics, science, or other school subjects (Darling-Hammond, 1994). Students from poor families and children of minorities have been awarded an education of less promise and less substance because of their poor performance on standardized tests.

> Clearly, the unintended negative outcomes brought about by the widespread policy use of IQ tests disproportionately disadvantaged minority populations. Despite Binet's original purpose to identify children in need of instructional assistance, the IQ test in this country led to Blacks and Hispanics being disproportionately placed in dead-end classes for the "educable mentally retarded." (Madaus, 1994, p. 86)

Misleading the Public

> Validation was once a priestly mystery, a ritual performed behind the scenes, with the professional elite as witness and judge. Today it is a public spectacle combining the attraction of chess and mud wrestling. (Cronbach, 1988, p. 3)

Until the last few years, despite questions about the validity of individual test items on standardized tests (Crouse and Trusheim, 1988; Hoffmann, 1962; Nairn et al., 1980; Owen, 1985), test takers were never able to see a list of the "right" answers after they had taken the exams. The Educational Testing Service (ETS) of Princeton, New Jersey, and other test developers published only a few sample questions, claiming that full disclosure would compromise the tests. In order to make the tests reliable,* they argued, many items had to be repeated from year to year, and the answers, therefore, had to be held back from public scrutiny. The ETS admitted that it was possible to construct new equivalent exams every year; however, it would be an expensive process whose costs would ultimately be borne by the test takers.

---

*Reliability in testing can be thought of as a synonym for stability, consistency, or dependability. Kerlinger's simile might be useful for an understanding of this concept. He writes: "A test is like a gun in its purpose. When we measure human attributes and abilities and achievements, we want to measure 'true' amounts of attributes that individuals possess. This is like hitting a target with a gun. With a test we want to hit the attribute. If a gun consistently hits a target—the shots cluster close together at or near the center of the target . . . we say it is reliable. Similarly with psychological and sociological measures. If they hit the target, they are reliable" (Kerlinger, 1979, p. 133).

Recognizing the power that standardized exams have over the lives of individual test takers, and not persuaded by ETS's arguments, New York and California enacted legislation that allowed test takers to see the answers after they had taken the exams. These truth-in-testing laws revealed ambiguity in test items. In some instances, more than one answer was correct. The ETS and other test makers took the issue to court, and in early 1990 a federal district court judge in New York set aside the test disclosure law on the grounds that it interfered with copyright laws. The truth-in-testing laws have cast doubt on the ability of tests to measure what it is they claim to measure and have opened up the issue of validity* to public examination.

There is good reason for public suspicion. In some cases, the results of standardized tests have been used intentionally to mislead the public. Take the case of the "magic mean," uncovered by a physician in West Virginia. According to newspaper accounts, he learned that the students in the state were performing above the national average on standardized tests. This intrigued him, considering that West Virginia had one of the highest rates of illiteracy in the nation. Further checking by the physician revealed that no state using the test was reported to be below the mean. The tests compared student achievement with outdated and very low national norms, and, thus, the results made even the worst test taker (and the school systems that bought the tests) appear to be above average. It was concluded that "standardized, nationally normed achievement tests give children, parents, school systems, legislatures, and the press inflated and misleading reports on achievement levels" (Cannell, 1987, p. 3).

Indeed, by the late 1980s, it was hard to find any school districts or states that scored below the mean on nationally normed standardized tests. These data have contributed to what has been termed the Lake Wobegon effect, after the mythical Minnesota town created by Garrison Keillor in which "the women are strong, the men are good looking, and all the children are above average" (Fiske, 1988; Mehrens and Kaminski, 1989; Phillips, 1990). This is, unfortunately, not an isolated example, and a great deal of caution is advised before drawing inferences about the quality of education from the data of standardized testing programs (Linn, 1993). For the past fifty years, psychometricians and companies that market tests have convinced the public that short-answer tests are objective, scientific measures deserving of public confidence and faith, when, in fact, these tests suffer from vagueness, ambiguity, imprecision, and bias. There is nothing scientific or objective about them; they are written, tested, compiled, and interpreted by highly subjective human beings (Owen, 1985).

---

*Validity refers to the ability of a test to measure what the test maker want to measure. Kerlinger (1979) uses the following example: "Suppose a group of teachers of social studies writes a test to measure students' understanding of certain social concepts: justice, equality, and cooperation, for instance. The teachers want to know whether their students understand and can apply the ideas. But they write a test of only factual items about contemporary institutions. The test is then not valid for the purpose they had in mind" (p. 138).

Bias Against Women

The results of standardized testing programs are further marred by their bias against women. Consider the Scholastic Assessment Exam (SAT), a test commonly taken by college-bound high school students. The ETS has encouraged colleges and universities to consider the SAT exam a scientific predictor of students' first-year grades in college. Consequently, SAT scores are often part of the data used by colleges in making admission decisions. According to the ETS, students with higher SAT scores should earn higher grades during their first year in college. One study, however, indicates that the SAT might be a gender-biased exam (Rosser, 1987). The gap between men's and women's scores on the test is 61 points. Female test takers scored 50 points lower on the math section and 11 points lower on the verbal section of the exam. If the SAT accurately predicted grade point average, male students would have higher first-year grade point averages than would female students. But this was not the case. Despite lower scores on the SAT, women earned higher grades than did men. The SAT does not predict what it is supposed to predict: success in college. The scores students get on SAT exams have less meaning than ETS has promised. Rosser concluded that because of sex bias on the SAT, women have less chance of being accepted to college, receiving financial aid, and being invited to join programs for the gifted. Because of an invalid exam, women are likely to earn less money and to lose out in appointments to positions of leadership.

Tests Drive School Curriculum

Standardized tests are terribly flawed, but despite their problems they continue to exert tremendous influence. Every teacher knows that testing drives the curriculum. What is tested is taught. No teacher wants his or her students to perform poorly on standardized achievement tests, and no school administrator wants his or her school to be ranked below others in the state or district. Everyone in education knows that, too often, the newspapers report the results of statewide testing in much the same way they report basketball standings. "We're Number One" or "County Schools Lowest in State" are not uncommon headlines in many local newspapers. To avoid invidious comparisons, instruction is geared to the test. Over time, material not tested tends not to be taught. Teachers and administrators fall victim to test makers' promises and the public's misplaced faith in testing. In truth, IQ tests are of little value in making educational decisions about children's education. Nationally normed achievement tests are often no better, and there is no compelling reason to subject students to large-scale multiple-choice exams.

National testing has become a national obsession. Encouraged by Bill Clinton, then governor of Arkansas, and then-President George Bush, the education community began to develop what were called "New World Standards" in each of the "five core subjects" (U.S. Department of Education, 1991, p. 11), and test makers madly scrambled to rush testing plans to the market. A national system of assessment was touted as a means to chart the progress of schools on their march to the new higher standards (Linn, 1993). However, Monty Neill of FairTest, among others, argued that all of the proposals to bring about school reform through renewed emphasis on assessment are based on premises not supported by an examination of recent history:

> During the 1980s, U.S. schoolchildren became probably the most overtested students in the world—but the desired educational improvement did not occur. FairTest research indicates that our schools now give more than 200 million standardized exams each year. The typical student must take several dozen before graduating. Adding more testing will no more improve education than taking the temperature of a patient more often will reduce his fever. (Neill, 1991, p. 36)

There is an antidote to standardized testing that does not sacrifice accountability. In every community, teachers, parents, and administrators should select appropriate content based on the students' interests, experiences, goals, and needs. Teachers should teach that content with all the skill at their command, and evaluate the extent of student learning with a wide variety of instruments. Students should be encouraged to demonstrate their ability to think, through written exercises, verbal expression, and informal papers, and they should be given ample opportunity to explain the reasons for their choices. The assessment of student learning requires that educators develop a broader, richer array of measures. Student achievement should not be reduced to a single numerical score. Multiple-choice tests cannot tell the story of academic success. Standardized testing is deceitful and biased; standardized tests should be abolished. A student's record of school achievement should include a rich portfolio of papers, essays, videos, poems, photographs, drawings, and tapes, not a series of test scores.

POSITION 2: EXPAND TESTING

Richard Herrnstein and Charles Murray argue that six firm conclusions can be drawn from the long history of research on standardized tests of cognitive ability:

1. There is such a thing as a general factor of cognitive ability on which human beings differ.
2. All standardized tests of academic aptitude or achievement measure this general factor to some degree, but IQ tests expressly designed for that purpose measure it most accurately.
3. IQ scores match, to a first degree, whatever it is that people mean when they use the word *intelligent* or *smart* in ordinary language.
4. IQ scores are stable, although not perfectly so, over much of a person's life.
5. Properly administered IQ tests are not demonstrably biased against social, economic, ethnic, or racial groups.
6. Cognitive ability is substantially heritable, apparently no less than 40 percent and no more than 80 percent. (Herrnstein and Murray, 1994, pp. 22–23)

Education was "rediscovered" as an issue of social concern in the 1980s and carefully examined. Researchers, critics, and government officials raised questions about the quality of teaching, student learning, and school leadership. Public education was rescued from years of neglect, dusted off, and reassessed. After a long period of inattention, it was no surprise that problems were discovered everywhere, from the head to the tail of the academic procession. The schools, it was generally concluded, were in need of reform. Academic standards had slipped and students were passing from grade to grade without having mastered the content that would allow them to be successful. Many educators recognized that the schools needed to set high standards for student achievement and to make scrupulously fair assessments of student performance or the United States would lose its competitive place in the world.

Previous generations of education reformers had concerned themselves with making education available to the children of all classes and races, and to a large extent they were successful. By the 1990s, a higher percentage of students were completing high school than ever before, but questions arose over what a high school diploma signaled. Instead of availability, the current generation of reformers is now forced to consider the quality of those school experiences. As Mortimer Adler (1982) argues, the legal mandates for education cannot be satisfied only by guaranteeing all children access to education. In order to satisfy the educational responsibilities of a democratic society, public education must demonstrate that each student acquires the requisite skills and knowledge. Educational outcomes no longer can be measured only in terms of quantity—years of schooling and the number of high school diplomas granted. Schools must guarantee that education has a demonstrably positive effect on students. They must show that students benefit from their years of attendance; that increased investment in schooling can be measured in the greater ability to read, write, and do mathematics; and that moving up the academic ladder from grade to grade is based on merit rather than social promotion.

The issue of educational quality raises a broad range of questions:

How good is the education provided students in grades K–12?

How do the students of today compare with former students?

How do students in School A or District A or State A compare with others?

How can prospective employers be assured that students who graduate from high school possess a minimum level of skills, knowledge, and ability?

How can taxpayers know that the dollars given to public education are being well spent?

If changes are made in public education, how can it be determined that they have contributed positively to learning outcomes?

Answers to these questions must be based on high-quality data. Schools need quantifiable measures of student performance and teacher effectiveness if they hope to maintain public support. Intelligent policy decisions must be based on objective information, and although no single means of data collection is sufficient, the data generated by well-designed standardized tests are crucial to an understanding of school outcomes. Good tests and good testing programs permit schools to gather information about curricula and students that is not available to them through other means. Without these data, schools cannot make appropriate decisions about the quality of the curriculum or the power of specific programs to produce academic learning by students.

Testing is the scientific base that supports decisions about the art of teaching. It permits measurement of the teacher's art, complementing, as well as assessing, classroom practice. Formal testing programs were introduced into schools in the nineteenth century to counter charges of examiner bias and subjectivity. Today, standardized testing programs also provide the yardstick against which society charts the progress and shortcomings of education, and their results are the form in which schools report the status of education to public officials and parents. Test and measurement experts are often at odds with others in education, and they have suffered abuse from critics who are skeptical about the power of testing and fearful of the ability of testing agencies to influence public policy. The purpose here is not to answer the critics or to submit a brief in support of the Educational Testing Service or the National Assessment of Educational Progress. Instead, we argue that (1) standardized testing is an essential tool for examining the measurable dimensions of education; (2) education has entered an era of accountability in which school officials must demonstrate that the money being spent for education is paying dividends in quality; and (3) new forms of performance testing allow test makers to augment standardized testing programs with "authentic" assessment techniques.

Testing for the Good of Schools

Standardized testing is an essential element of rational curriculum work. The data generated by testing programs help curriculum planners determine whether the measured outcomes of a given set of instructional inputs match the intended goals. In other words, tests can help educators find out if a specific program is working in the way it was designed to work. When taxpayers are asked to foot the bill for a new science program in the high school or a new math program in the elementary school, they should be informed of the likely effects of these programs. They should also have hard data by which to judge how well these programs have worked elsewhere. It is a simple matter of cost accounting and fiscal responsibility.

Effective change does not occur by chance. Educational decisions must be made about the progress of the students, the rate of achievement of proximate goals, and the best choice among the competing paths to the next objective. Education planners need to choose appropriate measures of student attainment. Impressionistic data are not sufficient; anecdotal evidence is not scientific. It is not enough that a program "seems to be working" or that the teachers "claim to like" this method or that approach. Schools need to have better answers to direct questions about the curriculum. At what grade level are the students reading? What do diagnostic and prescriptive tests tell us about a child's performance in academic skill areas? How much of the required curriculum have students mastered?

Standardized testing should not be viewed as a report card, but as part of an assessment system that permits schools to make decisions about curriculum and instruction. Standardized achievement tests are objective measures of performance. They are not designed to provide apologies for ineffective programs, nor do they offer arbitrary standards of excellence. Standardized tests are designed to measure the goals of education and to determine the extent to which the nation is meeting its responsibilities to provide a quality education to all children.

Shooting the Messenger

In 1991, Congress created the National Council on Educational Standards and Testing, and it charged the council with offering advice on the desirability of national standards and testing. Six months later, the council recommended that Congress take action to adopt high national standards for all schoolchildren and to develop a system to measure the extent to which students were meeting those standards (Linn, 1993). These recommendations have not yet been implemented fully. Until the United States establishes national standards and a national assessment system, determining the quality of education across state boundaries is especially difficult. At the present time, the United States has no national curriculum, and although education is essentially an enterprise run by the individual states, Americans have a right to know how well their children are being educated when compared with the children of other states and regions.

Since 1969, the federal government has financed an assessment program known as the National Assessment of Educational Progress (NAEP). Administered since 1983 by the ETS, the NAEP gathers data about the knowledge, skills, and attitudes of students across ten subject areas: art, career and occupational development, citizenship, literature, mathematics, music, reading, science, social studies, and writing. Tests are given to four age groups (ages 9, 13, 17, and young adults). Education planners need the information yielded by such tests in order to reform schools.

Unfortunately, much of the test data have been negative; schoolchildren appear to know less today than they did earlier in our history. Although these findings grab headlines, and cause a great deal of collective handwringing, they are not an end in themselves. The NAEP is designed to facilitate reconsideration of the quality of teaching and learning in public schools. Too often, the response to negative findings has been to blame the test makers instead of addressing the cause of poor scores. More energy has been expended attacking the validity of standardized testing than in examining the conditions revealed by the tests. It seems that it is easier to shoot the messenger than to consider an unpopular message.

In 1985, a project funded by the National Endowment for the Humanities and administered by the NAEP staff assessed students' knowledge of history and literature (Ravitch and Finn, 1987). The results were unequivocal: the 8,000 17-year-olds who took this exam were, in the words of the authors, "ignorant of much of what they should know." The sample was stratified for sex, race, ethnicity, geography, and private school attendance, in order to reflect a national population. Among all test takers, only 20 percent could identify Joyce, Dostoevsky, Ellison, Conrad, or Ibsen; fewer than 25 percent were able to identify Henry James or Thomas Hardy; only one in three knew that Chaucer was the author of *The Canterbury Tales;* 65 percent did not know what *1984* or *Lord of the Flies* is about. Three-quarters of the students did not know when Lincoln was president; one-third were unfamiliar with the *Brown* decision; 70 percent could not identify the Magna Carta.

Critics screamed that the test was not valid—that it did not measure knowledge of the history and literature students learn in school. This criticism cuts to the heart of testing (Wainer and Braun, 1987). The goal of psychometric testing is to provide policymakers with valid, reliable data on which to base decisions. Too often, criticisms of standardized tests come from people who are uninformed about the field of measurement. (Admittedly, this technical area seems to defy understanding by most of the general public and many educators.)

The National Assessment of History and Literature (NAHL) was certainly a valid exam. It was written in cooperation with public school teachers, and the majority of the questions were drawn directly from material covered in the textbooks and curriculum. Most of the questions were designed to cover fundamental facts that students of this age might reasonably be expected to know. Citing a handful of the literature questions—such as biblical references—relating to content not typically taught in school, critics raged that certain students were put at a disadvantage.

The detractors apparently were unmindful of the goal of the exam. The NAHL was not meant to grade students in the hope that many could be failed. It was designed to determine what students know so that the curriculum and the nature of instruction could be improved. The test did not try to identify individual or typical 17-year-olds. The test results were to be used as one body of objective data for considering what is learned in schools. The NAHL was not intended to replace teacher tests or to substitute the judgment of the test makers for the individual judgments of state legislators or curriculum workers.

Standardized test results cannot be ignored. One of the goals of the NAHL was to provide baseline data for future assessments in history and literature. Relatively little is known about these fields of instruction other than enrollment statistics. It is, frankly, shocking that the test has been attacked so viciously. Although testing is far from a perfect science, at present there are no measures that can compete with standardized tests for economically gathering valid and reliable data about what children have learned in school.

Admittedly, standardized tests, as a measure of educational achievement, are not without problems. Many of the goals of education are difficult to assess. The ability to communicate verbally and the possession of a healthy self-concept are hard to determine with paper-and-pencil tests. It is also well known among test developers that minimums tend to become maximums and that teachers tend to teach for the test. Not everything that is taught can be included on an exam, and material not tested has a tendency to disappear from the curriculum. Test writers do not want to dictate the curriculum, but schools and the public must realize that tests of minimum competencies cannot cover everything that is taught in schools. Despite the risk of skipping some learning outcomes that are significant and emphasizing others that may be less important, standardized achievement tests are a cost-effective means of ensuring quality education.

Opponents of standardized tests argue that too often the use of these instruments has resulted in discrimination against minority groups. Indeed, standardized testing is designed to discriminate, to make distinctions about what is known and by whom. If there were no differences in test scores—that is, if they did not discriminate among categories of test takers—the tests would be worthless. It is not a question of whether or not tests discriminate. Rather, do the tests discriminate fairly, and are the results of even the fairest tests used for unfair purposes? The fact that a particular racial, ethnic, or gender group outperforms others on a standardized test does not necessarily mean that the test is biased (Haertel, 1991). However, such performance differences should set in motion a careful review to determine whether there was any bias in the construction of the exam, its administration, or the areas it was designed to assess. Responsible test makers would not fail to do so.

Performance/Authentic Assessment

Much of the criticism directed at today's assessment may well be an attack on older forms of testing programs. Most of us are familiar with tests that indirectly measured what we knew. For example, a test maker who wanted to determine a student's woodworking ability might devise a test that was little more than a series of multiple-choice items. The student might be asked:

> Which of the following tools would be needed to make a wooden bowl? (a) A ball peen hammer. (b) A lathe chisel. (c) A screwdriver. (d) A wrench.

Other questions might probe the student's knowledge of various types of wood, appropriate procedures for using power tools, types of finishing materials, and safety procedures. These items, taken together, might indicate a student's knowledge of bowl making, but the student's score would tell the test maker very little about the student's actual ability to fashion a wooden bowl. A better measure of that ability would entail taking the student into a fully equipped woodworking shop and observing him or her set about making a bowl from a block of wood. This direct measure of performance would allow the test taker to demonstrate his or her actual ability in a real-life situation, and it would allow the test giver to ask why certain procedures were followed or others were omitted (Cizek, 1991).

Performance assessments of this type have become common not only in vocational education, but also in foreign language proficiency exams, as measures of writing ability, and in the sciences and mathematics. Performance or authentic assessments evaluate students' ability to complete-real life tasks. Used as part of the instructional process, the tests allow teachers to determine that students have mastered one set of skills before they move on to teach others. The NAEP first incorporated performance components in tests in 1990; in 1992, it experimented with having students establish writing portfolios as a way to assess their writing ability directly, and is planning to further expand the use of performance items. Performance assessment is one of the more exciting new developments in evaluation design. It promises to give educators at the local level answers to questions previously available only through high-inference or proxy measures of ability. Performance testing can tell teachers, parents, and students whether or not a child can write an essay, conduct a science experiment, or make a wooden bowl.

Performance-based assessments include portfolio reviews, students' oral and written presentations, and teachers' observations of students (Darling-Hammond, 1994). Test makers and psychometricians are eager to design assessment instruments that allow test takers to show what they know in authentic situations. Assessment programs are changing. In 1994, the verbal section of the SAT began to place greater emphasis on reading and reasoning; the mathematics section now places more emphasis on data interpretation and real-life mathematics, and students will be asked to demonstrate how they arrived at correct answers. "Multiple guess" no longer will be accepted as a valid synonym for multiple choice. The latest generation of performance-based tests is not being used to group students by ability or to measure them against arbitrary criteria; authentic assessment is designed to inform teachers about their students' abilities and improve learning for all students (Darling-Hammond, 1994). Performance testing is not new; it has been around in various forms for decades. However, it is not without its faults. Performance testing only recently has come into favor with education policymakers. The testing community is well aware of its strengths and weaknesses, and it urges educators not to discard standardized testing programs too quickly (Linn, 1993; Swanson, Norman, and Linn, 1995).

Since 1988, Vermont has been developing statewide performance programs in mathematics and writing, in order to generate data about student achievement. Careful reviews of the Vermont process suggest that such data may be very difficult, if not impossible, to obtain through performance evaluation alone. Scoring writing portfolios is particularly difficult. It is generally agreed that when evaluators want to determine the quality of students' writing, a review of their actual writing, collected over time, has clear advantages over a multiple-choice exam covering the rules of grammar and the mechanics of writing. However, unlike scoring standardized exams, the evaluation of writing samples is highly subjective. A single reviewer may not offer a reliable assessment of writing, and it is often difficult for two reviewers to agree on the quality of a written work.

A careful examination of a student's portfolio by two or more teachers would certainly produce a great amount of information about that student's writing ability and progress. However, it would not provide data that would permit comparison with other students in the state. To gather statewide comparative data, Vermont calls teachers together from various parts of the state and asks them to read portfolios from students who are not their own. An expensive process, this may make the assessment less subjective, but it does not solve all of the problems. For example, many teachers would like to reward effort, but objective portfolio reviews may not be able to gauge the quality of the effort given the student's ability. As researchers examining Vermont's portfolio experiment have noted:

> Clearly, the Vermont portfolio program has been largely unsuccessful so far in meeting its goal of providing high-quality data about student performance. The writing assessment is still hobbled by unreliable scoring, and the mathematics assessment has yet to demonstrate that it has addressed the vexing problem of validity that confronts performance assessments in general and unstandardized assessments embedded in instruction. (Koretz et al., 1994, p. 11)

The assessment of student learning always entails problems. Although policymakers would prefer assessments that are easy, accurate, and inexpensive, assessment designs must be complex in order to account for variations among students, teachers, and curricula (Linn, 1993). Performance/authentic assessment shows much promise, but it must be viewed with caution. It allows teachers to observe the effects of instruction directly; students demonstrate the extent to which they have mastered the subject being taught. However, performance testing alone does not provide data about how well students are performing compared with those in other districts, states, or nations. It permits students to exhibit real-world mastery of skills, but it does not solve the problem of comparing one student with others of the same age and ability.

Performance assessment is not a substitute for high-quality standardized testing programs. It offers the education community the promise of a fuller picture, but taken alone, the results instead provide a snapshot that is too grainy to be used to shape policy. As yet, there is no substitute for objective data, standardized tests, and other valid measures that allow test takers to know where they stand in comparison with others and permit policymakers to gauge the progress of educational change.

For Discussion

1. Traditionally, student performance has been measured by norm-referenced tests. This type of testing compares performance with a norm or standard established by a representative sample of students similar to the test taker. Although norm-referenced testing is popular with the public as a measure of school accountability, many educators prefer criteria-referenced performance measures. One such measure is Outcomes Based Education (OBE), in which student performance is compared against preestablished criteria. Students don't compete against one another in time-based competitive tests for a limited number of A's and B's. Instead, OBE assumes

that nearly all students can be successful in mastering specified goals; all students can get good grades. Students are given repeated opportunities to demonstrate that they have mastered instructional goals.

What do you see as the advantages and disadvantages of criteria-based and norm-referenced assessments? Who benefits from OBE? Are any students disadvantaged? Does norm-referenced assessment or criteria-referenced assessment have greater appeal for you?

2. Consider the following excerpt from the *PSAT/NMSQT Student Bulletin*, a guide to the test on which the National Merit Scholarships are based:

> Q. Might I find an error or ambiguity in a test question?
> A. It is unlikely. But if you think you do, tell the test supervisor as soon as possible. Immediately after the test, you may write to: College Board Test Development, Educational Testing Service . . . . ETS will send you a written response after your inquiry has been reviewed thoroughly by subject-matter specialists. If the response does not resolve your concern, you can request the Director of Test Development to initiate further reviews of your inquiry. If you still have concerns, you can request a formal review of your inquiry by an independent review panel . . . . (Educational Testing Service, 1994, p. 12)

> This process obviously is very costly for both the test maker and, ultimately, the students, who are paying the costs of test development. Can you justify this expense? Would you argue that test takers and their families have a right to see the correct answers for all the tests that students take in school?

3. Harold Rugg, a noted educator of another generation, proposed a "yardstick" to use in evaluating schools. Several of the items from that yardstick are included here for your consideration. Compare them with contemporary school objectives established by states and local districts. To what extent does Rugg's list represent the concerns of contemporary schooling? Are Rugg's objectives quantifiable? Are they considered significant in an era concerned with skills, objectivity, and comparability?

Rugg's Key Questions To Be Asked of Any School*

1. Is the general relationship of students and teachers one of friendly comradeship, of mutual respect for others as persons? Is it one in which the teacher assumes the role of mature guide and the student the role of learner, that is being guided by one who knows—the whole enterprise approached in the spirit of sincere, questioning inquiry?

2. Are the parents and teachers and administrators developing a theory of American culture upon which to build the school program?

3. How far does the school practice the concept of equality and functional interpretation of freedom of thought and expression?

4. Does the school help students to analyze the potential of a mixed and expanding economy? Or does it preach "back to the normalcy" of private enterprise and laissez faire? Or does it follow the line of least resistance and avoid the entire problem?

5. Does the school teach the implications of the interdependence of the peoples of the earth?

6. Is the school confronting frankly its responsibility in the continuing battle for consent? Does it confront students with the current pitfalls in understanding social conditions and problems?

*Only selected excerpts are presented here. For the original yardstick see: Harold Rugg, *Foundations for American Education*. Yonkers-on-Hudson, NY: World Book, 1947, pp. 808–813.

7. Does the school deal frankly and fully with the problems of propaganda and censorship?

8. Do the students understand that "he who owns the things that men must have, owns the men that must have them"?

9. Does the school invite representatives of various points of view and sources of knowledge and thought to help students in the study of such issues as property, employment, government, race, and religion? Or are these studies merely from books and other materials under the direction of the staff? Or are they ignored?

References

Adler, M. J. (1982). *The Paideia Proposal: An Educational Manifesto.* New York: Macmillan.

Callahan, E. (1962). *Education and the Cult of Efficiency.* Chicago: University of Chicago Press.

Cannell, J. J. (1987). *Nationally Normed Elementary Achievement Testing in America's Public Schools: How All 50 States Are Above the National Average,* 2d ed. Daniels, WV: Friends for Education.

Cizek, G. J. (1991). "Innovation or Enervation? Performance Assessment in Perspective." *Phi Delta Kappan* **72,** 695–699.

Cremin, L. (1961). *The Transformation of the School: Progressivism in American Education, 1876–1957.* New York: Knopf.

Cronbach, L. J. (1988). "Five Perspectives on Validity Argument." In *Test Validity,* edited by H. Wainer and H. I. Braun. Hillsdale, NJ: Erlbaum.

Crouse, J., and Trusheim, D. (1988). *The Case Against the SAT.* Chicago: University of Chicago Press.

Darling-Hammond, L. (1994). "Performance-Based Assessment and Educational Equity." *Harvard Educational Review* **64,** 5–30.

Educational Testing Service. (1994). *PSAT/NMSQT Student Bulletin.* Princeton, NJ: Educational Testing Service.

Fiske, E. B. (1988). "America's Test Mania." *The New York Times, Education Life,* April 10, pp. 16–20.

Garcia, G. E., and Pearson, P. D. (1994). "Assessment and Diversity." In *Review of Research in Education,* edited by L. Darling-Hammond. Washington, DC: American Educational Research Association.

Gardner, H. (1983). *Frames of Mind: The Theory of Multiple Intelligences.* New York: Basic Books.

Gould, S. J. (1981). *The Mismeasure of Man.* New York: Norton.

Gumbert, E. B., and Spring, J. H. (1974). *The Superschool and the Superstate: American Education in the Twentieth Century, 1918–1970.* New York: Wiley.

Haertel, E. H. (1991). "New Forms of Teacher Assessment." In *Review of Research in Education,* edited by G. Grant. Washington, DC: American Educational Research Association.

Herrnstein, R. J., and Murray, C. (1994). *The Bell Curve: Intelligence and Class Structure in American Life.* New York: Free Press.

Hoffmann, B. (1962). *The Tyranny of Testing.* New York: Crowell-Collier.

Jensen, A. R. (1969). "How Much Can We Boost IQ and Scholastic Achievement?" *Harvard Educational Review* **39,** 1–123.

Kerlinger, F. N. (1979). *Behavioral Research.* New York: Holt, Rinehart & Winston.

Koretz, D., Stecher, B., Klein, S., and McCaffrey, D. (1994). "The Vermont Portfolio Assessment: Findings and Implications." *Educational Measurement: Issues and Practice* **13,** 5–16.

Linn, R. L. (1993). "Educational Assessment: Expanded Expectations and Challenges." *Educational Evaluation and Policy Analysis* **15**, 1–16.

Madaus, G. F. (1994). "A Technological and Historical Consideration of Equity Issues Associated with Proposals to Change the Nation's Testing Policy." *Harvard Educational Review* **64**, 76–95.

Mehrens, W. A., and Kaminski, J. (1989). "Methods for Improving Standardized Test Scores: Fruitful, Fruitless, or Fraudulent?" *Educational Measurement: Issues and Practice* **8**, 14–22.

Nairn, A., and Associates. (1980). *The Reign of ETS: The Corporation That Makes Up Minds*. Washington, DC: Nairn and Associates.

Neill, D. M., and Medina, N. J. (1989). "Standardized Testing: Harmful to Educational Health." *Phi Delta Kappan* **70**, 688–697.

Neill, M. (1991). "Do We Need a National Achievement Exam? No: It Would Damage, Not Improve Education." *Education Week*, April 24, pp. 28, 36.

Ogbu, J. (1978). *Minority Education and Caste: The American System in Cross-cultural Perspective*. New York: Academic.

Owen, D. (1985). *None of the Above*. Boston: Houghton Mifflin.

Phillips, G. W. (1990). The Lake Wobegon Effect. *Educational Measurement: Issues and Practice* **9**, 3, 14.

Ravitch, D., and Finn, C. E., Jr. (1987). *What Do Our 17-Year-Olds Know*. New York: Harper & Row.

Rosser, P. (1987). *Sex Bias in College Admissions Testing: Why Women Lose Out*, 2d ed. Cambridge, MA: FairTest.

Swanson, D. B., Norman, G. R., and Linn, R. L. (1995). "Performance-Based Assessment: Lessons from the Health Professions." *Educational Researcher*, **24**, 5–11, 35.

Terman, L. M. (1922). *Intelligence Tests and School Reorganization*. Yonkers-on-Hudson, NY: World Book.

U.S. Department of Education (1987). *What's Happening in Teacher Testing: An Analysis of State Teacher Testing Practices*. Washington, DC: U.S. Government Printing Office.

———— (1991). *America 2000: An Education Strategy*. Washington, DC: U.S. Government Printing Office.

Wainer, H., and Braun, H. I., eds. (1987). *Test Validity*. Hillsdale, NJ: Erlbaum.

Wolf, J. B., Bixby, J., Glenn, J., and Gardner, H. (1991). "To Use Their Minds Well: Investigating New Forms of Student Assessment." In *Review of Research in Education*, edited by G. Grant. Washington, DC: American Educational Research Association.

Part III

How Should Schools Be Organized and Operated?

The six chapters of Part III have as their general theme the ways in which schools should be organized and managed. One of the areas explored is the role that teachers should play in schools. Among the oldest traditions of education is the view of teachers as the obedient servants of the state. Plato, who is often cited as the first philosopher of education, paid scant attention to the problems of teachers. His concern was the creation of a just society governed by the most able citizens. Education to prepare students for their place in society was under the heavy-handed control of the state. Schooling was compulsory up to age 20. The curriculum was scrutinized by censors and was to contain no reference to anything that did not serve public ends. Plato believed teachers should follow the curriculum. Any deviation could only be for the worse and was not to be allowed. He wrote:

In short, then, those who keep watch over our commonwealth must take the greatest care not to overlook the least infraction of the rule against any innovation upon the established system of education either of the body or of the mind. When the poet says that men care most for "the newest air that hovers on the singer's lips," they will be afraid lest he be taken not merely to mean new songs, but to commending a new style of music. Such innovation is not to be commended, nor should the poet be so understood. The introduction of novel fashions in music is a thing to beware of as endangering the whole fabric of society. (Cornford, 1968, p. 115)

Few people today would deny teachers the right to be innovative and creative in the classroom. Unlike Plato, most people believe in the

313

potential of progress and the value of change. However, many feel that the control of the curriculum remains the rightful province of the state or the community and not of the teacher. To empower teachers with authority over the curriculum is to disempower taxpayers, their elected representatives (boards of education), and school administrators.

Consider yourselves, for a moment, not as prospective teachers, but as taxpayers with children in public schools. Would you be comfortable paying hefty tax bills while having little or no say in the education of your children? Would you be willing to leave decisions about curriculum, textbooks, teaching methodology, and evaluation techniques to teachers who are not accountable to you? Or would you prefer to have these policy matters rest in the hands of school administrators and elected school boards who are responsible to you as a citizen and community resident? Clearly, there is a strong case to be made for community control of its schools.

It is argued with equal conviction that school reform has failed in the past largely because reformers have ignored the role of teachers. In order for schools to become more satisfying and more thought-provoking for children, they must first become better places for teachers. Teachers must be allowed to assume their rightful place as professionals with genuine authority in the school; they should control matters of curriculum, instruction, and policy. Teaching should be changed to enable teachers to assume a responsible role in shaping the purposes of schooling (Aronowitz and Giroux, 1985). As a prospective teacher, would you want to work for a school district that refused to listen to you about matters of curriculum and instruction?

The arguments about the organization and management of schools can be located along a continuum of political thought. The left, or liberal, end of the continuum includes those who tend to be sympathetic toward the rights of workers and teacher empowerment. It also includes those with positive views of unions and union involvement in school policy matters, as well as those who champion academic freedom for public school teachers. The right, or conservative, end of the continuum includes those who are more comfortable with the traditional exercise of authority in the schools. They oppose any attempt to weaken community control of schools by granting greater power to teachers. Those on the right tend to be less sympathetic toward unions, often viewing them as protectors of incompetent teachers and as unwise meddlers in the management of schools. Conservatives typically share a less than charitable view toward academic freedom for public school teachers, regarding it as an overused shield for spreading ill-founded and even un-American ideas in the classroom.

Of course, we need to be cautious about painting with too broad a brush. Unions tend to be on the left end of the spectrum—but former Presidents Reagan and Bush enjoyed great support among union members. Similarly, community control of schools is typically considered to be a plank in conservative political platforms, but the decentralization of New York City's school system in the 1960s was championed mainly by the left. Our goal is not to label school critics, but to make you more aware of the competing perspectives on education topics. As you think about what teaching should be, we ask you to consider the arguments of both left and right. Where do you now find yourself along the spectrum of opinion on each issue?

SCHOOL LEADERSHIP: TEACHER OR ADMINISTRATOR DIRECTED?

Teaching has been described as a "careerless profession," a job in which there is only limited opportunity for promotion or increases in authority and salary (Etzioni, 1969; Lortie, 1975). Upon graduation from college, most people pursue a series of work experiences and job-related career moves that bring additional responsibilities and greater remuneration. A few teachers—mainly those who move from classroom teaching through the principalship to central office administration—follow a similar ascent. However, most teachers do not have access to a promotion path that includes a series of increasingly rewarding positions, and teachers are often not allowed to participate in the reform and growth of education.

One teacher reported, somewhat tongue in cheek, that she had been "too busy to notice" that her husband, a hospital pharmacist, was participating in the development of his profession to a far greater extent than she was in hers. She slowly came to realize that her husband's work had allowed him to grow while her role as a classroom teacher had denied her

similar professional development. She noted that the knowledge base of pharmacy had expanded, as had its techniques. More important, the advances in the field were developed by practitioners and eagerly shared with colleagues across the country. She wrote:

> Meanwhile, in my school district, classroom lessons looked the way they had in the Fifties. Behind closed doors for the most part, teachers lectured, quizzed, and tested. Students "did" their workbooks and end-of-chapter questions, just as they had when I was in school myself . . . . I want a database, too. I want up-to-date bibliographies on issues that directly affect the students I teach. I need . . . access . . . to colleagues who are testing solutions to the same problems I encounter. (Swart, 1990, pp. 315–316)

Schools, unlike most other large workplaces, are characterized by a flat organizational structure, with most employees occupying a single, undifferentiated job category: classroom teacher. School districts typically do not offer enough routes out of the classroom (for example, guidance counselor, building principal, curriculum coordinator, department chair) to permit the career mobility common in other fields (Sikes, Measor, and Woods, 1985). The majority of teachers begin and end their careers as classroom teachers, without additional responsibilities or direct influence in running the school. Some sociologists have argued that because of its structure, teaching is an occupation that has better met the work needs of women than of men

(Lortie, 1975). Women, the argument goes, can begin teaching, drop out to raise a family, and return to the classroom when their children no longer need them at home.*

In the past, teaching and teachers' work were largely ignored as issues of public concern. If the public was satisfied with the quality of schools and the work of teachers, its satisfaction was expressed inaudibly. When schools appeared to be functioning well, communities rarely considered the problems of a teaching career. As long as student learning appeared to be high and student discipline was relatively unproblematic, few people outside of education concerned themselves with teachers' salary structure, the role teachers should play in schools, or the difficulty of attracting and retaining talented faculty.

By the 1980s, evidence suggested a variety of problems with public schooling. Educational expenditures had never been higher, but scores on standardized achievement tests were at all-time lows. Restive teachers demanded higher salaries, while the popular press delighted in printing stories of school violence, crime, and the numbers of poorly educated students. Studies criticized everything from student learning to teacher preparation (Boyer, 1983; Goodlad, 1984; National Commission, 1983; Sizer, 1984). The schools were said to be in crisis and the nation was declared to be at risk because of the poor quality of

teaching and learning. Teachers were held up to public scrutiny, and their work was weighed, measured, and assessed. Everywhere, researchers found dull, lifeless teaching; an absence of academic focus; bored, unchallenged students; and teachers mired in routine and paperwork. Implicit in this new focus was that teachers were not doing, or were not able to do, the job expected of them.

School problems were recognized by those on both sides of the desk. Neither immune to public criticism nor insensitive to school problems, teachers became increasingly dissatisfied with their work. A poll conducted by the National Education Association indicated that if they could start over, only 25 percent of the female teachers and 16 percent of the male teachers would again choose teaching as a career (*Status of the American Public School Teacher*, 1982). The Carnegie Forum (1986), among others, suggested that a major cause of teacher dissatisfaction was the structure of schools, and it predicted a diminished pool of high-quality teachers in the future unless schools are reorganized to make teaching more attractive.

It has been suggested that something is very wrong with the ways in which teachers' work and career paths are organized. In the late 1980s and early 1990s, nearly everyone advocated "restructuring" for school reform and sought ways to include teachers in making decisions about curriculum and teaching. According to Weiss, the arguments supporting the inclusion of teachers in decision making fall into three general areas: (1) Improved student performance: If teachers are given greater decision-making authority,

---

*Critics of this analysis note that it fails to account for the fact that women have multiple commitments, which include career and family. Teaching may permit women to meet multiple obligations, but that does not mean that teaching satisfies their career needs any better than it does men's (Feiman-Nemser and Floden, 1986).

they will use their special knowledge about teaching to develop innovative approaches that enhance student learning. (2) Increased teacher professionalism: Teachers will have enhanced status if they are recognized as part of the decision-making team. They will have a greater sense of responsibility for school problems, and they will have a deeper commitment to work for school improvement. (3) Better role models for students: Shared decision making presents teachers as active empowered workers. It provides students with role models for workplace democracy (Weiss, 1993, pp. 69–70).

Chapter 13 presents two positions on restructuring the work and role of teachers. Position 1 calls for teachers to exert influence well beyond the walls of their classrooms as the best means for improving their job satisfaction and performance. It recommends a restructuring of schools to grant teachers decision-making authority in organizing the curriculum, running the schools, and charting the reform agenda. Position 2 argues that the teacher empowerment suggested in Position 1 would be to the detriment of students and their communities. It argues that schools should consider teacher input, but they must be run by professional administrators in order to serve children, their parents, and the needs of the community.

ACADEMIC FREEDOM

If you view teachers as the leaders of schools, then you are likely to believe that their right to teach should be protected. If, instead, you see teachers as practitioners who have no leadership responsibilities, then you may be less willing to grant them the same degree of academic freedom enjoyed by those who teach in good universities. "Academic freedom," as applied to higher education, is the contemporary term for the classical ideal of the right to teach and learn (Hofstadter and Metzger, 1955). Socrates, charged with impiety and the corruption of Athenian youth, defended himself by claiming that he and his students had the freedom to pursue truth. All wickedness, he argued, was due to ignorance. The freedom to teach and the freedom to learn would uncover knowledge, eliminate ignorance, and improve the society. His fellow citizens were not persuaded, and Socrates was sentenced to death. Academic freedom has fared better; regularly battered, it has survived.

Although lacking a crisp, precise definition, "academic freedom," as the term is used in American higher education, typically refers to several related freedoms: (1) the freedom of professors to write, research, and teach in their field of special competence; (2) the freedom of universities to determine policies and practices unfettered by political restraints or other outside pressures; and (3) the freedom of students to learn.

It is argued that academic freedom ensures the freedom of the mind for both students and scholars and therefore is essential to the pursuit of truth, the primary mission of higher education (Kirk, 1955; MacIver, 1955). The university should be a marketplace of competing ideas. Students should be exposed to a diversity of views, and the classroom should be free of restraint and open to the regular and robust exchange of opinions.

The question here is not about academic freedom in universities, but whether academic freedom should be extended to those who teach in elementary and secondary schools. The word "academy" originally referred to the garden where Plato taught, and academic freedom came to be associated with institutions of higher learning. Public schools are unlike universities, and public school teachers and students have not automatically been given the same academic protection as their university counterparts. It has been argued that the comparative youthfulness of the students and the nature of instruction demand that public school teachers be more accountable to the community for what they teach and how they teach it.

The narrow conception of academic freedom, as a right enjoyed only in higher education, is undergoing challenges from professional associations of teachers and other groups interested in public education (Kaplan and Schrecker, 1983).* The American Civil Liberties Union (ACLU), for example, objects to any conception of academic freedom that limits it to university settings. The ACLU claims that academic freedom should be extended to the public schools, the authentic academic community for young people. "If each

new generation is to acquire a feeling for civil liberties," the ACLU argues, "it can do so only by having a chance to live in the midst of a community where the principles are continually exemplified" (*Academic Freedom in the Secondary Schools*, 1968, p. 4).

The courts have, on occasion, been highly supportive of academic freedom for public school teachers. Writing in *Wieman v. Updergraff* in 1952, Justices Frankfurter and Douglas argued that all teachers, from the primary grades to the university, share a special task in developing good citizens, and all teachers should have the academic freedom necessary to be exemplars of open-mindedness and free inquiry. Similarly, other courts have ruled that limiting academic freedom to postsecondary education would discriminate against students who do not attend college.

> To restrict the opportunity for involvement in an open forum for the free exchange of ideas to higher education would not only foster an unacceptable elitism, it would fail to complete the development of those not going to college, contrary to our constitutional commitment to equal opportunity. Effective citizenship in a participatory democracy must not be dependent upon advancement toward college degrees. Consequently, it would be inappropriate to conclude that academic freedom is required only in colleges and universities. (*Cary v. Board of Education*, 427 F. Supp. 945, 953 [D. Colo. 1977], quoted in Rubin and Greenhouse, 1983, p. 116)

The issue is not likely to be settled by the courts (O'Neill, 1984). Academic freedom and the extent to which it deserves to be extended to public

---

*Many national organizations are concerned with securing academic freedom for teachers in public schools. Students may wish to consult the positions on academic freedom taken by the American Association of School Libraries, the American Association of University Professors, the American Bar Association, the American Civil Liberties Union, the American Federation of Teachers, the American Historical Association, the American Library Association, the National Council for the Social Studies, the National Council of Teachers of English, and the National Education Association.

school teachers goes to the core of teaching, and it is properly a matter of education policy. The issue of academic freedom raises a series of difficult questions that must be addressed by school boards, local communities, and organizations of teachers and teacher educators: Who should be protected by academic freedom? Is it a right that can be extended automatically to all public school teachers? Does academic freedom clash with the community's right to determine what is taught to its children, and the manner of instruction? Who decides what is appropriate education for minor children? How do we best prepare our students for their role as citizens? Can higher education continue to claim academic freedom as the special province reserved for university experts (Hook, 1953)? Or do universities ignore threats to academic freedom in public schools at their own peril (O'Neill, 1987)?

Chapter 14 presents competing perspectives on the issue of academic freedom for public school teachers and students. Position 1 encourages a view of academic freedom as a right reserved for researchers in universities, which should not be extended to teachers in public schools. Teachers in elementary and secondary schools, it argues, need no freedoms beyond those guaranteed to all citizens by the Constitution. To give them more academic freedom could jeopardize their role as parental surrogates and political representatives of the society. Position 2 is more sympathetic to the empowerment of teachers. It defends academic freedom for public school teachers as a right essential to the search for knowledge and the freedom of mind necessary for the development of democratic ideals.

TEACHER UNIONS

Teacher unions are here to stay. That much is clear. What is not yet clear is whether they will turn out to be beneficial, harmful or merely irrelevant to the quality of education in American schools. (Finn, 1985, p. 331)

Are teacher unions necessary evils that must be accommodated in wage disputes? Are they potentially harmful to education, with the power to hijack the reform agendas of legislators and school administrators? Or are unions committed to working in a coalition—along with parents and administrators—that can turn failing school districts around? Your answers to these questions will help define your position on the continuum of opinions about school reform. Before discussing the arguments in Chapter 15, consider some of the background of teacher unionism.

Teachers have been organized for over 100 years, but the earliest organizations of teachers were not really unions. The National Education Association (NEA), for example, was established in 1857 to represent the views of "practical" classroom teachers and administrators. Annual conventions of the NEA were not union meetings, but settings for exchanges of ideas about teaching that typically avoided discussions of how teachers could influence decisions about their work or wages. The NEA was less concerned with the personal welfare of classroom teachers than it was with advancing the profession of education. In its early years, the NEA was a male-dominated organization *for* teachers that was led by school superintendents, professors of education, and school principals (Wesley, 1957).

As one critic of the NEA notes, the role of classroom teachers, especially women teachers, was "limited to listening" (Eaton, 1975, p. 10). Since the 1960s, the NEA has moved more aggressively to represent the views of all classroom teachers, advocating collective negotiations and encouraging its local affiliates to serve as bargaining agents for teachers.

Teacher unionism dates to the early twentieth century, when Chicago teachers organized to fight for better working conditions. In 1916, the American Federation of Teachers (AFT) was formed as an affiliate of the American Federation of Labor. Initially, the older NEA and the upstart AFT cooperated. The NEA focused on the professional and practical sides of teaching; the AFT concentrated on improving the economic aspects of teachers' lives (Engel, 1976). Over the years, local affiliates of the NEA and the AFT have become rivals in an effort to be recognized as teachers' bargaining agents. More than 80 percent of teachers nationally belong to either the NEA or the AFT, and more than 60 percent work under a formal collective bargaining agreement. (In comparison, fewer than 15 percent of workers in private industry belong to labor unions.)

Today, teacher organizations often bear a greater resemblance to professional associations (for example, the American Bar Association or the American Medical Association) than they do to labor organizations (such as the International Ladies Garment Workers Union or the United Automobile Workers). However, the leaders of the old AFT identified with unionized workers in other industries. They believed that problems common to all workers could be solved through cooperation and collective action. They wanted teacher organizations to provide economic benefits for their members, and they argued that teacher unions should also assist labor more generally by improving the education offered to children of the working class. Despite numerous efforts to organize teachers and to revitalize education, including the development of a workers' college and special public schools for workers' children, membership in the AFT declined in the 1920s and remained flat throughout most of the 1930s. Teachers were reluctant to join unions, and most school administrators were openly hostile toward unions. In the 1920s, fearing worker radicalism and union activity, many school superintendents demanded that teachers sign "yellow dog contracts," agreeing that they would not join a union.

The National Labor Relations Act (NLRA) of 1935 changed the status of unions by recognizing the right of workers in private industry to bargain collectively. Most labor historians consider this legislation to have been favorable to unions.* "Collective bargaining" refers to the process by which employees, as a group, and their employers negotiate in good

*Geoghegan (1991) argues that by bringing the federal government into union organizing and labor–management negotiations, the NLRA was ultimately harmful to unions. He claims that by embracing the state, unions did themselves in. The short-lived government support for unions during the 1930s was completely reversed by the 1980s, when antiunion sentiment contributed to their decline. Geoghegan argues that all labor laws should be repealed and that labor and management should be allowed simply to go at each other.

faith about wages and the conditions of employment (Lieberman and Moscow, 1966, p. 1). Employees are at a disadvantage in bargaining singly with employers, alone against the power and resources of management. Collective bargaining laws recognize the right of workers to join together and elect a bargaining agent (a union) that will negotiate with management. The NLRA required employers and unions to "meet at reasonable times and confer in good faith with respect to wages, hours and other terms and conditions of employment."

Questions about its constitutionality clouded the early history of the NLRA. The issue was eventually decided by the Supreme Court, which judged the act to be constitutional in 1937 (*NLRB v. Jones and Laughlin Steel Company*, 1937). This case was a major victory for organized labor, and it represented a great change in the thinking of the courts. Court rulings concerning the right of workers to engage in collective negotiations can be traced to the Philadelphia cordwainers case in 1806. In that case, the workers were found guilty of entering into a conspiracy (a union) to improve their wages. By the mid-nineteenth century, courts no longer believed that those who advocated collective bargaining were involved in criminal conspiracies (*Commonwealth v. Hunt*, 1842), but unions and collective negotiations were not given full legitimacy until the Supreme Court's 1937 decision.

The NLRA affects only workers in the private sector. Employees of federal, state, or local government are not covered, and the law does not guarantee collective bargaining for public school teachers. Schools are considered to be extensions of the state. School boards are, in a sense, state employers and, as such, they are excluded from federal labor legislation. It has been left up to the states to regulate employment relations in public education. Following the lead of Congress, the majority of state legislatures have taken action to recognize the rights of workers to organize and negotiate with employers. By the early 1990s, thirty-two states had laws legally protecting the rights of teachers to bargain collectively; six states had laws making collective bargaining illegal; and twelve states were officially silent, neither denying nor enabling collective bargaining, but instead leaving the decision to local school districts (Shanker, 1992).

The organization of teachers in New York City in 1960 is considered a watershed for public school teachers (Lieberman and Moscow, 1966, p. 35). The United Federation of Teachers (UFT), a local affiliate of the AFT was made up of several New York City teacher organizations. The UFT asked the board of education to recognize the teachers' right to bargain collectively and to conduct an election to determine which organization should represent them. The board was unsure how collective bargaining should be implemented, and it did not move swiftly. The union accused the board of stalling, and on November 7, 1960, the UFT declared the first strike in the history of New York City education.

It was a brief but effective job action. The next day the teachers were back in the classrooms. The board had agreed to hold elections and not to take reprisals against striking teachers. Union estimates put pickets at about 7,500, and it was claimed that another 15,000 teachers stayed home (Eaton, 1975, p. 165). The strike alerted the nation to the power of unions, and teachers began to recognize the advantages of collective negotiations, as well as the power potential of the strike. Collective bargaining changed the relationship between classroom teachers and administrators. It promised teachers more pay, better job security, and an audible voice in the conduct of education. As one labor historian puts it, "It essentially refined and broadened the concept of professionalism by assuring [teachers] more autonomy and less supervisory control" (Murphy, 1990, p. 209).

Reverberations of the New York City strike were felt nationally. The results encouraged teachers, and it sent the two largest unions, the NEA and the AFT, scrambling for members. The NEA has about two million teachers, about twice the number represented by the AFT. These organizations differ on specific issues. An examination of the views of each union can be found in the journal *The NEA Today* and the AFT's *American Teacher.* Regular columns by the AFT president appear in the *New York Times;* columns by the NEA president appear in the *Washington Post.*

Chapter 15 does not play out the debate between advocates of the NEA and supporters of the AFT, nor does it contain arguments about the morality or appropriateness of strikes by teachers. The issue here is not whether teachers should belong to professional work associations, but whether unions are good for the future of education. Position 1 argues that unions are undemocratic organizations that work against the best

interests of pupils, parents, and teachers. Collective bargaining is not for the public good, nor will it contribute to school reform. Collective bargaining should be restricted if schools are to serve the children and the community. Position 2 argues that unions have had a positive effect on education, and that collective bargaining and union influence should extend beyond wages and hours to include matters of school policy and personnel. This view holds that the success of future school improvement will be linked to the participation of unions in the reform agenda.

PRIVATIZATION

What are the reasons for the growth of the privatization movement? One is the allegedly greater efficiency of the private sector . . . . In the context of privatization, however, "increased efficiency" is not just a fiscal concept. Instead, it should be viewed as a response to widespread dissatisfaction with government service . . . . (Lieberman, 1989, p. 11)

School reformers fall into one of two general categories. Reformers in the first group, well represented in this book, find no fundamental problems with the basic governance structure of schools. They favor a tax-supported, state-run system of public education. Their proposed changes take the form of granting teachers greater authority, reconfiguring the curriculum, or redefining the role schools play in the community. The second group of reformers rejects these approaches as useless tinkering with a fundamentally flawed mechanism. They argue that the way schools are governed needs to be changed, and that the public sector should retreat from the business of education. Schools should be privatized; that is, many, if not all, of their essential services should be contracted out to private companies.

The term "privatization" means the transfer of activities from the public sector to the private sector. Essentially, this focuses attention on the ways in which governments deliver services. Public sector services are "made" by the government. For example, a city delivers protection to its citizens by organizing its own police force, hiring the officers, providing them with training, promoting the good ones, and firing the weak ones. The same city might choose instead to "buy" police services. It might accept bids from competing companies, each explaining how it would perform the appropriate service for the city. The city would enter into a contractual agreement with the company that offered the most promising police protection at the most affordable rate. If the private company proved to be corrupt, inefficient, or too expensive, it could be fired and replaced.

Many people share the belief that government has become synonymous with waste and inefficiency, and that the public would be better served if government utilized more private companies to provide services. State and municipal authorities, for example, have had a good deal of success in giving up their monopolies in certain areas—garbage collection and wastewater management, for example—and have realized greater economy through privatization (Clarke

and Pitelis, 1993). Chapter 16 raises the question of whether schools should be privatized. What would they gain through privatization and what would they lose?

The central question raised in this chapter asks whether or not the public might be better served if the state were to give up some or all of its monopoly over the control of education. Position 1 argues that public education has been a state-controlled monopoly for too long. Privatization would bring a greater range of choices to the public and unmatched innovation to public education. Position 2 maintains that privatization is unlikely to deliver the promised efficiencies and increases in quality, and that it represents a threat to the social and democratic goals of public education.

VIOLENCE IN SCHOOLS

> One in five high school students now carries a firearm, a knife, a club, or some other weapon to school every, single day. . . . Thirty-seven percent of students said they do not feel safe in schools. Sixty-three percent said they would learn more if they felt safer. Nearly 3 million crimes occur on or near school grounds each and every year. One-quarter of major urban school districts are forced to rely on metal detectors. Firearm violence kills an American child every 3 hours. (*Recess from Violence*, 1993, p. 2)

Violence and aggression have a long history in the United States. America was born of revolution. It has made heroes of frontier gunfighters and it celebrates wars and warriors. Americans have seen assassinations of national figures, racial lynchings, terrorist bombings, and riots by organized labor, farmers, and students. Until the 1930s, it was not possible to quantify the rate of violence, but since that time, the Federal Bureau of Investigation's *Uniform Crime Reports* document a dramatic increase in violent crime, including murder, forcible rape, robbery, and aggravated assault. The murder rate for all Americans is the highest in the industrialized world. At 9.4 for every 100,000 people, the incidence of murder in the United States is double that of Spain, the nation with the second highest murder rate, and four times that of Canada (Roth, 1994). In the past decade, statistics for violent crimes committed by persons under the age of 18 show that the murder rate rose by 60 percent, forcible rape increased by 28 percent, and aggravated assaults went up by 57 percent (Goldstein, Harootunian, and Conoley, 1994, p. 5).

Violent crimes are most often committed by men (who constitute 89 percent of those arrested for these crimes) and by members of racial and ethnic minority groups (Reiss and Roth, 1993, p. 4). The victimization rate for members of minority groups has also shown sharp increases. Since 1968, the murder rate for black Americans has risen 65 percent.

> A black person is now seven times as likely as a white person to be murdered, four times as likely to be raped, three times as likely to be robbed, and twice as likely to be assaulted or to have his car stolen. The total number of murders in the U.S.—about 22,000 last year—has remained constant since 1980, but murder now disproportionately affects the black community. (Elam, Rose, and Gallup, 1994, p. 42)

As a result of the reports in the media, the fear of crime also has seen a dramatic increase. Americans demonstrate this fear by their behavior. The middle class has abandoned the cities for the suburbs largely because of concerns about crime and the desire to find safer schools for their children. Now, even those who commute two hours or more a day do not feel that they have insulated their families from violence. One of their solutions is to buy handguns. About one-half of all householders own some type of firearm, a statistic that has not changed very much in the past thirty years. However, handguns, weapons purchased primarily for personal or home protection, are now found in one of every four homes (Reiss and Roth, 1933). The catalogue of one leading handgun manufacturer reads in part: "You work hard to do what's right for your family. Part of that commitment is providing security for yourself and them. How well you do that job might depend on how well you prepare. A Smith & Wesson compact pistol could be a vital part of your security plans." Elsewhere, the catalogue describes personal handguns "with a sleek feel, bobbed hammer and contoured trigger guard . . . designed for the contemporary woman." Other models aimed at women buyers feature "rosewood laminate stocks" and a "soft-side carrying case."

Violence is one of the most troubling problems facing American educators. Schools, once safe havens from the outside world, now must contend with acts of violence at every grade level. No longer confined to the inner city, violence against students and teachers has spread to the suburbs and small towns. With school violence on the increase, experts continue to debate its causes and how schools should handle violent students. Many teachers and criminologists argue that the time has come to crack down on the most violent offenders and expel them from school. They maintain that the job of the school is to teach academic subjects to those who are at least marginally willing to cooperate. Others argue that educators are responsible for helping students with whatever problems they bring with them to school, even if it means expanding the role of the school into nonacademic areas.

In 1994, pollsters gathering information for the 26th annual Phi Delta Kappa/Gallup poll asked people what they believed to be the greatest problems facing the schools. "Fighting/violence/gangs" shared first place with "lack of discipline." Responses to a question about the effectiveness of various measures to reduce violence indicate that people tend to believe that school violence can be controlled by various measures, ranging from stronger penalties for possession of weapons to conflict education for students (Elam, Rose, and Gallup, 1994, p. 42).

Position 1 in Chapter 17 argues that schools have an obligation to reduce school violence and that they already possess a range of effective strategies for doing so. Position 2 argues that the job of schools is not to protect the majority of students from the violent minority. The sole purpose of schools, they say, is academic: to pass on to succeeding generations the skills and abilities necessary for productive life. Time spent on conflict resolution and violence management strategies is time stolen from teaching academic subjects. Students who cannot control their behavior or who are a threat to the other students should not be allowed to be part of the regular school program.

SCHOOL REFORM: EXCELLENCE OR EQUITY

When schools are evaluated, questions naturally arise about the goals of schooling, and the extent to which the pursuit of some of its goals may exclude the realization of others. For example, can the schools be held accountable for delivering academic excellence while maintaining educational equity? Are the goals of excellence and equity so incompatible that, in the reform of public education, society is forced to choose one or the other (Herrnstein and Murray, 1994)?

"Excellence" typically refers to rigorous educational programs and high academic standards. Excellent schools set lofty expectations for students and encourage all students to fulfill them (Adler, 1982; National Commission, 1983). "Equity" refers to the role played by schools in furthering social justice. Equity demands that schools provide appropriate educational opportunity and democratic advancement for all children regardless of their academic ability (Aronowitz and Giroux, 1985; Bastian et al., 1986).

At first glance, it might appear that no conflict exists between excellence and equity; education should be able to help the less fortunate while contributing to the welfare of the most able (Glazer et al., 1987; Strike, 1985). If "excellence" is defined in such a way that anyone can become excellent, then everyone can be treated the same way. All students could be given a similar education; on the basis of merit, the best would achieve excellence and the rest would achieve varying degrees of adequacy.

Some critics argue that such a formula serves only to reinforce social inequities. Education for excellence, they claim, too often leads to schooling that is socially repressive. Students do not enter school with similar advantages. In kindergarten, the children of the poor perform at lower levels than the children of the wealthy, and the achievement gap between the two groups widens every year. Schools, it would seem, serve some children better than others. In the name of excellence, schools perpetuate social differences. These critics say that schools should serve everyone, not just those who begin school with comparative advantages. Education for equity would put schools more squarely in the fight for social justice and an expanded democracy. Equity demands curricula that serve the career and personal needs of all students equally well (Aronowitz and Giroux, 1985; Friere, 1973).

Previous efforts to reform schools have been guided by the assumption that education could not allocate sufficient human or fiscal resources to provide both equity and excellence. Therefore, public education has responded alternately to the social tugs of the competing camps. The decade of the 1950s was a period of elitism for schools. Prompted by Soviet advances in space technology, American social policy demanded that schools meet the challenge with enhanced programs in the sciences. New money was poured into schools, labs were added, and institutes were established to train science teachers at federal expense. The investment in excellence paid off in measurable ways. Scores on science achievement tests went up; increasing numbers of students—mainly male students— took science courses; and more students majored in science in college. The United States launched rockets and orbited satellites, and in 1969 a manned U.S. spacecraft landed on the moon and brought back samples of lunar rock.

The social upheavals of the 1960s led to other changes in schooling. The war in Vietnam, a renewed focus on poverty and civil rights, and cries for social justice were reflected in the school curriculum. Education was asked to become more inclusive. Students and faculty from varied cultural backgrounds demanded that the schools be excellent, not only for those bound for college, but for everyone. Academic requirements were changed to reflect the schools' new constituents. The core curriculum all but disappeared, and requirements in math and science were replaced by courses that were broader, more flexible, and, it was assumed, more relevant to the diverse social concerns of the students (Fantini, 1986).

It is difficult to measure the relevance of the curriculum or its ability to provide greater numbers of students with a more appropriate education. The quality of schools is measured by scores on standardized tests, and it came as little surprise that during the 1970s and 1980s SAT and ACT scores declined precipitously. Some saw this as a harbinger of doom; others were less shaken. Most of the decline in test scores can be attributed to the performance of newly empowered groups, such as women, minorities, and the poor, who previously had been excluded from college. Lower scores may only be a temporary downward phenomenon, a reflection of new students who are not yet accustomed to this format for displaying knowledge. It may ultimately be a reflection of progress, a sign that education is becoming more open and democratic.

In 1983, a new excellence movement was born. The National Commission on Excellence in Education's report *A Nation At Risk* declared the schools to be in crisis. The report said the nation's educational foundation was so badly eroded that the future of the society was threatened. In unequivocal language, the report announced, "If an unfriendly power had attempted to impose on America the mediocre educational performance that exists today, we might have viewed it as an act of war." The report was followed by several others, including those written or issued by Ernest Boyer (1983); the College Board Entrance Examination Board (*Academic Preparation for College,* 1983); John Goodlad (1983); the National Science Foundation (*Educating Americans for the 21st Century,* 1983); Theodore Sizer (1984); and the Twentieth Century Fund (*Making the Grade,* 1983). Several reports, reminiscent of John Gardner (1961), argued that our educational

system can provide students with both equality of opportunity and excellence in achievement (Adler, 1982; *Making the Grade,* 1983). Many in education greeted the reports with cautious optimism, praising the potential complementarity of educational excellence and educational equity (Fantini, 1986; Glazer et al., 1987; Shanker, 1984).

Critics of the reports have been more skeptical, maintaining that they are part of a neoconservative offensive in education. The endorsement of the reports by the political right (for example, the Heritage Foundation, Senators Orrin Hatch and Jesse Helms, former Secretary of Education William Bennett, historian Diane Ravitch) has aroused the suspicions of political liberals, who see the latest round of school reform as an elitist program designed to promote the success of the few at the expense of the many (Altbach, Kelly, and Weiss, 1985; Aronowitz and Giroux, 1985; Bastian et al., 1986).

Chapter 18 contains a debate over the excellence and equity goals of education. Position 1 argues that the primary purpose of education is to improve people's lives through knowledge, and that the quality of education can be measured only by its excellence. However, Position 1 finds no inherent conflict between excellence and equity in planning for future school reform. Position 2 argues that schools cannot be excellent and equitable at the same time. The new call for excellence, it argues, is a "sham," a smokescreen that promotes elitist and undemocratic goals in the name of reform. Position 2 holds that excellence is an inappropriate goal for mass public education in a democracy.

References

Academic Freedom in the Secondary Schools. (1968). New York: American Civil Liberties Union.

Academic Preparation for College. (1983). New York: College Entrance Examination Board.

Adler, M. J. (1982). *The Paideia Proposal: An Educational Manifesto.* New York: Macmillan.

Altbach, P. G., Kelly, G. P., and Weiss, L. (1985). *Excellence in Education: Perspectives on Policy and Practice.* Buffalo, NY: Prometheus Books.

Aronowitz, S., and Giroux, H. A. (1985). *Education under Siege: The Conservative, Liberal, and Radical Debate Over Schooling.* South Hadley, MA.: Bergin & Garvey.

Bastian, A., et al. (1986). *Choosing Equality: The Case for Democratic Schooling.* Philadelphia: Temple University Press.

Boyer, E. L. (1983). *High School: A Report on Secondary Education in America.* New York: Harper & Row.

Carnegie Forum on Education and the Economy. (1986). *A Nation Prepared: Teachers for the 21st Century.* Washington, DC: Carnegie Forum.

Clarke, T., and Pitelis, C., eds. (1993). *The Political Economy of Privatization.* New York: Routledge.

Commonwealth v. Hunt. (1842). Supreme Court of Massachusetts.

Cornford, F. M., ed. and trans. (1968). *The Republic of Plato.* New York: Oxford University Press.

Eaton, W. E. (1975). *The American Federation of Teachers, 1916–1961: A History of the Movement.* Carbondale: Southern Illinois University Press.

Educating Americans for the 21st Century: A Plan of Action for Improving Mathematics, Science and Technology Education for all American Elementary and Secondary Students so that their Achievement Is the Best in the World by 1995: A Report to the American People and the National Science Board. (1983). Washington, DC: National Science Foundation.

Elam, S. M., Rose, L. C., and Gallup, A. M. (1994). "The 26th Annual Phi Delta Kappa/Gallup Poll on the Public's Attitude Toward the Public Schools." *Phi Delta Kappan* **76,** 41–56.

Engel, R. A. (1976). "Teacher Negotiation: History and Comment." In *Education and Collective Bargaining,* edited by E. M. Cresswell and M. J. Murphy. Berkeley, CA: McCutchan.

Etzioni, A., ed. (1969). *The Semi-Professions and Their Organization: Teachers, Nurses, Social Workers.* New York: Free Press.

Fantini, M. D. 1986. *Regaining Excellence in Education.* Columbus, OH: Merrill.

Feiman-Nemser, S., and Floden, R. E. (1986). "The Cultures of Teaching." In *Handbook of Research on Teaching,* 3d ed., edited by M. C. Wittrock. New York: Macmillan.

Finn, C. A. (1985). "Teacher Unions and School Quality: Potential Allies or Inevitable Foes?" *Phi Delta Kappan* **66,** 331–338.

Friere, P. (1973). *Pedagogy of the Oppressed.* New York: Seabury Press.

Gallup, A. (1984). "The Gallup Poll of Teachers' Attitudes Toward the Public Schools." *Phi Delta Kappan* **66,** 97–107.

Geoghegan, T. (1991). *Which Side Are You On? Trying To Be For Labor When It's Flat on Its Back.* New York: Farrar, Strauss, & Giroux.

Glazer, N., et al. (1987). "Equity and Excellence in Education." *Harvard Educational Review* **57,** 196–199.

Goldstein, A. P., Harootunian, B., and Conoley, J. C. (1994). *Student Aggression: Prevention, Management, and Replacement Training.* New York: Guilford.

Goodlad, J. I. (1984). *A Place Called School: Prospects for the Future.* New York: McGraw-Hill.

―――― (1990). *Teachers for Our Nation's Schools.* San Francisco: Jossey-Bass.

Herrnstein, R. J., and Murray, C. (1994). *The Bell Curve: Intelligence and Class*

Structure in American Life. New York: Free Press.

Hofstadter, R. (1962). *Anti-intellectualism in American Life.* New York: Random House.

———, and Metzger, W. P. (1955). *The Development of Academic Freedom in the United States.* New York: Columbia University Press.

Hook, S. (1953). *Heresy, Yes—Conspiracy, No.* New York: Day.

Integrity and the College Curriculum: A Report to the Academic Community. (1985). Washington, DC: Association of American Colleges.

Jackson, P. W. (1969). *Life in Classrooms.* New York: Holt, Rinehart & Winston.

Johnson, S. M. (1988). "Unionism and Collective Bargaining in the Public Schools." In *Handbook of Research on Educational Administration,* edited by N. J. Boyan. New York: Longman.

Joyce, B. (1991). "The Doors to School Improvement." *Educational Leadership* **48,** 59–62.

Kaplan, C., and Schrecker, E., eds. (1983). *Regulating the Intellectuals: Perspectives on Academic Freedom in the 1980s.* New York: Praeger.

Kirk, R. (1955). *Academic Freedom: An Essay in Definition.* Chicago: Regnery.

Lieberman, M. (1989). *Privatization and Educational Choice.* New York: St. Martin's Press.

———, and Moscow, M. H. (1966). *Collective Negotiations for Teachers: An Approach to School Administration.* Chicago: Rand McNally.

Lortie, D. (1975). *Schoolteacher.* Chicago: University of Chicago Press.

MacIver, R. M. (1955). *Academic Freedom in Our Time.* New York: Columbia University Press.

Making the Grade: Report of the Twentieth Century Fund Task Force on Federal Elementary and Secondary Education Policy. (1983). New York: Twentieth Century Fund.

Murphy, M. (1990). *Blackboard Unions: The AFT and the NEA, 1900–1980.* Ithaca, NY: Cornell University Press.

National Commission on Excellence in Education. (1983). *A Nation at Risk: The Imperative for Educational Reform.* Washington, DC: U.S. Government Printing Office.

NLRB v. Jones and Laughlin Steel Company. (1937). 301 U.S. 1, 57 S.Ct. 615.

O'Neill, R. M. (1984). "Freedom of Expression: Schools and Teachers in a Democracy." In *The Foundations of Education: Stasis and Change,* edited by F. P. Besag and J. L. Nelson. New York: Random House.

———. (1987). "Higher Education's Responsibility." *Social Education* **51,** 435–437.

Recess from Violence: Making Our Schools Safe. (1993). Hearing Before the Subcommittee on Education, Arts and Humanities of the Committee on Labor and Human Resources. U.S. Senate, 103rd Congress, (313), First Session on S.1125, September 23, 1993. Washington, DC: U.S. Government Printing Office.

Reiss, A. J., Jr. and Roth, J. A., eds. (1993). *Understanding and Preventing Violence.* Washington, DC: National Academy Press.

Roth, J. A. (1994). *Understanding and Preventing Violence.* Washington, DC: National Institute of Justice.

Rubin, D. and Greenhouse, S. (1983). *The Rights of Teachers: The Basic ACLU Guide to a Teacher's Constitutional Rights,* revised edition. New York: Bantam.

Shanker, A. (1984). "Taking the Measure of American Education Reform: An Assessment of the Education Reports." *American Journal of Education* **92,** 314–324.

———. (1992). "United States of America." In *Labor Relations in Education, An International Perspective,* edited by B. S. Cooper. Westport, CT: Greenwood Press.

Sikes, P. J., Measor, L., and Woods, P. (1985). *Teachers' Careers: Crises and Continuities.* Philadelphia: The Falmer Press.

Sizer, T. R. (1984). *Horace's Compromise: The Dilemma of the American High School.* Boston: Houghton Mifflin.

Status of the American Public School Teacher: 1980–1981. (1982). Washington, DC: National Education Association.

Strike, K. A. (1985). "Is There a Conflict Between Equity and Excellence?" *Educational Evaluation and Policy Analysis* **7**, 409–416.

Study Group on the Conditions of Excellence in American Higher Education. (1984). *Involvement in Learning: Realizing the Potential of American Higher Education.* Washington, DC: National Institute of Education.

Swart, E. (1990). So, You Want To Be A "Professional"? *Phi Delta Kappan* **72,** 315–318.

Warren, D. (1985). Learning from Experience: History and Teacher Education. *Educational Researcher* **14,** 5–12.

Weiss, C. H. (1993). Shared Decision Making about What? A Comparison of Schools With and Without Teacher Participation. *Teachers College Record* **95,** 69–92.

Wesley, E. B. (1957). *NEA: The First Hundred Years.* New York: Harper and Brothers.

Wieman v. Updergraff. (1952). 244 U.S. 183.

CHAPTER THIRTEEN

School Leadership:
Teacher Directed or
Administrator Controlled

POSITION 1: FOR TEACHER DIRECTED LEADERSHIP

Nineteenth-century authors have left us with very unflattering characterizations of schoolteachers. Consider, for example, Washington Irving's description of schoolmaster Ichabod Crane:

> The cognomen of Crane was not inapplicable to his person. He was tall, but exceedingly lank, with narrow shoulders, long arms and legs, hands that dangled a mile out of his sleeve, and his whole frame most loosely hung together. His head was small, and flat at top, with huge ears, large green glassy eyes, and a long snipe nose, so that it looked like a weather-cock, perched upon his spindle neck, to tell which way the wind blew. To see him striding along the profile of a hill on a windy day, with his clothes bagging and fluttering about him, one might have mistaken him for the genius of famine descending upon the earth, or some scarecrow eloped from a cornfield. (Irving, 1880, pp. 478–479)

Despite his appearance, Crane enjoyed a modest popularity with most members of the community. "By hook and by crook," Irving writes, "the worthy pedagogue got on tolerably enough, and was thought by all who understood nothing of the labor of headwork, to have a wonderfully easy life of it" (Irving, 1880, p. 482). To the younger and rougher men of the town, however, he was a social outcast and the object of ridicule. Crane's courtship of Katrina Van Tassel ended abruptly when his rival, Brom Bones, masquerading as a headless horseman, smashed a pumpkin on the schoolmaster's head and drove him out of town.

Charles Dickens' teacher Thomas Gradgrind is an even less sympathetic character than Ichabod Crane. Crane urged his students along the path of knowledge with the aid of a birch, but he was conscientious, not cruel, and he administered justice with discrimination. Gradgrind, however, was a callous and pedantic martinet who prepared his students for a world of the grimmest practicalities. In a chapter titled "Murdering the Innocents," Dickens offers the following description of Gradgrind's teaching:

"Girl number twenty," said Mr. Gradgrind, squarely pointing with his square forefinger, "I don't know that girl. Who is that girl?"

"Sissy Jupe, sir," explained number twenty, blushing, standing up, and curtsying.

"Sissy is not a name," said Mr. Gradgrind. "Don't call yourself Sissy. Call yourself Cecilia."

"It's father as calls me Sissy, sir," returned the young girl in a trembling voice, and with another curtsy.

"Then he has no business to do it," said Mr. Gradgrind. "Tell him he mustn't. Cecilia Jupe. Let me see. What is your father?"

"He belongs to the horse-riding, if you please, sir . . ."

"Very well, then. He is a veterinary surgeon, a farrier, and horse breaker. Give me your definition of a horse."

(Sissy Jupe thrown into the greatest alarm by this demand.)

"Girl number twenty unable to define a horse!" said Mr. Gradgrind, for the general behoof of all the little pitchers. "Girl number twenty possessed of no facts, in reference to one of the commonest of animals! Some boy's definition of a horse. Bitzer, yours . . . .

"Quadruped. Graminivorous. Forty teeth, namely twenty-four grinders, four eye-teeth, and twelve incisive. Sheds coat in the spring; in marshy countries, sheds hoofs too. Hoofs hard, but requiring to be shod with iron. Age known by marks in mouth . . ."

"Now, girl twenty," said Mr. Gradgrind, "you know what a horse is."

She curtsied again, and would have blushed deeper, if she could have blushed deeper than she had blushed all this time. (Dickens, 1854, pp. 1–4)

Dickens' portrayal of Gradgrind was not meant as an assault on teachers; the novel is an indictment of the harsh factory system of nineteenth-century England and the schools that were all too willing to prepare students for work in them. However, Mr. Gradgrind is easy to dislike. Indifferent to his students' needs for esteem, insensitive to the imaginative side of childhood, and unaware of even the most rudimentary lessons of psychology, Gradgrind is hardly a flattering image of teachers.

"Unmarriageable Women and Unsaleable Men"

To a certain extent, Crane and Gradgrind represent the popular nineteenth-century image of schoolteachers, particularly male teachers. One historian notes that when Brom Bones smashed the pumpkin on Crane's head, "he was passing the symbolic judgment of the American male community on the old-time schoolmaster" (Hofstadter, 1962, pp. 315–316). During the last century, it was assumed that most of those who taught school would do so for only a short time. Women typically chose marriage and homemaking after a few years in the classroom. Ambitious men were expected to move from teaching to loftier, better-paying occupations. Classroom teaching was seldom chosen as lifetime work by the more able, and the treatment of teachers reflected the anticipated short-term job commitment. Teaching was considered as employment for workers who were "passing through," en route to more serious pursuits (Holmes Group, 1986, p. 32). (Even Ichabod Crane eventually abandoned teaching for a career in law.)

Teaching was seen as a good short-term job, but it was disparaged as a career choice, and those who chose to stay in the classroom for more than a few years often encountered social derision. In 1932, sociologist Willard Waller observed that teachers were not treated like other groups of workers. He noted that in small towns unmarried teachers were expected to live in a teacherage— a special boardinghouse for schoolteachers—apart from single adults who held nonteaching jobs. In barbershops and other male-dominated establishments, any exchange of ribald banter and off-color jokes would be suspended when a teacher entered. A male teacher was not accepted as "one of the boys." Waller also noted the popular prejudice against teachers commonly held by the wealthier and better educated members of the community. "Teaching," he wrote, "is quite generally regarded as a failure belt . . . the refuge of unmarriageable women and unsaleable men" (Waller, 1932, p. 61).

By the latter half of the twentieth century, the nature of the teaching workforce had changed dramatically. Today, more women and men look at teaching not just as a job they pursue in their youth, but as a lifelong career. Those who work in public schools must complete (in most states) five years of college education. Certification as a beginning teacher requires at least a bachelor's degree with a strong general education component, specialized academic course work, professional study, and practical experiences in schools. Many teachers have masters' degrees, and more than a few have doctorates. Today's teachers are unlike their nineteenth-century predecessors. They are well educated and able, and they pursue teaching as a career, not as a short-term job. They are experts in the practical matters of teaching and learning, and they rightfully expect to have a greater voice in all matters of education, including the management of schools and the planning of school reform.

1980s: Failure of Top-Down School Reform

In the 1980s, many states attempted to improve public education by adopting centralized accountability plans. These reform plans, typically stemming from legislative mandates, robbed local school districts of much of their control over the classroom and the curriculum (Carnegie Foundation, 1988). After only token consultation with local teachers or school administrators, officials of state departments of education determined what should be taught to all children and how student learning was to be assessed. School personnel were told what content was appropriate for their students. The state then administered exams—typically multiple-choice tests—to measure the extent to which student learning had taken place. To the surprise of very few teachers, the reforms of the 1980s failed to improve student learning. The reform plans had disregarded teachers' skills in curriculum planning, and discounted the teachers' knowledge about the students in their classes. Designed as accountability movements to ensure taxpayers that money for education was being spent responsibly and efficiently, statewide reforms hurt teachers by taking the school's curriculum away from them (Giroux and McLaren, 1986).

The teachers' loss of curriculum control was accompanied by an erosion of their freedom to choose the methods of instruction. Textbooks, basal readers, and curriculum packages, typically prepared for a national market, dictated classroom practice. Classroom teaching became dominated by "teacher-proof" materials with step-by-step instructions. Teachers were given objectives for their students; they were told how to present material; and they were instructed how to measure the impact of their teaching. As a result, teachers were taken out of their own teaching, and they were reduced to being semi-skilled, voiceless workers engaged in the mass production of education (Apple, 1982; Darling-Hammond, 1985).

Effective schools do not follow mechanical curricula. Effective teachers present lessons thoughtfully and reflectively, changing what they do in response to the ways in which students are learning. Successful schools are led by teachers who have control over resources, classroom time, instructional materials, and teaching strategies, and who make curriculum decisions (Glickman, 1991). Top-down administrative structures, state accountability programs, and teacher-proof curricula reflect a view of the school as a factory, where learning is mass-produced in standardized parts and teachers are workers on an assembly line. It should be obvious, however, that teaching is not like manufacturing and that it does not conform to models of mass production, but is a human enterprise that is unlikely to be effective without sensitive, intelligent teachers managing the operation. In teaching, planning cannot be divorced from execution; instructional methods and materials cannot be considered apart from the personalities and interests of students and teachers; and the most significant learning outcomes cannot be measured by standardized multiple-choice exams.

Past efforts to reform education seemed to ignore everything that had been learned about effective education. Top-down changes ignored the school-level variations that occur from district to district and from school to school. A single education design for all schools within a state disregarded the importance of including teachers in the process of change. Centralized school reforms ignored the obvious: for schools to be effective, every teacher must share in the authority to make essential curricular decisions about how to teach, how to pace instruction, and how to interact with students. As Darling-Hammond writes, good teaching "requires knowledge of and insight into the minds of students, and relentless imagination in forging connections that will make understanding the possession of the learner, not just the teacher" (Darling-Hammond, 1987, p. 354). Good teaching is more than the ability to follow instructions. Good teaching requires deep understanding of the ways in which children learn, a sophisticated knowledge of the subjects being taught, and command of a broad repertoire of instructional strategies (Holmes Group, 1986).

1990s: Shared Decision Making to Reform Schools

By the 1990s, a growing number of education theorists and researchers had come to realize that schools can deliver a better education by tapping the intellectual understandings and the creative energies of classroom teachers (Barth, 1990; Schlechty, 1990; Smylie, 1994). The current agenda for school reform is aimed at changing the governance structure of schools so that local teachers and administrators share the authority to make decisions about the students in their schools and the ways in which they are taught. Referred to as shared decision making (SDM) or school-based management (SBM), the reforms of the 1990s reflect the accumulated evidence as to what makes schools effective in teaching children (Marsh et al., 1990; Hatry et al., 1994). SDM/SBM is designed to involve teachers in the decision-making process of the school district. Although the level of teacher involvement varies from district to district, teachers in general are beginning to participate more and more in decisions about curriculum, instruction, personnel, and policy. They are slowly regaining their role as curriculum planners and decision makers. Schools are increasingly using teachers' talents, and teachers are more involved in selecting classroom materials, planning in-service workshops, designing evaluations, and helping new teachers to master the art and science of teaching.

SDM/SBM is a promising grass-roots phenomenon that is designed to harness the energy of teachers and administrators in reforming schools on the local level. No longer are schools being run from offices far removed from the places where students learn. For the first time in many years, teacher authority is on the rise. Teachers' knowledge about students and teaching is being transformed into educational policy. SDM/SBM involves more work for teachers; in addition to the demands of the classroom, they now contribute to the management and design of education. An expanded role in school management may not be right for all teachers, but those who choose to take on nonteaching tasks and participate in SDM/SBM do so because they believe that it will result in better education.

The logic of SDM/SBM rests on several interrelated assumptions:

1. Teachers have a great store of practical knowledge about students, curriculum, and instruction. SDM/SBM is good for students. It puts the control of education in the hands of the people who know them best: the classroom teachers.

2. Teachers must be treated as professionals in order to tap their talents, acknowledge their abilities, and improve their morale.

3. School reform is more likely to succeed when teachers are part of the decision-making process and assume a personal identification with school outcomes.

4. SDM/SBM is essentially democratic and fair. It provides students with role models who have a sense of ownership in their work and the power to make the workplace better (Lieberman and Miller, 1990; Weiss, 1993).
5. Teaching will become even more attractive when teachers assume greater authority in directing the course of schooling. Increasing numbers of talented undergraduates will choose teaching as a career in direct proportion to the authority given teachers to manage schools.
6. SDM/SBM is the final repudiation of the nineteenth-century view of teaching. It casts aside forever the view of teachers as social outcasts (Ichabod Crane) or martinets (Thomas Gradgrind). SDM/SBM recognizes the ability of teachers to participate in the management of the school.

Over time, the education community has come to realize that school reform depends on teachers who have expanded roles and responsibilities in the school and the opportunity to direct change. Research evidence suggests that when teachers are given responsibility for school change, there is a greater likelihood that the change will be positive and enduring (Roberts and Cawelti, 1984; Sarason, 1982). It is reasonable to predict that if schools are restructured so that teachers assume more responsibility for essential school processes—from curriculum to staffing and assessment—the education afforded students will be improved. Common sense tells us that people work harder and feel better about their work when they have a personal investment in what they do and a sense of identification with the product of their efforts (Foster, 1991). Teachers are likely to work toward the improvement of education in direct proportion to their involvement in school processes and decisions. The empowerment of teachers through SDM/SBM cannot help but pay dividends in improved education.

POSITION 2: FOR ADMINISTRATOR CONTROL

The formal participation of teachers in decision making was not the main mechanism that led to change. Rather in our sample it was usually the arrival of a reform-minded principal or superintendent . . . . New ideas appear to come mostly from administrators. Administrators are the innovators because they have the resources and the time to learn about new ideas, the opportunities to communicate widely, and the authority to bring the proposals to the attention of the school . . . . In most of the schools we studied, "empowered" teachers tend to use their power to slow the pace of change. (Weiss, 1993, pp. 80, 83, 89)

Exercising Authority for the Good of Students

To consider the restructuring of schools and the empowerment of teachers may be intellectually pleasing, but it ignores the demands placed on schools, the authority vested in administrative offices, and the research on school reform. The management of schools is not a power struggle between administrators and teachers; it is the exercise of authority necessary to establish the most appropriate conditions for learning.

"Authority" in this context means the legally designated exercise of responsibility. In public education, the state has given school administrators the authority to run schools and bring about effective instruction (Abbott and Caracheo, 1988). We generally assume that those given authority will use it properly to produce desired ends. If individual school administrators fail to provide quality education, they should be replaced. If, over time, administrative authority proves to be structurally unsound or unable to promote the conditions necessary for student learning, then the state can make changes in the authority structure of schools. However, research findings indicate no need for such changes. The solution for school problems, now and in the future, is most likely to be realized through the leadership exercised by school principals and superintendents.

Schools are complex institutions that seek to maximize student achievement and well-being. Good management principles demand that, in large organizations, one person or one small group of people must have the authority to direct corporate outcomes. It is part of American culture to view management as accountable for the success or failure of an organization. Parents know that this is the pattern found in government and industry, and they expect the same rules to apply to education. In schools, authority and responsibility rest with the administration. When parents have questions about academic achievement, school policy, or curriculum, they call the administrators. Parents demand accountability, and they expect school administrators to make sure that the teachers are managed appropriately and that education is conducted for the good of the children.

Good schools could not exist without good teachers, but excellent teachers alone are not sufficient to provide good education. In the same way that a winning baseball team is more than the sum of the athletic skills of the players, a good school is more than the total of the individual abilities of the teachers. The efforts of the baseball team and of the school must be organized and directed so that the whole will be at least as good as the sum of its parts. Some person or group of people will always have to manage the operation of schooling, measure its effectiveness, and chart its course. It is hard to manage and play simultaneously; these activities require complete concentration and separate sets of skills. Although managing a baseball team is not a perfect metaphor for administering a school, both managers share a downside risk: when the team or the school is not doing well, critics often vent their frustrations on the most visible leader, demanding the replacement of the manager or the principal.

Unfortunately, all is not well with the schools, but we cannot change the authority structure without considering the demands now placed on school administrators. School administration has become a complex task. It was considerably less difficult to manage schools in the past—in 1910 for example, when only 9 percent of the population completed high school, or even in 1950 when only 59 percent did so. In those days, motivated, bright students with supportive parents and college aspirations made high schools far easier to administer (Murphy, 1991). Today, with three out of every four students remaining in school for twelve years, school administrators must oversee programs for students who in previous generations would have dropped out or been forced out of schools. Administrators in the past did not have to contend with drugs, AIDS, guns, or students with children of their own. Society has visited all of its failings on schools, yet now demands that all high school graduates meet higher academic standards and acquire marketable skills.

Much to the credit of the field of educational administration, the preparation of school principals has been critically examined against these new social and academic demands. Administrators have taken a hard look at themselves, their work, and their training. It should not come as a surprise that after many years of neglect, a host of problems were uncovered. For example, researchers found that recruitment standards for prospective administrators had become inadequate. It was too easy to be accepted into programs of educational administration. Applicants for graduate programs in school administration scored a disappointing ninety-first out of the ninety-four groups of prospective majors taking the Graduate Record Examination. To make matters worse, program standards in educational administration were notoriously weak. Researchers concluded that, in the past, anyone who wanted to become a principal could do so (Hallinger and Murphy, 1991; Sarason, 1982).

School administrators not only assumed the lead in uncovering problems in the preparation of prospective principals, but they also proposed reforms that would guarantee that school leaders would be better educated and better prepared. The National Commission for Excellence in Educational Administration recommended, among other things, that some 300 universities and colleges cease preparing educational administrators and that licensure programs be reformed, made more rigorous, and linked more closely with the public schools (Hallinger and Murphy, 1991; Sergiovanni, 1991). These actions reflect well on educational administrators, who are eager to remain leaders in education reform.

Unbridled Teacher Power Is a Threat to Community Control

In addition to managing the enterprise, public school administrators must guarantee to the public that the schools are run in the best interests of the community. As Milton and Rose Friedman have pointed out, taxpayer support for public schooling in the United States was won on the promise that education would be controlled by the local community. Distrustful of the socialist philosophies that promoted state-controlled education in Europe, Americans would support public schooling only if it were to be part of a decentralized education system. The U.S. Constitution was designed to limit the role of the central government in education, and the states allowed the local communities to control schools. The schools were designed to be essentially democratic institutions, responsible to parents whose constant vigilance guaranteed the schools' service to community interests (Friedman and Friedman, 1979, pp. 154–155).

Over time, the power to run schools has shifted from the local communities to increasingly centralized authorities. The city, county, state, and federal governments, combined with the militancy of teachers have robbed local communities of most of their former control of the schools. Effective administrators must preserve community control over important aspects of children's education, and they must assure parents that the schools are still the servants of the community. Parents and other citizens rightfully fear the encroachments of big government and organized labor. They have seen the diminution of their authority and the rise of unseen professionals and bureaucrats who control more and more aspects of their lives. Government has become at once more remote and more controlling. One of the last areas over which citizens typically exercise a measure of real control is the public school system, and this is their right. The schools are in their neighborhoods and belong to them. Superintendents and principals must assure the community that education will not become the exclusive province of professional educators. Teachers already have a great deal of power. Giving teachers more power could only come at the expense of diminished parental control over education.

Teachers and administrators agree that parents should become more involved in the schools. Since the mid-1960s, educators and legislators have tried to shape policies that encourage the participation of parents, particularly those from low-income households. This has been no simple matter. Middle-class parents have responded quickly to teacher initiatives, but many poor and minority parents have not, and they have been labeled "hard to reach." These parents, often plagued by problems of their own, have less time, less energy, and less sympathy to give to schools. Many of them had not done well at school themselves, and they have been unresponsive and occasionally antagonistic to schools and teachers. Administrators can build bridges to the community that help the classroom teacher. Research demonstrates the key role played by school administrators in reaching out to parents and bringing them into schools to help teachers help children (Davies, 1991; Williams and Chavkin, 1989; Weiss, 1993). School administrators can act as brokers between powerful teachers and the often powerless members of the community.

Sacrificing Individual Freedom to Collective Power

In public education, "power" means the ability to produce or resist instructional outcomes. School boards and state departments of education have the power to deliver new programs of instruction, but teachers may disregard these initiatives by noncompliance. Schools are not run by the brute force of administrators, and it must be recognized that each teacher has a great deal of autonomy. When teachers close the doors to their classrooms, they have control over learning outcomes that is unmatched by anyone else in the school system, including the superintendent and the board of education. Teachers can control what students learn through the ways in which they pace instruction, group students, determine levels of difficulty, and establish the criteria for assessment. Teaching is now a very loosely supervised profession; any change in school structure is likely to cost teachers their freedom as individuals.

Classroom autonomy is one of the defining characteristics of the job, and one of the most closely protected. Teachers like the power to teach and to control instruction. Much to the frustration of administrators, attempts to diminish this autonomy—by introducing accountability measures or new curricula, for example—have met with resistance from teachers. For many teachers, the freedom to teach is among the most attractive aspects of the job. In the past, teachers purchased this power over their classrooms by relinquishing influence at the school or district level (Corwin and Borman, 1988). The current demands for restructuring schools require collective power for teachers to influence schools. Not only do such ideas run counter to the history of schools, but they also threaten teacher power in the classroom. If teachers were to become managers, they would have to relinquish the individual control over their own classrooms that they now enjoy.

Cries for restructuring schools are insensitive to teachers' freedom, and they ignore the contributions made to schooling by administrators. Educational administration is the art and science of applying specialized academic knowledge to the solution of school problems. It requires the sensitive manipulation of complex variables, including class size, instructional time, physical facilities, the curriculum, and the professional staff (Hoy and Miskel, 1978). At its base, school administration requires the experience of a teacher, or at least a deep appreciation of the teacher's art; in addition, it demands a strong knowledge of human behavior, management theory, school law, and organizational leadership. Administrators should understand teaching from a teacher's point of view, but they must also be able to lead teachers and to bring knowledge from administrative theory and research to bear on schools and the problems of teaching and learning.

The False Promise of Shared Decision Making

The public believes that effective administrators can change schools, and research evidence continues to document the successes of effective school leaders in improving education (Immegart, 1988; Leithwood and Montgomery, 1982; Manassee, 1985; Weiss, 1993). The problem with schools is not that they are headed by principals, and it is not likely that we could improve schools by handing them over to the teachers. In the final analysis, it is the administrators who are responsible for the schools, and they must exert the leadership and accept the consequences for the outcomes of schooling. Schools need effective leaders who can encourage learning, support and reward good teaching, make the schools satisfying places for students and teachers, and ensure that the community is served and the state's mandates are followed.

Although there is strong evidence that effective principals are the key to student learning, their potential in assisting in school reform has been ignored. For too long, the image of the public school administrator was that of the rigid disciplinarian who kept students in line with bluff and bluster, the retired coach who jollied up the board of education with sports talk and assurances that everything was operating smoothly. Based on models of management borrowed from industry, public school administration often has emphasized the control of teachers rather than educational leadership.

Faced with a set of difficult tasks and marginally prepared teachers, schools in the nineteenth century became enamored of industrial models of control and efficiency (Callahan, 1962; Tyack and Hansot, 1982). Although these methods now seem simpleminded or harsh and inappropriate for the establishment of intellectual and humane goals, there were few other models of organization from which to choose. Schools were organized from the top down. Teachers were to be managed "scientifically." Their jobs were laid out for them, defined for them, and simplified and routinized. In the name of efficiency, teaching was reduced to a series of steps that were managed and monitored by school administrators.

These conceptions of educational administration were abandoned long ago. The image of the bullying, despotic principal exists largely in memory, a fiction recreated by special interest groups that would like to seize control of the schools. The stereotype fails to acknowledge the changed nature of educational administration. Effective administrative leadership continues to be the most essential ingredient in school reform (Murphy, 1991; Weiss, 1993). The conflicting expectations for the schools as delineated by the state, the community, the teachers, and the students demand a specially trained group of managers. Without intelligent leadership from educational administrators, schools would be unlikely to meet any of their academic and social goals. Without specially trained, carefully selected administrators to lead education reform, change becomes less likely and educational anarchy looms as a reality. The future success of public education depends, in large measure, on the ability of administrators to bring together the needs of the community and the special talents of the classroom teachers.

No doubt, you have heard that bringing teachers into the decision-making machinery of the schools will lead to the solution of school problems. At first glance, a changed role for teachers may sound appealing. Shared decision making promises to expand the supply of good ideas and to bring front-line professionals into the discussions of school reform. However, the research evidence does not support the enthusiasm for decision making shared by teachers and administrators. Even in schools that have tried to empower teachers, most new ideas still come from administrators. Shared decision making does not improve teacher morale, nor does it necessarily lead to school reform or improved learning (Weiss, 1993; Smylie, 1994).

Administrators must lead school reform, but they are encouraged to include teachers in planning such reform. As one researcher notes:

> Despite the failure of [shared decision making] to live up to its hype, there is something intrinsically appealing about the notion that school administration derives its just powers from the consent of the governed, at least the adult governed. At a time when industry has moved toward greater worker partic-

ipation in management, it seems fair that teachers, too, have a say in conditions that affect their work lives. (Weiss, 1993, p. 87)

Good administrators will always recruit talented teachers to join them in their endeavor to improve the schools, but there is insufficient evidence to warrant turning over the actual control of schools to teacher leadership. Advocates of shared decision making seem to forget that teaching is a full-time, energy-draining job. To reserve part of a teacher's day for administrative work means that the teacher will have less time and less energy to teach. Schools are run for the benefit of the students, not that of the teachers. Research thus far does not support the claim that teacher management increases instructional effectiveness (Smylie, 1994). Unless shared decision making can be demonstrated to be good for students, school leadership should remain in the hands of school administrators.

For Discussion

1. Consider the "1930s Rules for Teachers" listed below. Are any of these rules appropriate for today's teachers? If you were given the authority to construct a new set of six rules to define the work of teachers, what would they be?

1930s Rules for Teachers

1 I promise to take a vital interest in all phases of Sunday-school work, donating my time, service, and money without stint for the uplift of the community.

2 I promise to abstain from all dancing, immodest dressing, and other conduct unbecoming a teacher and a lady.

3 I promise not to go out with any young men except insofar as it may be necessary to stimulate Sunday-school work.

4 I promise not to fall in love, to become engaged, or [to be] secretly married. I promise not to encourage or tolerate the least familiarity on the part of my boy pupils.

5 I promise to sleep at least eight hours a night, to eat carefully, and to take every precaution to keep in the best of health and spirits in order that I may better be able to render efficient service to my pupils.

6 I promise to remember that I owe a duty to the townspeople who are paying my wages, that I owe respect to the school board and the superintendent that hired me, and that I shall consider myself at all times the willing servant to the school board and the townspeople and that I shall cooperate with the town, the pupils, and the school.

2. Two competing views of school organization are presented in this chapter. The first view holds that schools are rigid top-down bureaucracies that define teachers as powerless workers with little influence. In the second view, schools are loosely organized and teachers have a great deal of autonomy and freedom in the classroom (Ingersoll, 1994). Which view of school organization is held by the teachers in schools familiar to you? Do the administrators in those schools share that perspective? If you can, interview several student teachers to learn their views of school organization.

3. Spend a day with a school principal. Observe what he or she does. Interview the principal about the nature of the job, the range of problems principals confront, and the demands on their time. What have you learned about the principal's role in the management of schools that you did not know before?

References

Abbott, M. G., and Caracheo, F. (1988). "Power, Authority, and Bureaucracy." In *Handbook of Research on Educational Administration*, edited by N. J. Boyan. New York: Longman.

Apple, M. W. (1982). *Education and Power*. Boston: Routledge & Kegan Paul.

Barth, R. (1990). *Improving Schools From Within: Teachers, Parents, and Principals Can Make the Difference*. San Francisco: Jossey-Bass.

Callahan, R. (1962). *Education and the Cult of Efficiency*. Chicago: University of Chicago Press.

Carnegie Foundation for the Advancement of Teaching. (1988). *Report Card*. Princeton, NJ: Carnegie Foundation.

Corwin, R. G., and Borman, K. M. (1988). "School as Workplace: Structural Constraints on Administration." In *Handbook of Research on Educational Administration*, edited by N. J. Boyan. New York: Longman.

Darling-Hammond, L. (1985). "Valuing Teachers: The Making of a Profession." *Teachers College Record* **66,** 209–218.

———— (1987). "Schools for Tomorrow's Teachers." *Teachers College Record* **88,** 354–358.

Davies, D. (1991). "Schools Reaching Out: Family, School, and Community Partnerships for Student Success." *Phi Delta Kappan* **72,** 376–382.

Dickens, C. (1854). *Hard Times, A Novel*. New York: Harper.

Foster, A. G. (1991). "When Teachers Initiate Restructuring." *Educational Leadership* **48,** 27–31.

Friedman, M., and Friedman, R. (1979). *Free to Choose*. New York: Harcourt Brace Jovanovich.

Giroux, H. A., and McLaren, P. (1986). "Teacher Education and the Politics of Engagement: The Case for Democratic Schooling." *Harvard Educational Review* **56,** 213–238.

Glickman, C. (1991). "Pretending Not to Know What We Know." *Educational Leadership* **48,** 4–10.

Hallinger, P., and Murphy, J. (1991). "Developing Leaders for Tomorrow's Schools." *Phi Delta Kappan* **72,** 514–520.

Hatry, H. P., Morley, E., Ashford, B., and Wyatt, T. M. (1994). *Implementing School-Based Management: Insights into Decentralization from Science and Mathematics Departments* (Urban Institute Report 93–4). Washington, DC: Urban Institute.

Hofstadter, R. (1962). *Anti-intellectualism in American Life*. New York: Random House.

Holmes Group. (1986). *Tomorrow's Teachers: A Report of the Holmes Group*. East Lansing, MI: Holmes Group.

Hoy, W. K., and Miskel, C. G. (1978). *Educational Administration: Theory, Research and Practice*. New York: Random House.

Immegart, G. L. (1988). "Leadership and Leadership Behavior." In *Handbook of Research on Educational Administration*, edited by N. J. Boyan. New York: Longman.

Ingersoll, R. M. (1994). "Organizational Control in Secondary Schools." *Harvard Educational Review* **64,** 150–172.

Irving, W. (1880). *The Sketch Book*. New York: G. P. Putnam's Sons.

Leithwood, K. A., and Montgomery, D. J. (1982). "The Role of the Elementary School Principal in Program Improvement." *Review of Educational Research* **52,** 309–339.

Lieberman, A., and Miller, L. (1990). "Restructuring Schools: What Matters and What Works." *Phi Delta Kappan* **71,** 759–764.

Manassee, A. L. (1985). "Improving Conditions for Principal Effectiveness: Policy Implications of Research." *Elementary School Journal* **85,** 439–463.

Marsh, C., Day, C., Hannay, L., and McCutheon, G. (1990). *Reconceptualizing School-Based Curriculum Development*. New York: Falmer Press.

Murphy, J. T. (1991). "Superintendents as Saviors: From the Terminator to Pogo." *Phi Beta Kappan* **72**, 507–513.

National Commission on Excellence in Education. (1983). *A Nation at Risk: The Imperative for Educational Reform*. Washington, DC: U.S. Department of Education.

Roberts, A. D., and Cawelti, G. (1984). *Redefining General Education in the American High School*. Alexandria, VA: Association for Supervision and Curriculum Development.

Sarason, S. B. (1982). *The Culture of the School and the Problem of Change,* 2d ed. Boston: Allyn & Bacon.

Schlechty, P. S. (1990). *Schools for the 21st Century: Leadership Imperatives for Educational Reform*. San Francisco: Jossey-Bass.

Sergiovanni, T. J. (1991). "The Dark Side of Professionalism in Educational Administration." *Phi Delta Kappan* **72**, 521–526.

Smylie, M. A. (1994). "Redesigning Teachers' Work: Connections to the Classroom." In *Review of Research in Education,* edited by L. Darling-Hammond. Washington, DC: American Educational Research Association.

Tyack, D. B., and Hansot, E. (1982). *Managers of Virtue: Public School Leadership in America*. Urbana: University of Illinois Press.

Waller, W. (1932). *The Sociology of Teaching*. New York: Wiley.

Weiss, C. H. (1993). "Shared Decisions About What? A Comparison of Schools With and Without Teacher Participation." *Teachers College Record* **95**, 69–92.

Williams, D. L., and Chavkin, N. F. (1989). "Essential Elements of Strong Parent Involvement Programs." *Educational Leadership* **47**, 18–20.

CHAPTER FOURTEEN

Academic Freedom: Teacher Rights or Responsibility

POSITION 1: FOR TEACHER RESPONSIBILITY

Teachers are the key to good education. They are also the key to poor education. When teachers in a school are excellent, the school is excellent. But not all schools are excellent, and many teachers are weak and ineffective. Some teachers are also zealots, eager to sell young people on their beliefs. Teachers are not immune to radical ideas, such as anarchism, atheism, and satanism, and they have a captive audience of immature minds; the concept of education is denied and there is a threat to society. Nevertheless, the state laws and their unions protect teachers, no matter how radical and socially detrimental their concepts are. This protection, under tenure laws and the false cloak of academic freedom, allows miseducation in the schools.

Tenure laws make it almost impossible to rid schools of poor or zealous teachers. And the claim that academic freedom gives teachers the right to do whatever they wish does not take into account the real history of academic freedom for scientists and scholars and the social responsibilities attendant on teaching in public elementary and high schools. Mandatory schooling for these young most impressionable children requires greater accountability from teachers than does voluntary education in colleges whose students are old enough to resist being brainwashed by their instructors.

No one would argue that good teachers should be treated like prisoners, without freedom to express creativity. They deserve respect and appreciation for their contributions to society. They deserve decent salaries and comfortable working conditions. And they deserve the protection that all American citizens have, under the Bill of Rights, of freedom of speech and association. Teachers do not, however, merit special treatment that protects them from being fired for insubordination or for subverting students, advocating radical ideas, or proselytizing.

Parading under the guise of academic freedom, this special treatment would give teachers license to engage in a variety of forms of educationally disruptive behavior. Forcing students to accept a teacher's view, when that view does not coincide with community or family values, is disruptive and unprofessional. Certainly, the teacher may have views that differ from community norms, but the classroom is not the place in which to express them. The pressures that a teacher can exert on students are many; teachers should not use their position to subvert parental ideas or to make students doubt basic values. Teachers should not be permitted to preach radical ideas in schools.

A child brought up to revere the family, to believe in marriage, to support the United States, and to respect people in authority will find it traumatic when a teacher seems to approve of such activities as participating in homosexual acts, child sexual abuse, anti-Americanism, or civil disobedience (Leo, 1993). Teachers should not have the unlimited right to damage children in this manner. This is a form of child abuse and cannot be condoned, and when it happens, the teacher should be dismissed. Stretching the idea of academic freedom to protect such a teacher is an affront to the traditional concept of academic freedom—protection for university scholars in the conduct of research in their specialties.

A license to teach is not a license to impose views on others. Corruption of the young is at the least a moral crime; it is ethically reprehensible. The majority of teachers accept this point and discharge their duties with integrity and care. For them, teaching is a calling to instruct the young in the knowledge and values of the society. This represents the best in the profession, and is a great support to the well-being of the community and nation. Unfortunately, some teachers do not subscribe to the values of their profession.

There are teachers who are caught in drug raids, who have cheated on their income tax returns, and who have committed robbery—but these are exceptions. Most teachers are not criminals. But when teachers do engage in criminal conduct, they are subject to criminal penalties and possible loss of employment. They are not given special treatment. However, there is another form of crime, intellectual crime, in which teachers may engage but for which they often seek special treatment in the name of academic freedom. Intellectual crimes include ridiculing student or family values, advocating antisocial attitudes, indoctrinating children in secular humanism, and influencing students to think or act in opposition to parent and community norms. These crimes may have an even greater devastating effect on children and the society than legal transgressions because they tear at the moral fiber of the nation. Their perpetrators should not have special protection. It is not an academic act to confuse and confound children about their families and their society; teachers who commit such crimes deserve no consideration under the rubric of academic freedom. Distorting the minds of the young is misteaching and should be penalized.

Some schoolteachers and their unions want to open a large umbrella of academic freedom to cover anything a teacher does or says. Their claims to protection are not justified, but they make school administrators wary. Administrators do not want the American Civil Liberties Union or other local vigilante groups interfering in school affairs. Thus, radical teachers often get away with their preaching and mind-bending for years because the administration is afraid to reprimand them. Instead, the problem is hidden. Parents who protest will be allowed to have their children transferred to other classes, but unsuspecting parents will fall prey to these unprofessional classroom Fagins. It takes a courageous and persistent parent to thwart such a teacher. Often, public disclosure of the teacher's actions will arouse the community and force the school officials to take action.

Radical teachers have also misused state tenure laws, which typically place excessive impediments in the way of efforts to dismiss a teacher. As a result, very few school districts find it worthwhile to try to fire even the most incompetent teachers, and radical teachers recognize this. Tenured teacher firings are very rare; the radical teacher merely has to sit tight until tenure, and then anything is permissible.

Tenure laws create burdensome requirements that save teachers' jobs, even when those teachers have demonstrated a lack of respect for parents, students, and community values. This is a travesty that demands correction. We need to abolish or change these laws to make it easier to dismiss teachers who behave in an irresponsible manner.

Schools Are Community and Family Agencies

Schools are not meant to be forums for teachers whose viewpoints differ sharply from those of the community. Instead, schools are intended to express and affirm community values. Malleable students are a captive audience; teachers must not have the right to impose contrary views on the young (McFarlane, 1994).

Teachers who abdicate their professional obligation to protect students from radical ideas deserve to be fired. Responsible teachers recognize this point; they deserve the general freedom of expression accorded all citizens under the Constitution, but not an additional license that would protect their jobs regardless.

Teachers are an important resource in society. They have the power to shape the ideas and behaviors of young people. They also serve as agents of the community to assure that the common culture is properly transmitted. The power and agency of teachers impose serious responsibilities on those who accept this role. Teachers derive their authority from the traditional presumption that they serve in the place of the parent and as agents for the community, and thus they must be concerned about parental rights and community sensibilities. Instruction that disrupts or erodes family and social values has no place in the schools, and should be grounds for teacher reprimand or dismissal. Academic freedom has sometimes been used as a defense for teachers who have deliberately engaged in challenging traditional values, but that is a smokescreen to hide subversive and irresponsible teaching. Responsible teachers deserve freedom in teaching, but academic freedom and teacher freedom are different topics.

There are two important considerations to bear in mind in any discussion of academic and teacher freedom in the schools. First, academic freedom has been reserved to provide limited protection to university-level scholars who are experts in their specialized fields, and it is inappropriate to apply the concept to teachers below college level. Second, teacher freedom is not unlimited or unrestrained; it is necessarily related to the tradition of teacher responsibilities.

There is no doubt that, within the limits of responsibility, teachers should have respect and some freedom to determine how to teach. That is, teacher freedom can be separated from academic freedom, which is intended to protect the rights of experts to present the results of their research. This separation does not denigrate teachers any more than it denigrates lawyers, doctors, and ministers as respected people who have no claim to special freedom in their work. Teacher freedom is protected by community traditions and the constitutional protection of free speech. Teachers do not need more than that.

The U.S. Constitution's protections of free speech for all citizens are more than sufficient for teachers. Under the Constitution, any of us can say what we wish to say about the government, our employers, or the state of the world, provided it is not slanderous, imminently dangerous, or obscene. Obviously, we cannot say false things about someone without risking suit for libel, and we cannot yell "Fire!" in a crowded theater or "Bomb!" in an airport without risking arrest. We must also accept the consequences for our other statements. It would be absurd to expect an employer to keep an employee who made public statements that reflected negatively on the company. Can you imagine the president of IBM guaranteeing the job of a salesperson who wrote a letter that advocated the purchase of Apple computers, or who sent a memo to colleagues complaining about a supervisor?

Public expression of controversial views, as in letters to a newspaper editor, is a right in America. Teachers, of course, have the same right. That does not mean that the teacher's job is safe, any more than are the jobs of people employed by private firms and who make controversial public statements. Keeping a particular job regardless of one's actions is not a right guaranteed by the Constitution. Anyone who wishes to make public statements must recognize the risks involved. Teachers, more than most citizens, should be aware of the responsibilities surrounding public discourse. Inflammatory comments by a teacher can lead to public outrage.

Schoolteachers should not expect job guarantees when they make negative comments about the schools, the community, or the nation. They also should not expect job protection when they use propaganda or inaccurate or provocative material to teach children. Private schools can expect their teachers to follow school and parent values because they have more latitude in dismissing teachers who are unsatisfactory. State tenure laws do not apply to them. Public schools have some constraints because of those tenure laws, but they should be more aggressive in weeding out the miseducative teachers. The public schools are public employers; the teachers are public employees. Each board of education has a responsibility to provide children with information, skills, and a set of social values and a moral code that strengthen the society. That responsibility cannot be abrogated by teachers.

Further, school is compulsory for children. The students are a captive audience, subject to the whims and eccentricities of the teacher. Students range in age from childhood to youth, and they are not yet mature. They are much more impressionable than the typical adult and easy prey for a manipulative teacher. Yet, many teachers expect that their jobs will be secure no matter what they say or do in public or in classrooms. They may call this academic freedom, but it represents license, not freedom.

Academic Freedom as a Function of Academic Position

Academic freedom protects scholars who recognize the academic responsibilities inherent in it. Scholars who have developed expert knowledge in a subject field may conduct research that challenges accepted views. This is how knowledge continues to be refined. Academic freedom provides that such scholars can publish or present their research without fear of losing their positions, but even these scholars have academic freedom only in those areas in which they have demonstrated expert knowledge. Academic freedom does not extend to everything they do or say. They have no greater freedom than any other citizen in areas outside their own expertise. An English professor who joins an activist group blocking traffic in an environmental protest has no claim to academic freedom for that activity. The professor is no different from any other citizen. Everyone's speech is protected by the Constitution, but a faculty job should not be. There is a difference between academic freedom and license, and no academic freedom should exist for those who indoctrinate others (Kirk, 1955, Hook, 1953; Buckley, 1951).

In specialized subject areas, where a scholar has demonstrated expertise, he or she may need the protection of academic freedom to publish or present research results that differ from those of prior research. Some few public school teachers may have developed this expert knowledge and are conducting research, but that is not true for the vast majority. As philosopher Russell Kirk has eloquently argued, not all subjects are equally deserving of academic freedom:

> The scholar and teacher deserve their high freedom because they are professors of the true arts and sciences—that is, because their disciplines are the fields of knowledge in which there ought always to be controversy and exploration; and their especial freedom of expression and speculation is their right only while they still argue and investigate. But if this body of learned men is trampled down by a multitude of technicians, adolescent-sitters, . . . and art-of-camp-cookery teachers (whose skills, however convenient to us, do not require a special freedom of mind for their conservation and growth) . . . then the whole order of scholars will sink into disrepute and discouragement. (Kirk, 1955, pp. 79, 80)

Unfortunately for teachers and for scholars, the idea of academic freedom has been abused. Attempts by teacher unions and lawyers to save the jobs of teachers who are incompetent or who espouse antisocial propaganda have clouded the positive idea of academic freedom. Academic freedom should not be used as a shield for incompetent, antisocial, or un-American teaching. Rather, the idea of teacher freedom related to teacher responsibilities is a much sounder approach to the protection of teachers and to the integrity of the society.

Law professor Stephen Goldstein (1976), in a well-reasoned article on this topic, argues that academic freedom is unsuited to elementary and secondary schools because of the age and immaturity of the students, the teacher's position of authority, the necessarily more highly structured curriculum, and the dominant role of the school in imparting social values. These factors, and others, cannot be dismissed easily. Elementary and secondary school teachers are different from university scholars in their training, their functions, their employment status, and their responsibilities. And the elementary and secondary schools have broad responsibilities to parents, the community, and the state that do not permit giving license to teachers to do what they wish. Schools and teachers serve in capacities that require support for and advocacy of social and family values. Academic freedom rhetoric does not diminish that significant responsibility.

Responsibility and Power in Teaching

Teaching is one of the most influential positions in society. In terms of the values and ideas that are carried from generation to generation, teaching is next to parenting in its power. In some respects, the teacher exerts more influence on the views and values of children than do parents. Parents have great control over what their children see and hear and do during the earliest years, but after the child starts school, the parent relinquishes increasing amounts of that influence to teachers.

Society gives teachers the authority to develop sound knowledge and values in children, and school is compulsory for that purpose. The child, being weaned from parental influence, looks to teachers for guidance. This is a heavy and important responsibility, one that merits serious consideration. Teachers bear duties to parents, to society, and to the child to provide a suitable education. They also have duties to the profession of teaching. It is that multiple responsibility that teachers and schools must recognize.

All rights and all freedoms are connected to responsibilities. Otherwise there is anarchy, where no social restraint exists. That is not freedom; it is a jungle without rules and without ethics. Civilization demands both freedom and responsibility. Within that civilization, teachers' freedom must be tied to their responsibilities, and their rights and freedoms are conditioned on their acceptance of those responsibilities. Teachers' freedom is supported and limited by responsibility to parents, to society, to the child, and to the profession.

Parents have rights and obligations to their children, which teachers and schools must not undermine. The provision of food, clothing, and shelter is a parental obligation that is only taken over by another social institution when parents are incapable. The parents have moral obligations and rights, including instruction in determining right from wrong, good from bad. Parents must train their children in ethical conduct by providing them with a set of socially acceptable behaviors, including integrity, honesty, courtesy, and respect.

Parents also have many legal rights and obligations in regard to their children. They are expected to take good care of their children, and, under the law, are given great latitude in providing that care. Parents are presumed to have the child's interests at heart. They are even permitted to exercise corporal punishment, more than any other person would be permitted to inflict upon a child, under the legal idea that the parent has broad responsibilities. The root of laws regarding parents' rights and obligations is that they are responsible for their children's upbringing, morality, and behaviors. Teachers act as surrogate parents in certain situations, and should not deviate from the norms of the good parent in the good society.

School as a Positive Parent Surrogate

The good society is made up of good families, and good schools are extensions of those families. This concept is quite different from the common idea that society is either the faceless government or just a collection of separate individuals. Social institutions confirm and sustain the family, even when specific families fail to live up to their responsibilities. Prisons, foster homes, mental institutions, orphanages, family welfare programs, reformatories, and court-mandated separations represent society's attempt to deal with these responsibilities when families fail. These institutions try to do a good job of surrogate parenting, but they have great difficulty because they are working with the results of a poor situation. Such institutions can be considered negative because they exist to correct problems in families and society.

Schools, however, are a positive social institution. They are specifically intended to continue the development of children, extending the family influence to produce good citizens and good members of future families. Children are not put in schools as punishment, or as a means for correcting family irresponsibility. The schools exist to supplement and expand the good family and the good society. Schools, therefore, must continue the cultural heritage by passing on positive social and family values to the young.

Teacher Responsibilities to Parents, Society, and Children

Schools, then, have a special obligation to be responsive to parents' concerns for their children. It is this reasoning that lies behind the legal concept that teachers act *in loco parentis*, or in the place of the parent. That concept, which has deep social and legal roots, protects teachers in their handling of student discipline and evaluation procedures. It also requires teachers to remain sensitive to parental interests in what is taught and done to their children. Parental rights and responsibilities extend beyond the time the children begin kindergarten. Children remain parental obligations until they become adults. Parents do not usually consider those obligations as merely technical requirements. They have strong emotional commitments to their children that transcend legal and social expectations. Parents want, and expect, the best possible for their children.

Teachers, standing in the place of the parents, take on similar responsibilities for the child's development and protection. Although teachers do not have the same innate responsibilities, beyond providing a safe and healthy classroom environment, they do have moral, ethical, and legal ones. In addition, they have formal educational responsibilities: they must teach the children the necessary knowledge and skills to get along in the society. Teachers discharge these responsibilities well by being responsive to parental concerns about the kind of knowledge and values taught.

Teachers cannot have license to do anything they wish to students, physically or mentally. No one today would argue that teachers should be permitted to abuse children physically, although some teachers are permitted to exert limited physical control over children to maintain an educational environment. For example, teachers can require students to remain seated, to change seats, to be quiet, to go to the principal's office, or to line up for activities. Teachers are properly prohibited from such abusive activity as striking students or using electric cattle prods. Good teachers would never contemplate such malevolent behavior; it is outside the standards of professional conduct.

Mental abuse of students is equally to be abhorred, but it is less easy to detect. The scars of mental abuse are not as obvious as physical damage. Mental abuse is no less harmful, however, to the student, the parents, and the society. It can consist of vicious verbal personal attacks, indoctrination in antisocial values or behaviors, or manipulation of children's minds against parents or morality. Parents have a right to insist that their children not be subjected to these tactics, but they are often unaware of them until after the damage has been done. Good teachers would not contemplate such misuse of their influential role in the lives of children; it would be unprofessional.

Parents have a right to monitor what is taught to their children, to expect the school to be accountable for it, and to limit the potential for damage to which their children might be subjected.

Teacher Responsibilities to the Society

The society, as well as parents, has a significant interest in the education of children. Schools were established to pass on the cultural heritage; to provide the skills, attitudes, and knowledge needed to produce good citizens; and to prepare children to meet their responsibilities in family, work, and social roles. Schools are social institutions, financed and regulated to fulfill social purposes.

Society has values, standards of behavior, and attitudes that the school is responsible for conveying to children. These standards have evolved over a long period, and represent our common culture. The school and the teachers are engaged by the society to ensure that social standards, and the ideals that these standards represent, are taught by example and in presentations.

Schools do not exist as entities separate from society, able to chart their own courses as though they had no social responsibilities. The schools were not intended to instruct students in antisocial, anti-American, or immoral ideas or behaviors, nor will society allow them to continue to do so.

Teachers are given a position of trust by society to develop the young into positive, productive citizens. Those few teachers who use their position to attempt to destroy social values or create social dissension are violating that trust. Those who sow the seeds of negativism or nihilism or cynicism are also violating that trust. The society has the right to restrict, condemn, or exclude from teaching those who harm its interests.

Teacher Responsibilities to Children

The paramount responsibility of teachers is to their students—the children of parents and the future adult members of society. It is because students are immature and unformed that the influence of teachers must be recognized, and that teacher freedom must be controlled by teacher responsibility. Teachers hold great potential power over the lives of children, and the disparity in authority between teacher and students needs to weigh heavily in teacher decisions as to what to teach and how. The teacher derives power from maturity, physical size, and position. The child is vulnerable.

In the forming and testing of ideas, attitudes, and behaviors, the child looks to the teacher for direction. Children are naturally curious and positive, but they cannot yet fully discern between good and bad, proper and improper. Much of what parents have not been able to teach during infancy and early childhood is given over to teachers for the formative period of twelve school years. Teachers have a responsibility to continue the moral and ethical education that good parents have begun. That is what character education is all about. In addition, teachers need to develop habits of thinking in students that will help them gain knowledge of, and learn to appreciate, the language, history, science, and art of their society.

Teacher Responsibilities to Their Profession

The profession of teaching has an extensive and illustrious history. It is based on the idea of service to children and to society. The teachers' code of ethics recognizes teacher responsibilities as singularly important. Teachers want to preserve and convey the cultural heritage to their students, along with a strong sense of social responsibility. Teachers can ask no less of themselves.

A basic responsibility of the teaching profession is to prepare young people for life in the society. That includes the teaching of social values and knowledge to students, and the teacher's personal conduct should exemplify the society's ideals. The teaching profession recognizes both the needs of the child and the needs of the society. Teachers have an obligation to their profession not to go beyond its bounds, and to reject those who would tarnish its reputation.

POSITION 2: FOR INCREASED ACADEMIC FREEDOM

A society cannot be free when its schools are not free. The continuing development of American democracy requires that academic freedom be further expanded in schools for both students and teachers. Ideas are the primary ingredients of democracy and education, and the realm of ideas is the basic realm protected by academic freedom. John Dewey (1936) noted over fifty years ago, "Since freedom of mind and freedom of expression are the root of all freedom, to deny freedom in education is a crime against democracy." Strong support for academic freedom for schoolteachers and their students should seem obvious to anyone who supports a free society.

One may wonder why this is considered a critical issue in education in the 1990s. Who could possibly be against academic freedom at this period of American life? Unfortunately, narrow-minded, backward-looking people have increased their efforts to restrict schools and to impose censorship on students and teachers. Zealots on different sides of political, economic, and religious fences have tried to use the schools as agents to impose their views and values on the young. They don't want opposing views or conflicting evidence presented, and they are against real critical thinking. That zealotry has increased the vulnerability of teachers who realize that good education involves dealing with controversial issues.

The good teacher who is willing to examine controversial topics runs risks far beyond those suggested in high-sounding slogans about academic freedom. Ominous overt threats and subtle pressure from administrators, parents, special interest groups, and peers are likely to cool this teacher's ardor for freedom of ideas. Ostracism or ridicule may also be encountered by the teacher who fulfills this basic educational responsibility. And teachers have been fired for doing what our society should expect all good teachers to do. All of these efforts, and more, are aimed at restricting the academic freedom of teachers and students and imposing censorship on the schools.

People for the American Way publishes a state-by-state annual report on censorship efforts in schools and libraries. The group cannot track all censoring activities because vast numbers are unreported, but their recent "snapshot" reports show an increase in incidents annually and a resurgence in right-wing attacks on academic freedom (*Attacks on the Freedom to Learn,* 1985–1994). The number of attacks on academic freedom more than doubled between 1982 and 1990. Other current studies confirm the fragile state of academic freedom in schools. Censoring of literature continues (*English Journal,* 1990; Hymowitz, 1991; Flagg, 1992; Waldron, 1993; Simmons, 1991, 1994); school boards and administrators keep trying to expand their control over instructional material (Mesibov, 1991; Daly, 1991); and courts render inconsistent decisions on the protection of teacher freedoms (Mawdsley and Mawdsley, 1988; Turner-Egner, 1989; Melnick and Lillard, 1989; Sacken, 1989; Pico, 1990; *English Journal,* 1990).

With the continuing attacks and the vulnerability of teachers and schools to censorship and political restrictions, is it worth the effort to have academic freedom?

The Essential Relationship of Academic Freedom to Democracy

Academic freedom is the "liberty of thought" claimed by teachers and students, including the right to "enjoy the freedom to study, to inquire, to speak . . . , to communicate . . . ideas" (*Dictionary of the History of Ideas,* 1973, pp. 9, 10). The question of academic freedom must be examined from the perspective of a society that prizes freedom and self-governance, even when those ideals are not always evident in the everyday practice of the society. It is the ideals of a society that education best serves. The nature of the academy, at any level, is interlinked with the goals of the society. A restrictive or totalitarian society demands a restrictive or totalitarian education system. A society that professes freedom should demand no less than freedom for its schools (Rorty, 1994).

The defining quality of academic freedom is freedom in the search for truth. This freedom should not be limited to a small elite corps of "experts," but should include students and teachers engaged in the quest for knowledge. The search for knowledge is not limited to the experts, including teachers, but is the purpose of schooling. There is also the risk that when experts control knowledge they will require conformity and not allow challenges or conflicting opinions. We may not like challenges to ideas we find comfortable, but those challenges are the stuff of progress. Without challenges to comfortable superstitions, we would not have had scientific achievements leading to medical and technical progress. Without challenges to the idea of royalty or dictatorial governments, we would not have had the idea of democracy.

There is one inescapable premise for democracy: people are capable of governing themselves. That premise assumes that people can make knowledgeable decisions and can select intelligently from among alternative proposals. Education and the free exchange of ideas are fundamental to the premise. To think otherwise is to insult the essential condition of democracy.

The U.S. Supreme Court demonstrated its commitment to the principle of academic freedom in a 1967 decision whereby a state law that mandated a loyalty oath for teachers was found unconstitutional. The Court noted that academic freedom is a "transcendent value":

> Our nation is deeply committed to safeguarding academic freedom which is of transcendent value to all of us and not merely to the teachers concerned. That freedom is, therefore, a special concern of the First Amendment, which does not tolerate laws that cast a pall of orthodoxy over the classroom . . . . The classroom is peculiarly the "marketplace of ideas." (*Keyishian v. Board of Regents,* 1967)

The democratic basis for academic freedom is part of that transcendent value. Democracy is now considered the most suitable way to organize American society. We find that increasing numbers of countries and peoples throughout the world are embracing democracy as an ideal, but the definition of a democratic society is still evolving. Self-governance emerged as a set of contrary ideas, actually at odds with the prevailing concepts of government, and became a compelling vision of a better social existence for the majority of people.

Similarly, academic freedom has evolved and expanded from a narrow and limited definition to embrace the general framework within which schooling takes place, and the work of teachers engaged in that process. Differences in state laws, and confusing court opinions, have produced a mixed view of what specific actions are legally protected under the idea of academic freedom (O'Neil, 1981). There has, however, been an expanding awareness by courts of the need for academic freedom in schools.

Nothing remains static. Change is constant in society and in education. Ideas about society and schools arise, are tested, and are expanded and improved or dropped. Democracy and academic freedom are evolving concepts. The basic principles are clear—for example, self-governance for democracy and enlightenment for academic freedom—but the practical definitions of these terms are under continuing development.

Propaganda and public deceit are practiced in all countries, including democracies, but citizens of a democracy are expected to have the right and the ability to question and examine in a manner that can expose those deceits, and then to act upon that knowledge.

Dictatorial regimes do not need, and do not desire, the mass of population to have an education that gives them the basis for judging from among alternatives and questioning the information presented. Totalitarian states maintain their existence by using raw power and threats, by utilizing censorship and restriction, and by keeping the public ignorant. Governments in democracies can attempt the same maneuvers, but they run the risk of exposure and replacement. The more totalitarian the government, the more it uses threats, censorship, and denial of freedom in education. The more democratic the society, the less it employs threats, censorship, and restriction of education. This litmus test of democracy is also a significant measure of academic freedom.

Academic Freedom and a Free Society

Because there has been a general misunderstanding of the central role of schools in a free society, teachers and students have often lived a peripheral existence in America. Teaching has been viewed as "women's work," and teachers as not deserving of the public trust to make wise decisions. States and communities impose restrictions on what can be taught and the methods of teaching to be used. Teachers and teaching materials are censored by school boards and administrators for dealing with controversial topics. Students are virtually ignored, are treated as nonpersons, or are expected to exhibit blind obedience. These conditions raise questions about American society and the vitality of academic freedom. Academic freedom, the essence of the profession of teaching, has been insufficiently developed in the society and in the education of teachers.

Educational Grounds for Academic Freedom

Where, if not in schools, will new generations be able to explore and test divergent ideas, new concepts, challenges to superstition, and propaganda? It is in schools that students should be able to pursue intriguing possibilities, under the guidance of free and knowledgeable teachers. Students can test ideas in schools with less serious risks of social condemnation or ostracism. In a setting where critical thinking is prized and nurtured, students and teachers can engage more fully in intellectual development. This is in the society's best interests for two fundamental reasons: (1) new ideas from new generations are the basis of social progress, and (2) students who are not permitted to explore divergent ideas in school can be blinded to society's defects and imperfections, and will be unable to participate as citizens in improving democracy.

There is no real threat to society when students examine controversial matters in school. Most young people encounter radical ideas in conversations with friends or in films, TV, and other media. In an educational setting, the opposing ideas can be more fully considered, and there is opportunity for informed criticism of each view. The real threat to American society is that controversial material will not be examined adequately in schools, and that students will come to distrust education and society as places for the free exchange of ideas. Teachers and students need academic freedom to fulfill their educational mission in a free society. Daly and Roach (1990) call for a renewed commitment to academic freedom to pursue these social and educational ends.

The primary purpose of education is enlightenment. Although teaching can be conducted easily as simple indoctrination, where the teacher presents material and students memorize it without thought or criticism, that leads to an incomplete and defective education. Teaching can also be chaotic, with no sense of organization or purpose. That, too, is an incomplete and defective education. Neither of these approaches to teaching offers enlightenment. Education consists of ideas and challenges, increasingly sophisticated and complex. Indoctrination stunts the educational process, shrinking the idea of knowledge and constricting critical thinking. Chaotic schools confuse the educational process, mix important and trivial ideas, and muddle critical thinking. A sound education provides solid grounding in current knowledge, and students learn to challenge ideas in the process of critical thinking.

Education that provides ideas and challenges and stimulates increasingly sophisticated critical thinking is necessarily controversial. Some of the challenges will not be popular, and critical thinking may raise questions about ideas with which the community is comfortable. Teachers who fear political reprisal for providing a sound education find themselves in an anomolous situation. These teachers need protection from politically powerful groups, from vocal special interests, and from shifts in popular political views. Students also need protection from these forces, as well as from incompetent and indoctrinating teachers. Academic freedom for teachers and students is essential to education.

The Center of the Profession

Academic freedom is at the heart of the profession of teaching (Nelson, 1990). Professions are identified by the nature of the work, the educational requirements for admission, and commonly held social ethics and values. Medical professionals work in the protection and improvement of health, have a specialized education in medical practice, and share a commitment to life. Attorneys work in the realm of law, have specialized training in the practice of law, and are dedicated to the value of justice. Teachers work to educate, have subject knowledge and specialized education in teaching practice, and share a devotion to enlightenment.

In earlier America, when teachers were not required to have a college degree and their main role was to provide minimal literary skills, there were severe limitations on their freedom in many places. With increasingly rigorous teacher credentialing regulations and improved professional study and practice, there are now no grounds for excessive restrictions on teacher's work.

The nature of teachers' work and their shared devotion to enlightenment require a special freedom, one not required for other occupations, to explore new ideas in the quest for knowledge. This freedom deserves protection beyond that provided to all citizens under the constitutional guarantee of free speech. Unlike other citizens, teachers have a professional obligation to search for truth, and to assist students in their search for truth (Zirkel, 1993). It is the practice of this profession, this obligation, that requires special protection from political or other interference. Teachers' jobs must not be at risk because they explore controversial material or consider ideas that are not in the mainstream. That is part of the process of free and liberal education, and is a basic condition of the profession.

Academic Freedom and Teacher Competency

The provision of academic freedom for teachers is not without limits or conditions. Neither every person certified to teach nor every action of every teacher warrants the protection of academic freedom. The basic condition for academic freedom is teacher competence. Incompetent teachers should not be given that extra protection.

Teacher competence is a mix of knowledge, skill, and judgment. It includes knowledge of the material being taught and of the students in class, professional skill in teaching, and considered professional judgment. It is more than just the accumulation of college credits and professional study. It includes a practical demonstration that the teacher can teach in a manner that shows subject and student knowledge, teaching skill, and judgment. As in other professions, competence is measured by peers and supervisors, and it continues to be refined. In teaching, initial competence is expected at the time of completion of the teaching credential program. That program includes subject and professional study and practice teaching under supervision. According to the laws of various states, teachers serve several years under school supervision and are granted tenure if they are successful. This long test of actual teaching should be sufficient to establish competence. Incompetent teachers should not get tenure.

Tenure and Academic Freedom

The main legal protection for academic freedom in schools is the state laws on tenure. Under tenure laws, teachers cannot be fired without cause. The tenured teacher who is threatened with firing must be provided with such due process conditions as a fair hearing and specific allegations of the grounds for the firing that can be addressed in a court. This protects tenured teachers from improper dismissal as a result of personality conflicts or politics. Grounds for dismissal, identified in the state law, often include moral turpitude, professional misconduct, and incompetence. The truth of the allegation must be clearly demonstrated and documented in order for the dismissal to be upheld. This is a reasonable treatment. It should be difficult to dismiss a tenured teacher who has demonstrated competence over a period of years. And teachers should not be dismissed on the basis of personal or political disagreements with administrators or others.

Nontenured probationary teachers also deserve the protection of academic freedom because they, too, are expected to engage in enlightening education. However, they do not have the same legal claims as do tenured teachers. Tenured teachers serve on "indefinite" contracts, which need not be renewed formally each year. Dismissal, or nonrenewal of the one-year contract, of probationary teachers can occur at the end of any given school term, often without any requirement that the cause for dismissal be stated by the school district. That leaves the nontenured teacher very vulnerable. Certainly, if the probationary teacher is not competent as a teacher, dismissal is appropriate. Dismissal for dealing with controversial topics in a competent manner should, however, be prohibited.

Obstacles to Academic Freedom

The compelling reasons supporting academic freedom notwithstanding, historical, political, and economic pressures have overwhelmed those reasons and have restricted teachers and students. American schools do not have an exemplary tradition in providing the academic freedom necessary to our democracy. Censorship, political restraint, and restrictions on freedom have a long and sordid history in the United States. Early American schools, under religious domination, imposed moralistic behavior on teachers, firing them for impiety or for not having sufficient religious zeal. In the nineteenth century, the number of public schools increased rapidly and many teachers had only limited education themselves; communities required strict conformity to social norms, and teachers could be dismissed for dating, dancing, drinking, visiting pool halls, or simply disagreeing with local officials.

In the first half of the twentieth century, religious and moralistic restrictions on teachers were replaced by political restraint and censorship (Pierce, 1933; Beale, 1936; Gellerman, 1938). College teachers often fared no better, and many suffered great indignities at the hands of college officials (Sinclair, 1922; Veblen, 1957; Hofstadter & Metzger, 1955). As the twentieth century draws to a close, it is clear that teachers have gained much in professional preparation and stature, but they are not yet free. Although teachers have more freedom now than when they were indentured servants in colonial times, significant threats to academic freedom continue to limit education and to put blinders on students.

A recent statement by the American Association of University Professors in support of academic freedom for precollege-level teachers identifies a variety of political restraints imposed on such teachers (AAUP, 1986). The *Intellectual Freedom Newsletter,* a publication of the American Library Association, keeps track of the many cases of school and library censorship across the United States. There have always been large numbers of such cases in local communities, but since 1970 the frequency of reported censorship incidents has tripled, and estimates suggest that for each incident formally reported, about fifty other censoring activities are unreported (Jenkinson, 1985). The National Coalition Against Censorship, affiliated with dozens of professional and scholarly associations, was formed recently because of the increase in censorship in America. Academic freedom remains a significant problem for American teachers. Continuing vigilance is required because of the continuing threats to this freedom.

The Censors and the Chill on Education

Topics that arouse the censors and those who want to control teachers vary over time. Socialism and communism were very visible in the 1920s and again in the 1960s. They surfaced again in the early years of the Reagan administration. Sexual topics and profanity are constant subjects of school censors. A more recent issue is the charge that secular humanism is taught in schools—a charge that teachers and materials are anti-God, immoral, antifamily, and anti-American. Among other current topics that stimulate people who want to stifle academic freedom are drugs, evolution, values clarification, economics, environmental issues, social activism and the use of African-American, feminist, or other minority literature (Jenkinson, 1990; Waldron, 1993; Japenga, 1994).

Publicized censorship and restraint activities have a "chilling effect" on school boards, administrators, and even many teachers (Whitson, 1993). The mere fact that there might be complaints if a teacher touches on a controversial topic leads to fear and sinister implications. Administrators issue informal statements warning teachers not to use certain materials, and over the teachers' grapevine, more experienced teachers suggest that younger teachers exercise extreme caution concerning anything remotely controversial. Daly (1991) found that few school districts had policies to protect teacher and student rights to academic freedom. As a result, there is an extraordinary amount of teacher self-censorship that denies to students and to society the full exploration of ideas. Many teachers avoid significant topics, or they neutralize and sterilize them to the point of student boredom. Academic freedom for teachers and students is not self-evident in America.

The Free Society Requires Academic Freedom

Despite the history of weak protection of academic freedom and the often powerful political pressures brought to bear to stifle it, attaining such freedom for teachers and students is worth the strenuous effort it demands. There are compelling democratic, educational, and professional grounds for expanding the protection of academic freedom for competent teachers and for students. And there are important social reasons why the public should support academic freedom in public education. Academic freedom is more than a set of platitudes, state regulations, and court decisions. It should be a fundamental expectation for schools in a free society. Academic freedom is the centering idea for the profession of teaching.

For Discussion

1. The definition of academic freedom may be hazy. Are the definitions of other major social ideas (justice, equality, democracy, authority, power) clearer and more precise? How is a definition of academic freedom related to definitions of these other terms?
2. Jenkinson (1990) identifies the following as myths related to censorship and other restrictions on academic freedom.
    a. The attacks mostly occur in the Bible belt.
    b. They occur more in rural communities.
    c. Parents want their children to think critically and read widely.
    d. Statewide adoption of texts avoids attack by censorial groups.
    e. Teachers should stick to literary classics because they are never attacked.
    f. Politically appointed boards censor more than do freely elected boards of education.
    g. Rational argument will prevail in dealing with censors and intellectually restrictive people.
    h. Censorship can't happen in my town.
    What evidence supporting these ideas have you encountered in your experience or in the news media? Do you agree with Jenkinson? What forms of censorship were discovered? Are all forms of censorship a threat to academic freedom?
3. Should there be any restrictions on what a teacher can cover in class? What set of principles should govern the establishment of those limits? Should students be given the same freedoms and limits? Is student age or teacher experience a significant factor in this determination?
4. Which, if any, of the following topics should be banned from schoolbooks as justified censorship?
    Explicit sexual material
    Sexism
    Racism
    Fascism
    Violence
    Anti-American views
    Socialism
    Antireligious material
    Inhuman treatment of people
    Animal, child, or spouse abuse
    What are the grounds for justifying censorship of any of these?

5. For the past decade, reports of efforts to restrict teachers have increased. The 1987–1988 report of People for the American way indicated that there was an "energized movement of extremists pressuring public schools on a broad range of fronts." That report identified 157 incidents of that kind of pressure in forty-two states:

Fifty in the south
Forty-six in the midwest
Forty-two in the west
Nineteen in the northeast

The most frequent topics during many years were:

"Satanism"—mostly in the west
Sex education—mostly in the south
Creationism—mostly in the midwest

The most frequent target was John Steinbeck's *Of Mice and Men*. Other most challenged authors were:

Judy Blume
Stephen King
J. D. Salinger

Other books challenged included:

All Quiet on the Western Front
Where the Wild Things Are

There were also challenges to:

Celebrations of Halloween
Meeting of Teens for Christ groups

The focus of attack shifted from secular humanism and globalism to offensive language and satanism and the occult. The 1994 report shows increased censorship.

What patterns show in these attacks? What are the likely consequences of such efforts to censor schools? What role should teachers play in learning about and responding to efforts at censorship? Should the censors be censored?

Source: Attacks on the Freedom to Learn, 1987–88; 1985–1994. Washington, DC: People for the American Way.

References

American Association of University Professors (AAUP). (1986). *Liberty and Learning in the Schools*. Washington, DC: AAUP.

Attacks on the Freedom to Learn. (1985–1994). Washington, DC: People for the American Way.

Beale, H. (1936). *Are American Teachers Free?* New York: Scribner's.

Buckley, W. F. (1951). *God and Man at Yale*. Chicago: Regnery.

Cheney, L. (1992). "Telling the Truth." *Humanities* **13**, 4–9.

Daly, J. K. (1991). "The Influence of Administrators on the Teaching of Social Studies." *Theory and Research in Social Education* **19**, 267–283.

———, and Roach, P. B. (1990). "Reaffirming a Commitment to Academic Freedom." *Social Education* **54**, 342–345.

Dewey, J. (1936). "The Social Significance of Academic Freedom." *The Social Frontier* **2**, 136.

Dictionary of the History of Ideas. (1973). I. Weiner, editor. New York: Scribners.

English Journal. (1990). "Censorship: A Continuing Problem." *English Journal* **79**, 87–89.

Flagg, G. (1992). "'Snow White' is the Latest Title Under Attack in Schools." *American Libraries* **23,** 359–361.

Gellerman, W. (1938). *The American Legion as Educator.* New York: Teachers College Press.

Goldstein, S. (1976). "The Asserted Right of Teachers to Determine What They Teach." *University of Pennsylvania Law Review* **124,** 1, 293.

Hentoff, N. (1991). "Saving Kids from Satan's Books." *The Progressive* **55,** 14–16.

Hofstadter, R., and Metzger, W. (1955). *The Development of Academic Freedom in the United States.* New York: Columbia University Press.

Hook, S. (1953). *Heresy, Yes—Conspiracy, No.* New York: Day.

Hymowitz, K. S. (1991). "Babar the Racist." *The New Republic* **205,** 12–14.

Japenga, A. (1994). "A Teacher at War." *Mother Jones* **19,** 17.

Jenkinson, E. B. (1985). "Protecting Holden Caulfield and His Friends from the Censors." *English Journal* **74,** 26–33.

――― (1990). "Child Abuse in the Hate Factory." In *Academic Freedom to Teach and to Learn,* edited by A. Ochoa. Washington, DC: National Education Association.

Jones, J. (1993). "Targets of the Right." *American School Boards Journal* **180,** 22–29.

Keyishian v. Board of Regents. (1967). 385 U.S. 589.

Kirk, R. (1955). *Academic Freedom.* Chicago: Regnery.

Leo, J. (1993). "Pedophiles in the Schools." *U.S. News and World Report* **115,** 37.

Mawdsley, R. D., and Mawdsley, A. L. (1988). *Free Expression and Censorship: Public Policy and the Law.* Topeka, KS: National Organization on Legal Problems of Education.

McFarlane, A. (1994). "Radical Educational Values." *America* **171,** 10–13.

Melnick, N., and Lillard, S. D. (1989). "Academic Freedom: A Delicate Balance." *Clearing House* **62,** 275–277.

Mesibov, L. L. (1991). "Teacher–Board of Education Conflicts Over Instructional Material." *School Law Bulletin* **22,** 10–15.

Nelson, J. (1990). "The Significance of and Rationale for Academic Freedom." In *Academic Freedom to Teach and to Learn,* edited by A. Ochoa. Washington, DC: National Education Association.

O'Neil, R. M. (1981). *Classrooms in the Crossfire.* Bloomington: Indiana University Press.

Pico, S. (1990). "An Introduction to Censorship." *School Media Quarterly* **18,** 84–87.

Pierce, B. (1933). *Citizens' Organizations and the Civic Training of Youth.* New York: Scribner's.

Rorty, R. (1994). "Does Academic Freedom Have Philosophical Presuppositions?" *Academe* **80,** 52–63.

Sacken, D. M. (1989). "Rethinking Academic Freedom in the Public Schools." *Teachers College Record* **91,** 235–255.

Simmons, J. (1991). "Censorship in the Schools: No End in Sight." *ALAN Review* **18,** 6–8.

――――, ed. (1994). *Censorship: A Threat to Reading, Learning, Thinking.* Newark, DE: International Reading Association.

Sinclair, U. (1922). *The Goose-Step.* Pasadena, CA: Sinclair.

――――. (1923). *The Goslings.* Pasadena, CA: Sinclair.

The Rights of Students, 3rd ed. (1988). Washington, DC: American Civil Liberties Union.

Turner-Egner, J. (1989). "Teachers' Discretion in Selecting Instructional Materials and Methods." *West's Education Law Reporter* **53,** 365–379.

Veblen, T. (1918, 1957). *The Higher Learning in America: Memorandum on the Conduct of Universities by Businessmen.* New York: Sagamore.

Waldron, C. (1993). "White Teacher's Use of *Ebony* to Teach Tolerance at Texas School Ignites Uproar Among Parents." *Jet* **84**, 10–16.

Whitson, J. A. (1993). "After Hazelwood: The Role of School Officials in Conflicts over the Curriculum." *ALAN Review* **20**, 2–6.

Zirkel, P. (1993). "Academic Freedom: Professional or Legal Right?" *Educational Leadership* **50**, 42–43.

CHAPTER FIFTEEN

Teacher Unions: Detrimental or Beneficial

POSITION 1: TEACHER UNIONS ARE DESTRUCTIVE

The National Education Association—which some years ago passed the Teamsters to become the country's biggest union—is the worm in the American education apple. The public may be only dimly aware of it, but the union's growing power has exactly coincided with the dismal spectacle of rising spending on education producing deteriorating results. (Brimelow and Spencer, 1993, p. 74)

Strikes, work slowdowns, and demeaning battles between teacher unions and school boards hinder rather than enhance education for the youth of the United States. With few exceptions, relationships between boards and unions are adversarial. Strikes and other less serious conflicts between boards and unions are never over the quality of education. Instead, they emanate from a "win what I want for myself, at any cost" mentality. (Streshly and DeMitchell, 1994, p. vii)

Self-Serving Unsupported Claims

Officials of teacher unions claim that when public monies are spent to improve working conditions for teachers, children are the ultimate beneficiaries. Their arguments are, no doubt, familiar to you: Public school students suffer because teachers are underpaid. The hard work of devoted teachers deserves greater compensation. Unless teachers are given higher salaries, not only will the current crop of teachers become discouraged, but the brightest college graduates will not go into education, and children will be taught by the less able. Union leaders similarly argue that teachers should be granted greater power in running the schools. They claim that teachers will be more effective if they are allowed to join administrators in all areas of school management, including curriculum development and the supervision and evaluation of teaching.

The logic of labor in these examples is simple: What is good for teachers is good for children. If the public wants better education for its children, the public should support the work of teacher unions to improve education through increased remuneration and greater autonomy for teachers. Collective bargaining practices, picket lines, work stoppages (strikes), and the expansion of union control over schools should be considered beneficial to the community, parents, and students.

Convincing? Not really. The public interest is not served by making schools good places for teachers. Schools are for children. The public's interest in education is not measured by teachers' job satisfaction, but by the quality of learning provided to students.

Despite the rhetoric, it has not yet been demonstrated that teacher unions have a positive effect on students. The implied causal link between increased teacher salaries and improved education has not been demonstrated. No experimental evidence exists to support the union claim that giving teachers more money pays off in better schooling. Researchers find negligible differences in achievement between students in union and nonunion schools (Eberts and Stone, 1984). In fact, it is not possible to evaluate the impact unions have had on any specific school or on any single group of teachers or students. For example, it cannot be known with any certainty how a group of unionized teachers would have fared economically over time if they had not joined a union (Brimelow and Spencer, 1993). Perhaps they would have done better in salary negotiations or would have been treated better by the board of education; perhaps not. There is no way to know. At best, gains by one group of teachers can only be compared with average gains made by their colleagues across the state or nation. Therefore, it is not possible to conclude whether unionization has helped or harmed a specific group of teachers. Similarly, there is no clear picture of the impact of compensation on teacher performance (Johnson, 1988; Stern, 1986). The public has been forced to accept the benefits of unionization on faith, an emotional appeal from unions that cannot be supported by scientific research, and which occasionally defies common sense. It is not likely, for example, that good teachers would become poor teachers without union representation, and it is fatuous to assume that collective bargaining can improve the teaching skills of weak teachers.

Not all teachers want to be represented by unions, and some refuse to join. However, teacher unions can force nonmembers to pay union dues. Referred to as "fair share" clauses in their contracts, unions have defended the practice in court, arguing that even if teachers do not want unions to represent them, they still have to pay to support union activities. One Indiana teacher, active in the antiunion movement, circulated a flier critical of the fair-share practice. His union sued him, but he was not silenced. One of his supporters argued:

We're supposed to hear no evil, see no evil, speak no evil when it comes to the unions . . . . But teachers are fed up with being controlled by the union. I think they're going to fight until they get some freedom. (Jane Ping, quoted in Richardson, 1994, p. 10)

From Bread-and-Butter to Policy Issues

Despite their history of heavy-handed tactics and the absence of hard data, unions claim that they have improved teachers' salaries. They argue that the union-wage effect is actually in the neighborhood of 5 percent to 10 percent, not enough to make teachers wealthy, they admit, but enough for them to keep paying their union dues, and more than enough to encourage unions to extend their influence in education beyond bread-and-butter work issues. In the past, union efforts were typically limited to traditional labor concerns: wages and hours, working conditions, fringe benefits, grievance procedures, organization rights, and such specific work-related issues as extra pay for extra duty. Over time, teacher unions began to demand a voice in policy issues, such as curriculum, class size, disciplinary practices, textbook selection procedures, in-service training, teacher transfer policies, and personnel matters—including hiring and the awarding of tenure (Kerchner, 1986). Today, affiliates of both the National Education Association (NEA) and the American Federation of Teachers (AFT) want teachers to be "empowered," and they demand that schools be "restructured" to accommodate teacher demands that go well beyond traditional bargaining agreements. Some union contracts have given teachers the right to make decisions about staffing, how money is spent, how teachers teach, and how students are to learn. Under the familiar guise that collective negotiations will result in better education for children, union leaders now argue that increased teacher participation in the decision-making and managerial aspects of schools will result in school reform.

No reasonable administrator would discount the advice of teachers or fail to involve them in professional decisions, but turning the schools over to teachers distorts the authority structure. No matter how it is packaged, capitulation to demands for teacher empowerment destroys community control of education. In most communities, school board members are elected officials, voted into office on the basis of their personal qualifications and their educational platforms. They typically work long hours, without pay, to ensure that appropriate education is delivered to the children of their friends and neighbors in the community. The school board appoints the superintendent of schools to implement local educational policies. On the recommendation of the superintendent, building principals are hired, a curriculum is developed, and teachers are recruited to implement the board's educational plan. School boards, as public employers, are given decision-making authority as a public trust, and this trust should not be shared with those who are not directly responsible to the electorate. If the board fails to deliver the education it has promised, its members can be voted out of office and the superintendent can be replaced.

The unions were not hired, and they may not represent the most effective classroom teachers. They should not expect that collective bargaining tactics will enable them to substitute their views of education for the judgment of the community. The unions are not suited to be district or school leaders, nor should they be given leadership authority. Over the years, teacher unions have become stronger, and teachers have increased their political power. But while teachers were winning, parents and the community were losing (Baird, 1984; Friedman and Friedman, 1979). If the unions are allowed to bargain collectively about issues of policy and curriculum reform, schools will become less responsive to the community and more an agency of the unions. Responsibility for running schools should be entrusted only to those who have been given that authority by the voters. Collective bargaining must not steal from the community the right to control the education of its children.

Unfortunately, representatives of the NEA and the AFT have been trained to regard local communities with disdain and to treat school boards as the enemy. In their pursuit of hegemony over the schools, unions have been willing to ignore the interests of the community, and unionized teachers have come to disregard the needs, the aspirations, and the future of the children they teach (Braun, 1972; Brimelow and Spencer, 1993). Educational policy should not be a matter of union concern. The district, through its elected board and board-appointed administrators, is legally accountable to the public for the quality of education it provides. The unions have no such responsibility or authority, and they should defer to those who do.

Apologizing for Bad Teachers

It is ironic that unions are demanding a greater role in the reform of schools; given their record, it can be argued that unions have caused more problems than they have solved. Unions have become apologists for teachers and an obstacle to school reform. On the one hand, unions love to praise the almost magical effect that good teachers have on children's lives. On the other hand, they fail to admit that weak teachers may be a cause of many of the schools' shortcomings. Everyone familiar with public schools knows that the quality of classroom instruction is highly variable. Nestled among the great teachers, and good teachers, and the marginally adequate are those who fail to convey enthusiasm for learning, and more than a few who have neither the personal qualities nor the skill and knowledge necessary to teach children. While the good teachers whet students' appetites for academic achievement, bad teachers kill interest, leave students with enormous gaps of information, and tarnish the reputation of the profession.

Unions talk about boosting teacher morale and teacher self-esteem, but they regularly oppose merit pay for good teachers. Some districts have proposed pay-for-performances plans under which unusually successful teachers—those who produce above-average learning gains in students—would receive larger raises, whereas those who evidence less success in developing student achievement would earn lower-than-normal raises. Typically, teacher unions reject these plans, claiming that the plans are "not fair" or that the concept of a "good teacher" is too subjective to be measured (Bradley, 1990). The public believes that schools are designed to treat each child individually and to make judgments about those who should be rewarded and those who should fail. It suspects that schools would benefit if similar judgments were made about teachers. Good teachers should reap the fruits of their individual talent; bad teachers should be fired.

In recent years, the popular press has not been kind to teachers. Stories of barely literate teachers and teachers who tyrannize students force parents to recoil in horror. Although these accounts represent but a tiny fraction of the nation's teachers, they are shocking, not only because of their perversity, but because the union consistently defends poor, and even dangerous, teachers. In one case, a Chicago teacher was known to punish bright students because they demanded more attention, and this made his work more difficult. His supervisors were alerted to the problem, but he was not fired. Under union rules, the teacher was allowed to transfer to another school (Freedman, 1987). Another case involved a special education teacher in New York City who was arrested, convicted, and sent to prison for selling $7,000 worth of cocaine to a colleague. After five years of litigation and board of education expenditures of over $185,000, the teacher still has a job in the school system. He was even able to collect part of his salary while he was in prison. This case highlights the difficulty of dismissing any unionized teacher who has been awarded tenure (Dillon, 1994).

Trade unionists in education are hard put to account for the number of poor teachers in their ranks. Typically, they place the blame either on weak university programs in teacher education or on public school administrators. The sad fact remains that too many schools have teachers who are not able to do the work expected of them. Unfortunately, because of unions and tenure laws, even the poorest teachers will probably stay on the job until retirement. Left to their own devices, unions are unlikely to rid the profession of bad teachers. The job of the union is not to improve the teaching profession, but to protect teachers. Given this goal, the unions can hardly refuse to fight dismissals, even when the teacher involved is obviously incompetent. As a result, it is nearly impossible to fire a tenured teacher. It is estimated that a typical school district would have to spend between $10,000 and $50,000 in legal fees to get rid of its worst teacher (Lieberman, 1985). In New York, it takes well over a year's time and costs the schools almost $195,000 to prosecute a single teacher accused of misconduct. In 1994, some 176 tenured New York City teachers and administrators were facing charges ranging from the commission of sex crimes and theft to chronic absence. All the accused had been transferred from their positions but were drawing full salaries while awaiting hearings (Dillon, 1994).

Union opposition to culling incompetents from the classroom has forced school districts to decide whether to spend money on new books and programs or on litigation. In many states, union rules have brought administrative actions against ineffective teachers to an absolute halt (VanSciver, 1990). Unions cry for greater involvement in the restructuring of schools, but their opposition to pay-for-performance plans and their refusal to allow the dismissal of tenured but incompetent teachers cast great doubt on their potential for reform. The public would be more supportive of unions if they were as concerned about the quality of teaching as they are about protecting individual teachers.

Resisting Change

Unions and teaching do not fit together gracefully. Unions are more appropriate for heavy industry, such as auto or steel production, where all workers perform similar tasks under much the same circumstances. The net effect of poor work or lazy workers is more destructive in teaching than in factory work. One bad steel worker might make co-workers' jobs more difficult, but he or she is unlikely to hurt the industry. A bad third-grade teacher may very well harm the education of children.

Unions are educational anachronisms. They may have been necessary at one time, in the early days of public schooling, but they have become obstructionist opponents of change. Teachers should be treated individually, not collectively. Good teachers should be recognized for their professional competence and financially rewarded according to the level of their performance. Weak teachers should be helped or weeded out, and labor negotiations should not consume the energies of schoolteachers and administrators. If union contracts were limited to basic issues—wages, hours, and working conditions—school reform would not be forced to march to the lock-step cadence imposed by collective bargaining. The record of teacher unions argues against their inclusion in the design of school reform. Unions may maintain that it is only coincidence that the rise of teacher unions in this country has been accompanied by rising costs of education and declining standards of student performance. However, parents and other members of the community have every reason to be suspicious of increasing union influence on the management of schools. School management and the design of effective schools are beyond the authority and the experience of unions.

POSITION 2: TEACHER UNIONS ARE BENEFICIAL

Unions take their form and function from the school districts where their members work. Even though they are adversaries, unions are utterly dependent on school districts for meaning and purpose. At their worst, unions and school districts are two prisoners manacled together slugging it out with their free hands. At their most productive, they are self-interested partners in a joint civic venture. (Kerchner and Koppich, 1993, p. 2)

Forcing Teachers to Unionize

In the early part of this century, teachers were trained to believe that sacrifice was the essence of their profession. Teachers worked long hours; their classes might number fifty or more students; their salaries were low; and schools were often poorly heated, poorly ventilated, and unsanitary. Female teachers were not allowed to go out unescorted (except to attend church) or to frequent places where liquor was served; and in many communities, when female teachers married, they were forced to resign from their jobs. In addition to living truncated social lives, teachers were assumed to serve at the whim of school boards, without any promise of tenure or of health or retirement benefits. They were not considered worthy of participating in book selection and were excluded from deliberations about the curriculum.

As school systems developed into large bureaucratic organizations, conditions worsened for teachers. School principals became administrators. Once referred to as the "principal teacher" or the "main teacher," the head of a school became a manager who shared few of the problems of teachers and none of their perspective. Most of the new school administrators were men; most of the classroom teachers were women. Administrators regarded teachers as inferior workers who needed to be told what to do. The authority to run schools was vested in the men in the administrative offices, and that authority was assumed to be unchallengeable by the teachers. Teachers eventually came to realize that what they were being asked to give up in the name of being professional was not good for them or their students, and that through collective action schools could be made better for everyone.

Teachers in general were never eager to join unions; they were forced to do so because the culture of administrative managers was at odds with the culture of working teachers (Jessup, 1978; Murphy, 1990; Urban, 1982). But many teachers urged their colleagues to use unions and collective bargaining to improve their working conditions and give themselves a voice in the improvement of education. The following letter, typical of the calls for teachers to organize, was written in 1913:

> On the ground that teachers do the every-day work of teaching and understand the conditions necessary for better teaching, we propose the following principles for the new organizations: Teachers should have a voice and a vote in determination of educational policies. The granting of legislative opportunity to the teachers would inevitably contribute to the development of a strong professional spirit, and the intelligent use of their experience in the interest of the public. We advocate the adoption of a plan that will permit all teachers to have a share in the administration of the affairs of their own school. In no more practical way could teachers prepare themselves for training children for citizenship in democracy . . . . ("A Call to Organize," *American Teacher*, December 1912, p. 140, quoted in Eaton, 1975, pp. 13–14)

The decision to join the labor movement no doubt was a difficult one for many teachers. Teachers tend to be politically conservative, first-generation college graduates who identify with management more than with labor (Aronowitz, 1973; Rosenthal, 1969; Zeigler, 1966). Strikes are anathema to most members of teacher unions (Rauth, 1990). The fact that the union movement has succeeded in recruiting teachers speaks well for unions; that most teachers now belong to some sort of union, despite a decline in union membership in other fields and continued middle-class antipathy toward unions, is evidence of teachers' faith in them. Today, thanks to progressive labor negotiations and contracts that go well beyond wages and hours, teachers are becoming the managers, students are seen as the workers, and learning is the product (Watts and McClure, 1990; Kerchner and Koppich, 1993).

Protecting Teachers' Rights

Unions have been good for classroom teachers. The research literature indicates that unions have had a positive effect on teachers' working conditions. As a result of collective bargaining, teachers' salaries have increased, and teachers have gained protection against unreasonable treatment by management. Unlike in the preunion days, teachers cannot be dismissed simply because they consume alcohol or change their marital status. Unions have also been good for education. They have put the faculty squarely in the front ranks of the battle for better schools and better education for children. Unions have allowed faculty to be heard collectively on matters of curriculum and school policy.

Teacher unions have always received some bad press. Some of it is traditional antilabor rhetoric, and some of it is simply misinformed. No doubt you have heard that unions are to blame for bad teachers and that unions have hurt education by protecting weak teachers who deserve to be fired. This is not the case. In fact, it is mystifying when unions are blamed for weak teachers. Before teachers are awarded tenure, they must graduate from state-approved teacher education programs, convince administrators to hire them, and survive an extended probationary period, typically from three to five years. Unions play virtually no part in any of these processes. Weak teachers may make it through the system, but they do so with no help from organized labor. Teacher unions are embarrassed by poor teachers in the same way that the American Bar Association and the American Medical Association are shamed by ineffective, corrupt, or lazy members in their ranks. No responsible union wants to protect incompetent workers.

In the mid-1990s, unions in several cities initiated a process to identify weak tenured teachers and refer them for help and possible dismissal. One union leader argues that peer review—the evaluation of teachers by teachers— is an appropriate role for unions. He says that it was a traditional function of medieval guilds, the forerunners of modern unions:

> Guilds began precisely *for* the regulation of practice. Middle management union people had bought the American legal model: not to judge but to defend. This kind of unconditional love and acceptance should be expected only from one's mother—not one's union. (Adam Urbanski, quoted in Birk, 1994, p. 10)

On the other hand, without union guarantees of due process, it is likely that many good teachers would be subject to dismissal for political or personal reasons. Therefore, unions protect all teachers' rights to a fair hearing when their jobs are at stake. Unions insist on protection of the due process rights of all teachers. Teachers should not be fired because of arbitrary or capricious actions on the part of administrators or members of the board of education. Unions recognize an obligation to stand behind teachers to make sure that any dismissal is a result of sufficient, demonstrable cause, not administrative whim, retribution, or discrimination. Union support guarantees fairness in the workplace.

You may have heard someone say, "Those who are good teachers have no need for tenure, and those who have need for tenure are not good teachers." This is dangerous rhetoric. Tenure is essential for the freedom to teach, and unions are proud to support teachers' rights to tenure. Without the academic freedom guaranteed by tenure, teaching would be too chancy for all but the independently wealthy or the hopelessly foolish. Tenure is among the more misunderstood aspects of teaching. It is not designed to provide teachers with a sinecure, a lifetime job free from the threat of dismissal. Tenured teachers can be fired for incompetence, but they cannot be dismissed for being critical of school policy or for using an instructional approach that the principal does not like. Tenure is essential to freedom of thought and action. It guarantees that teachers can use appropriate teaching methods and take reasonable academic positions in classrooms without fear of administrative reprisals. Tenure is the cornerstone of a merit system of employment. The unions' support of tenure helps to staff the nation's classrooms with practitioners secure in the knowledge that they are free to teach, governed by the norms of academic responsibility and unfettered by political constraints. It also assures the public that schools will remain forums dedicated to democratic processes and open inquiry.

Extending Workplace Democracy

Most school boards now accept the teachers' right to bargain over working conditions, but many remain unconvinced of the legitimacy of labor's voice in policy issues and matters of school reform. Some administrators argue that the traditional roles of school employees and employers must be preserved. Superintendents and principals should be the executives and managers, and teachers should be the workers; policymaking is the rightful province of the former and implementation is the only job for the latter. Administrators claim that policy should not be subject to the art of compromise, the democratic give-and-take of collective bargaining. Policymaking, they say, is not for teachers.

This is another flawed argument. Even if it were desirable to separate issues of policy from the conditions of teachers' work, it is not possible to do so. The concerns of teachers extend far beyond hours and wages. Classroom teachers are directly affected by a broad range of educational policy decisions. Restricting collective bargaining to bread-and-butter issues of working conditions, wages, and hours is naive to the ways in which schools function. Issues of school policy, from the adoption of a new basal series to the recruitment of a new building principal, influence every teacher's work. How could a teacher's work fail to be influenced by changes in the materials he or she uses in class? Textbooks, curriculum packages, the assessment of students, the evaluation of teachers, and school disciplinary policies all affect the daily lives of teachers.

Policies that regulate the school's organization are central to teaching and must be considered as the rightful province of collective negotiations. The education of children will be better served when teachers are given a voice in shaping policy and in making decisions about curriculum and personnel (Maeroff, 1988).

Unions have insisted that teachers be heard regarding the reform of schooling, but in doing so they are not depriving administrators of their authority. They are simply, in the best democratic sense, extending decision making to a broader constituency. Research suggests that workplace democracy has positive payoffs for schools. Collective bargaining about policy issues appears to produce a greater sense of professional efficacy in teachers; they feel better about their jobs, and they use their new authority to give more of themselves to the school (Johnson, 1988; Tuthill, 1990).

Unions' Stake in Education Reform

Unions have opened the door to teacher decision making, and teachers have used this right to join with management in the development of better schools. In education, labor and management are not necessarily adversaries; being pro-union does not automatically make teachers the enemies of administrators. No doubt, workers and management will always have separate perspectives, but these differences in outlook can be resolved through a negotiated contract. The adversarial roles of union and management are making way for more cooperative reform efforts that can better serve students.

Unions have always recognized their role in school reform, and they continue to insist that teachers be given a collective voice in bringing about better schooling. Teachers' direct daily contact with students provides them with powerful data about which policies and programs work and which ones do not. Teachers know what should be done to improve schooling, and their unions want them to use their knowledge to solve school problems. Affiliates of the NEA and the AFT have been active in involving teachers in school reform movements (Rauth, 1990; Watts and McClure, 1990; Kerchner and Koppich, 1993). Today's teachers demand more than a voice in school policies; they want a contract that guarantees that their voices will be heeded. One union contract, for example, requires each department or school in the district to

> develop a process for school improvement that truly engages teachers . . . in defining problems and opportunities, brainstorming alternatives, gathering and analyzing data, proposing and evaluating solutions, and making decisions with respect to the design and delivery of the instruction program in that school or department. (From the 1989–1992 contract negotiated between the Bellevue [Washington] Education Association and the Bellevue School District, quoted in Watts and McClure, 1990, p. 769)

Unions also realize that unless teaching becomes a better job, it will be increasingly difficult to keep good teachers in the classroom. A sad fact of teaching is that too often the best teachers leave the field after only a few years. Lured by more lucrative careers or seduced into administration, where they can effect change while being paid more, many of the most able teachers look for ways out of the classroom soon after landing their first teaching jobs.

The Rochester, New York, teacher union has been trying to keep teachers in the classroom by granting them more authority to run the schools. The union-conceived "career ladder plan" is designed to tap the knowledge of the best teachers. Senior teachers with at least ten years of teaching experience and five years in the district assume leadership functions in the school that combine administrative work with classroom instruction. The plan calls for selected teachers to spend half their time working in administrative or supervisory capacities and the other half teaching in the classroom. Their out-of-classroom work includes serving as mentors for new teachers and working as curriculum developers and consultants in such specialty areas as math, reading, and science. For their additional responsibility, and their eleven-month contracts, these teachers receive a 20 percent pay differential based on their regular salary. The Rochester teacher union has made it clear that it wants teachers to work in a decision-making capacity in the schools. Teachers are no longer willing to be merely advisors. They will assume greater responsibility, but they want greater authority and a salary structure that reflect their new role in schools. By the early 1990s, some Rochester teachers were earning as much as $70,000 a year, more than twice the national average.

The union model is designed to recognize exceptional teaching skills honed by years of experience. The most experienced teachers, like the most able surgeons and attorneys, not only should be the best paid, but they should also be glad to take on the most challenging cases. The president of the Rochester union wants his lead teachers to assume a "Clint Eastwood" attitude. They should say, "I'm a good teacher. I've seen it all. Give me any student or program that is the toughest challenge, and if I can't do it, it can't be done." Such attitudes put teachers where they belong: designing policy for, and participating in, the fight for better schooling. Unions and unionized teachers are the keys to the future of education. In the past, unions have used their collective bargaining power to improve schools and to make teaching a better job. Unions are eager to continue the education reform agenda; they want to use their power to improve the quality of teaching and learning.

For Discussion

1. Assume that you are a tenured teacher attending a meeting with other teachers from your school district to decide whether or not to unionize. What arguments could you make to convince your colleagues to join a union? What arguments could you make to discourage them from joining a union?
2. Some authors make the distinction between older "industrial-style teacher unionism" and a new style of union, referred to as a "union of professionals." Examine the contrasting sets of union mottos. Is it clear how they reflect a change in the union position concerning work in schools? Can you add other sets of contrasting mottos?

Industrial-Style Unionism	Union of Professionals
a. "Boards make policy, managers manage, teachers teach."	"All of us are smarter than any of us."
b. "It's us versus them."	"If you don't look good, we don't look good."
c. "Any grievance is right."	"The purpose of the union is not to defend its least competent members."

(Kerchner and Koppich, 1993, p. 10)

3. The laws of many nations give teachers the right to strike. Strikes by teachers are legal, for example, in Australia, Canada, France, Germany, Greece, Israel, Italy, Mexico, and Sweden. However, in the United States, strikes by public employees are legal in only four states (Hawaii, Montana, Oregon, and Pennsylvania). In all other states, strikes by public employees, including teachers, are illegal (Shanker, 1992, p. 287).

   The strike is undeniably labor's most powerful weapon. What arguments can you offer to support the right of teachers to strike? What arguments would you use to deny teachers the right to strike?

4. In Japan, the *Nikkyoso* (Japan Teachers Union) enjoys general support from teachers, and plays a significant role in decisions involving education policy matters and bread-and-butter job issues. Although the union takes strong positions, it does not use confrontational tactics. The Japanese traditionally dislike confrontation, preferring instead to base decisions on consensual agreements between labor and management. The writings of Prince Shotuku Taishi (604 A.D.) reflect the cultural traditions of harmony and shared decision making.

   Decisions on important matters should not be made by one person alone. They should be discussed with many. But small matters are of less consequence. It is unnecessary to consult a number of people. It is only in the case of weighty affairs, when there is a suspicion that may miscarry, that one should arrange matters in concert with others, so as to arrive at the right conclusion.

   Harmony is to be valued, and an avoidance of wanton opposition to be honored . . . . When those high above are harmonious and those below friendly, and there is concord in the discussion of business, right views of things gain acceptance. Then what is there which cannot be accomplished?*

   Compare the cultural values reflected in these quotes with American values concerning leadership and followership in the workplace. Do you think shared harmonious decision making could become part of the culture of American schools? What advantages or disadvantages would it offer?

References

Aronowitz, S. (1973). *False Promises: The Shaping of American Working Class Consciousness.* New York: McGraw-Hill.

*Quoted in B. Duke (1986). *The Japanese School: Lessons for Industrial America.* New York: Praeger, pp. 30–32.

Baird, C. W. (1984). *Opportunity or Privilege: Labor Legislation in America.* Bowling Green, OH: Social Philosophy and Policy Center.

Birk, L. (1994). "Intervention: A Few Teachers' Unions Take the Lead in Policing their Own." *The Harvard Education Letter,* November/December, p. 10.

Bradley, A. (1990). "Rochester Teachers Reject 'Accountability' Contract." *Education Week,* October 3, p. 4.

―――. (1991). "Administrators in Los Angeles Form a Bargaining Unit." *Education Week,* March 20, p. 1, 16.

Braun, R. J. (1972). *Teachers and Power: The Story of the American Federation of Teachers.* New York: Simon & Schuster.

Brimelow, P., and Spencer, L. (1993). "The National Extortion Association." *Forbes* **151,** 7, 72–84.

Dillon, S. (1994). "Teacher Tenure: Rights vs. Discipline." *The New York Times,* June 28, pp. 1, A15.

Eaton, W. E. (1975). *The American Federation of Teachers, 1916–1961: A History of the Movement.* Carbondale: Southern Illinois University Press.

Eberts, R. W., and Stone, J. A. (1984). *The Effects of Collective Bargaining on American Education.* Lexington, MA: Heath.

Freedman, M. (1987). "Difficulty of Firing Bad Teachers: Continuing Embarrassment for Schools." In *ENS Special Report.* Employers Negotiating Service, May 20.

Friedman, M., and Friedman, R. (1979). *Free to Choose.* New York: Harcourt Brace Jovanovich.

Jessup, D. K. (1978). "Teacher Unionization: A Reassessment of Rank and File Education." *Sociology of Education* **51,** 44–55.

Johnson, S. M. (1988). "Unionism and Collective Bargaining in the Public Schools." In *Handbook of Research on Educational Administration,* edited by N. J. Boyan. New York: Longman.

Kerchner, C. T. (1986). "Union-Made Teaching: Effects of Labor Relations." In *Review of Research in Education, Vol. 13,* edited by E. Z. Rothkopf. Washington, DC: American Educational Research Association.

―――, and Koppich, J. E. (1993). *A Union of Professionals: Labor Relations and Educational Reform.* New York: Teachers College Press.

Lieberman, M. (1985). "Teacher Unions and Educational Quality: Folklore by Finn." *Phi Delta Kappan.* **66,** 341–343.

―――, and Moscow, M. H. (1966). *Collective Negotiations for Teachers: An Approach to School Administration.* Chicago: Rand McNally.

Maeroff, G. I. (1988). *The Empowerment of Teachers: Overcoming the Crisis of Confidence.* New York: Teachers College Press.

Murphy, M. (1990). *Blackboard Unions: the AFT and the NEA, 1900–1980.* Ithaca, NY: Cornell University Press.

Rauth, M. (1990). "Exploring Heresy in Collective Bargaining and School Restructuring." *Phi Delta Kappan* **71,** 781–784.

Richardson, J. (1994). "Two Indiana Suits Put Teachers and Union at Odds." *Education Week* **14,** 1, 10.

Rosenthal, A. (1969). *Pedagogues and Power: Teacher Groups in School Politics.* Syracuse, NY: Syracuse University Press.

Shanker, A. (1992). "United States of America." In *Labor Relations in Education, An International Perspective,* edited by B. S. Cooper. Westport, CT: Greenwood Press.

Stern, D. (1986). "Compensation for Teachers." In *Review of Research in Education,* edited by E. Z. Rothkopf. Washington, DC: American Education Research Association.

Streshly, W. A., and DeMitchell, T. A. (1994). *Teacher Unions and TQE: Building Quality Labor Relations.* Thousand Oaks, CA: Corwin.

Tuthill, D. (1990). "Expanding the Union Contract: One Teacher's Perspective." *Phi Delta Kappan* **71,** 775–780.

Urban, W. J. (1982). *Why Teachers Organized.* Detroit: Wayne State University Press.

VanSciver, J. H. (1990). "Teacher Dismissals." *Phi Delta Kappan* **72,** 318–319.

Watts, G. D., and McClure, R. (1990). "Expanding the Contract to Revolutionize School Reform." *Phi Delta Kappan* **71,** 765–774.

Zeigler, H. (1966). *The Political World of the High School Teacher.* Eugene OR: University of Oregon Press.

CHAPTER SIXTEEN

Privatization of Schools: Boon or Bane

POSITION 1: PUBLIC SCHOOLS SHOULD BE PRIVATIZED

One of the most interesting innovations sweeping across the world in the 1990s is the idea of privatization. Privatization, the process by which public provision of services is changed to the private sector, will also be the movement of the twenty-first century. This concept is consistent with the tradition and evolution of market-based economics and private enterprise that have made the United States a model for other nations. There is now worldwide recognition of private enterprise as the key vehicle for improving the life of citizens while becoming more efficient with available funds and resources. The resounding collapse of the Soviet Union illustrated defects in economic structures that depend on governmental organization and operation. Now there is a race to see which nation will provide leadership in private development.

In a global environment that is increasingly competitive, the United States must maintain its leadership. To continue expensive and plodding public services in the face of increasingly private operations throughout the rest of the industrialized world puts us at a severe disadvantage. The nation deserves better. Further, the burden borne by taxpayers as a result of inefficient governmental management of services has become excessive while actual service falls. Privatization of public services offers significant benefits in worldwide competition, including lower taxes, customer-based service, and greater efficiency.

Schools are basic to the national interest and international competition. America's leadership depends on top-quality, well-educated people, that is, successful students from achievement-driven schools. The talents and vision of such people are limited by cookie-cutter schools that offer less than the most current and efficient approaches to education. The private sector of the American economy, where survival demands innovation and efficiency, offers an avenue for reshaping and restructuring American schools for the global competition of the twenty-first century. This idea has been recognized at the highest levels.

Privatization Is in America's Interest

The President's Commission on Privatization was established by President Reagan to explore the separation between public and private delivery of goods and services and to recommend which public services could be transferred to the private sector. The commission's report, *Privatization: Toward more Effective Government* (1988), expressed a concern about government-operated services:

> The American people have often complained of the intrusiveness of federal programs, of inadequate performance, and of excessive expenditure . . . government should consider turning to the creative talents and ingenuity in the private sector to provide, whenever possible and appropriate, better answers to present and future challenges. (p. xi)

The report identified the essential ways to privatize as (1) selling off government assets, (2) contracting work out to private companies, and (3) giving vouchers to purchase private services. In a long and well-documented presentation that used testimony from some of America's most eminent scholars, the commission noted its primary interest in "the American consumer who is in need . . . of education; of loans for school, home, farm, or business; of transportation; of health care; of other social services" (p. xi). Obviously, members of the commission considered education one of the most significant public services, and one seriously in need of improvement.

With regard to education, the commission found that:

> The recent record of educational achievement has fallen far short of the basic goals that Americans set for their schools. . . . Despite substantial public spending on education—at all levels of government—the nation's schools were not producing commensurate results—educational report cards have turned the 1980s into a decade of dissatisfaction with schools. (*Privatization*, 1988, p. 85)

The commission's report showed that taxpayer spending on public schools doubled during the prior two decades, but educational results have been far less than would be expected from that level of public financial support. For comparison, expenditures per student in private education are about two-thirds the per-student costs of public education. Although the nation spends heavily on public schools, average SAT test scores declined in the 1980s. These scores have only haltingly started to increase, and a massive infusion of tax dollars over the past decades has not been shown to have any effect on them. The National Assessment of Educational Progress (NAEP) and other tests of basic skills also show poor performance by American students. In the international arena, comparative studies of test scores show that U.S. students rank at the bottom among industrialized democracies (Finn, 1995; Mandel, 1995). Public schools are not getting any better by following the patterns of the past. Pumping more taxpayer money into those schools is not likely to alter their long-term deficiencies. Emily Feistritzer (1987) showed several years ago that there is no apparent correlation between education spending and student achievement. At no additional cost, privatization can improve schools, teacher motivation, and student learning.

Clearly, the decline in the standards of American education at the same time that school costs were rapidly increasing was of great concern to the commission. Public schooling is one of the areas that could be improved by the application of expertise in management, cost control, and performance. Schools are a public service that could be helped by drawing on the creative talents of the private sector.

The most significant commission recommendations for reforming education involve providing diversity in school choice, giving parents vouchers to be used at private schools, and allowing private schools to participate in other federal programs. While these are important ideas and should be further pursued, they may be insufficient to stem the obvious decline in public education. Although the commission was accurate in its assessment of problems in public schools and its determination that significant change was needed, it did not go far enough in its recommendations for privatizing schools. There are many reasons to seriously question the continuation of public education as it is has been organized and operated (Geiger, 1995).

Further Reasons for the Privatization of American Public Schools

There is no doubt that schools exert great influence on America's future and the nation's role in the global marketplace. International competition requires the United States to remain on the cutting edge of innovation or suffer future decline. If the public schools, as now constituted, are not up to the task, we need to find other ways to continue to improve America's status. This is one strong reason to move toward privatization of the schools. Beyond the obvious necessity of assuring America's place as a world leader and correcting long-term performance problems in public education, there are at least three other reasons that privatization of schools is an idea whose time has come.

1. Improving Schools for Our Children

The most important reason to involve private enterprise in schools is our children. Our primary resource deserves the best schools we can provide. Well-run schools, where success is the motivating purpose, are appreciated by both students and parents. When educational results make us ashamed of our schools, children and parents are understandably reluctant to support or take pleasure in them. The faceless bureaucracy created for government-operated schools not only overwhelms local budgets, but it also does not respond to complaints. Private enterprise could not survive with that approach; its success is linked to increasing efficiency and customer satisfaction.

Privatization will also increase accountability, making school staffs responsible for meeting performance standards for the benefit of children. Accountability, a keystone of private enterprise, offers the means to clearly identify problems and to reward performance in schools. Instead of weak and vague educational jargon that hides poor school practice, private enterprise sets specific goals and measures the performance of schools in meeting them. Schools that work will be rewarded; those that don't work will be changed or closed.

The Edison Project, an innovative approach to school privatization, contracts with public schools to operate them without an increase in costs, but with better results and, in addition, makes a profit. The Edison purposes are clear and direct: "to offer the best education in the world," "to welcome all students," and "to operate at an affordable price" ("An Invitation to Public School Partnership: Executive Summary," the Edison Project, undated). This puts the focus on student achievement. The enterprise includes strict performance conditions in its contracts, which can be terminated on short notice if the results are not satisfactory. What public school operation gives the public the same performance contract? Educational Alternatives Inc. (EAI), the other major private contractor for public school operations, also puts performance conditions in its contracts and focuses on improving student work.

2. Breaking the Public School Monopoly

A second reason for privatizing schools is to balance the monopoly that public education has had in the United States. This will offer democratic choices to parents who are concerned about the education of their children but have had to send them to a state-specified school. Choice of schools is certainly in the best interest of children and their parents, but it also creates a condition where schools have to be competitive in order to attract students and the financial support needed.

The public schools have established a monopoly over taxpayer-supported education in the United States. Law professor John Coons (1987) describes the U.S. education system as a "state-run monopoly" rather than as a system of public schools. He argues that these state-run schools strip families of the authority to choose their children's schools by limiting them to local public school boundaries. Public schools have no competition, and their access to public funds to educate children is legally protected. The comparatively few private and parochial schools in the nation are currently prohibited from receiving taxpayer money. As a result, they serve different and more selective audiences than do their public counterparts; they don't compete for the taxpayer dollar. Without competition, the public schools have developed into self-protective havens where performance is not a high priority.

The public schools have been a monopoly for far too long, and they suffer the results of lack of competition. They have institutional hardening of the arteries, bloated and inefficient operations, and slow bureaucratic response to public concerns. These schools have little reason to provide better public service, increase their efficiency, require higher standards, or eliminate layers of bureaucracy. Privatization offers the means to bring customer satisfaction and state-of-the-art efficiency to such schools, without the self-serving bureaucracy. Of course, the public schools do not welcome the idea of privatization, and their unions will fight it at all costs (Shanker, 1994a, 1994b).

3. Increasing Productivity

Third, privatizing will increase productivity in the public schools, a place where productivity has not changed for a century. In most public school districts, the schools are operated much the same as they were when our grand-parents were students. Private industry could not operate in this manner without suffering financial collapse. Expensive, labor-intensive public schools with inflated administrations sap local and state finances. Improvements in technology and communications have revolutionized American business and provided manifold increases in productivity, but there has been virtually no change in the public schools. Computers and other forms of high technology speed up all forms of industry, but the schools continue to take the same costly approach as before. Improved productivity is necessary in the modern world; no nation can afford the luxury of wasting time and resources. Improved productivity is consistent with the best thinking in economics and the best use of public money.

Public schools exemplify wasteful public agencies where productivity has declined while costs have escalated. In high-cost, high-maintenance buildings, students attend classes about six hours a day for about one-half of the calendar year. Teachers still teach about twenty-five students per hour in separate classrooms using multiple copies of costly printed textbooks, similar to the way in which teachers taught at the beginning of the twentieth century. Those teachers, no matter how good or bad they are, are paid according to a standard scale, earning from about $25,000 to $60,000 per year for only nine months' employment. The one-size-fits-all teacher pay scale depends on seniority, not on how well each teacher teaches or how well students learn. Excellent teachers are paid the same as poor teachers, just because they have the same seniority.

It is a lock-step system, out of touch with contemporary business management. The current management of schools follows an archaic and costly pattern, under regulations influenced by the education establishment early in this century. There are many small schools with separate administrations and budgets for providing essentially the same services. New Jersey, for example, has more than 600 separate school districts. In some states, even tiny schools are mandated to employ a school principal, and often a superintendent and other staff. In large districts, there are multiple, well-paid school administrative officers who never teach a student and who seldom visit the district's schools. The organizational structures of schools are more similar to those of early inefficient factories than they are to the structures of modern corporations.

Public schools are managed through an old-fashioned system that relies on politics to get more tax money, elaborate and expensive lobbying efforts in state legislatures to improve teacher salaries and keep teacher unions in power, and coziness with state education agencies to maintain the status quo. Increasing state regulation only serves to further bloat school administrations. And all this is practiced without being required to give full accountability. The failings of public schools are revealed in the low test scores of American students as compared with those of other nations, in the discourteous behavior of students, and in low public esteem.

The schools are mired in bureaucracy and self-protective traditional thinking. They are not efficient institutions. Instead of attempting to keep costs down while improving quality, a standard that business sets, schools simply obtain increased tax funds without improved productivity. They continue to be shelters for inefficient public employment.

There are numerous places to increase productivity in this antiquated system of education. The school day and school year are expensive links to America's agricultural past. Most industrialized nations keep students in school for longer days and for more days of the year, which is part of the reason why we have not done well in student achievement. The traditional form of small-group instruction, with one well-paid teacher for each class of twenty-five students, does not account for striking advances in communication technology or flexible management. It increases school staff, but does not add to student learning. Interactive computers linked with major libraries and scholars would use excellent but scarce resources better. The lack of salary recognition for teachers who provide better performance limits their motivation to seek more innovative and efficient ways to prepare students. Similarly, administrators with make-work jobs or infrequent contact with the direct work of the schools are not likely to be enthusiastic about improving their productivity. The inertia of low productivity is built into the current public schools; private enterprise offers a fresh approach.

What Can Privatization Provide for Schools?

Any market-driven enterprise must be capable of flexibility and diversity to be able to compete well. This idea applies to schools as well. There are a variety of ways that privatization can be established in the public schools. Private operation of schools, when undertaken in any of a number of structures, can shift easily to meet changing conditions.

In complete privatization, a private organization would take charge of the schooling operation, under rigorous contracts with the local board of education to guarantee performance or face dismissal. Included in complete privatization would be such activities as:

Managing the school(s)

Hiring, organizing, and evaluating the teaching and support staff

Developing the curriculum and purchasing teaching materials

Providing in-service assistance to teachers

Evaluating student learning

Communicating with parents and the community

Setting up the school's physical plant and facilities

Providing custodial and ancillary maintenance

Arranging for health and food services

Accounting for the budget and school financing

The public schools are complex organizations with many areas in which privatization could make operations more efficient and successful. In public–private partnerships, the school board hires private managers to run the public schools under five-year contracts that include specified performance standards and provision for the board to fire the managers with ninety days' notice. Although complete privatization offers some distinct advantages for districts to hold private managers responsible and accountable for student learning, it is possible to identify many segments of current school operations that could be handled well by private contract in ways that would benefit the students and the taxpayers.

Some public schools now contract for selected services that are too costly or too cumbersome to handle under public control. Public school boards have been the providers of education since the beginning of the American republic, but now they are becoming the purchasers of educational services provided by private enterprise. Many school districts have contracted for bus services for years. Contracts for major building repair and maintenance have also been common. Some districts contract with computer corporations for payroll and accounting services. Others have found that contracting with popular fast-food companies, such as McDonalds, to provide school lunch service offers many benefits in that they are more cost-effective, and more acceptable to students, and sometimes their food is more nutritious than the standard school-cafeteria food.

Private contracts for specific services, from the provision of food to top management, have proved their value to students, school officials, and taxpayers. Piecemeal privatization of school services has been working well in many schools. Now, private operation of individual schools, and even entire city school districts, is developing.

Charter school programs, under which a state government grants specific charters to groups to organize or take over schools, are now legal in at least eleven states. The Massachusetts charter school law allows profit-making companies to apply for charters. The Edison Project, developed by business entrepreneur Chris Whittle, recently won three charters to operate public schools in Massachusetts as part of its plan to establish up to 200 public, but for-profit, schools nationwide. Whittle's Channel One, the privately sponsored television channel for schools, has been operating successfully in a number of school districts as another example of the privatization of schools.

Privatizing the Schools: An Example

There are many examples of privatizing parts of school operations, such as custodial, bus, or cafeteria service. There are also examples of privatization of individual schools, such as charter schools and the contracts given to EAI, a private firm headquartered in Minneapolis, to operate individual schools in Baltimore and in southern Florida. But no city had completely privatized its schools until Hartford, Connecticut, took that step in 1994.

Hartford has experienced the problems common to many cities, including crime, traffic, drugs, and middle-class flight. One of the poorest cities in the wealthy state of Connecticut, it operates under the fiscal restraints characteristic of urban areas. But with a school budget of about $200 million annually, about half of which comes from the state, Hartford can afford to spend about $9,000 per student each year for public education, as compared with a national public school average of about $6,000 per student. Even so, students in the Hartford schools score among the lowest in the state on standardized tests and have a dropout rate that is among the highest in the state. Almost three-quarters of fourth-grade students need remedial help in basic subjects. Less than half of the ninth-grade students stay in school long enough to graduate. And all this occurred, despite the large amount spent per pupil and the fact that Hartford teacher salaries, averaging over $52,000 per year, are among the highest in the state and the nation.

Obviously, school costs and student results were highly inconsistent. These school problems had extended over a decade, during which a variety of attempts at reform had come and gone. Finally, in October 1994, the Hartford public school system was privatized through a contract with EAI. *Education Week* (1994) reported that this contract was the first in America to "entrust all aspects of a school system's operations, including its budget, to a private firm" (p. 14).

The Hartford school system's problems, its size, and its diverse population offered an excellent opportunity to show what privatization of schools could do. It may take several years before we can adequately judge the Hartford experiment, but it is remarkable as the first of its kind and represents one of myriad possible ways to approach the privatization of schools.

The Privatization Movement: A Global Context

Schools are not the only public agency that could be improved by privatization. In fact, the worldwide privatization movement is already in progress, rapidly improving services in many other agencies, such as public transportation and communication. Schools are an important, but later developing, part of this movement, and the effort to privatize them should be viewed in the larger context.

The global political economy has changed since the end of the cold war, as there is increasing recognition of the values inherent in free market private enterprise. Privatization is a concept in keeping with the demonstration that communism and socialism are defective political systems. Communism robs people of their individuality and socialism robs them of their personal motivation. The former communist and socialist nations of the old Soviet bloc realize that privatization of wasteful and bureaucratic state-owned industries is the only way to improve their economies and the lives of their people.

As the Soviet Union collapsed in the 1980s, Russian and other former communist governments tried to embrace capitalistic economics by replacing public ownership with privately held and operated businesses. This experiment has been slow and difficult because of the many years of communist rule and the serious economic decline caused by state socialism policies. Economic analyses (Earle, Frydman, and Rapaczynski, 1993; van Brabant, 1992; Vickers and Yarrow, 1991) show the various difficulties encountered in such nations as

Hungary, Poland, Czechoslovakia, and Russia in their massive effort to restructure a failed system, but economists generally recognize the need to privatize in order to compete in the global market. Earle, Frydman, and Rapaczynski, for example, note:

> After decades of experience with malfunctioning command economies and unsuccessful attempts to improve their performance through moderate "market socialist" reforms, the countries of Eastern Europe and the former Soviet Union are struggling to radically transform their economic systems. (p. 1)

In addition, members of Russia's old ruling Communist Party have undermined and attempted to destabilize the shift toward capitalism. If the Russian people can persist in their short-term sacrifices, they will be far better off than they were under communism. Had Russia pursued more complete privatization more quickly, it would now be stronger and more economically competitive. In 1990, formerly communist East Germany had almost 14,000 state-owned businesses, and just four years later, the number was fewer than 150 (Protzman, 1994b). Private enterprise and marketplace competition are replacing inefficient government-controlled business enterprises.

Other nations are engaging in massive privatization of publicly owned industries. Several South American countries are privatizing, among others, telephone companies and airlines, as well as mineral development. Great Britain, suffering under Labour Party governments and socialistic economics for several decades, more recently privatized many of the industries that had been publicly owned and operated. The British economy has improved significantly. Privatization is an idea whose time has come for industries in many nations.

The competition that is a hallmark of private enterprise requires efficient operation and consumer satisfaction—two elements that are lacking in government monopolies. Under privatization, it is possible to maintain and improve public services while cutting taxes. In addition, private enterprise is built on the human desire to succeed and to get credit for it. It is a system that motivates people to achieve more and rewards those who show improved work. It is no wonder that the process of privatization is sweeping the world, creating increased global competition.

The key to continued world leadership is constantly to search for better ways to do things. We should not be content with old structures and the myths that support them, if those structures are no longer efficient. Just as an old car must be replaced when it costs more to repair it than it is worth, some social agencies must be reviewed to see if they are as efficient as possible alternatives. It may be romantic to keep an old car, but it may not be wise economically. Similarly, public agencies should be looked at regularly in terms of their efficiency and effectiveness.

Revitalizing the Public Sector: Improving Schools

Privatization is a valid idea for any public sector enterprises that have become stagnant. The purpose of public agencies is to provide needed services where private enterprise has been unable to do so. That historical concept does not mean that public agencies, once established, must always be continued as such. The standard against which we must measure all public enterprises is whether the quality of service they afford is the best we can get for the price we pay as taxpayers. If public agencies don't measure up against what could be accomplished in the private sector, they should be replaced. That is the essence of privatization. Public agencies outlive their purposes and become an inefficient drain on public funds if they are not well monitored. They become complacent and bloated, protected from the marketplace.

Denis Doyle (1994), a senior fellow at the Hudson Institute, argues:

> While it is the business of the public to provide public service, the question before us should be, Does government need to own and operate the means of production to see that the service is provided wisely and well? To which our answer must be, "Only rarely and in special circumstances." (p. 130)

Doyle submits that the police department and currency issuance must be kept in public hands, but construction of public roads, buildings, and bridges already is performed mainly by private contractors, as is true with trash collection and maintenance in many cities. Further, contracting out for services is just good business for many public agencies. In particular, Doyle singles out public schools as places where entrepreneurship clearly is needed to provide innovation and confront conventional ways that have been too unproductive and conformist. He points out that "the uniformity of the school system, once thought to be a virtue, is clearly a liability in the modern era" (p. 129).

Public schools are key examples of a public agency that deserves constant critical review for the quality of its service to the society and its public costs. The schools consume more taxes than any other agency in local communities, and they also account for the largest part of state budgets. That favored financial position should have made American schools the best in the world, but we all know such is not the case. The evidence shows that public schools spend increasing amounts of taxpayer money while becoming more and more mediocre. This is a downward spiral whose direction must be reversed. Privatizing schools is one strong alternative to the spend-and-decline model we have seen in education during the latter half of the twentieth century.

Historically, it could be argued, the public schools made a contribution to the development of the nation by providing access to education for many people and offering basic literacy and Americanization to immigrant children. There is certainly good reason to continue to provide mass education for all students in this modern and globally competitive age, but there is no reason that such schools must be owned and operated by the government. The government school is an anachronism of a bygone period, held over because of romantic ideas about tradition. It is one holdover we will look back on one day and wonder why it lasted so long and cost so much to maintain. Government schools have come to represent high cost, low efficiency, and bureaucratic layering. It is time to shake up the bureaucrats and consider innovative ways to improve our schools at less cost. Privatization offers that to schooling.

POSITION 2: PUBLIC SCHOOLS SHOULD BE PUBLIC

There is a strange notion expressed in newspapers and business magazines that private operation of public services is superior to public operation. That notion, widely supported in the corporation-oriented mass media, suggests that greed offers more to a society than does social responsibility. Inherent in the privatization concept is the presumption that if something makes a profit, it must be good for us. This encourages privateering more than it does public good.

Now there is a call to privatize the public schools. That call, a siren song that advertises lower costs and better test scores, shifts attention away from the fundamental social purposes of public education in a democracy. These basic purposes, however, must be the centerpoint of any substantial debate over privatization. Such purposes serve as appropriate criteria against which the public and private operation of schools can be measured. The focus of the debate should be to determine whether public or private control is more likely to move us toward fulfilling those purposes. There is, unfortunately, a lack of long-range social perspective in the pressure to privatize schools (Hunter and Brown, 1995).

There is also a lack of balanced treatment of each side in the call to privatize schools for the shortsighted goals of attaining higher test scores and saving money. The call magnifies problems that have confronted public schools for more than a century, while it hides the significant and historical defects of private enterprise. Public schools have been subjected to a relentlessly negative campaign during the past decade, despite a tradition of service and good work in difficult social and financial conditions. Private enterprise, however, enjoys a positive reputation generally, despite its history of high cost and low ethics, the cavalier treatment of employees and the public, and declarations of bankruptcy when in trouble. These points are not well presented in the public discourse on privatization. Much of the debate over the privatization of public schools revolves around shallow advertising that capitalizes on negative images of public schools, unsupported claims of cost savings, and a paternalistic aura that corporations know best. To address the lacks in long-range perspective and balance in treatment, we present two major points: (1) public schools serve significant public purposes, and (2) privatization operates under a number of myths that hide its unpleasant history and characteristics. The conclusion, that public schools must not be sacrificed to private profiteering, follows.

The rush to privatization demands serious questioning of rationales, practices, and potentials. In certain situations and under strict public regulation, it may be reasonable to provide some aspects of public services, such as food service in school lunchrooms, through private contracts. But wholesale privatizing is an extremely hazardous approach to dealing with public services. In areas as important to the future of the society as education, privatizing may destroy the soul of democratic life.

Privatizing and the Democratic Purpose of Public Education

To be self-governing, a democracy requires a well-informed, active, and free population. The primary ideals of democracy in the United States include improvements in justice, equality, and freedom. Within those high social ideals, the overriding purpose of public education is to prepare students for active and knowledgeable participation in society. In schools, student preparation involves the development of language facility, social knowledge, ethical conduct, and sound critical thinking—all in a context of the accumulated wisdom of the arts and sciences. Standardized test scores, of course, reveal relatively little about this significant curriculum or the social purposes served by public schools. Further, these instructional topics, and the related extracurricular life of the school, are baseless without the root purpose of improving civilization by a focus on justice, equality, and freedom. To lose sight of that grand democratic ideal by diverting attention to trimming costs and raising test scores is to undercut the fabric of American society.

This relationship between democratic society and the need for publicly operated schools has been widely recognized throughout history. Aristotle, the first western political philosopher, clearly recognized the necessity to provide schooling for all citizens in order to preserve a democracy (*The Politics*, 1988). Jefferson (1939) understood the close relation between a democracy's requirement for knowledgeable citizens and common schooling. Among the most compelling statements for public education in a democratic society is John Dewey's *Democracy and Education* (1916). In recent years, leading political theorists have restated the significance of public education to democracy (Gutmann, 1987).

The civilizing goals of improving justice, equality, and freedom are central to the idea of public school, but not to private enterprise. Clearly, we have a long way to go in public education to meet these high standards; minorities and women have not had equal opportunities or freedom in schools. But we are improving significantly in this area, and we continue to pursue those goals in public education. Privatizing, with its attendant emphasis on cutting costs and improving test scores, is less likely to expand opportunities in school for the weakest or most disadvantaged. When you take seriously the need to educate the whole society, and not merely the elite, you improve the society, but you may not increase average test scores or cut the school budget.

In addition to strong efforts in public schools to meet social obligations to improve justice and equality, there is a necessary condition of freedom of inquiry to fulfill the claim of democracy. Education for knowledgeable self-governance liberates us from ignorance, including the ignorance intended by propaganda and censorship. Public education for all citizens, then, requires student and teacher freedom of inquiry and practice in critical thinking about social problems. But free, critical study of social problems may not be a goal of corporation-operated schools. The open examination of controversial topics, necessary in democratic society, may conflict with corporate agendas and an ethos in which business knows best.

Not only has the common schools tradition in the United States been a keystone of democratic society by offering individuals the opportunity to develop skills and knowledge to be self-governing, but the schools have also provided a community-centered service responsible to that community in a variety of ways. Privatization threatens that tradition. Dayton and Glickman (1994) pointed clearly to one aspect of the threat:

> A fundamental problem with the privatization movement is that it views public education as merely another individual entitlement and ignores the vital public interests served by common public schools. Public education is democratically controlled by the elected representatives of the People. Ultimately it is the People who decide how public education funds are expended. Privatization systems use public funds, but limit public control. Allowing private control of public funds circumvents the democratic control and interests of the People. (p. 82)

A significant question regarding the privatization of public schools is whether private management is likely to take justice, equality, and freedom as the schools' most important purposes. Public education may have some difficult problems, but its purposes are clear and positive. Can the private sector be trusted to foster justice, equality, and freedom?

Recent Examples of School Privatization: Reasons for Resistance

The two most prominent efforts to privatize public schools in the United States have already shown fraying at the edges and questionable practices that should cause the public to be skeptical of the whole process (Toch, 1995; Saks, 1995).

The Edison Project

The Edison Project, the most widely advertised effort to take over public schools and turn a profit from their operation, was established by Christopher Whittle in 1991. Whittle, a strong advocate of free market economics, was known for comments that were "unbelievably hostile to the public school world" (*New York*, 1994, p. 53).

Using Whittle's funds for startup, with the expectation that investors would seize the money-making opportunity, the Edison Project proposed to build new schools. That idea changed quickly to an effort to contract with public school systems for the complete operation of existing schools. Whittle had claimed that the Edison Project would be operating 200 private schools by 1996, and would be educating two million children by the year 2010. He also pledged personally to finance the education of 100 "Whittle Scholars" for a year at the University of Tennessee (*New Yorker,* 1994). The widely publicized project now appears unable to meet any of the projections made at its initiation.

In 1992, Whittle persuaded Benno Schmidt, then president of Yale University, to become the Edison Project's chief executive officer, reportedly "in exchange for equity in the new company and a salary that insiders estimate at around 1 million dollars" (*New York,* 1994. p. 53). The *New York Times* (Applebome, 1994a) reported Schmidt's salary as $800,000, but whichever figure is accurate, Schmidt's move from one of education's highest paid positions as Yale president (with a salary in the range of $150,000) to private enterprise had certainly profited him. A $1 million executive salary compares with the average public school educator's salary of about $40,000 and the salaries of the highest-paid public school administrators of about $150,000. How can privatization, with executive salaries at this level, bring cost savings to taxpayers?

Taxpayer financing has not adequately provided the good salaries and working conditions deserved by those who serve the public in education, but money is not the primary motivation for their commitment to social improvement. Taxpayers realize a bargain when good teachers agree to stay in public education. Providing million-dollar salaries to privatizing school executives, while proposing to lower the costs of school operation, suggests mirrors-and-smoke accounting or major cuts in the most direct services to students. This means even lower pay and higher workloads for teachers and counselors, increased saving on textbooks and materials, and the cutting of other services. This corporate model—excessively highly paid executives and exploited workers vulnerable to the executive's budget cuts—benefits an elite few, but has not benefited society in general.

There should be no confusion about who is going to be paying executive salaries after private corporations take over the public schools. The formula calls for public funds. Can private business show the way to better finance schools with public funds, make a profit, and preserve educational quality? The financial management of Whittle's corporation may provide a perspective. By 1994, Whittle Communications had reached a state of financial collapse. *The New Yorker* magazine (1994) featured a long story detailing this collapse under the title "Grand Illusion," and subtitled with the line, "But the biggest surprise may be that it took so long for anyone to know that things had gone so wrong" (p. 63). That story described Whittle's reputation on Madison Avenue as a "legendary salesman" and one whose "most striking quality may be his charm" (p. 63).

Whittle had earlier established Channel One, a private television channel that "gave" TV equipment to schools on the condition that students be required to watch that channel and its commercials daily. Needing capital to try to save his other ventures, Whittle sold Channel One to K-III Communications. K-III owns *Seventeen* magazine and the *Weekly Reader,* a school newspaper, and is itself under the control of the same corporate body that also controls RJR Nabisco. That relationship raised some concerns about corporate interests and influence when the *Weekly Reader* carried a story on "smokers' rights" (*Wall Street Journal*, 1994). But the larger concern is about the broad effort to commercialize public education under corporate control.

The Edison Project's sudden shrinking and its financial difficulties illustrate some of the defects inherent in the privatization scheme. Venture capital, with its high risk and potentially high reward for a few, is not the best model for organizing public schools in a democracy. Public schooling's long-term goals of knowledge and ethical conduct based on justice, equality, and freedom are socially constructive. Are those goals best served by those most known for being legendary salespeople and hostile to public schools? A public education system based on charm and advertising is inconsistent with the democratic purposes of education. The potential damage to youth and to the society is too great.

Another Privatization Experiment

The second most visible effort to privatize public schools is that of EAI. That organization obtained the first contract for the private operation of an entire public school district, the Hartford, Connecticut, schools. The controversial decision was described as the result of a city "torn between a desperate plight and a radical plan" (*Time*, 1994, p. 48). Hartford's schools suffered from problems similar to those of many urban districts: the results of neglect, intensified social problems, and the high costs of maintaining old schools and senior staffs. Per-student expenditures were higher, at about $9,000, than those of the average district in the state, but student test scores were low and the dropout rate was high. The board of education chose EAI to undertake a five-year contract to pay the bills, shape the curriculum, train the teachers, and then keep whatever money was left in the public school budget, about $200 million per year, as profit.

One question posed in the *Time* article was, "what will be the driving motive: Improving schools or improving EAI's bottom line?" (p. 49). In commentary raising serious questions about the Hartford deal with EAI, Judith Glazer (1994) posed the idea that "American education is for sale" to "profit-making companies whose bottom line is not education but the strength of their financial performance for their stockholders" (p. 44). Glazer makes a strong point that if Hartford's school problems had become so dire as to necessitate the schools' being turned over to a private corporation, why didn't the public hold the state governor, state legislature, city council, and local school board accountable for neglect of their duties to provide quality public schools?

EAI's record in school privatization is sketchy. In 1992, the corporation obtained a contract for $135 million to take over a few schools in Baltimore. EAI agreed to improve instruction and to make school operations more efficient, with any unspent funds going to the company as profit. Judson (1994) reports that the school district uses its public budget to pay EAI the city's average amount per student, or about $6,000. In fact, most non-EAI schools actually receive less than the average total student expenditure because the costs of maintaining the central district offices are figured into the averages, but are not counted against EAI's budget. Thus, EAI actually gets about $1 million more per school per year than other schools.

EAI improved physical facilities at the schools, but spent "more than the average amount of money" and "had not begun to deliver on its promise, that private enterprise can do a better job for less in running big-city public schools" (Judson, 1994, p. A13). Albert Shanker (1994b) stated that EAI changed some arrangements after the agreement, putting special education students in regular classrooms and then replacing special education teachers with "interns," recent college graduates paid $7 per hour with no benefits.

With regard to student test scores, EAI initially reported that scores in EAI schools in Baltimore had increased considerably, but an examination of the scores by the *Minneapolis Star-Tribune* found that EAI had inflated the data (*Newsweek*, 1994). EAI later acknowledged its error; data show that standardized test scores in the EAI schools have actually gone down (Judson, 1994). After the incident was publicized, the eight schools used to make comparative evaluations with EAI schools were changed by dropping the three non-EAI schools at which students did very well (Shanker, 1994a). This change should make EAI school test scores compare better, but not because of improved education. Surprisingly, for all the fanfare about business hard-nosed accountability for performance in private enterprise, the Baltimore contract does not set any performance standards for EAI to meet (Judson, 1994) and the comparative evaluation program has been compromised.

Privatization and Private Enterprise

The Edison Project and EAI provide examples for considering the privatization of public education. In those areas in which private enterprise is supposed to afford the best leadership (efficiency, financial acuity, accountability, performance), these private ventures do not measure up. Instead, there is evidence of financial manipulation, wastage and inefficiency, and insufficient public accountability, and there is no demonstration that instruction was actually improved and at a lower cost. Further, the actions of the school privatizers so far should make the public very suspicious when these corporations report the results of their work or their financial positions. The social purposes of public education, of course, are not addressed in these examples. Where is the concern for justice, equality, and freedom?

Private entrepreneurship is one of the values American society holds dear. We prize the brave individuals who risk their financial security to bring new ideas and products to the public marketplace. Thomas Edison and Alexander Graham Bell are considered heroes who endured sacrifices and hard work to emerge as successful inventors and businessmen. Private entrepreneurs encourage innovation, experimentation, and development. This is often to the advantage of the society, as well as to the economy. But private entrepreneurship also is marked by unethical and illegal practices, including fraud and scams, graft and corruption, "Let the buyer beware" as common corporate philosophy, and irresponsible pollution of the environment. The robber baron mentality permeates much of private enterprise, where payoffs and hidden conspiracies for fixing prices or market control are simply ways of doing business. The primary value is personal greed. In these forms, private enterprise has shown little regard for social responsibility.

Some of the practices of private enterprise, and their eroding effect on public servants, were the grounds for President Eisenhower's warnings about military–industry entanglements long before public disclosures of military spending made the United States an object of international ridicule: $2,000 screwdrivers and $500 toilet seats under Pentagon contracts with private industry. Incompetent private operation and lack of adequate governmental regulation have cost taxpayers billions in government bailouts of Chrysler, Lockheed, and savings and loan associations. Yet, there remains an aura of respectability about private enterprise that implies that it is better than public operations.

Myths of Privatization

Clever packaging in a period when people distrust government and are concerned about rising taxes has made privatization popular. There are, however, several presumptions on which privatization is based, that simply are false or are seriously questionable. These presumptions are not expressed or challenged in the popular media. They are the myths of private enterprise, and they deserve to be fully examined before the public purse is opened even wider to private operations.

Myths about privatization:

1. It is more efficient, so it can save tax money while providing good service.
2. It is market-driven and responsive to the consumer.
3. It is based on performance, rewarding the productive and cutting out the incompetent.
4. It is successful as a worldwide movement.

Examining the Myths of Privatization

Efficiency

Efficiency is one of the main claims of private enterprise. It is almost an article of faith, but the claim collapses when subjected to scrutiny. The purposes for being efficient, the narrow and self-serving corporate definition of efficiency, and the practices associated with business all provide evidence that real efficiency is a myth.

Efficiency is a means, not a goal. The mere act of being efficient is inadequate as a rationale for social policy. There has to be a social purpose for striving to make human activities efficient. In a democratic society that respects the environment and aspires to equity for its members, efficiency can be a worthwhile pursuit, but effectiveness is more important. Efficient use of resources, human and other, should aim to preserve and improve the environment. Efficient operation of social services should have the purpose of improving the lot of society as a whole, not that of just one class of people. That statement of purpose suggests the kind of social benefit measure that needs to be applied to efficiency. Does the efficiency improve civilization by increasing the quality of justice, equality, and freedom?

Against this measure, the superficial type of efficiency of the private sector is found wanting. The profit motive defines efficiency as a cost-saving way to increase corporate income. Saving time by requiring dangerous shortcuts may appear to be efficient, but may simply be foolhardy. Efficient slaughter of wild animals, once a pastime of the wealthy, sped the decline of endangered species. Efficient mining of coal and other minerals by surface cuts led to permanent land scarring and pollution. Efficient demolition to clear land for real estate development has destroyed natural beauty, good agricultural land, and older architectural delights. The wall trophies and the loss to future generations may not be worth the price of efficiency.

Efficient manufacturing has created toxic waste, workplace accidents, worker health problems, overproduction, and waste. The actual social costs of this business form of efficiency are seldom calculated. The environmental and human costs of industrial efficiency are hidden elements unaccounted for in the search for profit. In addition, the private sector is often subsidized by the public through corporation-friendly policies on taxes and the use of natural resources.

A related concern is whether the captains of industry are themselves efficient and productive. Do they seem to practice what they preach for the public sector? Are the homes, cars, boats, and planes of the wealthy evidence of efficiency? Do they lead lives that model efficiency and social improvement? Although it is possible to find examples among the wealthy of people who make significant contributions to the improvement of society and who strive for efficient and productive lives, that is not the standard. Lives of excessive consumption and waste, with little obvious concern for the general quality of life in the society, is the more typical example. Large homes, expensive cars, servants, yachts, exclusive clubs, private planes, and legal and financial assistance to take advantage of tax loopholes typify those who gain from private enterprise. These are not the accoutrements normally found among public school educators, whose lives are devoted to public service. Conspicuous consumption is a characteristic of private enterprise, not of public employment.

Market-Driven and Consumer Responsive

Another myth is that the private sector must be better because it has to compete in the open marketplace and please its customers. However, it should be clear that there is no free and open market in the current economy. The marketplace itself is a myth. Price-fixing, monopolistic trusts, special interest legislation, weak regulatory agencies, and other corporation-protective practices skew the market to the benefit of the biggest corporations and the politically adept business people. Lobbying, graft, buyouts, control of the regulating authorities, and an "old boys' network" combine to deny newcomers equal opportunity in the market. Gaining control of the market to keep others out, not free competition, is the purpose of most corporate strategies. When that doesn't work well, corporations appeal to the government for special treatment or subsidies, or they undergo bankruptcy, which hurts small investors but leaves the executives wealthy. The free market does not happen.

Consumer responsiveness is another figment of the imagination with regard to private enterprise. Marketing to increase consumerism is a high priority in the private sector, but the primary purpose is to increase profits, not to please the customers. Enticing consumers to buy things they do not need is one of the purposes of advertising. Making consumers believe they are getting a good deal is the job of the sales force. But making sure that manufacturers provide complete information, fully back up warranties, don't mislead customers, and meet minimal safety requirements is the job of government through laws, consumer affairs departments, and the courts. Consumer protection and satisfaction is a public concern, fostered by decades of consumer manipulation by private enterprise. Every consumer has experienced traumatic confrontations with corporations over such common practices as their making errors, furnishing poor-quality goods or services, being unwilling to correct or replace an item, using bait-and-switch tactics, providing weak warranties, listing conditions of sale in fine print on contracts, and inflating credit charges. Private enterprise is ill-suited to take real consumer satisfaction seriously. The record of much private business in consumer affairs is one of enticement, profit, and resistance to customer complaints once a sale has been made.

Performance-Based, Rewarding Merit, and Cutting Incompetence

One of the most interesting myths about private enterprise is that it is rigorous about performance, expecting increased productivity and not condoning incompetence. But performance, in business terms, is merely selling more products at less cost with more profit. That is not a focus on quality. Presumably, performance-based systems would not reward underperformance, but the business news is filled with stories of CEOs whose corporations underperform, but who still receive large salary increases and bonuses. Nor does the myth of performance-based corporations square with the ideas that most people have about corporate life: incompetence occurs regularly and at high levels, office politics is more important than quality of work, and you can't challenge higher-level decisions even when they are obviously wrong.

If U.S. businesses are so committed to performance, why was there a decline in its quality of manufacture and share of the world marketplace? Why are corporation stockholder meetings a façade to cover the actions of a small group of board members, while good ideas from ordinary stockholders are essentially excluded? Why is the business of consumer advocate offices increasing, and why don't corporations encourage strong consumer protection laws? Why are the most meritorious employees often forgotten while the connected get quick promotions? These and other points suggest that performance is not always in the corporation's interest, and is not a major principle of big business.

The Successful Worldwide Movement Myth

The vaunted privatization of public services in many nations has been unraveling. Britain's problems with the privatization of public services illustrate the public loss for private gain. After World War II, Britain moved to public ownership of many enterprises to provide better accessibility to mass education, health care, and social services. Fifteen years of the Thatcher and Major governments produced privatization, and public services are under assault.

Ellingsen (1994a) examined this privatization program and found: "Britain's passion for privatization has produced no payoff for the public . . . the public is starting to realize not only that the sell-offs have made millionaires of those who run former state enterprises, but have cost consumers something like $9 billion" (p. 21). The minister responsible for most of the privatization, Lord Parkinson, admitted after retirement that auctioning public businesses had not gone as planned; private shareholders did well, but the customers did not. British Telecom, auctioned in 1984, had embarrassingly high profits while customers paid about $1 billion more than necessary. Water authorities, after privatization, saw profits soar while "customers are paying an extra $640 million for service that, as yet, has not fundamentally improved" (p. 21).

As a result of privatizing, London Electricity executives saw their salaries rise from averages well below those of the private sector from $2 million to over $4 million annually for each of the twelve top officers. One executive retired on a $3 million pension, about $200,000 per month for each month he was in the privatized corporation. Under privatization, British Gas doubled the chief executive's salary to more than $1 million. Public utilities were sold at excessively low prices that allowed quick profits, and executive income was linked to those profits in a charade claim of performance—all essentially at taxpayer expense. Some government ministers left public service to become members of the boards of the newly privatized companies (Ellingsen, 1994a). The greed of privatization has transformed the benevolent post–World War II British welfare state into a nation marked by increased separation between the social classes, illegal child labor, hidden sweatshops, and crime and drugs (Ellingsen, 1994b).

Australia's experience with privatization also was problematic. Although studies concluded that a Sydney harbor tunnel was not economically viable, a private firm was proposed as a cost-saving approach to build and operate one. After two years of private operation, it is now reported that taxpayers will pick up a previously unreported tab of $4 billion to cover extra expenses during the thirty-year life of the private contract. Following that disclosure, alarms were sounded about other privatization efforts because of secrecy, hidden costs, and lack of adequate scrutiny of private contracts for public services, such as hospitals, prisons, airports, railroads, and water services ("Why Parlt must Scrutinize Projects with Private Sector," 1994; "Auditor Criticises

Secrecy on Public Works Contracts," 1994; "Public Funds, Public Works," 1994). The public services employees' organization warned that a proposed bill to privatize state utilities (gas, electricity, and water) could lead to the destruction of the public sector without adequate protection for consumers or public funds or the provision of quality service ("Competition May Kill Utilities: ACTU," 1994).

Citizens of other nations have also suffered under privatization. In Eastern Europe and the former Soviet Union, privatization created high unemployment, extraordinary inflation, pyramid schemes that enriched a few and resulted in financial disaster for the many, and social unrest (van Brabant, 1992; Earle, Frydman, and Rapaczynski, 1993; *New York Times*, 1994b).

Ideology or Sound Thinking?

Having studied the economics of public service privatization for over six years, Sclar (1994) dismissed the claims that it would save money while improving services. He found that to be ideological hype, a starkly conservative agenda that is unsupported by research and in practice. He suggests that real competition in the global marketplace will require an improved public infrastructure, not its decimation by privatization. The undercutting of public services, an increase in actual total costs, and windfalls for the well-connected do not offer a quality of life for average Americans that encourages global leadership. Sclar concludes: "Finally, it is the public sector that is the dispenser of social justice. It is difficult to envision America sustaining itself as a progressive democracy with that role impaired" (p. 336).

In a system of democratic capitalism, where the relationship between the public and private sectors is delicate, there are many tensions. Private enterprise has some virtues and advocates, but it creates severe economic disparity among people and carries a history of exploitation. Similarly, public enterprise offers virtues and has supporters, but creates tax burdens and has a history of bureaucratic bungling. Each sector serves different needs of individuals and of the society at large. Increasing the proportion controlled by the private sector comes at a cost to the public. For a democracy, the cost of privatizing public education is too high.

For Discussion

1. On what basis should the decision be made as to which services are better provided through private or public agencies? Who, or what body, should be empowered to make that decision?
2. Shanker (1994b) noted that a public–private venture called "performance contracting" was started twenty years ago during the Nixon administration to save the public schools. The idea was for private firms to contract to improve test scores of students in specific subjects. The result, says Shanker, was scandalous: repetitive test taking or drill teaching of answers to test questions because the companies were good at marketing, but knew little about education. If there is to be privatization of the public schools, what conditions should be established or regulated?

3. The Milwaukee parental choice program, a voucherlike plan that uses state funds for sending a small group of children from poor families to private schools, has been evaluated in three independent studies. The evidence shows that parents in the privatization program are more satisfied with school than are those who are not in the program, but the evidence also shows that there is no difference between public and private schools in actual student achievement. What could account for these findings? What implications can be drawn from the evidence? What does this say about privatization ideas?

4. Discuss the following proposition: Even if it costs more to better educate children under private operations, this would clearly show the public the need to better finance schools to improve them. Either way, it is a benefit to education.

References

Applebome, P. (1994). "A Venture on the Brink: Do Education and Profits Mix?" *The New York Times*, October 30, p. 28.

Aristotle. (1988). *The Politics*. S. Everson, editor. Cambridge: Cambridge University Press.

"Auditor Criticises Secrecy on Public Works Contracts." (1994). *Sydney Morning Herald*, October 18, p. 1.

Brett, C. (1994). "Education in No-Zone Land: The Price of Free-Market Learning." *North & South* **102,** 75–88.

"Competition May Kill Utilities: ACTU." (1994). *Sydney Morning Herald*, October 29, p. 39.

Coons, J. (1988). "Testimony, Hearings on Educational Choice. December 22," Cited in *Privatization: Toward More Effective Government*. Washington, DC: U.S. Government Printing Office.

Dayton, J., and Glickman, C. D. (1994). "American Constitutional Democracy: Implications for Public School Curriculum Development." *Peabody Journal of Education* **69,** 62–80.

Dewey, J. (1916). *Democracy and Education*. New York: Macmillan.

Doyle, D. (1994). "The Role of Private Sector Management in Public Education." *Phi Delta Kappan* **76,** 128–132.

Earle, J., Frydman, R., and Rapaczynski, A. (1993). *Privatization in the Transition to a Market Economy*. New York: St. Martin's Press.

Education Week. (1994). "Even as Whittle Falls on Hard Times, Edison Model Leaves Wichita Hopeful." *Education Week* **14** (11), 12, 13.

Education Week (1994). "The New Politics of Education: School Districts for Sale." Commentary. *Education Week* **14**:44+.

Ellingsen, P. (1994a). "Making Profit in Private." *Sydney Morning Herald*, November 26, p. 21.

———— (1994b). "Rule Britannia—A Nation of Despair." *Sydney Morning Herald*, October 29, p. 28.

Feistritzer, E. (1987). "Public vs. Private: Biggest Difference Is Not the Students." *The Wall Street Journal*, December 1, p. 36.

Finn, C. (1995). "The School," Commentary. 99:6–10.

Geiger, P. E. (1995). "Representation and Privatization." *American School and University*, **67,** 28–30.

Gibbs, N. (1994). "Schools for Profit." *Time*, October 17, pp. 48–49.

Glazer, J. (1994). "The New Politics of Education: Schools For Sale." *Education Week* **14,** 44–ff.

Gutmann, A. (1987). *Democratic Education.* Princeton: Princeton University Press.

Hunter, R. C., and Brown, F. editors. (1995). "Privatization in Public Education." *Education and Urban Society* **27,** 107–228.

Jefferson, T. (1939). *Democracy.* New York: Greenwood Press.

Judson, G. (1994). "Hartford Hires Group to Run School System." *The New York Times,* October 4, pp. B1, B6.

Leslie, C. (1994). "Taking Public Schools Private." *Newsweek,* June 20, p. 7.

Mandel, M. et al. (1995). "Will Schools Ever Get Better?" *Business Week,* April 17, pp. 64–68.

New York. (1994). "Has Benno Schmidt Learned His Lesson?" *New York,* October 31, pp. 49–59.

New Yorker. (1994). "Grand Illusion." *The New Yorker,* October 31, pp. 64–81.

"Public Funds, Public Works." (1994). *Sydney Morning Herald* (editorial), October 18, p. 18.

Privatization: Toward More Effective Government. (1988). Report of the President's Commission on Privatization. Washington, DC: U.S. Government Printing Office.

Protzman, F. (1994). "East Nearly Privatized, Germans Argue the Cost." *The New York Times,* August 12, pp. D1, D2.

Saks, J. B. (1995). "Scrutinizing Edison." *American School Boards Journal* **183,** 20–24.

Sclar, E. (1994). "Public-Service Privatization: Ideology or Economics?" *Dissent,* Summer, pp. 329–336.

Schmidt, P. (1994). "Hartford Hires E.A.I. to Run Entire District." *Education Week,* **14:** 1, 14.

Shanker, A. (1994a). "Barnum Was Right." *The New York Times,* October 23, p. E7.

———— (1994b). "A History Lesson." *The New York Times,* March 6, p. E7.

Time. (1994). "Schools for Profit." *Time,* October 17, pp. 48–49.

Toch, T. (1995). "Taking Public Schools Private: A Set Back." *US News and World Report* **117,** 74.

"Tunnel Payout Climbs to $4bn." (1994). *Sydney Morning Herald,* October 17, p. 3.

van Brabant, J. V. (1992). *Privatizing Eastern Europe.* International Studies in Economics and Econometrics, No. 24. Boston: Kluwer Academic Press.

Vickers, J., and Yarrow, G. (1991). "Economic Perspectives on Privatization." *Journal of Economic Perspectives* **2,** 111–132.

Wall Street Journal. (1994). "A KKR Vehicle Finds Profit and Education a Rich But Uneasy Mix." *The Wall Street Journal,* October 12, p. A11, A12.

"Why Parlt Must Scrutinize Projects with Private Sector." (1994). *Sydney Morning Herald,* October 18, p. 19.

CHAPTER SEVENTEEN

School Violence: School or Social Responsibility

POSITION 1: SCHOOLS CAN CURB VIOLENCE AND EDUCATE

I believe that school is primarily a social institution. Education being a social process, the school is simply that form of community life in which all of those agencies are concentrated that will be most effective in bringing the child to share in the inherited resources of the race, and to use his own powers for social ends . . . . I believe that education, therefore, is a process of living and not a preparation for future living. (Dewey, 1897, "My Pedagogic Creed," reprinted in Dworkin, 1959, p. 22)

We didn't call ourselves gangs. We called ourselves clubs or *clicas*. In the back lot of the local elementary school, about a year after Tino's death, five of us gathered in the grass and created a club—"The Impersonations" . . . . It was something to belong to—something that was ours. We weren't in the Boy Scouts, in sports teams or camping groups. The Impersonations is how we wove something out of the threads of nothing. (Rodriguez, 1993, p. 41)

John Dewey helped define the relationship between the community and its schools. Schools are extensions of the community. When social problems overwhelm the community's resources, schools are expected to lend their strength and assistance. Schools share in the burden of caring for the community's children and of equipping them with the skills and habits necessary to survive and succeed. Schools take the highest ideals of the community and translate them into academic and social programs for all children. As Dewey wrote, "What the best and wisest parent wants for his own child, that must the community want for all its children" (Dworkin, 1959, p. 54).

Dewey recognized that the social conditions of his day were changing and that schools had to adjust to new demands placed on the communities. In a speech delivered in 1899, he said, "It is useless to bemoan the departure of the good old days of children's modesty, reverence, and implicit obedience, if we expect merely by bemoaning and by exhortation to bring them back. It is radical conditions which have changed, and only an equally radical change in education suffices" (Dworkin, 1959, p. 37).

The industrial revolution had upset the traditional nature of the community and the nature of work. As a result, families had changed, and they were not able to carry out the full range of their former functions. Schools had to expand their role to go beyond providing instruction in reading and arithmetic and to help children adjust to the "radical conditions" of the day. Helping children adjust to the problems of a new industrial economy imposed a great burden on public education in the late nineteenth century. Helping children understand and overcome the radical conditions of the late twentieth century may require even greater effort, but it is not a problem the schools can shirk. The community's problems are the school's problems.

The Violent Community

Violence is among the most "radical conditions" now confronting the nation and its school-age children. Violence increasingly affects the daily lives of children, and violence prevention and aggression management have become the business of schools. As one teacher notes:

> Five years ago, I noticed the topics at teachers' conventions had begun shifting from curriculum matters to coping skills. Workshop sessions had cute names and suggested strategies for redirecting aggression, signing good-behavior contracts, and letting the group decide the consequences of inappropriate behavior. As the years passed, session names became a little more serious and so did the topics—"coping skills" became "survival skills." Now, sessions like "Legal Rights of Teachers," "Sex Harassment in the Schools," "Dealing with Violent Students," and "Gang Signs and Symbols" get more attention than ever before. (Mahaffey, 1994, p. 82)

America is violent. It has been violent for a long time, and violence threatens to increase. Messages of aggressive behavior enter the world of children no matter how hard families may try to protect them. These messages flow not only from children's direct experiences, but also from news reports of violence, as well as from film, music, and advertising. War toys line the shelves of stores; cartoon heros destroy cartoon villains; music videos hint darkly at anger and destruction; and computer games allow interactive simulations of murder and mayhem.

Television brings a steady volume of vicarious violence into living rooms. Over 97 percent of American households have at least one television set, and it is estimated that young children watch an average of four hours of television a day. Each year, they are likely to watch passively, and typically without adults present, acts of violence at unprecedented levels. The American child will see an estimated 8,000 murders and 100,000 acts of televised violence before leaving elementary school (*TV Violence*, 1993). It's hard to know how viewing violence affects children, but some authorities note that we are raising a generation of children unlike any others. The media expose them to more aggressive acts than children were exposed to in the past, and "they are taken away from other things they could be doing, should be doing and have been doing for generations before the advent of television—like playing, interacting with other children and participating in family and community life" (Carlsson-Paige and Levin, 1990, p. 10). While the schools alone cannot overcome the problems of violence, they are central in the struggle to protect children and to teach them that physical aggression is not the preferred solution to problems.

Violence inevitably flows from the community into the children's daily lives (Moore and Anderson, 1995; Dill and Haberman, 1995). Many children have nightmares that stem from the violence in their lives. Increasing numbers of students report that they do not feel safe in their schools (Harris et al., 1994). Ronald Stephens, executive director of the National Schools Safety Center, in testifying before a congressional subcommittee remarked, "Literally, our children are dying to come to school. . . . A lot of former fistfights are being replaced by gunfights; the former fire drills are being replaced by crisis drills, and even by the new drive-by shooting drills" (*Recess from Violence*, 1993, p. 37). Although violence is more prevalent in urban areas and among the poor and minorities, no one in any neighborhood is immune from it. School violence affects young women as well as young men and children as young as 10 years of age (Goldstein, Harootunian, and Conoley, 1994). Testifying before a congressional committee, Mia Robinson, then an 11-year-old student in Washington, D.C., was asked what she thought about a proposal requiring all public school students to wear uniforms. She replied, "I think uniforms are a great dress code for school because most of the children out here nowadays are getting picked on for what they wear or shot for the tennis shoes they have on their feet" (*Recess from Violence*, 1993, p. 34).

While the overall rate for crimes of violence has been fairly stable, for school-age children, violence is on the rise. Adolescents account for the highest victimization rate in crimes involving a handgun. A recent survey showed that the rate for persons 16 to 19 years of age was seventeen times that for those 65 and older (U.S. Department of Justice, 1994, p. 5). Crime and victimization rates are highest among urban minorities. Statistics indicate that "the lifetime risk of being murdered is about 32 per 1,000 for black males and 18 per 1,000 for native Americans. By contrast, it is 6 per 1,000 for white males and 3 per 1,000 for white females" (Roth, 1994, p. 2). Teachers, especially those in schools serving predominantly low-income and minority children, report steady increases in violence (Elam, Rose, and Gallup, 1994). Overall, it appears that more children are exposed to higher levels of violence in their lives than ever before, and more children are demonstrating more aggressive behaviors in school than did children of earlier generations. Reports of increasing childhood aggression are especially troublesome considering the research that links children's inability to manage their aggression with their future violent behavior as adults (Caspi et al., 1994; Reiss and Roth, 1993; Goldstein, Harootunian, and Conoley, 1994).

Schools and Violence

Violence takes many forms in public school (student-to-student, student-to-teacher, and teacher-to-student violence), and while we do not wish to minimize its significance or dismiss it as a media creation, we do not want to make you fearful of becoming teachers. Nor do we want to make the problem of violence seem intractable. The vast majority of teachers are not worried about their personal safety in schools. In a Louis Harris survey of public school teachers, 99 percent reported that they felt "safe" or "very safe" at work (Harris et al., 1993). The survey indicates that the problem of violence may be felt more acutely by students than by teachers: 4 percent of students reported feeling not very safe; 3 percent said they did not feel safe at all. Students who had been the victims of school violence were far more negative about school and teachers than were students who had not been victimized (Harris et al., 1994).

The bad news is easy to report. The statistics are alarming: violence is increasing; too many children feel unsafe in schools; many schools have to invest in metal detectors and guards instead of books and field trips. The good news is harder to quantify, but it should be reassuring: school programs can make a difference in preventing childhood aggressive behavior and future adult violence (Curcio and First, 1993; *Recess from Violence,* 1993; Reiss and Roth, 1993).

Violent behavior is one of the most frequently studied phenomena of the late twentieth century. The social and behavioral sciences have learned a lot about the subject, and there is every reason to assume that schools can be successfully proactive in stemming the tide of violent behavior and in protecting children and society from the violent among us. Research indicates that certain factors predispose children to violent behavior. Children who are at risk for violence typically "bring to school a pattern of behavior that makes it difficult for them to establish trust, autonomy, and social competence" (Wallach, 1993, p. 4). The factors most often found to make up this pattern include: (1) excessive viewing of violence on television; (2) repeated examples of bullying behavior; (3) evidence of poor parenting, such as abuse, neglect, or lack of nurturing; (4) a history of harsh or erratic discipline at home; and (5) an inability to develop friendships in school (Reiss and Roth, 1993, pp. 7–8). These are, of course, only statistical correlates of violent behavior. Not all of the rough and uncontrolled kindergartners become violent junior high school students. However, children who exhibit several of these factors are at risk for later violence.

Schools have been developing programs to prevent or manage the problem of violent behavior. The range of programs is very wide. Some programs focus on the physical aspects of the school, such as installing better lighting and metal detectors. Other programs are designed to make control of aggression part of the curriculum. Most programs try to involve the community, and all of them require special training for teachers, ranging from aggression management to self-defense classes (Goldstein, Harootunian, and Conoley, 1994).

In addition to school-based programs, policymakers are now debating the role that schools should play in contending with violence in the larger community. They recognize that the school must reach out to the community and extend education beyond the walls of the classroom in order to confront the problems of children. For example, it is well known that violent behavior is learned, and that children of abusive parents often use excessive physical punishment in disciplining their own children. One policy under consideration would require parents of aggressive, potentially disruptive children to attend school-sponsored parenting classes. Another outreach proposal would encourage pregnant women who grew up in physically abusive homes to take special parenting classes provided by schools (Reiss and Roth, 1993).

The best violence prevention programs use the academic power of the schools to bring support to the community. The problem is complex and there are no simple solutions. The National Education Association (NEA) argues that reliance on external controls (for example, metal detectors, school guards, body searches) provides only an artificial and short-lived relief (*National Education Association*, 1992). To solve the problem of school violence, children must learn how to understand and control their anger and practice using nonviolent problem-solving techniques in their daily lives. Schools can help students manage their aggression by teaching alternatives to violence through violence prevention curricula.*

Violence Prevention Curricula

Consider a few violence prevention strategies suggested by national organizations. They are illustrative rather than prescriptive. Many schools are now using school-wide conflict resolution approaches in which children are taught

---

*Schools are now experimenting with hundreds of new curricular interventions designed to reduce violence. You are encouraged to examine examples in your community or to contact one of the following national centers for more information.

Centers for Disease Control and Prevention, Division of Violence Prevention, National Center for Injury Prevention and Control
Mail Stop K-60
4770 Bufford Highway, N.E.
Atlanta, GA 30341-3724
(404) 486-4646

Center for the Study and Prevention of Violence, Institute for Behavioral Science, University of Colorado at Boulder
Campus Box 442
Boulder, CO 80309-0442
(303) 492-1032

Education Development Center Inc.
Center for Violence Prevention and Control
National Network of Violence Prevention Practitioners
55 Chapel Street
Newton, MA 02160
(617) 969-7100

to handle their own disputes and to assume responsibility for helping other children find peaceful resolutions to their disagreements. It is disarmingly simple and effective. First, children are taught that problems are inevitable, and in most disputes, both sides are apt to believe that they, and they alone, are in the right. Conflict resolution approaches, such as those recommended by the NEA, encourage students to listen to each other and to take responsibility for ensuring that the conflicts in their lives are resolved by conversation and negotiation rather than by physical means.

When a playground dispute occurs, an older child, who has been trained by the teachers, asks both parties to tell their sides of the story. Certain ground rules are agreed to beforehand: no yelling, no cursing, no interrupting, no put-downs of the other person. The older student, acting as a conflict manager, seeks to have the disputants solve their own problems. If they cannot, the conflict manager tries to help. A teacher or administrator is always available. The goal is to provide a caring community in which all children can feel safe, where problems can be resolved, and where everyone is responsible for the well-being of others. Caring communities teach children to handle problems without resorting to violence (*Violence in the Schools*, 1993; Brendtro, L., and Long, N, 1985). By practicing mediation techniques, participants also learn to be good communicators and thoughtful problem solvers. One student trained as a mediator said that the program "informed me on how to be a better listener and taught me how to help other people solve their problems." Another participant said, "I got a chance to understand people and the ethics of helping people solve problems" (Morse and Andrea, 1994, p. 82).

Secondary school students are often encouraged to use role-playing techniques to examine critical incidents in their lives. The goal is to have students see how simple, commonplace events can escalate into violence. In the following example, written by eighth-grade students, one young woman taunts another.

"I heard that she was at the movies with your boyfriend last night. All over him."

"I wouldn't take it," adds another girl.

"She doesn't need your boyfriend. What was she doing with him anyhow?"

The young women simulate pushing and shoving. They break off from the simulation with self-conscious laughter, recognizing that in real life the angry words they scripted would often escalate into real acts of violence. The classroom teacher applauds the students' effort, and the class examines what had taken place. A rumor had been spread; it led to an exchange of words; verbal accusations threatened to become physical. In real life, it could easily have resulted in injury. The teacher asks: How could this have been avoided? What did others do to make the situation worse? What should they have done to help (*Violence in the Schools*, 1993)?

For too many children, violence is a way of life. School programs can and do help students find alternatives to violence. According to Rodney Hammond, an authority on school violence: "The most effective violence prevention interventions tend to be very structured programs that focus on teaching the behaviors that tend to prevent the development of violence coping strategies and that work intensively with youth over a sustained period of time." He adds, "Slogan campaigns and scare tactics simply do not work" (*Recess from Violence*, 1993, p. 41). Violence prevention curricula are quite new and their successes have not yet been carefully evaluated or scientifically assessed. However, as one school administrator notes, "It makes a difference in my school, and I have a reduction of 10 percent in some problems. These materials are O.K. by me, and I don't need researchers to say it works" (Lawton, 1994, p. 10).

Every school should adopt an appropriate set of strategies for interdicting and managing violence in the lives of students. Antiviolence can be an important strand running through the social studies, language arts, and other curriculum areas. School programs for reducing overly aggressive behavior show great promise, but for many children they may not be sufficient. Teaching students mediation skills, for example, is not likely to erase completely the violent patterns already established in the lives of many children. These young people need greater, more intensive support than teachers alone can provide. Violence is a learned response, and because it is learned, it can be unlearned (Noguera, 1995; Sautter, 1995). Schools, working with social service agencies and psychologists, can replace antisocial behaviors with prosocial behaviors and provide positive role models for children.

The absence of appropriate parental supervision is a strong predictor of trouble with school discipline. Often thought of as a problem confined to the poor, it is now recognized that increasing numbers of the nonpoor suffer from the absence of appropriate role models in their lives. Students from all social classes need sources of support other than the family. Many colleges and universities provide help by matching volunteer mentors with at-risk students. The mentors act as role models, older brothers/sisters, and surrogate parents. They offer help with homework and they teach study skills. They are models of problem solvers who do not resort to violence and examples of success who have not succumbed to the temptations of crime. Above all, they offer at-risk children a caring, thoughtful person in their lives. The importance of their presence cannot be overestimated. Children at risk for violence have had too few positive role models. Research indicates that "the involvement of just one caring adult can make all the difference in the life of an at-risk youth" (Sautter, 1995, p. K8).

Schools cannot curb violence by themselves, but by working with other agencies, they can reach out to potentially troubled young people in the community, provide support for them, and offer them a real promise of a less turbulent future. Schools can also reach out to new mothers in the community, especially pregnant teenagers and others who are at risk of providing poor role models for their children, and teach them the skills they need to pass on to those children. Schools can join with social welfare agencies to help families teach children to resolve social conflicts without violence. The process is likely to be slow and expensive, but if it does not begin in school, the future social and personal costs are likely to be greater. These children and their problems will not go away or get better by themselves. To paraphrase John Dewey, what the best and wisest parents in the community want for their children should be made available to all children through the power of the schools. To do less is to betray the schools' social responsibilities for improving community life.

POSITION 2: SCHOOLS MUST ELIMINATE THE VIOLENCE IN ORDER TO EDUCATE

> What means does civilization employ in order to inhibit the aggressiveness which opposes it, to make it harmless, to get rid of it, perhaps? . . . Civilization . . . obtains mastery over the individual's dangerous desire for aggression by weakening and disarming it and by setting up an agency within him to watch over it, like a garrison in a conquered city. (Freud, 1930/1961, pp. 78–79)

You don't have to be a Freudian psychologist to understand the relationship between aggression and civilization. Humans are born with instincts toward aggression and the pursuit of narrow self-satisfaction. Civilization requires individual renouncement of base instincts and the pursuit of loftier goals. In a normally functioning world, parents teach their children the importance of managing their impulsiveness and harnessing their aggressions. Parents are supposed to pass on the values of a civilized society to the next generation.

Traditionally, parents teach their children using all of the psychological tools at their disposal. Parents can dispense praise to reward appropriate behavior, and they can use punishment to discourage inappropriate behavior. Reward and punishment are common child-rearing techniques, but middle-class parents typically rely more on psychological than physical discipline. They know that nothing rivals the psychological pain endured by children when parents make them feel guilty about some action. Even as adults, many people cringe at the memory of parents who chastened them for misdeeds not by beating or scolding them, but by saying, sotto voce, "You disappointed us"; "We trusted you"; "You let us down." Parental discipline of this sort has social as well as personal ends. Through their parents' teaching, children develop a conscience; they learn how to behave, to channel their aggression, to curb their violence, to live with others. In short, children learn from their parents how to behave in a civilized manner.

Decline of Family Values

To argue that these are not normal times would be to belabor the obvious. The family is in disarray and family values are all but lost to many Americans. Thirty percent of all children and 70 percent of minority children are born to single mothers. Too often, there is no family to teach family values. Too many children show up at the doors of the nation's schools with only a vague sense of right and wrong, no self-discipline, and a limited ability to get along with other children. Increasing numbers of today's youth claim that the counterculture or gang life offers a sense of belonging, worth, and purpose denied to them by their families. Freud defined civilization as the sum of achievement and self-control that distinguishes us from our animal ancestors (Freud, 1930/1961). Unfortunately, too many children bring to school little evidence of civilization. Human achievements in science, the arts, and the imagination and intellect are likely to be lost on these children.

Not only are traditional family values neglected, but in their place the contemporary home environment may substitute values that are destructive of civilized ends. Consider one example, admittedly an extreme case, but one that is unfortunately becoming more common. A 5-year-old girl complained to her mother that she was being picked on by another child. The girl's mother had also been victimized as a child and she did not want her own daughter to suffer in the same way. The mother locked her daughter out of the house and told her that she was not to come back unless she could present the mother with her tormentor's two front teeth. The young girl did just that; she attacked the other child, knocked out the teeth with a rock, and gave them to her mother (Natale, 1994, pp. 38–39).

Children do not show up for the first day of kindergarten as blank slates. Their environments have etched upon them a wealth of experiences. Some children are ready to begin school. They come from families in which their parents have invested tremendous amounts of time and energy in them. The children are self-controlled. They demonstrate appropriate mastery over their emotions, an enthusiasm for learning, and a respect for the authority of the teacher. These children are ready for school. Others are not. Victims of poor parenting or no parenting at all, they come to school insufficiently prepared to learn and unable to adequately control their behavior. Teachers spot them easily. They are overly impulsive, physically aggressive, and uncooperative. They are not likely to do well in school, and they are destructive of, if not a threat to, the education and well-being of other children. Psychologists predict that "undercontrolled" 3-year-old children will tend toward delinquency when they enter adolescence (Caspi et al., 1994, p. 188).

We are not trying to alarm you. Only a small percentage of students exhibit aggressive behaviors or other traits that predict adult violence. Potentially violent students represent only 1 percent of the children who enter school. The majority of students whom teachers identify as "problems" are so described for reasons other than their potential to do physical harm to others or themselves.* Our focus on violence is to draw attention to an extreme problem of schools and society—a problem that threatens to become worse.

*Brophy and McCaslin list twelve types of "problem" elementary-school-age students examined in the research literature:

1. Failure syndrome: These children believe that they cannot do schoolwork. They often avoid work or give up easily. They expect to fail, often saying, "I can't do it."

What responsibilities do schools have to teach children who are not able to control their aggression? This is a difficult question. None of us wants to be indifferent to children, but schools are not social welfare agencies. Teachers are not social workers or psychiatrists. They are educators trained to teach children reading, math, social studies, and other important skills. It is not reasonable to expect schools and teachers to function as therapists, nor can they be expected to serve as parents. Some school administrators want to turn their schools into "around-the-clock social service centers," teaching parenting skills to adults and conflict resolution techniques to children. The principal of one Brooklyn, New York, high school wants to build dormitories, funded at public expense, for students who do not have stable homes (*Violence in Schools*, 1992). Proposals such as this are unwarranted extensions of school authority and result in outrageous expenses of doubtful worth. Schools already consume too many tax dollars in order to provide basic education. To indulge the whims of educators and transform schools into social service agencies violates common sense. Schools are designed to provide basic instruction. They cannot and should not try to be ersatz families. Values are learned at home or not at all. To ask schools to teach those things once taught at a mother's knee is to invite failure.

Who Are the Potentially Violent?

We know who is likely to commit crimes, the early experiences that lead to violent behavior, and the personal and family traits that tend to protect chil-

2. Perfectionist: These children are unusually anxious about making mistakes. They have unrealistically high self-images, and they are never satisfied with their performance. They often hold back from class participation unless they are very sure of themselves.
3. Underachiever/alienated: These children do the minimum to get by. They do not value or enjoy schoolwork.
4. Low achiever: These students have difficulty with schoolwork even when they are willing to try. Their problem is low potential or lack of readiness.
5. Hostile-aggressive: These students express hostility through direct, intense behaviors. They intimidate and threaten other students. They are easily angered, and they may hit and push other students or destroy property.
6. Passive-aggressive: These students indirectly express their opposition and resistance to the teacher. They disrupt classrooms surreptitiously and use subtle noncompliance.
7. Defiant: These children want to have their own way. They may resist the teacher verbally, saying "You can't make me," or "You can't tell me what to do." They resist nonverbally by posturing, frowning, and sometimes by being physically violent toward the teacher.
8. Hyperactive: These children squirm, wiggle, jiggle, and show excessive and almost constant movement. They are often out of their seats and bother other children.
9. Distractable: These children have very short attention spans. They are unable to sustain attention and concentration.
10. Immature: These children have poorly developed self-control, social skills, and emotional stability.
11. Peer rejected: These children are often forced to work and play alone, although they seek acceptance by other students.
12. Shy/withdrawn: These children avoid personal interaction with other classmates. They are quiet and do not call attention to themselves. (Brophy and McCaslin, 1992, pp. 62–63)

dren from becoming violent adults. Unfortunately, research has not yet developed a strong knowledge base on which to base violence prevention programs (Reiss and Roth, 1993). No one knows how to prevent potentially violent children from becoming violent adults. Schools now embracing one violence management curriculum or another are doing so without adequate evidence of its effectiveness. In most cases, these programs are likely to be a waste of taxpayers' money. Many of the causes of violence are not in the control of schools (Weishew and Peng, 1993). Violent children become violent adults, and if children have not learned to control their aggression by the time they come to school, it may not be possible for them to disentangle the patterns of violence that took shape in their earlier years.

In a perfect world, all children would arrive at school free of tendencies toward violent behavior. If it were in our power, we would have all children raised in loving, drug-free, nurturing homes. They would have bonded with an adult who dispensed love freely and taught them that they belong to someone and that someone belongs to them. The children's earliest experiences would have shown them that disagreements are part of life, but that discord can be settled through calm discussions rather than rancor or violence. We would like all children to have high IQs. We would like them all to have parents who are literate adults, who are not addicted to alcohol or drugs, who consult books about child rearing, and who read stories to their children. We would like all children to have had limits put on their television viewing. We would like children to learn that firearms are part of an American tradition and that bearing arms is an American right, but that gun use is dangerous. We would like all these things and more, but social policies cannot create them. Too many children are born to single mothers who are unprepared for the task or are unable to give them what they need to be successful in life. Drug addiction, crime, and poverty are beyond the control of the schools. Short of taking children out of undesirable home situations and having them raised by substitute parents or social agencies, there is little that schools can do but accept increasing numbers of unprepared and potentially disruptive students. Although public schools must work with all students, they do not have to mix the disruptive and the potentially violent with other students, nor do they have to encourage violent students to stay in school until graduation. Let's look at what we know about potentially violent children and what is reasonable for schools to do about them.

Schools and Violence

Overly aggressive children should be identified in kindergarten and trained to work on anger control. Although the school cannot replace the family, it can provide some of the things found in the homes of self-controlled high-achieving students. For example, school discipline policies should incorporate the reward-and-punishment system utilized by middle-class parents. Students should learn that appropriate behavior will be rewarded with teacher praise and special privileges and inappropriate behavior will result in the loss of praise and privilege. Aggressive children who have been exposed to a great deal of violence on television could be made aware of the prosocial models the medium offers (for example, Mr. Rogers). This would be reasonable, inexpensive, and not too intrusive on the privacy rights of students or their parents.

No one believes that schools by themselves can solve problems of violence (Lawton, 1994). The influences of early family experiences are pervasive (Caspi et al., 1994). Unfortunately, schools may not be able to correct the course of children who come from chaotic family environments. Research provides little encouragement about the success of school interventions in preventing violence, and the research may simply be confirming what is public knowledge. In 1994, one item of the Gallup poll of the public's attitude toward the public schools asked respondents to rate the importance of various factors as a cause of school violence. Listed in order of frequency, the public rated the following factors as "very important" (Elam, Rose, and Gallup, 1994, p. 44):

1. Increased use of drug and alcohol among school-age youth
2. Growth of youth gangs
3. Easy availability of weapons
4. A breakdown in the American family
5. Schools' lack authority to discipline that they once had
6. Increased portrayal of violence in the media
7. Inability of school staff to resolve conflicts between students

Note that the first six responses are beyond the control of schools. It is not until the fifth item that schools are mentioned. The public recognizes that society has visited many of its problems on the schools, including the vexing problem of school violence. However, the public is not convinced that solutions to the problem are within the schools' power. Asked to rate various measures for their potential effectiveness in reducing violence, 88 percent of the respondents listed first, "stronger penalties for possession of weapons by students." At the bottom of the list, mentioned by 51 percent and 45 percent of respondents, respectively, were "courses offered by the public schools in how to be a good parent" and "conflict education for students" (Elam, Rose, and Gallup, 1994, p. 44).

The public shows eminently good sense. Most people realize that schools have a narrow role to play in society: schools are designed to provide students with an academic education. This is no easy task in the best of times, and probably is never accomplished to the satisfaction of anyone who knows about schools. Providing a sound academic education should be the primary, if not the exclusive, concern of schools. Schools should leave social problems to other agencies (social workers, probation officers, police officers). If the society wants social problems solved, it should solve them directly and not look to the schools for their solution. Welfare laws that reward unwed teen-age mothers and a system of taxation that penalizes the working poor have a more direct bearing on children than does school curriculum.

Of course, schools should try to help all children, but they should not impede the progress of well-behaved students. It is reasonable for schools to try every measure to help young children adapt to school and school discipline. But let's face it, some children will never adjust to the academic demands and the self-discipline required for academic success. This tiny percentage of students should not be the focus of school attention and a constant drain on school budgets. If these students have not learned to control themselves by early adolescence, schools should waste no more time or money on them.

Alternative Schools/Shock Camps

What should be done with undisciplined, troubled adolescents? Although it might seem draconian, alternative schools and shock camps offer promising options other than public schools for violent students. Educators have long recognized that alternatives to public schools are sometimes necessary to serve special populations of students—teen-age mothers, for example, or the physically disabled. Now educators are considering alternative schools for violent or potentially dangerous youths (Portner, 1994; Newman, 1995). Based on a military model, these programs emphasize discipline in order to shock participants toward a better path. Currently, forty-seven shock camps operate in twenty-seven states for criminal offenders, and over 1,000 alternative schools have opened in the past several years to serve youths who are heading for violence and criminality. The state of Florida is developing alternative schools for juvenile offenders (Portner, 1994); New York City is opening alternative schools for violent children (Newman, 1995). Alternative schools and shock camps have a lot to offer young people. For the first time in their lives, young men and women learn to lead orderly and regimented lives. As one writer describes it, shock camp residents at one facility "get up at dawn for calisthenics and run a mile, work all morning at a lumberyard, attend afternoon counseling and academic sessions, partake of all meals in silence, speak only when spoken to and endure more physical training before lights out at 9" (Yen, 1994, p. 10).

Do these programs work? It may be too early to tell how effective this behavior modification model is in instilling appropriate values and self-discipline in their graduates. Some studies indicate that young people graduating from shock camps have a recidivism rate of 50 percent—that is, half of all shock camp graduates return to crime. Obviously, shock camps are less than perfect, but their success rate should be compared with a 70 percent recidivism rate for all violent youths (Sautter, 1995). Shock camps show promise. They protect the majority of students by removing the violent minority, and the camps don't burden schools with tasks for which they are unsuited. Shock camps and alternative schools for the disruptive are certainly less agreeable than regular public schools, and they should be. Students need to know that violence will not be tolerated and that repeated antisocial behaviors will guarantee them a life that is far less pleasant than life in school. There is no greater deterrent to behavior than the guaranteed risk of punishment. As one criminologist notes:

> Human actions are governed by incentives and disincentives. We are attracted by the hope of pleasure or gain, deterred by the fear of pain. . . . [Crime] can

be deterred by disincentives—the fear of pain, the threat of punishment. . . . Whenever the risks of punishment fall, the crime rate rises. (van den Haag, 1994, pp. 30–31)

The schools have brought much of the problem of violence onto themselves. John Dewey and the progressive education movement of the 1920s introduced a child-centered curriculum in the schools. That movement was responsible for the slippage of academic standards and the gradual erosion of school discipline. The traditional authority of the teacher as the keeper of order and the transmitter of academic knowledge has given way to a focus on the child and the child's wants and needs. Progressive education helped produce educational anarchy. Sociologist Jackson Toby argues, "When I went to school, it was unthinkable to hit a teacher or say something [rude] to a teacher. If you have teachers in control and students afraid of teachers, they behave themselves. Now teachers are afraid of students" (*Violence in Schools,* 1992, p. 794).

The child-centered approach of the 1920s paved the way for the misguided educational egalitarianism of the 1960s. The progressives expanded the schools to include vocational and home economics programs in order to encourage students to stay in school. School attendance increased as schools filled with students who previously had dropped out or were forced out. By the 1960s, school success was more likely to be measured in graduation rates than in student learning. School administrators became reluctant to expel even the most disruptive students, and the problem has become worse. As Toby points out: "Most schools in most big cities have given up and keep kids in school who are sufficiently troublesome that it's very difficult to maintain an educational program" (*Violence in Schools,* 1992, p. 789).

Schools should focus less on the problem students and more on the well-behaved students and those with the greatest academic potential. It is cruelly ironic that schools pay more attention to and spend more money on the potentially violent than on the academically gifted. Schools are bending over backward to help the socially disadvantaged, but in doing so, they are disadvantaging the most academically able. Less than one-tenth of 1 percent of federal expenditures on public education goes to programs for gifted children's education (Brimelow, 1994). The gifted deserve greater school support. "It needs to be said openly: The people who run the United States—create its jobs, expand its technologies, cure its sick, teach in its universities, administer its cultural and political and legal institutions—are drawn mainly from a thin layer of cognitive ability at the top" (Herrnstein and Murray, 1994, p. 418). This group suffers when education focuses on the nonacademic and when teacher and administrator energies are devoted to solving problems of school safety instead of attending to the design and delivery of high-quality academic education. Because the elite serve the whole country, failing to allow them to develop their individual potential does a great disservice to all of us. As one veteran teacher, tired of trying to discipline unruly students, told us, "Teach the best, shoot [expel] the rest."

You may well ask whether expelling problem students is likely to increase their inclination toward further violence and criminality. It's hard to know.

Research indicates that future dropouts have high levels of criminal behavior while in school, but there is some evidence that after they drop out of school, they have less trouble with the law (Herrnstein and Murray, 1994). Schools often add to the problems of young people. Many students who do not succeed academically feel frustrated. Others feel confined by school rules and the abrasiveness of school crowding (Noguera, 1995; Sautter, 1995). Some students might do better in an environment other than the school, and schools should find a place for those students. We have suggested identifying potentially violent students and introducing interventions in their curriculum, but at some point school remedies must end and other agencies must be brought in—alternative schools and shock camps, for example. The social functions of public education should not compete with academic responsibility. Schools are academic institutions designed to teach cognitive skills. Students who have not learned to play by the rules of civilized behavior—self-discipline, order, respect for others—have no place in school.

For Discussion

1. Thanks to television, the typical American child sees 100,000 acts of violence and 8,000 murders by the end of the sixth grade (*TV Violence*, 1993). Surveys indicate that American preschool children watch an average of twenty-seven hours of television per week, and about half of American families set no limits on how much television their children can watch (Centerwall, 1994). How does television viewing affect children? Anecdotal evidence of parents and teachers links violent television programming to violent behavior in children (Carlsson-Paige and Levin, 1992). One psychiatrist writes, "It has been demonstrated that long-term exposure of preadolescent children to television is a major cause of violence in later life. It could be concluded that television is not suited for preadolescent children" (Centerwall, 1994, p. 194).

   The National Association for the Education of Young Children (NAEYC) wants to regulate television programming aimed at young children "to limit media exposure to violence and restrict practices that market violence through the linkup of media, toys, and licensed products" (NAEYC, 1993, p. 82).

   Media representatives argue that such regulation would amount to censorship and a violation of the First Amendment's guarantee to freedom of the press. They argue that "violence on the home screen *follows* the violence in our lives"; it does not cause violence (*TV Violence*, 1993, p. 281).

   Which position do you support? If you support the NAEYC point of view, would you favor regulations that limit children's exposure to video games that encourage aggressive behavior? What about music videos that suggest danger and violence?

2. Several years ago, a 4-year-old child in California was playing with his grandfather's loaded .22-calibre handgun when it went off. The boy shot himself in the heart and died almost instantly. The boy's grandfather was charged under a California law that holds adults responsible for injury or death resulting from negligently stored firearms. Similar laws are on the books in Florida, Iowa, Connecticut, Maine, Virginia, New Jersey, Wisconsin, Maryland, and Hawaii. These laws are supported by members of Handgun Control, Inc., an organization advocating stricter control of firearms.

   Representatives of the National Rifle Association (NRA) argue that to prosecute the gun owner if children are injured with the adult's gun is a misguided use of governmental authority. They argue that homes are filled with dangerous items: pesticides, cleaning fluids, kitchen knives, and matches, to name a few. Children must be taught that guns and many other things found in the home are dangerous. Families have a responsibility to teach children about safety. In the case cited above, prosecuting the grandfather of the deceased 4-year-old only visits additional tragedy on an already suffering family (*Violence in Schools,* 1993).

Do you support the NRA position or the position of Handgun Control, Inc.? If you support the NRA position, would you go so far as to argue that the school curriculum should include lessons on firearm safety?

3. The NAEYC recommends against the use of corporal punishment in schools. It argues that the "use of corporal punishment in such situations teaches children that physical solutions to problems are acceptable for adults and that aggression is an appropriate way to control the behavior of other people. The institutional use of corporal punishment should never be condoned" (NAEYC, 1993, p. 83).

What policies concerning corporal punishment are there in your state and local school district? What are your personal views about corporal punishment as a form of discipline? If some parents approve of the teacher's use of physical punishment and prefer that their children be disciplined in this manner, should the teacher accede to the parent's wishes?

References

Brimelow, P. (1994). "Disadvantaging the Advantaged." *Forbes* **154,** 52–57.

Brendtro, L., and Long, N. (1995). "Breaking the Cycle of Conflict." *Educational Leadership* **52,** 52–56.

Brophy, J., and McCaslin, M. (1992). "Teachers' Reports of How They Perceive and Cope with Problem Students." *The Elementary School Journal* **99**(1), 3–68.

Carlsson-Paige, N., and Levin, N. (1990). *Who's Calling the Shots? How to Respond Effectively to Children's Fascination with War Play and War Toys.* Philadelphia: New Society Publishers.

Caspi, A., et al. (1994). "Are Some People Crime-Prone?" *Criminology* **32,** 163–196.

Centerwall, B. S. (1994). "Television and the Development of the Superego: Pathways to Violence." In *Children and Violence,* edited by C. Chiland and J. G. Young. Northvale, NJ: Aronson.

Curcio, J. L., and First, P. (1993). *Violence in the Schools: How to Proactively Prevent and Defuse it.* Newbury Park, CA: Corwin.

Dill, V. S. and Haberman, M. (1995). "Building A Gentler School." *Educational Leadership* **52,** 69–71.

Dworkin, M. S. (1959). *Dewey on Education.* New York: Teachers College.

Elam, S. M., Rose, L. C., and Gallup, A. M. (1994). "The 26th Annual Phi Delta Kappa/Gallup Poll of the Public's Attitudes Toward the Public Schools." *Phi Delta Kappan* **76,** 41–64.

Freud, S. (1930/1961). *Civilization and Its Discontents,* translated and edited by J. Strachey. New York: Norton.

Goldstein, A. P., Harootunian, B., and Conoley, J. C. (1994). *Student Aggression: Prevention, Management, and Replacement Training.* New York: Guilford.

Harris, L., and Associates. (1993). *Violence in America's Public Schools.* New York: Metropolitan Life Insurance Co.

———— (1994). *Violence in America's Public Schools: The Family Perspective.* New York: Metropolitan Life Insurance Co.

Herrnstein, R. J., and Murray, C. (1994). *The Bell Curve: Intelligence and Class Structure in American Life.* New York: Free Press.

Lawton, M. (1994). "Violence-Prevention Curricula: What Works Best?" *Education Week,* November 9, pp. 1, 10–11.

Mahaffey, F. (1994). "Eliminate Violence in the Classroom." *Utne Reader,* January/February, pp. 82–83.

Moore, M. and Anderson, J. W. (1995). "Wars Young Victims." *Washington Post National Weekly Edition,* May 8–14, pp. 6–7.

Morse, P. A., and Andrea, R. (1994). "Peer Mediation in the Schools: Teaching Conflict Resolution Techniques to Students." *NASSP Bulletin* **78,** 75–82.

NAEYC Position Statement on Violence in the Lives of Children. (1993). *Young Children* **48,** 80–85.

Natale, J. A. (1994). "Roots of Violence." *The American School Board Journal,* March, pp. 33–40.

Newman, M. (1995). "Disciplinary Schools Planned for Students Carrying Weapons." *The New York Times,* March 8, pp. 1, B4.

Noguera, P. A. (1995). "Preventing and Producing Violence: A Critical Analysis of Responses to School Violence." *Harvard Education Review,* **65,** 189–212.

Portner, J. (1994). "A New Breed of School for Troubled Youths." *Education Week* **13,** 30–31.

Recess from Violence: Making Our Schools Safe. (1993). Hearings before the Subcommittee on Education Arts and Humanities of the Committee on Labor and Human Resources. U.S. Senate, 103rd Congress, First Session on S.1125 (September 23). Washington, DC: U.S. Government Printing Office.

Reiss, A. J., Jr., and Roth, J. A. (1993). *Understanding and Preventing Violence.* Washington, DC: National Academy Press.

Rodriguez, L. J. (1993). *Always Running, La Vida Loca: Gang Days in L.A.* Willimantic, CT: Curbstone.

Roth, J. A. (1994). *Understanding and Preventing Violence.* Washington, DC: National Institute of Justice.

Sautter, R. C. (1995). "Standing Up to Violence." *Phi Delta Kappan* **76,** K1–K12.

TV Violence. (1993). In *CQ Researcher.* Washington, DC: Congressional Quarterly.

U.S. Department of Justice. (1994). Firearms and Crimes of Violence: Selected Findings from National Statistical Series, February 1994 MCJ-146844. Washington, DC: Department of Justice.

van den Haag, E. (1994). "How to Cut Crime." *National Review,* May, pp. 30–35.

Violence in Schools. (1992). In *CQ Researcher.* Washington, DC: Congressional Quarterly.

—————— (1993). National Education Association (video), Teacher TV Episode No. 15. West Haven, CT: National Education Association.

Wallach, L. B. (1993). "Helping Children Cope With Violence." *Young Children* **48,** 4–11.

Weishew, N. L., and Peng, S. S. (1993). "Variables Predicting Students' Problem Behaviors." *Journal of Educational Research* **87,** 5–17.

Yen, M. (1994). "A Shock That Seldom Jolts." *The Washington Post National Weekly Edition.* November 28–December 4, pp. 10–11.

CHAPTER EIGHTEEN

School Reform: Excellence or Equity

POSITION 1:
EXCELLENCE IS A PUBLIC DECEPTION

Introduction

How many times have you seen a school identify itself as an inferior school? Do you recall hearing school officials refer to their school as mediocre or below average? When school innovations are announced, does the school proclaim the changes to be common or average? Are there examples of schools that aim just to be good or fair or decent? Most schools, instead, claim excellence as their goal, excellence as the reason for change, and excellence as their official identity. Just as we have had grade inflation and price inflation, we have also had language inflation.

Excellent schools produce excellent students who become excellent readers and excellent college students. Readers of this text may see themselves as examples of the truth of that statement. The defect, of course, is that excellence comes to have no meaning because it encompasses all meanings when overused. Using excellence as a synonym for success diminishes its comparative value. At the same time, the undercurrent of comparative weight carried by the term "excellence" is deceptive when used to evaluate the complex quality of schools. What is an excellent school? Who should determine that? What criteria should be used? Is excellence the best measure of education? In a somewhat satirical, but insightful, article, Linda Weltner (1994) captured the nonsense of the excellence standard; she notes that mediocrity allows people to experience the simple joy of doing things without the intimidation (and superficiality) of an imposed standard of "excellence."

Excellence is the catchword of the education reform movement at the end of the twentieth century. It is an overused and ill-used word. Unfortunately, the excellence movement in education is a sham and a deception, despite its popularity. In addition, there is a hidden agenda, beneath the soft rhetoric, that should alarm American citizens and make them angry. First, we will explore the nature of the excellence movement, and then offer a critique.

If you doubt that "excellence" is the key word of the government's 1990s school reform agenda, consider the evidence. Most of the major newspapers and weekly newsmagazines feature stories on school reform as part of the schools' effort to become excellent. *Education Week* ("American Education's Newspaper of Record") has devoted front-page space in many issues to the "excellence" movement and has chronicled, state by state, the various school reform activities identified as moving toward excellence. Even Burger King, noted for its concerns for quality, sponsors national awards for excellence in education.

The professional education literature is filled with such stories. *Educational Leadership* has devoted entire issues and many articles to "excellence." *Phi Delta Kappan* has featured whole issues and presented numerous articles on it. The most widely read publications in education have used or overused the term in the past few years.

One indicator of the increasing overuse of "excellent" is the number of times it has been featured in the professional literature. The *Education Index* lists current articles appearing each month in the most widely circulated journals on education. At the end of the 1970s—for example, July 1977 to June 1978—there was no separate "Excellence" category. And of the thirty-four articles listed under the category of "Education: Aims and Purposes," not one used "excellence" in its title. Five years later, in academic year 1982–1983, there also was no separate category of "Excellence," and no articles under "Aims and Purposes" with excellence in their titles. But the next year, 1983–1984, the category "Excellence" had to be added, and eleven of sixty-seven articles cited under "Education: Aims and Purposes" used the word "excellence" in their titles. By the end of the decade, the "Excellence" category had become a fixture because of the number of articles on that topic. By 1995, "excellence" was so trite, it declined in usage.

The situation is similar in the *Current Index to Journals in Education* (CIJE), another reference work to professional literature. Before June 1983, there was no separate category for articles on excellence. By December 1984, there were two categories: "Excellence" and "Excellence in Education." By the end of the decade, a new and third category, "Excellence (Quality)," had been added.

The widely publicized Report of the National Commission on Excellence in Education, *A Nation at Risk,* appeared in 1983. The risk to America, the report suggested, was a school crisis that threatened America's military and business competitiveness in the world. No significant evidence that there was a crisis was presented, but this politically important document contributed the oft-quoted phrase that schools were developing "a rising tide of mediocrity." The answer to the risk, the report said, was excellence, even though it did little to define the term or to explain how we would know excellence when we saw it. Now we find that the so-called crisis in American education was not real, and that the government suppressed a solid study showing that the schools were better than the report had claimed (Bracey, 1993; Tanner, 1993).

Where was the standard of excellence in this fiasco? Certainly the government did not behave with excellence.

Given all of this publicity, one would think that there actually is a massive excellence movement in education in America. That might indicate some level of agreement on what excellence is and how we are moving toward it. Advocating excellence is easy. It sounds desirable, but in determining what constitutes excellence as it appears in schools, we must raise some critical questions.

What Constitutes the Excellence Movement in Education?

Current indicators of excellence in education are illustrated by a list of "reform" regulations and activities that have been described in recent articles:

Mandatory kindergarten

State-mandated tests for grade-to-grade promotion, graduation, and school-to-school comparisons

Longer school days and school years

Emphasis on homework and mastery of skills

Limits on time students spend on extracurricular activities

Increased course and grade requirements for high school graduation

Increased college admission requirements

Increased state control of teacher education

State-required tests to obtain teacher licenses

This list summarizes much of the excellence movement in education. There are several important points to note in examining the list.

This excellence movement seems intent on making school a dull, lifeless, unexciting drudgery that focuses on a series of test hurdles and gates that separate students and label them for life. Little in the literature on excellence speaks of improving the quality of school life for students and teachers, encouraging creativity, and enhancing the joy of learning. Little speaks of the need to correct disadvantages among children, to equalize opportunities, or to bring minorities more fully into the American mainstream through education. The movement mainly presents a restrictive and negative list of increasing requirements that is likely to increase the gap between those who already have economic advantage and those who do not. Cuban (1994) argues that the national standards overlook one-third of our schools, mostly inner-city places where the sham of excellence in education without adequate financing is apparent.

It is no wonder that we now face increasing student dropout rates, especially for minorities, and a decline in the number of minority candidates for teaching credentials. The excellence movement is taking its toll on democracy.

Most of the items on the excellence list of reforms are new state mandates, inserting the state bureaucracy more fully into control of the schools. In the

1990s, there is a major effort to expand this idea from state to national control through tests and curriculum determination. This increasing centralization of control limits the possibilities of variation and flexibility among schools. In addition to the obvious conformity it entails, the movement threatens school district autonomy and academic freedom because it becomes easier to exert state or national control over the curriculum and teaching methodology.

Also, the list shows that there is increasing infatuation with simplistic numbers from test scores, rather than with the deeper quest for quality in education. Because test scores have become so important, tests exert excessive influence on the school curriculum, teacher activities, and teacher and school evaluation. School boards and administrators force teachers to teach to the test. Teachers drill students to score higher. If the tests were universally valid, actually showing what students know, there might be some grounds for more testing. Instead, the tests are seriously limited and generally invalid; they are mainly devices that reduce schooling to a series of comparative numbers to make political, not educational, decisions easier. Testing and quantitive changes in the time spent are the primary indicators of this so-called excellence movement; the qualitative concerns for which education was established are ignored. It is easy to measure excellence by using invalid standardized tests, but it is absurd.

State legislatures have underfunded education for decades, but escape blame for school problems by blaming the victims of this situation. Minorities and members of lower socioeconomic classes are penalized by the shift from equity to excellence. Teachers are deprofessionalized by state requirements that diminish teacher rights to make academic decisions. Although there has been some effort to improve teacher salaries, it does not make up for years of neglect, and does not compensate for the deprofessionalizing and antidemocratic nature of most of the "excellence" agenda (Barber, 1993).

What is the real meaning of "excellence" in schools? There are serious questions with regard to the definition, the direction, and the virtue of setting excellence as the school purpose in a society that aims to be free and democratic.

Excellence and Elitism

"Excellence" is a word that separates people. To excel is to be superior to others, to stand above them, to outdo them. Excellence requires some form of elite. And Lasch (1994) argues that the threat to democracy comes now from the elite in America: "Simultaneously arrogant and insecure, the new elites regard the masses with mingled scorn and apprehension" (p. 41). The excellence movement, largely supported by the elite, may be just another way to deal with the masses by undercutting their education and differentiating their quality on grounds that have little to do with real quality.

The idea of excellence begins with the premise that some people are superior to others, and the only question is how to find ways to measure those differences. The measure must separate people, labeling some excellent and others by other titles. We can then have categories of people: excellent, very good,

good, poor, rotten failures. If you are in the "excellent" category, you may be happy to have the others below you. If you are in the "poor" category, you may not be so content, and you may not have an escape. There is a necessary elitism in the term "excellence." And that elitism may rest only on the desire of an elite group to maintain itself.

Assume for a moment that we are members of a group of foot fetishists. What we are going to measure is the length of people's feet—the longer, the better. Feet are easy to measure, and we can set the "excellent" category to mean those with feet at least 18 inches long. Very few will be excellent, but we have a clear though absurd measure. Those identified as excellent on this measure are likely to protest any effort to lower the requirement. If some egalitarian concerns prompt us to expand the "excellent" category to include those with feet that are 9 inches long or longer, we have not added to the quality of the definition, but only to the quantity of people who can now be called excellent. This approach clarifies the measure and the category to some extent, but it has no real meaning in the complex workings of the society, no matter how many people are included. Relative foot size may be of great significance to shoe manufacturers, but it has little to do with the broad context of everyday life.

Similarly, the measures we have of excellence in schooling are usually severely limited, weak, and simplistic symbols that convey far more than they should. Various state tests of "achievement," SAT scores, grades, or other single-score indicators hide as much knowledge of students as they reveal. These indicators are often biased in language, in content, in form, and in intent. They typically show that those who were born into advantaged families and have proper training do well, while those who were born into disadvantaged families and have more limited economic environments do poorly.

Excellence based on these indicators is not excellence, but luck. Worse, the measures become labels that separate and identify those who will succeed and those who will not. Even though the measures have little relation to real life in a complex world, they become the stamps society accepts, and individuals begin to believe in them. Those stamped as failures begin to see themselves that way, and they become failures. Those from the already elite groups remain elite because they control the images of success and failure. That means they must control the measures, the symbols, and the rituals that give power in the society. And they utilize convoluted logic and language to try to convince a presumably democratic society that elitism is a way of moving toward the basic democratic values of justice and equality. This is the sham of the excellence movement.

Mystification in Educational Reform

The excellence movement relies on mystification. Mystification is a process that uses vague and ambiguous terms, seemingly objective symbols, and politically dramatic rhetoric to confuse and hide real purposes. The movement's inability or unwillingness clearly to define adequate criteria for excellence, and its attempts to argue that excellence and equality are easily compatible, are examples of vague and ambiguous language. Objective-appearing symbols include the overuse of tests, despite questions as to their validity, and the separation and labeling of people by comparative test scores. Dramatic political rhetoric appears in national reports that claim, without examining conflicting evidence, that the nation is "at risk" and subject to international decline because of schools.

Mystification serves the interests of those in the dominant class. It is a means to undergird and protect the power base of elites. Techniques of mystification are used to persuade the public that the ruling elite are naturally endowed and best suited to further the interests of society. In hierarchical societies, most elite positions are reserved for those who claim a birthright monopoly on such characteristics as excellence, nobility, or refinement. The definition of "excellence" includes vague and mysterious qualities that the elites are presumed to already have. Not all citizens are equally eligible, since the elites have early and continuous advantage. And the elites control the measures and the gates for admission. A democracy, however, is intended to provide equality and justice in real opportunities for all. One should expect much more social mobility in a democracy, but that mobility is a threat to the elites. Mystification, in a democracy, uses terms that sound democratic, but hide the latent purposes of elitism.

This is of particular importance because the political rhetoric that surrounds necessarily elite terms like "excellence" either must boldly announce that the advantaged will get increased favoritism, or it must tread very lightly on the required hierarchical separation. In a nominally democratic society, the goal of excellence must be expressed subtly in order to retain public support. It is theoretically and linguistically possible to have justice, equality, and freedom for all. But how can there be excellence for all and the term still retain its implications? If all are excellent, then excellence has no meaning. The essence of the term "excellence" requires elitism.

Manifest and Latent Goals of Excellence

A manifest goal of an excellence movement is to achieve excellence, that is, to increase or enhance the separation among people according to some criteria identified as fitting a definition of "excellent." That goal may be stated in terms that attempt to incorporate large proportions of a society, like "better than we were" or "better than other contemporary societies." There is, thus, a necessary presumption that we were of lower quality in previous times or other places. A statement of goals for excellence may also lead to a separation among people for social benefit, as in special advantages for the best and brightest to assure excellent future leadership.

Often, manifest goals are cloudy and disguise the potential consequences of separatist requirements, as when advocates of merit salary systems for teachers presume that we all agree on what merit is and how it is measured. Interestingly, most current literature and the National Commission report do not refer to the previous excellence movement for schools, which followed the launching of *Sputnik* in 1957. That movement contained much of the same mystification rhetoric; it advocated testing and dull routine in school life, and elitist control of the contemporary movement. It also suffered the same inability to set clear criteria for excellence, to expand democracy, to enhance opportunities, and to provide for quality in education (Bracey, 1994; Tanner, 1993).

Latent goals of the excellence movement are based on such grounds as social-class interest, racism, free-enterprise capitalism, and political power. These latent goals include:

Reasserting social control

Preserving the status quo

Maintaining certain elites

Redressing a shift toward progressive egalitarianism

Reasserting the influence of business and industry

The current reform efforts aimed at "excellence" are a collection of restrictions and requirements that will do little to improve democracy, justice, or equality. The previous excellence movement only reinforced gross inequalities in the amounts of public tax money available for schools. Wealthy suburbs gained significantly, while poor urban schools suffered even more. Excellent schools were arranged for the well-to-do, while deficient schools were provided to the poor. The drive for progressive equity in schools, drawing from ideas of the 1930s and 1940s, was slowed.

Current efforts appear to be repeating this phenomenon. The government restricts funds for equalizing opportunities, such as Head Start, Title 1, and higher-education loans, while initiating projects to reward high test scores and "meritorious" students. Progressive equity policies expanded in the 1960s are the victims of efforts to provide protection for elites, under the title of "excellence," in the 1990s. Is it the society or the elites that have chosen excellence over equity?

The sham of the excellence movement in education will become known as its dimensions are realized by an educated and critical public.

POSITION 2:
EXCELLENCE IS THE ONLY REFORM

Schooling requires accountability to students, parents, taxpayers, and the general society. Schools, as the social agency that involves the most people for the longest period of their lives at the greatest cost, are accountable to many constituencies. Students deserve to know they are well served and will be prepared to function at the highest level in society. Parents need to know that their children are being taught knowledge, skills, and values, and in safety. Taxpayers must be shown that the high cost of schooling is worth it. And the society properly expects that schools will fulfill their mission of providing society with well-educated citizens. In America, the public has a right to expect high-quality performance; it is a standard suited to America's role in the world. To meet these expectations, American schools must establish high goals and continuously work to achieve them.

Excellence is the goal we should use in education as the basis for planning, and as the main criterion against which to judge the schools. The goal of excellence sets our vision high, but still provides an ideal that incorporates the flexibility to change as conditions change. Excellence is the appropriate educational goal for a nation that has already achieved world recognition in establishing a democracy, in science, in the arts, in literature, in business and industry, and in protecting human rights. For America, there can be no lesser goal for the schools.

The primary purpose of education is to improve the lives of people through knowledge. That is also a fundamental purpose of any democratic and progressive society. To be satisfied with less is to move away from democracy and progress. Improvement is, therefore, the key to educational reform. Obviously, it does not make sense to advocate reforms that do not intend to improve on the way things are. Why would one want reform that made things worse?

But improvement is elusive without a sense of direction, and it can be so minor that it is virtually unmeasurable, or it can be very extensive. The issue, then, is to determine criteria against which to evaluate reforms. In effect, we should ask how far we should go in reforms in education. And how do we know which reforms are going in the right direction?

These questions need to be addressed in terms of our long-range goal. This goal sets the basic agenda, and allows us to plan the strategies and tactics that will nudge schools toward the achievement of that goal.

This would seem to be a goal about which there would be no argument. Excellence, one would think, is what we all would want. But there is dispute that needs review.

The Naysayers

Some people argue that America should not set excellence as the goal for schools because it makes the school too rigorous, too "academic." They want the schools to be a place of free play for children, where little work is required. This may sound like a pleasant purpose for schools and for children, but it is misleadingly pleasant. Little is gained without a struggle. Freedom without purpose is really slavery to personal whims. The schools form the new generation of citizens in the society. We cannot allow schools to become playgrounds, or America will suffer. Excellence requires effort and achievement. Our children deserve more credit and more challenge.

Other people don't want to change the schools because they fear the challenge of excellence. They are not accustomed to having their work reviewed, and they resent any intrusion that holds them responsible for good work. They have found a sanctuary in the bureaucracy and do not want exposure. Reform toward excellence threatens their jobs or their convenience. They do not want to be evaluated; they do not want to exert energy; they do not want to be accountable. Despite the evidence of weakness, the schools resist change. There is good reason to shake up this group. It is more than a question of mere job productivity; the resisting ones are holding back students, parents, and the society.

School is too important to leave to those who are satisfied with less than excellence. Some of the resistors will respond when they see that reforms are coming in any event. Others will begin to fade as their inadequacies are revealed by the reforms. Resisting change is a losing proposition for all concerned. It is a prescription for atrophy in schools and in society.

Some distrust excellence because it is an unknown. They have seen school fads come and go, without improvement. Their argument is that if the schools won't change, it is hopeless to pursue reform. They have become accustomed to mediocre performance in schools, but do not know how to alter the situation. They have watched test scores drop. They have read of high school graduates who are illiterate. They have observed deficiencies in student knowledge of American history. And they know students who have trouble with simple math and scientific principles. They are frustrated with the state of the schools, but complacent. Complacency, especially in the face of declining quality, will simply speed the decline of the schools. Since change is always happening, these people stand against the tide. Standing still while everything else moves leaves you further behind. While this group may not like the decline of schools, they are unsure of what excellence would mean. But they are, at least, open to setting a new agenda for the schools.

A final group of naysayers believes that excellence in education is somehow undemocratic. This is a substantial argument, since equality is popularly believed to be part of democracy. How can we have equality and still have excellence? Not everyone can be excellent, they claim, so using excellence as a criterion will only separate people, and then they will not be equal. That idea is interesting, and deserves fuller consideration than that given to the other arguments of the naysayers.

Excellence, Equality, and Equity

It is a smokescreen to suggest that excellence and equality are opposites. Excellence does not automatically deny equality. To be equal does not mean that we cannot be different. Differences are necessary in nature. Similarly, equality can function well when the goal is excellence. We do not have to choose one or the other. In fact, the democratic idea of excellence that is advocated here as a goal for the schools actually improves equality. It is by setting the goal of excellence that everyone is given the chance to develop their individual potentials. Excellence provides the opportunity for all to be excellent. That is the best form of equality, an excellent society. Although this ideal has not yet been achieved, it is an ideal that is worth pursuing. That is the excellence agenda.

We can try for excellence in our daily work activities. A cabinetmaker who carefully fits fine-surfaced pieces of wood together can be proud of workmanship that represents excellence. A stockbroker who examines company financial statements with care and diligence before making recommendations can also demonstrate excellence. Street sweepers who recognize their contributions to the beauty of a city and make special efforts to do a first-class job can be excellent. Store clerks, bankers, florists, computer operators, politicians, artists, hairdressers, librarians, and all those in other occupations can show excellence in their work. When people take pride in going beyond the mediocre, the resulting product is of higher quality. The benefits accrue to the individual and to the society. Excellence becomes a great motivator, with intrinsic and extrinsic rewards. We feel better about our work, and we do better work.

Forms of Equality and Equity

Some of the dispute over excellence and equality occurs because of differences in the way equality is viewed. There are several ways to look at equality.

Equality of condition means that everyone has or gets an equal amount of something. If we had an apple pie to divide among eight people, we could cut eight equal slices so that each person would have equality of condition with regard to the pie.

There is also an equality based on claim. This form of equality presumes that everyone has the same power to claim equal portions of things, but may elect not to exercise that claim. If we cut the pie into eight equal pieces, and one person gave his or her slice to another, we no longer have equality of condition. One person has two slices and another has none. But we would have equality of claim. Each person could have claimed an equal piece of pie.

Equality of opportunity is similar to equality of claim. If we notified all eight people that the pie would be cut at noon, and only seven people showed up by that time, we could cut the pie into seven equal slices and the eighth person would have none, having given up the opportunity to have a piece. There was equal opportunity, but equal condition did not result.

Equality determined by justification suggests that there are rational grounds on which to justify unequal conditions. There may be sound reasons to slice the pie into unequal parts. If one person is diabetic and can't eat pie, this could be a good reason not to divide it equally among all eight persons. If one person does not like apple pie, that may alter the division. If one person cannot eat a whole slice and another can eat more than one slice, an unequal division is reasonable. If the group agrees to give half of the pie to two people who missed out on pie the last time, this is a justification for inequality in pie slices. This is the basic notion of equity, that things may be divided unequally if there is a reasonable justification for doing so.

Equity, the Reasonable Approach to Equality

A democratic society can attempt to provide equity. Equity is based on fairness or justice. Equity permits inequality when it is fair to do so. There are times, as in our attempt to correct the racial discrimination of years ago, when we need to provide extra help for those who have been victimized. That extra help is unequal since not everyone gets the same amount of it. But it is considered the fair, or equitable, way to proceed. Programs of assistance in welfare, in tax relief for those with low incomes, in special college scholarships for disadvantaged minorities, and in many other unequal distributions of financial support are considered fair as examples of equity in society.

Equality of condition has never occurred, and it is unlikely to ever develop. Despite efforts in some socialistic countries, there is no example of completely equal treatment for all people of a society. Socialist governments attempt to make some things appear equal by requiring conformity and stifling individual initiative, but inequalities persist. Commissars and internationally competitive athletes were better treated than were typical workers in the old Soviet bloc nations. The obvious failure of socialism in the current world tellingly marks the weakness of equality of condition.

Humans are simply born unequal, and we grow unequally. We have unequal mental and physical characteristics. We have unequal desires, needs, and interests. This is a natural condition. Since we have inherent inequality of condition by endowment, we can't change that by trying to manufacture equality of condition, dividing everything into equal portions.

Equality of claim, of opportunity, and of justification all permit some inequality. These views of equality can fit into the concept of equity. If we provide that all persons have a claim to equal treatment under the law, that is fair, even though not everyone will necessarily have equally sound cases or equal amounts of time or equal lawyers and speaking ability. It is fair to provide equality of opportunity for everyone to succeed, by offering free public education, special help for those who want to take advantage of it, and access to public information and assistance, even though not everyone will get, or want, an equal amount. If we give special assistance to some groups and individuals because there is social justification for special treatment, that is fair, even though not everyone will get an equal distribution. The fairness of this approach to equality is the root of equity.

School Reform for Excellence and Equity

The promotion of excellence and equity at the same time in schools is difficult, but worthy. Essentially, there are two major premises for this approach to reform in education. One offers clear and open opportunity for all to achieve; the other sets standards for performance. Both elements are needed in improving schools.

First, public schools need to remain open to all who can benefit, and they should especially encourage those who are making the most effort to do well in schoolwork. Schools should make this point very clear in their communications with the community and in their organization and operation. This principle should be obvious to the society and to the students. We need to be sure that everyone understands that access to schools is open, but there is an expectation for performance. All are welcome, but learning is valued and disruption is not tolerated. Equality of opportunity occurs when everyone understands the focus of the school and is able to take advantage of what schools offer.

Second, the schools need to emphasize excellence in academic quality. This should include giving extra help to those who have had difficulty, but who desire to succeed and who show potential. It should also include extra help for students whose exceptional talents can be expanded and enriched. These youngsters, sometimes called gifted and talented, are the students who are likely to become leading figures in society as adults. They deserve to have their abilities honed, and the society will reap the benefits in the future. It is a social and educational tragedy to hold back our brightest and best in their development because a school is misguided in its idea of equality. Equity would suggest that our best need the best.

Developing Excellence

High-caliber students develop in the company of others of high quality. Excellent tennis players want to play with other excellent players because they improve their skills that way. Excellent carpenters want to work with excellent carpenters because they can learn and improve. But weak tennis players and carpenters learn more when they are with others who are only slightly better than they are. If there is too much difference between the levels of quality and talent, the weak ones become embarrassed and drop out, and the talented ones are restricted in their development because of the time spent with the weaker ones. The development of excellence in schools requires some separation to utilize real peer encouragement and initiative.

Excellent students must also have excellent teachers and administrators. We should be able to leave that unsaid, since it is so obvious. But in many schools, high-ability students are not challenged by their teachers, and are managed by administrators who impede their progress. Reforms are needed in teacher and administrator education. We must provide adequate rewards for teaching and school administration, but we must expect high-quality performance. Further, we must give extra rewards to truly exceptional teachers and administrators in order to motivate their pursuit of excellence in education. Excellent educators serve as ideal role models for the academic development of students who have the basic talent and who make the effort.

Effort and Excellence

An important point needs to be made with regard to the need for effort in our move toward excellence. Innate intellectual differences among people and luck are unsuitable grounds for giving educational advantages to some youths over others. Simply because a person is born with high intelligence is not a sufficient basis for special treatment if that person does not work to develop those inherited traits. Similarly, the mere luck of being born into an upper-class family should not entitle a person to favored treatment in schools. We need to motivate and encourage students toward success in academic activities, but some may forsake their talents or rely primarily on family status. Neither position is compatible with the movement toward excellence in education. And neither is consistent with the concept of equity in the distribution of special advantages in schools.

Those who are intellectually lazy and those who believe that wealth deserves favor are not making the kind of contribution needed for the excellent society.

Excellence and Equity in Schooling Reform

The movement toward excellence in education includes school reforms that:

Provide access to schools for all who can benefit

Set high standards of performance

Hold schools accountable for their academic work

Reward merit in students, teachers, and administrators

It is clear that excellence is the most appropriate goal for a progressive democratic society and its schools. Without such a goal, schools are adrift and will decline. It is to society's benefit that schools continually strive for excellence. That striving will require extra effort and may involve some discontent. Some of the discontent can be easily dismissed, but the concern about equity is important. It is incumbent on the schools to demonstrate that the reforms leading to excellence are also equitable.

Excellence and equity are very compatible when educational excellence offers equality of opportunity for all students to become high achievers. Further, some inequality of condition is fair and equitable because the entire society gains from the nurturing of the most talented. This helps in America's search for excellence.

For Discussion

1. How should excellence be defined? If it is possible to be excellent at fascism, excellent at dictatorship, excellent at creating death and destruction, then being excellent is insufficient without some values to guide the purpose for excellence. What are legitimate values that should undergird the striving for excellence in American society? How are these values addressed in the movement for excellence in schooling?
2. Which of the following data show excellence in America? Which show equity?

Infant mortality:	Ranks 21st among nations (lower than Spain, Ireland, Japan, Hong Kong, Germany, and France).
African-American infant mortality:	Ranks thirty-second.
Prenatal care for mothers:	25 percent do not or cannot afford to receive it.
African-American prenatal care:	39 percent do not receive it.
Immunization against polio:	Ranks seventeenth among nations (lower than Albania, Botswana, Tunisia, and Sri Lanka).

Health insurance:	Almost 40 percent of children have no coverage.
Poverty:	20 percent of all children under age 18 are poor; 33 percent of those with parents under age 30 are poor.
Income gap:	The gap between rich and poor is wider now than at any time since the Census Bureau started keeping records (1947). The poorest 20 percent of the population get only 3.8 percent of total American income.
Child abuse:	Increased 90 percent between 1981 and 1986; remains high in 1990s.
School dropout rates:	Among poor families, 28.5 percent
	Among nonpoor families, 10.5 percent
	White females, 14 percent
	White males, 13 percent
	Black females, 14 percent
	Black males, 17 percent
	Latino females, 32 percent
	Latino males, 35 percent
Preschool program enrollments:	56 percent of those with incomes above $35,000 had children enrolled; 25 percent of those with incomes of $10,000 or less had children enrolled.
High school graduation rates:	Whites, 74 percent
	Blacks, 58 percent
	Latinos, 52 percent
Arms Exporting:	Ranks first among nations.
Military expenditures:	Ranks first among 142 nations.
Nuclear reactors:	Ranks first among nations.
Military aid to other countries:	Ranks first among nations.
Population per physician:	Ranks twenty-second among nations.
School-age children per teacher:	Ranks twentieth among nations.

Sources: State of America's Children 1991. Washington, DC: Children's Defense Fund, 1991; Ruth Leger Sivard, World Military and Social Expenditures, 1993. Washington, DC: World Priorities, 1993.

3. Being opposed to excellence sounds un-American. What case, in addition to the ones presented in the chapter, can be made that being against excellence is in the American tradition?

References

Astin, A. (1990). "Educational Assessment and Educational Equity." *American Journal of Education* **98,** 458–478.

Baptiste, H. P., et al., eds. (1990). *Leadership, Equity, and School Effectiveness.* Newbury Park, CA: Sage.

Barber, B. (1993). "America Skips School: Why We Talk So Much About Education and Do So Little." *Harper's Magazine* **287,** 39–47.

Bracey, G. (1994). "The Fourth Bracey Report on the Condition of Public Education." *Phi Delta Kappan* **76,** 114–127.

Bracey, G. (1995). "The Assessor Assessed: A 'Revisionist' Looks at a Critique of the Sandia Report." *Journal of Educational Research* **88,** 136–144.

Bridgman, A. (1985). "States Launching Barrage of Initiatives, Survey Finds." *Education Week,* February 6, pp. 1, 31.

Carnoy, M. (1983). "Education, Democracy, and Social Conflict." *Harvard Educational Review* **53,** 398–402.

Cuban, L. (1994). "How Can a 'National' Strategy Miss a Third of our Schools?" *Education Digest* **59,** 12–17.

Excellence in Education: Blue Ribbon Schools Program. (1990). Office of Educational Research and Improvement. Washington, DC: U.S. Department of Education.

Finkelstein, B. (1984). "Education and the Retreat from Democracy in the United States, 1979–1980?" *Teachers College Record* **86,** 275–282.

Finn, C. E. (1984). "The Excellence Backlash: Sources of Resistance to Educational Reform." *The American Spectator* **17,** 10–16.

Fisher, L. (1990). "Equality: An Elusive Ideal." *Equity and Excellence* **24,** 64–72.

Gardner, J. W. (1961). *Excellence: Can We Be Equal and Excellent Too?* New York: Harper & Row.

Glazer, N. (1987). "Equity and Excellence in Education: A Commentary." *Harvard Educational Review* **57,** 196–199.

Husen, T. (1985). "The School in the Achievement-Oriented Society: Crisis and Reform." *Phi Delta Kappan* **66,** 398–402.

Lasch, C. (1994). "The Revolt of the Elites." *Harper's Magazine* **289,** 39–49.

———— (1995). *The Revolt of the Elites and the Betrayal of Democracy.* New York: Norton.

Lewis, J. (1986). *Achieving Excellence in Our Schools.* Westbury, NY: Wilkerson.

Marcoulides, G. A., and Heck, R. H. (1990). "Educational Policy Issues for the 1990s: Balancing Equity and Excellence in Implementing the Reform Agenda." *Urban Education* **25,** 304–316.

McNett, I. (1984). *Charting a Course: A Guide to the Excellence Movement in Education.* Washington, DC: Council for Basic Education.

National Commission on Excellence in Education. (1983). *A Nation at Risk.* Washington, DC: U.S. Government Printing Office.

Peters, T., and Waterman, R. H. (1982). *In Search of Excellence: Lessons from America's Best Run Corporations.* New York: Harper & Row.

Raywid, M. A. (1990). "The Evolving Effort to Improve Schools: Pseudo-Reform, Incremental Reform, and Restructuring." *Phi Delta Kappan* **72,** 139–144.

Schaefer, T. E. (1990). "One More Time: How Do You Get Both Equality and Excellence in Education?" *Journal of Educational Thought* **24,** 39–51.

Tanner, D. (1993). "A Nation Truly at Risk." *Phi Delta Kappan* **75,** 288–297.

Weltner, L. (1994). "The Joys of Mediocrity." *Utne Reader* January/February, pp. 99–101.

Index

Abbott v. Burke, 42, 51*n*
Abramowitz, M., 36, 42, 51*n*, 64, 81*n*
Abstinence, 266
Academic freedom, 314, 317–319, 345–364
  and communities, 314
Academics
  in curriculum, 185–201, 203, 222
Academies
  Greek, 318
Accountability
  and curriculum, 241–242
  and excellence, 425
  school, 381
  for teachers, 345–364
Active learning, 212
Adler, M., 14, 20, 21*n*, 242, 260*n*, 303, 311*n*, 325, 329*n*
Administration, 315–317, 331–344
Adopt-a-school, 283–284
Affirmative action, 48–51, 160–184
African-Americans, 44, 50, 72–73, 225–227
Afrocentrism, 226
Aggressiveness, 409
Ahlquist, R., 271, 279*n*
Aid to families with dependent children, 32, 35–36
AIDS, 205
Altbach, P. G., 327, 328*n*
America 2000 (*See also* Goals 2000), 281, 287
American Association of University Professors (AAUP), 360, 362*n*
American Civil Liberties Union (ACLU), 29, 318, 346–347
American Federation of Teachers (AFT), 321–322, 367
Americanization, 9

Anderson, D., 262, 267, 279*n*
Anglo-American students, 229
Annenberg, W., 114
Anselm's Ontological Argument, 252–253
Anson, R., 177, 181*n*
Anti-American, 274–275
Anti-communism, 13
Anyon, J., 190, 200*n*, 273, 279*n*
Apartheid, 135
Apple, M., 4, 8, 21*n*, 200*n*, 224, 225, 240*n*, 275, 279*n*, 288, 291, 293*n*
Applebome, P., 68, 81*n*, 392, 400*n*
Aristotle, 187, 200*n*
Armor, D., 47, 51*n*, 149, 157*n*
Arnold, Matthew, 224
Aronowitz, S., 5, 21*n*, 228, 239*n*, 256, 260*n*, 273, 279*n*, 314, 325–326, 328*n*, 371, 376*n*
Arts in education, 268
Asian-Americans, 228–229
Asante, M. K., 226–227, 233, 239*n*
Atkins, A., 15, 25*n*
Authentic Assessment, 307–308
Australia, 398–399
Authoritarian, 214

Baird, C. W., 368, 377*n*
Bamberger, J., 212, 221*n*
Banks, J., 16, 21*n*, 225, 226, 239*n*
Barbanel, J., 111, 122, 123, 129*n*
Barber, B., 257, 260*n*, 422, 433*n*
Barnett, S., 116, 129*n*
Bartlett, D., 32, 51*n*
Barton, P., 111, 129*n*
Barzun, J., 109, 129*n*
Basic education, 186, 203–222
  and skills, 280–287

Bastian, A., 15, 21*n*, 32, 51*n*, 89, 98, 105*n*, 121, 129*n*, 253, 260*n*, 325, 328*n*
Beale, H., 359, 362*n*
Begley, S., 212, 221*n*
Bell, D., 117, 129*n*
Benefits, 74–75
Bennett, C., 152, 157*n*
Bennett, W., 14, 123, 129*n*, 262, 279*n*
Bensman, D., 138, 157*n*
Berger, J., 123, 129*n*
Berliner, D., 2, 21*n*
Bernstein, A., 33, 51*n*
Bernstein, N., 1, 21*n*
Bernstein, R., 50, 51*n*
Berthoff, D., 148, 152*n*
Besharov, D., 36, 51*n*, 71, 81*n*
Bestor, A., 208, 221*n*
Bill of Rights, 143, 345
Binet, A., 297
Birk, L., 372, 377*n*
Bissinger, H., 141, 157*n*
Blau, P., 284, 293*n*
Blits, J., 175, 181*n*
Block, F., 32, 52*n*
Bloom A., 225, 234, 240*n*
Bluestone, B., 30, 52*n*
Board of Education of Oklahoma City v. Dowell, 45, 52*n*
Boaz, D., 88, 105*n*
Bok, D., 33, 52*n*
Bond, J., 160, 182*n*
Bourdieu, P., 191, 200*n*
Bowles, S., 112, 129*n*
Boyer, E., 14, 21*n*, 188, 200*n*, 316, 328*n*
Bracey, G., 2, 21*n*, 420, 425, 433*n*
Bradley, 114, 129*n*, 369, 377*n*
Bradley, L & G., 47, 52*n*
Bradley v. Milliken, 145, 157*n*
Brameld, T., 6, 21*n*
Braun, R. J., 368, 377*n*
Brentro, L., 407, 417*n*
Briggs v. Elliott, 142, 157*n*
Brimelow, P., 365, 366, 377*n*
Broadfoot, P., 199, 200*n*
Brody, J., 58, 81*n*
Brophy, J., 411, 417*n*
Brown v. Board of Education of Topeka, 11, 21*n*, 43, 44, 52*n*, 132, 157*n*, 192, 200*n*
Bruck, C., 32, 52*n*
Bryant, W., 72
Buckley, W. F., 349, 363*n*
Bureaucracy
   in schools, 383–384
   and unions, 371–372
Bush, George, 84

Business, 196–198, 281–294
   ideology, 287–294
   influence on schools, 281–294
   intrusion into schools, 287–288
   as a model for schools, 281–294
   and privatization, 379–401
   roundtable, 281
   and school control, 196–198
   and technology, 285
Butts, R. F., 245, 260*n*

Cage, M., 171, 260*n*
California, 42
Callahan, R., 273, 279*n*, 288, 292, 298, 311*n*
Calvita, K., 290, 293*n*
Cannell, J. J., 300, 311*n*
Canon of knowledge, 234
Capitalism, 118–119, 197–198
   and schooling, 117–131, 275–276
Carlson, K., 7, 23*n*, 121, 129, 201*n*
Carnegie Foundation, 116, 129*n*
   forum, 316
Carnoy, M., 191, 200*n*
Carson, C. C., 2, 21*n*
Carter, S., 170, 179, 182*n*
Cary, L., 177, 182*n*
Cary v. Board of Education, Denver, 318
Caspi, A., 404, 410, 417*n*
Caywood, C., 211, 221*n*
Celis, W., 40, 52*n*, 121, 124*n*, 145, 157*n*, 250, 260*n*
Censorship (*See also* Academic freedom) 5, 359–360
Centerwall, B. S., 416, 417*n*
Chambers, G., 10, 21*n*
Channel One, 385, 392–393
Charter Schools, 37, 385
Chavez, L., 172, 182*n*
Cheney, L., 244, 254, 260*n*
Cherryholmes, C., 190, 200*n*
Child development, 215
Children
   poor, 57–83
   and violence, 402–418
Children's defense fund, 220
Chinn, P. C., 225, 240*n*
Chira, S., 4, 58, 66, 71, 81*n*, 102, 105*n*, 120, 123, 129*n*
Chmelynski, C., 100, 105*n*
Choice, 36–40, 84–107
Christensen, B., 263, 279*n*
Christenson, R. M., 5, 21*n*
Christian coalition, 6–8
Church-state, 10
Churchill, Winston, 118

Citizenship, 270, 318
  and school, 99–100
Civics, 266
Civil rights, 227–228
  and welfare, 60
Cizek, G. J., 307, 311n
Clark, J., 86, 106n
Clark, Kenneth, 148, 157, 181, 200n
Clark, M. A., 271, 279n
Clark, T., 323, 328n
Class struggle, 273–274
Clinchy, B. Mc., 3, 21n
Clinton, William, 36, 161
Clymer, A., 175, 182n
Cohen, D., 58, 74, 81n
Cohen, R., 37, 51, 52n
Cohen, W., 32
Coleman, J., 117, 129n
Collective bargaining, 320–322, 365–378
College Entrance Examination Board, 14, 21n
Colorado, 39
Colson, C., 264, 279n
Colvin, R., 124, 129n
Committee for Economic Development, 30,
  55n, 117, 129n
Commonwealth v. Hunt, 321
Communism, 285
Community control of schools, 314
Competence
  and academic freedom, 358–359
  and corporations, 397–398
  technological, 282–283
Competitiveness, 281–287
Conant, J. B., 11, 21n, 108, 129n
Conard, B. D., 137, 157n
Conformity, 270
Conservatives, 6–8, 13–14
  and teaching, 314
Constantine, J., 148, 157n
Controversy
  and academic freedom, 347–349, 344–346
Coons, J. E., 86, 106n, 114, 382, 400n
Cooper, D., 20, 21n
Corcoran, T., 116, 129n
Cornbleth, C., 228
Cornford, F. M., 313, 328
Corporations,
  and corruption, 287–294, 394–395
  and schools, (See Business) 287–294
  threat to schools, 287–291
Corruption
  and business, 287–294
Corwin, R., 103, 106n
Coughlin, E., 35, 47, 52n, 65, 69, 81n
Counts, G., 6, 21n
Cowan, A., 32, 52n

Crabtree, C., 244, 247, 253, 260n
Crain, F., 283, 293n
Cremin, L., 9, 21n, 297, 311n
Critical
  literacy, 256–257
  theorists, 190
  thinking, 203–222, 270–271
  views, 190
Criticism, 1–21
Cronbach, L. J., 299, 311n
Crouse, J., 160, 182n, 199, 200n, 299, 311n
Cuban, L., 250, 260n, 421, 433n
Cultural
  assimilation, 229
  bias in testing, 166, 296
  diversity, 162
  heritage, 203–204
  reproduction, 274–275
Curriculum, 185–201
  control, 190–192, 241–261
  and corporate influence (See Business)
  local, 241–261
  national, 241–261
  and testing, 301–302
  and values, 263, 267–268

Daley, S., 109, 129n
Daly, J., xvi, 354, 357, 360, 362n
Darling-Hammond, L., 15, 22n, 298, 299, 311n
Davis, Kinglsey, 263
Dawes, R., 167, 182n
Dayton, J., 391, 400n
Decentralizing schools, 189, 314
Deem, R., 192, 200n
deLone, R. H., 31, 52n
Democracy, 17–19
  and academic freedom, 317–319
  and elitism, 422–423
  and knowledge, 272
  and privatization, 390–391
Dennison, G., 12, 22n
Dentler, R. A., 149, 157n
deParle, J., 33, 36, 52n, 61, 63, 81n
Dershowitz, A., 66, 81n
Desegregation, 43–48
Dewey, John, 5, 6, 18, 22n, 214, 221n, 340, 354,
  362n, 400n, 402
DeWitt, K., 152, 157n
Dialectic reasoning, 19–21, 277–278
Diegmueller, K., 256, 260n
Dill, V. S., 404, 417n
Dillon, S., 123, 130n, 369, 377n
Disadvantaged, 160–184
Disciplines, 203–222
Discrimination, 160–184

Diversity, 1–21, 94–95
  and multicultural education, 223–240
Downs, A., 139, 157*n*
Doyle, D., 388, 400*n*
Drop-outs, 205
Drive-by-shooting, 404
Drug Education, 1
D'Souza, D., 15, 22*n*, 172, 182*n*, 235, 240*n*
DuBois, W. G. B., 152–153, 157*n*
Duckworth, E., 212, 221*n*
Dugger, C., 6, 52*n*, 65, 67, 74, 81*n*
Duke, David, 161
Dworkin, M. S., 402, 417*n*

Earle, J., 386–387, 399, 400*n*
Eaton, W. E., 320, 322, 328*n*, 371, 377*n*
Eberts, R. W., 366, 377*n*
Economic
  competitiveness, 241, 379
  school issues, 27–56
Edin, K., 80
Edison Project, 382–386, 391–393
Edsall, T. and M., 176, 182*n*
Educational Alternatives Inc., 382–386,
  393–394
Educational politics, 1–3
Educational Testing Service, 299
Edwards, H. H., xvi
Efficiency, 322
  and privatization, 395–396
  and schools, 322–323
Egalitarians, 27, 119–120
Eggleston, J., 199, 200*n*
Ehrenreich, B., 61, 70, 81*n*
Eichenwald, K., 32, 52*n*
Elam, S., 102, 106*n*, 141, 147, 152*n*, 242, 260*n*,
  325, 328*n*, 404, 413, 417*n*
Elconin, M., 98, 106*n*
Elitism, 253–254
  and excellence, 422–423
Ellingson, P., 398, 400*n*
Ellwood, D., 60, 81*n*
Elmore, R. F., 101, 103, 106*n*
Employment
  and affirmative action, 164–166
  and education, 283–284
  opportunities, 164
Empowerment, 270–280
Ennis, R., 212, 221*n*
Entrepreneurship, 388, 394–395
Epperson v. State of Arkansas, 100, 106*n*
Equality
  and excellence, 325–327, 419–433
  and liberty, 27–51

Equality, (*Continued*)
  of opportunity, 108–117, 325
  and privatization, 390–391
Equalizing education, 108–117
Equity, 108–117, 325–327, 419, 433
Erikson, E., 4, 22*n*
Ethics
  and values, 270–271
Ethnic prejudice, 160–171
Etzioni, A., 315, 328*n*
Eurocentrism, 230–231
Evaluation (*See* Testing)
Excellence
  in education, 325–327
  and equity, 325–327, 419–433
  and multicultural studies, 11–13
Experience, 211–222

Falwell, Jerry, 264, 279*n*
Faludi, S., 160, 182*n*
Family
  Support Act, 60
  values, 262–269
Fantini, M. D., 89, 97, 106*n*, 326, 328*n*
Farber, B., 90, 106*n*
Feiman-Nemser, S., 316, 328*n*
Feistritzer, E., 380, 400*n*
Feldman, S., 192, 200*n*
Feminism (*See* Gender, Women)
Feulner, E. J., 286, 293*n*
Finance, 40–43, 108–131
  and public schools, 380
Finkelstein, B., 289, 293*n*
Finn, C., 14, 22*n*, 203, 221*n*, 242, 260*n*, 319,
  328*n*, 380, 400*n*
Fischer, J., 115
Fisher, E., 15, 22*n*
Fisher, I., 68, 82*n*
Fiske, E., 15, 22*n*, 188, 200*n*, 279*n*, 300, 311*n*
Fliegel, S., 38, 52*n*, 85, 106*n*
Flagg, G., 354, 363*n*
Foderaro, L. W., 46, 52*n*
Forgotten Half, 282, 293*n*
Formisano, R., 140, 157*n*
Fox-Genovese, E., 233, 240*n*
Free enterprise
  and schools, 290
Freedman, M., 369, 377*n*
Freedom (*See also* Academic freedom)
  of inquiry, 317–319, 345–364
  and school organization, 142–143, 317–319
  of speech, 348
  student, 270–280, 317–319, 345–364
  and teachers, 271–272, 287, 317–319, 345–364
Freeman, J., 120, 130*n*

Freeman v. Pitts, 45, 46, 52*n*
Freire, P., 191, 196, 200*n*, 256, 260*n*, 278, 326, 328*n*
Freud, S., 409, 410, 417*n*
Friedenberg, E. Z., 12, 22*n*
Friedman, M. and R., 30, 38, 53*n*, 90, 106, 368, 377*n*
Fuller, B., 36, 53*n*
Fullilove v. Klutznik, 50, 53*n*

Galbraith, J. K., 79
Gallagher, W., 74, 82*n*
Gallup
　A. M., 102, 106*n*, 141, 157*n*
　Polls, 3, 51, 147, 325
Galton, F., 297
Gangs, 402
Garcia, G. E., 297, 311*n*
Gardner, H., 211, 221*n*, 298, 311*n*
Gardner, J., 12, 22*n*, 327, 328*n*
Garms, W. I., 118, 130*n*
Gates, H. L., 144, 157*n*, 223, 225, 226, 230, 240*n*
Gays, 171
Geiger, P. E., 381, 400*n*
Gellerman, W., 359, 363*n*
Gender (*See also* Women, Sexism), 160–184
Genetics, 59–60
Geoghagan, T., 320, 328*n*
Georgia, 42
Gibbs, N., 35, 53*n* 62, 68, 71, 82*n*, 110, 130*n*
Gilbert, T., 283, 294*n*
Gilder, G., 30, 53*n*
Gintis, H., 112, 129*n*
Ginzberg, E., 98, 106*n*
Giroux, H., 5, 15, 22*n*, 190, 196, 200*n*, 228, 239*n*, 271, 279*n*
Gladwell, M., 163, 182*n*
Glass, G., 73, 77*n*
Glass ceiling, 169
Glasser, I., 29, 53*n*
Glazer, J., 393, 401*n*
Glazer, N., 87, 93, 106*n*, 144, 157*n*, 326, 328*n*
Glenn, C., 92, 106*n*
Global society, 194, 379, 386–387, 398–399
Gluck, C., 249, 260*n*
Goals 2000, 3, 287
Goertz, M., 40, 53*n*
Goldstein, A. P., 404, 417*n*
Goldstein, S., 350, 363*n*
Gollnick, D. M., 225, 240*n*
Goodlad, J., 14, 22*n*, 212, 221*n*, 316, 328*n*
Goodman, E., 35, 53*n*
Goodman, P., 12, 22*n*, 215
Goodson, I., 223, 240*n*

Gordon, L., 34, 53*n*, 60, 82*n*
Gottfredson, L., 74, 82*n*
Gould, S. J., 297, 298, 311*n*
Government interference, 142–144
Graff, G., 257
Graglia, L., 176, 182*n*
Graham, P., 10, 22*n*
Granovetter, M., 149, 157*n*
Grant Foundation
　Commission on Work, Family and Citizenship, 31, 53*n*, 283, 294*n*
Green v. County Board of New Kent County, 44, 53*n*
Greene, E., 257, 260*n*
Greene, M., 3, 22*n*, 186, 200*n*, 271, 279*n*
Griggs v. Duke Power Co., 166–7, 182*n*
Grimshaw, J., 192, 200*n*
Gross, J., 109, 130*n*
Guinier, L., 161, 182*n*
Gumbert, E., 297, 311*n*
Guthrie, J., 118, 124, 130*n*
Gutmann, A., 390, 401*n*

Hacker, A., 168, 171, 177, 179, 182*n*
Haertel, E. H., 307, 311*n*
Hahn, R. O., 21*n*
Hammond, R., 407
Handguns, 324, 404
Hanushek, E. A., 124, 130*n*
Harp, L., 42, 53*n*
Harrington, M., 34, 53*n*
Harris, L., 404, 405, 417*n*
Hartford, 385–386, 393
Harty, S., 292, 294*n*
Harvey, P., 63, 82*n*
Havighurst, R., 41, 54*n*
Hawley, W. D., 15, 22*n*, 137, 157*n*
Haydon, G., 2, 70, 280*n*
Hayek, F. A., 119, 124, 130*n*
Hedges, L., 124, 130*n*
Helms, Jesse, 237
Henig, J. R., 102, 106*n*, 250, 260*n*
Henneberg, M., 65, 82*n*
Hentoff, N., 12, 22*n*, 215, 221*n*
Herbers, J., 115, 130*n*
Herrnstein, R., 34, 52*n*, 63, 82*n*, 140, 157*n*, 181, 298, 302, 311*n*, 325, 328*n*, 415, 417*n*
Hicks, J., 178, 182*n*
Hidden curriculum, 189–190
Hinds, M., 46, 53*n*
Hirsch, E. D., 225, 231, 240*n*, 242, 244, 253, 260*n*
History
　standards, 247–253
　and values, 266

Hobson v. Hansen, 41
Hochschild, J. L., 136, 157*n*
Hoffman, B., 295–296, 299, 311*n*
Hofstadter, R., 192, 201*n*, 317, 329*n*, 359, 363*n*
Holmes, S., 161, 174, 182*n*
Holt, J. 11, 22*n*
Holt, R., 15, 22*n*
Homosexuals, 172
Hook, S., 319, 329*n*, 349, 363*n*
Hopwood v. Texas, 50, 174, 182*n*
Houston, W., 118
Housing, 138–140
Howe, H. H., 250, 260*n*
Humanism (*See also* Secular humanism), 232
Hunter, R. C., 389, 401*n*
Huxley, Aldous, 19, 22*n*
Hymowitz, K. S., 354, 363*n*

IBM, 50
Ideology, 4–8
    and knowledge, 272–273, 276–277
    and privatization, 399
Illich, I., 8, 22*n*
Imperialism, 253–254
Indoctrination
    and curriculum, 247
Industrial Revolution, 198, 403
Inequality (*See* Equality)
Inert ideas, 218
Ingraham, L., 178, 182*n*
Integration (*See also* Segregation), 43–48,
    132–159
Integrationists, 132–141
Intellectual Freedom (*See* Academic freedom)
International education
    and business competition, 282
IQ tests, 77, 288–290
Islam, nation of, 73

Jackson, Jesse, 132
Jacobs, J., 177, 182*n*
Jaffe, J., 238, 240*n*
Japenga, A., 360, 353*n*
Jaschik, S., 46, 50, 53*n*
Jaynes, G., 68, 82*n*, 168, 182*n*
Jefferson, Thomas, 390, 401*n*
Jehl, D., 36, 53*n*
Jencks, C., 39, 53*n*, 111, 130*n*, 168, 183*n*
Jenkinson, E. B., 360, 361, 363*n*
Jensen, A. R., 298, 311*n*
Jersey City, 134
Jessup, D. K., 371, 377*n*
Johnson, D., 73, 82*n*

Johnson, K., 139, 158*n*
Johnson, Lyndon B., 48
Johnson, S. M., 366, 374, 377*n*
Johnston, R., 248, 260*n*
Jones, A., 249, 260*n*
Jones, C., 141, 158*n*
Jordan, K., 41, 53*n*
Judeo-Christian ideals, 267
Judson, G., 155, 394, 401*n*
Justice (*See also* Equity), 289, 390

Kadish, J., 70, 82*n*
Kaestle, C., 9, 22*n*
Kagan, D., 244, 260*n*
Kagan, J., 74, 82*n*
Kansas City, 145
Kaplan, C., 318, 329*n*
Kaplan, G. R., 7, 22*n*
Karier, C., 9, 23*n*
Kaus, M., 29
Katz, M., 9, 23*n*, 192, 201*n*
Kean, T., 242, 260*n*
Kearns, D. T., 89, 106*n*
Keilor, Garrison, 300
Kelly, G. P., 327, 328*n*
Kelly, V., 63, 82*n*
Kemmerer, F., 93, 106*n*
Kemper, V., 38, 53*n*
Kennedy, John F., 48, 164
Keniston, K., 31, 53*n*
Kerchner, C. T., 93, 106*n*, 367, 370, 374, 377*n*
Kerlinger, F., 299, 312*n*
Keyes v. School District No 1, Denver, 44, 53*n*,
    135, 158*n*
Keyishian v. Board of Regents, 355, 363*n*
Kidder, R., 270, 280*n*
Kilborn, P., 169, 183*n*
King, W., 114, 130*n*
Kinsley, M., 15, 23*n*
Kirk, R., 317, 329*n*, 349, 363*n*
Kirp, D., 38, 53*n*, 85, 106*n*, 135, 147, 158
Klein, J., 62, 82*n*, 178, 183*n*
Kluger, R., 43, 44, 53*n*
Knapp, M., 124, 130*n*
Knowledge, 185–201
    and curriculum, 185–201
    mainstream control, 275–276
Kohl, H., 12, 22*n*
Kotlowitz, A., 110, 130*n*
Kozol, J., 12, 23*n*, 38, 109, 113, 114, 130*n*
Kristol, I., 29, 54, 120, 130*n*
Krugman, P., 119, 130*n*
Kurtz, P., 20, 53*n*
Kuttner, R., 28, 54*n*

Ladson-Billings, G., 227, 240*n*
Lamar, J., 165, 183*n*
Lane, R. E., 4, 23*n*
Larew, J., 165, 183*n*
Lasch, C., 288, 294*n*, 422, 433*n*
Lawrence, F., 256, 260*n*
Lanton, M., 408, 413, 418*n*
Leadership
  school, 315–317
Learning, 211–222
Lefelt, S., 112, 130*n*
Lesbians, 171
Leslie, C., 165, 183*n*
Leo, J., 7, 346, 363*n*
Leusner, D., 69, 82*n*
Levi, E., 49
Levin, H., 97, 106*n*, 123, 130*n*
Levin, T., 64, 82*n*
Levine, D. U., 41, 54*n*
Lewis, N. A., 72, 82*n*, 122, 130*n*
Liberals, 6–8, 28
  and education, 262, 270–280, 314
Liberal arts, 189
Liberation, 195–196
  education, 270–280
Libertarian, 27
Liberty
  and equality, 27–51
Lieberman, M., 39, 54*n*, 87, 106*n*, 321, 359*n*,
  369, 377*n*
Limbaugh, R., 69, 82*n*, 176
Linden, E., 70, 82*n*
Lindsay, D., 93, 102, 106*n*
Linn, R. L., 300, 302, 305, 309, 312*n*
Linton, T., 7, 23*n*, 201*n*
Literacy, 185–201
  and curriculum, 194–195
  and knowledge, 186–187
Local control, 110–112
Lortie, D., 315, 329*n*
Loury, G., 172, 183*n*
Lubman, S., 178, 183*n*
Lucas, 117, 130*n*, 136, 158*n*
Lukas, J. A., 153
Lynd, A., 11, 23*n*

McCall, N., 72, 82*n*
McCarthy, M. M., 124, 131*n*
McCarthyism period, 11, 71, 195
McCloud, L., 48, 54*n*
McEvoy, A., 15, 23*n*
McFadden, R., 68, 82*n*
McFarlane, A., 264, 280*n*, 347, 363*n*

McGroarty, D., 93, 106*n*
McGuffey Readers, 6, 269
MacIver, R., 317, 329*n*
McKeown, M. P., 41, 54*n*
McKinley, J., 123, 131*n*
McLarin, K., 136, 158*n*
Madaus, G., 295, 289, 312*n*
Madden, N., 125, 131*n*
Maeroff, E., 374, 377*n*
Magnet, M., 71, 82*n*
Magnet schools, 37–38
Maguire, D., 174, 183*n*
Mahaffey, F., 403, 418*n*
Mahard, R. E., 136, 158*n*
Mainstream ideas, 6–8
Male domination (*See* Sexism)
Mandel, M., 15, 23*n*, 86, 294*n*, 380, 401*n*
Mann, D., 283, 294*n*
Manno, B., 16, 23*n*
Margaronis, M., 255, 260*n*
Marina, A., 287, 294*n*
Marriott, M., 150, 158*n*
Marrou, H., 191, 201*n*
Marx, Karl, 33–34
Mass Media, 198
Massachussetts School Laws, 263
Mawdsley, R. D. and A. L., 354, 363*n*
Mead, L., 29, 54*n*
Mediocrity, 251, 419
Mehrens, W. A., 198, 201*n*, 300, 312*n*
Meier, D., 38, 54*n*, 85, 106*n*
Melnick, N., 354, 363*n*
Men (*See* Women)
Mental abuse, 352
Mercer, J., 171, 183*n*
Mesidov, L. L., 354, 363*n*
Metz, M. H., 111, 131*n*
Metzger, W. P., 359, 363*n*
Meyer, A. E., 232, 240*n*
Michigan, 40
Mill, John Stuart, 257, 271, 280*n*
Miller, W. H., 281, 294*n*
Milliken v. Bradley, 44, 46, 54*n*
Mills, N., 48, 54*n*
Mink, G., 36, 54*n*
Minorities, 132–159
  and national curriculum, 246
Missouri v. Jenkins, 46, 54*n*
Mitchell, A., 69, 75, 82*n*
Monoculturalism, 227–228
Monopoly of schools, 85–86, 323, 382
Mooney, C. J., 239, 240*n*
Moore, M., 404, 418*n*
Moral choice, 271
Moral education, 187

Morality
 and schools, 187, 262–280
Moran, B., 39, 54*n*
Morgan, J., 63, 82*n*
Morse, P. A., 407, 418*n*
Mosle, S., 148, 158*n*
Moynihan, D. P., 15, 23*n*, 144, 158*n*
Multicultural education, 12–13, 193–194,
 223–240
 and public schools, 223–240
Multiracial (*See* Multicultural education)
Murphy, M., 322, 329*n*, 371, 377*n*
Murray, C., 29, 31, 54*n*, 63, 69, 74, 77, 82*n*, 140,
 158*n*, 298, 311*n*
Muslims, 73
Mystification, 272–273, 423–424
Myths, 271–272

NLRB v. Jones and Laughlin Steel Company, 321
Nairn, A., 249, 312*n*
Nasar, S., 22, 54*n*
Natale, J. A., 410, 418*n*
Nathan, J., 15, 23*n*, 37, 54*n*
National Assessment of Educational Progress
 (NAEP), 305–306, 380
National Association for Advancement of Col-
 ored People (NAACP), 148
National Association of Manufacturers, 164
National Coalition Against Censorship
 (NCAC), 360
National Commission on Excellence in Educa-
 tion, 13, 23*n*, 188, 201*n*, 203–204, 22*n*
National curriculum, 305–306
National Education Association (NEA), 319,
 322–323, 365, 405
National goals, 301
National Labor Relations Act, 320
National Science Foundation, 14, 23*n*
Native Americans
 and testing, 296
Neill, A. S., 12, 23*n*
Neill, D. M., 296, 299, 312*n*
Neill, M., 254, 261*n*, 302, 312*n*
Nelson, F., 117
Nelson, J. L., 7, 23*n*, 201*n*, 357, 363*n*
Nelson, L-E., 32, 55*n*
Neo-conservative, 6
Neo-liberal, 6
New England Primer, 263
New Jersey, 42
New World Standards, 301
New York, 229
Nixon, Richard, 48, 84
Nocero, J., 119, 131*n*

Noddings, N., 3, 23*n*
Nolan, K., 3, 24*n*
Novak, M., 15, 23*n*

Oakes, J., 191, 201*n*
Occams Razor, 253
Ogbu, J. U., 148, 149, 158*n*, 298, 312*n*
Ohanian, S., 213, 222*n*, 249, 261*n*
Oklahoma City, 45
Olson, L., 37, 54*n*, 96, 107*n*
O'Neill, R. M., 318, 319, 329*n*, 356, 363*n*
O'Neill, T., 126, 131*n*
Open Education, 12
Oregon, 39
Orfield, G., 45, 54*n*, 88, 107*n*, 133, 138*n*
Orwell, George, 255
Outcomes-based education, 309
Owen, D., 199, 201*n*, 299, 300, 312*n*

Paglia, C., 14, 23*n*
Parents
 choice, 84–107
 rights, 86–87
 surrogates, 351
Particularism, 233–234
Patterson, O., 246
Patterson v. McClean Credit Union, 162, 183*n*
Peace education, 205
Pear, R., 36, 54*n*, 64, 82*n*
Peat Marwick Main & Co., 122
Pedagogy
 liberation, 276–277
Peltis, C., 325, 328*n*
Peltzman, S., 203, 222*n*
Pennsylvania, 46
Pentagon
 and military spending, 290
People for the American Way, 354
Performance, 303
 and privatization, 397–398
 assessment, 307–308
Perry, R., 235, 240*n*
Perry, T., 228, 240*n*
Peterkin, R., 99, 107*n*
Phelps, R., 248, 261*n*
Phillips, G. W., 300, 301*n*
Phillips, K., 33, 54*n*
Piche, D., 41, 53*n*
Pico, S., 354, 363*n*
Pierce, B., 359, 363*n*
Pitsch, M., 39, 54*n*
Plato, 5, 6, 277, 313
Pluralism (*See* Multicultural education)

Polakowa, V., 79
Political correctness (*See* Multicultural education)
Political restraint (*See* Academic freedom)
Politics in education, 1–4
Poor people, 57–83
  and testing, 57–58
Popenoe, D., 58, 82*n*
Popkewitz, T., 190, 201*n*
Portfolios, 308
Portner, J., 414, 418*n*
Postman, N., 252, 261*n*
Poverty (*See also* Welfare), 33
Prejudice, 160–171
Presseisen, B., 15, 24*n*
Private enterprise, 394–399
Privatization, 134, 322–323, 379–401
  international, 386–387, 398–399
  myths, 395–399
Progressive education, 10–11, 203–222
Progressivism, 5, 10
Propaganda, 356
Property tax, 40–43
Protzman, F., 387, 401*n*
Psychometrics (*See* Testing)
Purdy, M., 58, 82*n*
Purpel, D., 7, 9, 15, 24*n*

Quotas (*See also* Affirmative action), 160–184

Rabkin, J., 263, 280*n*
Racial
  quotas, 48–51, 160–184
Racism, 9, 43–48
Radical, 5–8
  teachers, 347
Rafferty, M., 8, 24*n*, 266, 280*n*
Ramsey, N., 282, 294*n*
Rationalism, 232
Rauth, M., 371, 374, 377*n*
Ravitch, D., 14, 24*n*, 203, 222*n*, 225, 231, 240*n*, 253, 261*n*, 306, 312*n*
Rawls, J., 65, 83*n*
Raywid, M. A., 85, 107*n*
Reactionaries, 274–275
Reagan, Ronald, 4, 380
Redburn, T., 66, 83*n*
Reeves, R., 164, 183*n*
Reiss, A. J., 324, 329*n*, 404, 405, 412, 418*n*
Reform, 1–21
  and business values, 289–290
  and curriculum, 187–189, 203, 222
Regents of the University of California v. Bakke, 49, 54*n*

Relativism, 264
Religion
  and values, 264–265
Resnick, L., 3, 24*n*, 253
Restructuring schools, 316–317, 367
Reynolds, A., 124, 131*n*
Reynolds, W. B., 152, 158*n*
Richardson, J., 367, 377*n*
Richmond v. A. J. Crosson, 50, 55*n*
Rist, R., 146, 158*n*
Roberts, S. V., 262, 280*n*
Robinson v. Cahill, 42, 43, 55*n*
Rochester, New York, 375
Rodriguez, L. J., 402, 418*n*
Rorty, R., 355, 363*n*
Rosen, J., 164, 183*n*
Rosenberg, R., 149, 158*n*
Rosenthal, A., 371, 377*n*
Rosser, P., 301, 312*n*
Rossow, L., 50, 55*n*
Rotberg, I., 115, 131*n*
Roth, J. A., 324, 329*n*, 404, 418*n*
Roth, R. A., 20, 24*n*
Rothenberg, R., 6, 24*n*
Rothman, R., 251, 261*n*
Rubin, D., 318, 329*n*
Rubin, L., 121, 129*n*
Rugg, H., 310
Russell, B., 18, 24*n*
Rychlak, J. F., 20, 24*n*

SAT Exam, 5, 166, 301
Sack, K., 35, 55*n*, 74, 83
Sacken, D. M., 354, 363*n*
Sadker, M. and D., 160, 183*n*
Safety (*See also* Violence), 323–324
Safire, W., 14, 24*n*, 32, 55*n*
Saks, J. B., 391, 401*n*
St. John, N. H., 47, 55*n*, 149, 158*n*
Samuelson, R. J., 75, 203, 222*n*, 242, 261*n*
San Antonio Independent School District v. Rodriguez, 42, 55*n*, 121, 131*n*
Sautter, C. R., 15, 25*n*, 409, 414, 418*n*
Schlesinger, A., Jr., 231, 240*n*
Schmidt, B., 392
Schmidt, P., 136, 145, 158*n*
Schofield, J. W., 137, 159*n*
School
  administration, 313–330
  choice, 36–40, 84–107
  and community, 402
  desegregation, 132–159
  finance, 40–43, 108–131
  and income, 57–83

School, (*Continued*)
 organization, 313–330, 375
 privatization, 134, 322–323, 379–401
 problems, 1–21
 reform, 1–21
 reorganization, 141
 violence, 323–324
School-based management, 375
Schorr, J., 39, 55*n*
Schandler, B., 38, 53*n*, 107*n*
Schwarz, P., 250, 251, 261*n*
Schwebel, M., 254, 261*n*
Sclar, E., 399, 401*n*
Searle, J., 235, 236, 239, 240*n*
Secular humanism, 7, 86–87, 264–265
Segregation, 43–48, 132–159
 de jure, 132–133
Self-esteem, 149
Serrano v. Priest, 42, 55*n*
Sewall, G., 208–209, 222*n*, 282, 294*n*
Sex education, 1, 206–207, 266
Sexism, 9, 160–184
 and testing, 301
Sexton, P. C., 114, 131*n*
Sexual prejudice, 160–171
Shanker, A., 39, 53*n*, 96, 101, 107*n*, 236, 240*n*,
 241, 243, 261*n*, 321, 329*n*, 382, 394, 401*n*
Shapiro, W., 92, 107*n*
Shaw, P., 204, 222*n*
Shelton, B., 146, 159*n*
Shils, E., 4, 24*n*
Shock camps, 414–416
Shor, I., 271, 280*n*
Sikes, P. J., 315, 329*n*
Simmons, J., 354, 363*n*
Simon, W., 25, 55*n*
Sinclair, Upton, 8, 24*n*, 292, 294*n*, 359, 363*n*
Site-based management, 317
Sizer, T., 14, 24*n*, 212, 222*n*, 248, 261*n*, 316,
 330*n*
Skills, 203–222
Slavin, R., 125
Sleeper, J., 168–169, 183*n*
Smith, Adam, 29, 55*n*
Smith, F., 1, 24*n*
Smith, M., 12, 24*n*
Smith, V., 148, 159*n*
Smothers, R., 148, 159*n*
Snider, W., 85, 107*n*
Sobol, T., 226, 230, 240*n*
Social class
 and excellence, 424
 and IQ, 77
 and SAT scores, 57–58

Social construction of reality, 230–231
Social mobility, 9
Social services, 58–59
Socialization, 270
Socrates, 8, 277
Soltow, L., 284, 294*n*
Soviet economy, 146
Sowell, T., 172, 183*n*, 262, 280*n*
Spring, J., 41, 55*n*, 192, 201*n*, 273, 280*n*
Sputnik, 11
Standardized testing, 198–200, 295–312
Stanley, W., xvii, 6, 15, 24*n*, 186, 190, 201*n*
Staples, B., 72, 83*n*
Starr, P., 173, 183*n*
Stasz, C., 168, 183*n*
State takeover of schools, 134
Steele, C., 137, 159*n*
Steele, S., 72, 83*n*, 177, 183*n*
Steinfels, P., 6, 24*n*
Stern, D., 366, 377*n*
Stevens, M., 37, 55*n*
Stimpson, C., 178, 183*n*
Streshly, W. A., 365, 378*n*
Strike, K. A., 16, 24*n*, 326, 329*n*
Strikes
 teacher, 366
Student
 failure, 204
 freedom, 317–319, 345–364
 performance, 303
Sugarman, S. D., 86, 106*n*, 114
Suro, R., 121, 131*n*
*Swann v. Charlotte-Mecklenburg Board of Educa-
 tion*, 44, 55*n*
Swanson, D. B., 312*n*
Swart, E., 315, 330*n*
Szabo, J. C., 209, 222*n*, 281, 294*n*

Takaki, R., 224, 240*n*
Tanner, D., 2, 29*n*, 420, 425, 433*n*
Tashman, B., 98, 107*n*
Tawney, R. H., 191, 201*n*
Tax credits, 39
Taxman v. The Board of Education of Piscataway,
 50, 55*n*
Taxpayers, 314
Taylor, W., 41, 55*n*
Teachers
 accountability, 314, 345–364
 careers, 315–317
 education, 370–371
 empowerment, 313–314, 345–364
 freedom, 317–319, 345–364

Teachers, (*Continued*)
　and leadership, 313, 330
　and privatization, 383
　role, 313, 345–364
　salaries, 370–371, 383, 392
　and school choice, 89–90, 100–101
　unions, 100, 319–322, 365–378
　and values, 268–269
Technology, 285–286
Teenage pregnancy, 205
Television
　and violence, 403–404
Tenure, 345–346, 369, 373
　and academic freedom, 345–364
　and unions, 373
Testing
　and academic subjects, 198–200, 295–312
　and bias, 296, 301
　and coaching, 166
　and curriculum, 198–200, 301–302
　standardized, 198–200, 295–312
Texas, 42
Thomas v. Stewart, 42, 55*n*
Thurmond, S., 265, 280*n*
Thurow, L. C., 34, 55*n*, 116, 131*n*
Tice, T. N., 212, 222*n*
Tien, C-L., 163, 183*n*
Toch, T., 391, 401*n*
Tocqueville, A. de, 30, 52*n*
Towns, E., 265, 280*n*
Traditionalism, 5–6, 185–201, 203–222
　and values, 262–280
Traub, J., 150, 159*n*
Travers, R. M. W., 199, 201*n*
Treaster, J., 109, 131*n*
Trowbridge, R., 103, 107*n*
Tuition tax credits, 39
Turner, M., 156
Turner, R., 46, 55*n*
Turner-Eigner, J., 354, 363*n*
Tuthill, D., 374, 378*n*
Twentieth Century Fund, 14, 42*n*
Tyack, D., 4, 9, 24*n*, 195, 201*n*
Tyler, R. W., 124, 131*n*

Uchitelle, L., 33, 55*n*
Ulich, R., 9, 24*n*
Unions, 319–321, 365–378
United Steelworkers of America v. Weber, 49, 55*n*
Urban, W., 371, 378*n*
Urbansky, A., 372
Urofsky, M., 164, 165, 170, 183*n*

Values, 27–51
　and academic freedom, 346
　clarification, 265
　and curriculum, 266–267
　education, 270
　and violence, 409–410
Van Biema, 60, 83*n*
Van Brabant, J. V., 386, 399, 401*n*
Van den Haag, E., 415, 418*n*
Van Sciver, J. H., 369, 378*n*
Van Tassel, P., 114, 129*n*
Veblen, T., 359, 363*n*
Vergara, C., 110, 131*n*
Verstogen, D., 42, 55*n*
Violence, 402–417
　prevention, 406–409
　in schools, 323–325
Vobejda, B., 66, 83*n*
Vouchers, 38, 85–107
　and private schools, 85–86

Wainer, H., 167, 183*n*, 306, 312*n*
Waldron, C., 354, 360, 364*n*
Wallach, L. B., 405, 418*n*
Walsh, M., 37, 55*n*
Wards Cove Packing Co. Inc. v. Antonio 162, 183*n*
War on Poverty, 144
Watt, J., 6, 25*n*
Watts, G. D., 372, 374, 378*n*
Webster, W. E., 14, 24*n*
Weiler, K., 192, 201*n*
Weinraub, B., 37, 55*n*
Weis, L., 327, 328*n*
Weishew, N. L., 412, 418*n*
Weiss, C. H., 317, 330*n*
Weiss, P., 113, 131*n*
Welfare, 28–29, 34–36, 57–83
Wells, A., 47, 55*n*
Welter, R., 9, 25*n*
Weltner, L., 419, 433
Wesley, E., 319, 330*n*
West, C., 162, 184*n*
White flight, 45, 133
Whitehead, A. N., xv, 218, 222*n*
Whitehead, B. D., 1, 25*n*, 266, 280*n*
Whitson, J. A., 354, 364*n*
Whittle, C., 391–393
Wilentz, D., 139, 159*n*
Wilkerson, I., 140, 147, 159*n*, 178, 184*n*
Wilkinson, J. H., 45, 56*n*, 142, 150, 159*n*
Will, G., 68–69, 77, 83*n*
Wilson, W. J., 133, 159*n*, 172, 184*n*

Winerip, M., 111, 131*n*
Wingert, P., 126, 137*n*
Winkler, K., 14, 25*n*, 253, 261*n*
Wolf, J. B., 298, 312*n*
Women (*See* Gender, Sexism, Affirmative
    action)
  and affirmative action, 160–184
  and jobs, 315–316
  and test bias, 301
Workers
  and democracy, 289, 373–374
  education, 289–290

Workers (*Continued*)
  and schools, 99
  and teacher unions, 365–378
Wraga, W., 95, 107*n*

Yen, M., 414, 418*n*
Young, M. F. D., 190, 201*n*, 275, 280*n*
Yuppies, 13

Zeigler, H., 371, 378*n*
Zirkel, P., 358, 364*n*
Zook, J., 171, 184*n*

Date Due

8/15/02			
AP 25 '05			